STEPS ON THE PATH TO ENLIGHTENMENT

STEPS
ON THE PATH TO
ENLIGHTENMENT

A Commentary on Tsongkhapa's
Lamrim Chenmo

Volume 3: The Way of the Bodhisattva

GESHE LHUNDUB SOPA
with Beth Newman

WISDOM PUBLICATIONS • BOSTON

Wisdom Publications
199 Elm Street
Somerville MA 02144 USA
www.wisdompubs.org

Library of Congress Cataloging-in-Publication Data for Volume 1
Lhundub Sopa, Geshe, 1925-
   Steps on the path to enlightenment : a commentary on Tsongkhapa's
Lamrim chenmo / Geshe Lhundub Sopa ; David Patt, senior editor ; Beth
Newman, editor.
       p. cm.
Includes bibliographical references and index.
   ISBN 0-86171-303-6 (alk. paper)
   1. Tson-kha-pa Blo-bzan-grags-pa, 1357-1419. Lam rim chen mo. 2.
Lam-rim. I. Patt, David. II. Newman, Beth. III. Tson-kha-pa
Blo-bzan-grags-pa, 1357-1419. Lamrim chenmo. IV. Title.
   BQ7950.T754L359 2003
   294.3'444--dc22
                           2003017363

ISBN for volume 3: The Way of the Bodhisattva
0-86171-482-2

12 11 10 09 08
5   4   3   2   1
Cover and interior design by Gopa&Ted2, Inc.
Set in DiacriticalGaramond 10.5/13.
Photos of Geshe Sopa © C&N Photo, www.candnphoto.com.

Wisdom Publications' books are printed on acid-free paper and meet the
guidelines for permanence and durability set by the Council of Library
Resources.

Printed in Canada

Table of Contents

Foreword

THE *Great Treatise on the Stages of the Path to Enlightenment (Lamrim Chenmo),* composed by Tsongkhapa and explained here by Geshe Lhundub Sopa, is a commentary on the *Lamp for the Path to Enlightenment* by Atiśa. The primary goal of these teachings is to discipline and transform the mind. These texts have their source in the sutras and the other teachings of the Buddha himself, but their special virtue is that they convey the thought of the Buddha in a format that is easy to apply in actual practice.

The authors of these wonderful texts composed them in order to help all living beings. Since they developed the altruistic attitude to benefit mother sentient beings, we too should follow their example, irrespective of our own weak situation.

The Buddha and the great teachers who followed him gave clear instructions on how to proceed from a state of suffering to a state of peace and happiness. Following such teachings of the great masters of the past, Atiśa summarized them in his famous text, the *Lamp for the Path to Enlightenment.* It is a wonderful text, and Atiśa's disciples such as Dromtonpa and Potowa put what it teaches into practice. It was then transmitted through the Kadam lineages, finally coming down to Tsongkhapa.

He was an unparalleled scholar, who composed the *Great Treatise on the Stages of the Path to Enlightenment,* the marvelous text explained here in the manner of the great masters of Nālandā monastic university. We are indeed fortunate after so much time to have access to such a great work and to be able to read and think about what it contains. With this publication of Geshe Sopa's commentary, Tsongkhapa's words are brought to life and illuminated for a modern audience, continuing the lineages of scripture and realization that the Buddha set in motion more than 2,500 years ago.

The two principal aspects of practice described here are a proper understanding of emptiness and the awakening mind of *bodhicitta.* A correct understanding of the view of emptiness is very important, for whether you are taking refuge, or cultivating the awakening mind of *bodhicitta,* all other practices are enhanced by such an understanding. At the same time, it is extremely important that our insight into the ultimate nature of reality is supported by compassion and the awakening mind of *bodhicitta.*

In my own case, regardless of my limited capacity, I try my best to develop these two minds: the wisdom understanding emptiness, and *bodhicitta*—the wish to achieve enlightenment for the sake of all sentient beings. Merely trying to approach and cultivate these two minds brings greater peace and happiness. The development of these two minds is really the heart of Buddhist practice. It is the essential meaning of this *Stages of the Path to Enlightenment.* If we were to examine all the sutras and words of the Buddha, along with the subsequent treatises that are commentaries on them, we would find that they can be summed up in these two practices. Therefore, we should study these teachings motivated by an aspiration to achieve enlightenment for the sake of all sentient beings.

Today, Buddhism is spreading throughout the Western world, encountering new cultures and new languages. During such a period of transition it is very important that the Dharma be transmitted by scholars and practitioners who possess a deep and vast understanding of the teachings, because that is the only way to protect the authenticity and purity of the teachings.

Atiśa exemplified this role by bringing the pure teachings from the great monastic centers of North India and establishing them in Tibet in an authentic and complete form that was, at the same time, suitably adapted to the Tibetan personality. He reestablished monasticism in Tibet and emphasized ethical conduct as the heart of Buddhist training. He dispelled the many misconceptions and erroneous customs that had entered the practice of the Dharma in Tibet. In this way he reestablished the pure Buddhadharma in many places where it had been lost, and enhanced it where it survived.

Requested by Jangchub Ö to give a teaching that would be beneficial to the Tibetan people in general, Atiśa composed the *Lamp for the Path to Enlightenment,* which condensed the essential points of both sutras and tantras into a step-by-step method that would be easy to follow. This text inaugurated the grand tradition of the study and practice of the stages of the path method in Tibet. Atiśa also worked with his Tibetan students on the translation of many texts from Sanskrit into Tibetan and so made a rich contribution to the flourishing of Buddhism in the Land of Snows.

Geshe Sopa, the author of this commentary on the *Lamrim Chenmo,* was one of the several good students of Geshe Lhundrub Tabke and was therefore chosen to debate with me during my final examination. Geshe Lhundrub Tabke, who became the abbot of Sera Je, was in turn one of the several good students of Geshe Tsangpa Lhundrub Tsondru, who was a renowned scholar at the time of the Thirteenth Dalai Lama and later ascended the throne of

Ganden Tripa. Geshe Sopa is therefore the third generation of high-quality scholarship commencing from Geshe Tsangpa Lhundrub Tsondru and he continues the excellent tradition today.

He is an exemplary heir of Atiśa's tradition conveying the pure Dharma to a new world in an authentic and useful way. He has been a pioneer among those bringing Buddhism to the West. He left for America in 1962. In due course, Geshe Sopa was invited to the University of Wisconsin, where he became one of the first Tibetan language instructors at an American university. He later rose to become a tenured faculty member, and his career as a Professor of Buddhist Studies eventually spanned more than thirty years.

All Tibetans should feel honored and proud that Geshe Sopa, a man from far-away Tibet, could rise to the highest levels of Western academic attainment largely on the basis of his Tibetan monastic education combined with his own brilliance and personal qualities. Publication of this excellent series of books is a fitting tribute to an illustrious career.

Tenzin Gyatso, the Fourteenth Dalai Lama

Editor's Acknowledgments

WITH DEEP GRATITUDE I offer respectful thanks to my teacher, the venerable Geshe Lhundub Sopa, a human embodiment of all the buddhas and bodhisattvas.

The third volume of *Steps on the Path to Enlightenment* is a concrete example of the kindness of the guru. Here Geshe Sopa patiently explains for contemporary students the nature of the Mahayana path. Starting with an in-depth discussion of the motivation to attain enlightenment, he progresses through detailed instructions on how to develop the attitude of bodhicitta: the desire to attain complete buddhahood in order to benefit all other sentient beings, to a description of the perfections: the actions we undertake once we have generated bodhicitta. While this volume gives an overview of the entire Mahayana path, the next two volumes of this series will provide thorough explanations of the last two perfections: meditative stabilization and wisdom.

It is only through the kindness of my teachers that this work was made possible. Everything that is correct and helpful in this text is a result of the compassionate, patient instruction of Geshe Sopa and my other virtuous friends; any mistakes are my own.

I was exceptionally fortunate to be able to listen to these teachings when they were originally offered in Madison, Wisconsin, USA over the course of many years. It has been a privilege to be part of the effort to make these instructions available to many more people through the composition of this series.

Thanks are due to a number of individuals. In addition to being an inspiring teacher and exemplary practitioner, Lama Thubten Zopa Rinpoche made the successful completion of this project possible through his unstinting moral and financial support. I am especially grateful to David Patt for inviting me to participate in this project. The staff of Wisdom Publications, particularly Tim McNeill and David Kittlestrom, have demonstrated admirable patience and help throughout the project. Jon Landaw's careful copy editing identified and removed ambiguity. My husband, John Newman, answered many technical questions, provided advice and support, and kept me on track for the many years the work on this volume required. Friends and members of Deer Park Buddhist Center in Oregon, Wisconsin gave me warm friendship, continual encouragement, and generously offered places to stay when working in Madison.

I pray that I, and all others who read this work, will be able to put these teachings into practice and quickly attain enlightenment for the benefit all sentient beings. In this way may we repay the kindness of our teachers.

> Bodhicitta is supreme and most precious.
> Where it has not arisen may it arise.
> Where it has arisen may it never decline,
> And only grow stronger and stronger.

Sarva Mangalam

Beth Newman
Sarasota, Florida
Fall 2007

Technical Notes

REFERENCES

All works mentioned are referenced by their titles in English. Although there are many ways to render a particular title, we have employed the versions used in Cutler's translation of the *Lamrim Chenmo—The Great Treatise on the Stages of the Path to Enlightenment*—to make it simple for the reader to use both works.

At the first mention of a particular work we provide the title in its language of composition. Again, although scholars may find some irregularities, for the ease of the general reader we have followed the Sanskrit titles as they appear in *The Great Treatise on the Stages of the Path to Enlightenment.* The bibliography allows readers to find an English title and see the same title in Sanskrit (if applicable) and/or Tibetan.

PRONUNCIATION

Terms from Sanskrit and Tibetan that have become part of the English language appear without diacritic marks or Tibetan spelling.

Tibetan technical terms and names are spelled phonetically for ease of use of non-Tibetan speakers. Sanskrit technical terms that are not commonly used in English appear in this work with diacritic marks. These terms appear in the glossary in English alphabetical order.

The following rough guide to Sanskrit pronunciation is from *The Wonder That Was India,* by A. L. Basham.

The vowels *ā, ī, ū, e, ai, o,* and *au* are long and have approximately the same pronunciation as in Italian, or as the vowels in the English words *calm, machine, rule, prey, time, go,* and *cow,* respectively. The vowels *a, i,* and *u* are short and equivalent to the vowels in the English words *cut, bit,* and *bull.* Ṛ is classed as a short vowel and pronounced *ri* as in *rich.*

The aspirated consonants *th* and *ph* are pronounced as they are in the words *pothole* and *shepherd;* they are never pronounced as the English *thin* or *photo.*

C is pronounced *ch* as in *church*. Ś and ṣ are both generally pronounced as English *sh* as in *shape*. The distinction between the other subdotted retroflex consonants *(ṭ, ṭh, ḍ, ḍh, ṇ)* and the dentals (without subdots) is not important to the general reader.

STYLISTIC NOTE

Steps on the Path to Enlightenment is based on an oral commentary on Tsongkhapa's *Lamrim Chenmo* that Geshe Sopa gave to his students over the course of more than a decade. In turning Geshe-la's presentation into a series of books the editors have chosen to use an informal second-person voice. In contrast, the Tibetan language generally leaves person understood and is often rendered with an abstract third person: "one can do this" or "one should do that." We chose the second-person style in order to preserve something of the oral nature of the original and to create a more intimate bond between the author and the reader. The intent of Tsongkhapa and of Geshe Sopa was to give those who wish to embark on the path to enlightenment advice on how to proceed. This advice is offered here in the direct address of a teacher to his students.

STRUCTURE OF THE BOOK

The outline of headings in this book is drawn from Tsongkhapa's own outline of the *Lamrim Chenmo*. The chapter breaks and the format of the outline correspond to *The Great Treatise on the Stages of the Path to Enlightenment*, the English translation of the root text. The chapter numbers of this book correspond to volume 2 of that root text translation. The full outline for this volume is reproduced in the appendix.

Introduction

DURING HIS LIFETIME, Śākyamuni Buddha gave 84,000 teachings, each one an antidote to a human problem. Like a skilled doctor he diagnosed our problems and prescribed the medicine to alleviate it. Because we do not suffer from just one type of illness, there are many hundreds of volumes of Buddhist teachings, on many different subjects, from various points of view. The collected teachings are like a vast pharmacy; each teaching is a different medicine tailored to cure a specific disease.

Since Buddha passed away a long time ago, it can be difficult nowadays to sort out all his instructions. Fortunately, other great teachers put this advice into practice themselves and then organized it for their students. Tsongkhapa composed the *Lamrim Chenmo (Great Treatise on the Stages of the Path to Enlightenment)*[1] in order to draw out the essence of all the Buddha's teachings and arrange them in a practical, easy-to-follow format. The term *lamrim* literally means "stages of the path." The lamrim method is designed to lead a practitioner from the very beginning of his or her interest in spiritual practice all the way to perfect enlightenment. Drawing from the scriptures, Tsongkhapa explains what to do first, what to do next, which method is for which purpose, and how to practice at each stage.

The point of all these teachings is to transform our current state of dissatisfaction into one of true happiness. Buddhism, like every religion, teaches that real happiness is something more than ordinary pleasure. The lamrim teachings are not relevant for someone preoccupied with the fleeting enjoyment of the present life. Possessions, fame, and power are not spiritual goals. Unlike animals, humans have the capacity to attain something far superior to temporary pleasures. Tsongkhapa follows the great Indian master Atiśa in identifying three goals of spiritual practitioners: a good rebirth, complete freedom from cyclic rebirth, and the omniscience of enlightenment.

Although the teachings speak of three different spiritual goals, reached by three different paths, by people with three different levels of motivation, in practice these are not as distinct or divergent as they first appear. The various Buddhist teachings are not contradictory, and the paths do not lead in different directions. The paths progress from one to the next. To attain the highest goal of perfect enlightenment or buddhahood one starts by engaging in the practices designed to lead to the first goal, in the middle one takes up the practices leading to the intermediate goal, so that eventually one can practice the path leading to the final goal. It is like following a road to a destination: to get from here to there you must travel the whole route, but you can break your journey into stages with intermediate destinations along the way.

The lamrim explains how to reach all of these goals. Thus, the most valuable thing we can do in life is to study it and put the teachings into practice. That is why I taught this method for so many years. This is the third volume of five in the series *Steps on the Path to Enlightenment: A Commentary on Tsong-khapa's "Lamrim Chenmo."* A very brief overview of the lamrim will help to put this volume in context.

A GOOD REBIRTH

The first two volumes of this series outlined how to achieve the first two spiritual goals: a good rebirth free from the suffering of the lower realms and total emancipation from samsara, or cyclic existence. A good rebirth and individual liberation from samsara are considered lesser aims because they are pursued for the benefit of the practitioner alone. These goals and the practices to reach them are common to both Hinayana and Mahayana Buddhism. When we call the Hinayana the "lesser" or "smaller" vehicle, it is because its practices carry only the individual practitioner to freedom. In contrast, the "great vehicle" or Mahayana carries an enormous load—all living beings. The Mahayana practitioner practices the path to perfect him- or herself so that he or she will be able to help all others. Yet another reason the Hinayana is considered to be a lesser vehicle is because liberation from samsara, as incredibly wonderful as it is, still is limited in comparison to the knowledge, power, compassion, and love of a fully enlightened buddha. But the Hinayana is "small" only compared to the Mahayana; compared to the way beings ordinarily live their lives, the Hinayana path is truly great and profound.

To seek a good rebirth requires us to become disillusioned by the pursuit of temporary gratification in this life. To do this, we need to become cognizant of the inevitability of death. Only after recognizing the fleeting nature of life do people become worried about what will happen to them after they die. According to Buddhism, happiness and suffering do not occur randomly, without causes. The causes are our actions, the *karma* we create, which will result in our future experiences. Karmic causation is a law of nature; we must be convinced that sooner or later our positive actions will yield happiness and our negative actions will bring us trouble and misery. If we engage in negative actions, we are creating the causes for misery in a future life.

Once we are born in inferior conditions, things tend to go from bad to worse. Our habituation to negative actions leads us to do harmful things. Those actions will yield a less-fortunate rebirth, and if that life goes poorly, the next rebirth will be even worse. It is important to consider the truly unpleasant results that can come about from our actions. If we are not aware of the misery that awaits us, we will do nothing to prevent it. So the question becomes, what can protect us from the misery of unfortunate rebirths?

The only real refuge is the Triple Gem: Buddha, Dharma, and Sangha. Buddha is a supreme teacher instructing us how to prevent the kind of suffering that we fear most—rebirth in the lower realms. The Dharma is the method itself. It explains how to completely reverse our negative habits and lead a pure life so that our wholesome actions will increase and ensure happy results. The Sangha consists of fellow practitioners who help us put the method into practice because they are following it themselves. In short, taking refuge involves properly following valid spiritual teachings. Those seeking a good rebirth must therefore act in a positive manner. There is no other way to cure the deep sickness of suffering in cyclic existence.

A strong and stable focus on using this life to create the causes for better lives in the future is the beginning of the spiritual path. It is the mark of a person who has developed the attitude of a person of small spiritual capacity. The goal is "small" because rebirth within the upper realms is a relatively short-term objective. A high rebirth will not last forever; it is not something definitively, permanently good. It is a valid goal, however, because a good rebirth—particularly a so-called perfect human rebirth—is a necessary foundation for further spiritual progress.

Freedom from Suffering

Persons of intermediate spiritual capacity aspire to attain complete emancipation from all contaminated rebirths. They strive to develop a strong and spontaneous desire to be free from even the higher rebirths. Therefore they contemplate the suffering of the upper realms in great detail. The way to develop revulsion for the defects of every type of life in samsara is to understand the twelve links of dependent origination and the four noble truths: the truth of suffering, the truth of the cause of suffering, the truth of the cessation of suffering, and the truth of the path to cessation. If we do not think about the faults of what we currently label "happiness," we will have no desire to be free from it. Further, if we do not consider which causes result in misery, which causes result in happiness, and how causation works, we will not understand the method to cut the root of samsara.

Why do we suffer cyclic rebirth? In general, the primary causes of misery are the three poisonous mental afflictions: ignorance, desire, and hatred. Of the three, ignorance is the most fundamental, since it is the cause of the other two. In brief, ignorance is a totally mistaken conception about oneself and the external world. We grasp at things as truly existing, but our selves and phenomena do not exist in the way that they appear to us. Based on this mistaken perception, attachment or aversion for the object arises.

The most pernicious ignorance is the way we misconceive of ourselves. We believe that we are truly real, and on the basis of this mistaken perception, we become obsessed with our own welfare. We become attached to what we desire, crave security, and fear losing what we have. So much mental turmoil springs from the ground of this ignorance, including all the other branches of the mental afflictions, such as jealousy, pride, anger, and attachment. Together, ignorance and the other mental afflictions lead us to act selfishly. Our self-centered physical, verbal, and mental actions then tie us to every type of misery.

The measure of someone who has developed the attitude of a person of intermediate spiritual capacity is the continuous and spontaneous desire to be free from samsara and its causes. This is not a thought that comes up just for a moment. It is not something that is strong one day and forgotten the next. Of course it is good to have even short-lived, occasional thoughts of renunciation, but that is not enough to produce the goal desired here—complete, definite, and unalterable freedom from rebirth in samsara. Renunciation of samsara is a thought that must spontaneously arise all the time and dominate all other thoughts and actions: day and night we must want to be free from the cycle of rebirth.

Therefore the person seeking freedom is not only very concerned with understanding what binds us to samsara; he or she must also comprehend what leads to emancipation. In general the path to freedom consists of the three trainings: ethical discipline *(śīla)*, concentration *(samādhi)*, and the wisdom that realizes the true nature of reality *(prajñā)*. Wisdom, the direct realization of the nature of the person and phenomena, is what eliminates ignorance. By eliminating ignorance we get rid of all the causes of misery and suffering. Wisdom can only be developed by a stable and concentrated mind. Mental stability, in turn, is only attained on the foundation of ethical discipline. In this way ethical discipline, concentration, and wisdom work together and result in emancipation from suffering or even complete enlightenment.

Ethical conduct is basic training; it is the front line in the battle against our worst enemy—the mental afflictions. They are the enemy because they make us do negative things that directly and indirectly harm us. If they dominate the mind, we are powerless to create pure good karma. If we do not reduce the mental afflictions, we will wander in samsara forever. So, in order to practice ethical discipline, we have to recognize and then fight this enemy in all its major and minor forms. We have to know how the mental afflictions function, their faults, and the benefits of being free from them. This is not just book knowledge; we have to be aware when and how the mental afflictions arise in the mind. We have to be mindful so that we can apply the antidote to them. We want to be able to stop them before they arise, catch them early, or at least slow them down by doing some other virtuous thing. For this reason, ethical discipline is discussed in detail in the context of the practices of the person of intermediate spiritual capacity.

THE PRACTITIONER OF THE GREAT VEHICLE

The latter two trainings are part of the practices of the person of great spiritual capacity. In this volume we learn how to develop the motivation and engage in the practices to attain the highest goal: complete and perfect enlightenment. The motivation to practice the Mahayana rests on the foundation of the previously discussed basic practices. We engage in the practices for those of small and intermediate spiritual capacity because only when we clearly understand the nature of our situation and its causes can we expand our perspective and see that our parents, relatives, friends, and all other sentient beings are in the same condition. Only when we strongly desire emancipation from our current state can we expand our scope and desire to free others as well. A person with great spiritual capacity sees that if we engage in religious practice and succeed in attaining only our own emancipation, we would leave all other sentient beings in misery. How could such a selfish state of affairs make us peaceful and happy? Wanting others to be from suffering and wishing that they too have the highest perfect emancipation and happiness is the seed of the attitude of a person of great spiritual capacity.

The practitioner of the great vehicle is someone who has taken on a great responsibility; his or her objective is to ensure that all sentient beings attain freedom and happiness. How can we achieve that goal? Right now we can help others on a small scale, but our ability to help is limited and imperfect. What kind of power, knowledge, abilities, and circumstances are required to help all other living creatures attain a blissful, liberated state? No one, not even a buddha, can just place another sentient being in a state of buddhahood. Nor can anyone wash away the negative actions of another sentient being. No one can pluck out the root of others' misery as if it were a splinter, or insert one's own realizations into their minds.

The only way to lead others to perfect happiness is to show them the way to remove their ignorance and mental afflictions. If we have not done so ourselves, how can we help others to do it? Only when we are perfect ourselves can we perfectly help others. Therefore, a Mahayana practitioner dedicates all his or her actions, life, and mental effort to becoming a fully enlightened buddha. This motivation is called *bodhicitta,* the desire to attain complete enlightenment in order to be able to benefit all sentient beings. Even though the primary objective of bodhicitta is one's own enlightenment, the goal of omniscience and perfect freedom from samsara is not one's own selfish pleasure. The Mahayana practitioner's desire for enlightenment comes from pure compassion and love for all others; he or she knows that attainment of buddhahood is the most effective way to help all other sentient beings who are miserable and in need of assistance. When this attitude arises spontaneously, all the time, and without effort, one has developed bodhicitta and become a bodhisattva.

Bodhicitta is the central practice of Mahayana Buddhism. The Buddha taught two Mahayana vehicles: the *Paramitayana,* also called the *Sutrayana* because it is the path following the sutras, and the *Vajrayana,* the tantric vehicle. Bodhicitta is the doorway into both vehicles. It is the essential motivation behind every practice on both Mahayana paths. Since bodhicitta leads us to buddhahood, it fulfills both our own and all others' wishes. In that sense bodhicitta is often praised as being the essence of the great variety of teachings taught by the Buddha. From this point of view it is the most important spiritual practice; it is where we should expend our greatest effort.

Bodhicitta is the method side of the Mahayana path. It is with bodhicitta that wisdom—one's realization of emptiness and the four noble truths—becomes powerful enough to lead to buddhahood. Hinayana practitioners must also develop wisdom to attain liberation, because the insight that directly apprehends the true nature of reality is the destroyer of ignorance. But wisdom alone is not enough to result in the omniscience of enlightenment. Wisdom is like a sharp blade, but even a power tool needs a power source, a sturdy handle, and other things to be effective. In this case the power and direction are provided by the spontaneous attitude of bodhicitta; with bodhicitta everything we do, in every moment, is for the benefit of others. Whether awake or asleep, walking, eating, reading, doing a religious practice, or meditating, every activity becomes a Mahayana practice. With bodhicitta all our actions are virtuous, and every moment we accumulate great merit. Without bodhicitta, even the highest esoteric tantric practices are mere worldly magic, whereas with it they are the quickest path to enlightenment.

THE WAY TO DEVELOP BODHICITTA

It is easy to understand what bodhicitta is; but it is difficult and takes a great deal of practice for this attitude to arise spontaneously and constantly. We can achieve it, however, and in the *Lamrim Chenmo* Tsongkhapa explains two methods to develop it. The first is called the *sevenfold cause-and-effect personal instructions.* Originally taught by the great master Atiśa, this method includes six successive steps, the causes, that culminate in bodhicitta, the result. The first step is to recognize all sentient beings as having been our mother. The second is to recognize all our mothers' kindness toward us. We usually don't think of how kind they are, but when we follow the outline in the instructions, we may be so amazed and grateful for their kindness that we want to cry. The third step is a desire to repay their kindness. These first three causes together produce the fourth, a special affectionate love for all mother sentient beings. Based on affectionate love, the fifth step, compassion, arises. Compassion is the desire to free all sentient beings from the unbearable suffering of samsara. When compassion becomes exceptionally strong, it is more than a simple wish that others be free from misery; it becomes a determination to take personal responsibility to free others from suffering. This special type of compassion, called the *superior thought,* is the sixth cause, and it directly gives rise to bodhicitta, the result.

The second method of mental training to develop bodhicitta was taught by Śāntideva; it is called *exchanging self and others.* Exchanging self and others does not mean that you become someone else and that person becomes you; it also does not mean that you hand your happiness over to others and take their misery in exchange. That cannot be done; what we can do is reverse our mindset. We can replace our self-centered desire for our own happiness with a wish for others to have happiness. The practice of exchanging self and others is to replace selfish egotism with sincere caring for others.

You may think this is impossible, but it is possible because both selfishness and loving compassion are relative—they are dependent upon thought. The basis for this practice is a correct perception of the dependent, relative nature of reality. This may sound daunting, but in fact we are all quite familiar with this on an ordinary level. Consider how we usually think about other people; if we concentrate only on the negative things they did in the past, are doing in the present, and might possibly do in the future, we make them seem so completely horrible that we cannot stand to be around them. If at some point these repulsive enemies give us a nice present or praise us, we may begin to reconsider our opinion. We try to forget the negative things and add up the positive things they have done for us and for others. We may come to like them a little bit, and after a while they may become our best friends. Then, even if they do negative things, we do not notice. Where before we saw the others as evil, now we see them as wonderful. Where before we could not stand to hear their names, now we cannot bear being apart from them for a moment. This change is a result of our thought process. If we can change our thinking 180 degrees like this toward one person, why not toward all sentient beings? Everyone can change. We simply need to learn the proper method and then practice it. We have the capability; if we use our intelligence and put in the effort, we can become completely compassionate and develop bodhicitta.

THE PERFECTIONS

Bodhicitta is the foundation of Mahayana practice, but as wonderful and necessary as it is, it is not enough on its own. Bodhicitta is just a thought; we have to put our intention into action. Simply wanting to go somewhere does not get us there; we must make preparations and actually travel. To fulfill our intention to take on the responsibility to alleviate all the suffering of all others, we must make a great effort to attain buddhahood. There are an almost incalculable number and variety of actions that must be done to perfect oneself and become a buddha. These activities are organized in various ways to make them easier to practice: two collections, three trainings, six perfections, or ten perfections. Tsongkhapa says that the six perfections—generosity, ethical discipline, patience, perseverance, meditative stabilization, and wisdom—are the most practical way to approach the activities of a bodhisattva.

The first three perfections—generosity, ethical discipline, and patience—enable us to control our senses and keep our actions pure. The fourth perfection, perseverance, is joy in the practice of virtue even when one is tired, sick, or the task is difficult. The fifth perfection deals with harnessing the mind and developing the ability to concentrate on whatever we wish for as long as we want. We need this powerful mental instrument in order to practice meditating on the sixth perfection—the perfection of wisdom. Wisdom—understanding the true nature of the self and other phenomena—is essential in order to break the chains of ignorance and attain liberation and enlightenment. This volume includes an extensive explanation of the first four perfections and a summary of the perfections of meditative stabilization and wisdom. The last two perfections are such important and complex practices that the next two volumes of this series expand on them in great detail.

Each perfection supports and is part of the practice of the others. To attain perfect enlightenment we need all the perfections because they encompass every aspect of method and wisdom. The first five perfections are the method and the sixth is wisdom. Why do we need the combination of method and wisdom to attain perfect enlightenment? Because to go anywhere we must both be able to see where we are going and have the physical ability and energy to travel there. If we have wisdom but lack the method, it is like being able to see where we want to go but having no means of travel. If we have the method practices but lack wisdom we are blind; we cannot see if we are on the right path or walking into danger. If we practice all six perfections, we have a perfect vehicle that will carry us to buddhahood.

Intended for Practice

The point of the Mahayana teachings is mental and spiritual development. Think about what you read in this volume with an open mind. Do not simply accept these ideas with blind faith, or reject these ideas out of hand. When you first encounter a new idea, you may not understand all the details. You may have doubts and questions, but the second time you come across the concept you will understand more. In order to make things clear for contemporary students, I have added examples, quoted other texts, and mentioned various interpretations of Tsongkhapa's text. As you read this commentary you may want to read the *Lamrim Chenmo*[2] itself and examine my explanation in light of Tsongkhapa's words.

You may become enthusiastic about what you read here, but if you do not practice these teachings they will not help you very much. Test the instructions by applying them in your daily life; see if they provide useful antidotes to negative patterns of behavior and help you develop better ways of relating to others. Only with long-term practice can we become more patient and compassionate, and have less animosity and attachment. Remember, Mahayana practice is not only for one's own achievement; the key is benefiting other sentient beings. The emphasis of these teachings is developing concern for others, trying to help them and not harm them. Even while we are trying to reach our own perfection, our main focus is on other sentient beings. When the mind is strongly directed in this way, our attitudes and behavior will definitely change. Every situation can be an opportunity for spiritual practice if we apply the Buddhist teachings intelligently. No matter what happens we will be calm and loving. When the mind is positive and strong, we will act accordingly, and as a result others will naturally like us more. They will want to be near us so they can learn the method as well. This volume concludes with the way to draw others to us in order to teach them the practices we have mastered.

In summary, we can develop the bodhisattva motivation to attain complete enlightenment in order to save all others from drowning in the ocean of samsara. In order to prepare ourselves to benefit others, we must train day and night to accumulate merit and wisdom. All the necessary methods are contained in the practice of the six perfections. The Buddha himself practiced, fully accomplished, and then taught these perfections. All the great bodhisattvas and spiritual masters from the Buddha to the present have practiced them and handed them down to us.

Right now we have every condition needed for Mahayana spiritual practice. If we use this opportunity, emancipation and even buddhahood are within reach. Even if we just improve a little bit, it is certainly something to rejoice about; it is a sign our practice is succeeding. If we gradually and systematically apply ourselves to the stages of the path in this and future lives, we will definitely achieve perfect, complete enlightenment and will provide the greatest help to all other living beings.

❖ 1 ❖

The Stages of the Path for Persons of Great Capacity

3) Training the mind in the stages of the path for persons of great spiritual capacity
   a) Showing that developing bodhicitta is the only entrance to the Mahayana
   b) How to develop bodhicitta
      i) How bodhicitta depends on certain causes to arise
         a' The way to produce bodhicitta depending on four conditions
         b' The way to produce bodhicitta depending on four causes
         c' The way to produce bodhicitta depending on four powers

———❖———

THE KIND of existence we have right now is the most excellent and powerful type of life. According to Buddhism most sentient beings do not have a life like this; most are born in the hells, as spirits, or as animals. Even if they are human their lives are often not peaceful or fortunate. In those circumstances they are not able to accomplish what they desire—everlasting peace and happiness. But we have a wonderful situation: we have physical and mental abilities, wealth, teachers, teachings, and other environmental conditions conducive for practice. From a spiritual point of view this is the most difficult type of life to attain. For a long, long time we may not have had a life with qualities like this; we have it now, but soon we will lose it and many eons may pass during which we will not have anything like it again. Because a human life of leisure and fortune gives us the opportunity to achieve a religious goal, it is not something to squander on temporary sensual pleasure; we should use it instead to gain everlasting bliss. We have everything we need, both external and internal, to succeed in achieving the highest spiritual goals. Even if we do not achieve our final goal, we can accomplish a great deal in this life.

Usually we waste our time because we do not appreciate the positive conditions that we have. This life is like a wish-granting jewel. How should we use it? While we can use it to benefit just ourselves, we can go beyond our selfish pursuits and use it to benefit all sentient beings. We all suffer in samsara; life after life, again and again, we endure birth, aging, sickness, and death. We cycle up and down without choice. Consider whether there is any method for all beings to attain freedom from this situation. If there is such a method, is it possible for us to follow it successfully? We need to study to learn how to use our fortunate life to achieve liberation.

Spiritual practitioners can be divided into three levels from the point of view of their fundamental goals.[1] The most basic spiritual goal is a high rebirth; a person striving for this goal engages in religious practice in order to prevent him- or herself from falling into lower rebirths in the future. A desire for complete emancipation from all suffering, not just from the lower rebirths but from the entire unsatisfactory cycle of samsara, is the intermediate spiritual goal. An individual of intermediate spiritual capacity fully comprehends the suffering nature of all samsara. Suffering is not just one small thing; there are many, many types of misery. This distress is not something of short duration; it is not something that lasts only a few years or even one lifetime. We have suffered in these many different ways since beginningless time. Realizing that he or she will continue to suffer endlessly into the future unless countermeasures are taken, a person with intermediate spiritual capacity engages in the three trainings: ethical conduct *(śila)*, meditative stabilization *(samādhi)*, and wisdom *(prajñā)*. It is through these practices that we can become free of uncontrolled rebirth.

But even their own liberation from samsara is not enough for those with great spiritual capacity. They see that all other sentient beings are in the same miserable situation—they all create the causes of misery and undergo the resulting suffering. Spiritual practitioners of great capacity feel intense compassion for these poor beings and decide to take on the responsibility to help them eliminate their suffering. However, even the practice of the three trainings does not completely equip them to help all others. Personal liberation from uncontrolled rebirth is not enough. They must attain complete enlightenment, because without the perfect qualities of a buddha they will not be able to save all other living beings. The great teacher Atiśa explains the nature of an individual of great spiritual capacity as follows:[2]

> Someone who wants to completely eliminate
> All the suffering of others,
> Having compared it to one's own,
> Is a person of great spiritual capacity.

Tsongkhapa quotes Aśvaghoṣa's *Compendium of the Perfections (Pāramitā-samāsa)* to make a similar point:[3]

> They completely abandon the two lower vehicles,
> Which have no means to fulfill the aims of the world,
> To enter the vehicle compassionately taught by the Buddha
> That has only one flavor—helping others.

By properly understanding the nature of reality we see everything as if it were a dream. We recognize that under the power of karma and the mental afflictions sentient beings are sometimes born in the lowest hells, sometimes have an intermediate birth, and are sometimes born in the highest kingdom of the gods. They cycle without control because they are dominated by ignorance. Not seeing things as they truly are, they act badly and their evil actions bring them suffering. How could it be right to work for just our own bliss when all living beings are like exhausted travelers who have used up their provisions and are wandering the wrong way in search of a place to rest? If we attain perfect enlightenment we will be like an oasis that satisfies the wishes of fatigued sentient beings; we will be able to provide everything necessary to alleviate their problems and misery. One of the key spiritual attitudes for the being of great spiritual capacity is the desire to help others have blissful happiness. This mindset is the essence of all the great variety of instructions taught by the Buddha. As Aśvaghoṣa says:

> When you see happiness and unhappiness as a dream
> And that the faults of ignorance cause sentient beings to degenerate,
> How could it be right to strive for your own goals
> While forsaking joy in pure actions that accomplish others' goals?

As Mahayana practitioners we must first recognize the adverse experiences we will have to confront if we continue to drown in the ocean of samsara. Then we must see that all other sentient beings are in the same situation. Other sentient beings do not have the eye of wisdom; they cannot distinguish what should be done and what should not be done. They are in great danger because they are acting in ways that will lead them to disaster in their next life. If they fall down to the lower realms they may not be able to get out for millions and millions of lifetimes. They are in a pitiable situation. Imagine your mother blindly stumbling along a path on the edge of a precipice. If she takes a misstep she could fall to her death. How could you see this and not help her? If you have the ability to lead her to safety but let her walk on by herself it would be utterly shameful, even evil. Bodhisattvas are not like that;

they clearly see all sentient beings stumbling through life unable to discern what is dangerous. They perceive each one of these pitiful beings as their own dear mother who is about to fall into great misery because she is blind to the true nature of things. They know it is not right to lack compassion for others; they know it is not right to avoid helping others. As a result they do everything they can to benefit other sentient beings.

The same text continues:

> When a prince of the lineage that benefits worldly beings
> Sees others stumbling, their wisdom eye tightly shut,
> How could that bodhisattva not have compassion arise?
> How could he not make an effort to remove their ignorance?

A bodhisattva is a prince in the lineage of the victorious one, the Buddha. This means that the bodhisattva is destined to become a buddha. Bodhisattvas have special qualities—they have developed bodhicitta and have realized or are striving to realize śūnyatā. Bodhisattvas see that most sentient beings lack the wisdom necessary to become free from suffering. There is no way a bodhisattva can be comfortable for even a moment without doing something to assist others. All day and all night a bodhisattva's body, speech, and mind are focused on benefiting others.

This kind of practice is the great vehicle, the Mahayana. It is the way to bring all other sentient beings to enlightenment. Someone who carries the burden of helping others attain their utmost desires is the most excellent type of person. It is not very admirable to be proficient at doing things only for yourself. Even some animals are very good at taking care of themselves and defeating others. I have heard stories about birds that steal other birds' eggs and drop them on a rock to kill the fledglings before they hatch. Later when that killer bird builds a nest, to get revenge the first bird comes and drops its eggs on the very same rock. But it is the nature of a truly excellent person that all his or her actions are for the benefit of others. Such people give happiness even to those who have harmed them. The great yogi Śāntideva says that such a person is a source of happiness and peace:[4]

> I bow down to the body of someone
> Who has produced this precious mind.
> I take refuge in this source of happiness
> That gives bliss even to those who have harmed.

Usually if we injure others they respond by trying to damage us more. But bodhisattvas never retaliate no matter how much harm others do to them. They understand that when others want to injure them it is because they are unhappy and under the power of ignorance. It is as if they have taken a drug that has made them insane. Wise people do not get angry if a friend or a loved one attacks them. They know something must be seriously wrong inside to make the person act that way, so the sick person becomes an object of even more love and compassion. Bodhisattvas cannot be happy until the other person is cured, so they try to give others peace and happiness. There are many stories about the Buddha before he attained enlightenment that illustrate this point. Once five flesh-eating demons begged for his body. As he gave it to them the bodhisattva thought, "By giving my body to satisfy these creatures, in the future may I be able to lead them to emancipation. May they become my first disciples when I attain buddhahood." Although the demons did appalling things, the bodhisattva's love and special dedication caused them to be the first to hear his teaching of the Dharma when he delivered his first discourse at the Deer Park in Sarnath.

The mind under the power of bodhicitta is dominated by compassion and love. Kind affection is always the source of both temporary and everlasting peace and happiness for individuals and the world in general. As a result of actions done purely for the benefit of other sentient beings we will accomplish our goals. This will occur naturally, even if we do not want something good for ourselves. For example, if you plant some apple seeds you will naturally get trees with leaves, flowers, and branches. You are planting to get apples, but you get the leaves anyway. Similarly, with the great method of the Mahayana you can accomplish many things. The Hinayana method is not like this; if we work only for our own purposes, not only will we not be able to place others in a state of happiness and freedom, we may not even achieve our own goal.

Think about the benefits of bodhicitta because the more good qualities you see, the more you will want to obtain this precious mind. Hearing, recollecting, and, of course, truly integrating Mahayana practice into your life will help you and other sentient beings. Even on first hearing about the Mahayana attitude we can begin to eliminate aspects of selfishness. Gradually, as we recollect the nature of bodhicitta and make an effort to dedicate our actions to helping other sentient beings, we can alleviate other kinds of suffering. And it goes without saying that we will ultimately attain the highest freedom and omniscience. Therefore, now that we have the opportunity to practice the Mahayana, we should think, "Wow! What an excellent chance! If I were a cat, a dog, or a pig I would not have an opportunity to practice.

This human life gives me the ability to accomplish this path." This thought should make you very happy. A bodhisattva relishes how very worthwhile this kind of life is because it enables him or her to take on the responsibility of benefiting other sentient beings. With this type of thought we enter the Mahayana path.

Seeing the beneficial qualities of the Mahayana path draws us toward it. Then we have to consider how to practice this path. What causes, conditions, and methods produce bodhicitta? Where can we obtain them? Detailed answers to these questions are found in the teachings. Aśvaghoṣa's *Compendium of the Perfections* says:

> The supreme vehicle is accomplished by pure wisdom.
> It comes from omniscient buddhas.
> This vehicle is like an eye for worldly beings;
> It is like moonlight and the light of the rising sun.

To reach the destination at the end of the best path of practice we must eliminate ignorance. Pure wisdom is the main instrument to accomplish that. *Pure* can have many meanings. In the Mahayana context *pure wisdom* means wisdom free from selfishness. The various stages of wisdom are purified by combining them with compassion, love, and the great Mahayana method of bodhicitta.

Where did we get this method? It comes from the victorious ones, the omniscient buddhas. They taught others this technique based on their experience of successful practice of the path to enlightenment. At first wisdom comes from extensive study—we learn from a teacher and from books. After we have learned about the goal and the method to attain it, we analyze what we have studied. We establish our understanding by independent examination. Once we understand things through the first two techniques, we meditate on these topics.

The Mahayana vehicle is like an eye for those who have no sight because it illuminates the world. There are two natural sources of light: at night the moon sheds a cool light, and then the rising sun burns away darkness. The brightness of the method side—compassion and love—is like the moon. The wisdom that comprehends true reality is like the sun because it destroys the darkness of ignorance. Since Mahayana practice combines the highest method and highest wisdom, it is the principal cause for our own and others' enlightenment.

Intelligent people examine the benefit of a goal before they begin a task. Only if they find that the result is worth it will they try to attain it. Here we have to become convinced about the good qualities of the Mahayana goal. Our enthusiasm about beginning to practice the path is dependent upon thinking about its benefits again and again. Seriously following the path—in other words, actually doing the practices—requires great respect for the method. Therefore it is important for beginners to learn about the qualities of the Mahayana, analyze them, and finally integrate them into the mind through meditation. Blindly entering the Mahayana path does not have great benefit. If we do not know what we are doing and why we are doing it, our practice will be hesitant and weak. With the respect that comes from wisdom, our motivation to enter the path will be strong.

Now we can look at how a person with great spiritual capacity enters the Mahayana path and then engages in its practices.

3) TRAINING THE MIND IN THE STAGES OF THE PATH FOR PERSONS OF GREAT SPIRITUAL CAPACITY

Practice is training the mind. An ignorant mind creates all our pain and trouble. Each vehicle of the Buddhist path has various levels of practice to gain control over the wild untamed mind. The Mahayana path as explained in the lamrim has three stages of practice:

a) Showing that developing bodhicitta is the only entrance to the Mahayana
b) How to develop bodhicitta (chapters 1–6)
c) How to learn the bodhisattva deeds after developing bodhicitta (chapters 7–14, and volumes 4 and 5 of this series)

It is most important to understand what the Mahayana path is and how to embark on it. Therefore Tsongkhapa first explains that the main door to the path is bodhicitta. What is bodhicitta? The details will come later, but in essence *bodhicitta* is the thought to attain perfect enlightenment in order to save all other sentient beings. The second section explains how to produce this thought. We have sophisticated mental abilities; if we use them properly, even this short life provides the opportunity to produce this attitude. Bodhicitta is a special positive mindset, but it is not enough. We should actually do something to help others. The third topic explains what we should do after generating bodhicitta. Bodhicitta is the motivation that propels us to do various activities called the bodhisattva deeds. Thus, the final section details how a bodhisattva should think, speak, and act until he or she attains enlightenment.

a) Showing that developing bodhicitta is the only entrance to the Mahayana

The Mahayana path of practice has two main divisions: the Paramitayana, also known as the Sutrayana, and the Tantrayana, also known as the Mantrayana. There are an almost measureless number of Mahayana practices, but only one determines whether you have entered the Mahayana path; if you have it you have entered the path, but if you do not have it you have not entered either part of the Mahayana path. What is that special thing? The gate of entry is bodhicitta. As soon as you have a spontaneous wish to attain perfect enlightenment in order to save all other sentient beings you have entered the Mahayana path and become a bodhisattva.

Without bodhicitta, no matter what you do you will not be on the Mahayana path. Even if you meditate on śūnyatā or practice great tantric rituals, they are not part of the Mahayana path if they are done out of selfishness, wanting to be free of demons, desiring a long life, or yearning for wealth. Tsongkhapa said if bodhicitta rises once, but then we lose it and practice with some other motivation, we have left the Mahayana path. Our practices will fall into the Hinayana or some other tradition. The Buddha taught this in various sutras, and many other great teachers explained this in the śāstras. This point can even be proved logically.

The great bodhisattva and yogi Śāntideva said in *Engaging in the Bodhi-sattva Deeds (Bodhisattva-caryāvatāra)*:

> The moment someone produces bodhicitta,
> Even the most pitiful being in the prison of samsara
> Will be called a son of the sugatas[5]
> And worshipped by worldly men and gods.

As soon as someone produces bodhicitta, even if that being is in a lower rebirth, the buddhas will call him or her their child. Such a person is virtually a prince in the line of buddhas. In a worldly context the duty of a prince is to prepare himself to become a leader of many people. It is not for his own sake that he engages in training; to be a world emperor he has to become worthy of his subjects' respect. In a similar way, but on a higher level, the king of the Mahayana is the Buddha. Spontaneously wanting to become the leader and protector of all sentient beings is like being born a son or daughter of the Buddha. This person's duty is to attain perfect enlightenment in order to help all sentient beings. It is in this way that he or she becomes worthy of the worship of all beings in the world. So the moment we produce this thought we can rejoice and say:

> Today I was born in the lineage of the Buddha;
> From now on I am a prince of the Buddha.

The *Life of Maitreya (Ārya-maitreya-vimokṣa)* says that there is no comparison between bodhicitta and any other religious practice. The text uses the analogy of a diamond—the most precious of all stones—to show that if we possess this attitude we are great bodhisattvas even if we have not yet started doing any of the bodhisattvas' measureless deeds:

> Even a broken diamond is superior to all special golden ornaments. It does not lose the name *precious stone* and it can reverse all poverty. Similarly, noble child, even those who are not exerting themselves in the precious diamond practices after producing the mind to attain omniscience, they still overshadow all the golden ornaments of the good qualities of śrāvakas and pratyekabuddhas. They do not lose the name *bodhisattva* and can reverse all the poverty of samsara.

Bodhicitta is the desire to attain omniscience or perfect enlightenment in order to help all other sentient beings reach that state. Those with this desire generally take the bodhisattva vow; they formally promise to act in accord with their wish until all sentient beings attain enlightenment. No matter how much trouble or suffering ensues, they ignore themselves and work for others. Even without taking the vow or engaging in bodhisattva actions, this mere intention outshines any practice of virtue by the śrāvakas and pratyekabuddhas. The greatest virtuous practices of the Hinayana practitioners cannot compare to the thought of bodhicitta because bodhicitta is the antidote of all others' lack of happiness and joy.

Nāgārjuna says in the *Precious Garland (Ratnāvalī)* that bodhicitta is the root of the tree that bears the fruit of enlightenment for oneself and other beings:

> If I and all sentient beings in the world
> Wish to attain highest enlightenment,
> We must have its root:
> Bodhicitta as firm as the king of mountains.

All the branches and flowers of the Mahayana come from the root of bodhicitta. They cannot grow without it. Our bodhicitta should not be shaky or arise for just a few minutes. If it is not established as firmly as a mountain, we will lose it as soon as we face some difficulties.

Tsongkhapa quotes a few of the many sutras and śāstras that point out the importance of producing bodhicitta and then making it firm. In the *Tantra Bestowing the Initiation of Vajrapāṇi (Vajrapāṇi-abhiṣeka-mahā-tantra)* Mañjuśrī asked Vajrapāṇi:

> The mandala of great mantras is very extensive and profound. It is difficult to measure its depth. It is the most secret of secrets. It is not suitable to teach to ordinary sentient beings. Vajrapāṇi, you gave this most rare teaching that has not been heard in the past. So, to what type of disciple should this be taught?

Mañjuśrī's question is: "To whom can we teach the great and secret tantric Dharma?" In an ordinary sense certain activities are dangerous so we keep them secret from children. Although a machine may be useful, it also can be destructive so we do not want children touching it until they reach a certain level of maturity. In the same way tantric teachings are not suitable for just anyone; the practices are complex and most people have many obscurations. Until disciples reach a suitable level of spiritual development, instead of being helpful these teachings are dangerous. Vajrapāṇi then explains to Mañjuśrī who can be taught this practice:

> Mañjuśrī, when those who have begun the practice of meditating on bodhicitta come to attain it, they are bodhisattvas. They are practicing the bodhisattva deeds to enter the door to the secret mantra. They may enter the mandala of secret mantra that is bestowed with a great wisdom initiation. But those who have not fully actualized bodhicitta should not enter. They should not be shown the mandala.

Vajrapāṇi is saying that you can give the initiation to enter the mandala to anyone who has attained bodhicitta. *Attainment of bodhicitta* means that the wish to attain enlightenment for the benefit of other sentient beings arises spontaneously and unshakably all the time. Someone who attains bodhicitta is a bodhisattva and is ready to engage in tantric practice. Those who have not attained bodhicitta should not undertake tantric practice. Actually not only does *secret* mean that those who lack bodhicitta should not enter the mandala, they should not even be shown it.

According to the great Mahayana tradition, there are two levels of the teachings: outer and inner. The inner refers to a higher more technical level that requires great skill to practice. It necessitates prior training. For example, if you want to fly to the moon you have to know how to operate many complex machines before take-off. A child or ordinary person may want to go, but because they are not prepared it would be very dangerous to let them have the controls. For similar reasons the Mahayana path has two levels. First one practices the Paramitayana to learn the various methods, especially bodhicitta. Only after engaging in those outer practices is one prepared to engage in the very powerful practices of the Tantrayana. Why? Because if someone's mind is completely under the power of bodhicitta, their motivation is always to eliminate others' problems and give them happiness. Whatever that person does will be wholly positive. In contrast if someone is self-centered, whatever he or she does brings harm to him- or herself and others. If people motivated by selfishness do tantric practices there could be great negative consequences. So in ancient times tantric teachings were strictly controlled. Spiritual teachers had close contact with their disciples and strictly monitored what they practiced.

Tsongkhapa says that it is not enough to say that a practice is a part of the Mahayana. If the outer Mahayana practices—such as reading Mahayana texts—or inner Mahayana tantric rituals are done with a selfish attitude they are not Mahayana practice. The key to Mahayana practice is bodhicitta. Some people claim to be Mahayana practitioners; however their practice is superficial because they merely understand bodhicitta but have not produced it in their hearts. One must have all the characteristics of bodhicitta fully developed in the mind to be a real Mahayana practitioner.

Therefore bodhicitta is the most essential practice among all the Buddha's teachings. If you churn milk eventually you will get the essence of it: butter; similarly, if you shake out the teachings it is bodhicitta that will emerge because the essence of the Dharma is nonharming. In general Hinayana practice entails refraining from harming others; this frees the practitioner from creating negative causes and experiencing the resultant suffering. In addition to this, a Mahayana practitioner takes on the responsibility to bring others happiness and clear away their misery. This attitude is far beyond the ordinary. If this thought dominates you, not only is there no way you would harm others, all your actions will only benefit sentient beings. If you have bodhicitta your activities will lead to the highest bliss for all. Once this thought is as firm and unshakable as a mountain there is no limit to what you can do. As long as you do not have it everything you do is small because you cannot accomplish great things with an inferior approach. It is a difficult attitude to produce, but it is most beneficial. It is worth the effort no matter how long it takes to develop. Many former great sages and famous teachers in India spent years and years, sometimes their entire lives, studying with many teachers and employing numerous techniques in order to produce this precious thought.

The *Array of Stalks Sutra (Gaṇḍa-vyūha-sūtra)* explains the greatness of bodhicitta through many analogies. Let's look at just one example: "Bodhicitta is the seed of all the excellent qualities of buddhahood." It is important to have a clear understanding of this statement. We know that everything grows from a principal cause with many supporting causes and conditions. For example, to grow an apple tree, the special or uncommon cause is an apple seed. But you also need water, soil, fertilizer, sunshine, and many other things to bring any kind of seed to sprout and grow. If these common causes converge with rice seeds, rice will grow; if they come together with barley seeds, barley will grow. It is the seed that is specific to a particular type of plant. It is similar for spiritual attainments: a particular cause brings its own special result, but certain conditions are necessary for all accomplishments. All the causes and conditions necessary for the attainment of liberation or buddhahood are included in the method and wisdom sides of practice. The uncommon cause is the method side. There are so many practices on the method side: compassion, love, charity, ethical discipline, patience, and so on. The key method to attain the Mahayana goal of enlightenment is bodhicitta. That is why we say that bodhicitta is the seed that sprouts into buddhahood.

The wisdom side, direct realization of śūnyatā, is not an uncommon cause because even if you are just seeking your own liberation from samsara you must have the wisdom that eliminates ignorance. Realization of the true nature of reality is a necessary cause for attaining all three definitively good spiritual goals: the liberation of śrāvakas, pratyekabuddhas, and bodhisattvas. Wisdom is common to all; it is like the water or fertilizer in the horticultural example. If we lack the realization of śūnyatā, all our effort in other practices will not yield our objectives. If we have wisdom then we can accomplish our temporary and final goals.

The union of a particular method with wisdom leads to a specific accomplishment. Bodhicitta leads directly to the Mahayana goal: buddhahood. Maitreya says in the *Sublime Continuum (Uttara-tantra):*

> Aspiring to the Mahayana is the seed.
> Wisdom is the mother for producing buddhahood.

In this passage the phrase *aspiring to the Mahayana* means the desire to attain enlightenment for the benefit of other sentient beings. So it specifically refers to bodhicitta. Many sutras and tantras say that wisdom is the mother and the method of bodhicitta is the father, or seed, of buddhahood. The analogy of a father and mother can be explained many ways, but in an ordinary sense we say that both are necessary to produce children. The seed comes from the father and a child develops in the mother's womb. In ancient times lineage was determined by the paternal side. A mother was considered a common cause for a child. If she had children with three different men—one Chinese, one Mongolian, and one Tibetan—one child would be deemed Chinese, one Tibetan, and the other Mongolian. Although the children shared the same mother, each child's lineage is uniquely dependent upon its father. Similarly the realization of śūnyatā is like a mother or the common cause for the śrāvaka, pratyekabuddha, and Mahayana goals.

From the point of view of emancipation, all three goals are freedom from samsara. The root of samsara is a special kind of ignorance: grasping the self. To get rid of that ignorance one needs the wisdom that realizes selflessness: the true nature of reality. So wisdom is a common cause for all of them. This wisdom married to a particular method will bring a specific goal; wisdom wedded to bodhicitta brings the Mahayana goal of enlightenment while wisdom joined to wanting one's own freedom from samsara will bring the lower goal of nirvana. It is in this sense that the perfection of wisdom is called the mother of those who enter the Mahayana and the Hinayana. Thus the great Ārya Nāgārjuna praises the perfection of wisdom by saying that all śrāvakas, pratyekabuddhas, and bodhisattvas rely on it:

> Buddhas, pratyekabuddhas, and śrāvakas
> Must rely on a single path to liberation.
> You definitely taught us that
> There is no other path.

Thus the distinction between the paths is the method side of their practices. Bodhicitta is what makes the Mahayana far superior. The Mahayana motivation is to attain enlightenment in order to save other sentient beings from suffering and lead them to perfect happiness. It takes almost limitless time and effort to fulfill that responsibility. The Hinayana attitude and goal are much narrower. A sutra says that if you put the Mahayana and Hinayana side by side it would be like comparing all the oceans to the little bit of water collected in a cow's footprint.

Nāgārjuna also said in the *Precious Garland:*

> In the instructions for the śrāvakas you did not teach
> The aspiring mind of bodhicitta,
> Or activities completely dedicated to others,
> Because how could they become bodhisattvas?

The point of this quotation is that the distinction between the Mahayana and the Hinayana is the method side. Some teachings, such as wisdom, are for both Hinayana and Mahayana disciples, but other instructions were taught solely for the benefit of Mahayana practitioners. Hinayana followers are not taught to develop bodhicitta because they shrink away from the necessity to practice great activities for eons solely for the benefit of others. They are afraid and primarily concerned with their own liberation, so there is no purpose to teaching them the bodhisattva practices for the time being.

One of Tsongkhapa's main points is that in order to achieve the Mahayana goal we need both the method and wisdom sides of practice. We cannot lack either one. Tsongkhapa says that in his time there were many people who claimed to be Mahayana practitioners but did not practice the most essential teachings of either side. They did not really produce bodhicitta. They thought it was enough to quickly say the words, "I will attain enlightenment in order to benefit others," at the beginning of their recitations or meditation sessions. This demonstrates a very limited understanding of the Mahayana Dharma. Even when simply reciting Mahayana texts, it is most important to spend as much time as possible generating bodhicitta before starting. If an activity is dominated by this warm, compassionate attitude, the whole session will become part of the Mahayana path. In addition some people thought that the main antidote to ignorance is merely *samatha*—a concentrated mental state without any constructive thought. Do not be mistaken; mere stabilization of the mind is not superior insight. A blank peaceful mind is not emancipation nor will it lead to liberation because it will not destroy egotistic thoughts. To eliminate ignorance you must have the realization of selflessness.

If you want to be a Mahayana practitioner and take responsibility for other sentient beings' emancipation in addition to your own, you must train in the practice of bodhicitta along with wisdom. Maitreya said in the *Ornament for Clear Knowledge (Abhisamayālaṃkāra):*

> Through wisdom you will not abide in samsara.
> Through compassion you will not abide in peace.

There are two extremes that a Mahayana practitioner should fear and avoid: falling into samsara and falling into the peace of nirvana. Hinayana practitioners—those who only want their own emancipation—are worried about remaining in the misery of samsara. They want to escape from this wretched cycle of repeated life and death and it is the realization of śūnyatā that cuts the bonds tying them to samsara. But being in samsara is not the main fear of bodhisattvas; their primary fear is that if they attain their own emancipation they will never wake up from that peaceful state. In general peace is something worthy of attainment, but bodhisattvas dread being so satisfied with their own cessation of misery that they will not care about other sentient beings' dismal states.

So for the bodhisattva remaining in either samsara or nirvana is a dangerous extreme. In fact the latter is more serious for bodhisattvas because their main goal is to become a buddha in order to fulfill their vow to take responsibility for other sentient beings. How do they avoid the extreme of absorption into their own peace and happiness? The main technique is meditation on great compassion: the wish to free all sentient beings from samsara. Bodhicitta is grounded in this compassion. This is the method to attain buddhahood. Buddhas are free of the two extremes; they are free from samsara and in addition, because they are dominated by compassion and love, they engage in activity until all sentient beings are fully enlightened.

To understand how compassion works let's look at an ordinary example. If your parents were in a miserable situation, how could you be happy and comfortable? Consider that from beginningless time all sentient beings have been as compassionate toward you as your mother. They continue to suffer, so what good would it be if you attained your own emancipation from suffering? What is your own peace worth? How could you be happy while your mother sentient beings are in terrible pain? The great teacher, the bodhisattva Togme Zangpo, said:[6]

> They have cared for me from beginningless time,
> So what could I enjoy if mother sentient beings are suffering?
> Therefore, in order to liberate limitless sentient beings,
> Producing bodhicitta is the bodhisattva practice.

Selfishness is the great enemy of bodhisattvas because it will make them lose their compassion. To prevent this bodhisattvas have to be aware of any tendency toward a selfish attitude. It is the main object rejected by bodhisattvas.

The children of the conquerors who are authorities on the actual meaning of the Buddha's teachings are amazed when anyone produces bodhicitta. In wonder they put their hands together and bow down to all who have developed this precious mind and become great Mahayana practitioners. These great bodhisattvas are not impressed when someone develops the power to fly, foretell the future, see distant objects, or overpower other beings. In contrast ordinary people are like children and respect superficial qualities; they are astounded when someone can shoot water or fire from his or her fingertips. But these are common powers that result from mental techniques on an ordinary level of meditative concentration. They can be produced even when the mind is still dominated by selfishness. Instead of being beneficial to all sentient beings, these supernatural powers may be harmful. Compared to bodhicitta, which is like a wish-fulfilling jewel, there is nothing great about them. Bodhicitta brings peace and happiness to all sentient beings. It is most difficult to produce spontaneously, but there is no better way of thinking. We should make every effort to produce bodhicitta and then develop and strengthen this key practice of the Mahayana.

It is not only Tsongkhapa who says this; the great Indian Mahayana yogi Śāntideva says in *Engaging in the Bodhisattva Deeds:*

> Others do not even think about their own goals.
> So this thought to benefit all sentient beings
> Is the most precious of all attitudes.
> It is most marvelous when it newly arises.

It is rare for people to want to attain enlightenment even for themselves. So wanting to attain perfect enlightenment solely for the benefit of other beings is particularly remarkable. Among all possible attitudes it is the most valuable. When this mind-set arises for the first time we should rejoice, "Now I've got it; this is the most marvelous thought."

The same text says:

> What other virtue is like this?
> What other friend is like this?
> What other merit is like this?

Bodhicitta is the most powerful virtue. There is nothing better for the accumulation of merit. Other practices such as meditating, reading sutras, or reciting mantras create a certain amount of merit, but not like bodhicitta. Every moment of every action motivated by bodhicitta creates an incredible amount of merit. Because bodhicitta is dedicated to the benefit of all sentient beings, even one small act of kindness to one sentient being, if motivated by bodhicitta, creates as much merit as the number of sentient beings in the universe.

Bodhicitta and people dominated by bodhicitta are our best friends. There is no other friend like these because they only want us to have good things and to be free from suffering. If we want a true friend who can bring us lasting benefit, we should bring bodhicitta into our mind. Therefore Śāntideva also says:

> I bow down to the person
> Who has produced this holy, precious mind.

There are many analogies to praise the beneficial nature of bodhicitta. The sun and the moon are commonly understood to have great value, but bodhicitta has even more superior qualities. The great Śāntideva says:[7]

> This mind is the rising moon
> Cooling the torment of the mental afflictions.
> It is the powerful great sun
> Clearing away the mist and darkness.

Sentient beings suffer feverish heat from the mental afflictions. Bodhicitta is the remedy because it sheds cool light like the moon. Bodhicitta is also like the bright rising sun; it clears away the darkness of ignorance and burns away the mental afflictions. All sentient beings want happiness and to be free from suffering but they do not know how to obtain them. Bodhicitta provides all temporary happiness in samsara and leads to the final bliss of nirvana. It does not harm you or anyone else.

Tsongkhapa said that it was for this reason that the great master Atiśa held Serlingpa to be his most important guru. If we categorized Serlingpa from the standpoint of his philosophical view, Atiśa would be his superior because Atiśa had a realization of the highest view of the Madhyamaka while Serlingpa held the Yogācāra view. Although Serlingpa had not realized the subtlety of the Madhyamaka view of śūnyatā, Atiśa felt Serlingpa was the kindest of his many spiritual teachers. Why? Because he gave Atiśa teachings on bodhicitta. Atiśa studied and practiced with him for a long time and finally realized bodhicitta based on this great guru's instructions. Atiśa's main practice was bodhicitta. In Atiśa's biography it says that whenever he heard the name Serlingpa he immediately put his palms together in reverence. Sometimes tears would spring to his eyes because he had such profound respect for his teacher's kindness.

The import of this historical example is that bodhicitta is the essence of the Mahayana spiritual path. The amount of effort it takes to produce bodhicitta is immaterial. We must strive until this thought arises spontaneously and naturally no matter how much work it takes. If you have bodhicitta, even tossing a small morsel of food to a crow will be a bodhisattva activity. Giving a crumb to a single bird with the motivation of benefiting all mother sentient beings is not a small thing; it is a Mahayana practice. If someone does not have bodhicitta, he or she may be giving gifts hoping to gain something in return, such as riches or his or her own emancipation. With such a selfish motivation, even offering a buddha the whole universe filled with precious gold and jewels would not be part of the Mahayana path. In short giving a tiny thing with the motivation of bodhicitta is far superior to giving magnificent gifts without it.

The great sage Śāntideva writes:[8]

> Merely the thought to help others
> Is greater than making offerings to the buddhas.
> So what need is there to say anything about
> The thought to attain the aim of all beings without exception?

With bodhicitta even the desire to help others in ordinary ways—with food, clothes, or shelter—is more virtuous than worshipping the buddhas. So there is no need to say anything about the great merit that comes from the wish to help each and every sentient being attain their most desired goal: ultimate happiness. The goal of Mahayana practice is not just others' temporary happiness; it is to provide them with the highest, everlasting, blissful peace. Wanting this for all sentient beings creates thousands of times more merit than making offerings to the buddhas. Here generosity, the first of the six bodhisattva perfections, is given as an example. You should understand that this also pertains to the other perfections: ethical discipline, patience, joyous perseverance, meditative stabilization, and wisdom.

Whatever is done with bodhicitta is a bodhisattva practice; if it is not motivated by bodhicitta, then even if you practice pure conduct or meditate for eons it is not bodhisattva practice. This is true from the point of view of both the sutra and tantra: bodhicitta is critical for the practice to be part of the Mahayana path. Tantric techniques—meditating on a mandala, meditating on yourself as the deity, or even the highest completion stage practice of meditating on the veins, channels, winds, and drops—are very powerful because the realization of the emptiness of these objects is joined to bodhicitta. The same tantric techniques done without bodhicitta will not be Mahayana practices.

Tsongkhapa gives a secular example to further explain this point. In ancient times people had to use hand scythes to harvest grain. If you wanted to harvest the grain efficiently you did not just hurry out into the field with any old tool. First you sat down and carefully sharpened the scythe's blade. With a sharp blade you could cut many stalks in a few minutes; if the scythe were dull the work would be very hard and take a long time. Similarly, if you have not properly developed the precious mind of bodhicitta, then no matter how long you practice the other virtues it will be like trying to harvest grain with a dull scythe. You work a long time and bring in only a small amount of merit. If your bodhicitta arises continuously and spontaneously, however, it is like very quickly harvesting a large area with a sharp scythe.

Bodhicitta also burns up enormous amounts of negative karma in an instant. It is a powerful purification because it is the very opposite of harmful action. All negative actions involve harming others. Out of attachment and selfishness we become angry with others, take their lives, hurt them, steal their property, cheat them, lie to them, and so on. Negative karma—like deliberately killing your parents or an arhat—has consequences that are long-lasting and deep-seated obstacles to emancipation. What could overcome this hindrance other than vowing to take responsibility to eliminate others' suffering? When a desire purely to benefit all others, not just your relatives and friends, is spontaneous, everything you do creates great merit and destroys prior negative actions. Not only that, bodhicitta causes small merits created in the past to become enormous, merit that had degenerated to become never-ending, and large merits to become inexhaustible. No other virtue can do that. Śāntideva says this in verse:

> Other than the mind aspiring to complete enlightenment
> What other meritorious action can completely overcome
> The inexhaustible results of powerful sinful actions?

Bodhicitta is like the fire at the end of an eon which incinerates everything animate and inanimate in the universe. The oceans dry up and the elements are destroyed so completely not even ashes remain; all that is left is empty space. Similarly, bodhicitta is the fire that completely destroys the negative karma we created in the past. Even if we have done mountains of negative deeds, the power of bodhicitta can obliterate them in a moment. If you think, "That is a little bit exaggerated. How could bodhicitta get rid of so many negative things at once?" Śāntideva answers by alluding to a story from the sutras:

> Merely thinking, "I want to alleviate
> The headaches of sentient beings,"

Is a great and beneficial thought.
It creates incalculable merit.

So what needs to be said about the desire
To alleviate the incalculable unhappiness
Of each and every sentient being,
And the wish that they have limitless good qualities?

You need to know the background story for these stanzas to make sense. Many of you may have heard this story about a young man named Dzawai Pumo. His father was a merchant who traded for jewelry and other precious things. He would travel across the ocean and bring back goods to sell, then he would sail off again to get more. But when Dzawai Pumo was a child his father and all his wealth were lost at sea.

In ancient times it was customary for a boy to follow his father's profession when he grew up. But Dzawai Pumo's mother kept his father's occupation a secret from him because she did not want her son to enter the same dangerous line of work and risk the same fate that had befallen her husband. However when Dzawai Pumo grew up he wanted to know what his father's occupation had been, and when he eventually found out, he decided he would also become a seafaring merchant. His mother tried to stop him but nothing she said had any effect. Finally, on the day he was planning to leave, she lay down across the doorway in a last desperate attempt to block his departure. But Dzawai Pumo was not to be denied. Even though it was considered highly disrespectful for a son even to stretch out the sole of his foot toward one of his parents, he stepped on his mother's head to make his escape.

Then he boarded a boat and headed across the ocean. The wind carried him to a strange island. He stayed there quite comfortably for a long time. The inhabitants took care of him and there were many beautiful women there for him to enjoy. This pleasurable experience was the result of his prior merit and virtue. One day he went to another part of the island. There he saw a very dark and forbidding house, it seemed to be made of iron and lacked an entrance. As he drew near he heard screaming—a very disturbing noise—and wondered what was inside. Suddenly, because of his karma, a doorway opened and he went in. As soon as he entered the door closed behind him and he was trapped.

Now that he was inside he saw that the house was filled with many people screaming in pain. They all had a wheel of blades spinning on their head causing their brains and blood to spurt out! Dzawai Pumo asked, "What is happening here? How did this come about?" A god appeared and told him that the suffering he was witnessing was the karmic fruit for having stepped disrespectfully on the head of one's mother's. "Oh no," Dzawai Pumo thought. "I have done the very same thing myself," and he became very afraid that he would have to suffer in the same way.

As soon as he had this thought, what he dreaded came to pass: A wheel affixed with sharp blades appeared on his head and began to whirl around. Immediately he generated the compassionate wish, "May all the suffering results arising from this type of negative action ripen on me alone." In this way he wished that everyone there, and anyone else who had created the cause to suffer this way, might be free from this particular misery. As soon as he had that altruistic thought, the entire vision of suffering disappeared. He did not experience any pain and no one else was left imprisoned there; it was as if they were all suddenly released.

Dzawai Pumo's special wish, which had such a dramatic effect, was to take upon himself all the pain of just this particular kind of agony; it was not a thought to relieve *all* the misery of *all* sentient beings. In contrast, a person with bodhicitta does not desire to alleviate merely *one* kind of problem. Bodhicitta is the aspiration to relieve every aspect of all the measureless suffering that exists. This wish includes every single sentient being without exception.

From the positive point of view, bodhicitta is the desire to give happiness to each and every sentient being, as Śāntideva expresses in the following stanza:

> All other virtues are like reeds;
> Once they bear fruit they die.
> Bodhicitta is like an ever-bearing tree;
> The fruit is never exhausted, there is always more.

Reeds that grow on mud flats near water are hollow. They do not flower and bear fruit more than once. All virtues other than bodhicitta are like that: once the main result of that virtuous karma is experienced, the karma is exhausted; it is finished bringing results. But bodhicitta is like a fruit tree because it yields fruit not just one time but again and again. Creating the fruit does not kill the tree and picking the fruit does not finish it forever. No matter how much it produces, more comes. The results of even a simple act of charity, if done for the purpose of attaining enlightenment in order to benefit others, will not be exhausted until buddhahood is attained. And this is not just your enlightenment; the results of bodhicitta will last until *all* sentient beings attain enlightenment. There are other examples like this from the sutras. For example, if you mix a drop of water in the ocean, that drop will not be drained until the entire ocean is gone.

To summarize how bodhicitta is the main gate to the Mahayana path we can look at what Tsongkhapa says in the *Condensed Lamrim (Lam rim bsdus don):* [9]

> Bodhicitta is the central support for the Mahayana path.
> It is the foundation for the great waves of bodhisattva deeds.
> It is the alchemy that transforms the two accumulations.
> It is the treasury holding all virtues together.
> Knowing this, the heroic bodhisattvas
> Hold this precious attitude as their central practice.

Bodhicitta is the most important of all the many practices necessary to attain enlightenment. Bodhicitta holds the Mahayana path together the same way that a central pillar holds together the support structure of a tall tower. There are many practices that we can do to accumulate merit and wisdom, but for these practices to become causes for enlightenment they must be done with bodhicitta. Without bodhicitta, no matter how intensely or how long we do things such as meditating on śūnyatā, giving charitable gifts, or practicing morality, we are creating causes for a lesser result. Bodhicitta is like an alchemical elixir that turns iron into gold because it transforms every activity so that it is for the benefit of other sentient beings. With bodhicitta, everything we do—even eating or sleeping—becomes a virtue. Why? We need a precious life, like this human one, to attain enlightenment for the benefit of other sentient beings. We have to take care of this body so that we can use it. Therefore when bodhisattvas eat or sleep their motivation is to keep up their strength so they can attain their goal of helping other sentient beings. And this pertains, of course, to all other activities as well; every action motivated by bodhicitta is virtuous.

The bodhisattva practices are called *great deeds.* Bodhicitta is the foundation of these deeds, which comprise the path to enlightenment. Once we have this perfect attitude, all merits, virtues, happiness, and peace flow to all sentient beings like the unceasing and powerful waves of the ocean. The bodhisattvas who practice these deeds are heroes. Even if they must practice for eons, they will endure any necessary discomfort because they are completely devoted to the welfare of others. They are willing to sacrifice themselves for the benefit of others because they understand that bodhicitta is a treasure of virtues; it creates the cause for many, many good things. Thus these heroes hold this precious attitude as the center of their practice. It does not matter how much effort over how many lifetimes it takes to produce bodhicitta, it is worth it because until one has it there is no Mahayana practice. If one is motivated by selfish desires and does not care for other sentient beings nothing one does is part of the Mahayana path.

Now we move on to the second topic: how to produce bodhicitta.

b) How to develop bodhicitta

There are four parts to the explanation of how to produce bodhicitta:

   i) How bodhicitta depends on certain causes to arise
   ii) The stages of training the mind in bodhicitta (chapters 2–4)
   iii) The measure of producing bodhicitta (chapter 4)
   iv) How to adopt bodhicitta through ritual (chapters 5–6)

Bodhicitta will not arise randomly by itself. There are specific causes and conditions necessary for it to come into the mind. So, first we will look at what those causes and conditions are, and then we will look at how to put those causes and conditions in place. The third subject concerns how to know when bodhicitta has really arisen. Lastly, although we generally say that bodhicitta is produced through mental training, a particular kind of bodhicitta comes from a special ritual. The fourth topic is a discussion of this ritual and the particular type of bodhicitta created when one repeats the ritual vow three times after a spiritual teacher.

i) How bodhicitta depends on certain causes to arise

There are three subtopics to explain the causes and conditions from which bodhicitta arises:

   a' The way to produce bodhicitta depending on four conditions
   b' The way to produce bodhicitta depending on four causes
   c' The way to produce bodhicitta depending on four powers

a' The way to produce bodhicitta depending on four conditions

The term *bodhicitta* can be broken down into the syllables *bodhi*, meaning the highest realization or enlightenment, and *citta*, meaning mind or thought. So in various sutras and śāstras the meaning of bodhicitta is simply *the thought to attain buddhahood.* When those scriptures say that bodhicitta arises depending on four conditions they mean that four kinds of thought can arouse the desire to attain enlightenment. Bodhicitta can be produced in dependence upon any one of these thoughts, but it does not always rise from them. Further, when bodhicitta does rise from one of these thoughts, it is not complete bodhicitta. When the word *bodhicitta* is used to mean only "wanting to attain buddhahood," the term is referring to what we call *nominal bodhicitta;* this definition does not cover *complete and perfect bodhicitta.* The four conditions for producing the nominal desire to attain enlightenment are taught in different sutras with varying degrees of emphasis. The causes and conditions for real bodhicitta—that is, for developing complete and perfect bodhicitta—will be explained later in this text according to Maitreya's *Ornament for Clear Knowledge.*

The first condition for producing nominal bodhicitta is directly seeing or hearing from others about the inconceivable powers of buddhas, bodhisattvas, or other high spiritual beings. When someone becomes aware of those fabulous qualities, he or she may think, "Wow! That is really something. I want to have the power to perform miracles like that!" In other words, this is a desire to attain buddhahood because the person wants those amazing qualities for him- or herself. The second condition for nominal bodhicitta is reading or listening to teachings that describe enlightenment, the buddhas, and bodhisattvas. Although the person may not have directly seen or heard about these qualities from another person, his or her study produces admiration and faith in them. Based on this trusting faith a person desires to attain the same state.

The third condition is to become aware that the holy Dharma, particularly the Mahayana, is disappearing from the world. Even if someone has not read the scriptures, he or she may see some sign that indicates that the end of Dharma practice is near. Further, because such people realize that the Dharma can truly benefit others, they decide to attain enlightenment so that the teachings will continue to exist for a long time. The fourth condition is a recognition that not only is the Dharma disappearing, but times are bad in general. We live in a degenerate era, dominated by the mental afflictions of ignorance, shamelessness, envy, stinginess, and so forth. In some periods of history people have had more virtuous thoughts than we have. In a period like ours, where evil attitudes predominate, it is rare for people to develop the desire to attain even their own freedom. It is even more challenging to produce bodhicitta than to develop an aspiration for the Hinayana goal. Seeing how uncommonly rare it is, someone may be stimulated to think, "If I produce this Mahayana motivation I can teach it to others. Maybe others will follow my example and practice bodhicitta, too."

The third condition is almost complete bodhicitta. It is a desire to attain enlightenment because one finds it unbearable that the method that sentient beings use to attain freedom will soon vanish. One decides to attain enlightenment because if the Dharma remains in the world then sentient beings' misery can be eliminated. This is not totally complete bodhicitta because the primary motivation is distress over the disappearance of teachings. The desire to attain enlightenment in order to preserve the Mahayana teachings is different from desiring to attain enlightenment in order to free all others from suffering.

Therefore, because the desire to attain enlightenment that arises from any of these four conditions is not a desire to help others founded on great love and compassion, we can only loosely refer to them as the causes for bodhicitta. These conditions yield a desire to attain the highest goal *for oneself.* In contrast, complete bodhicitta rises because one cannot bear seeing that all sentient beings have been suffering from beginningless time and that the end of their misery is nowhere in sight. In order to save all these living beings, one desires to attain enlightenment as quickly as possible. Thus real bodhicitta has a double purpose. Its main purpose is to free other sentient beings from misery and lead them to the highest bliss; the secondary purpose is to attain enlightenment oneself because until one does so one cannot accomplish the main goal. In other words, the direct or immediate objective of bodhicitta is to attain enlightenment oneself so that one will be able to accomplish the primary goal of liberating all others.

An example of the difference between a direct and a primary objective will make this clearer: "I will go to the supermarket so that I can make a delicious dinner." Going shopping is my direct or immediate goal. I need to complete this direct objective in order to accomplish my primary goal: making a wonderful meal. In the case of bodhicitta, it is in order to obtain your primary goal—saving other sentient beings—that you vow to attain your own enlightenment. Real bodhicitta must have both of these goals.

Bodhisattvas need to reverse two misconceptions about what is necessary for accomplishing both the primary and direct goals. The first mistake is to be satisfied with mere emancipation as the perfect goal for oneself. The second misguided idea is to think that one's own liberation will be enough to liberate other sentient beings. The more serious mistake is to think that one's own emancipation from samsara is enough to be able to help all sentient beings perfectly. If people believe the Hinayana goal of personal peace and freedom is totally satisfactory, they will only worry about creating the causes for their own freedom from suffering; they will not be concerned with others' sorrow and misery. If that selfish aspiration arises in a bodhisattva's mind, he or she will lose the desire to attain enlightenment in order to save other sentient beings. Not only will they lose bodhicitta, without great compassion and love for other sentient beings they will lose the bodhisattva vow. To prevent this they must recognize that the perfect qualities of buddhahood are necessary to truly benefit others. Only by developing faith in a buddha's qualities of knowledge, power, and so forth will they come to aspire to the highest goal of perfect enlightenment in order to attain the qualities necessary for accomplishing the primary goal. In this way training in compassion and love reverses the wrong thought that their own peace is enough to complete the goal of saving other sentient beings from misery.

This line of thinking will not reverse the first misconception—that it is enough to attain mere emancipation to accomplish your own goal. Why is the attainment of emancipation from samsara not even personal perfection? Because the wisdom and method of the Hinayana nirvana are not absolutely perfect. Hinayana arhats attain freedom from samsara by eliminating attachment and other mental afflictions through direct realization of the four noble truths. Although they eliminate the mental afflictions—sometimes referred to as *passions*—they have not gotten rid of the more subtle *knowledge obstacles.* Therefore they attain some portion of cessation, but it is not completely perfect cessation. They have a kind of knowledge, but because they still have knowledge obstacles they are not omniscient like a buddha. They cannot read every aspect of a buddha's mind nor can they see certain subtle aspects of karmic causation. In contrast the wisdom of Buddha has no subtle or gross obstacles.

Furthermore, only a completely enlightened buddha has the perfect method side: great love and compassion. Although Hinayana arhats are free from all bad conditions in samsara such as famine, ill health, and natural disasters, they are not free from the bad conditions of peace. In general the peace of nirvana is wonderful because it is freedom from misery, but it is a big obstacle for bodhisattvas because it is selfish. Once practitioners attain nirvana they happily remain in calm meditation without doing anything useful for others. They forget about all the other sentient beings still suffering in samsara.

In short, bodhisattvas see both the extreme of samsara and the inactive extreme of peace as frightful. They recognize the need to attain the qualities of a buddha's dharmakāya in order to complete their own highest goal.[10] When one sees that only enlightenment has absolutely perfect qualities, one will not follow the Hinayana path because it does not lead to this perfect result. The main way to prevent falling to the extreme of peace is the Mahayana method of compassion, love, and bodhicitta. These awaken Hinayana practitioners and arhats to actively work for the benefit of other sentient beings. In other words we need to combine the method to become free from samsara with the antidote to falling into peace. To do this we begin by developing faith in the good qualities of a buddha. Through this we come to see that buddhahood is the only perfect state to benefit others and it is indispensable even for our personal goal. Although merely thinking "I want to attain enlightenment for the benefit of other sentient beings" is bodhicitta, for this thought to arise completely and spontaneously it must be grounded in a realization of *why* we must attain buddhahood. When one clearly understands the necessity for enlightenment one will not be practicing with blind faith. A strong desire for highest enlightenment because it will accomplish both one's own and others' goals is complete bodhicitta.

So bodhicitta is not a simple thing. Tsongkhapa clearly explains that we should avoid confusion about the term *bodhicitta* when we read the scriptures. Here and there the term is used in a general way to refer to only a portion of complete bodhicitta. It is similar to the way we may talk about a bolt of cloth that is burned on one end by saying, "The bolt of cloth is burned." To be precise, the whole bolt is not burned; just one edge of it is ruined. Nevertheless, we ascribe the quality of being burned to the bolt in its entirety.

In some places the word *bodhicitta* is used to refer to the thought: "I want to attain buddhahood because it is so wonderful." This is similar to the discussion of bodhicitta arising from the first two of the four conditions, where the desire for buddhahood arises because of an attraction to various qualities of a buddha. This is part of complete bodhicitta but not all of it. In other passages bodhicitta is used to refer to making the vow, "I will lead all sentient beings to enlightenment" or, "I want all sentient beings to be free from misery." The positive desire to help sentient beings is also part of bodhicitta, but again it is not all of it. Complete bodhicitta has two aspects: you have to attain buddhahood yourself because if you are not perfect you cannot lead others to perfection. Therefore the immediate goal of bodhicitta is your own goal of perfect enlightenment. The main goal is to help other sentient beings perfectly by leading them to enlightenment. So complete bodhicitta is wanting to attain perfect buddhahood, not only to help other sentient beings but also to accomplish your own goal. Desiring either one of those goals can be counted as a kind of bodhicitta, but as individual thoughts they are not complete bodhicitta. Maitreya's definition of bodhicitta in the *Ornament for Clear Knowledge* expresses this dual goal:

> Bodhicitta is: for others' welfare
> The desire to attain complete enlightenment.

In summary the bodhicitta arising from the four conditions is not complete. True bodhicitta is striving to accomplish both your own and others' attainment of enlightenment.

b' THE WAY TO PRODUCE BODHICITTA DEPENDING ON FOUR CAUSES

Some scriptures mention that bodhicitta can rise from four types of causes or various possible environments and human qualities that are conducive for practice. The first cause refers to the type of family into which one is born. If you are born into an excellent family, all the necessary conditions that make spiritual development easy to achieve are present. If you are not born into such a family, you may encounter temporary obstacles to your practice. For example, in ancient India if you were born into a low caste you were cut off from religious instruction. If you find yourself in such a difficult situation you can think, "Even if I do not attain bodhicitta in this life, I can create the causes to do so in the future. By creating merit and dedicating it with special prayers I will obtain a life that is fit for spiritual development." The second cause presumes one is born into a good family; it is the good fortune of having a spiritual teacher who helps one produce bodhicitta and practice the path.

These first two causes are external conditions: family environment and a teacher. The next two are internal qualities. The third cause is to naturally have some compassion for other sentient beings. Some people are instinctively compassionate; they can easily produce bodhicitta. Others are not naturally compassionate and need to engage in various practices to produce patience, love, and compassion for others. The final cause is to not become discouraged by difficulties. There can be a lot of adversity when one tries to help others. One must be able to endure many uncomfortable situations without sorrow because one knows that one is doing something for the benefit of others. One of the sutras says that an arhat's experience of the bliss of emancipation cannot compare to the joy bodhisattvas feel even when they experience hardship while working to benefit other sentient beings. A bodhisattva, dominated by compassion and love, is far happier and does not become disheartened.

These are some of the main causes for bodhicitta. With these causes one's bodhicitta will be powerful and no type of bodhisattva activity will be difficult.

c' THE WAY TO PRODUCE BODHICITTA DEPENDING ON FOUR POWERS

The first power is a desire to attain buddhahood that rises through one's own ability. The second is when bodhicitta arises in dependence upon the power of others. In other words someone else convinces you that you can produce it. The third is the power of causes created in a previous life. In a prior rebirth you engaged in Mahayana practices so you have a predisposition for them now; as soon as you hear about the Buddha or bodhisattvas you naturally have a powerful inclination to attain buddhahood. The fourth strength is the power of training in this life. Even if you do not have the power of habits created in prior lives, if in this life you make an effort to listen to the instructions of a holy teacher, analyze them, and concentrate on them again and again you will eventually able to produce bodhicitta.

Asaṅga taught the way to produce bodhicitta from the four conditions, four causes, and four powers in the *Bodhisattva Levels (Bodhisattva-bhūmi)*. The various ways in which these conditions, causes, and powers are grouped can result either in bodhicitta that is firm or bodhicitta that is a bit unstable. The four causes and four conditions in combination or individually united with the first power—one's own power—will result in strong and steady bodhicitta. Bodhicitta will be less sound when it arises in dependence upon the four causes and conditions combined with the second power—someone else convincing you to practice—or combined with the fourth power—making a lot of effort for a long time. This does not mean that such bodhicitta is bad. It can become firm. But in general the bodhicitta created through your own power or the power of predispositions is more stable than the bodhicitta that depends upon the urging of others and your effort during this life. Even if you do not succeed in producing bodhicitta despite making a great effort throughout your life, your exertion will not be fruitless. Whatever you do becomes a predisposition; it is like having planted a seed so that in the next life you have the power to grow. You will have the ability to start practice in another life almost from where you left off.

We live in a degenerate time. *Degenerate* in this context means faulty or rotten. From the spiritual point of view, the teachings are in a degenerate state; they are like old food that does not have much nutrition or taste. After the Buddha's time slight defects have been introduced into the pure teachings. People have less ability to achieve spiritual goals and less power to engage in earnest practice. Conditions in the world are also less conducive to religious practice. Thus the teachings are slowly weakening and getting close to extinction. They are like the setting sun; they shone for many years but are now close to disappearing. In short, the situation is very bad. Sentient beings have more mental afflictions, the pure teachings are scarce, and it is difficult to practice. As a result there is less religious practice, less spiritual development, and fewer and fewer arhats and bodhisattvas. It has become difficult to hear about the special thought of bodhicitta. It is very rare for people to produce bodhicitta from the depths of their hearts. Nevertheless we need this kind of spiritual practice. If many people developed compassion, love, and bodhicitta there would be no fighting, no suffering, and no problems in the world.

Because this is a very difficult time one should rely on a spiritual teacher. Listen to the Mahayana scriptures, but do not just listen—think about them, try to understand them, and meditate on them. Make an effort to do these things, but not just because you are urged by someone else. It does not help much if you do it because someone tells you to or because everyone else is doing it. Do not do these practices just because it is the custom of your family, town, or country. You should do these practices from a deep feeling in your heart. Use your own understanding and effort to plant the seed of bodhicitta. You must establish the root of bodhicitta because the entire Mahayana path depends upon it. With bodhicitta even giving someone just a penny becomes a great Mahayana practice; one hour of keeping pure conduct with bodhicitta becomes a great bodhisattva deed; reciting a mantra or listening to teachings become a great Mahayana action if done with bodhicitta. But without bodhicitta there is no bodhisattva activity at all.

Real bodhicitta with all its characteristics is wanting to attain enlightenment, not for your own pleasure, but in order to lead all mother sentient beings to buddhahood. Complete bodhicitta has this double purpose: you want to attain your own enlightenment so that you can accomplish your key goal: freeing sentient beings from samsara. This thought cannot just rise once, occasionally, or be superficial. It has to rise spontaneously and effortlessly from the depths of your heart. Then it will be the type of thought makes you a bodhisattva. It takes a lot of effort and practice to have this kind of thought. It is not easy. It may take your whole life. It may take several lives. Once you produce real bodhicitta other activities can be done easily. Even things that are physically difficult can give you great joy because you know that your pain is going toward accomplishing something worthwhile. So now we move on to how to train the mind to develop bodhicitta.

Compassion, the Entrance to the Mahayana

ii) The stages of training the mind in bodhicitta
    a' The training based on the sevenfold cause-and-effect personal instructions in the lineage descended from Atiśa
        1' Developing certainty about the order of the stages
            a" Showing that the root of the Mahayana path is great compassion
                1" The importance of great compassion in the beginning
                2" The importance of great compassion in the middle
                3" The importance of great compassion at the end
            b" How the six other personal instructions are either causes or effects of compassion
                1" How the first four personal instructions—recognizing all living beings as your mothers through affectionate love—are causes of compassion
                2" How the superior thought and bodhicitta are the effects of compassion

---

I N OUR CURRENT STATE we do not have the ability to help all other sentient beings all the time. Only a buddha—someone with perfect love, compassion, power, and who is free from all obstacles—can truly benefit all others. So the heart of the Mahayana is bodhicitta: wanting to attain perfect enlightenment in order to save other sentient beings. If bodhicitta is spontaneous and continuous a practitioner's attainment of buddhahood is not too far off because there is almost no chance for him or her to engage in a negative action. Every one of a bodhisattva's actions is motivated by the desire to benefit others whereas nonvirtuous actions are motivated by a wish to harm others directly or indirectly. Every moment of every action motivated by bodhicitta creates great virtue and destroys or reduces the potential of many prior negative actions. Further, once bodhicitta is firmly established all the rest of the Mahayana practices follow. So the best thing to do with our human life is to practice bodhicitta.

Śāntideva places great emphasis on the importance of cultivating bodhicitta. He says this attitude should be as unshakable as Mt. Meru, the mountain that is the central axis of the world:[1]

> I must consider again and again:
> I have attained this fortunate life after a long time.
> Likewise I must hold this attitude
> In mind as unshakable as Mt. Meru.

It is not easy to attain what we have now: a human life with the opportunity to practice the Dharma. It would be shameful not to take advantage of these fortunate circumstances because we do not know what will happen in our next life—we might be reborn as a dog! But we should not simply accept the scriptural praises of bodhicitta and follow the instructions with blind faith. We should study with an open mind to learn about the goal, whether it is possible to achieve it, and the steps to follow to reach it. We must not leave this as mere intellectual understanding; we must use what we learn and by practicing these teachings make our human life useful.

It is not difficult to understand what bodhicitta is. However, it is not easy to make bodhicitta spontaneous and as stable as a mountain because from beginningless time we have been dominated by the opposite type of thoughts: self-centeredness, self-pity, and self-cherishing. No matter what is going on we are only concerned with our own situation. Our minds are like wild elephants drunk with self-centered egoism. If anything looks like it might harm us we try to destroy it. We fight any interruption to our happiness. We kill others to save ourselves. But our attempts to influence the external world have not worked; we have only created more problems and suffering for ourselves. Yet this powerful elephant of the mind can be tamed. We can reverse our habitual selfish inclinations and develop universal compassion free from partiality. When unbiased compassion arises bodhicitta is easy to attain. So compassion is an essential part of Mahayana practice. Thus the question becomes, "How do we first develop compassion and then train the mind to develop bodhicitta?"

ii) THE STAGES OF TRAINING THE MIND IN BODHICITTA

The Buddha gave many instructions and many great sages and yogis achieved high spiritual levels by following them. Then based on their experiences they wrote manuals to teach others. Many of these are still available. The *Lamrim Chenmo* arranges these traditional teachings to make them easier for us to practice. Tsongkhapa divides this topic into two sections; each one explains a method to produce bodhicitta that comes down to us from a different famous Indian teacher:

a' The training based on the sevenfold cause-and-effect personal
   instructions in the lineage descended from Atiśa
b' The training based on the bodhisattva Śāntideva's text (chapter 4)

The sevenfold cause-and-effect method was practiced by the great teachers Candrakīrti, Candragomin, Kamalaśīla, and Atiśa. When the great teacher Atiśa, Dipaṃkaraśrījñāna, came to Tibet, he wrote the *Lamp for the Path to Enlightenment* to organize these instructions in a concise way. The second method of training comes from the great Indian teacher Śāntideva. In *Engaging in the Bodhisattva Deeds* that great Mahayana yogi explains the method called exchanging self and other. These two systems are slightly different so Tsongkhapa explains them both. Even though much time has passed and our lifestyle and culture are very different from those of India and Tibet, these teachings are still topical and useful. You can transform your mind if you take them down from the shelf and put them into practice.

a' The training based on the sevenfold cause-and-effect personal instructions in the lineage descended from Atiśa

The order of the causes is determined by the result, bodhicitta, and without bodhicitta one cannot attain highest enlightenment. Therefore, before going into detail on how to practice each step in turn, I will summarize the causes in reverse order: the superior thought, compassion, love, a desire to repay the kindness of all other sentient beings, recollecting the kindness of all others, and seeing all sentient beings as one's mother.

Remember, bodhicitta is the desire to attain perfect enlightenment for the benefit of other sentient beings. Bodhicitta rises from the superior thought, a special kind of love and compassion. Superior love is taking responsibility for the happiness of all others. Superior compassion is thinking, "I will take responsibility for eliminating the suffering of other sentient beings." This is far greater than kindly thinking, "How nice it would be if others were happy and free from misery." Once we decide to take on the responsibility to free others from misery and lead them to bliss, we see that attaining enlightenment is the only way to do it. So bodhicitta rises directly from this superior thought.

The superior thought rises from compassion. As the result of practicing compassion, the wish that all sentient beings be free from misery will become so powerful that we decide to take responsibility to free others from suffering.

Compassion rises from love. In general we can say that compassion focuses on freeing others from negative circumstances while love focuses on bringing them positive things such as happiness. This type of love arises simultaneously with compassion. In the context of the sevenfold method to develop bodhicitta, however, the love that is the cause of compassion is feeling that other sentient beings are very attractive. This is not the ordinary worldly "love" of attachment or sexual desire. It is affectionate love—a feeling that others are so wonderful that you cherish them more than yourself. It is more like the kind of love a mother has for her only child or that a young child feels for his or her parents. When someone we love this way experiences pain we strongly wish to free that one from suffering and to help him or her have joy. Even now we may experience this type of love in relation to one or two people. But for this type of love to be the basis for great compassion, it must arise for all sentient beings equally. Universal love is extremely important; it is the key to developing bodhicitta in both systems.

How does affectionate love that is equal toward all arise? Usually we feel affection for those who have done us great kindness. When others are generous or helpful we want to repay their benevolence. So the love that finds all others attractive comes from a desire to repay the kindness of all other sentient beings. You may think, "If love depends upon the desire to repay the kindness someone has extended toward me, how can I feel this for my enemy? He has never done anything nice for me." The key is to put enough effort into remembering the kindness of all others. We have to train ourselves to recollect how all other sentient beings have been immeasurably kind to us.

Recollecting their kindness comes from seeing all sentient beings as our mother. A mother's love for her child is an example of the dearest kindness. There is no one in the world kinder to you than your mother: she gave you life, she was your first friend, and she protected you from harm. Of course there can be ugly parental relationships but the essential nature of the relationship between mother and child is pure kindness and love. Through yogic techniques we can come to understand that every sentient being, other than oneself of course, has been our mother. According to Buddhism we have all been each others' father, mother, and child because we have taken birth an uncountable number of times. There is no one about whom we can say, "This person has never been my mother." The only difference between these beings is time: in the present lifetime there is one person who is your mother, but in past lives others have given you birth. This has not been the case just once; all other beings have been your mother hundreds, thousands, even a countless number of times. This is a difficult subject to master, but through meditation we can come to see that there is no difference between our dear mother and any other sentient being. When we focus on the kindness of our mothers we will want to repay their kindness; we will feel a strong, powerful universal love. All the other causes rest upon this understanding.

So the six causes start with seeing all sentient beings as your dear mother. Second is to recollect their kindness. Third is to want to repay their kindness. Fourth is a special affectionate love for all sentient beings. Fifth is great compassion. Sixth is the superior thought. The superior thought is such powerful compassion and love that you want to take on the responsibility to clear away all the misery of all sentient beings by yourself alone. This directly leads to bodhicitta. So usually in the sevenfold method we say there are six causes for one result. But there is a foundation for these six causes: equanimity. If you count equanimity as a cause, we have seven causes and one result.

You can spend a long time meditating on each of these subjects to develop bodhicitta. The *Lamrim Chenmo* explains the details of each of these topics in two major headings:

1' Developing certainty about the order of the stages
2' The actual training in these stages (chapter 3)

The order of the stages of practice is important because if one does not understand the method, one cannot practice it. The order of these causes is explained both backward and forward so that we develop a firm understanding of them. Starting with a backward explanation we begin with the result and learn how it depends upon a preceding cause. Then we look at how that cause is the result of a prior cause, and so on. Going forward we examine how this is a basis for that, and how that supports the next one.

1' DEVELOPING CERTAINTY ABOUT THE ORDER OF THE STAGES

The first subtopic has two divisions:

a" Showing that the root of the Mahayana path is great compassion
b" How the six other personal instructions are either causes or effects of compassion

a" SHOWING THAT THE ROOT OF THE MAHAYANA PATH IS GREAT COMPASSION

Great compassion is one of the most important subjects in the entire lamrim. It is called the root of the Mahayana path because all the other practices stem from it. Everybody has some compassion, but it is partial—it only extends toward a particular person or two. In this system we develop great compassion. *Great* refers to both the object of compassion—all sentient beings—and the desire to take on the responsibility for alleviating their misery. Great compassion is critical in the beginning of Mahayana practice, in the middle while you are training as a bodhisattva, and even after you attain enlightenment. The importance of compassion is taught in terms of the following three subtopics:

> 1" The importance of great compassion in the beginning
> 2" The importance of great compassion in the middle
> 3" The importance of great compassion in the end

1" THE IMPORTANCE OF GREAT COMPASSION IN THE BEGINNING

We have already talked about how the gateway to enter the Mahayana path is the continuous and spontaneous rise of bodhicitta. Only if we are deeply moved by compassion for all sentient beings' misery will we make a commitment to free them from suffering. Great compassion motivates a bodhisattva to do everything necessary to attain enlightenment for the benefit of other sentient beings. The Mahayana is called the *great vehicle* because it carries a huge load: all sentient beings. Every Mahayana practice is geared to the enormous task of liberating all sentient beings. Great compassion is the most rudimentary distinction between Hinayana and Mahayana practices. If others' suffering does not bother us sufficiently, a desire to attain enlightenment for the sake of eliminating their problems cannot arise. If we do not want to take on that responsibility we will not have entered the Mahayana path. Even if we claim to be practicing the Mahayana, without great compassion we have not begun the practice of the Mahayana.

Tsongkhapa quotes the *Teachings of Akṣayamati Sutra (Akṣayamati-nirdeśa-sūtra)* to show that great compassion is the most essential element of the Mahayana path. In this sutra the Buddha says to Śāriputra that the great compassion of bodhisattvas is inexhaustible. In other words, the benefits, qualities, and importance of great compassion are limitless because it runs through the entire Mahayana path. The Buddha says compassion is analogous to our human life-force. The gross distinction between life and death is breathing in and out. As long as we are breathing there is life. Even when breathing stops there is still a subtle internal air-energy called *prāṇa*. The vital life-force is a subtle mind that rides on this air-energy. When that leaves the body you die; when that enters a mother's womb there is the start of a new life. Without this vital life-force at the start, there is no life as a human being. Similarly, great compassion precedes the Mahayana because without great compassion there is no bodhicitta and without bodhicitta it is not possible to undertake the bodhisattva vow and practices. If we do not do those practices then buddhahood is not possible. Another way to look at this is if you want a particular kind of fruit you have to plant the right type of seed; in the same way, buddhahood grows from the seed of great compassion. In the beginning great compassion is the seed that will sprout into bodhicitta—the wish-granting tree of the Mahayana path. Without being nourished by compassion in the middle, the tree cannot grow and produce fruit. At the end the ripe fruit, buddhahood, nourishes others every moment of every day.

Tsongkhapa refers to another sutra, the *Foremost of Gayā (Gayā-śīrṣa)*, to reinforce this point. A sutra's name can be based on the person to whom the sutra was taught or the particular place the teaching was given. This sutra is named for the place where it was taught: the city of Gaya. A person in Gaya asks Mañjuśrī, "What is the source of a bodhisattva's practice? What is the object of a bodhisattva's practice?" Mañjuśrī replies, "The beginning of the bodhisattva practice is great compassion. Great compassion arises with sentient beings as its object." We first have to think about the problems of sentient beings in detail. When we see their suffering we will want to free them from their misery. So the place where compassion arises is sentient beings.

Once great compassion arises the vow to attain perfect enlightenment in order to free all sentient beings from samsara will follow. As soon as that vow spontaneously arises we have entered the Mahayana path. From that time on we have committed ourselves to working for the benefit of other sentient beings. We vow to do whatever needs to be done to attain buddhahood so that we can liberate them. But we cannot leave this as a mere promise; we have to carry it out. How do we do that? We must train in the accumulation of merit and the accumulation of wisdom in order to reach enlightenment. Wisdom is realization of śūnyatā, the true nature of reality. The accumulation of wisdom eliminates all ignorance and mental obstacles. But no matter how sharp our wisdom, it needs an assistant: the method side of practice. For example, in order to cut down a tree we must have a handle for a sharp axe blade. The accumulation of merit and wisdom is difficult; it may take many eons of hard work. But because of their great compassion bodhisattvas joyfully work for however long it takes.

Compassion is the cause for bodhicitta; it is the foundation for the bodhisattva vow. Like the earth, which supports everything animate and inanimate, every aspect of the Mahayana depends upon the support of great compassion. Without powerful compassion it is impossible to begin the great bodhisattva training.

2" THE IMPORTANCE OF GREAT COMPASSION IN THE MIDDLE

Of course it is difficult to take on the great responsibility to help all other sentient beings, but it is not as difficult as actually engaging in the bodhisattva's practices. In the middle—from the time of taking the vow up to attaining enlightenment—compassion supports practitioners through many hardships. There are numberless sentient beings and they behave so badly: they are rude, abusive, and tough to deal with. Until we attain buddhahood there are so many things to learn and practice. The time it takes to accomplish these things is almost measureless and the difficulties one encounters seem almost limitless. When one sees all this it is difficult to keep one's commitment. For example, one day a beggar came and asked an arhat, who was one of the Buddha's disciples, for his flesh. The arhat had developed bodhicitta and was trying to practice charity so he cut off one of his fingers and gave it to the beggar. But this sacrifice did not satisfy the beggar. The arhat became discouraged and thought, "How can I help all sentient beings when I cannot even satisfy one of them?" In this way he lost his bodhicitta and veered onto the Hinayana path. It is easy to give up feeling responsible for others and think, "It is better to work for my own freedom," when things become difficult.

Great compassion is necessary for preserving our commitment to attain enlightenment to help all other sentient beings. It keeps us from becoming selfish and forgetting other sentient beings. Compassion's object is the alleviation of other sentient beings' problems. By recalling other sentient beings, their tribulations, and our relationship to them, we will be able to keep our vow. Meditating on great compassion again and again will make us stronger and stronger. Instead of focusing on our own sorrows we will joyfully, without any reservation, work for the benefit of others. We will never be discouraged. We will experience a special kind of happiness.

Firm compassion is not easily shaken. Tsongkhapa quotes the first *Stages of Meditation (Bhāvanā-krama)* by the great Indian scholar Kamalaśīla to reinforce this point:

> Moved by great compassion bodhisattvas do not look out for themselves. They strive to greatly benefit others. Therefore to amass the two accumulations they enter into activities that are difficult, take a long time, and incur great hardship.

The meaning of this passage is that we have the capacity to do enormous things if we train ourselves to see the benefit of an action. There are a lot of examples of how someone with a limited objective can do things beyond the ordinary. Boxers fight because they want fame or money. They may be knocked down several times, but they get up to fight again. Because of their mental strength they view getting bloody as a type of decoration. If the boxer saw this as a form of punishment, he would not be able to take even one punch. Similarly bodhisattvas can accomplish amazing feats because of their practice of love and compassion. The *Intense Power of Faith Sutra (Śraddhā-balāvadhāna-sutra)* says:

> When you have great compassion you can take on any type of suffering and give up any type of happiness in order to ripen other sentient beings.

All sentient beings have the potential to become perfect buddhas. They can develop bodhicitta and the highest enlightenment. We have not matured into buddhahood yet. Right now we are dominated by selfishness, anger, and so on. Our minds are like muddy water, but the mud can be separated out to leave the water completely pure. With great compassion comes great courage; bodhisattvas accept whatever hardships arise. They give up their pleasure if it will benefit other sentient beings. Tsongkhapa says that if bolstered by compassion we too engage in these difficult endeavors, we will attain enlightenment without delay. It is not far away.

3" The importance of great compassion at the end

Great compassion is important even after achieving highest enlightenment or buddhahood. If practitioners lack great compassion at the end of the path, they would be like a Hinayana arhat and remain absorbed in the great peace and happiness of their own liberation. They would not engage in activities to bring relief to other sentient beings. But there is no way that someone with great compassion can enjoy the great peace of the Hinayana goal. Because of their great compassion buddhas will not cease to act for as long as there are suffering sentient beings. Buddhas will stay involved with sentient beings until the end of samsara. The middle *Stages of Meditation* by Kamalaśīla says:

> Because buddhas are dominated by great compassion, even though they have obtained their own goal with every aspect of their own perfection, they remain until there are no more beings in samsara.

Great compassion is the cause for a buddha's nonabiding nirvana. The term *nonabiding* means it is beyond the two extremes—it rests neither in samsara nor in the peace of the Hinayana arhats. Samsara is one extreme; the other is the extreme of peace. Buddhas avoid both extremes. Their activities for the benefit of others continue all day and all night, for as long as there are sentient beings in need.

In the first stanza of the *Commentary on the "Middle Way" (Madhyamakā-vatvāra)* Candrakīrti uses an agricultural example that I mentioned earlier. In order to produce a harvest, in the beginning you must have the seed, in the middle you have to water it, and at the end you have the enjoyment of fully ripened grain. Similarly, in order to enjoy the final harvest of buddhahood, great compassion is important in the beginning, middle, and end:

> I praise great compassion in the beginning
> Because it is the seed of this supreme harvest,
> The water that nourishes its growth over time,
> And the desired ripened fruit of the harvest itself.

In Candrakīrti's time it was customary to begin a text with an homage. Depending on the book's subject matter, the homage would address all the buddhas or a particular buddha like Mañjuśrī. But Candrakīrti writes that he bows down to great compassion. Why? Because compassion is the source of all buddhas, bodhisattvas, and the Mahayana and Hinayana arhats. From great compassion in the beginning and the middle, bodhisattvas finally attain buddhahood. Out of compassion at the end, the buddhas teach other sentient beings. When sentient beings partake of the Dharma teachings they too achieve various attainments.

There are a number of similes in the sutras for the primacy of great compassion. An ancient Indian example is that compassion is like a cakravartin king, an emperor of the world, with his entourage. Wherever an emperor goes, his ministers, army, and symbols of rule go as well. Great compassion is the king of all Mahayana practices. Wherever it is the rest of the Mahayana practices follow. Another comparison is how life starts at conception. Once the critical elements and life-force come together in a mother's womb, the physical and mental organs of the fetus begin to develop. Great compassion is like this essence of life; once you have it the practices of the six perfections and the ten stages of the bodhisattva path will gradually and naturally grow. Tsongkhapa comments that while many scriptures say that great compassion is the essence of the path, this can be proved with logic too. Through logic and scripture we should develop a firm understanding that great compassion is the root of bodhicitta and hence the supreme teaching.

For this reason the *Compendium of the Teachings Sutra (Dharma-saṃgīti-sūtra)* says that in the beginning we should not try to do many different things. We should make a great effort to perfect just one practice because accomplishment of the rest of the training will naturally follow. What is this thing? It is great compassion. In Tibet there was a practitioner named Shangna Chung who kept requesting a special teaching from Atiśa. One day Shangna Chung said to the great lamrim Geshe Dromtonpa, "Every time I ask for instruction, Atiśa only says, 'Give up worldly attitudes. Meditate on bodhicitta.' This is all I get. He never tells me anything else." Dromtonpa, Atiśa's direct disciple, laughed and told him that this was Atiśa's most essential teaching. Dromtonpa knew that giving up enjoyment of the pleasures of this life and developing bodhicitta was the most important lesson to learn.

People are always looking for some kind of superior practice. If you think that there is something deeper, higher, and more profound than great compassion you are under a huge misconception. All the practices will be in the palm of your hand if you have great compassion. If compassion for all sentient beings is invariable and spontaneous, deciding to do something to help them immediately follows. Then bodhicitta develops because we come to see that there is no way we can alleviate others' suffering and bring them happiness other than to attain enlightenment. With great compassion we become able to do all the bodhisattva practices. Thus great compassion is the essence of the path; it brings about buddhahood and fulfills our desire to help others. To bring this firmly to mind we need to purify obstacles by doing virtuous practice, and studying texts such as the *Array of Stalks Sutra* and various commentaries. Otherwise our practice will be difficult; we will run here and there doing this and that—none of which are essential.

The great Śāntideva puts the situation this way:[2]

> The great protectors with limitless intelligence
> Examined what is most helpful to others:
> Those who want to free others from samsara
> Should produce and firmly practice bodhicitta.

Buddhas are the great protectors of sentient beings. To lead us to the far shore of the ocean of samsara they used their incredible insight to determine the best practice they could teach us to do. They determined that bodhicitta is the great prize for those who want to liberate themselves and others from this world of suffering and danger. It is the instrument to free all sentient beings from samsara. It is the most valuable of all precious things. Once we have bodhicitta we can quickly achieve our own and others' goals.

Tsongkhapa concludes this discussion about compassion being the root of the Mahayana teaching with a quotation from Mātṛceṭa's *Praise in One Hundred and Fifty Verses (Śata-pañcāśatka-stotra)*. Mātṛceṭa is another name for Aśvaghoṣa. He was a non-Buddhist who became a great and famous Buddhist teacher. He composed many praises of the Buddha. A stanza from one of them reads:

> Your mind is precious;
> It is the seed of complete enlightenment.
> You are the only hero who realizes the essence;
> Other beings just understand partially.

Mind here refers to the Buddha's realization of the essential attitude of bodhicitta. No one else understands it as he does; everyone else has only a partial understanding. Great yogis see that the common conception of a hero— someone with a weapon and many dead bodies around him—is wrong. There is nothing spectacular in destroying external enemies or responding to provocation by hitting back or killing others. Our enemies will eventually die even if we do not try to kill them. Since they will die sooner or later without any effort on our part, fighting them is just like trying to kill a corpse. There is nothing heroic about that. It is foolish.

As Śāntideva says: [3]

> Ignoring all external temporary misery
> They conquer the inner enemies: hatred and so forth.
> That victorious one is a real hero;
> Attacking the rest is like killing a corpse.

A genuine hero is someone who conquers the real enemy: the self-centered attitude. The Mahayana teachings are instructions on how to become victorious over this egotistic selfishness and attain the two goals: placing others in a state of freedom and enjoyment and our own perfection. There is no way we can accomplish the first goal until we have completely subdued our internal enemies. Until we have attained buddhahood we cannot help others to that state. So bodhicitta is the thought: "I must become a perfect buddha in order to liberate all other sentient beings." That thought is necessarily preceded by great compassion.

b" How the six other personal instructions are either causes or effects of compassion

The other elements of the sevenfold method are either causes for compassion or the result of compassion. The first four are causes: recognizing all sentient beings as your mother, recollecting their kindness, wanting to repay their kindness, and affectionate love. The fifth is compassion itself. The superior thought is a stronger, special type of compassion. Bodhicitta is the result of the superior thought. So this discussion has two parts:

> 1" How the first four personal instructions—recognizing all living beings as your mothers through affectionate love—are causes of compassion
> 2" How the superior thought and bodhicitta are the effects of compassion

1" How the first four personal instructions— recognizing all living beings as your mothers through affectionate love—are causes of compassion

First we will look at how great compassion rises from affectionate love. Then we will examine how the first three causes produce this kind of love.

In general compassion is the desire that some other living being be free from distress. The wish for someone to be without misery comes from a recognition that the other person is in difficult straits. Sometimes compassion does not arise easily. Sometimes strong compassion may arise but fades quickly. At other times compassion is stable but not very strong. For compassion to arise naturally and be both strong and stable, we must find that suffering sentient being attractive. In other words, if we have no affection for someone we will not feel compassion for him or her. Compassion therefore depends on the loving attitude that precedes it.

What should this affectionate love be like? If something is precious to us, we do not want to lend it to anyone for even a few minutes. If it gets lost or slightly damaged we are ready to collapse in misery. When we feel this way about others, we strongly wish for them to be free from sorrow. Our desire for them to be happy and prosperous also depends on this attitude. For strong and stable compassion this other person must be as dear to us as an only child is to his mother. If her child is missing for just a few moments a mother feels terror. A mother wishes for her darling child to have happiness, a long life, wealth, fame, and pleasure. Note that the term *love* refers to two distinct feelings. It is used for both for the feeling of affection—that this being is very attractive—and for the result that comes from this feeling—the wish for the other being to experience happiness. Affectionate love—the feeling that someone is attractive—precedes compassion and the other type of love.

If we feel strong affection for all sentient beings, then compassion for all sentient beings will be easy to develop. This is not simple, however; it is difficult to feel affectionate love for even one person. Sometimes it is difficult for children to feel affection for their mother; occasionally it is difficult for a mother to feel affection for her child. If this is so, then of course it is far more difficult to feel affection for *all* sentient beings. Nevertheless it is not beyond the realm of possibility. We can learn to produce affectionate love for all beings by employing two different methods of mental training: the first three steps of the sevenfold cause-and-effect personal instructions passed down to us from Atiśa and the system explained by Śāntideva. Both systems stress that affectionate love is necessary for great love and great compassion to arise.

Tsongkhapa says that we can see from our own experience why affectionate love is necessary for great love and compassion. Generally we divide people into three categories: friends and relatives, enemies, and a neutral category of strangers somewhere between the other two. How do we feel when someone in each of these groups is suffering? When a relative or a friend has a problem, we find it uncomfortable, perhaps even unbearable. But when we hear that our enemy is in trouble we often experience a type of enjoyment. As for what we feel when someone we do not know is suffering, we generally do not care one way or the other. We are not sorry nor are we happy; we simply remain a neutral spectator.

Why do we feel distressed when our friends or relatives are miserable? Because we have affection for them. The depth of our affection determines how strongly we desire that they be free from suffering and have happiness. If we have deep affection for someone we are very concerned even if he or she catches a little cold. We want to do whatever we can to help this dear person recover. If we feel a small or medium amount of fondness for someone then our discomfort when this person suffers will be of corresponding intensity. We feel the opposite toward those we label as our enemies. Not only do we do not have any desire to relieve their misery, we often wish that they were even more wretched. We find these people so unattractive that we want them to have problems all the time. For those whom we consider strangers, we have no special feeling one way or the other because we do not find them either particularly attractive or unattractive. These different attitudes do not arise based on the qualities within the other person; there is no compelling external reason behind our various reactions. Instead, it is our mind that finds that person attractive or unattractive. We make a decision to either like or dislike this person.

Therefore in order to produce affectionate love for all sentient beings we learn to expand the warmest affection we are familiar with to all others. The closest people to us at the beginning of life are our parents. Later we develop love for our siblings and then for our friends. The deepest affection is ordinarily found between a mother and child. There are many reasons we have strong feelings of love for our mother. She brings us into existence; first she carries us in her womb and then she gives birth to us. She nourishes and cares for us until we can fend for ourselves. She does everything for us. She is our best friend. Therefore the symbol of affectionate love is a mother who has only one darling child. She has the warmest spontaneous love for her child all the time. She finds her child absolutely adorable. Nothing compares to the depth of love that she has for her only child. This is the reason we start the sevenfold method by meditating on all sentient beings as being our dear mother.

Next we meditate on the kindness others have shown us. We naturally appreciate others' thoughtfulness and consideration. If we become aware of others' benevolence toward us we naturally feel affection for them. So if we recognize other sentient beings as having been our mother, we can think in detail about how much kindness they have shown us. Then we will want to repay their kindness. These meditations and resultant feelings go step by step. If the first one is strong, the second will be strong. If we meditate on these three steps in succession—seeing others as our dear mother, recognizing their kindness, and wanting to repay their kindness—then a strong feeling that they are attractive will arise. This will not be a superficial feeling; it will be a deep affectionate love.

But we do not stop when we find all others attractive. Based on affectionate love, we develop great compassion: the desire that all sentient beings be free from suffering. The other type of love—wanting all sentient beings to have the highest bliss and happiness—arises simultaneously with great compassion. Once again, to be very clear, the *Lamrim Chenmo* clearly distinguishes between love and affectionate love. The love that wants all sentient beings to have happiness is not a cause of great compassion. Affectionate love is the cause of both great compassion and the love that wants all others to have happiness.

2" HOW THE SUPERIOR THOUGHT AND BODHICITTA
ARE THE EFFECTS OF COMPASSION

Great compassion is one of the main causes of bodhicitta. As a consequence of great compassion the superior thought arises. In turn the superior thought is the direct cause of bodhicitta. Now we look at this second causal relationship.

You may wonder why compassion does not directly result in bodhicitta. Isn't great compassion enough? When you have it don't you want to attain buddhahood for the benefit all sentient beings? Why do you need something extra, the so-called superior thought, in between compassion and bodhicitta? Actually the superior thought is not anything other than great compassion. It is simply exceedingly powerful great compassion; it is compassion so strong that it deserves another name.

By training the mind in the first four causes, the twin desires of great love and great compassion arise. Such immeasurable love and compassion are common to those who practice the śrāvaka and pratyekabuddha paths. Hinayana arhats also want all sentient beings to be free of misery and to have happiness. But Mahayana great love and compassion do not consist of merely thinking how wonderful it would be if all sentient beings had happiness and were free from misery. Mahayana great love and compassion involves taking on the personal responsibility to give all others the highest happiness and eliminating their misery. It is not just wishing; it is taking up the burden to make it happen oneself. This kind of great compassion is the superior thought; it is deciding, "*I* must remove all sentient beings from samsaric misery. *I* must provide them with happiness." Because the Hinayana arhat does not take on this task, the superior thought is far beyond the Hinayana attitude of immeasurable love and compassion.

Thus in the context of the two vehicles *great compassion* can mean different things. In Sanskrit the term *great compassion* is *mahākaruṇā; mahā* means great and *karuṇā* means compassion. In some scriptures the distinction between Hinayana and Mahayana compassion is that Hinayana practitioners develop karuṇā but not mahākaruṇā. Other texts state that the Hinayana path embraces great compassion, but it does not include taking on the burden to liberate others oneself. If we examine the object of Hinayana compassion, we find it comprehends all sentient beings. It is universal compassion and so, from this point of view, Hinayana arhats do practice great compassion. Their compassion is measureless because they want all sentient beings to have freedom.

Immeasurable compassion like this is even found in some other religions. So if we are concerned only with the perspective of the object, great compassion is not particular to the Mahayana. But if the meaning of *great* also includes the attitude of the subject, then *great compassion* includes taking personal responsibility to free all sentient beings from misery and leading them to enlightenment. This is not a mere wish. Nor are we relying on someone else to take care of matters. Instead, we are thinking, "I'll do it." This is unique to the Mahayana. So when the Mahayana path refers to great compassion it includes greatness from the point of view of both the object and the subject.

The great compassion and love common to the Hinayana path is not enough to bring about bodhicitta. The mere wish or thought, "How nice it would be if all sentient beings were free from misery and that all sentient beings were happy," is not powerful enough to be a direct cause for the desire to attain enlightenment in order to benefit all other sentient beings. The kind of love and compassion that directly leads to bodhicitta includes taking personal responsibility to accomplish others' emancipation and bring them to happiness. The label *superior thought* indicates this special great compassion and love. The superior thought is at the top of the scale of compassion. It cannot be superficial; it is intense and must be produced from the depth of one's heart. That is why the superior thought is labeled as a separate category in the sevenfold method. However there is nothing wrong with saying that great compassion is the cause of bodhicitta. The superior thought is not something distinct that arises in between great compassion and bodhicitta.

In the *Questions of Sāgaramati Sutra (Sāgaramati-paripṛcchā-sūtra)* the Buddha gives an example to help us understand the differences between these types of compassion. When a merchant householder's wife gave birth to a much desired only son, the parents cherished the baby. They saw only his good qualities; they perceived no faults in him. This dear baby grew into an attractive child. Because young children run around heedless of danger, this little boy fell down into a deep sewer. When his mother and other relatives saw that the toddler had fallen into the hole in the ground, they screamed, mourned, and cried for help, but they remained above ground. This did not mean that they did not love their child; they did, but they did not have the courage to go down into the deep pit. When the child's father arrived and saw that his only darling boy had fallen into the sewer, he too immediately desired to free him. He had more courage than the others and without any disgust for the filth or fear of the deep, he took upon himself the responsibility to rescue the child and jumped down to save him.

We all have seen situations like this on the news but here it is an analogy for great compassion. The deep, dirty sewer is a symbol for the three realms of samsara: the desire, form, and formless worlds. The only child represents all sentient beings who have fallen into samsara. The mother and other relatives who want to save the child but do not have the ability or courage to do so are like Hinayana practitioners. They have compassion and want others to be free from samsara but do not have the bravery to act for others' sake. It is only the father—the merchant householder symbolizing the bodhisattva—who has the courage to take full responsibility to lead all sentient beings out of samsara. He is the only one with the superior thought.

Once this superior compassion, which takes full responsibility to save others, rises, practitioners survey their current situation. They realize that at present they do not have the ability to free even one sentient being from samsara. Not only that, even if they became a śrāvaka or pratyekabuddha arhat there would still be limits to their ability to help others. By becoming such arhats they will be free of samsaric misery themselves and perhaps will be able to help some creatures, but they will not be able to lead all sentient beings to omniscience. Having concluded this, these practitioners think in the following manner: "I want to make the wish all sentient beings have for temporary and final happiness come true. I definitely am going to do this. But how can it be done?" They realize that only a buddha is free from all obstacles and has perfected all the necessary qualities of knowledge, ability, and power necessary to complete this task. With the attainment of buddhahood they see that they will be able to complete this altruistic task as well. This causes them to think, "I must first attain buddhahood myself in order to help all other sentient beings." When this desire to attain buddhahood for the benefit of other sentient beings spontaneously arises, it is bodhicitta. This is the relationship between the superior thought and bodhicitta.

In summary, you have to understand the general order and function of the six causes in the production of bodhicitta. The root of bodhicitta is the superior thought, a special type of great compassion. So compassion is the most important cause. Great compassion is the result of the other causes. The famous teacher Puchog Jampa Tsultrim says:[4]

> Equanimity is the ground moistened with love.
> Compassion is the seed. Nourished by warm superior thought,
> The sprout of bodhicitta branches and extends the two accumulations
> Until you attain the final fruit of the three bodies of a buddha.

Equanimity is not discriminating between sentient beings based on attachment for some and hatred toward others. Without equanimity one's mind is rough; there is no smooth basis to support love and compassion equally for all others. For example, to grow a good crop we have to level the ground for planting. Then we need to water the prepared ground; affectionate love is the moisture for the mental continuum. Compassion is like a freshly planted seed in the moist soil. The attitude of mercy that wants to take responsibility to free all sentient beings from their suffering is the seed of the Mahayana. This refers to the superior thought bringing about bodhicitta, the sprout. Once bodhicitta sprouts in the mind, the leaves and flowers of all the bodhisattva activities come forth. The two accumulations of merit and wisdom grow like branches higher and higher. The final result is the fruit: the buddha's body, speech, and mind, or the three bodies of dharmakāya, saṃboghakāya, and nirmāṇakāya.

⊹ 3 ⊹

The Sevenfold Cause-and-Effect Personal Instructions

2' The actual training in these stages
    a" Training the mind to strive to accomplish the goals of others
        1" Establishing the foundation for producing this attitude
            (a) Achieving impartiality for all sentient beings
            (b) Having affection for all sentient beings
                (i) Cultivating a recognition that all beings are your mothers
                (ii) Cultivating a remembrance of their kindness
                (iii) Cultivating the wish to repay your mothers' kindness
        2" The actual production of this attitude
            (a) The cultivation of love
            (b) The cultivation of compassion
            (c) The cultivation of the superior thought
    b" Training the mind to strive for enlightenment
    c" Recognizing bodhicitta, the fruit of the training

2' THE ACTUAL TRAINING IN THESE STAGES

BEFORE we seriously start to practice a particular technique we need to understand the context into which that method fits. In this case we must be familiar with what bodhicitta is, the number and importance of its causes, and how the causal relationships work. When we understand these topics we can begin to work in a step-by-step fashion. Even if it takes our whole life to master just the first step, we will have begun an essential practice. There are three subdivisions to the discussion of how to actually train the mind in these stages:

a" Training the mind to strive to accomplish the goals of others
b" Training the mind to strive for enlightenment
c" Recognizing bodhicitta, the fruit of the training

Bodhicitta has two objectives: a goal for others' sake and a goal for you, the practitioner. The primary objective is that all sentient beings become free from misery and attain enlightenment. The individual practitioner's immediate aim is to attain perfect enlightenment for him- or herself. Only if we attain complete buddhahood will we be equipped to benefit others. The third topic describes how to know when we have succeeded in attaining bodhicitta.

a" TRAINING THE MIND TO STRIVE TO ACCOMPLISH THE GOALS OF OTHERS

The *others* referred to in this subtopic are all sentient beings. Sentient beings need our help. They are seeking happiness, protection from suffering, and freedom from problems. It does not matter what situation they are in right now, high or low they all have some kind of misery. They want something that lasts but none of their efforts gives them what they desire. It is up to us to become someone who can truly help them. A Mahayana practitioner's goal is to free all mother sentient beings from misery and to provide them with blissful happiness. We are promising more than just temporary enjoyment; giving everlasting happiness entails leading them to enlightenment or nirvana. In other words, this section is about developing great compassion. So training the mind to strive for others' goals explains how to produce great compassion and the superior thought. This training can be divided into two parts:

1" Establishing the foundation for producing this attitude
2" The actual production of this attitude

1" ESTABLISHING THE FOUNDATION FOR PRODUCING THIS ATTITUDE

At present we do not have a good foundation for great compassion because we have so much attachment toward certain people and so much hatred toward others. The basis of great compassion is two attitudes: affectionate love and equanimity. True affectionate love does not discriminate between others. So before developing love we practice equanimity in order to remove all the rocks from the mental field. Then we can moisten the mind with affectionate love enabling the seed of compassion to germinate. Therefore there are two parts to the foundation for great compassion and great love:

(a) Achieving impartiality for all sentient beings
(b) Having affection for all sentient beings

We do not need to sit in unmoving isolation to do these meditation practices. We can work on transforming our mental processes anytime simply by thinking about these methods and bringing to bear our own experiences. We can do this while we are walking around, eating, or enjoying being with other people.

(a) ACHIEVING IMPARTIALITY FOR ALL SENTIENT BEINGS

Equanimity or *impartiality* does not imply that all sentient beings are equal. We cannot make them alike and the point of this practice is not to even wish that they become the same as one another. There are three different uses of the term *equanimity* on the Buddhist path. The first is in the context of developing single-pointed concentration. This use of the term equanimity *('du byed btang snyoms)* is to do something without making a sharp distinction. It refers to not being discriminatory and leaving the mind alone when it is functioning properly. We put forth effort to place the mind only when it is not properly focused, otherwise we do nothing. The second use of the term *equanimity* is from the point of view of feeling. There are three basic types of feeling: unhappiness, happiness, and a neutral, equanimous feeling *(tshor ba btang snyoms)*. The third type of equanimity is in the context of the preparatory practice of the four immeasurables: equanimity *(tshad med btang snyoms)*, compassion, love, and joy. The latter is the groundwork for the Mahayana training of equanimity that we are discussing here.

Before a meditation session we practice the type of immeasurable equanimity that was explained for persons of small and intermediate spiritual capacity in the context of the six preparatory practices.[1] This is the prayer that all sentient beings come to see each other without the partiality of hating some and being attached to others. It is thinking how nice it would be if they had no biased wish that some be happy and others be miserable. But this type of equanimity is not enough to be the basis for great compassion. The Mahayana practice of immeasurable equanimity is to train one's own mind, not to pray for others to have equanimity. Mahayana practitioners engage in analytical meditation to come to see that there is no reason to divide sentient beings into unequal categories. If we do not take the antidote to partiality—

being attached to some, hating others, and ignoring the rest—our compassion and love will be discriminatory. Without equanimity we will have compassion for some sentient beings but not for others. If we try to generate compassion before mastering equanimity the result will not be the great universal compassion that is the essential Mahayana attitude. This is why we train the mind in equanimity.

It is not easy to find a mental bulldozer to level the mental ground, but there are various ways to do it. We could start by thinking about all sentient beings and try to level out our feelings. A way to do this is to imagine directly in front of you all those you find most unattractive—your enemies. Then to one side put those you find most dear, and on your other side put the neutral ones. Next examine the reasons you feel hatred, attachment, or indifference. Finally compare all these beings all at once.

This method does not work very well for beginners because meditating on general categories does not prepare one to put equanimity in practice in specific, real-world situations. A more effective way to develop equanimity is to work on feeling equanimity for one category at a time. This technique is based on how the human mind naturally functions. We always have some reason for dividing people into categories. However the reasons for our attraction or aversion are not founded on reality; we grasp some superficial aspect of the person in question and then exaggerate its apparent goodness or badness. Based on such ignorant and twisted perceptions we see some people as disagreeable and others as agreeable; as a result we take sides and strong feelings of hatred or attachment arise. Therefore the way to remove attachment and hatred is to develop wisdom and see things as they actually are. With this understanding we can logically examine the reasons we feel a certain way toward others and can counter those unfounded opinions.

The easiest place to begin is with those we have no reason to like or hate. It is easier to feel equanimity for those who have not done anything beneficial or harmful to you. After developing equanimity for those neutral people, we take our friends as the object of meditation. After we have developed equanimity for our friends we consider our enemies. Finally when we feel the same toward strangers, friends, and enemies we can put all sentient beings together and meditate on them all at once.

That is the procedure, but what should we meditate on to get rid of attachment and hatred? In the middle *Stages of Meditation* Kamalaśila gives us two things to consider: why sentient beings are equal from *their* side and why there is no reason for us to discriminate from *our* side. We start by thinking about sentient beings from their side. All of them, whether they are our friends or enemies, equally want to have happiness. None of them want any problems, disagreement, or suffering; on this basis there is no difference between them. If we think about this deeply we will realize that they are equal. Because there is no point of difference from their side there is no reason for us to hold some lovingly close, hatefully push away others, or be carelessly indifferent toward others. The second reason is from our side. From beginningless time we have been born in samsara; there is no way to count the number of births we have had. Because of karma we have been born high and low, up and down, back and forth, in every type of life in the six realms. We did not have the same mother and father or friends and enemies in each of these lives. We have had various relationships with each and every sentient being. There is not one that has not been our mother hundreds of times. All of them have been our dear friends. Each of them has been our worst enemy. So to which ones should we be attached? Which of them should we hate? There is no way to make this distinction objectively.

This is the basic way to think. We should contemplate these karmic relationships in much more detail by considering our own experience and stories from the scriptures. For example, once there was a couple living with the man's elderly parents. When the old father passed away he was reborn as a fish in a pond behind the house. When the old mother died she was reborn as a dog that became the family pet. When the family's enemy died he was born as the couple's child. Neither the husband nor wife knew about these rebirths. They felt so much love and lavished so much care on their baby, their previous enemy. They caught the fish that had been the man's beloved father, cooked, and enjoyed eating him. The dog, who had been the man's mother, begged for some of the fish, her former husband. The couple got angry and beat the dog, but finally they gave her the bones to eat. In one way this is laughable; in another it is something to cry over. Arhats can see these karmic connections and know their relationships with others differ only with respect to time. Through internal debate, analytically pitting the view that intuitively feels that our enemies are always our enemies, etc., against the view that recognizes that our relationships with others are in a constant state of flux, we too can come to an understanding that all beings are equal in relation to us. The purpose of this meditation is to lessen our strong partiality. Even a slight evening out of our sharply biased beliefs would be a big achievement.

In order to loosen our attachment to friends or relatives we should think, "They have been my enemy in the past. They have done even more horrible things to me than my present enemies." To loosen our hatred we should think, "Many times these people have done the same type of loving actions that my friends do." The *Daughter Like the Finest Moon's Discourse Sutra* (*Candrottama-dārikā-vyākaraṇa-sūtra*) says:

In the past I killed all of you.
All of you have chopped me to bits.
We go back and forth as enemies and killers,
So why should you feel so attached also?

Thinking this way is the antidote to strong attachment. The word *also* in the last line of the stanza implies that this same line of thought is the antidote to hatred. Usually we hate our enemies because directly or indirectly they have done something to injure us. But those we love have done the same things to us in other lives. There is no certainty about enemies and friends across lifetimes. We have had so many lives from beginningless time that at some point we have been each and every living being's enemy. If we think about sentient beings one by one, we cannot find one we did not kill in a prior life. We cannot come up with even one who has not been our enemy and killed us. We have all been meat for others: they have killed, chopped, cooked, and eaten us. And we have done the same to all of them. Even during one life, an enemy can become someone we dearly love while someone we cherish can become our most powerful adversary.

A yogi can clearly see that all beings are equal in this way. We, however, are confused and so our attitudes and behavior swing back and forth: first killing, then loving, then hating, then feeling tenderness, and so on. Based on faulty reasoning all sentient beings continue to change how they feel about each other. So ask yourself, "Why should I be so attached to certain people thinking, 'These are my relatives and friends?'" Through analysis we can come to see that there is nothing real, absolute, or externally existent in the other person that is the basis of our discrimination; our attitude toward others simply reflects how we happen to think about them at any given moment. There is no underlying reason to be attached strongly to some and to hate others.

The point is not to eliminate the categories of enemy, friend, or stranger. In the beginning we are not attempting to reject specific enemies or friends. We are not trying to think, "This person, whom I have considered my enemy, is not my enemy; this person is my friend, or is neutral to me." We are using these categories to try to understand the reasons for our feelings. Then we can reduce our attitude of hatred and attachment toward these objects. When we become accustomed to this through meditation we will smooth the rough aspects of the mind. Our attitudes become more equal and our mind turns away from hatred and attachment. This meditation does not remove attachment and hatred from the root. It just pushes them down temporarily. The root of ignorance has to be removed later. However, once equanimity is established, you can develop a positive attitude of love and compassion toward all.

(b) HAVING AFFECTION FOR ALL SENTIENT BEINGS

Kamalaśila's middle *Stages of Meditation* says that our typical attitude is as hard as rough arid ground. Practicing equanimity smoothes the ground out and is therefore the foundation for the development of all positive qualities. Once we have cultivated equanimity we are ready to generate positive attitudes toward all sentient beings by engaging in meditations to develop affectionate love. Tsongkhapa elaborates that just as clearing away stones readies a field for planting, equanimity removes attachment and hatred from the mind making it serviceable. However, the ground is still dry and everyone knows that seeds need water in order to germinate and grow. Traditionally in Tibet the first watering of the fields is called *pouring gold* because it is so crucial. To ready the mind for planting the seed of compassion, it has to be moistened by the love that finds all sentient beings attractive. Only then can we plant the seed of compassion that will grow into bodhicitta and the Mahayana path. The seed in this example can be understood both as the potential for producing the sprout of great compassion and that great compassion itself, for such compassion is the seed of bodhicitta and the Mahayana.

Tsongkhapa says that it is important for us to understand the techniques to bring the mind to the positive side as taught in the *Stages of Meditation.* Equanimity and affectionate love are not easy to produce. We naturally have a tendency to discriminate among sentient beings. We care for some and hate others because we are so concerned about ourselves. It is difficult to put these feelings aside even temporarily much less to completely subdue them and feel equanimity for all sentient beings. It is even more challenging to find all sentient beings as attractive as a mother finds her only child. Nevertheless equanimity and affectionate love can be produced through meditation. In the sevenfold cause-and-effect method there are three successive practices to develop affectionate love for all sentient beings:

   (i) Cultivating a recognition that all beings are your mothers
   (ii) Cultivating a remembrance of their kindness
   (iii) Cultivating the wish to repay your mothers' kindness

Affectionate love naturally rises from these three causes; it is not necessary for there to be a separate meditation called *cultivating affectionate love.* By engaging in these three meditations one by one, a warm feeling cherishing all sentient beings will evolve by itself. This is not a partial, biased love; it values all sentient beings equally. To generate this feeling we must first recognize that all sentient beings have all been our mother. Then we think about how much kindness each one has shown us every time she has been our mother. After we see her kindness we will want to do something to repay her. We get to a point where we feel we cannot live without doing something in return. This progression of feelings occurs even in ordinary social interactions: if someone gives you food or some other desirable thing, you feel obligated to repay them. Through these meditations we create a feeling that is much deeper and wider than this ordinary experience. We begin by thinking about our mother in this life. When we have seen her kindness and desire to repay it, we expand our meditation to include thinking about our father. After we develop these three realizations in regard to him, we expand our focus further. Finally we recognize all sentient beings as our mother. We concentrate on all their kind actions, the ways in which they helped us when we were helpless. Now we, in turn, want to protect them; we cannot stand seeing their pitiable situation. We cannot repay their kindness by some simple gift of food or clothes. The best way to repay their countless acts of benevolence is to help them to become permanently free from misery and to have unalterable happiness.

None of these topics is easy to master. Each one may take a long time to perfect. The goal may be very far away but we have the capacity to reach it. The hard part is the beginning because we have habitually thought in a different way for most of our lives. Our stubborn tough mind is so entrenched in the opposite way of thinking that we need many techniques, a lot of time, and a great deal of effort to bring about these positive attitudes. Our customary thought patterns are so strong that when we first try to change, our positive thoughts are like a candle flame in the wind. If we only do these practices once in a while or only for a short time it seems that the candle will easily be blown out. However, if we take these practices seriously and engage in these meditations continuously, our positive attitudes will become stronger and stronger. Why? Because our old mind-set was built upon an unstable foundation—self-centeredness, attachment, and hatred based on a misconception of the *I*. The old way of thinking was based on ignorance, but this positive way of thinking is based upon reality.

The wisdom that looks at the reality of the self or *I* can destroy all faults from their root. The methods for achieving each of the stages of meditation are explained in the teachings. We must listen to the teachings on these methods, evaluate our experiences, use logical reasoning, and then meditate again and again. These techniques will bring about a strong attitude of universal affectionate love because it will have wisdom as its foundation. When we accomplish this, bodhicitta will not be too far away.

(i) Cultivating a recognition that all beings are your mothers

The concept to understand is that all sentient beings are the same as your dear mother of this lifetime. The only difference between them is time; in other respects their relationship to you is the same. You have one mother in this lifetime and the others were your mother in different lifetimes. How do you come to this realization? The start of the meditation is to consider that samsaric rebirth has no beginning. This is a very different view from Western culture's premise that there is a beginning—some first cause—that created the universe. You were probably taught that either material causes or God was the creator. According to Buddhism there is no beginning. Why would there be such a beginning? There would have to be a reason for this kind of a commencement. The Buddha did not create the world or sentient beings and there is no other being who created all of this either.

This is a complicated subject, but in short Buddhists say that although there is no beginning, samsara can come to an end because all sentient beings can achieve buddhahood. The mental continuum has no beginning and no end, but samsara—the impure mental continuum—is conditioned, so it can come to an end. A big question that comes up in this connection is the following: Is there life after death? And there are many closely related queries as well. Does the mind go on after death? Is the mind destroyed when the body dies? Do the body and mind both disappear without continuation? Does life come from a prior life? And so forth.

Some of the basic presuppositions behind all Buddhist practices have to do with the beginningless mental continuum, karma, and the mental afflictions. According to Buddhist logic there is a continuum of rebirths because life is a constant mental flow. The continuation of life is a continuum of mind. Consciousness does not arise from just physical conditions; its cause is a similar preceding consciousness. Without a prior moment of consciousness there is no way for consciousness to arise. Therefore the mind, or consciousness, has existed beginninglessly and this mental stream continues endlessly into the future. While it is true that mind is temporarily related to a particular body, it is basically different from the body.

The tantric systems explain that the essence of life is a subtle mind in combination with a very subtle form of physical energy. A particular life comes into existence from both physical causes and the subtle mental continuum.

The different physical features or shape of a particular life are due to karma, temporary conditions, the environment, and other physical factors in combination with the mind. The physical material cause for a birth comes from the parents. However the mind does not arise as a result of the union of the parents' sperm and egg; it is a continuation from a prior mind. If we track back from one moment of mind to the previous moment of mind, we see that the mind of a baby as it emerges from his mother's womb must have had a moment of existence before that. Then we look at consciousness in the mother's womb. The first moment of consciousness in the womb also had to come from a prior consciousness—a moment of the consciousness in the intermediate state, or *bardo*. The first moment of consciousness in the bardo was preceded by the last moment of consciousness, just before death, of another life.

The last moment of the bardo mind results in a moment of consciousness that combines with the father's sperm and the mother's egg—the start of the next life. If merely physical conditions caused consciousness—simply the combination of the sperm and egg without some other unique special cause—then a child's mind should be identical to his or her parents' minds. An intelligent father would always have an intelligent child. However skillful, intelligent, or dull the parents are, their children should be the same. However we see all the time that three children from the same parents have very different mental abilities.

Obviously some aspects of the mind are more closely related to the physical organs than others. It is definitely true that external physical factors have an effect on the mind, but the essence of the mind is completely different from matter. Do not be confused by statements such as, "The main cause of visual consciousness is the eye organ." This simply means that the physical organ affects consciousness a great deal. For example, the clarity of an image to visual consciousness depends upon the condition of its physical sense organ, the eye. This physical organ, however, is not the material cause of visual consciousness. In this sense *material* does not mean matter; it means *key* or *primary*. The physical organ has a special secondary role, but it is not the primary cause of consciousness. The primary cause for a moment of mind is another moment of mind, just as a seed is the primary cause for a sprout.

Other aspects of mind are deeper and more subtle and have less of a connection with the physical body. In deep sleep the physical body almost appears to be dead, but the mind is still actively functioning. In tantric practice, you can learn to do meditations during which the subtle mind leaves the gross body temporarily and later re-enters it. At some point in the future the body and mind will separate at death. A corpse does not have consciousness but this does not entail that the mind has been destroyed. At death the continuum of the physical body is over but the mind goes on to the intermediate state. In short, the next moment of mind has as its material cause the present moment of mind.

Since there is no beginning to cyclic existence there is no beginning to life and death. We have taken birth, aged, become sick, and died again and again, continuously, since time without beginning. We have been in many situations: sometimes high, sometimes low, and sometimes in the middle. The impure causes and conditions of karma and the mental afflictions have caused us to cycle throughout the desire, form, and formless realms.[2] There is no type of life in samsara that we have not experienced. We have taken every type of birth in every possible realm of existence: human, animal, hell-being, hungry ghost, and so forth. And even within a particular realm, such as the human or the animal realm, we have experienced many different types of life as a result of many different types of karma. It is necessary for us to become convinced that we have taken every type of life, in every place, in every realm. There is nowhere we have not been born and no type of body we have not had.

Each time we are born in samsara from a womb we have a mother and father. It therefore follows that over countless lifetimes we have had countless parents and relatives. No one can point to a sentient being who has not been his or her mother in another life. Similarly, no one can say, "I have not been that sentient being's child." There are no exceptions. Furthermore, this has not been the case just once; every living being—other than yourself, of course—has been your mother many, many times. Nāgārjuna said that if you took all the matter on earth and made tiny balls the size of juniper seeds, there would not be as many balls as the number of times each sentient being has been your mother. Every sentient being has been your mother more times than you can count.[3]

Asaṅga expresses this by quoting a sutra in his *Levels of Yogic Deeds (Yoga-caryā-bhūmi)*:

> It is difficult to find in the long, long past a place where you have not been born, not gone, or not died. It is difficult to find any sentient being who in the distant past has not been your father, mother, brother, sister, preceptor, the one who gives you vows, your spiritual teacher, or stood in a teacher's stead.

The mind of a buddha is free from ignorance and obstacles so nothing blocks him or her from seeing reality. Omniscient ones can look into the past and see where we have been born. They understand karma so they can see how present events are the results of actions done in former lives and how the karma we are creating in this life will bring results in future lives. The Buddha said he did not see any sentient who had not been your father, sister, and so forth. We do not see these connections because we are blinded by ignorance. We do not recognize our prior mothers because of the changes that have taken place over time. In fact, sometimes people do not even recognize their mother of this life!

The purpose of the first meditation topic is to become convinced that all sentient beings have been your mother, not only once but countless times. Not only have they been your mother in the past, they will be your mother countless times in the future. Although we have had every possible relationship with every sentient being, we begin by concentrating on all beings as our mother because it will make the rest of the steps toward developing affectionate love easier. Without a fundamental understanding of others' kindness, the basis for the rest of the steps does not exist.

It is not difficult to see that in any one life a mother nourishes and develops her child; she is her child's best friend. Of course advanced yogis and bodhisattvas can see all the relationships they have had with all others. They know that without other sentient beings' kindness there is no way to exist. However that is not very obvious to beginners. In fact it is sometimes said that karmic causality is more difficult to understand than the ultimate truth, śūnyatā. There is no definitive way to explain the particular causal relationship between past lives and this life, this life and future lives, or a specific good or bad karma and its result in a specific experience. At our present level many of these relationships can only be understood in general; we are not able to say, "This has definitely happened because of that."

The present subject is often particularly difficult for westerners. Many have a negative reaction to the ideas of karma and rebirth because of their cultural or religious heritage. They do not even want to listen to an explanation of this philosophy. They think these ideas are stupid and the people following them are foolish, naïve, and gullible. If you close your mind and think, "There is no way any of this can be true; I do not even want to bother considering it," you are shutting the door to the path to emancipation. This closed-minded attitude will be a big obstacle to spiritual development. I am not saying you should simply accept these things as true; blind faith will not work either. It would be wrong to accept these ideas without critical examination. I am simply pointing out that people born into a culture that accepts reincarnation and karma do not question it much. They grow up with stories about how many beings attained the highest state over a series of lives. Everyone around them has a basic trust in these principles. Even if they do not understand these things clearly they feel it must be true that they have had many different relationships with others in other lives. As a result it is easier for them to develop compassion and love according to these instructions. In contrast, Westerners have to employ many techniques to develop faith in this world-view. So if you are very skeptical about the truth of beginningless mind and rebirth, to gain a general understanding of these ideas I suggest that you begin by listening to teachings, reading and studying scriptures, and examining what past teachers and thinkers said and did. Try your best to disprove the concept of beginningless rebirth by using sound and clear inferential reasoning. By simply investigating this topic in a systematic manner you might find that you start to develop some measure of trust in these ideas. As your mind begins to open a bit you can further develop your understanding through meditation.

The continuum of mind is like the stream of a river. The stream can go in many ways. In some places it combines with contaminants; in other places at other times it is clear. There are infinite combinations. If you have a strong understanding of how all sentient beings have been and will be your mother, every time you see another living creature you will feel, "This is one of my mothers." Your attitude toward them will be similar to your love for your present mother. On this basis the meditations on your mothers' kindness and wanting to repay their kindness will naturally follow. You do not have to convince other people that this is the case; you must be sure yourself. If you are not convinced the subsequent steps will be difficult. The practice of meditation and the path system work by gradually joining the mental continuum to a special environment and conditions. You will not succeed if you try to do everything at once or skip some steps. Once a particular step becomes spontaneous you can try the next set of practices. As the impure conditions are eliminated the mind's nature of clarity and purity comes to the fore. Finally the pure perfect nature of buddhahood is attained. It is not simple, but it can be done.

(ii) Cultivating a remembrance of their kindness

The Kadampa Geshe Potowa said that we should first meditate on the kindness of our present mother because if we start there it is easy to bring to mind the kindness of other sentient beings. From our mother we move on to thinking about our father, our relatives, our enemies, and finally all sentient beings in general.

To begin, clearly visualize your mother in front of you. For the first few times as a continuation of the previous meditation think, "This person has not only been my mother in *this* life. Because I have been born in this world life after life from beginningless time, she has been my mother countless times in the past." Then begin to think about the kindness she has shown you each time she has been your mother. A mother's job is to protect her child from harm as much as she possibly can. She does whatever she can to benefit her child and make him or her happy. This person, your mother, has done this over countless lives.

Consider your present mother's kindness as an example. In this life, she held you in her womb for nine months. From the time she knew she was pregnant she made every effort to support the fetus so it could be born alive and healthy. She sacrificed her enjoyment and customary habits in order to benefit her unborn child. Even before she saw her child she began to worry about him or her. When a human baby is first born it can do nothing. It is totally helpless, almost like a little worm. A mother protects her child from cold by warming it with her body; she holds it carefully with all ten fingers; she nurses it with her milk; she gives her child appropriate food and drink at the proper times. Sometimes she feeds the infant with food from her own mouth to give it a special kind of pleasure.

This last action is not common in contemporary Western countries because you have so much wealth and so many items specially prepared for the care and feeding of babies. But not everyone has access to all these things and yet people around the world are able to care for their infants, often with far less than you may think is necessary. For example, in Tibet a mother would clean the skin below her baby's nose with her tongue in order not to hurt her child's delicate skin. They had cloth they could have used to wipe their baby's nose, but they used their tongue instead to protect their offspring from even the slightest injury. And everywhere mothers carefully clean their child's bottom without any feeling of disgust.

There are so many dangers to an infant; every day, hundreds of times a day, a mother protects her child from hunger, thirst, heat, cold, animals, falling down, and so on. Without his or her mother a child would face certain injury and death; it would be difficult for a baby to survive even a few hours without her care. In a poor family a mother will short-change herself in order to provide for her child's comfort. Sometimes she will even threaten others, steal, or engage in other shameful activities for her child's benefit without considering her own reputation. She exhausts herself for her child. When her child is sick she cares for him or her with seemingly limitless love and affection. When her child is in pain, she wishes she could experience it instead. And if her child should die a mother experiences sorrow beyond description. She feels that if given a choice she would sacrifice her life rather than let her child die. From the samsaric point of view there is no one as kind as our mother. In every sense our mother is our best helper, friend, and protector.

Sometimes people think, "Oh, my mother is not like that." We tend to forget most of her kind actions and all that she did for us. Even if we do remember a few of the things she did for us, we tend to discount them. We think that as soon as we were able to stand up and walk we took care of ourselves with no help from our parents. We think, "I did all this; she had nothing to do with it." Ignorance like this is extremely powerful. If we come up with reasons to support a negative interpretation of things it is easy to be drawn into a destructive attitude.

A mother's nature is to be concerned about safeguarding her child for as long as it needs protection, but sometimes ignorance may influence her attitude for the worse. Ignorance may bury all the pure motherly kindness she felt when the child was first born. Children are also under the power of ignorance. When a child grows to be stronger and cleverer than the mother, it can lead him or her to adopt a mistaken attitude and to engage in destructive actions. Slowly distance develops between mother and child. The child forgets every good thing about his mother and concentrates on the negative aspects of what is just a temporary situation. The mother may also come to see nothing good in her offspring. Eventually a mother and child can come to hate one another. Animosity can become so strong that a child may want to kill his mother or a mother may want to kill her child. This is how ignorance creates problems. It can make a yogi cry to see how the most sincere and loving friendship in the world can be destroyed by ignorance. This kind of situation should not happen, but it does all the time when people are completely defeated by their inner enemy.

We can make our positive thoughts of love powerful by considering how a mother takes care of her child, how she worries about her child, how she wants her child to develop, and how much more she loves the child than herself. A child's primary thought is of his mother; when frightened a child seeks his mother first. She is naturally the child's first friend. When we think about the mother-child relationship we can see how many positive things she has done for us and how full of kindness she is. This is true not only of human mothers; even animal mothers behave the same way. They are far less competent and intelligent than humans, but still they love and protect their children. Last year I watched some robins build a nest in the corner of my porch. The mother and father bird worked so hard to build that nest. Every day they went back and forth hundreds of times gathering little sticks to build a solid structure and then bringing soft things, one hair at a time, to make the inside comfortable and smooth. Once the eggs were laid the robin parents took care of them. They protected the nest from enemies, chasing away other birds and predators. When the chicks hatched the mother brought them food, then picked up their droppings and threw them away.

Animals will fight to protect their offspring even though they may be injured or killed. When I was a child in Tibet several youngsters and I had to go after the cows way up on a hillside. There we found a large bird nest with eggs. We wanted to bring the eggs home. The mother bird was quite big so we picked up sticks to chase her away. But she fought to keep us from getting her eggs. Finally we saw that another big bird was coming, perhaps the father, and we became afraid he too would attack us so we all ran away. Usually birds fly away if humans come near, but to protect her eggs this bird was ready to fight.

Birds are not the only animals that demonstrate such care and concern for their offspring. There is a story about a highwayman who robbed horse caravans coming from Amdo to Lhasa. One time during an attack a pregnant mare was slashed with a big knife. As the horse fell to the ground her wound caused her to give birth, and soon the mare and her foal were lying in the dirt next to one another. Even though the mare was dying, she used her last bit of strength to lick the colt and try to help it. This vivid example of motherly love touched the thief so deeply that he vowed that he would never rob and kill again.

There are so many examples of a mother's love. Just look around. You can observe this love in animals, but a human mother generally uses a much wider range of skills in caring for her child. Usually we do not pay attention to how many hardships a mother undergoes for the sake of her child. Tsongkhapa says there are things that may be beyond their ability, but mothers do whatever they can to protect their children. And a mother does not only take care of her child while it is still an infant; she is concerned about her child's long-term future as well. She wants him or her to be happy and healthy, to be respectable and famous, and to have all the good things in the world. She endures a great deal of mental suffering on this account. Desiring her child's success she may scold him to correct his behavior. She may fight with her child. She may punish him harshly. Out of ignorance the child may think his mother is acting cruelly. And of course the mother is also under the power of ignorance so it is not surprising when she behaves in a mistaken and even destructive manner.

We should try to gain a proper understanding and appreciation of the entire situation. Think about these teachings, examine them point by point, and bring in details from your own experience to build up a powerful affectionate attitude toward your mother. Seeing her as a truly kind and loving friend is not something false or imaginary; you are training yourself to see the real thing. Do not forget her kindness or let your relationship be destroyed by selfish concerns arising from ignorance. With this kind of meditation try to recover the positive feelings you once had for your mother until thinking about her kindness almost makes you cry. This is very important because the goal of this yogic technique is to comprehend our close relationship with all sentient beings by starting with our present mothers.

Next we think about how kind she was to us in other lives, too. When we feel this way about her in regard to other lives, we can move on to thinking about other sentient beings. Understanding that relationships have gone back and forth over many previous lives, we think that our father, other dear friends, and our relatives have all been our mother. They have shown the same type of loving kindness toward us that this life's mother has. Then we expand our thoughts to include those who are neutral. Finally we bring in those who seem to be our enemies. We think, "Right now my enemies may be doing these hurtful things, but in the past they have been such kind mothers to me." Gradually animosity will fade as our wisdom grows. After we feel this way about our enemies, we will be able to extend this positive way of thinking further and further until it encompasses all sentient beings in the ten directions.

This understanding will not arise without employing a method. Right now under the power of ignorance, egotism, and selfishness we feel hatred, anger, jealousy, pride, and conceit. But the mind is trainable; we can develop another—a completely opposite and much more beneficial—way of thinking. Using logic and yogic techniques we can develop the pure love felt between a mother and child for all sentient beings. Meditation means to accustom oneself to something by bringing it to mind again and again. In these analytical meditations we use reason to examine a topic from many points of view. Every person has different skills but everyone uses his or her intelligence to make deductions from direct experience, observation, listening to others, hearing teachings, and formal logic. All of these are different approaches we can use to train our mind in the proper manner. When meditating we do not just think over and over again, "My mother is kind, my mother is kind, my mother is kind." That type of single-pointed concentration will not get us anywhere.

These analytic meditations may be difficult in the beginning but they will become easier and stronger as we proceed. Realizations cannot be achieved in one day. Success takes more than a little work, using more than a single reason, in more than just a few meditation sessions. It may take a long time to develop complete certainty in the object of meditation, but we should meditate until we succeed. Yogis practice this way. If you just read this book and do not do any analytical meditation on your own, your mind may become tough. In the future if you read or hear about this topic, you may think, "I know this already; I do not need this." The teachings cannot help someone whose mind is as hard as iron. This method can transform your mind a hundred percent. There is no other method than this to develop the mind. So now that we have the opportunity we should examine as closely as possible the line of reasoning explained in the lamrim. The more we deliberate on these points, the stronger our understanding and attitude of affection will be. In the beginning we may simply follow the outlines provided in the scriptures, but eventually those words will be the horse that carries the mind along the path of spiritual development. We will eventually be able to actualize affectionate love from the depths of our hearts. If we do this, our positive attitude will become irreversible; ignorance and other wrong views will be powerless to overcome it.

(iii) Cultivating the wish to repay your mothers' kindness

After developing a strong recognition of all our mothers' kindness we begin to think about how to repay that benevolence. What kind of repayment? How will we settle up? It is not easy to repay the almost measureless kindness of all sentient beings. Something small and temporary like a good dinner is not going to be enough. Repayment in full would be to provide them with everlasting happiness and permanent freedom from samsaric suffering. Is this possible or not? If it is you will want to do it. This is how compassion, love, and bodhicitta can be produced from this repayment mind-set.

In the *Guru Puja (Bla ma mchod pa'i cho ga)*, Panchen Losang Chökyi Gyaltsen says we begin by seeing the benefits of cherishing others:[4]

> Having seen that the door to all good qualities
> Is the thought to place all cherished mothers in happiness,
> Even if others rise up as my enemy
> May I be blessed to cherish them more than my life.

If we recognize that all sentient beings have been our kind mother we will find them so dear that we want to help them and give them happiness. This type of spontaneous loving attitude will make all our actions virtuous. It is the door to both temporary and ever-lasting good qualities. Once we have this attitude, even if all sentient beings joined together to do us injury our compassion for them would simply grow stronger. We would know that they are suffering a type of mental illness; they are dominated by ignorance and egotism. Their polluted self-centered thoughts make them act this way.

When we focus on the importance of *I and mine,* or *me and my property,* we try to dominate external things as much as possible. Whether someone actually says, "No one in the world is more important than me," is not the issue; this is the kind of thought that governs most sentient beings. Self-cherishing leads us to do selfish actions. Those actions result in many problems both near and far: between a husband and wife, between children and parents, between families, towns, and countries. Misery and suffering can make us so crazy that we attack others. When Buddhist yogis see others acting this way they think, "What can I do to help them?"

The stanza above is a prayer to succeed in developing bodhicitta through this Mahayana practice. Remember that bodhicitta combines our own and others' goals: the primary goal is to free all others from suffering and lead them to enlightenment and our personal goal is to attain enlightenment ourselves. We must attain enlightenment because that is how we will accomplish our main purpose. In order to train the mind to produce bodhicitta we have to separate these two goals and work on them individually. We do not emphasize wanting to attain our own enlightenment in the beginning. First we focus on wanting to free all sentient beings from misery and leading them to happiness and everlasting bliss. Then in order to accomplish that goal for others we engage in the training to become enlightened ourselves. When we develop this attitude and join it to the wisdom of understanding reality, the attainment of enlightenment is not too far off. This loving and compassionate attitude is a wish-fulfilling jewel for us and everyone else. If one person develops this attitude, it will influence others. If everyone were to have this attitude there would be no trouble or misery in the world; there would be no fighting and all problems would be completely solved.

It is definitely possible to attain selfless bodhicitta. With a few simple techniques we can stop many negative tendencies from arising and develop this positive attitude. How? First think about how all sentient beings are born and die due to the power of karma. We change so much with each rebirth in different realms that we do not recognize each other as having been each other's loving parents, children, and so on. In reality we are all very closely related to one another. Every other being has done so much for us and shown us so much kindness. They are all in big trouble and suffering the deep misery of birth, aging, sickness, and death in samsara. They have no protector. It would be shameful to have no concern for them and leave them to suffer alone without any help. A person who has no gratitude for the kindness shown to him or her is shameless. If we ignore our mother sentient beings, forget their kindness, and just try to get out of samsara ourselves, we are the most disgraceful type of person. If we think about this properly, eventually we will have an almost spontaneous appreciation of their past kindness and a respectful desire to repay it.

Candragomin says in *Letter to a Student (Śiṣya-lekha):*

> There is nothing more shameful than working for your own liberation
> If you recognize but ignore those reborn in a changed state—
> Your dear relatives who have fallen into the deep samsaric ocean
> And are tossed about by the strong currents of suffering.

Imagine seeing one of your close relatives—your brother, for example—fall into a deep river. He is not able to get out and the current is about to carry him away. If you had the ability to help him out of this predicament it would be terribly cruel just to sit by and let him drown. All sentient beings—whether they are humans, gods, animals, or hell denizens—are under the power of karma and the mental afflictions. They have fallen into the oceanic currents of samsaric misery. They have no power to help themselves; even those in the higher realms are in serious danger of falling into a lower rebirth.

Because sentient beings change from life to life we do not recognize them. Once your mother is reborn into a new life, her form changes to something else, but she is still your mother. If she has been reborn with the ugly little body of an insect, ignorance causes you look upon her as having no relationship to yourself. We forget that all our dear relatives are in the same type of suffering situation. It is simply a lack of knowledge that causes us to hate others and have no pity for their misery. But now we have received teachings and have the intelligence to understand the situation properly. We also have the best opportunity to do something for them. So what could be more shameful than to claim to be a Mahayana practitioner but only try to free yourself from suffering? There is nothing in the world more dishonorable than a bodhisattva who works only for his or her own happiness and liberation. A Mahayana practitioner should think, "These beings have been so kind to me. I can repay their kindness in this lifetime. I *must* do so."

The mind will not conform to this way of thinking right away. It is used to running wild because we did not meet with spiritual teachers or these instructions in most of our past lives. So this time, which is perhaps the first time, trying to train the mind will be like taming a wild elephant. It may take a long time, but it is possible.

It is helpful to think about both the positive and negative reasons for generating the compassionate wish to repay the kindness we have received from others. Consider how we view ourselves: a human who is trying to practice the Mahayana Dharma. We recognize the great kindness that all mother sentient beings have shown us and remember that right at this moment these poor mother sentient beings are experiencing external and internal conditions of suffering. We are in a better position than they are: we are grown up, understand some of the teachings, have many skills, and are physically fit. We can use all these attributes to help our mothers. How could it be right for us to ignore the past kindness they have shown us? Even low-class people—thieves, and murderers—consider it bad manners to ignore others' past kindness. So we should feel a special kind of responsibility to repay in the most complete way possible the kindness that our mothers have shown to us. This thought should rise strongly.

Candragomin's text continues:

> A child in his mother's lap is not able to do anything for himself.
> He drinks milk that flows due to his mother's love.
> He depends upon her love, which persists despite many hardships.
> Who, even of the most reprehensible classes, could abandon her and be
>   happy?

> With loving thoughts a mother takes great care
> Of the child residing in her womb and the baby when born.
> Who, even among the most disreputable, could be happy
> Abandoning his ignorant mother who has no protection from suffering?

An infant cannot even nurse without its mother's help. A mother endures many hardships doing whatever she can for her child's sake. She loves her child so much that she smiles even if she has nothing to smile about. She gives her child the ability to succeed in life. Therefore it is considered disgraceful, even by the worst types of people in the world, if a successful adult who was a beloved only child pretends not to know his mother, much less help her, when she has fallen into bad straits. But this is exactly what we have done. We have been dominated by egotistic self-cherishing; we held ourselves to be more important than anyone or anything else. Directly or indirectly all our thoughts and actions have been under the control of this enemy. The most powerful weapon to subdue selfish egotism is bodhicitta. Therefore the primary practice of Mahayana practitioners is to cherish others so much that they strive to attain enlightenment in order to help them solve their problems.

The *Praise of Infinite Qualities (Guṇāparyanta-stotra)* says:

Sentient beings blinded by ignorance have little intelligence,
But as my father or son they lovingly helped me with wealth and honor.
Think, "Abandoning them to work for my own liberation is not my way."
Make prayers to lead those who lack a leader to definite freedom.

In other texts yogis remind themselves of what they have to do, but here a teacher instructs his disciple that it is terrible to forget the kindness of others. Although sentient beings are blinded by ignorance, when they are our relatives they lovingly give us wealth, respect, and whatever else would help us. We have to fight the ignorant selfish attitude that wants blissful emancipation just for ourselves. What good is personal pleasure when those who have had so much compassion for us from beginningless time are in deep trouble? Could we truly be happy when those who love us are suffering? Although the stanza literally says we should pray, it means we should dedicate our merit to the primary goal: permanent freedom from suffering and the highest bliss for all sentient beings.

When we are convinced that we could not enjoy ourselves without repaying the kindness of others we will not be able to stand not doing something. What should we do? The usual manner of social recompense can become the cause of more trouble. Giving a small gift or fighting on someone's behalf might appear to help someone temporarily, but actually it may increase their samsaric desire and mental afflictions. It does not lead to everlasting peace.

In *Heart of the Middle Way (Madhyamaka-hṛdaya)* the yogi Bhāvaviveka says:

Moreover, in the past I was possessed
By the evil spirit—ignorance.
As if I had irritated their wounds,
I made the misery of suffering beings worse.

A wound is a source of pain. If you bring something sharp in contact with a wound, it hurts even more. Bhāvaviveka says to himself, "Mother sentient beings are like patients wounded by samsaric suffering. In the past because of my hatred, jealousy, and attachment I did not do anything to lead them to freedom and blissful happiness. In a half-hearted attempt to help them I just did a little of this and a little of that. It looks like I did as much as I could to make their suffering worse!" He continues his thought as follows:

In other lives many others
Helped me with love and respect.

What other than emancipation
Can repay their beneficial actions?

Wise people think they are in great debt if they have not done anything to repay someone's kindness to them. Tsongkhapa says it is taught that not repaying the kindness of others is a heavier burden than carrying the weight of the world's oceans and mountains, whereas repayment is worthy of praise by the wise. Temporary assistance is not the best thing we can do to repay others. To truly repay their kindness we need something unique: peace, happiness, and bliss that will last. Therefore the only way really to help others is to lead them to complete emancipation from samsara. That liberation is everlasting and pure; it cuts off the repeated cycle of birth and death. If we give them this we will repay everything they have done for us in countless lives.

A bodhisattva takes upon him- or herself responsibility to repay the kindness of sentient beings. It is a huge burden, but bodhisattvas know that from beginningless time up to now everything we did was for ourselves and our own purposes. These selfish actions made us suffer, made others miserable, and we have nothing left to show for it. Now, as it says in *Verses from the Nāga King's Drum (Nāga-rāja-bherī-gāthā)*, we can work to benefit others rather than ourselves:

The oceans, mountains, and earth
Are not a great burden for me.
However not repaying others' kindness
Is a great burden for me.

Those whose minds are not distracted
Know and want to repay others' kindness.
Whatever they do is not wasted.
That is worthy of great praise by the wise.

To sum up Tsongkhapa gives an analogy that explains how we should think about repaying the kindness of others. Imagine that your dear mother has gone crazy or blind and is wandering along a dangerous road. Perhaps she is walking toward a cliff where one wrong step could result in a terrible plunge downward. Who should she be able to rely upon in that situation? If you, her beloved child, are able to lead her to safety, it is your responsibility to do so. It is right in every way that you should help her in her time of need. All sentient beings are in a similar situation. Because of the mental afflictions their minds do not function normally; it is as if they are sickened by a disease or addled by a drug. Not only are they mentally ill, they are blind; ignorance prevents them from seeing their situation properly. They do not see the danger they are in; they cannot see what is right. Every day of their life is spent walking toward great peril. After death something very dreadful will occur because they did not see where they were going. There is no one to lead them in the proper direction. If there were someone who could help them it might be okay, but there is not. They are in imminent danger of falling into a lower rebirth. A yogi sees this state of affairs very clearly and strongly desires to do something to help these mother sentient beings.

We can become a leader of sentient beings. From the teachings we can learn how to develop a desire to repay their kindness by giving them freedom from samsara and attainment of the highest happiness. We should think, "Now is the time for these mother sentient beings to depend upon me. They should expect this from me." We can show them that what they thought was helpful is really harmful because actions under the power of attachment, hatred, jealousy, and pride are stepping-stones to the misery of samsaric rebirth, usually in the lower realms. Even if, with our help, they are unable to achieve full emancipation from samsara, at least we can show them a path to a higher rebirth from where they can work to achieve liberation.

When this kind of thought becomes strong our actions will follow suit. So it is important to establish this attitude in the beginning. It is difficult to do, but no matter how long it takes we should work on it until we succeed. Even if we do not attain enlightenment in this life, our future lives will be improved by creating great merit. Wherever we are born others will naturally trust and love us.

Śāntideva's *Compendium of Trainings (Śikṣā-samuccaya)* also expresses these ideas:

> Crazed by mental afflictions and blinded by ignorance,
> We stumble dangerously every step
> Along a path traversing many precipices.
> This is always the basis of my own and others' suffering.
> All travelers are equal in misery.

Sentient beings are called *travelers* or *go-ers* because they move from one rebirth to the next in samsara. This stanza is usually quoted to show how everyone is equal because we are all in this pitiful suffering situation. However it is also appropriate to conclude the discussion of the first three points of the sevenfold cause-and-effect personal instructions: seeing all sentient beings as your mother, recognizing their kindness, and repaying their kindness. Once these are in mind, it is easy for affectionate love to arise. The next topic is how to actually produce bodhicitta.

2" THE ACTUAL PRODUCTION OF THIS ATTITUDE

Generating the actual intention to accomplish the goal of others' enlightenment has three parts:

(a) The cultivation of love
(b) The cultivation of compassion
(c) The cultivation of the superior thought

Love, compassion, and the superior thought all have others, not oneself, as their object. Since the desire to help others is the goal of these attitudes, they are called *the attitudes that seek others' goals.* These three are the basis for the development of spontaneous bodhicitta. First we generate love that wants all sentient beings to possess everlasting happiness. After this we develop compassion that wants all sentient beings to be free from misery from the root. Out of great compassion and love arises the determination to take responsibility to bring sentient beings to the highest happiness and lead them from suffering. This superior thought is more than a mere wish; it is actually taking responsibility to act. The superior thought is like a wise young man who sees the trouble faced by his family, decides that it is his duty to help them, and dedicates himself to carrying out this task.

(a) THE CULTIVATION OF LOVE

Actual love arises after one feels affectionate love for all sentient beings equally without discrimination. Usually when people talk about whom they sincerely love they are referring to a few or even just one sentient being. The love developed here has all sentient beings who do not possess happiness as its object. There are three subjective levels of this attitude. First one thinks, "How nice it would be if all mother sentient beings possessed happiness." Slightly stronger is the second level of thought: "May all these beings possess happiness." Finally one thinks, "I will make sure they possess happiness." This is a gradual process; we progress from thinking how nice it would be if they were happy, through wishing that they had happiness, to finally taking responsibility to ensure their happiness.

Tsongkhapa refers to the *King of Concentrations Sutra (Samādhi-rāja-sūtra)* to show that there is no comparison to the enormous amount of merit that comes from sincere love for all sentient beings. The sutra says that if you constantly fill the entire universe with expensive and lovely things and offer them to the supreme field of merit—the buddhas and bodhisattvas—great virtue would result. In many ways this is the supreme way to create merit; it is the best from the point of view of the object to whom you are presenting the offering, the superb quality of the offering itself, and the fact that you are making this offering constantly. But this merit still does not compare to the merit created by great love. Nāgārjuna says something very similar:[5]

> The amount of merit created
> From filling millions of worlds
> With offerings for the great beings
> Cannot compare to that of the loving mind.

The *Array of Qualities in Mañjuśrī's Buddha-realm Sutra (Mañjuśrī-buddha-kṣetra-guṇa-vyūha-sūtra)* compares the merit created by meditating on love to the merit created in a pure land. Certain yogis practice a special kind of higher training on the path of meditation called *absorption of cessation ('gog pa'i snyoms 'jug)*. This is a special kind of meditative absorption that arrests the mind and mental factors. It would require a lot of explanation to describe this āryan practice, so let's simply say that it is not something an ordinary sentient being can do. As a result of this practice, even though the yogis are not yet buddhas, they are born in the Buddha Buddeśvara's pure land and experience great peace and happiness. There they can keep their religious vows for eons. Of course, if one kept pure morality in a buddhafield for hundreds of thousands of years one would create a great deal of merit. However this sutra says that you create much more virtue as a human even if just once, just for a moment, you sincerely want all sentient beings to have happiness. If this is the case for an instant of love, what needs to be said about the amount of merit we would create if we had this attitude day and night for a long time? The reason one creates less merit in the pure land than in the human realm is because the Buddha's power of prayer and dedication affects those born in a pure land so it is not difficult for them to keep pure religious conduct for ages. In contrast, in our short human lifetimes there is so much internal and external turmoil that to produce love in this environment is very rare and quite difficult.

Everyone is trying to achieve some kind of goal. If you are striving for your own temporary enjoyment it is not considered religious practice. It is ordinary activity that may cause trouble directly or indirectly. Dharma practice is compassionate by nature. The goal of compassionate activity is not to injure others; one always tries to avoid harmful attitudes and actions that destroy others' happiness. Thus the most basic level of Dharma practice is to keep away from the ten nonvirtuous actions. All of the Hinayana virtuous practices are based on not harming others. Through the practice of nonharming one can accomplish the goals of those with lower or intermediate spiritual aspirations—to have a better rebirth or to gain liberation in this or future lives. One creates far greater virtue if, in addition to not harming others, one provides them with excellent and blissful things. Instead of being concerned only with oneself, one is focused upon benefiting others. Thus love and compassion are the foundation of Mahayana practice.

Tsongkhapa quotes from Nāgārjuna's *Precious Garland* to elaborate this point:

> There is no comparison between the merit
> Created from one short moment of love
> And that from offering three times everyday
> Three hundred pots of the best food.

Producing love for sentient beings even for a short time creates greater merit than making vast and extensive offerings. Nāgārjuna explains this with an example that people of his day could easily understand. In ancient India the best foodstuffs were cooked in small clay pots. He says that the merit created by offering others three hundred pots of this food three times a day cannot compare to the merit created from an instant of love.

The next stanza of this text discusses eight beneficial results that arise from meditating on love:

> Even if you do not attain liberation,
> There are eight benefits from love:
> Deities and men come to love you,
> They also will protect you,
> You will be happy and have much physical pleasure,
> Poison and weapons cannot harm you,
> You attain your goals without much effort,
> And will be reborn in the Brahmā realms.

Love is the opposite of wanting to harm others. If you love others they will want to assist you. This does not mean that if a person is not angry and selfish it necessarily follows that everyone around him will be calm and loving. However meditating on love is the best protection from harm because sincere love only benefits others and makes it easy to accomplish your goals. For example, just before the Buddha attained enlightenment many demons tried to prevent him from succeeding, but because he was meditating on love he did not get angry at them. Overpowered by his love, the demons' weapons could not harm him; their arrows turned into flowers. Finally, if one practices love and is then reborn in samsara, it will be in one of the higher rebirth realms. The *Brahmā realms* are another name for the four limitless absorptions of the form realm. The *final Brahmā* refers to the highest state of buddhahood.

The great Mahayana practitioner Śāntideva also explains the benefits of love:[6]

> Whatever misery there is in the world
> Arises from pursuing one's own desires.
> Whatever happiness there is in the world
> Comes from desiring others to be happy.

Self-cherishing, which is a lack of love and compassion, is the cause of all misery. The opposite is also true; even in a worldly sense happiness comes from concern for others. Even if you are not seeking fame or respect you will gain them if you have sincere concern for your family, town, or country. If everyone in the world wanted to help others and give them happiness, there would be no disharmony, fighting, or trouble. Even in a temporal sense there would be happiness and peace. Buddhahood, the final goal of enlightenment, arises from the desire for others to have happiness, perfect compassion, and wisdom. Therefore the highest Buddhist practice is to eliminate one's selfishness and cherish others.

Even though it is difficult to produce sincere love we should make an effort to do so. We can accomplish this aim; as humans we have the opportunity to succeed. There are many historical examples of great sages, buddhas, and bodhisattvas who accomplished this spiritual practice. They were no different from us; they were all ordinary humans when they started to practice. At first, even if they do not come from your heart, at least say the words, "How nice it would be if all sentient beings were peaceful and happy."

In the *Compendium of Trainings* Śāntideva advises us to recite various stanzas from the *Sutra of the Golden Light (Suvarṇa-prabhāsa-sūtra)* because they are about how to put love into practice. For example:

> May the sound of great drum of the *Pure Golden Light*
> Pacify the suffering of the lower realms, the anguish of death,
> The misery of poverty, and all suffering,
> Here in the three realms of the trichiliocosm.[7]

The point of repeating words from this sutra, other scriptures, and prayers is to put their ideas into your mind. What does this stanza mean? The *Sutra of the Golden Light* is like a big drum that makes a relaxing and enjoyable sound. Recitation of this sutra's explanation of love, śūnyatā, and so on, makes music that pervades the three samsaric realms—the desire, form, and formless realms. We dedicate the merit of reading this sutra aloud by praying, "By hearing the great drum of this teaching may all sentient beings be freed from all types of misery." To create great merit it is important to think about what you are saying; do not just say these words because you like their sound. Try to feel the meaning of the words; then you will be doing a meditation along with your recitation. Uniting thought to the repetition of prayers will bring a special result. You will have succeeded in this practice when a feeling of love arises spontaneously and sincerely within you.

There is a progression to follow when meditating on love. The process is important, Tsongkhapa says, because if we do not follow the right order our love will be superficial. We start by meditating on those we already love: our friends, relatives, and parents. After love rises strongly for those who are dear to us, we take neutral beings as our object. *Neutral beings* are those who are neither our enemies nor our friends. We practice feeling love for them until our love is sincere. Then we use the same techniques and meditations to develop love for those whom we usually dislike or consider to be our enemies. Remember it is the mind that makes a distinction between friend, enemy, and neutral persons; there is no individual who is ultimately one or the other. Once we have the same degree of love for our enemy, friends, and neutral persons, we can move on to all mother sentient beings. If we work through these stages our love will be sincere. If we start meditating in a generalized way about all sentient beings, we will find love lacking when particular situations arise.

The way to meditate on love is similar to the manner of meditating on compassion. Where compassion is wanting sentient beings to be free from misery, love is wanting them to possess happiness, enjoyment, and bliss. So here we look at sentient beings, beginning with our relatives, and see that they do not even have worldly happiness. They are not looking for the highest spiritual bliss; they simply want the commonplace kinds of happiness, wealth, and pleasure that they currently lack. Think about this in detail and in various ways. Go back and forth, first thinking that sentient beings lack a specific thing and therefore they suffer this or that type of misery, and then wishing that they have the cause of happiness. Think this way again and again and you will come to feel like a mother whose dear child is in need of many things. A mother wants her child to have the things that will make him or her happy; she sincerely desires to help her child obtain those things.

This explanation is short and lacks many details. Love can be approached in many ways. Wherever we go and in connection to whatever we are doing we can consider how sentient beings lack peace and happiness and make them the object of our love. When you start thinking this way you will find an object everywhere. Beginning is difficult; it takes skill in meditation. However if you follow the steps of this technique the desire that all sentient beings have bliss will eventually arise spontaneously.

When you feel this kind of real, powerful love you will begin to consider taking on the responsibility to help them have happiness. You think about this until the desire to take responsibility to help all others arises strongly. Then ask yourself, "How can I provide them with happiness?" The great saint Śāntideva provides the answer to this question:[8]

> Leaders of beings with measureless wisdom,
> Upon analysis have determined the best method
> To free beings from their suffering state:
> It is to firmly rely upon precious bodhicitta.

Only buddhas can guide others to freedom from all suffering because only they have perfect wisdom and compassion. They know every possible method to lead sentient beings to safety. When the omniscient buddhas considered what the best method would be for us to use to free others from suffering, they determined that it is bodhicitta: the desire to attain enlightenment in order to benefit all other sentient beings. Why? Because it is not possible to help others perfectly until one is equipped to do it. We need wisdom; we need to understand their problems, the kinds of practices and paths suitable for them to follow, and how to attain the highest perfection. Along with wisdom, we have to have the ability and power to help them. Even knowledge and power are not enough; we have to have compassion as well. Otherwise we might just sit around and all our power and knowledge would be unhelpful to others. In order to have the combination of wisdom, power, and compassion that can perfectly help all sentient beings without discrimination we must attain the state of highest enlightenment. Until then our ability to help is limited. Even if we try to help others, our help will be partial, extending only to some, or it might help in some ways but harm in others.

Great love and compassion are the direct causes of this mind-set. The next step toward desiring to attain a perfect state in order to help others is to cultivate compassion.

(b) THE CULTIVATION OF COMPASSION

Great compassion is wanting all sentient beings to be free from suffering. In other words the object of great compassion is any living creature suffering any type of misery. If you want emancipation from suffering for yourself and others you have to know what suffering is. Otherwise you may think, "I do not need liberation because I am not suffering." Ordinary sentient beings are like children: we only see what is right in front of us. We identify suffering only as obvious sharp pain and we desire just ordinary happiness. Unaware of the more subtle aspects of misery we do not see the need to pursue religious goals and emancipation. We see no danger looming in the future.

So what is suffering? To make it easier for us to comprehend the many types of misery endured by sentient beings, the Buddha sometimes summarized this vast subject into three types: the suffering of suffering, the suffering of change, and pervasive suffering. (See volume 2, chapters 5–7.) The first one, the suffering of suffering, is easy to understand. It is ordinary misery such as physical pain and mental distress. The second type of suffering, the suffering of change, can be understood on both an ordinary level and more subtly. Most people do not like change; that is the ordinary understanding of the suffering of change. But great sages see that even what we usually call happiness is actually misery. For example, we usually think it is pleasurable to get warm in the sunshine when we are cold. But heat is also the cause of misery. Instead of getting more and more enjoyment as we sit in the sun, we start feeling miserably hot and want to go somewhere cold. All worldly pleasures are impure because they contain the seed of misery. They are not perfect sources of delight. From the yogi's perspective, therefore, because ordinary enjoyment changes it is actually suffering.

The third type of suffering, pervasive suffering, is the most subtle of the three. The term *pervasive* applies to our body and mind; both are completely saturated with suffering. Just being born is suffering because it is caused by a combination of karma and the mental afflictions. The great yogis and bodhisattvas see that our delicate bodies are always ready to be a cause of pain and trouble. The body in and of itself is not obviously painful, but it is the basis of pain. For example, just a little bit of heat, cold, a tiny needle, or rich food can make us miserable. It is as if the body were a big wound or a sore. Sometimes a wound does not hurt, but the slightest touch can make it extremely painful. Even life as a deity in the form or formless realms is caused by karma and therefore afflicted with pervasive suffering. Those gods enjoy a long and peaceful life but they have no control over it. Their temporary high state will soon be over. Every moment shortens the remainder of their life and moves them closer to death; every moment they use up their good karma. They are still subject to karma and the mental afflictions so they are in danger of falling down to lower rebirths. That is the nature of life; this is the nature of the subtle misery of pervasive suffering.

Without studying this subject we only recognize the first type of suffering and usually just in relation to ourselves. It takes more knowledge to see that we are suffering from the other types of misery as well. Even if we are aware of the other two, we often try to ignore them. But the object of great compassion is any sentient being enduring any of the three types of suffering. So the practice of great compassion does not only focus on those who have immediate pain; it encompasses all beings who are born in the three realms of samsara under the power of karma and the mental afflictions. Therefore, those who practice the Dharma examine all types of suffering and its causes. They see that the way to eliminate suffering is to remove its causes. Not only do they recognize that cessation of suffering is possible, they see there is a path to get to that cessation. Understanding the four noble truths will make one's practice stronger and more meaningful.

The subjective aspect of compassion is the practitioner's attitude toward the object of compassion. There are three levels to wanting others to be free from misery. The most basic level is to think how nice it would be if all sentient beings were free from suffering. The next level is a dedication prayer; one wishes, "May they be free from misery." And finally on the third level one takes responsibility to free sentient beings from suffering. Hinayana practitioners develop the first two levels of compassion. They see the misery of sentient beings and think how wonderful it would be if they were all free from it. They may dedicate merit and prayers to this end, but they do not take personal responsibility to make that occur. In contrast, the third aspect of compassion is the focus for Mahayana practitioners.

A way to understand this difference is through the analogy of seeing a child fall into a pool of quicksand. Hinayana practitioners would be like the person who thinks, "How wonderful it would be if this child could get out of this horrible mud. I hope somebody will be able to save the child from drowning." They have ordinary compassion; they strongly wish for a good result but they do not take responsibility to accomplish it themselves. Mahayana compassion is like what the drowning child's father feels. He feels worse for the child than if he were in trouble himself. Without question he will jump right in and strive to free his child. Taking on the responsibility to free others from suffering is a mark of the Mahayana, the great vehicle. So while in general we can identify three levels of compassion, in the context of the sevenfold cause-and-effect method, we are referring only the last one—taking responsibility to free others from suffering.

Do not think that this is some minor ancillary practice or something only for beginners. It is the heart of the Mahayana. It may take your whole life to develop this strong compassion; it may take more than one life to spontaneously generate the intention to take responsibility to free all sentient beings. You will reach that level, but it develops gradually from following the same method we use to develop love and equanimity. The order is to start with those we already have sympathy for—our parents, children, or friends. We think about their problems and feel so much sympathy for them that we want to take responsibility to help them. After that feeling is quite well developed, we change our focus to those who are neither our enemy nor our friend—those about whom we are neutral. We concentrate on their difficult situations until we have as much pity for them as we do for our dearest friends. Then we can move on to those we do not like, the people we consider to be our enemies. We slowly work to see that they are the same as our most beloved spouse. When we recognize that, we can look at all three categories simultaneously. On one side we visualize our friends, on the other our enemies, and in the middle the neutral ones. We contemplate their equality and feel equal sympathy for them; we want them to be equally free from misery. Then we can generalize this to a desire to free all sentient beings anywhere in the ten directions.

Tsongkhapa's advice on how to develop great compassion follows the recommendations in the *Sutra on Knowledge (Abhidharma-sūtra)* and Kamalaśila's *Stages of Meditation*. Kamalaśila was a great Indian teacher who was instrumental in bringing Buddhism to Tibet. He wrote the *Stages of Meditation* to explain how those with great spiritual capacity should practice compassion. In that text he says that if we try to develop great compassion for all sentient beings in general from the start, our compassion will stay superficial. It may appear that we have developed great compassion, but when we think about a particular sentient being our compassion evaporates! We can get angry; we find some people we do not like. So we begin by working on our feelings about individuals: our friends, then those toward whom we are neutral, and finally our enemies. Later as our practice develops we can start with our enemies, move on to those who are neutral, and then consider our dear friends. We have to go back and forth in order to experience deeply a shift in our attitude. We have to feel compassion and love equally for beings in all three categories because in reality there is no one out there who is ultimately our enemy or dear friend. Gradually, through practice, we can generalize more and more until we can include all sentient beings and our compassion becomes spontaneous. Then no matter who confronts us, whether a group or individuals, we will have equal compassion and love for all.

This method presumes we have already developed the recognition that all sentient beings have been our dear mothers. Here we consider that all these mother sentient beings are caught in the great trap of samsara: sometimes they are born in a better life, sometimes they cycle down to the lower realms, other times they occupy an intermediate position. Even during one lifetime they undergo so many ups and downs without any control. They experience the general misery of samsara—birth, aging, sickness, death, meeting undesirable situations, and separating from what they desire—as well as the specific suffering of the each of the six realms.[9]

Tsongkhapa says that sometimes people think that bodhisattvas do not need to contemplate samsaric suffering. They have the mistaken idea that meditation on suffering is meant only for those with intermediate spiritual capacity who must understand the nature of misery in order to desire their own escape from it. It is true that from a realization of the truth of suffering Hinayana practitioners develop the thought of renunciation—the strong and spontaneous desire for freedom from suffering for themselves forever. However, this does not mean that meditation on suffering is not suitable for bodhisattvas. On the contrary, bodhisattvas have to see the nature of suffering even more clearly than Hinayana practitioners because before one can produce great compassion that desires to eliminate all others' suffering, one must understand the faults of suffering in relation to oneself. Only after we see our own suffering and develop renunciation can we have true sympathy for others experiencing the same miserable state.

The meditations on suffering prescribed for those of intermediate spiritual capacity cannot be skipped; if we try to start by thinking about others' suffering and not our own, we will not develop compassion from the heart. Therefore those on the Mahayana path need to think about the suffering of samsara in hundreds and thousands of ways because one's compassion and love is in proportion to one's understanding of others' suffering. If we do not see that others have a problem, or just acknowledge that they have a little difficulty, the strength of our compassion will be weak. Meditation on suffering in great detail brings a special urgency, power, and spontaneity to love and compassion.

This method of mental training works because it is based on how the mind functions. The more we think about how wonderful something is the more we will desire it. It does not matter if our reasons are right or wrong, the more we focus on its various past, present, and future benefits, our attachment for it becomes stronger and stronger. Hatred works the same way, and so does love and compassion. Therefore we need to think about many aspects of suffering to make our compassion strong. We consider these for a long time to make our compassion stable. Most of us, however, do not want to contemplate the misery of our lives. We are like someone stuck in jail but we see our prison as a nice place. Not wanting to know the reality of one's state of affairs leads to greater problems. The sutras, great teachers, saints, and yogis explain that if we do not know our problems, how can we find the appropriate solution?

Here I have presented Tsongkhapa's brief explanation of samsaric suffering. It is suitable to review a short summary for an overview of the practices, but do not be satisfied with just that. You will impoverish yourself if you are satisfied with hearing a little bit here and there; you make yourself weak by relying on just a simple short meditation text and ignoring the great books of scripture. If you want to progress you must meditate on the details that support these general points. For a more extensive account of how to meditate on suffering, you should look at Asaṅga's *Bodhisattva Levels* and other great texts.

Study and understanding will give you confidence. You do not need to sit in unmoving solitude to do this kind of meditation. Think about what is taught in the scriptures and apply it to what is occurring around you. When you begin to realize the truth of suffering, everywhere you look you will see it immediately. When you are out in traffic look at other people hurrying around. Think about their misery; they would not be rushing so much if they did not have so many problems. If you look at them with ignorance you do not see the rushing as suffering; you may even think it is enjoyable and want to race after them! This pertains to whatever you are practicing. You must try to understand it clearly, examine it well, and open your wisdom eye through experience. Wisdom is seeing the truth and seeing the truth is always good. Without a broad and deep understanding of suffering you will not realize that the foundation of the Mahayana path is great compassion. If you focus on just one small aspect of suffering you will not see the whole picture. You should not be satisfied if you feel some compassion and love for a single object for a short time. A vague, unclear experience of compassion will not lead anywhere.

How do you know when great compassion arises? It is easy to check if you are close to becoming a bodhisattva. In the first *Stages of Meditation* Kamalaśīla says that the key factor for measuring your progress is whether compassion for all sentient beings arises spontaneously, naturally, and effortlessly by itself. In the beginning by making a conscious and concerted effort we may feel compassion for a few short moments, but it is not strong and does not last. Spontaneous compassion is similar to the feeling that a mother has for her one darling child. She loves that child from the depths of her heart. Whenever her child experiences pain or is in a difficult situation, she fervently wants him or her to pull through. Does this desire arise just once a day, once in a while? No, it is in her heart all the time no matter what she is doing. She does not need to make an effort to think about it; it arises naturally. Great compassion is to feel this way for all sentient beings. Examine yourself to see if you have this attitude for all sentient beings all the time or not. In the beginning it will not be there at all. Through this practice you become more and more aware of others' problems and your compassion will become stronger and stronger. Changing your feelings is a mark of great success. That is the sign of becoming a great saint or bodhisattva.

As you develop compassion you will begin to avoid all negative attitudes and faulty actions. Not only that, you will wipe out the negative karma that you have amassed in the past. All negative thoughts and actions are in relation to other beings. Hatred and injuring other living beings are the causes of misery. Great compassion is the opposite; it is wanting others to be free from suffering all the time. When this positive thought is spontaneous, it is so strong that there is no opportunity for anger or other evil attitudes to arise. When we eliminate malicious attitudes we will not engage in evil actions. When evil actions are eliminated, there is no cause for future miserable results. There also will be no conditions that are appropriate for the ripening of prior negative karma. Without negative causes and conditions there will not be any suffering. Even though you are not looking for your own happiness, you will be happy. Even if you pray to suffer in order to help other sentient beings, you will not because you have destroyed the causes of suffering. I cannot express how delightful it would be if everyone in just one family—a father, mother, and children—had compassion for each other. It is so much more wonderful when compassion is for all sentient beings; it brings everyone the benefits of happiness, peace, and prosperity. In this way great compassion is a real, everlasting friend for you and other sentient beings.

How do you know when real love or bodhicitta has arisen? It is similar to knowing when you have succeeded in developing great compassion—they must be spontaneous. Tsongkhapa quotes the *Stages of Meditation* to expand on this point:

> Therefore, because of the strength of your experience of great compassion you vow to lead all sentient beings. So bodhicitta, which has the nature of aspiring to complete unsurpassable enlightenment, arises without effort.

Great compassion necessarily precedes bodhicitta. When we meditate on great compassion we look directly at sentient beings and want to free them from misery. By accustoming ourselves to that thought over and over again, our compassion becomes powerful. Then we look at ourselves and recognize that although we want to draw other sentient beings out from the ocean of samsara, we cannot do it. What do we have to do in order to be able to accomplish that task? We think, "To equip myself to do whatever is necessary to help sentient beings I need method and wisdom. I must be free from all obstacles. There is no solution other than to attain enlightenment."

In Tibetan the desire to attain perfect enlightenment in order to benefit other sentient beings is *jang chub gyi sem (byang chub gyi sems)*. This term can be broken down into its syllables. Enlightenment is *jang chub. Jang* means to be purified of all obstacles and their causes; every negative has completely ceased. *Chub* is to realize reality and truth; it is omniscience, knowing everything. With omniscience you know exactly what to do to help all other sentient beings because you see their problems and the best way to solve those problems based on their capacity and desires. *Sem* means *thought;* in this case the thought is desiring enlightenment. The measure of bodhicitta is when this desire arises naturally, without requiring deliberation or effort. Later I will explain that there are two types of bodhicitta: aspirational bodhicitta *(smon sems)* and active or engaging bodhicitta *('jug sems)*. Here bodhicitta is the former: the wish to attain buddhahood as quickly as possible.

The spontaneous bodhicitta drawn forth from great compassion is not an accomplishment of the higher āryan stages of the path. It is not even an achievement related to the first few āryan bodhisattva stages. This is something that occurs at the very, very beginning of the bodhisattva path; one enters the Mahayana path when aspirational bodhicitta arises. The bodhisattva path has five levels or sub-paths: the paths of accumulation, preparation, seeing, meditation, and no further training. Spontaneous aspirational bodhicitta marks entry into the path of accumulation.

Asaṅga's great work, the *Mahayana Compendium (Mahāyāna-saṃgraha)*, which collects the essence of the Mahayana teachings, says:

> When the good and the wish are powerful,
> Firmly stable, and always increasing,
> A bodhisattva begins to practice
> Over three countless eons.

In some contexts the term *good*, which appears in the first line of the stanza, can be understood to refer to positive karma. But here it is referring to the great compassion and love for all other sentient beings that precedes bodhicitta. The *wish* is bodhicitta itself: the desire to attain enlightenment in order to benefit other sentient beings. That wish will be firm when it arises from great love and compassion. It will not disappear and will only become better and better. When someone develops those qualities he or she becomes a bodhisattva. So bodhicitta is at the very beginning, before one even begins to practice the Mahayana.

According to the sutras, after bodhicitta spontaneously arises it takes over three countless eons to accumulate the merit and wisdom necessary to attain enlightenment. *Countless* does not mean the length of time cannot be measured; it is the name of a very large number: ten to the sixtieth power. It could take that long to accumulate merit but the length of time is not the principal concern here; the issue is the amount of merit that must be amassed. During the first countless eon a bodhisattva accumulates merit by practicing the first two paths: accumulation and preparation. There are ten higher bodhisattva stages, called āryan stages, which begin when one enters the path of seeing. The first through the seventh āryan bodhisattva stages are the paths of seeing and part of the path of meditation; these are practiced during the second countless eon. The last three āryan stages—the eighth, ninth and tenth, collectively called the *three pure stages*—are the last part of the path of meditation and are practiced during the last countless eon. After that the practitioner enters the path of no further training, the state of buddhahood itself.

So it is clear, Tsongkhapa says, that the bodhisattva beginning three countless eons of accumulation must already have aspirational bodhicitta. He scolds us because some people mistakenly believe that they have attained bodhicitta even if they have not developed great compassion. They think that if they simply dedicate their virtues by saying, "I must attain buddhahood for all sentient beings, so for that purpose I create this merit," they have attained bodhicitta and are engaged in its practice. If, however, they have not trained in the essential practices to develop bodhicitta, then they are merely saying the words with conceited pride. It does not mean that it is not good to say them. It is good to do this as a mental exercise, but it is not real bodhicitta. It is a complete misunderstanding to think that bodhicitta will arise if you say the words but do not practice the actual method to develop it.

Those who have reached a higher level of the path really know the essence of the Mahayana teaching. They find it laughable when people expect someone will confer buddhahood, spiritual achievements, and powers upon them when they meditate on a deity or do some recitations. Of course we need some outside help, but no one can cram enlightenment into us the way we stuff a statue with mantras written on bits of paper. Bodhicitta and other qualities have to be developed through our own effort.

Training the mind is not easy. Just having this thought occasionally does not make one a bodhisattva. Sometimes bodhisattvas practice great love, compassion, and bodhicitta for many eons. Therefore there is no need to say that those who actually have bodhicitta have trained themselves for a long time. Their understanding is not superficial; they worked until it became a sincere and spontaneous attitude. Many teachers and teachings say that the central practice is developing bodhicitta. Tsongkhapa makes it clear that this should not be understood to mean that we should not do any other practices. Bodhicitta is one of the essential teachings and we must practice it to enter the Mahayana, but this does not mean we should not do anything else.

The term *bodhicitta* can be understood quite widely. There are many types of bodhicitta. At the very beginning our bodhicitta is artificial. Beginning practitioners generally want their own freedom and enjoyment; others' goals are far from their thoughts. It takes great effort to learn the techniques, study the teachings, and practice them over and over until we have an overwhelming consideration for others. By making an effort we can sometimes produce a sincere attitude for a short time. It is not spontaneous so it is not the real thing, but artificial bodhicitta is a step toward real bodhicitta. We can produce artificial bodhicitta by listening to teachings, reading religious books, or seeing a specific example of misery in the world. *Engaging in the Bodhisattva Deeds* explains that after one produces artificial bodhicitta through these methods one takes the bodhisattva vows. Then one is committed to trying to produce bodhicitta three times every day by thinking in a specific way; in addition one begins work on the real training to produce bodhicitta. We practice various meditations and exercises for a long, long time to produce actual, spontaneous bodhicitta. Eventually love, compassion, and bodhicitta will naturally and spontaneously arise. Until they are spontaneous we have to work on our practice. It is like becoming an expert in a sport; in the beginning the movements are difficult, possibly even painful, and can almost seem impossible. But with practice they become effortless. Developing spontaneous bodhicitta may take your entire life; for some people it may take several lives. It depends on your capacity and previous connection with this subject matter.

Śāntideva organized his text *Engaging in the Bodhisattva Deeds* according to this order of practice to develop bodhicitta: first generating artificial bodhicitta, then producing bodhicitta through ritual, and finally engaging in the meditative training. The first chapter of the text presents the benefits, necessity, and importance of bodhicitta. Then after that the text discusses the importance of purification, compassion, and accumulation of merit through the seven-limb prayer. Then comes a chapter that deals with taking hold of bodhicitta through ritual and receiving the bodhisattva vow. After these early chapters the text explains how to keep the precepts and practice the bodhisattva path. In separate chapters Śāntideva discusses the practice of the first four perfections: generosity, ethical discipline, patience, and joyous perseverance. Then in the chapter on the fifth perfection, meditative stabilization, he gives an extensive explanation of how to produce bodhicitta through the method called *Exchanging Oneself and Others*. If we follow this process our bodhicitta will have the proper characteristics.

The sixth perfection, wisdom, is also important. Although people know that both method and wisdom are necessary in combination to achieve any spiritual result, many misunderstand the practice of wisdom. They think that realization of śūnyatā, emptiness, means emptiness of mind. In other words they think the mind should be blank. Some sutras contain expressions like "unclouded by thought" or "a mirror that does not reflect anything," but they are not to be taken literally for the practice of the path. The expression *an empty mind* is sometimes used to describe practitioners when they reach nirvana or have a direct realization of śūnyatā. At that point practitioners have gone beyond ordinary thought and have a direct understanding of the truth. In that sense *doing nothing and thinking nothing* means they are not involved in any worldly enjoyment, desire, hatred, jealousy, or pride.

Analytical thought is necessary to reach those high stages of spiritual development. Whatever we do requires thought. The *Ornament for Clear Knowledge* explains in detail how to practice the method side. The emphasis throughout its eight chapters is the path system—how to develop the mind step by step to produce bodhicitta. These special instructions on the causes needed to attain enlightenment explain bodhicitta from twenty-two varied perspectives. We should not drop these key practices and make the mind blank. It is disastrous to think that all thoughts, whether good or bad, are obstacles to attaining enlightenment. If one believes that all practices that involve thinking are impediments, one tries to push away every thought that comes up, even compassion. Thinking nothing entails doing nothing. This type of thinking and doing nothing completely misses the essence of these powerful Mahayana practices. It does not lead one anywhere near enlightenment. If you want a deeper understanding of this you should study the stanzas of this root text and the commentaries on it written by the great Indian pandits.

(c) The cultivation of the superior thought

The superior thought is exceedingly powerful compassion and love that takes full responsibility to free others from misery and lead them to the highest happiness. Earlier in the context of repaying sentient beings' kindness we looked at this idea a little bit. Remember we develop affectionate love for all sentient beings by concentrating on three topics: that all beings have been our mother, how kind they have been, and that we should repay them. Then upon considering that all these dear sentient beings desire happiness, lack everything they need, and suffer all sorts of undesirable circumstances we thought, "How nice it would be if they were free from misery; how wonderful it would be if they had the highest happiness." There is no question that something should be done for all sentient beings. Now we consider that it is not enough for us just to think this way and we resolve to take responsibility for helping them. This resolve is called the *superior thought* because you do not rely on any one else to help others, you take responsibility to do it yourself.

To seriously practice the superior thought you might do a long meditation session four times a day, as if you were taking a dose of medicine every few hours. In fact the literal meaning of the Tibetan word for a meditation session *(thun)* is *dose*. During a meditation session all other activities are pushed aside and one fully engages the mind on a specific topic. For successful progress one should keep the subject in mind after the meditation session too. If we only consider a topic during meditation sessions and let the mind go its habitual negative direction at other times, we are not reinforcing positive development. By keeping the meditation subject in mind when we are cooking, walking, or eating we condition the mind so that when we go back to another session our meditation will be more powerful. Kamalaśīla's second *Stages of Meditation* says: "You should meditate on compassion for all sentient beings all the time, whether you are sitting in meditation or engaged in any other behavior." By doing this wherever we go, we will see the problems, desires, misery, and dissatisfaction of sentient beings. Everything will contribute to the increase of our desire to help others. Our compassion and love will start like a small fire that we feed with some paper and kindling so that it becomes a large blaze. The *Stages of Meditation* specifies practicing compassion this way, but this advice applies to every topic of meditation—śūnyatā, patience, or anything else—all should be carried over to other times. Then your spiritual progress will be quicker and greater.

The great teacher Candragomin says:

From beginningless time the field of the mind
Has been soaked by the bitter water of the passions.
It is not easy to make this sweet once again:
A few drops of good qualities will not be enough.

Just a sprinkle of sugar cannot make the sour taste of a bitter lemon sweet. Similarly a few good qualities will not transform a mind that has been soured by the mental afflictions. The nature of the mental afflictions is always bad. Hatred, jealousy, pride, and attachment always have a bitter taste; they only bring misery, suffering, and trouble. Those negative mental habits have been with the mind for a long, long time so trying to change is very difficult. It is not enough to do just a short meditation on love, compassion, bodhicitta, or śūnyatā. Even a few days of meditation on these meritorious qualities is not enough for real change. These Mahayana practices are excellent, but it is wrong to expect quick results. Sometimes for a couple of days people practice so intensely that they forget to eat. But when they do not get quick results, they are so disappointed that their practice completely falls apart. This does not mean that a short meditation on compassion or love does not have any effect. Even one short moment of this meditation has great benefit and creates enormous amounts of merit. But the scale of change needed to transform the mind takes a long time and requires a lot of reinforcement. It takes firm and constant effort to change. We have to start small and build from there. We cannot do the big things until we have done the small ones. Back to the example, a single grain of sugar will not do anything to change the taste of the lemon. But slowly as we add sugar grain by grain—two, three, four, a hundred—eventually the sweet taste dominates the sour. It is important to try at the beginning and then to continue our efforts. We can make the mind free of ignorance and empowered by compassion, love, and bodhicitta. Buddhahood is a completely positive mind without any impurities whatsoever.

b" TRAINING THE MIND TO STRIVE FOR ENLIGHTENMENT

The superior thought is the direct cause of bodhicitta. It is such powerful compassion and love that one takes on the responsibility to free all sentient beings from misery and to make them happy. One decides, "this is my job." Just wanting to take responsibility is not enough. Drawn out of love and compassion we begin to search for the answer to the questions, "How can I free all these sentient beings from misery? What can I do to make them have blissful happiness?" How can we carry out this responsibility? Right now we cannot do it. Right now we cannot even help one sentient being perfectly, much less all of them. Why? We cannot do it because we are just like everyone else: handicapped by the mental afflictions, karma, suffering, and obscurations. In order to help all other sentient beings perfectly, without discrimination, and without error we have to know their situations, their problems, and the methods to solve their problems. We also need the power to do whatever is needed. We must be free of obstacles ourselves to help others become so. Therefore the best thing to do is to quickly obtain buddhahood in order to help other sentient beings. So beginning bodhisattvas must focus on their own goal: their direct object is buddhahood because it is the indirect way to benefit others.

Buddhahood is something we attain for ourselves but we do so in order to benefit others. This may sound convoluted but it is a pattern we see wise people follow every day. Wise people do not focus only on their own problems; their concern is for their family or perhaps even wider—for their country, or peace and happiness throughout the world. When they see a problem they think, "Something should be done about this. I should do something about it." They realize that to be able to effectively change things they must attain an influential position such as a president or a prime minister. Then they seek to attain that specific goal. They are striving for a personal goal in order to be able to benefit others.

There is an old Tibetan story that illustrates this. Once there was a family with a lot of children living in an area struck by famine. The family had no food for a long time and everyone was dying of hunger. One day the father was able to acquire a small chunk of meat. As he was carrying it home he thought, "This is not very big. If it is shared among everyone, each portion will be so small it will not help anyone much at all. What should I do?" He thought, "A father has the responsibility to free his family from misery. Right now I cannot search for food to feed them because I am so weak from hunger I can barely walk. If I were stronger then I could help them. Therefore the best thing I can do is eat all of this myself so that I become able to help them." He ate the meat and was able to walk a long distance to get enough food to free his entire family from hunger.

Similarly bodhisattvas are striving to fulfill others goals. They do not want to waste time because others cannot wait. From making an effort in the practices explained previously we have seen it is necessary to attain enlightenment in order to benefit others. To make this desire unshakably firm, we must have faith in what we are seeking. We have to learn about the nature of enlightenment, its qualities, what it can do, and why it is necessary to fulfill our own, and others' goals. Tsongkhapa makes a similar point in the context of taking refuge in the Three Jewels of the Buddha, Dharma, and Sangha. There he explains how the qualities of each of the objects of refuge have the power to protect us. If we do not know these details our faith in the objects of refuge will not be meaningful. In the present context if we do not really know what buddhahood is, our search for it could be selfish or even meaningless. To do any good our faith must come from thoroughly understanding the qualities of enlightenment. (To review the qualities of a buddha's body, speech, mind, and actions, refer to the discussion of the objects of refuge [volume 1, chapter 11]). When faith arises through wisdom it will support one's desire to attain those qualities in order to save sentient beings. The stronger one's faith the firmer one's intention to attain the goal will be. Our practice will be as powerful as our intention. We will draw energy from our heartfelt desire to attain the qualities of a buddha as soon as possible in order to benefit other sentient beings. When we are sure that buddhahood has what we need to attain our goal to help others, our desire to attain enlightenment as soon as possible will arise spontaneously day and night.

In the *Stages of Meditation* Kamalaśila says that the scriptures teach that the best way to produce the desire for enlightenment is through our own realizations. This will be much more powerful than relying on someone else's writing, instruction, or opinion. We may have a few moments of bodhicitta that come from relying on others, but it soon disappears. We should concentrate again and again on why we want to attain that perfect, highest goal. The perfect omniscience of buddhahood is necessary for the accomplishment of both our own and others' goals. Without it, neither will be accomplished. Therefore bodhisattvas are willing to endure any necessary discomfort to attain their goal. They do whatever they can, mentally, physically, and financially to attain buddhahood themselves.

c" RECOGNIZING BODHICITTA, THE FRUIT OF THE TRAINING

The training to produce bodhicitta is difficult but identifying whether one has bodhicitta or not is not very hard. Tsongkhapa does not explain the definition of bodhicitta in detail here because it was already discussed in the context of the quotation from the *Ornament for Clear Knowledge* above. In brief, the measure of bodhicitta is when a desire to attain highest, perfect enlightenment for the sake of others comes to mind spontaneously all the time. A person dominated by that thought is a bodhisattva and all his or her actions are Mahayana practices because everything he or she does is to attain perfect enlightenment for the benefit of other sentient beings. We have to practice until this thought is spontaneous. This might not take some people too long. It may take others many years. It may take many lives for some people. But until that spontaneity is achieved we have not entered the Mahayana path. We have not become bodhisattvas.

There are a number of divisions of bodhicitta. In the *Ornament for Clear Knowledge* twenty-two different names or divisions of bodhicitta are explained based on its various aspects, stages, or qualities. In *Engaging in the Bodhisattva Deeds* Śāntideva following the *Array of Stalks Sutra* explains that there are two types of bodhicitta: aspirational or wishing bodhicitta and active or engaged bodhicitta.

> Just as you understand the distinction
> Between wishing to go and going,
> The wise understand the division
> Of these two in sequence.

If someone really wants to go to a place, let's say New York City, her longing to go there came from thinking about the various qualities of the city. Her desire to go there may be strong and constant, but it is only a thought. She has decided to go there to see the sights, but has not done anything about it. This is analogous to aspirational bodhicitta. When she gets up and takes the first step on her journey, she is taking action. This is active bodhicitta. Sometimes you will hear this second type of bodhicitta called *entering bodhicitta* or *engaged bodhicitta* because it is actually entering into engaging in activity.

The scriptures and great teachers have explained these two types of bodhicitta in various ways. Tsongkhapa explains that the thought, "I must attain enlightenment as quickly as possible for the benefit of sentient beings," is aspirational bodhicitta. After generating this wish, it becomes active bodhicitta when we take the bodhisattva vow. The *Lamrim Chenmo* is explicit that whether one engages in the bodhisattva's deeds or not is not the point of difference between the two types of bodhicitta. The distinction is whether one has taken the vow; until one takes the vow a person is practicing aspirational bodhicitta even if he or she engages in various other practices. Tsongkhapa quotes Kamalaśīla's *Stages of Meditation* to make this point. Some other great teachers who followed Tsongkhapa cite other sources that state that in addition to taking the vow active bodhicitta also includes the practice of the six perfections: generosity, ethical discipline, patience, joyous perseverance, meditative concentration, and wisdom. In either case, aspirational bodhicitta is at the beginning; the desire to attain buddhahood in order to benefit other sentient beings precedes taking the vow. Active bodhicitta is taking the bodhisattva vows and then engaging in the accumulation of merit. In order to attain enlightenment one needs a great accumulation of merit from the practice of various virtuous actions and a realization of wisdom developed through intensive yogic meditation. With active bodhicitta one is actually moving toward the desired goal of being able to do many things for the benefit of others.

There is a lot of scholarly discussion about the definitions of aspirational and active bodhicitta. For example, is active bodhicitta merely having the vow, or are some other things required? Does a buddha have both of these types of bodhicitta or not? If a bodhisattva is meditating on śūnyatā, is bodhicitta present in his or her mind or not? People have only one mind so if it is focused on śūnyatā, bodhicitta cannot be present, can it? I do not want to get into these questions here, but this gives you an idea about some of the possible issues to discuss.

❖ 4 ❖

Exchanging Self and Other

————◆————

b' THE TRAINING BASED ON THE BODHISATTVA ŚĀNTIDEVA'S TEXT

ŚĀNTIDEVA was the great Indian teacher who wrote *Engaging in the Bodhisattva Deeds*. In the first nine chapters of that text Śāntideva gives a detailed explanation of bodhicitta beginning with its benefits, followed by the practices to generate it, and finally how to take the vow and practice the six perfections. Bodhicitta in this system is the same motivation explained before: the desire to attain enlightenment in order to benefit other sentient beings. However, Śāntideva's method to produce this intention is different. He says we should begin by contemplating the many benefits of bodhicitta, in particular that it is the antidote to selfishness. When we clearly see the disadvantages of selfishness and the advantages of bodhicitta we are at the beginning of the practice called *exchanging self and other*. There is a body of literature and oral teachings on this method called *mind training* (blo 'byong). These instructions, which came from India and were further developed in Tibet, are about how to transform our ordinary mind-set into bodhicitta. To elucidate this method Tsongkhapa explains some of the key stanzas from *Engaging in the Bodhisattva Deeds* in three main sections:

1' Contemplating the benefits of exchanging self and other and the faults of not exchanging self and other
2' The ability to exchange self and other if you accustom yourself to the thought of doing so
3' The stages of meditating on how to exchange self and other

Exchanging self and other implies an attitude shift. From the beginningless past until now each of us has felt, "I am the most important thing in existence." Everything we did or thought was for us alone. This selfishness creates disharmony among families, disagreements between friends, and even wars. Śāntideva advises us to switch our selfishness to concern for others because actions motivated by cherishing others will bring peace, harmony, and finally the attainment of enlightenment. It is the cause of attaining all of our temporary and final goals. When we are convinced of the many advantages of cherishing others and the disadvantages that come from selfishness we will have the desire to change our attitude.

The second topic deals with the question of whether this attitude shift is possible. Sure there are methods outlined in the teachings, but if they do not work why waste time and effort practicing them? The ordinary mind comes up with a negative response; it acknowledges the good and the bad but tells us that change is impossible. However we can shift our attitude if we make enough effort to become accustomed to this way of thinking. Just as we can train the body to do difficult athletic movements, we can also train the mind. The Tibetan word translated into English as "meditation" *(goms)* includes the idea of becoming familiar with an idea through repeated concentration on it. Even though right now one hundred percent of the mind is on the selfish side, it can be changed if we practice the proper techniques again and again.

The third topic outlines the way to bring about the change. The actual practice is called *giving and taking (tong len)*. This is mentally giving up all our possessions, even our merit, and taking all the misfortune and misery of others onto ourselves. This practice can sometimes be done with the breath. When we breathe out we imagine giving all good things to others, and when we breathe in we imagine taking in all their misery.

These three are very important topics, so to supplement the *Lamrim Chenmo* I will bring in information from other sources, particularly Pabongka Rinpoche's lamrim teachings annotated by Trijang Rinpoche in *Liberation in Our Hands (Rnam grol lag bcangs)*. Although based on the *Lamrim Chenmo*, Pabongka Rinpoche's text divides this subject into five topics: the equality of self and others, the faults of self-cherishing, the benefit of cherishing others, the contemplation on the exchange of self and others, and the way to practice this exchange through the meditation on giving and taking.

1' CONTEMPLATING THE BENEFITS OF EXCHANGING SELF AND OTHER AND THE FAULTS OF NOT EXCHANGING SELF AND OTHER

Pabongka Rinpoche said that although we can produce bodhicitta with the sevenfold cause-and-effect method, Śāntideva's method is more powerful because it incorporates the special technique of exchanging self and other.

Śāntideva says:

> Anyone who wants to quickly save
> Himself and others,
> Should practice the secret teaching
> Called exchanging self and other.

In ancient India exchanging self and other was considered to be a secret instruction. *Secret* means the teachings are not to be given to just any disciple; certain people are appropriate recipients for the teaching and others are not. Do not think that this indicates a lack of compassion for some students. Some aspects of this practice are difficult; they can be dangerous rather than helpful to some people. These teachings could make some beginning practitioners develop a wrong view or give up their practice, thinking it is not possible to succeed. The instructions are therefore only given when a student reaches a certain level of spiritual development.

When Atiśa came to Tibet he taught this practice to only one person, Dromtonpa. Later Dromtonpa taught this method to just a few of his disciples, primarily Geshe Potowa. Potowa also did not teach this technique publicly. He selected for instruction only his two most suitable students: Geshe Langri Tangpa and Geshe Sharawa. Later on Geshe Chekawa heard about this special technique and wanted to learn it. He looked all over for a teacher but could not find anyone. When he finally heard of someone and went to see him, he was too late—that person had already passed away. Eventually he met and studied with Geshe Sharawa. As a result of his difficulties Chekawa decided that the teachings should not be kept secret any longer. He taught this holy practice publicly because it is so beneficial and if it were kept secret it could be lost to the world.

Śāntideva says this practice is so powerful because:

> Whatever happiness there is in the world
> Comes from wanting others to be happy.
> Whatever misery there is in the world
> Comes from wanting happiness for yourself.

According to Buddhism every experience is the result of karma. Whatever happiness we experience is the result of virtuous actions that were directed toward others. By definition good actions do no harm and provide others with happiness. If we care about others we do positive things such as making charitable donations and we avoid negative actions such as killing, stealing, and lying. One result of these actions is that during our life others will respect us, and in the future we will be born into an honorable family. Even if we are born into a place where people are experiencing many problems, we will not have those difficulties because of our past virtue. In short, wishing that others have happiness causes all good things to occur.

Evil actions are also created in relation to others. They stem primarily from wanting good things for ourselves alone. Ignorance—attachment to the self—creates selfish desire. We feel that the purpose of others is to serve us and make us happy. If they do not, it makes us unhappy. We get angry if anything or anyone prevents us from obtaining what we desire. When we see others with better possessions we jealously want to destroy what they have or get them for our own. As a result of these types of thoughts we are led into disagreements and fights. Thus all the misery there is in the world comes from a desire for one's own happiness. There is nothing to blame on others; without our own mischief there would be no negative result for us to experience.

The great Panchen Lama Losang Chokyi Gyaltsen says in the *Guru Puja* that self-cherishing is like a chronic disease:[1]

> Seeing that grasping the self is a chronic illness
> That is the cause of undesirable suffering,
> May I be able to bitterly hold it to blame
> And destroy the demon of self-cherishing.

It is so uncomfortable to suffer from a disease throughout life. Chronic self-cherishing makes us even more miserable. Our selfish attitude has led us to act badly toward others. Even when we did nice things—giving gifts, making friends, helping our parents—at the root we wanted something for ourselves. Directly or indirectly we aimed at our own benefit. Actions dominated by selfishness may bring some temporary satisfaction, but in the end they always bring much misfortune. In other words our past selfishness is the cause of all our current problems. Geshe Chekawa said, "Put all the blame on one thing—the selfish attitude."[2] Nevertheless we usually think that the cause of our problems is something external. We believe that happiness can be found outside ourselves and that an external enemy is causing us to suffer. Such thoughts as, "Someone else has done this to me" or "Others have injured me," or "That has harmed me" have arisen in our mind over and over again from beginningless time and they have never brought us peace. We do not recognize the real enemy who causes our problems because we always look for it outside. We label others our enemies or blame evil spirits. It is true that if we are stabbed or poisoned the direct cause of our pain was someone or something else. Occasionally, however, we may make a mistake and hurt ourselves, or we may be injured in an accident. An accident does not mean there is no cause. So who is at fault? Was it a weapon by itself? Was a human or nonhuman primarily responsible? A yogi sees that the real evil demon is the self-centered attitude in the mind.

The source of all fear and every miserable situation is selfish egotism. There is a little bit of difference between the egotistic view and selfishness; in this practice, however, we put them together as one. One is like the king and the other like the minister. The evolution of the problem begins with the wrong conception of *I, me,* or the *self.* This does not mean there is no self at all; the problem is that we make a fundamental mistake: we think the self exists as it is perceived. We perceive it incorrectly without knowing it. Then we grasp at *I* or *me* as essentially important. Desire, attachment, hatred, pride, conceit, and all the other mental afflictions are the branches, flowers, and fruit of this wrong view. We think everything should focus upon us—all services and good things should be for *me.* Then of course we try to gain enjoyment, fame, wealth, and everything else that we feel is necessary for this *me.* We become angry if we see that something might prevent us from getting those things or if anyone else gets something better. These feelings make us think, act, and speak in negative ways. Everyone is subject to this problem; we all act from selfishness. We all have this powerful devil inside us. It has been in charge for a long time. Until we remove this evil demon we will have no happiness or peace; we will always be subject to fear and problematic conditions.

Śāntideva puts it this way:[3]

> In the world, all of the harm,
> Fear, and suffering that exist
> Arise from the self-centered attitude.
> What good is this great devil for me?

Misery does not occur without a cause. The source of all our problems is individual selfishness; there is no omnipotent causal agent somewhere out in space responsible for our suffering. Every negative experience—from the worst type of rebirth to minor annoyances in the human realm—is the result of karma motivated by selfishness. The big negative karmas, such as killing or stealing, can yield a terrible result: we can be born into a miserable life in the lower realms. After that horrible rebirth ends, some residual bad karma can remain to be experienced even in a human life. That is why others may injure us now even though we have not done anything to them.

Some humans are afflicted with suffering or poverty from birth. Other people are born into wealth but end up miserable. Many are afflicted with a temporary illness, worry about an enemy, fight with others, battle cold, or fear punishment from the law. All these conditions are results of previous karma stemming from the desire to have something good for oneself. Not caring about others' problems, we want everything our own way. That selfish, self-centered attitude can produce friction between children and parents or between husbands and wives. On a larger scale strife happens between neighbors, towns, cities, and countries so that finally we have world wars. There is no end to the problems and trouble. It all starts with being concerned about *I* and *mine*.

Everyone is selfish. It does not matter if someone has high social standing or is on the lowest economic level. Even those in the best circumstances—rulers with all kinds of wealth, fame, and power—suffer when they see a powerful country that rivals their own. Such a ruler can be more miserable than a beggar who possesses only the clothes on his back and a handful of food. The beggar might be satisfied with enough food to eat and a place to sleep for the night, while the wealthy ruler might experience no contentment at all. But do not think that the poor are exempt from this problem; they also suffer from selfishness. They may become thieves or murderers to get what they desire. When they are caught, who punishes them and puts them in jail? No one except their own selfishness. The root cause of their suffering is their prior negative actions done without caring for others' misery.

These are not just words; it is the truth. Serious practitioners develop faith in karma and its results by considering various examples until they see that everyone everywhere is affected by his or her prior deeds. If we investigate carefully we too will see that our evil thoughts and negative actions are the primary causes for whatever bad things happen to us. Other people or creatures may be the immediate cause for our miserable experiences, but if we ourselves had not done something selfish in the past, there is no way that this present injury could occur. With repeated reflection we will begin to understand the disadvantages of selfishness in detail.

Now that we have identified the real enemy, we can begin to target it. Bodhisattvas do not feel animosity toward any other sentient being, but they are very angry at this wrong attitude. They see selfishness as the enemy, want to destroy it within themselves, and help other people eliminate it as well. Instead of letting selfishness control them, Buddhist practitioners work to control it. To do this we have to be convinced about the disadvantages of selfishness. Gaining this conviction will not come about if our understanding is superficial, unsupported by a detailed investigation of these disadvantages. Only when we have a deep understanding will we want to begin to change our attitude. Developing the attitude that cherishes others is the method. When combined with a realization of the truth it is the destroyer of misery and suffering.

On this topic Śāntideva says:

> There is not a need to say too much:
> Children act for their own goals;
> Buddhas strive for others' goals.
> Look at the difference in the result.

Ordinary beings are like children. They see what is right in front of them but completely miss the underlying danger. From beginningless time up to now ordinary beings have worked for their own selfish purposes, looking out for themselves without caring for others. On the other hand great sages have attained the highest happiness and emancipation by acting in the opposite way. Look at the many lives of the Buddha Śākyamuni outlined in the Jātaka tales. After the Bodhisattva worked to produce the thought that selfishness is the enemy, he produced compassion, love, and bodhicitta. He then practiced only to benefit others. When necessary he even gave up his life. There is not too much that needs to be said about the result of his actions in comparison to the results of ordinary beings' selfish actions.

All the past buddhas, bodhisattvas, and arhats started out like us. They were dominated by ignorance and the enemy: self-cherishing. They recognized that selfishness is the cause of all trouble and decided to change. They no longer obeyed their egotistic view. They came to want everything for the benefit of others and ignored their own happiness. They attained high spiritual states by exchanging their self-cherishing attitude for a mind-set that treasures others. If we persist holding on to the thought, "I am the most important," we will continue the same routine of misery and problems. To experience anything different our attitude has to change.

Śāntideva says:

> If you do not really exchange
> Your happiness with others' suffering
> You will not attain buddhahood
> Nor will you have happiness in the world.

This does not literally mean, "You take my happiness and give me your misery." There is no way to do that. The method does not involve trying to change externals by building something, sending out armies, or fencing in boundaries. The change Śāntideva is talking about is a shift from selfishness to caring for others. We have always obeyed our self-centered feelings but we can change this habit. We can cherish others the way we have revered ourselves. We can treat others the way we used to treat ourselves and view ourselves as we previously viewed others. Tsongkhapa says it is very important to develop familiarity with the view that the door to all misfortune is thinking only of oneself and that cherishing others is the source of all excellent things. This is the case even in the world. We all know that those working solely for their own purposes will not succeed in social situations but that those who throw aside their own welfare to help others become famous even if they do not seek renown.

Pabongka Rinpoche uses many analogies to help us understand this point.[4] He says selfishness is like a fire that catches hold and gets bigger and bigger, incinerating our family, our country, and the whole wide world. Selfishness is like a butcher; it slaughters our chance for a high samsaric rebirth—much less the possibility of emancipation—because it destroys our merits. It is the root of negative thoughts and so eliminates the possibility of doing any meritorious actions. It brings us down to the lowest conditions in samsara. The self-centered attitude is also like a great thief. Thieves carry a bag in which they place others' valuables, destroying the happiness of those whose possessions are stolen. Selfishness carries a bag filled with the three poisons: ignorance, desire, and hatred. What is it stealing? It is stealing the fruit of our merit and virtues.

Pabongka Rinpoche also says that selfishness is like a farmer who works hard planting seeds to get a bountiful crop. Selfishness plants negative actions in the field of ignorance, and the harvest we reap is to be born into samsara and have all kinds of trouble from birth until death. Selfishness is the great master of greed. It tries to acquire good things even if that requires fighting with spears, knives, guns, or other weapons. Fighting only brings destruction to ourselves and others, but greed forces us to do it. Selfishness makes a person shameless. Shamelessness is the worst personality trait because we do bad things without ever considering, "If I do this other people will hate it." Selfishness is like a demon with empty hands. It makes us run around trying to gain satisfaction, but no matter how hard we work we have nothing to show for it. From beginningless time we have been born in various situations, sometimes high, sometimes low, and sometimes intermediate. In all those lives we have tried to benefit ourselves but we are still in the same situation.

We do not know where we are going to be reborn. We have made no progress toward our goal of peace and happiness.

Śāntideva says:[5]

> Mind! You have only wanted selfish goals.
> Even though you have worked for countless eons,
> Enduring all kinds of hardships,
> All you have accomplished is suffering.

Pabongka says that under the power of selfishness we are suspicious of others when there is no need for mistrust. We become jealous when we see any one who has better qualities or education than our own. When we see someone we consider to be our equal we feel antagonistic competitiveness. We look down on those who are our inferiors. Instead of being happy when someone praises us we become conceited and proud. We get angry if someone blames us or says something bad about us. This is how selfishness functions to bring us nothing but suffering.

Selfishness is sometimes called a bad omen. In Tibet when people saw a sign that something dreadful would occur, they made a ritual offering to chase away the evil spirit before it could cause problems. But this kind of ceremony will not help to eliminate the real bad omen—selfishness. It takes mental training to purge selfishness. The antidote to selfishness is learning to look at things in a different way, but we will not desire to change our attitude until we see the faults of the self-centered mind-set. And we will not want to develop concern for others until we see the benefits of cherishing others. Only when we see both sides—the disadvantages of one and the advantages of the other—will we stop following the orders of that demon of self-cherishing.

This situation is illustrated clearly in Śāntideva's example of a master and a servant:[6]

> You cannot even achieve the goals of this life,
> Let alone a goal beyond this world,
> When a servant does not do his work
> And the master does not give him his pay.

A self-absorbed worker just wants his paycheck and has no concern for his employer's affairs. A self-centered employer wants his employee's help but does not care about the person working for him. As a result of their selfishness the worker does not do his job well and the employer does not treat the worker well. Because neither one is concerned with the other, there is no way for either of them to get what they want. However if the employer and employee were concerned for each other they would both get what they desire. The employee would do his job properly out of love for his employer. Concerned for his worker's happiness and welfare, the employer would commend him, pay him the proper wages, and give him extra presents.

A bodhisattva practices giving up selfishness because without doing so there is no way to get rid of misery completely and attain liberation from samsara. Śāntideva says:[7]

> If you do not completely give it up
> There is no way to get rid of misery.
> Similarly, if you do not let go of something on fire
> There is no way to avoid being burned.

If we hold a flaming torch it will eventually burn down to our hands. The self-cherishing attitude burns us, therefore a bodhisattva tries to throw it down.

But how do we begin to cherish others? The famous *Seven-Point Mind Training* by Geshe Chekawa says, "Meditate on the great kindness of all beings." Even simple things in this life are the result of the kindness of others. Consider how many sentient beings labored so that we can eat a piece of toast for breakfast. Someone had to plant the wheat, work in the field, harvest it, mill and transport it, and use the flour to bake bread. Our clothes, house, and everything involved in living depend on other sentient beings. On a more profound level, a high rebirth and a long life are the results of having avoided killing others. Wealth is the result of prior generosity. Patience brings us a life where everyone likes us and wants to be near us. To attain enlightenment we must perfect our virtuous conduct and develop universal love and compassion; this requires us to interact with other sentient beings. Therefore we should cherish others because we depend upon them for ordinary enjoyment, good future rebirths, and attaining enlightenment. One reason why the method of exchanging self and other is a more powerful means to develop bodhicitta than the seven cause-and-effect personal instructions is because it takes into account the present and future happiness that results from the kindness of sentient beings. In the earlier method we recollect only others' past kindness. We may forget the past, but we are always concerned about our future.

Thus we start this practice by looking at how the mind works, how we are motivated to act, and the effects of our actions. Through this training we can determine how we will act, how we will speak, and how we will think. Each time a selfish thought arises we should think, "Here comes my enemy," and knock it down point by point. Instead of obeying the enemy, we decide to be kind and helpful to others. At first we may extend this kindness to just a few people, but by gaining familiarity with the various meditation topics we can extend it more and more widely. By considering these topics deeply we will eventually be able to actualize them. These meditations are great, great practices. They were taught by the Buddha and bodhisattvas in many sutras and tantras because they lead us to emancipation. As the great teacher Togme Zangpo says in *The Thirty-Seven Practices of Bodhisattvas:*[8]

> All misery rises from wanting your own happiness.
> Perfect enlightenment is born from thinking of others.
> Therefore, my happiness and others suffering
> Should be completely exchanged. This is the bodhisattva practice.

2' THE ABILITY TO EXCHANGE SELF AND OTHER IF YOU ACCUSTOM YOURSELF TO THE THOUGHT OF DOING SO

We may think that these teachings about the benefits of cherishing others sound nice. We may even be convinced that self-cherishing is very disadvantageous. However the most we are willing to concede is, "I would like to help others but the main issue is my happiness. I will help others along the way to getting good things for myself. It would be great if I could completely eliminate selfishness and cherish others all the time, but is that even possible?" We know it is a self-defeating thought, but we cannot help thinking, "It is hopeless. Forget about getting rid of selfishness." This attitude prevents us from even trying to begin to practice.

The answer to the question, "Is it possible to eliminate self-cherishing?" is "Yes." And there are logical reasons to prove it. First of all the human mind has a special and precious characteristic: the capacity to change. The mind is not permanent or absolute. With repeated practice the mind can become so accustomed to a new mode of thought that it will become the natural way to think. For example, if we consider a person to be our enemy it is because we have thought about what he or she did or said. Animosity builds up because we dwell on the following nine reasons this person is so horrible: "He did this bad thing to me in the past; he is doing it now; he will likely do so in the future. He did this bad thing to my friend in the past; he is harming my friend now; he will do so in the future. He did this good thing for my enemies in the past; he is helping them now; he will help them in the future." Considering these things in detail over and over again as if it were a meditation, we become more and more upset until even in our dreams we fear and hate this person. It gets to the point where we cannot tolerate being near him. Just hearing his name makes us frightened and angry.

However if that person says a couple of nice things to us and brings us a present, we may think, "He is not so bad after all. Actually he is kind of nice." Our former bad opinion of him starts to loosen up. As we become more friendly we put a positive spin on the bad things of the past, "Maybe he did that to help me learn something." We start to add up positive things and even if he does something negative we ignore it. Slowly we forget what had gone on before. After a while this person who was our worst enemy becomes our dear friend. We are happy to hear his name. We do not want to be apart from him for even a few minutes. The other person is the same; what changed was our attitude. It may have seemed impossible that we would come to love our enemy, but we did. We have all seen this happen.

If we can change our thinking 180 degrees—from animosity to heartfelt love—in regard to one person, why can't this happen with every sentient being? The mind follows the train of thought to which it is most accustomed. Right now we see everything through the veil of ignorance. Unless we apply the antidote to our selfish, egotistic perception, the internal enemy will win every time. If we make the mind more familiar with a new way of thinking we can get to the point where we consider others the way we had thought about ourselves and ourselves as we had considered others. We will come to take the side of others in every situation. We will be afraid that we will get something good instead of them. When we have something better than others we will become jealous on their behalf. It will not be as difficult as you may think because the nature of the mind is pure. For a long time our minds have been like clear water muddied by wrong attitudes. Water can be made into many things depending upon what we put into it: coffee, tea, or poison. Like water, the mind can be purified. We simply have never tried. If we do not change now, it is because we are still not trying. We put ourselves down when we decide it is too difficult, give up, and turn away. The great Śāntideva says:

> You should not turn away because it is difficult.
> From making an effort to become familiar to this,
> You will be very unhappy when someone is not present,
> Where before even his name made you afraid.

This is analytical meditation; we put our wrong attitude on one side, wisdom on the other side, and argue back and forth. We build the wisdom side up so that it is the winner. Once we are more familiar with the positive side we will not stray from it. Why? Because the reasons to cherish others explained here are based on a valid experience of reality. Our old selfish way of thinking is unstable because it is based on superficial perceptions and an incorrect, habitual way of thinking. Wrong thought after wrong thought, all based on ignorance, have no firm foundation so they can be removed. In contrast, the wisdom that realizes the truth about sentient beings, their qualities, and causality is unshakable. Wisdom together with compassion and love is much stronger than ignorance. It can be built up limitlessly until it is so perfect that no unfriendly attitude can intrude. Then we will be free from selfishness. We will always want happiness for others. We will not be able to bear it when others have the smallest amount of misery. In fact Śāntideva contends:

> It will not be difficult to consider
> Your body like others' and others' your own.

Now the negative side of the mind will say, "How can it be right to think this way about another person's body? No one else's body is my body. My body is not someone else's." This subject is not simple. It requires a rather involved answer. In some meditations we examine the phenomena we perceive with our senses from an ordinary perspective. In other meditations we employ a deeper analysis of the fundamental nature of reality: emptiness or śūnyatā. Here we must use a deeper analysis and examine the ultimate nature of self and other.

We are attached to certain things because we are accustomed to considering them as our own. It is this thought pattern that leads us to cherish our body so much more than any other body. From the time of our birth we were aware of our body and as we grew we continued to identify it as *mine*. That association is so strong that we think we are identical to our body. The concept of *I* or *me* is based on this body of flesh and bone. Employing analytic meditation we deconstruct this thought process. Consider the fact that we did not bring this body with us intact from a previous life. The primary physical cause for the body was the union of our mother's egg and father's sperm. Because our physical existence was conceived from parts of our parents' bodies, there is nothing absolutely independent or inherent about our body. The body exists dependent upon others' bodies, but as is the case with our favorite article of clothing, once we acquired it we became so attached to it that we think, "This is mine." In technical terms we say that based on the five aggregates of body and mind we conceive of an inherently existing *I* and develop a self-centered attitude.

When a meditator has a realization of śūnyatā he or she sees this clearly. Then it is easier to see how we can cherish others' bodies the same way we do our own. If we become accustomed to this way of thinking we too can produce that attitude. Śāntideva says this in *Engaging in the Bodhisattva Deeds*:

> You can become accustomed to think about others
> Just as you think, "This is mine"
> About the drop of semen and blood
> That came from others.

Once we clearly see the benefits of changing our selfish attitude, the disadvantages of not changing, and recognize that we can change, we will actually begin the meditation on exchanging self and others.

3' THE STAGES OF MEDITATING ON HOW TO EXCHANGE SELF AND OTHER

According to Pabongka Rinpoche before we can change our attitude from self-cherishing to cherishing others we must be convinced about the equality of all beings. *Equality* does not mean everyone is on the same level. In this context it refers to the fact that everybody wants happiness and no one wants suffering. There is no difference between us from that point of view.

The great Panchen Losang Chokyi Gyaltsen says:[9]

> No one wants the slightest amount of suffering.
> No one is satisfied by even the best happiness.
> There is no difference between myself and others
> So may I be blessed to rejoice in others' happiness.

No matter how much happiness we have, we always want more. Nothing in the world satisfies us because what we really want is supreme everlasting happiness and peace. So how will we get this? We have a choice. We can either try to attain happiness for ourselves and forget about others, or we can try to give everyone happiness. Usually we think that, between the two, our own happiness is more important. But we must recognize that the way we have gone about getting the happiness we want has not worked. In contrast bodhisattvas and all the great sages who have attained emancipation practiced cherishing others. Life after life they fought against the egocentric attitude and selfishness. They worked for others' benefit and in that way they attained freedom.

Now that we know what works, we too should apply the antidote to selfishness—the method of exchanging self and other. What does Śāntideva mean by *exchange self and other*? And what does it mean when other sources say, "Make yourself other; make others yourself?" These statements do not mean that we should train ourselves to think, "Other beings are me, and I am them." Nor does it mean that our *I* is theirs and their *I* is ours. It means that we replace the attitude that we alone are important with an attitude that cherishes others. Our orientation becomes one of caring for others the way a mother nurtures her dear child; we neglect ourselves and care for others. Even in an ordinary sense we have seen wise and noble people who sacrifice themselves for their family or a good ruler who is only concerned about the welfare of his or her subjects.

The many exhortations in the teachings to trade our happiness for others' misery do not mean that we should give our happiness away like loose change. The exchange involved here is a mental training. It means we cease not caring about others' suffering and make our primary goal others' happiness. To begin to do this we pay attention to our self-centered attitude and come to see that it directly and indirectly brings suffering. When we analyze this situation according to the outlines in the teachings we will recognize that our self-cherishing attitude is our worst enemy. Making an effort to satisfy our selfish desires is serving this foe. In contrast, cherishing others is our true friend because it brings many temporary and everlasting advantages. This attitude will bring only harmony, happiness, and enjoyment to ourselves and others. So for the sake of our own happiness we no longer want to serve that enemy. We resist. We work against the internal enemy in the same way we previously struggled against exterior adversaries. We come to see cherishing others as a wish-granting jewel or a god that grants beneficial boons to everyone. Therefore we decide to think about how we can benefit others.

The *Lamrim Chenmo* and many other texts present elaborate explanations for why we should change our attitude and how to actually do so. In brief, the only way to totally alleviate our own and others' misery and attain perfect happiness is to become a buddha. And it is in order to attain a buddha's enlightenment that we decide to engage in the practice of exchanging self and other. There are two obstacles to this practice. The major one is ignorance. It is not easy to comprehend fully what *ignorance* and its opposite, *wisdom,* denote, but even at the beginning of our practice we must have a general understanding of these terms.

Ignorance is not simply not knowing some little thing. Ignorance is a subtle, fundamental mistake—grasping the *I,* or the *self,* as inherently and independently existent. This is an error because objects do not exist exactly as they appear to our sensory perceptions. In other words we do not see things as they really are.

We perceive ourselves as having an identity that is ultimately different from others. Even if we do not adhere to a specific philosophical system, our perception is that our *self*, or *I*, and others exist as absolutely and inherently separate entities. Because the *I* appears to be completely real and independent we hold it to be so. Once we make this wrong assumption about *me*, our self-centered attitude proceeds to label everything else—our body and so on—as *mine*. In other words, as soon as we grasp the self as a completely different entity from all others, selfish desires and hatred arise. Happiness and misery are qualities; their support is a sentient being. It appears that the bases supporting others' misery and our happiness are as completely distinct as the colors blue and yellow. Others seem far distant, with almost no relation to us.

Ignorance brings us so many difficulties; nevertheless we do not regard it as a problem. Ignorance is why we have so many conflicts with others; all jealousy, pride, hatred, and the other negative attitudes are rooted in the wrong assumption that the *I* is absolutely existent. Because it is the fundamental cause of all the trouble in the world, both Hinayana and Mahayana Buddhism put a tremendous emphasis on understanding the opposite of ignorance: the wisdom of śūnyatā, or *anātma*—the emptiness or lack of a personal self. The antidote to ignorance is understanding that there is no ultimately, inherently different self and other; an inherent duality of self and other is a belief superimposed onto reality. This does not mean, however, that there is no difference between you and other beings on the day-to-day phenomenal level of reality.

The great sages with insight into śūnyatā see something different than we do; they see that the self exists as a dependent arising. The self is a relative concept; it does not objectively, absolutely, inherently exist. We can approach their understanding of the self by considering the way we conceive of *this side* or *the other side* of a mountain or river. Even though the two sides seem utterly distinct, where is the reality of *this side* and *the other side*? It depends upon where we are standing; it is dependent on thought. This side of a mountain is only *this side* in comparison to *the other side*. If one side of the mountain were absolutely and inherently *the other side* then even if we were standing there it would still have to be *the other side*. In actuality, when we go over to the other side, it becomes *this side* and where we were before becomes *the other side*. People on the far shore of the river think that the side they are on is *this side*, while people over on this side think that those people are on *the other side*. There is no ultimate *this shore* or *the other shore* that exists independently of where we are. Neither of them is inherently real because their nature is dependent upon our perception and each other. They are relative concepts like long and short.

Another example of how ignorance perceives an ultimate difference between what is close and what is far away is our concept of nationality. When I was young and living in Tibet, Tibet was my country and the United States was the other. It was outside and so far away that I hardly even knew about it. Now I think of the United States as my country. How did this change? The two countries did not change. Neither was absolutely *my* country or some *other* country.

This is the Madhyamaka view of reality. It is not easy to understand, but here is a succinct way of expressing the gross level of śūnyatā: The appearance of an ultimate distinction between an independent self and others is not valid because self and other are mutually dependent. Śāntideva says in the *Compendium of Trainings*:

> By becoming accustomed to the equality of self and others
> Bodhicitta will become firm.
> Self and others are dependently established;
> They are false, like this shore and the other shore.
>
> That shore is not in itself the *other* shore;
> In relation to someone else it is *this* shore.
> The self is not established in and of itself;
> In relation to someone else it is other.

We must train ourselves to perceive the self and other in the correct way. The proper understanding is the realization of emptiness. When we comprehend emptiness correctly we will turn away from believing that the self ultimately, inherently exists exactly as it appears. We will be like someone who understands a magic trick is an illusion. The audience is fooled when a magician makes a stick appear to be an attractive woman. They believe she really exists and so have many ideas about her. Some in the audience may desire her, others may criticize her, and so on. But as soon as they see that she is just a magically created illusion, every idea built on top of the premise that she is a real woman disappears. Similarly when yogis and bodhisattvas directly realize the emptiness of the self, the base of all the mental afflictions is removed. Everything based on ignorant grasping collapses when we realize the true nature of the self. Attachment and the other afflictions do not disappear the instant we see emptiness, but if we continue to meditate on śūnyatā, ignorance and the mental afflictions will fade away.

The second obstacle to training in the practice of exchanging self and other is thinking, "That other person's misery does not affect me so why should I do anything about it? It is somebody else's problem." This is a common attitude. We do not care when other people suffer because it does not hurt us. Their problems are nothing to us because we believe that we are completely independent and unconnected to them. The Buddhist response is another analytical meditation directed against believing in an ultimately existent, inherent self. Thinking that we do not need to help others because the self and other are absolutely separate is as ridiculous as thinking our hand does not need to pull a thorn from our foot because they are different entities.

Does it make sense, in relation to oneself, to think, "Since a completely different person will exist in the future, why should I worry about saving money for retirement?" You may object to this analogy and say, "The duality of self and other is not the same as the difference between my youth and old age. There is continuity between my youth, old age, and next life, so even though tomorrow's problems do not affect me today, I will do what is necessary in order to prevent my suffering in the future. In contrast others are absolutely different from me. There is no connection between us so I do not need to worry about them." Stated slightly differently, old age is different from the present but there is an identity relationship to the whole continuum of life. The idea of a whole with parts is similar. A hand and foot are parts of the body; they are both part of *me*. Even if we do not put this into words, we feel that there is a central thing and single continuity that is *me*. We believe this continuum has a real substantive nature. We feel that there is an ultimate whole person. However if things were ultimately existent in and of themselves then other causes and conditions could not affect them. They would be permanent and impossible to change. If things were absolutely, inherently existent there would be only one way to think about them.

Phenomena such as a continuum and a whole do not actually exist in the way we perceive them. A continuum changes moment by moment. Is there something holding these moments together like a long rope? No, there is no absolute real bridge between our past, present, and future. The continuity is imputed by conceptually putting these moments together. In the same way there is no inherently existing thing into which we can fit our youth and old age. There is also no ultimately real whole body. The body is an aggregation of many parts—torso, feet, hands, and so forth. The mind adds a label to all these parts and we grasp it to be an independent, absolutely real *whole*. But that whole entity depends upon the mind perceiving the parts. Reason shows us that the whole is not independent of its parts. The whole and the continuum exist dependently, not absolutely. There is no essence there, just a phenomenal relativity.

In exactly the same way the self exists as a dependent origination. The *I*, the self, or the person, is established in dependence upon different parts, causes, and conditions. We identify a person based on the combination of the body, mind, emotions, and so forth. But an absolute, real person—you, your friend, or your enemy—existing as solidly distinct as it appears to the mind cannot be found in an ultimate sense. How do we exist? We can softly establish the *self* as imputed on a collection of parts. There is no absolutely real so-called *self* or *other* deep down beneath this imputation. The mind imposes the continuity of a self-sufficient whole upon a combination of causes, conditions, parts, and moments. It appears that something is absolutely there, but it is a mistake to hold on to this appearance as a discrete absolute existent.

There are many examples to explain how the self does not exist the way we perceive it. It is like being terrified of a poisonous snake when we see a piece of rope coiled in a dim corner. We misperceive it and make it into a big thing, screaming "Snake!" But if we search we will not find a snake even in the tiniest piece of that rope. A magician can use a stone to create a frightening illusion. To the audience this thing seems objectively real; it is scary and so they react with fear. But what appears to exist is not there in reality. Emptiness is also taught in the sutras with the analogy of a wagon; today we would use the example of a car. We believe that a car absolutely exists. So long as we do not analyze it, there is something solid and identifiable as a car. However when we look in detail at the nature of the car, we find there is nothing actually real and independent. Our usual thought *car* is based on many things: a color, door, floor, roof, engine, and so on. What is the real car? What is so special about *my* car that I care so much about it? The door is not the car. The floor is not the car. The roof is not the car. The steering wheel is not it either. Maybe the engine? But the engine has many parts—so where is the engine? We cannot find it in between the nuts and bolts. Maybe the shape? No. So where is the car? It disappears when we look for it. It is empty of truly, absolutely existing. This does not mean there is no car. The car exists phenomenally or relatively. It is nominally acceptable, understandable, and functional. It is a dependent origination.

There will be much more detail on this subject in volume 5 of this series. I have introduced this topic here only because otherwise it is unclear why Tsongkhapa quotes these stanzas by Śāntideva in this context. Tsongkhapa's point is that yogis use wisdom to distinguish between phenomenal and ultimate truth in order to reduce their egotistic self-centered attitude. They look for the inherent nature of the self and find emptiness: śūnyatā. They develop wisdom because if they incorrectly grasp reality it is not possible to practice love, compassion, and bodhicitta properly. Method and wisdom have to be joined together perfectly to negate evil attitudes effectively. Only by correctly understanding the phenomenal nature of things can we function well. When a yogi realizes śūnyatā, he or she is like a magician who sees the illusion he has created but knows it does not exist as it appears. The magician is not attached to the illusion. The magician knows there is no inherent existence and that the appearance of an ultimate thing is a creation of the mind. Because our attitude toward self and others is based on how we grasp them, if we change our perception we can feel for others what we had in the past felt only for ourselves.

Now that we understand the obstacles we are ready to begin the practice of exchanging self and other. The way to start is to meditate on the many faults of selfishness and the benefits of caring for others. We contemplate that from beginningless time the self-centered attitude has led us up and down, life after life, and every life has had so many highs and lows. The majority of the time we have been in the worst states of existence, experiencing great suffering. Sometimes we have a slightly better type of life, but overall selfishness has created miserable lives during which we had many unpleasant experiences. Even this human life is full of suffering, dissatisfaction, and problems. We do not know what will happen tomorrow much less in our future lives. What is wrong? Why are we still in such an unfortunate situation after spending countless lives striving for something better? It is because we pursued the wrong method to achieve perfection. For innumerable lives, over eons and eons, we have done the same selfish things to achieve our self-centered goals. Not only have we not achieved what we sought, we have caused ourselves so much misery, uncertainty, and trouble. There is no doubt that if we had done as much for others as we did trying to benefit ourselves, we would have attained buddhahood many lifetimes ago. When we sincerely love others our actions are meritorious and are the cause for accomplishing our goal. We become perfect and can benefit countless other sentient beings. Many have become buddhas and bodhisattvas by changing their attitude.

Meditating on the faults of self-cherishing is very effective and powerful. It brings meaning to our lives. We do not have to sit alone in a cave to do this meditation. When we are in a crowd we can examine ourselves and infer what is going on in other people by observing their behavior. We will see that the source of everyone's problems is the self-centered attitude. We will see through our own pride, anger, and jealousy. We can knock it down: "Now I see you! Selfishness, you are my enemy. You are controlling these people, too. They are nice but you make them crazy." If we meditate this way we will gain knowledge everywhere we go throughout life. It is important to approach this issue from many different points of view and use many different examples, because until we are convinced we will continue to follow the side of ignorant self-cherishing. When we consider enough reasons we will grow certain that the only function of selfishness is to cause problems. Then slowly we will change our routine habit of self-cherishing.

The actual practice is to recollect that the supreme enemy is the self-centered attitude and to inspect the mind to see whether it is present. Wisdom is like a spy in the mind constantly checking, "Is the enemy winning or am I winning?" Here *I* means the wisdom side. We try to place ourselves on the wisdom side. We want to change sides by switching from concern for *me* to concern for sentient beings. As soon as our spy detects that a big enemy operation is going on, we try to combat it. We make an effort to refrain from initiating negative actions. If we have already started something selfish, we try to discontinue or at least reduce it. We do not want to let selfish thoughts and actions become larger and greater. Of course in the beginning this is a very difficult struggle. It is like a little child trying to battle a grown man. The self-cherishing side is so strong and firmly established in the mind. It has many, many friends; attachment, pride, jealousy, hatred, and so on are like an army of its allies. In order for wisdom to win we have to try to conquer all of them. This is difficult but it is not impossible. We can completely overcome them.

How? A Mahayana practitioner should be aware of what his or her mind is doing. In addition we should always recollect what we should and should not be doing. We must compare what we are doing to what we should be doing all the time. The great teacher Togme Zangpo said:[10]

> In brief, whatever your course of action,
> Ask, "What is the state of my mind?"
> With continuous recollection and introspection
> Benefit others. This is the practice of bodhisattvas.

Great practitioners do not use this mental spy to investigate others. They are checking themselves to make sure that a pure attitude is in place. They must know if deceitful or evil thoughts arise when they are dealing with others. Even though it may look as if we are helping someone, if the self-centered attitude is present in our mind then we are just cheating others and ourselves. If we see something wrong, false, or evil we have to fight it. We have to eliminate the negative, try to reduce it, or try to replace it with something else. Constant daily introspection is critical. Without this mental spy we may be able to concentrate when sitting alone in a meditation room, but once we get up our mind may run wild. We have to be constantly vigilant. Mindfulness and introspection are the bodhisattva's way to benefit others.

Śāntideva says that employing this method is evidence that we understand the way to exchange self and others. Many of you know that Śāntideva was one of the great Indian Mahayana Buddhist yogis. He meditated this way all the time, day and night. To his contemporaries, however, he looked like he was not doing anything. He seemed lazy because he lay on his bed for hours. Everyone called him names and said he only thought about three things—eating, defecating, and sleeping. Actually he was doing the most important and difficult work—training his mind. *Engaging in the Bodhisattva Deeds* came almost spontaneously from his meditative experience. It became clear to others that he was a great meditator when they heard the words of that precious text. If we learn the method he taught and combine it with our own wisdom, our meditations will be fruitful as well.

Śāntideva says:

> This selfishness has injured me
> Many hundreds of times in samsara.

> Mind! Wanting your own benefit,
> You endured great hardships
> Over the passage of countless eons,
> But all you accomplished was misery.

This is an angry meditation. However this is not aggression toward others stemming from selfish ignorance. That type of anger is precisely what we are fighting against. It is only because virtuous anger looks like ordinary anger that we apply that label to it. However here anger is not a negative thought because it is based on wisdom. We scold the mind with sharp words; we are hostile to the selfish attitude. We desire to destroy that obstacle to true happiness and liberation with whatever method we can. Whatever we do to injure the self-centered attitude is not negative.

Śāntideva says:

> If in the past
> You had worked for others,
> It would be impossible to be in a situation like this
> Which lacks the perfect happiness of buddhahood.

The happiness of enlightenment is everlasting and perfect. It is not like the happiness that we experience now. Ordinary worldly happiness becomes the cause of misery. We call it happiness but it is part of the suffering of change. We experience impure happiness because of self-cherishing. If in the past we had cherished others, we would no longer be in this situation. We would be experiencing the happiness of buddhahood.

After we recognize the disadvantages of self-cherishing and how that attitude dominates us, we try to annihilate it. The way to destroy it is to take sides. Do not continue the habit of taking your own side! We have seen that when we try to protect our *I* we encounter many obstacles. We worry, get angry, fight for our own happiness, and misery builds up exponentially. Instead we train the mind to desire to benefit others. To counter selfishness we train ourselves to practice generosity. Where in the past we took from others, now we wish that they could have our possessions, our body, and even our merit. It is not possible for our virtues to ripen for others, but we wish that it were possible because we would be willing to give them away to help others. We decide that we will use our body to serve others and to give them our wealth, property, and possessions.

This does not mean you should go crazy and give away everything you have right now. These instructions are not advising you to run out and feed your body to a tiger. There are steps in the practice of the bodhisattva vows. In the beginning we must train ourselves mentally. We are not allowed to give away our body or life until we reach a certain point in the mental training. When that time comes we will not experience the slightest uneasiness or difficulty in giving away our bodies. We will feel great joy. But for a long time before that, we have to train the mind by imagining giving our body and wealth to others again and again. So here these instructions are not to be taken literally. *Giving your body* means that you think that your body is no longer yours with which to pursue selfish goals. You contemplate that since you mentally gave your body to others, they own it. Therefore it should not be used to injure them; it should only be used to help them. Your body must work for their welfare not for your benefit. For the time being it is enough to train yourself mentally to use your body and wealth in whatever manner is beneficial for others. Exercise your mind in this practice again and again. Śāntideva said this in verse:

> You, mind, must understand:
> "I belong to others."
> Now you should think about nothing other
> Than the welfare of all sentient beings.
>
> Because my eyes and so on belong to others,
> It is not right to use them for my own purposes.

Since these eyes and so on are for their benefit
It is not right to use them in the opposite way.

From now on we should not act as we did in the past. Then even when we did something nice—such as giving others gifts or praising them—our intent was to gain something for ourselves. Now we change that completely around. Even when we do something for ourselves—like eating or sleeping—we are nourishing the body so that we can use it to help others. We think about how to solve others' problems all the time.

This practice requires us to be constantly aware of our mental state. We must recognize when we lose the thought that our body, possessions, and so forth belong to others. We need mindfulness to know when we have reverted to thinking that our body is our own, to be used for our own purposes, and to work against others. For example, if someone says bad things to us or comes to attack us, the selfish attitude arises pretending to be our friend. It influences us to use our body or speech to injure others because it seems as though those actions are going to help us. This is normal; it is the way we have thought from beginningless time up until now. But now consider how this manner of thinking caused us limitless harm in the past. If we follow that past pattern of behavior we will continue to experience inexhaustible misery. Now that we clearly see what selfishness does we should not continue to obey it. We should reject it as completely wrong. Do not be confused about who is the friend and who is the enemy. Try to negate that old way of thinking.

Śāntideva writes about this training in the following series of stanzas:

You destroyed me in the past,
But that was another time.
Now I see through you; wherever you go
I will destroy all your arrogance.

You refers to the egotistic selfish attitude which is the cause of all trouble. The yogi says that in the past the selfish attitude compelled him to do wrong actions that resulted in disasters in his present life and in many other lives. When he did not recognize the cause of his problems, selfishness had power over him. But no longer. He says, "You have no more power over me because I understand causality. Right now you may be proud of your control over me, but I will overcome you." In other words practitioners build up a positive attitude; under the power of love they care for others rather than themselves.

Now you should cast away the attitude
Of concern for your own welfare.

Because I have sold you to others,
With no regret you should voluntarily serve.

The author reminds himself to be humble and serve others gladly from now on. With the positive aspects of his mind he dedicates his body, speech, and everything he previously thought of as his own to others. Therefore he should not be discouraged when doing whatever needs to be done for others. The thought of doing something for oneself should be completely eliminated. It is like signing a contract; once we say that we will do something, we will have a problem if we do otherwise.

If I become careless,
And do not give you to sentient beings,
You will definitely hand me over
To the guardians of the hells.

If we let selfishness arise it will lead us to create many negative actions and make us miserable again. Since beginningless time selfishness has put us in jail, led us to hell, and caused every conceivable type of suffering.

Thus, in the past you gave me to them,
So I suffered for a long time.
Now I remember my resentment;
I will destroy the selfish attitude.

Our attitude should be the opposite of what it was in the past. Then we were controlled by selfishness; we wanted bad things to happen to others instead of to us and we wanted every good thing that others had. Now we should try to cherish others as much as possible. A bodhisattva takes responsibility for all other sentient beings, dedicating him- or herself to solving their problems and leading them to higher rebirths, emancipation, and finally perfect enlightenment. A bodhisattva becomes an instrument to achieve these goals through this training. This practice is extremely virtuous; even a single moment of it is beneficial to other sentient beings. Therefore we should attempt to produce an attitude that cherishes others.

The cause for being able to hold others as more important than oneself is recollecting their kindness. In the sevenfold cause-and-effect method we recollect the kindness of sentient beings by thinking of each one as our mother. In this practice we contemplate how all sentient beings have been helpful to us. Every one of our goals—from minor temporary objectives to the highest spiritual states—is only achieved with help from others. Tsongkhapa gives us an agricultural example. Farmers value a good field and high-quality seed because together they will result in a bountiful harvest. Farmers make a great effort to clear their fields, amend the soil, water the plants, weed, and so on because the quality of their harvest depends upon it. Similarly, sentient beings are a field of merit or virtue. If we use this merit field properly the results will be many good things in this life and we will be reborn in the higher realms. The practices of generosity and the other perfections can only be accomplished in dependence on this field of sentient beings. Thus highest enlightenment as well grows from the field of sentient beings. If we are certain that all these desirable results come about only in dependence upon sentient beings, we will feel their importance and cherish them.

Śāntideva says:

> From sentient beings and buddhas
> Alike we accomplish buddhahood.
> So just as we honor the buddhas
> Why don't we treat sentient beings?

Enlightened beings have marvelous qualities and give teachings to help us achieve our objectives. Therefore Buddhists honor them, make offerings to them, and take refuge in them knowing that there will be positive results by doing so. Sentient beings are just as essential to our happiness and spiritual progress because without sentient beings we could not develop bodhicitta or practice any of the bodhisattva deeds. Sentient beings are the object of all of these practices. Therefore we should honor sentient beings for the same reason we worship the buddhas; both are indispensable for attainment of our goal.

Because it is important to concentrate on how all good things come from sentient beings and all misery comes from treating sentient beings incorrectly, let's look at this in a bit more detail. Consider that even during this life there are positive results when we do something favorable for others. Destructive, injurious, or harmful actions may seem to gain us something, but this gain is temporary. The end result will always be greater misfortune because others will desire revenge. From a longer perspective, if we kill someone the result will be rebirth in the three lower realms and after that, if we are born human, we will be miserable throughout life. Maybe we will have a life-long sickness or experience harm similar to what we had committed. If we steal from others we will be born in a lower realm and after that, if we are born human, we will have difficulties, worries, and shortages of food, clothing, and shelter. The opposite is also true. If we try to save someone in danger or otherwise care for others, we will be reborn as a human or a deity. We will have a long life because we saved others' lives. If we help others by providing them with material goods, in the future we will be wealthy. In summary we will have as many negative rebirths as the negative actions we do out of selfishness and we will have higher rebirths if we love and cherish others.

The following stanzas from Nāgārjuna's *Essay on the Spirit of Enlightenment (Bodhicitta-vivaraṇa)* expand upon this point:

> Good and bad rebirths in samsara
> Are desirable and undesirable results
> That come about from benefiting
> Or harming other sentient beings.

Sentient beings are a sensitive area. On the one hand it is most dangerous to do something wrong in relation to them. On the other hand if we do positive things for them we will experience good results. If we think about them this way we will do nothing to harm others. We will strive to make everything we do favorable to others because every good thing in samsara and beyond comes from doing meritorious things for other sentient beings. There is no other cause.

> If depending upon sentient beings
> One can attain the highest state of buddhahood,
> Why be amazed that there is nothing
> In the three worlds other than
> Benefiting others to bring forth
> All human and heavenly wealth
> Used by Brahmā, Indra, Rudra,
> Or a protector of the entire world.

We cannot be born as a human being, a high worldly god, or cakravartin king if we have not done positive things for others. The great worldly gods—Brahma, Indra, Viṣṇu, and the others—have wealth, sensual enjoyment, certain powers, and people worship them. All of this came from prior actions benefiting others. As with meritorious actions, nonvirtuous actions have others as their object. The result of nonvirtuous actions is suffering. None of the extreme miseries of the lower realms occurs without a cause, and that cause is harming others. Of course there are many levels of harming others; the severity of the result depends upon the action.

Hell denizens, animals, and hungry ghosts
Endure so much misery.
Every experience of these sentient beings
Arises from having harmed other beings.

The misery of being tormented,
Hungry, thirsty, and fighting each other,
Is inexhaustible and difficult to escape.
That is the result of harming others.

These stanzas provide us with the logical foundation for the development of kindness and love. Sometimes people think that analytical thought is an obstacle to practice. They think meditation is stopping mental activity and therefore all this logic will not get us anywhere. Rejecting analytical meditation is wrong. It is true that sometimes we have to calm the mind down because our thoughts are running wild without control. In that sense we learn to stop thought in order to stabilize the mind. But once single-pointed concentration is mastered we must use the mind to gain control over our negative attitudes and destroy them from the root. As we meditate on the natural law of causality we will decide that the only actions left for us to do are those beneficial to other sentient beings. Eventually based on analytical meditation we will engage in positive actions from the heart without any pretension. We will become a wish-granting jewel for other sentient beings. Then even if we are not seeking a positive effect for ourselves it will come to us because we are benefiting others.

Whether one practices for the benefit of sentient beings or not is the defining difference between the Mahayana and Hinayana. Let me be clear about this. Hinayana practitioners do some practices beneficial to others, but their primary goal is their own emancipation. Their attainment of emancipation is far superior to any ordinary experience—they are free from samsara. However, they are not completely perfect; they have not attained buddhahood. Their lower achievement is a result of not practicing solely for the benefit of others.

Thinking about one's own goal all the time is selfish. It is one of the main enemies of a bodhisattva. We have to pray to cease that attachment. The shift to cherishing others will not come about instantly. Sometimes people complain, "I did some meditation, but I am still self-centered." To experience change takes many, many meditations over a long period of time because egotistic selfishness is so strong within us. Life after life from beginningless time we have never considered a perspective other than selfishness. Thus our egotism is as firm as a mountain. It is not easy to shake it; it is not easy to remove. But slowly, little by little, even a mountain can be completely eroded away. Even though we may not see any immediate effects, if we keep cutting selfishness down bit by bit we will succeed. In the beginning we do not practice well because we have only a vague understanding of the goal, the practices to attain it, why the practices work, and so forth. Gradually our understanding of this system will become clearer and stronger. This in itself is a great improvement. It is a great practice. We will be aiming for the right target.

Nāgārjuna says:

> Make an effort to abandon as if it were poison
> A lack of attachment for sentient beings.
> Because śrāvakas lack this attachment,
> Don't they attain a lower enlightenment?

Usually we say attachment is wrong and that we should get rid of it. But in this stanza the term *attachment* is not ordinary selfish desire. Here it refers to compassion and love for other sentient beings. A lack of this positive attachment for others should be avoided. A lack of concern for others and selfishness are both poison. A bodhisattva knows those negative attitudes should be eliminated as soon as they arise. On the other hand, Nāgārjuna continues, bodhisattvas see the advantageous results that come from cherishing others and the disadvantages that come from acting the opposite way. They understand that by never ceasing to benefit other sentient beings they will attain highest buddhahood. How could a person who sees this be attached to his or her own purposes for even a moment? That would never happen. Mahayana practitioners never give up their love for others in any situation. Life after life, for eons and eons, they strive for enlightenment in order to help all sentient beings. They attain the highest result because out of love for others they create all the necessary merit and wisdom.

Nāgārjuna continues:

> By never giving up other sentient beings
> Perfect buddhas attained enlightenment.
> Thus when they comprehend the results
> Arising from helping or not helping,
> How could they remain self-centered
> For even a single moment?

This is what we should do, too. However we will not have the strength of mind to cease our old pattern of selfishness if we do not study this topic, listen to lectures, and think about it. It is important to examine this subject from many points of view. Consider logical reasons, scriptural explanations, and examples from daily life to become convinced that selfishness is our worst enemy. Tsongkhapa comments that highest enlightenment is the result of bodhicitta. Spontaneous bodhicitta rises from compassion for others. Compassion comes from seeing sentient beings' problems, wanting to free them from their suffering, and wanting to help them have happiness. So, without caring for others compassion will not arise, without compassion bodhicitta will not arise, and without a spontaneous desire to become a buddha we cannot attain enlightenment. Bodhisattvas meditate to see this causal relationship clearly and do whatever needs to be done to develop compassion. Eventually their desire to take responsibility to free others from misery and lead them to emancipation will be firm. This means that no matter what occurs they will not lose their compassionate intention to help others. In fact, instead of losing their compassion, adverse conditions heighten bodhisattvas' compassion. They engage in the most difficult activities without hesitation because when compassion is strong even difficult tasks become easy. Their activities are like a great ocean wave, flowing naturally without conscious thought to benefit others. In contrast, when we act naturally it is for our own selfish purposes. Our egotism is so strong and powerful we do not need to think—we naturally strive for our own benefit. When a bodhisattva's practice of compassion becomes spontaneous it is beyond control; the bodhisattva has no choice to act in any other way.

Again Tsongkhapa quotes from the *Essay on the Spirit of Enlightenment:*

> With a root of firm compassion,
> Bodhicitta is the sprout from which grows
> The fruit of enlightenment solely to benefit others.
> This is the what bodhisattvas always practice.

> When this becomes firm through practice,
> Out of fear for the suffering of others
> They cast away their happiness and peace
> And even enter the Avīci hell.

> This is marvelous; this is worthy of praise;
> This is the holy manner of the best people.

Those without powerful compassion always have difficulties. No matter how great a person or deity they may be, they fear adverse consequences for themselves. Bodhisattvas are the opposite; they find it unbearable when others suffer. They have no fear of physical suffering or losing their property. They would even go to hell without a moment of hesitation if it would be beneficial to others.

Up to this point Tsongkhapa has been presenting the way to develop bodhicitta according to the sutras and famous Indian Mahayana practitioners such as Śāntideva, Asaṅga, and so on. Now he explains how to do this based on the Tibetan oral tradition. The oral tradition is comprised of collections of sayings, not formally written books. One such collection is the *Sayings of the Holy Kadampas (Bka' gdams kyi skyes bu dam pa rnams kyi gsung bgros thor bu)*. The Kadampa geshes—including Geshe Chengawa, Geshe Potowa, and Geshe Sharawa among others—were eleventh and twelfth century yogis following the teachings of Atiśa Dipaṃkaraśrījñāna. They lived in an area called Pempo, a big river valley surrounded by mountains north of Lhasa. Each geshe practiced in his own retreat, a mile or so away from the other retreat places in this region. Sometimes the geshes sent their disciples back and forth to relate interesting comments about their practices, the target, and goal. Sometimes they got together and talked. They were famous for their special way of practicing and expressing their ideas. Their stories and advice are often quoted in the lamrim literature. In Tibetan they are often amusing, but because of cultural differences they sometimes do not come across as humorous when you translate them into English.

The first special oral teaching mentioned by Tsongkhapa is a saying attributed to Atiśa himself. When Atiśa was teaching in Tibet he said, "You Tibetans know of bodhisattvas who do not know how to practice love and compassion." In other words, Atiśa did not know of any bodhisattva like this, but the Tibetans thought they did. The Tibetans were wrong because without a practice of love and compassion there is no bodhisattva. Atiśa continued, "Well then, what is the proper way to practice? You should practice in order from the beginning." Sometimes people want results right away. They want to be a bodhisattva now; they do not want to take the time to develop compassion and love. This cannot be. If you want to become a bodhisattva you must create the causes for bodhicitta: compassion and love for all sentient beings. Partial compassion and love is insufficient. Just a few minutes or a day of powerful love for others is also not enough. Love and compassion have to arise spontaneously, all the time, for all others equally. Until that occurs we are not bodhisattvas. We have to do many practices and meditations in the right order to reach this point. We cannot jump right into being a bodhisattva; we must train in the progressive stages explained in the lamrim.

Another Kadampa geshe was Langri Thangpa. He said about himself and another geshe Shawopa:

> We two, Shawopa and I, have eighteen human skills and one horse skill. So in all we have nineteen. The human skill is that after producing bodhicitta, everything we do is practice for the benefit of other sentient beings. The single horse skill is to do, in a straightforward manner, everything possible to harm the self-cherishing attitude, which prevents bodhicitta from arising, does not let it abide if it does arise, and hinders its increase. The central practice is to do whatever you can to benefit others.

There have been disagreements about the meaning of this saying because Geshe Langri Thangpa did not enumerate each individual skill. Some of the geshe's followers specified eighteen practices. But others say that this is a case where a number simply indicates *a lot* or *many*. For example, we have a saying in Tibetan, "He (or she) is someone who does nine things." This means that the person will do anything, good or bad, without any discrimination. So the meaning here is that a bodhisattva's skill has no bounds because he or she is acting for limitless sentient beings. Such bodhisattvas do whatever is necessary to benefit others. In this way they are like a person who does anything and everything without bias: if they need to injure himself, that is fine; if it will benefit others, they will give up their life. There are no limits. Bodhisattvas are eager to do whatever they can to help others.

There are many activities we can do to help others, but there is just one thing to fight against. A bodhisattva always tries to push down and destroy egotistic selfishness. This attitude keeps us from producing compassion, love, and bodhicitta. Even if positive attitudes arise a little bit, selfishness can destroy them. Even if compassion and love remain in the mind, selfishness will not let them increase. As long as self-centeredness is strong, it is the enemy of the bodhisattva and all other sentient beings. Geshe Langri Thangpa says that we should face off against our selfishness and fight it with every possible method all the time. Benefiting others is our center; in other words it is the heart of our practice. This is the training. Even a little reduction in selfishness is helpful; it shows our practice is succeeding.

The next anecdote is about Dromtonpa. Geshe Dromtonpa was one of Atiśa's great Tibetan disciples. When he met Atiśa he was a nomad and already an older man, but he became a great yogi and bodhisattva. He remained a layman and was a leader of the Kadampa teachers. Geshe Dromtonpa said another great yogi came to see him and said, "I have such and such meditative concentrations, like absorbing the inner energy-wind *(prāṇa),* and so on." Dromtonpa responded, "Even if you have a concentration that cannot be broken by someone beating a huge drum near your ear, if you do not have love, compassion, and bodhicitta, you may be born in a place that necessitates confession day and night."

The other yogi is referring to advanced tantric practices involving the breath, the inner energy-wind, and the energy channels *(nāḍī);* these practices result in a particularly powerful form of meditative concentration. In this type of meditation practitioners stop mental activity. First they stop their sense consciousnesses; then they go deeper and stop gross mental consciousness, and finally their mind becomes more and more subtle until consciousness completely ceases. They are not dead, but consciousness stops through the power of meditation. They can survive a long, long time in this state if particular things are done to their body.

Dromtonpa is not disparaging deep meditation in general. However, he is warning that if yogis produce this type of deep meditation without compassion and love it will result in a common samsaric level of peace. In their next life they might be born in a high place on earth or in one of the four heavens of the form realm. Those born in form realm have long lives that are predominantly mental, not physical. Deities there remain in a deep, natural meditation on the subtle mind. The fourth or highest level of the form realm is called No Perception *(asamjñasamapati)* because the deities there have no conscious perception at all. From a worldly point of view this is a good rebirth. However, although a life there is long and has no mental or physical suffering, it is not free from samsara. It is just a temporary peaceful heaven. In fact, from a spiritual point of view this type of rebirth is considered to be unfortunate because it lacks the leisure for religious practice. If we are born into this heaven we will be conscious at the first moment of rebirth but then the rest of that life is like being asleep. We stay unconsciously absorbed in peace for many eons; during that time there is no opportunity to create the causes for better future experiences. We do not wake up until the result of our prior karma is exhausted. That is the moment of death from that realm and from there we will be reborn. The life after one in the No Perception heaven is often a lower rebirth because those deities create no merit and still have all the negative karmic seeds they had created before. So Dromtonpa cautions the yogi that if he selfishly develops this kind of advanced concentration, he may have to confess his negative actions day and night to prevent being born somewhere like this.

In a worldly sense a human life is not such a great thing: it is mostly misery with only little happiness mixed in. Birth, aging, sickness, death, and all kinds of undesirable things fall upon us. We only rarely meet with desirable experiences. Our body is so delicate that even the smallest change in circumstances can greatly harm us. However this short and fragile life is better than a life in the form realms. Humans can comprehend the causal nature of suffering. We can achieve complete freedom or even buddhahood if we make an effort and use our intelligence under the guidance of a genuine teacher. In contrast, buddhas do not even appear in the form realms because teaching the Dharma there is never successful. Those deities there have no experiences to relate to teachings on karma. Causation and suffering sound like fiction to them. They see no purpose to religious practice and, as a result, they waste their lives. Therefore a serious practitioner always chooses a human life over a life in the form realms.

Khamlungpa was another famous Kadampa teacher. To others he looked sad because he stayed in solitary places and cried and cried. His meditation practice was love, compassion, and how to solve the problems of sentient beings. He said, "When we, as lords, act from the heart toward sentient beings, they naturally come to us that way." The meaning of this statement can be understood in both a positive and negative way. Khamlungpa says that if we sincerely do something without any other consideration, others respond accordingly. If we love all other sentient beings, they naturally will return our love. They will want to be with us. We will not need to look for friends; they will come to us with trust and respect. In contrast, if we push or attack others, they will respond to us the same way. We may want them to love us, but we create the cause for the opposite result.

If we plant the roots of a tree firmly in the ground, the wind cannot blow it over easily. Whether or not someone is a Mahayana practitioner depends on whether he or she has planted the root of the Mahayana practice: compassion. If compassion, love, and bodhicitta are firmly planted in the mind, one becomes a bodhisattva. We should continually examine ourselves to see if we are developing as a result of our practice. Have we become better and changed? Is our practice stronger and less easily shaken? Have we become better in dealing with others? It is good if there is noticeable development; it is bad if nothing has happened. If we see good things happening, we should continue to push ourselves that way. If we are still in the same old condition, we should see what else we can do.

In the beginning, when our practice is shaky, it is important to be in a suitable situation. We should go to a spiritual guru for guidance. We should try to be around others who are doing this kind of practice so we can imitate and follow them. We should combine outside conditions with our efforts. For example, we should read the scriptures rather than something like a novel. Reading nonreligious works that focus on worldly conflicts and extol aggression might cause beginners to feel that they, too, should indulge in anger or that people who refrain from killing are weak. In short our choice of friends, teachers, books, and other circumstances are important for our development. Also for this purpose we should accumulate merit through prayer, meditation, and other activities. When a negative mental state arises we should purify it with confession, ritual recitations, and meditation. If we train this way, we will plant the seeds of positive predispositions that will germinate and grow later. It is definite that if we create the causes we will establish the conditions to reach our goal. In the beginning it may be uncomfortable and we may feel uneasy, but it will not always be so hard. When we see the reasons for following these practices, doing them can give us joy. Having confidence in our goal and what we are doing to reach it will make us peaceful and happy. Mental joy is greater than physical pleasure. There is no comparison.

To conclude this section, Atiśa said:

> Those who wish to enter the door of Mahayana,
> Should strive for eons to produce
> Bodhicitta which, like the sun and moon,
> Clears away darkness and pacifies suffering.

The sun and the moon shed light that eliminates the dark. In addition, sunlight ripens plants and moonlight is cooling. Similarly, bodhicitta clears away the darkness of ignorance and pacifies suffering. There are two types of bodhicitta: *phenomenal bodhicitta* and *ultimate bodhicitta.* Phenomenal bodhicitta—the desire to attain enlightenment to benefit others—is like the cooling light of the moon, giving respite to those burning with suffering. Ultimate bodhicitta—realization of śūnyatā—is the wisdom that severs the root of ignorance and is therefore like the sun, which destroys all darkness. Making an effort to produce these two types of bodhicitta is the right thing to do even if it takes eons of practice.

iii) THE MEASURE OF PRODUCING BODHICITTA

Understanding when you have produced bodhicitta has been explained previously as part of the sevenfold cause-and-effect personal instructions under the heading: "Recognizing bodhicitta, the fruit of the training." (chapter 3)

❊ 5 ❊

The Ritual for Adopting Bodhicitta

iv) How to adopt bodhicitta through ritual
    a' Attaining what has not been attained
        1' From whom you should take this ritual vow
        2' Who can take this ritual vow
        3' How to take part in the ritual
            a" The preparation for the ritual
                1" Performing the special practice of going for refuge
                    (a) After decorating the place of the ritual and setting up representations of the Three Jewels, arranging the offerings
                    (b) Supplications and going for refuge
                    (c) Stating the precepts of refuge
                2" Amassing the collection of merit
                3" Purifying your attitude
            b" The actual ritual
            c" The conclusion of the ritual

---

iv) How to adopt bodhicitta through ritual

TRAINING THE MIND to cease egotistic self-centeredness and develop great compassion is one of the most valuable human activities. When we begin to wish to solve others' problems and seek ways to help them find perfect freedom, we realize that in our present situation we cannot fulfill these compassionate aims. We see that we must attain buddhahood as soon as possible because only then will we be able to benefit others perfectly. Bodhicitta is the bodhisattva's primary motivation because it is the best method to eliminate one's own misery, ease the suffering of others, and place everyone—

yourself included—in pure and everlasting blissful happiness. As the great Śāntideva says:[1]

> Those who wish to destroy the hundreds of types of samsaric misery,
> Desire to clear away the unhappiness of sentient beings,
> And also want to experience hundreds of types of happiness,
> Should never let go of bodhicitta.

We have now looked at two methods for developing bodhicitta. In both systems one first studies the details of the method. From teachers and scriptures such as the *Lamrim Chenmo* we learn the techniques of meditation to develop the mind. Then one puts them into practice. Through personal experience of either of these systems one can develop spontaneous bodhicitta. There is a third way to develop bodhicitta; it can be produced ritually by taking a vow in front of one's teachers, the buddhas, and bodhisattvas. Atiśa says that we should take the vow once we have determined the importance of bodhicitta and have a strong wish to develop it.

> Those who wish to train after they develop bodhicitta
> Accustom themselves with effort for a long time
> To the four immeasurables, love and so forth,
> Thereby clearing away attachment and jealousy
> And produce bodhicitta through a pure ritual.

Training to produce bodhicitta through a ritual has three subdivisions:

a' Attaining what has not been attained
b' Protecting what you have obtained from degenerating (chapter 6)
c' The method to restore bodhicitta if it does degenerate (chapter 6)

The first topic explains how those who have not yet developed bodhicitta can perform a ritual to produce it. Not only do we want to produce bodhicitta, we want to promise to keep it by making a vow in front of witnesses. Therefore the second topic is how to protect bodhicitta if one already has it. The special precepts of the bodhicitta vow are the way to guard against weakening or losing bodhicitta. Last is an explanation of how to recover if one has taken the vow and broken some of the precepts. It explains what to do if we lose our bodhicitta, thinking that we cannot do this practice and give up.

a' ATTAINING WHAT HAS NOT BEEN ATTAINED

The ritual to produce bodhicitta that has not yet arisen has three subtopics:

    1' From whom you should take this ritual vow
    2' Who can take this ritual vow
    3' How to take part in the ritual

1' FROM WHOM YOU SHOULD TAKE THIS RITUAL VOW

The person leading the ritual will be your preceptor so you should make sure that he or she is qualified. When a teacher is going to give precepts to a disciple, he or she must have the vows and precepts in question. In this case the preceptor must have the bodhisattva vows.

2' WHO CAN TAKE THIS RITUAL VOW

What kind of person can take this vow? The *Lamrim Chenmo* explains that it should be someone who has studied and practiced and so has some understanding about the nature of bodhicitta, the method to develop it, and the stages of the path. It is not necessary to have already developed spontaneous bodhicitta. What is required is a sincere desire to develop bodhicitta. To feel enthusiasm for practicing bodhicitta from the depths of one's heart one has to have heard and studied the lamrim teachings. That enables one to see this attitude as precious and very desirable to obtain. In short we can say the type of person who can take this ritual vow is someone really "turned on" by bodhicitta.

3' HOW TO TAKE PART IN THE RITUAL

In this section Tsongkhapa explains the ritual itself. Traditionally a ritual has three parts:

    a" The preparation for the ritual
    b" The actual ritual
    c" The conclusion of the ritual

a" THE PREPARATION FOR THE RITUAL

The preparation consists of three parts:

1" Performing the special practice of going for refuge
2" Amassing the collection of merit
3" Purifying your attitude

Because the ordinary mind is full of negativity and impurity there are things we need to do to prepare to take part in the ritual to generate bodhicitta. Even in ordinary situations we clean up and decorate our home if we invite someone special, say a high official or a teacher, to visit. The king of Mahayana spiritual practice is bodhicitta. If we invite this noble attitude into the mind, we first have to do some mental cleaning. We cannot make these preparations completely on our own. We need assistance so we take special refuge in the Buddha, Dharma, and Sangha. In addition because this kind of attitude does not come easily to anyone, we need a wealth of virtuous mental qualities to create the potential for bodhicitta to arise. Finally after taking refuge and accumulating merit we need compassion and love. Therefore just before the actual recitation of the ritual we purify our attitude by going through one of the thought processes to develop bodhicitta, either the seven cause-and-effect personal instructions or exchanging self and others. After these preparations we will be ready to take part in the ritual.

1" PERFORMING THE SPECIAL PRACTICE OF GOING
FOR REFUGE

There are different ways to take refuge in the Three Jewels based on a practitioner's level of motivation and his or her goal. Here we take a special Mahayana refuge. In ancient India and later in Tibet the way to take this refuge had three parts:

(a) After decorating the place of the ritual and setting up representations of the Three Jewels, arranging the offerings
(b) Supplications and going for refuge
(c) Stating the precepts of refuge

(a) AFTER DECORATING THE PLACE OF THE RITUAL
AND SETTING UP REPRESENTATIONS OF THE THREE JEWELS,
ARRANGING THE OFFERINGS

A suitable place for the refuge ceremony is free from potential disruptions. In particular it should be secluded from those who might try to disturb the ceremony because they think that taking refuge is wrong. When one has chosen a location, it should be cleaned up. Cleaning a temple has many levels of meaning: the most obvious is that one is simply making dirty things clean again. A deeper symbolic meaning is that one is purifying the negative aspects of the mind. Mental purification is the real cleaning job. I will not go into detail about this here because the preparatory practices are taught in detail in the beginning of the *Lamrim Chenmo*. (In this series, see volume 1, chapter 5.) Once the place for the ritual is clean it should be decorated. One should ornament it with religious banners and arrange various offerings in a beautiful way. For example, in different places around the room one should place nice smelling things such as scented water, incense, powdered sachets, and sweet-smelling flowers. There is a traditional item made from five products of a cow: milk, butter, yogurt, dung, and urine. If you have this you can set it out, but it is not necessary.

Symbolic representations of the three objects of refuge should also be set out. To represent the supreme teacher, the Buddha, you can use whatever image of the Buddha you have, whether it is a carving, molded statue, or a painting. Atiśa says that this image should have been consecrated previously. The Dharma is the teachings so it is represented by a scripture such as the *Verse Summary of the Perfection of Wisdom in Eight Thousand Lines (Ratna-guṇa-saṃcaya-gāthā)*. If you do not have this text you could use the *Heart Sutra (Prajñapāramitā-hṛdaya)*. To represent the Sangha, the spiritual community of bodhisattvas, you can display the images of various bodhisattvas found in different thangkas. When arranging these symbolic representations it is nice if you have valuable images and books to use, but it is not at all necessary for you to go to some foreign country to purchase expensive items for your altar. Remember that these things are just images; they are not the real buddhas and bodhisattvas. Even without any of these representative objects present one can take refuge while imagining the Three Jewels in front of one. The main thing is the mind.

In front of the representations of the objects of refuge one should set out various offerings: lights for their eyes to see, music for their ears to hear, incense for their noses to smell, food for their tongues to taste, and beautiful ornaments for their bodies. This is not ordinary jewelry: every crown, earring, bracelet, and so on is symbolic of a specific perfect quality or knowledge. Therefore the ornaments worn by peaceful deities are different than those of the wrathful deities. If you do not have these things, you can offer whatever lovely things you have—banners, canopies, flowers, and so forth. In addition one should prepare as an offering a beautiful seat for the spiritual teacher who will be the preceptor of the ceremony. During the ritual of taking refuge and generating bodhicitta one imagines the preceptor to be the Buddha. In that way one takes the vow directly from the Buddha.

It is to honor the Buddha that one prepares an attractively decorated, high throne.

The Buddha, Dharma, and Sangha do not need these offerings; they are not hungry and do not want anything. However we need to accumulate the good fortune of positive predispositions. In order to do that we make offerings, show our respect, and take refuge. Some earlier teachers said that before the ritual one should also make offerings to spirits, monks, and nuns in order to accumulate merit. This is a more extensive practice, but it is important that one does as much as one can to plant meritorious seeds in the mind.

There is a Tibetan story about Atiśa regarding the importance of making elaborate offerings. When Atiśa came to Tibet from India, he first went to the Mangyul and Ngari area in western Tibet. Later he went to Samye in central Tibet. In both regions when Atiśa conferred the bodhicitta ritual he told the Tibetans, "Poor offerings will not produce bodhicitta." Atiśa was not implying that he wanted good things for himself; he was explaining that the disciples needed the merit that comes from enthusiastic physical, verbal, and mental preparation. It was important that the disciples did not think that worship and offerings were inconsequential. These ritual preparations are for the purpose of developing bodhicitta, the principal cause for attaining perfect buddhahood for the benefit of all sentient beings. We must bear in mind that bodhicitta is truly wonderful and that one is extremely fortunate to have the opportunity to generate it by participating in a ritual led by a lama. It is to make oneself ready for this wonderful opportunity that one offers whatever one can to the buddhas and bodhisattvas, purifies oneself, and accumulates merit.

If we do not have much to offer, the *Sutra of the Auspicious Eon (Bhadrakalpika-sūtra)* says we can make the smallest and simplest offerings. The sutra relates a story about the thousand buddhas in our eon of time. Before these buddhas attained enlightenment they were bodhisattvas who produced bodhicitta through ritual. Some of them made a lot of offerings in the ritual but others had nothing to offer at all. The only thing one bodhisattva had was a string that had unraveled from a piece of cloth. However even that little thing was a suitable offering because it was presented with sincere respect. If you do have things that could be offered, however, you should not pretend that you have nothing. Sometimes when people see others do elaborate offerings they are surprised. Their disbelief is almost like jealousy. Even if our friends say, "How can you do that?" we should do as much as we can with a joyful attitude of trust and faith.

After setting out all the offerings, one should do the ritual to invite the buddhas, bodhisattvas, and deities from their pure lands. Then one recites a mantra called the *Clouds of Offerings Formula (Dharma-megha-dhāraṇi)* to bless and magically increase the offerings. You do not need to worry about meager offerings because they become extensive by reciting this mantra three times.

Next the disciples bathe and dress up. When we go to a party we wash and put on our best clothes. There is not much to gain from a party but nevertheless we put a lot of effort into getting ready for one. In contrast by participating in this ritual we are going to accomplish one of the most meaningful goals of a precious human life. So it is a great day for which we should dress up with great joy and excitement. These preparations from the disciples' point of view might not mean too much to you right now; do not worry if you are new and feel a bit in the dark.

When everyone is seated the guru explains the field of assembly to the disciples. Remember that in one's imagination the buddhas, bodhisattvas, the Sangha, and one's spiritual teachers have been invited to the ceremony. This assemblage of high spiritual beings is the focal object of our offerings, honor, and refuge. Just as farmers plant their fields in spring to yield a great harvest in autumn, we plant seeds of merit by making offerings to this merit-field so that we will obtain the perfect fruit of a buddha's qualities. So here the lama explains the good qualities of this exalted field so that the disciples will have faith in the assembly. We should have the desire to attain that high spiritual position; we should want to follow the same path and do the same practices that the beings in the field of assembly did so that we can benefit others as well. With this kind of great faith we should imagine ourselves sitting in front of the buddhas and bodhisattvas while doing the ritual that follows. There are many ways to do this. One can imagine the entire assembly in front of just oneself, or one can mentally emanate many bodies so that a replica of one's body is in front of each member of the assembly.

After that we do the seven-limb practice. The seven limbs are the basic practices that form the foundation for more advanced training. They are very effective for purifying prior negative actions, accumulating new merit, and increasing the merit already accumulated. It is important to understand the purpose of each limb and how to practice it properly. If you do not know these things then these practices will be nonsensical activities that do not achieve anything. I will only summarize these extensive practices here because they were explained in detail earlier. (See volume 1, chapter 5.)

The purpose of the first two limbs—obeisance and offerings—is to create merit. The first limb is to bow down to the buddhas and bodhisattvas with one's body, speech, and mind. Paying homage with the body can be any physical gesture of respect. We use speech to praise them. Mental obeisance is to have faith in what they are, what they represent, and to have a desire to attain their qualities. The second limb is to make offerings. Here I am using the phrase "to make offerings" to translate the Sanskrit word *puja*, which literally means "to please." To please the buddhas we can offer ordinary items to their five physical senses and their mental sense, but the best way to please the buddhas and bodhisattvas is to act in accordance with their wishes. Their primary goal is for everyone to have peace, happiness, and freedom from misery. They teach sentient beings what to do and wish they would practice what they were taught. Thus our practice is the best offering; it makes them the most happy.

The third limb, confession, is for purification. We confess all the negative and sinful things we have done in the past, particularly actions that were purely selfish, careless, or harmful to others. The two most critical aspects of confession are (1) to feel such strong regret for those nonvirtuous actions that (2) one vows never to do them again. This is similar to feeling great remorse because you ate something to which you are so allergic that it is like poison. If you got really sick from eating something like that, would you ever eat it again? No. Without the combination of regret and vowing not to do that action again, whatever else we do for purification—for example reciting mantras, making offerings, or meditating—is not confession.

The fourth limb is to admire one's own and others' virtues. When we have done good things we should be happy. We should think about the wonderful things the buddhas and bodhisattvas have done for the benefit of sentient beings. Instead of feeling jealous or envious, we should also admire the things ordinary people do for others, such as protecting the weak, caring for the sick, giving to the poor, and meditating to achieve goals that will benefit others. Admiring others' virtuous actions is one of the great ways to accumulate merit. This is something we can do sitting or lying down. We do not have to do anything but think about others' merits and admire them. We can even admire our own everyday positive actions. If we did a virtuous action yesterday, and today feel happy that we did so, the power of that seed of merit will increase. On the other hand, if we regret the good things we have done, that seed of merit is damaged and becomes weaker. If we admire the merit of others who are on our own spiritual level, we gain almost the same amount of merit that they do. If we admire the merits of a higher bodhisattva, we gain less than they do, but our merit still increases significantly.

The fifth and sixth preparatory practices are both requests. The fifth limb is to request the buddhas, or directly ask your teacher if you have one, to turn the wheel of Dharma. We ask them to teach until the end of samsara so that all sentient beings may have happiness and peace. The teachings are like medicine for those suffering from the sickness of misery. Imagine yourself and all other sentient beings appealing to the buddhas and bodhisattvas, "Please give us the medicine we need to cure our suffering." The sixth limb is to ask the buddhas and bodhisattvas to remain. We beg them not to pass away and disappear until all sentient beings are completely freed from samsara. Buddhas do not experience death the way ordinary sentient beings do. They can do what they wish; they could disappear at any time or they could stay forever. However sometimes it is helpful to others if they appear to be born, get sick, and die. We ask them to live a long life and give teachings because making these requests creates merit.

The seventh and final limb is dedication. Dedication makes the merits we have created go in a certain direction. This is important because we could simply dedicate our virtuous actions to our own future happiness, a long life, wealth, or freedom from samsara. We could dedicate our merit to peace in the world. Or like a bodhisattva we could pray, "May these merits be the cause for me to attain enlightenment so that I can benefit all sentient beings as soon as possible." This is not dedicating one's virtues to become enlightened for one's own enjoyment; it is a desire to quickly attain enlightenment because it is the best way to help others. If you do not know how to dedicate your merits, it is enough to say, "However the buddhas and bodhisattvas have dedicated their merits, may my virtues be dedicated that way too." There is a verse in the *Prayer of Samantabhadra (Samantabhadra-caryā-praṇidhāna)* like that.[2] The great teacher Atiśa said that there are two important parts of every practice: in the beginning one's motivation and at the end the dedication. In short, every time we do a practice we should dedicate the merit we have created.

The seven-limb puja is a common Buddhist practice included in many prayers and tantric rituals. There was some scholarly debate about how to recite it during the ritual for generating bodhicitta. Some early Tibetan teachers said that if one is following the lineage transmitted through the great teachers Nāgārjuna and Śāntideva, one should recite the entire seven-limb puja during the ritual. However if one was following the lineage transmitted from Asaṅga, one should only recite the first two limbs: obeisance and offering. Why did they believe that one lineage instructed us to recite the entire prayer and not the other? Because these teachers felt that confession should not be done when generating bodhicitta. To truly confess one must feel regret and sorrow about prior negative actions, but when one is about to produce bodhicitta one should be joyful. Therefore they believed the sadness of confession did not fit into this practice. That is not correct. Atiśa says to do "obeisance, offering, and so forth" in the ritual to generate bodhicitta and confer the bodhisattva vows. "And so forth" here means that the other limbs of the practice are also to be included. He clearly explains what to do in this ritual in the *Stages of the Activities of the Guru (Guru-kriyā-krama):* "You should do the seven limbs before you generate bodhicitta." Further, if it were true that sorrow prevents compassion and bodhicitta then it would mean that one could not generate bodhicitta following Nāgārjuna's and Śāntideva's system either because they advocate confession. Regret cannot block bodhicitta in one system and not in another. So disciples and the lama preceptor should sit together and do the seven-limb puja slowly and thoroughly.

(b) Supplications and going for refuge

Sometimes people say to a spiritual teacher, "Please give me refuge." Nobody can actually give you refuge. What they can do is give the ritual of taking refuge. We must understand why we take refuge, how the three objects of refuge protect us, and the way to take refuge. Without this understanding no matter how many millions of times we say, "I take refuge," it will not work. We will create only a small amount of merit. However if we correctly take refuge the Three Jewels will save us. They will protect us on a temporary level and lead us higher and higher until we reach enlightenment.

To begin one imagines the guru leading the ritual to be the Buddha. The Buddha was the perfect teacher; he gave these teachings originally and so here one imagines him as one's own spiritual teacher. Before taking refuge one bows down three times and makes a mandala offering as a request. The mandala symbolizes the whole universe with all its continents, mountains, oceans, rivers, and precious things. If you do not have a mandala set you can make the hand gesture signifying holding the universe in your hands. It is a Tibetan custom to request a teaching by offering a mandala because it represents the first turning of the wheel of the Dharma. After the Buddha attained enlightenment he remained silent for seven weeks. Then the god Brahma came and offered a golden mandala requesting that the Buddha teach sentient beings. Because of this request the Buddha began to turn the wheel of the Dharma.

When making the request one should sit with the right knee on the ground, the left knee up, and palms pressed together. One prays for help producing bodhicitta. The lama leads the disciples through the request; they repeat the words of this request after him. The only thing they change is substituting their own name where the vow says, "… whose name is such and such." Disciples repeat the following request three times:

Just as prior buddhas, arhats, perfectly enlightened ones, and great bodhisattvas who have attained the high bodhisattva levels first produced the thought of attaining enlightenment, Preceptor, please help me, *whose name is such and such,* to produce the thought of unsurpassable complete and perfect enlightenment.

The past buddhas and bodhisattvas are our example. What did they do to attain their high spiritual states? They produced spontaneous bodhicitta. According to the sutras, it is after they produced bodhicitta that they began three countless eons of accumulating merit by engaging in the bodhisattva activities and dedicating the resulting merit for the benefit of sentient beings. So the beginning of the path to these high spiritual stages is the generation of bodhicitta. The entire Mahayana—the stages of the path and the fruit of highest enlightenment—grows from the ground of bodhicitta. So one prays, "Please help me to produce bodhicitta just as they did in the past."

After this request one takes a special form of refuge. When taking refuge we must define the object from which we are seeking protection. In Buddhism we go for refuge to the Buddha, Dharma, and Sangha. In general the Buddha is the one who has attained perfect enlightenment and has completely destroyed all ignorance. Taking refuge in the Dharma is a little more complicated. The Dharma is not something external that will carry us to a wonderful place; the Dharma is within us.

The Dharma has two aspects: the cessation of suffering and the way to attain that cessation by practicing the path. This specifically refers to the latter two of the Four Noble Truths: the truth of cessation and the truth of the path. From our practice of the path, the mental afflictions are removed. When attachment, hatred, and so on are eliminated we will have attained the supreme Dharma, the truth of cessation, which is complete freedom from misery and the causes of misery. Thus the two aspects of the Mahayana Dharma are: (1) the path that removes selfishness and the egotistic attitude in order to benefit other sentient beings and (2) the cessations that come from the practice of this path.

You may not be familiar with this use of the term "cessation." When an obstacle or a problem is completely, irrevocably removed there is what we call a *cessation.* The highest cessation is enlightenment; a buddha has completely destroyed all gross and subtle obstacles. Prior to attaining buddhahood there are many different levels of cessation. On each of the ten bodhisattva stages bodhisattvas remove certain obstacles. When an obstacle is removed a bodhisattva has that portion of the truth of cessation. Even bodhisattvas at the highest levels have very subtle mental stains to remove and cessations to attain. For example, even though they do not get angry, they have a predisposition for anger until they attain enlightenment.

The way to achieve the cessations is to practice the path. The truth of the path is the practice of meditation realizing the true nature of phenomena in general, the true nature of one's self in particular, and the practice of bodhicitta. As one becomes accustomed to this view and method one gradually removes ignorance, wrong views, wrong perceptions, and wrong attitudes. In other words, when we take refuge in the cessations we do not get it all at once. We remove obstacles slowly; first the gross levels are ceased then more subtle things are removed.

Removing obstacles from the mind is a process similar to that involved when cleaning a very dirty shirt. First we rinse the garment in water to remove the most obvious dirt; this gross filth is the easiest to remove. Then to remove stains we have to add some soap and rub the cloth. There are some spots that still may not have come out; we have to really scrub with special detergent to remove those. The most subtle stains may be hidden; the shirt may look clean, but it is not completely decontaminated. It takes a lot of effort to remove these last stains. Similarly we can subdue the roughest mental obstacles without too much effort. Gradually the mind will become purer and we engage in different practices to remove more subtle mental stains. In summary the path and the cessations are the real refuge.

The Sangha is the third object of refuge. The rough definition of the ordinary Sangha is "those who believe and follow the teachings." If we associate with such people they will help us to develop a practice to remove suffering. They are our spiritual friends; they can be nuns, monks, and bodhisattvas. But here in this ritual we take refuge in the Mahayana Sangha. A Mahayana Sangha can consist of just one person so long as he or she has bodhicitta. It is good if there is more than one member, but one is enough. It does not matter if that person is a layperson or ordained, a man or a woman, a deity, or a bodhisattva in the form of an animal.

Ārya bodhisattvas are the best type of Sangha; these are bodhisattvas who have directly realized śūnyatā. They are on one of the ten bodhisattva stages and are irreversibly on the path to enlightenment. Sometimes a lower bodhisattva may give up because the behavior of certain sentient beings is so unpleasant, or because helping all sentient beings equally is so difficult, or because their own limitations are depressing. A combination of many factors may make them think, "I can't do this. I won't be a bodhisattva. I am going to take care of myself instead." But a bodhisattva who has attained an irreversible stage knows that he or she will never turn back. If our spiritual community consists of this type of person we will learn only pure, good things from them. They will never lead us in the wrong direction. By imitating a member of this high Mahayana Sangha we will attain freedom from misery and develop high Mahayana qualities. It is difficult to know who is an ārya bodhisattva, but we pray to meet and follow this type of person.

When we take refuge it is important for our attitude to be like a patient who is under the care of a skillful doctor. When we trust the doctor and the treatment prescribed, it does not matter if he or she gives us a painful injection, tells us to eat awful tasting things, or surgically removes pieces of us here and there. We will assiduously follow this person's instructions in order to be cured. Spiritual refuge is similar. The Buddha is like a doctor; he gives us the right medicine to cure all misery. The Buddha cannot put his knowledge into our minds or take our misery away with his hands. Instead, he can teach us and show us the path. The Dharma is the real cure, our real protection. As much as we take this medicine, that much of our misery will be removed. If we lack faith and do not put the Dharma into practice our refuge will not work. The Sangha helps us to follow the teachings that lead to the cessations. We should treat them as valued nurses. Good nurses know what the doctor's prescription means, why it was given to the patient, what the medicine will do, and what the patient is supposed to do. They stay with their patients and help the patient follow the doctor's orders. Do not imagine a big, cold hospital; these nurses are really compassionate and friendly people who know the system. Trusting the Buddha, Dharma, and Sangha in this manner is the way to take refuge. With these three objects of refuge we have all that we need to attain enlightenment for the benefit of other sentient beings.

For how long does one take refuge? You take refuge from now until you attain enlightenment. Atiśa said that when we engage in the ritual we must firmly resolve that we will never give up until we attain enlightenment. Why does one take refuge? The reason we take refuge is important. We could take refuge for simple things: a long life, health, wealth, fame, or our own liberation. But the special aspect of the Mahayana refuge is that its purpose is to save all other sentient beings. By taking refuge in this way we not only eliminate our own suffering, we attain enlightenment in order to help all others as well. The main enemy from which a bodhisattva needs protection is selfishness. To completely eliminate this obstacle a bodhisattva needs the highest realization of śūnyatā and bodhicitta. This is the Dharma that must be our refuge on every stage of the path. Without all three refuges we cannot develop the many good qualities and eliminate all the mental afflictions and their latencies on progressive levels of the path. Therefore our attitude should be, "For the benefit of other sentient beings, until I attain enlightenment I take refuge in these three. I rely on them, I have trust in them."

After disciples have made these preparations, they bow down to the preceptor three times. Then they sit in the manner previously explained—with one knee up and palms together—to show physical respect. After that they repeat after the preceptor the following words of refuge three times. As before, they replace the words "…who am called such and such" with their name:

> Preceptor please pay attention to me. I, *who am called such and such,* from now until I attain the essence of enlightenment, take refuge in the buddhas, the enlightened ones who are supreme among humans.

> Preceptor please pay attention to me. I, *who am called such and such,* from now until I attain the essence of enlightenment, I take refuge in the supreme teachings, the Dharma, which is the peace of freedom from attachment.

> Preceptor please pay attention to me. I, *who am called such and such,* from now until I attain the essence of enlightenment, I take refuge in the supreme assembly, the Sangha of ārya bodhisattvas who have reached the irreversible path.

Tsongkhapa notes that these ritual words of taking refuge are a little different than those often recited. Here we appeal to the preceptor before taking refuge in each of the Three Jewels. Also the words of the Dharma refuge are a bit unusual in that they specify attachment as the cause of misery. Of course hatred, jealousy, and so on are also causes of misery, but here attachment symbolizes all the mental afflictions. Tsongkhapa gives us the ritual this way because this is exactly how Atiśa recited the ritual words of refuge.

(c) STATING THE PRECEPTS OF REFUGE

Taking refuge means one has promised to rely on specific objects. This promise entails doing some things and not doing others. Returning to the medical analogy, these precepts are similar to a doctor's prescription, specifying certain things to do and certain things to avoid. In the course of the ritual to generate bodhicitta the spiritual teacher explains the precepts of refuge. Tsongkhapa does not give detailed advice about these precepts here because he explained them earlier. (See volume 1, chapter 12.) However, because at this point in the ritual the teacher will explain the precepts, I will briefly go over a few of the main pieces of advice again.

There are individual precepts for each of the Three Jewels and some that are common to all three. Here let's look at actions that should not be done in relation to each of Three Jewels. Taking refuge in the Buddha means we should not rely on someone who denies the Buddhist teachings, practices, and cessations. When you take refuge in the Buddha you trust him to be a skillful doctor. Someone who tells you, "He is no doctor; he cannot do anything to help you," is trying to destroy your practice, wanting to lead you in the opposite direction. Although we should not trust the advice of people with this extreme view, it does not mean we must steer clear of general friendships with them. Similarly, when we say, "I take refuge in the Dharma," it means we are trying to eliminate our own and others' misery. Therefore we should avoid harmful activities of body, speech, and mind, which result in suffering. The actions to avoid after taking refuge in the Sangha are very similar to those we should not do after taking refuge in the Buddha; we should try to avoid companions who lead us away from or hinder our serious practice of the path.

Now for the things that we should do after taking refuge. When we take refuge in the Buddha we should honor him as our teacher because we recollect what enlightenment is and how taking refuge can help us. To show respect we should venerate images of a buddha because they are representations of the perfectly enlightened body, speech, and mind. We should keep statues and paintings in a high place, decorate them, and place offerings before them. After taking refuge in the Dharma we should pursue our practice to develop realizations. To achieve a particular cessation we must remove the cause of its opposite misery; therefore every means to remove the mental afflictions should be taken up. Along with reliance on actual practice, we should respect the scriptures and books that explain the Dharma. In Tibet we conscientiously cared for religious books. If a page came loose and blew away, we would not step on it. We would retrieve it and put it in a high place. We did not store books with shoes. It is not just for ornamentation that Tibetans keep a piece of cloth under books; it is a way to show our respect for what the book represents. After we take refuge in the Sangha we should have respect for those who practice and teach others to engage in meritorious activities. Buddhist monks and nuns exemplify the practice to attain complete liberation. They have completely renounced ordinary worldly life; they wear unique garments and cut off their hair to symbolize their renunciation of the causes of misery. Understanding the meaning of these symbols, we should respect even a piece of the cloth that is part of a monk's or nun's robes. This is similar to westerners' veneration of the clothing of saints. These small actions add up to a strong practice; they reinforce our refuge in the Three Jewels.

2" AMASSING THE COLLECTION OF MERIT

Earlier in the bodhicitta ritual, before taking refuge, one does the seven-limb puja to accumulate merit. After taking refuge one should recite this prayer again. In other words we should honor and make offerings to our direct and indirect spiritual teachers both before and after taking refuge in the Three Jewels. The *Commentary on the Difficult Points of the "Lamp for the Path to Enlightenment" (Bodhi-mārga-pradīpa-pañjikā)* says that we should do the seven-limb puja while recollecting the kindness of the buddhas, bodhisattvas, our past and present spiritual teachers, and their lineages if we know them. It was customary in Tibet to recite the short version of the seven-limb puja found in the *Prayer of Samantabhadra*. These stanzas are in the *Preliminary Practices (sByor chos)*. Or one can follow the longer version of the seven-limb puja found in Śāntideva's *Engaging in the Bodhisattva Deeds*. It is good to recite this latter version because it has more detail about whom we are honoring, the mundane and supramundane offerings, and the way to practice compassion, confession, taking refuge, dedication, requesting, and so on.

3" PURIFYING YOUR ATTITUDE

The purpose of the ritual is to produce a special mind-set: a desire to attain perfect enlightenment in order to save all other sentient beings. As we have seen, in order to produce bodhicitta we have to think about certain things beforehand. It is no different here; simply saying the words of the ritual three times will not make bodhicitta arise. The mind is the critical element. So just before one produces bodhicitta by repetition of the ritual, the preceptor and disciples should review the steps of one of the two methods to produce bodhicitta: the seven cause-and-effect personal instructions or exchanging self and others. Atiśa's *Lamp for the Path to Enlightenment* says we should recollect a summary starting with producing affectionate love for all sentient beings. Then as much as we can we should think about their misery—birth, aging, sickness, death, the inability to get what they desire, constantly encountering undesirable circumstances, and so on. Then, for the purpose of freeing all of them from that suffering, we decide, "I will quickly attain enlightenment in order to solve all of their problems." Our desire to take responsibility for others will only be as strong as our compassion and love. If we do not see their problems clearly, our compassion will be weak and our bodhicitta will be faint. It is proper to engage in the ritual when we deeply desire to help all mother sentient beings have happiness and be free from suffering. So we must study, learn, and meditate on these practices beforehand so that we can bring them forcefully to mind at this time. This completes the preparations for the ritual.

b" THE ACTUAL RITUAL

The actual ritual to produce bodhicitta is to repeat specific words three times after the preceptor. The ritual has a special kind of karmic force because one mentally, physically, and verbally engages in the practice. One adopts the previously described stance in front of the person leading the ritual. Kneeling with the right knee down, left knee up, and clasping the hands is not very comfortable and is quite different from our usual way of sitting. In Asia it is a way to show respect, demonstrate seriousness, and build up physical merit. If someone is ill or has physical problems, that person may sit in whatever way he or she is able. One's posture is not the key thing, but it does contribute to one's attitude. Following the words of the teacher and repeating them three times creates verbal merit. One prepares the mind as just explained. Then one imagines the preceptor as Buddha himself and visualizes all the buddhas and bodhisattvas in the space behind him. They are witnesses to the ritual.

When we ritually make a vow to produce bodhicitta it is not enough to simply wish to attain enlightenment in order to benefit all sentient beings. Atiśa's *Lamp for the Path to Enlightenment* says we make an irreversible promise to have bodhicitta always, without cease, until attaining enlightenment. This is a powerful intention to hold this precious mind, never giving up until reaching the goal. There is a great difference between producing bodhicitta with or without this intention.

Tsongkhapa makes it clear that there are different levels of bodhicitta. Earlier we talked about two types of bodhicitta: aspirational bodhicitta and active bodhicitta. Now we divide the first type into two. Remember aspirational bodhicitta is a determination to attain enlightenment for the benefit of other sentient beings; it is analogous to strongly desiring to go to a place, but prior to taking a step in that direction. There are two types of aspirational bodhicitta: one is making the promise always to hold bodhicitta by repeating the ritual words three times, and the other is without that vow. Tsongkhapa says that if you are not able to train in the precepts of the vow for aspirational bodhicitta, then do not make the special promise during the ritual. Instead during the ritual you can think, "For the benefit of all mother sentient beings I will *try* to attain enlightenment." This is not taking the vow. It is when you add, "Until attaining enlightenment I will *never* give up this thought for the benefit of sentient beings" that you take the vow. So the ritual for developing aspirational bodhicitta is for both those who can promise to train in the precepts and for those who cannot. In other words the ritual to produce aspirational bodhicitta can be combined with the bodhisattva vow, but it is not essential to take the bodhisattva vow. Aspirational bodhicitta can be produced with or without the vow.

The other type of bodhicitta, active bodhicitta, is actually to engage in activities to attain buddhahood. This involves taking the bodhisattva vow and doing the many practices described in the precepts. Thus by definition there are not two levels of active bodhicitta depending on whether or not one takes the vow. If one does not take the bodhisattva vow one cannot produce active bodhicitta through a ritual. Some people do not understand this difference between aspirational bodhicitta and active bodhicitta. The ritual for the former can be done with or without the vow, but the latter requires the vow. Because of this misunderstanding some people think that the ritual books followed by the lineage of Nagarjuna differ from those who follow Asanga. They think one lineage says that it is necessary to take the vow to practice active bodhicitta and the other disagrees. This is a great mistake. Both the lineage that comes from Nāgārjuna and the lineage that comes from Asaṅga agree that in order to produce active bodhicitta through a ritual one must take the bodhisattva vow. Further, Tsongkhapa says that it is wrong for beginners to recite daily prayers that contain the ritual for active bodhicitta if they do not understand the precepts in general and particularly what it means to break the rudimentary precepts. Many prayer books contain prayers and rituals without explanations about what the precepts mean. Those who have compiled these books have led others to make a great mistake.

Simply producing aspirational bodhicitta is a great thing and creates great merit. In the *Advice to the King Sutra (Rājāvavādaka-sūtra)* the Buddha teaches an Indian king that people who cannot engage in the bodhisattva practices according to the vow should develop aspirational bodhicitta. The great Indian teacher Kamalaśila cited this sutra in the first of his three books on the stages of Mahayana meditation. The first *Stages of Meditation* says that aspirational bodhicitta has great benefits and should be practiced even by those who cannot keep the precepts of the bodhisattva vow. Although those who take the bodhisattva vow and those who do not can engage in the ritual for producing aspirational bodhicitta, you should understand that when one takes a tantric initiation one must take the bodhisattva vow.

Now we have reached the ritual itself. The ritual is to kneel as explained before and repeat after the preceptor:

> All buddhas and bodhisattvas residing in the ten directions, please listen to me. Preceptor, please listen to me. Through the roots of the

merit that I, *who am called such and such,* create from the nature of generosity, ethical discipline, and meditation in this life, the next life, and many more lives, the merits that I make others create, and those I create by admiring the virtuous acts of others—just as previous *tathāgatas,* arhats, perfectly enlightened buddhas, and great bodhisattvas who reside on the high stages produced the special intention to attain perfect enlightenment—I, *who am called such and such,* will produce the aspiration for perfect complete enlightenment from now until I attain perfect enlightenment. I will free all those beings who have not been freed. I will liberate those who are not yet liberated. I will give relief to those who have no relief. I will lead those who have not yet attained the highest emancipation to the highest emancipation.

In the ritual we model ourselves upon the buddhas and bodhisattvas. They reached high spiritual levels because they produced bodhicitta and dedicated many lives to activities for the benefit of sentient beings. When we promise, "I will free all those beings who have not been freed," we are giving our word to help arhats—those who are already free from the mental afflictions—eliminate the more subtle obstructions to omniscience.[3] Pledging to liberate those not yet liberated is to undertake freeing others from samsara. Finally we vow to give relief to those in the three lower realms of samsara. We wish to relieve them from that suffering and help them be reborn as a human.

Tsongkhapa said that although it is not clearly stated that we should repeat the ritual words of taking refuge and generating bodhicitta three times after the preceptor, it is necessary to do so. These instructions are for engaging in the ritual in front of a guru or preceptor. However if you cannot find a preceptor you can do it by yourself. In that case you imagine Buddha Śākyamuni and many other buddhas and bodhisattvas in front of you. You make salutations to them, and do all the elements of the seven-limb puja exactly as you would if you had a preceptor. The only difference in the ritual is that you do not say the words, "Preceptor, please listen to me." You say the rest of the ritual words three times. You may take the ritual from someone the first time and then every day you can repeat this ritual by yourself.

c" THE CONCLUSION OF THE RITUAL

At the conclusion the preceptor explains the precepts that go along with the vow. He or she gives the students detailed advice about what they should do and what they should avoid.

⚜ 6 ⚜

Maintaining Bodhicitta

---

b' PROTECTING WHAT YOU HAVE OBTAINED FROM DEGENERATING

To protect our bodhicitta we should understand the precepts because they describe what we should and should not do. Tsongkhapa explains the precepts in two sections:

1' The training in the precepts that cause you not to weaken your
    bodhicitta in this lifetime
2' The training in the precepts that cause you not to separate from bodhi-
    citta in future lifetimes as well

1' THE TRAINING IN THE PRECEPTS THAT CAUSE YOU NOT TO
WEAKEN YOUR BODHICITTA IN THIS LIFETIME

There are four subtopics within this subject:

a" The training in the precept to recall the benefits of bodhicitta in
    order to increase the strength of your enthusiasm for it
b" The training in the precept to generate bodhicitta six times each day in
    order to increase actual bodhicitta
c" The training in the precept not to mentally abandon the living beings
    for whose sake you develop bodhicitta
d" The training in the precept to accumulate the collections of merit and
    sublime wisdom

Great joy comes from seeing the benefits of bodhicitta. This happiness will
help us maintain bodhicitta because it makes us enthusiastic about further
practice. In addition, in order to increase bodhicitta we should try to produce
it by repeating the words of the ritual three times every day and three times
every night. Another tactic to maintain our bodhicitta is to learn how to not
give up on sentient beings. Because the purpose of bodhicitta is to save others from misery and lead them to the highest happiness, losing hope is very
detrimental to Mahayana practice. Even if we do not have natural sympathy,
we must keep trying. Finally, to be successful in this endeavor we have to be
fortunate. In other words we must have the accumulations of merit and wisdom. We accumulate merit by generosity, saying prayers and mantras, making offerings, performing obeisance, and so forth. We accumulate wisdom by
increasing our understanding of reality.

a" THE TRAINING IN THE PRECEPT TO RECALL THE BENEFITS
OF BODHICITTA IN ORDER TO INCREASE THE STRENGTH
OF YOUR ENTHUSIASM FOR IT

When we clearly see the benefits of bodhicitta no hardship will deter us from
practice. We will be like businessmen who take risks and endure many
difficulties with pleasure because they foresee a large profit. It is the same with
bodhicitta. In chapter 1 Tsongkhapa discussed the importance and benefits

of bodhicitta in extensive detail. Here he mentions them once again as a means to increase our keenness to practice. If you have not developed bodhicitta before, understanding the benefits cannot come from your own experience. So in the beginning he advises us to learn about the benefits of bodhicitta by reading the scriptures and listening to a spiritual teacher. Following Atiśa, Tsongkhapa refers us to the *Array of Stalks Sutra* because it provides many analogies to explain the benefits of bodhicitta. Although we have gone over these earlier, here are a few brief examples to refresh your memory.

Bodhicitta is like a seed that will grow into huge tree whose every part— trunk, branches, leaves, flowers, and fruit—is medicinal. The seed of bodhicitta grows as the Mahayana path and ripens into the fruit of buddhahood. Bodhicitta is a condensation of all the Mahayana practices and prayers. It is the heart of all the bodhisattva practices for the benefit of sentient beings. With bodhicitta any practice or prayer becomes a Mahayana practice. Just as in literature a few introductory lines summarize the contents of a text, bodhicitta is a synopsis of Mahayana practice. There are almost countless practices necessary to attain perfect buddhahood in order to lead all sentient beings to perfect happiness and peace, free from all misery along with its causes. So implicit in bodhicitta there are many subjects, stages, and instructions for a long period of practice. In this sense bodhicitta is the linchpin of the entire Mahayana path; without it the entire structure falls apart.

Now Tsongkhapa discusses the benefits of the first type of bodhicitta— aspirational bodhicitta—a desire to attain enlightenment for the benefit of other sentient beings. The other type of bodhicitta—active bodhicitta—is actually doing something to accomplish that wish so it has even greater benefits. However the *Bodhisattva Levels* by the great teacher Asaṅga explains that merely developing a sincere and firm aspiration to attain buddhahood in order to help other sentient beings has two immeasurable benefits: one becomes a holy field for accumulating merit and one holds all meritorious virtues without any danger of damage or injury. To understand the first benefit we look at an agricultural analogy. All crops grow in dependence upon the earth, and whatever we plant in a field with good soil will yield a good harvest. Similarly the happiness of all sentient beings is founded upon bodhicitta. Those who have bodhicitta are a field producing merit for others. The power of the field causes actions directed toward it to have great results. So even small virtuous actions, such as a little gift given to someone with bodhicitta, yield enormous merit. Of course a person motivated by bodhicitta also creates great merit. There is a great difference between doing something motivated by bodhicitta and doing the same thing with a selfish incentive. Someone with bodhicitta is like the father of all other sentient beings because he or she lovingly devotes all his time and energy to caring for others.

This first benefit is also expressed in a stanza from *Engaging in the Bodhisattva Deeds:*

> The moment one produces bodhicitta,
> Even the most pitiful being in the prison of samsara
> Will be called a child of the buddhas,
> And worshipped by men and gods in the world.

As soon as aspirational bodhicitta arises one becomes worthy of more reverence than arhats, those who have attained freedom from samsara. Although someone with aspirational bodhicitta has not achieved nirvana, bodhicitta makes him or her superior to those who have eliminated their mental afflictions and attained liberation for themselves alone. The *Play of Mañjuśrī Sutra (Mañjuśrī-vikrīḍita-sūtra)* explains that as soon as bodhicitta arises one is like an infant prince who from birth is acknowledged to outshine ordinary people with much greater knowledge and maturity. This baby has not developed his qualities yet, but he will grow up to be the leader of all his people. Similarly as soon as one produces the thought of bodhicitta one becomes a child of the buddhas and will mature into an enlightened Dharma king guiding all sentient beings. One is no longer an ordinary being because one has a great and noble intention to save all beings from their problems and lead them to the highest happiness. When that thought arises sincerely and spontaneously one becomes a holy person in whom others can take refuge. Such a person is worthy of honor. A desire for honor and respect could inspire one to produce bodhicitta, but that is a very different motivation.

The second benefit of aspirational bodhicitta is that it protects one from harm. Humans, animals, or invisible spirits will not be able to hurt us because the best protection from harm is to suppress hatred and develop altruism. All our problems are the result of egotistic self-centeredness. In contrast, when we have compassion and rejoice in others' happiness it is very difficult for them to hurt us. They cannot do it. Deities, dharma protectors, and other beings will protect us when we consistently desire to benefit others. Sincere and spontaneous bodhicitta provides double the number of guards that protect a cakravartin king. Even when not actively practicing—such as when we are sleeping, working, or involved in some ordinary situation—bodhicitta prevents any evil spirit from hindering us.

Another aspect of the second benefit of aspirational bodhicitta is that it makes common spiritual achievements easy to attain. Certain yogic practices, mantras, and spells result in four miraculous powers: the power to pacify sickness or injury; the power to extend life; the power of wrath that protects one from evil; and the power of control. These powers are called *common* because they arise from both Buddhist and non-Buddhist practices. In addition, one does not need to be an advanced spiritual practitioner to attain these powers; even ordinary people can achieve them if they put some effort into the practice. However if you have bodhicitta you do not even have to practice to get them. If you have not accomplished them before attaining bodhicitta, they just come into your hands when you do develop it. The goal of bodhicitta is not these common powers, however; it is the uncommon achievement of enlightenment. Thus when a bodhisattva has these powers he or she will use them to benefit others. Without bodhicitta these powers can be dangerous; they may be the cause of injuring others and indirectly they will harm their possessor.

There are so many other benefits of bodhicitta. Bodhicitta also protects those living around bodhisattvas. The power of bodhicitta brings about an environment of peace and harmony where fear, famine, sickness, disasters, and harm created by evil spirits will not occur. If frightening things already exist they will slowly be cleared away. The bodhisattva's power of bodhicitta blesses a place so it takes on the atmosphere of a shrine or object of worship. Areas where few people are practicing bodhicitta have many more problems.

Some benefits accrue to a bodhisattva individually. New bodhisattvas who have not reached an āryan stage may have some past heavy karma that cannot be reversed or they may break a vow that leads to rebirth in a lower realm. However the power of their bodhicitta prevents them from suffering there like ordinary beings. They do not remain in the lower realms long; they rebound like a ball to a better rebirth. Their time in the lower realm will benefit the other sentient beings there because it makes these bodhisattvas want to attain buddhahood even more quickly. Their experience of misery is like pouring oil onto a fire; their compassion becomes even stronger. In their next rebirth these bodhisattvas will not suffer much from illness. The power of bodhicitta shortens the duration and reduces the strength of any type of harm or injury. Bodhicitta gives one physical and mental strength; bodhisattvas do not tire easily when giving teachings or doing other things for the benefit of other sentient beings.

There are various types of sentient beings. Because of their previous karma some people are low and weak, some intermediate, and others are naturally superior. Some people lean toward selfishness while others are naturally loving and compassionate from a very young age. They do not need to be taught to enjoy helping others. Such people are not yet bodhisattvas, but they have strong karmic tendencies from past practice making them ready to develop bodhicitta. Therefore even if we do not succeed in our present attempt to develop spontaneous bodhicitta, mental training in this life will make us more compassionate and less selfish in the next life. When we meet the right circumstances we will easily develop bodhicitta. If someone develops bodhicitta in one life, it will rise again with much less interference in his or her next life. Such people naturally do far less negative activity because their intent to harm others is very, very low. Their minds are dominated by a desire to benefit others. They are very patient, calm, and gentle; they can bear any attempt made to injure them, never retaliate, and respond only with helpful actions. When bodhisattvas see someone harming another being, they feel the pain as if it were their own. This is what makes them unhappy. Bodhicitta is the antidote to faults such as anger, jealousy, deceit, and concealing one's own shortcomings. Even though these negative attitudes are not totally eliminated when we first develop bodhicitta, they will be reduced. They may arise every once in a while, but if and when they do they will not be very strong or long-lasting; we will quickly become able to eradicate them from the root.

If the merit that resulted from bodhicitta were physical it would not fit into the world. Its benefit has no measure because merit created with the intention to help all sentient beings will fill all space until every sentient being attains enlightenment. The *Questions of the Householder Vīradatta Sutra (Ārya-vīradatta-grha-pati-paripṛcchā-nāma-mahāyāna-sūtra)* says:

> If the merits of bodhicitta
> Had a physical mass,
> They would fill all space,
> And there would be more left over.
>
> Someone may offer all the buddhafields,
> Filled with as many precious jewels
> As there are grains of sand along the Ganges,
> To the savior of the world,
>
> But superior to that offering,
> Is putting your palms together
> Wanting to attain enlightenment to save others.
> This is no limit to the merit in this.

Tsongkhapa tells a story about the great teacher Atiśa to illustrate the benefits of bodhicitta. This anecdote was not part of the literary tradition; rather it was commonly known in Tibet and passed orally from one person to another. While Atiśa was circumambulating the great stupa at Bodhgaya, he thought about how best to attain enlightenment as quickly as possible. He had a vision of various small statues rising up and asking the bigger images, "How should those who want to attain enlightenment quickly train?" The bigger ones answered, "They should train in bodhicitta." Then when Atiśa went upstairs in the temple he saw two women, an older one and a younger one. The younger woman asked her elder the same question. She replied, "The quick method to attain enlightenment is bodhicitta." From then on Atiśa had an especially strong conviction that bodhicitta is one of the most important practices of the Mahayana path.

Tsongkhapa concludes that we too must understand the importance of bodhicitta. In summary, bodhicitta is key; it is the special instruction of the Mahayana because the essence of the path is condensed within it. It is like a great treasury containing everything we desire: all spiritual powers and religious goals. It is what makes the Mahayana distinct from the Hinayana; practitioners of the lower vehicle take responsibility for their own liberation but Mahayana practice is motivated by a desire to help all sentient beings. Any practice—even tantric practices—are part of the Hinayana if they are done for one's own purpose. With bodhicitta even a small act of charity is for the benefit of all. Bodhicitta is the noble support that enables bodhisattvas to accomplish great deeds. Bodhisattvas will stay in hell if it will free just a single sentient being. The great yogi Śāntideva says:[1]

> Therefore if you train your mind
> To feel joy when others' misery is pacified;
> Just like swans enter a lotus covered lake
> You can even go to the depths of hell.

A bodhisattva's happiness is based on knowing that others are free from suffering. If bodhisattvas see that something will benefit others, they will do it without hesitation, even if it involves entering the worst, most miserable hell. They jump in as happily as swans land on a beautiful lake covered with lotus flowers. Buddhas and bodhisattvas know that bodhicitta is the crucial practice for attaining enlightenment.

Śāntideva says in *Engaging in the Bodhisattva Deeds:*

> After many eons of examination
> The buddhas see that this is most beneficial.

We too should meditate on this over and over so that it becomes clear and firm in the mind. This will increase our joy in the practice of bodhicitta. Then our practice of bodhisattva activities will continue for many many eons without decrease.

b" The training in the precept to generate bodhicitta six times each day in order to increase actual bodhicitta

Even if we cannot actually produce bodhicitta, we should say the ritual words six times every day. If one has the time this should be done with a meditation. By making this effort we may be able to produce bodhicitta for a short time. However it is not enough just to produce bodhicitta; we must not lose it. Even that is not enough; we have to increase it. Therefore this topic has two subsections:

1" Not giving up your development of aspirational bodhicitta
2" The training to increase aspirational bodhicitta

1" Not giving up your development of aspirational bodhicitta

When we take the vow to produce aspirational bodhicitta, we promise never to give up our desire to attain buddhahood until we actually attain it. This does not mean that the bodhicitta produced through the ritual must always be present. That would be impossible for beginners. In the beginning especially it takes a special effort for this thought to arise. Most of the time we will not have this thought; when we eat, sleep, or do other things it will not be present. Therefore we try to produce it six times during the day and night. So *giving up* does not mean that bodhicitta is not present. *Giving up* is to take the vow and later decide that you cannot keep it. You deliberately go back on your word to help others and decide to attain something just for yourself.

A variety of conditions can discourage one so much that one reaches the breaking point and gives up. One may be disheartened about how many sentient beings there are, and that they are so crude physically, mentally, and verbally. It may be depressing to think about the very long time it will take to help all of them equally. Or one may be daunted by the difficulty of accumulating immense amounts of merit and wisdom. When you contemplate these things you may think, "This is impossible. This is not for me."

To prevent this we consider the faults of giving up. Giving up this vow is one of the most powerful negative actions. The sutras contain many teachings about the bad consequences that result when one gives up bodhicitta from the heart. It is far worse for a Mahayana practitioner to drop the bodhicitta vow than it is for fully ordained Hinayana monks or nuns to break one of their root vows. Tsongkhapa quotes from the *Verse Summary of the Perfection of Wisdom in Eight Thousand Lines*:

> Despite practicing the ten virtues for eons,
> If desire for your own Hinayana arhatship arises,
> You have a moral fault; your conduct has degenerated.
> Losing bodhicitta is a heavier fault than a prātimokṣha downfall.

Hinayana practitioners vow to refrain from negative actions of body, speech, and mind in order to attain their own emancipation from samsara. They are very careful not to kill, not to touch certain things, not to eat certain things, to avoid sensual pleasures, and so on. Breaking one of these root vows is very negative karma; it will prevent liberation. The practice of the ten virtuous actions is also part of a bodhisattva's ethical conduct. But even if a bodhisattva has practiced the ten virtuous actions for millions of eons, this ethical discipline will be severely damaged if he or she desires Hinayana arhatship after having taken the bodhicitta vow.

Conduct is primarily mental. If one has self-centered goals, every activity—including keeping the vows—is Hinayana conduct. Wanting emancipation for oneself is selfish; it is the bodhisattvas' worst enemy. If a Mahayana practitioner is selfish, he or she has lost the religious conduct of a bodhisattva. Therefore the most important aspect of bodhisattva ethical conduct is to resist selfish thoughts and not to lose bodhicitta. If someone has bodhicitta, even if he or she engages in activities forbidden by the prātimokṣa vows, the special bodhicitta vow is not damaged. Whatever is done while keeping the bodhisattva vow—even indulging in the five sensual enjoyments—does not make one lose the key to the perfection of ethical discipline. The same sutra continues:

> The wise understand the perfection of ethical discipline remains
> Even if bodhisattvas enjoy the five sensory objects,
> Because with the thought to attain omniscience for others' sake
> They have taken refuge in the Buddha, Dharma, and noble Sangha.

If we give up bodhicitta we will wander a long, long time in the lower realms. Śāntideva says:

Having the intent to give
Even a few ordinary things,
Then deciding not to give them,
Is said to be the cause to become a hungry ghost.

If you invite all sentient beings
To unsurpassable happiness
And then you deceive them,
How can you go to a pleasant rebirth?

Stinginess makes someone change his or her mind after thinking, "I will give a little food or money to those poor people." The sutras teach that miserliness about such small items is the cause to be reborn as a hungry ghost. What we promised to give all sentient beings in the bodhicitta vows is not some small thing. From the heart we have invited all mother sentient beings to be our guest at the feast of the highest enlightenment. We decided to attain buddhahood in order to give them a banquet of extraordinary happiness. If later we renege thinking, "I do not want to give them the everlasting supreme bliss of enlightenment," we have deceived all sentient beings. The result of breaking a promise to give something extraordinary to benefit all others is much greater than the result of simple miserliness involving one or two people. So if we create this karma how could we go to a high rebirth? We will definitely go to a low rebirth.

The great yogi Śāntideva also says:

Bodhicitta arising in my mind
Should be viewed just like
A blind man accidentally finding a jewel
In a heap of garbage.

How happy a poor man will be if he finds something precious in a trash bin. Consider how much he will appreciate it and try to protect it from loss. Similarly producing the precious mind of bodhicitta, even just once through a ritual, is very, very rare. Usually the mind is like a heap of garbage containing so much attachment, hatred, jealousy, and pride. We are egotistic and self-centered with almost no concern for others' happiness and well-being. It is difficult for a pure desire to attain buddhahood in order to save others to arise from this rubbish. Even if one is introduced to the idea of bodhicitta, it is still difficult to produce. So we should think, "It is amazing, almost accidental, that this precious attitude could be found by someone like me." We should have great joy in this rare occurrence. Once we find bodhicitta we should make an effort not to lose it. Promise yourself that you will not drop it for even a moment. This is how to practice so as to not let your bodhicitta degenerate.

2" THE TRAINING TO INCREASE ASPIRATIONAL BODHICITTA

It is not enough just to produce bodhicitta and not lose it. We have to become accustomed to this attitude so that it arises spontaneously all the time. The more we practice, the stronger and more sincere our bodhicitta will become. This is the purpose of the advice to produce this thought three times during the day and three times during the night. If we try again and again to produce bodhicitta sincerely from the heart, we will finally actualize this mindset. This will not happen without practice and effort. How do we do this? We do it as explained before: through the extensive ritual. If that is too much, a shortened means is to visualize the field of assembly—the buddhas and bodhisattvas—in front of you and make whatever offerings and reverence you can. Then because the main cause of bodhicitta is love and compassion, we should think about the misery of all sentient beings and how their relationship to us is the same as that of our mother.

The ritual to produce bodhicitta can be the short stanza we often recite:

> Until I attain enlightenment I go for refuge
> To the supreme Buddha, Dharma, and Sangha.
> By whatever I have done such as giving and so on
> May I attain buddhahood in order to benefit other beings.

When reciting these words we should remember that taking refuge is for more than just oneself. To attain enlightenment to benefit all sentient beings we need help from the Buddha, Dharma, and Sangha. We pray that whatever merits we created in the past will help us achieve this goal. Merely saying these words six times a day is adequate, but much more serious meditation should be done to produce this thought strongly. This is how to try to increase bodhicitta every day by means of ritual.

c" THE TRAINING IN THE PRECEPT NOT TO MENTALLY ABANDON THE LIVING BEINGS FOR WHOSE SAKE YOU DEVELOP BODHICITTA

To abandon living beings is to think, "I will never do anything for this person again." After taking the bodhicitta vow we should try never to have this thought. We should not give up on others; we should be like a kind guru who takes care of his or her disciples just as a loving father manages every detail to enable his son or daughter to follow in his footsteps. We should guard our bodhicitta from the point of view of its object, benefits, ritual, increase, and not forgetting it. This topic is not found in the root text of the *Lamp for the Path to Enlightenment* or the precepts of the ritual itself. However Atiśa's commentary says that we should take care of other sentient beings by helping them, leading them, and encouraging them to practice to attain enlightenment. Tsongkhapa says that this instruction does not contradict the meaning of the root text so it should also be practiced.

d" THE TRAINING IN THE PRECEPT TO ACCUMULATE THE COLLECTIONS OF MERIT AND SUBLIME WISDOM

One has to be very fortunate in order to succeed in developing and maintaining bodhicitta. *Fortunate* means that one has a wealth of virtue. Therefore after we have taken the ritual vow to produce bodhicitta, we should accumulate merit every day in order to maintain and increase it. I have talked about how to accumulate merit before in terms of an upper field of merit and a lower field of merit. In brief to create merit in regard to the upper field—the buddhas, bodhisattvas, the Three Jewels, and things connected with them—we make prostrations, recite praises and prayers, make offerings, and do various other things to honor and please them. To create merit with respect to the lower field—sentient beings who are sick, poor, and so forth—we help and support them in various ways. These are general examples of how to create mental, physical, and verbal virtuous actions. Tsongkhapa says that he did not find a particular source for this advice, but previous gurus have taught this and he agrees that it is very beneficial.

2' THE TRAINING IN THE PRECEPTS THAT CAUSE YOU NOT TO SEPARATE FROM BODHICITTA IN FUTURE LIFETIMES AS WELL

The point of the practices discussed so far is to increase and maintain bodhicitta in this life. The second topic is how to not lose bodhicitta in future lives. There are two subtopics regarding how to continue to develop bodhicitta in the future:

a" The training in the precept to eliminate the four black practices that weaken bodhicitta b" The training in the precept to adopt the four white practices that keep bodhicitta from weakening

The term "black" as used here indicates that something is negative or sinful. There are four black actions that weaken or make one forget bodhicitta in future lives. Even if one has developed bodhicitta through sincere practice and has not lost it completely, these black actions will destroy future positive conditions for developing bodhicitta. Then even if one tries to develop bodhicitta it will be very difficult because one has created powerful opposition. There are also four positive, or white, actions that will keep bodhicitta intact until one attains buddhahood. The *Kāśyapa Chapter (Kāśyapa-parivarta)* of the *Ratna-kūta Collection (Ratna-kūta-dharma-paryāya-śata-sāhasrika-grantha)* explains that these four black and four white actions are special instructions for aspirational bodhicitta. Tsongkhapa says we should try to avoid the black ones and practice the white ones in order to have bodhicitta in our future lives.

Before we begin to discuss these actions in detail it will be helpful to have a summary. The first black practice is to deceive people who are helping you along a path of spiritual practice. The second is to make someone regret his or her interest and endeavor in Mahayana practice. The third is to verbally abuse those who have entered the Mahayana path. The fourth harmful activity is to deal with other people in a deceitful, insincere way. The white practices are the antidotes of the black ones; they are the way to eliminate the black actions.

a" THE TRAINING IN THE PRECEPT TO ELIMINATE THE FOUR BLACK PRACTICES THAT WEAKEN BODHICITTA

The first black action—deceiving those who are helping one practice the path—should be understood in terms of the object of this activity—those who are deceived—and the types of actions that are deceitful. The people deceived are one's abbot, preceptor, spiritual teacher, and any holy being who compassionately desires to help one progress spiritually. These categories of people may be somewhat confusing. According to the Vinaya, the difference between an abbot and a preceptor is as follows. When people decide to become a monk or nun they go to someone who can help them through the ordination process; an abbot is the one who takes primary responsibility for arranging to bring the aspiring practitioner into the Sangha. A preceptor is the monk or nun who leads the ritual recitations at the time of taking the ordination vows. The preceptor can be, but is not necessarily, the same person as the abbot; in fact there may be several different preceptors involved.

A spiritual teacher is one's own lama, and it is not necessarily the case that your spiritual teacher and the preceptor are the same individual. Last are those who may not have a direct relation to you but have many good qualities and are noble spiritual beings.

What type of action in relation to these people is considered to be the first black action? It is to deceive them, meaning to mislead them intentionally. Sometimes, without knowing it, we may do something that gives someone a wrong impression; that is not considered to be an example of deceit here. One must have the intent to mislead, otherwise it will not be the first black action. In addition, the method one uses to deceive others must be by telling a lie; misleading someone in some other way will be considered in another section. Tsongkhapa says that the first black action is exclusively verbal because according to the *Compendium of Trainings* avoiding intentional lying is the first white practice. The white practices are the antidotes to the black ones; since the antidote is verbal the action it is counteracting must also be verbal.

As an example of this first black action Tsongkhapa mentions verbally deceiving one's teachers and so on. If we have broken certain rules or done bad things, our abbot or teacher may bring it up in conversation in order to help us change our behavior. They may kindly inquire, "Are you doing such and such a thing? This is not something that should be done." Or they may say in a sterner fashion, "You did such and such a thing, didn't you?" If we say something sneaky to mislead them we are engaging in this black practice. But deceit does not have to be in regard to one's faults; it is the intention to be misleading in respect to anything. For example, when we decide to do something that we do not want our spiritual teacher to hear about, we may say to our friends, "Do not repeat this because the Geshe will hear." This karma will result in not meeting with the teachings, a teacher, or honest and helpful friends in the future.

The second black action is to make someone who is trying to practice feel that he or she is doing something wrong. The object of this action is a person who is contentedly practicing or wishes to practice. The action is intentionally making that person feel remorse or uncomfortable about virtuous actions that he or she had no regret about before. According to the *Commentary on the Kāśyapa Chapter (Kāśyapa-parivarta-ṭīkā)*, this is trying to discourage someone who is correctly practicing the same practices that you are doing, such as upholding the the prātimokṣa or the bodhisattva vows. The strict interpretation is that simply having the intention to cause regret completes this black action; it is not necessary that the other person actually lose confidence, or wonder if he or she is doing something wrong. In other words, this black action is judged to be complete based on the actor's intention, not on whether the object toward whom it is directed is deceived. According to some other commentaries, however, completion of this action requires a bit more than intent; one must at least confuse the other person a little. Of course everyone agrees that it is a black action if one succeeds in making someone feel regret about Dharma practice. This is the opposite of bodhicitta; instead of wanting to lead other sentient beings along the path to enlightenment, one is trying to discourage their practice on the path. This is a powerful negative action.

The third black action is to denigrate those who have entered the Mahayana path. The object of the action is people who have developed bodhicitta with a ritual and still possess it. Others say it includes those who have produced bodhicitta with a ritual in the past but do not possess bodhicitta at present. The meaning of the sutras is not obvious because the *Commentary on the Kāśyapa Chapter* simply says that the person to whom you say these disparaging words is a bodhisattva. Other sections of the *Commentary* explain that the term *bodhisattva* indicates someone who has entered the Mahayana, possesses the bodhisattva vows, and is training in the bodhisattva deeds. However Tsongkhapa says that a bodhisattva should be understood to be someone who possesses bodhicitta. So his conclusion is that the object of this action is someone who possesses aspirational and/or active bodhicitta.

The motivation for this maligning speech is hatred. According to the *Commentary on the Kāśyapa Chapter* one does not have to speak angrily directly to a bodhisattva; one can complete this action by saying nasty things about a bodhisattva to someone else. The *Commentary* explains that in the latter case it is not necessary that the people to whom one is speaking have bodhicitta, but they must understand the unpleasant things one is saying about a bodhisattva. Therefore talking to a baby or small child in this way will not complete this action. It will still be a negative action, but this specific black karma will not be complete. However if you say derogatory words about a bodhisattva to someone who understands them, the action is complete. There are several types of negative speech included here. The first is disparagement; this is a general negative comment about a bodhisattva's faults, saying for example that he or she engages in bad behavior. It is not specific about a particular type of bad conduct. The second type of speech is to insult. Insults are sharper than disparagement because a particular type of bad conduct is specified; an example of this would be to say, "He engaged in sexual misconduct." The third type of speech is libel; it is even more specific. Here one lists details about the specific type of behavior, who was involved, when, and where the action took place. All three types of speech are degrees of criticism. If one angrily says any of these abusive words about a person who has bodhicitta one creates the third black action.

The third black action is easy for us to commit in the course of our daily activities because we have no way of knowing who is a bodhisattva and who is not. If we were sure that someone was not a bodhisattva we could say something critical about him or her with less severe karmic results, and we could be careful about what we said about bodhisattvas. Earlier Tsongkhapa explained that the sutras contain many accounts about how very bad it is to criticize bodhisattvas out of anger. (See volume 2, chapter 2.) Bodhisattvas are potent objects; if we do good things in relation to them it will create great merit, while even a small negative action in relation to a bodhisattva will result in very negative effects. The sutras teach that just thinking critically about a bodhisattva for a moment will destroy the merit that one accumulated over many kalpas and can result in an eon of suffering in a lower rebirth. The *Sutra on the Magic of Final Peace (Praśānta-viniścaya-prātihārya-sūtra)* says that no activity other than angrily criticizing another bodhisattva has the power to cause a new bodhisattva to fall into hell. The power of bodhicitta protects bodhisattvas so that if they fall into a low rebirth they come out quickly. However if abusing another bodhisattva with anger is so detrimental to new bodhisattvas, consider how severe the negative effects of this action will be for ordinary beings. Even if a bodhisattva does not fall into hell, angry abuse of another bodhisattva creates an obstacle to quick progress on the path because one powerful angry thought wipes out the eons of merit that made him or her ready to attain the next stage of development.

The *Verse Summary of the Perfection of Wisdom in Eight Thousand Lines* says:

> If a bodhisattva who has not yet obtained the prophecy for his
>   enlightenment
> Becomes angry and argues with a bodhisattva who has obtained his
>   prophecy,
> For as many eons as there were moments that he had this faulty thought
> He will have to wear the armor of practice before advancing on the path.

When a bodhisattva attains a certain level of spiritual development the Buddha prophesizes when he or she will attain enlightenment. The *Ornament for Clear Knowledge* and the *Perfection of Wisdom Sutras* explain there are three points on the path where a bodhisattva's attainment of buddhahood may be predicted. Some bodhisattvas' enlightenment will be forecast while they are still on the path of preparation, before they attain the āryan stage. Other bodhisattvas will have their buddhahood foretold when they attain the path of seeing and become āryan bodhisattvas. The last type of bodhisattva receives a prophecy when they reach the eighth bodhisattva stage. The first line of the above stanza refers to a bodhisattva whose enlightenment has not yet been prophesized; this means a brand new bodhisattva—one who has just entered the path of accumulation, the very beginning of the bodhisattva path.

Since bodhisattvas have taken responsibility to free all sentient beings from suffering, getting angry with a bodhisattva is like getting angry at everybody. Thus anger—the opposite of compassionate love—is an especially powerful negative action when directed at a bodhisattva. The *Lamrim Chenmo* says that if new bodhisattvas get angry at a bodhisattva who has received his or her prophecy, the result will be that they must to go back to the start of the path and practice for as many eons as the number of moments they were angry. Progress before reaching the āryan stages of the path is generally slower than after one achieves the path of seeing. If one is not practicing tantra the bodhisattva path will take three countless eons; in that case the accumulation of merit on the first two paths will take a countless eon. So one powerful moment of anger can destroy all the merit one creates on the path of accumulation and the path of preparation. This makes the attainment of enlightenment very distant. Therefore Tsongkhapa urgently advises us to be especially careful when relating to bodhisattvas because they are a great field for increasing either the negative or positive effects of an action. If we get angry we should immediately confess it and vow not to do so again.

Tsongkhapa quotes from the same short perfection of wisdom sutra:

> One should always recollect that this thought is not good.
> If it arises, confess it and vow not to enjoy it in the future.
> This is the way to practice the Buddha's Dharma.

Because anger is extremely powerful and destructive, we should immediately feel great regret and confess the specifics either to the object of our anger or to the buddhas and our gurus. Confession alone, however, is not enough. We must vow to never do this again in the future. Together these two are the way to purify negative actions. If we recognize hatred as poison and acknowledge our past faults, we will not give anger the opportunity to arise again. Without this attitude we will have no antidote to anger. Letting anger arise will make our compassion powerless and weak. Not only will the compassion that has already arisen degenerate, it will very difficult to produce it again even if we try for a long time. This indicates that the root of bodhicitta is cut off, because without compassion there is no bodhicitta. If we train the mind to resist anger our practice will get better and better. We can increase the positive qualities of the mind without measure by developing constructive conditions and eliminating negative ones.

In the second chapter of the *Commentary on the "Compendium of Valid Cognition" (Pramāṇa-vārttika-kārikā)*—in the course of proving past and future lives, emancipation, and perfect enlightenment—Dharmakīrti mentions the ability of the mind's positive qualities to increase. He says:

> If there are no harmful negative conditions,
> The mind is completely perfectible.

The subject of this syllogism is compassion and love. The thesis is that if there is no opposition to compassion and love the mind will become completely one with their nature. At the beginning of practice there is much resistance to compassion and love in the mind; they are like a little fire whose flames can be easily doused out. However the mind's nature can be compassionate. A buddha's mind is completely under the power of compassion and love; no negative attitude can destroy it. It is limitless. In contrast, ordinary physical things can only be increased to a limited extent. For example, let's say you are training yourself to do a long jump. In the beginning perhaps you can jump just a few feet. As you practice you go further and further. But no matter how much you exercise, the length of your jump cannot increase beyond a certain point. Another constraint on physical improvement is that each time you jump it takes effort. The effort you made in your previous jump does not help you with the new jump; you have to make a fresh start.

Another example of ordinary things' limitations is the effect of heat on water. As we heat water in a pot the water will get hotter but it is not going to become limitlessly hot. Eventually the heat makes the water disappear; it boils away until eventually the pot is dry. The increase of the quality—the heat—destroys the basis—the water. The mind is different. The nature of consciousness is the basis and the quality we want to develop is compassion. If you strive to eliminate anger and develop compassion, both the mind and compassion will increase limitlessly. Unlike the case of heating water, as compassion rises consciousness does not go down; it increases too. Eventually the mind will become fully perfect; it will be an enlightened mind with perfect knowledge, compassion, and love.

Dharmakīrti also says:

> Because their nature is similar, a prior moment
> Is a seed that increases naturally.

> So if you practice, how could those attitudes—
> Compassion and so on—remain the same.

The nature of the mind is a continuum; each moment is similar to and conditions the next one. In the beginning meditating on compassion will take some effort. But each attempt gives more strength to the next one. The next attempt builds on the former and compassion becomes greater and lasts longer. The seed of prior practice naturally brings an increase. The *Commentary on the "Compendium of Valid Cognition"* explains in detail that it is possible to have complete perfection of compassion, love, and bodhicitta.

This is true for any kind of mental quality; even a wrong consciousness such as attachment or anger can become spontaneous and unlimited. For example, if you meditate over and over on how wonderful, beautiful, and desirable something is, your mind will become powerfully attached to that object. Then attachment will arise spontaneously without requiring any effort. Anger works the same way. With effort any mental quality can become dominant. Hinayana practitioners meditate for a long time on the ugliness and impurity of the body. Eventually they see its true nature: the contamination of the aggregates, impermanence, and selflessness. This realization disgusts them; it makes them want to escape samsara as much as we want to get away from a pile of excrement. We do not have to think about it; an impulse to vomit and the desire to move away arise naturally and spontaneously.

The fourth black action is dealing with other sentient beings deceitfully instead of having a superior thought. Here "superior thought" does not refer to a high level of compassion; it means being straightforward, earnest, and pure in relation to others. According to the *Commentary on the Kāśyapa Chapter,* superior thought is a natural attitude that is the opposite of deceit. It is how bodhisattvas should interact with others. The object of this black action is any other sentient being and the activity is doing anything deceitfully. In Tibetan the term translated "deceit" is made up of two syllables: *yo* and *gyu. (g.yo sgyu).* On its own the first syllable means "trying to hide your faults." The second syllable means "pretending to have a special quality that you do not have." Asaṅga says in the *Compendium of Knowledge (Abhidharma-samuccaya)* that both aspects of deceit are motivated by desire for material possessions, honor, and wealth for oneself. So among the three poisons, deceit is part of both attachment and ignorance. Neither aspect of deceit emphasizes anger. An example of such deceit is a merchant who cheats when measuring out a certain weight of grain. Today in the west we may not have this problem, but in ancient times, despite the use of balance scales and standard weights, some grocers found ways to give less than what the customer paid for. As another example of deceit Tsongkhapa tells of a person named Gyalwa Yenjung who wanted to send someone to a place called Ragma, but first he told the person that he was being sent to Tölung, a place not as far away. After the man traveled to Tölung, Gyalwa Yenjung sent word that it would be easy enough for him to just continue on to Ragma.

In conclusion some of the four black actions destroy all one's merit and others will force one down to hell. In addition, one will face obstacles that make bodhicitta very distant. Fortunately there are antidotes to these black actions, the four white deeds, which are explained next.

b" The training in the precept to adopt the four white practices that keep bodhicitta from weakening

The first white action is to avoid any kind of intentional lie. Lying is deceiving: it is the opposite of straightforwardness, kindness, and love. Mahayana practitioners should not lie to any sentient being for any purpose—not even to make a joke or to save one's own life. However saying something untrue if you do not know that it is untrue does not count as lying. The black action is to lie deliberately and the white action is to avoid consciously telling falsehoods. The object of this white action is every sentient being, not just bodhisattvas. Thus it is the antidote to lying in general and in particular to the first black deed: deceiving one's guru, preceptor, and so on.

The second white action is to be earnest and truthful toward all other sentient beings. So again the object is all sentient beings. The activity is to have a superior attitude of sincerity and honesty. This is the direct antidote to the fourth black deed—deceiving others.

The third white practice is to praise, honor, and respect bodhisattvas as much as we can. The object is all bodhisattvas. The activity is to try to perceive that they are perfect teachers like Buddha Śakyamuni. We respect the Buddha because all his actions were compassionate and for our benefit. Our attitude toward bodhisattvas should be the same because they manifest as buddhas for us. We should praise their good qualities in the four directions. This does not mean we must travel around! Instead it means that whenever we have the opportunity we should praise the qualities of bodhisattvas. This also does not mean that we should exaggerate. We should praise whatever qualities that we are aware of. This is the opposite of and antidote to the third black deed: criticizing a bodhisattva in general or in detail.

Criticizing and lacking respect for bodhisattvas is the reason that there is no sign of our virtue increasing even though we seem to be practicing. In fact, more often than not there is a sign that our merit is decreasing. Even though we do a bit of positive activity here and there, we promptly destroy it. The *Compendium of Trainings* says that if one is able to avoid animosity and angry thoughts toward bodhisattvas, one will steer clear of many negative actions that destroy merit. So we are supposed to think in a positive way about bodhisattvas. But who is a bodhisattva? Our problem is that without knowing it we are continually involved with bodhisattvas; we get angry at them, do them injury, or say bad things about them.

Since we cannot tell who is a bodhisattva and who is not, how can we avoid these serious mistakes? The way to avoid such negative actions is called the *practice of pure perception*. This is training the mind to perceive the pure nature of everything that appears. Instead of thinking there are not any bodhisattvas around and being careless in our relations with everyone, we should treat all sentient beings as if they were bodhisattvas. The attitude we should have toward every living being is that they are our teacher or a manifestation of the Buddha. We should respect and honor them. We should be truthful. Pure perception is difficult, but many Buddhist yogis do this type of practice. Many other religions also have this type of practice; even some monotheists train themselves to see everything as a manifestation of God. This practice of pure perception is very similar to the tantric practice of pure perception wherein one perceives every place as a mandala, every being as a deity, and every sound as a mantra. This practice of the imagination is wonderfully effective for the accumulation of merit. It does not matter if a thing is completely contaminated; if we see it as pure we will not create any evil actions and will only be involved with virtue.

The fourth white action is trying to help others as much as we can by leading them to the Mahayana path. The object is all the sentient beings we are trying to ripen. This means that we are trying to make them suitable vessels for Mahayana practice even though they may be attracted to the Hinayana path of self-emancipation. Thus this white action is trying to lead those who desire to enter the lesser vehicle—a path to their own salvation without involving benefit to others—to the Mahayana path so that they can become a beneficial savior of all sentient beings. We should try as much as we can, but it is not our fault if someone does not develop the Mahayana attitude of bodhicitta no matter what we do. Success in leading every being to the Mahayana would be an impossible standard to meet. So not succeeding despite compassionate effort is not a fault. The essence of this practice is wanting from the heart to lead others to highest happiness. It is therefore the antidote to the second black activity: making others regret their practice of the Mahayana. Here one avoids anything that would make others unhappy or have regret about their practice.

This is the way to ensure that one never loses bodhicitta in future lives. In the *Sutra Requested by a Lion (Ārya-siṃha-paripṛicchā-nāma-mahāyāna-sūtra)*, the Buddha was asked, "What kind of practice is the cause for not losing bodhicitta in all lifetimes?"

> What must one do to have
> Bodhicitta in all future lives—
> Keeping this thought even during dreams,
> To say nothing of when one is not asleep?

The Buddha responded that wherever we live and wherever we go, we should make an effort to lead others to practice the path to enlightenment. If we do this as much as we can, we will never lose bodhicitta. It will come naturally and spontaneously even during our dreams.

> Lead townspeople and villagers,
> And others wherever they live,
> To enter the path to enlightenment.
> Then you will never lose this thought.

According to the *Array of Qualities in Mañjuśrī's Buddha-realm Sutra* another way to not lose bodhicitta in future lives is to conquer conceit, pride, and envy of others' virtues and good qualities. If one lacks bodhicitta one is dominated by selfishness. Selfishness—envy and not sharing with those that we know are in need—is the opposite of bodhicitta. So the practice is to apply their antidote. We should try to avoid miserliness by sharing our wealth, food, and clothes with those in need. We should not hold on to our possessions because we are worried about our own well-being. We should try to feel happy when others are prosperous and in good health. We should work on the mind this way even when we are engaged in ordinary activities, says the *Cloud of Jewels Sutra (Ratna-megha-sūtra)*. We can do this when we are eating, lying down, and especially when walking around. When we go out we have a lot of opportunity to practice because we encounter so many sentient beings. They all have problems and are trying to get something. By looking at what they lack and seeing what they search for we can practice developing bodhicitta all the time. It is also important to generate bodhicitta before every virtuous activity, such as saying prayers, meditating, giving charitable donations, and whatever else we do to create merit. Recollecting one's desire to attain perfect enlightenment in order to help other sentient beings will block a low motivation of expecting something in return for oneself. If, for one's whole life, one practices these four things—avoiding pride, jealousy, and miserliness while developing altruistic joy—one will not lose bodhicitta in future lives.

Now we have completed the discussion about the method to obtain bodhicitta if one has not yet attained it, and the method not to let the bodhicitta one has attained degenerate in this and future lives. The next topic is what we should do if we lose the bodhicitta that we have generated through a ritual vow.

c' THE METHOD TO RESTORE BODHICITTA IF IT DOES DEGENERATE

In this section Tsongkhapa explains the parameters of the aspirational bodhisattva vow in detail. He draws from sutras, commentaries, and logical analysis to make a clear distinction between the rudimentary downfalls that cause us to completely lose bodhicitta and those actions that merely weaken aspirational bodhicitta. He does this by contradicting the following common misperceptions:

> You give up your aspirational bodhicitta if you let a certain amount of time pass after engaging in the four black activities, if you mentally abandon sentient beings, or if you cast away your bodhicitta thinking, "I cannot attain buddhahood." If you come to regret these within a certain period of time, they become a cause to weaken your bodhicitta. If your practice of generating bodhicitta six times per day and amassing the two collections weakens, that will be a cause for weakening your bodhicitta. If a cause of abandoning bodhicitta occurs you must recite the ritual for generating bodhicitta. If a cause merely for degenerating bodhicitta occurs, reciting the ritual is not necessary; confession is sufficient.

Contrary to these assertions Tsongkhapa says that as soon as one thinks, "I cannot attain enlightenment," one has given up aspirational bodhicitta. No time need elapse after thinking this way. Further, the four black activities are not causes to give up bodhicitta in this life. We should avoid them now because they are causes for not having bodhicitta in future lives. It is true that the four black activities will weaken our bodhicitta in this life, but they are not rudimentary downfalls. If they were root downfalls, then lying as part of a joke and letting a little time pass without feeling regret would destroy bodhicitta and the bodhisattva vows. However, these four black actions are not taught as components of the fourteen rudimentary downfalls of the bodhisattva vow in any sutra or commentary.

Unlike the many rules in the Vinaya that specify when certain actions should or should not be done, none of the bodhisattva vows depend upon time. For example, the Vinaya states that if fully ordained monks eat after noon they are breaking their vow. However in the context of keeping or breaking the bodhisattva vows, the time at which something is done is not relevant. Further, it is incorrect to consider the passage of time as a measure of a fault becoming a rudimentary downfall. This misconception is based on some passages in the *Questions of Upāli Sutra (Upāli-paripṛcchā-sūtra)*. In this sutra within a discussion of the three levels of practitioners, the disciple Upāli asks the Buddha to explain certain issues about time in regard to purifying a broken vow. The Buddha explains that the best practitioners immediately purify their faults; if they break a vow in the morning they purify it before noon. Intermediate practitioners purify their faults during the next period of the day; for example, a morning infraction would be corrected in the afternoon. Lesser practitioners leave purification for a later time. The sutra's comments about the heaviness of the fault depending on how long someone waits to purify it should not be understood to apply to the bodhicitta vows. Tsongkhapa does not go into the correct way to interpret this sutra and the bodhisattva vows here because he does so in the *Basic Path to Awakening (Byang chub sems dpa'i tshul khrims kyi rnam bshad byang chub gzhug lam)*, an extensive commentary on Asaṅga's explanation of the conduct entailed by the bodhisattva vows in the *Bodhisattva Levels*.

In the lamrim system mentally giving up on sentient beings is abandoning bodhicitta. This is becoming discouraged and thinking, "There are so many sentient beings. How could I possibly help them? I cannot do this." One also loses aspirational bodhicitta by thinking, "In general I want to help all sentient beings, but I will make an exception about this one. I do not want to help that particular sentient being." Thinking that we would never benefit a particular sentient being is abandoning bodhicitta because bodhicitta is the desire to attain enlightenment in order to benefit *all* sentient beings without exception. If we exclude one particular sentient being then the whole is lost. How can we logically make an exception of one or two sentient beings? If we could make exceptions, first we would single out one, then a second, then a third, and on and on until hundreds or thousands were excluded. Then where is our bodhicitta?

In regard to this and other precepts of bodhicitta, Tsongkhapa goes into some technical detail based on the *Commentary on the Difficult Points of the "Lamp for the Path to Enlightenment."* There is some discussion about whether this commentary was written by Atiśa. Because certain points in this commentary are dissimilar to Atiśa's explanations in other places, followers of Dromtönpa do not accept this commentary to be Atiśa's work. However Nagtso Lotsawa's followers believe this commentary was written by Atiśa. Nagtso was a great Sanskrit scholar; he translated many books, was sent to India to invite Atiśa to Tibet, and interpreted for Atiśa as they traveled from India and remained in western Tibet for about three years. This was before Dromtönpa met Atiśa. According to Nagtso, this commentary was a hidden teaching that was not revealed to everyone. Tsongkhapa says that earlier scholars also assert that Atiśa wrote the root text, *Lamp for the Path to Enlightenment,* and its commentary in Purang in western Tibet. However the commentary written there was supposedly a much shorter work than the present one. Perhaps the initial translator or later followers added to the original text some of what they heard Atiśa teach later at Samye Monastery in central Tibet. Tsongkhapa says that because others added to Atiśa's work, we find mistakes in some passages. However, there are also some excellent explanations in it. Therefore Tsongkhapa says that sometimes he cites the commentary and at other times he rejects the view of the commentary and shows the mistakes for what they are.

Tsongkhapa says that the passage in the commentary regarding the precepts of aspirational bodhicitta taken with a vow is not correct. First let's look at what the commentary says and then we will examine what Tsongkhapa says about it. The commentary says that the great Indian teachers and scholars like King Indrabhūti, Nāgārjuna, Asaṅga, Āryaśūra, Śāntideva, Candragomin, Śāntarakṣita, and so on had different views regarding the precepts of aspirational bodhicitta. Some say that the precepts include everything that is to be practiced by beginner bodhisattvas, by bodhisattvas who are a little more advanced, and by bodhisattvas on the first through seventh āryan stage. Others say everything taught in the sutras concerning bodhicitta should be considered precepts of aspirational bodhicitta. Yet others say the precepts for aspirational bodhicitta are only those taught for beginner bodhisattvas who have just entered the path of accumulation. Other scholars do not accept that there are specific precepts specifying one thing or another. Some say that the precepts for aspirational bodhicitta are the precepts of taking refuge and in addition the four black and four white actions. The commentary concludes that because all of these teachers' systems are based on the sutras, they are all acceptable despite their differences. Therefore the commentary advises us to hold the system that is given to one by one's spiritual teacher.

Tsongkhapa says that the commentary's conclusion is not reliable. The various systems are contradictory because they conflate the precepts for aspirational bodhicitta with those for active bodhicitta. The two are not the same. It would not be sufficient for those engaging in the bodhisattva deeds to simply avoid the four black actions and practice the four white actions in addition to the precepts of refuge. Further, it is not necessary for those with only aspirational bodhicitta to practice every precept taught in the sutras or all those taught for practitioners engaging in the bodhisattva deeds. Therefore, Tsongkhapa's opinion is that the only precepts for those with aspirational bodhicitta but who have not yet taken the vow, are giving up aspirational bodhicitta and mentally abandoning sentient beings. Until you take the bodhisattva vows you cannot break the vows; however doing those types of actions is nonvirtuous and contradicts your commitment to practicing virtue. Therefore you should confess those faults using the four powers.[2] This should be done according to the instructions given with the precepts for active bodhicitta.

7

An Introduction to the Six Perfections

c) How to learn the bodhisattva deeds after developing bodhicitta
  i) The reason why you must learn the trainings after developing bodhicitta
  ii) Demonstrating that you will not become a buddha by learning either method or wisdom separately

———※———

UP TO THIS POINT we have followed the extensive discussion in the *Lam-rim Chenmo* about how to produce and maintain the motivation for practicing the Mahayana path. To briefly review, the first subject was how to develop compassion and love equally for all living beings. Based on the wish to free all sentient beings from their misery and for all to have happiness, we learned how to produce bodhicitta. *Bodhicitta* is the wish to become perfect so that without error or favoritism one can lead all sentient beings to enlightenment. When bodhicitta arises spontaneously and continuously it dominates one's life. Every aspect of thought and behavior will be governed by this attitude and one will engage in real Mahayana practice. The great yogi Śāntideva says in *Engaging in the Bodhisattva Deeds:*[1]

> The primary view of the sons of the conqueror
> Is bodhicitta. After producing it they hold it firmly,
> And without any distraction
> They always persevere in their practice.

Bodhicitta has two aspects. *Aspirational bodhicitta* is the desire to attain buddhahood for the benefit of others; this is the foundation of Mahayana practice. However, merely a good thought, even one as excellent as aspirational bodhicitta, is not enough. We need the motivation, but once we have decided to take full responsibility to help others, we must do more than think about it. We must take action. The second aspect, ~~active bodhicitta~~, is what we should do when this excellent thought arises spontaneously; we take and keep all the bodhisattva vows. So one way to understand the words *hold it firmly* in the stanza above is that bodhicitta is held through the ritual of the vows. The ritual contains a promise, made in front of all the buddhas and bodhisattvas, to do all of the activities necessary to attain buddhahood. What kind of activities should we do? Many sutras explain how to progressively accomplish over ten stages the almost countless activities required to accumulate merit and remove internal obstacles in order to become enlightened. The rest of the *Lamrim Chenmo* explains which of these many practices are crucial and how we should practice them.

c) How to learn the bodhisattva deeds after developing bodhicitta

Tsongkhapa breaks this topic into three parts:

> i) The reason why you must learn the trainings after developing bodhicitta
> ii) Demonstrating that you will not become a buddha by learning either method or wisdom separately
> iii) Explanation of the process of learning the precepts (chapters 8–15 and volumes 4 and 5)

Tsongkhapa first shows the reason why we must engage in these practices after producing aspirational bodhicitta. Next he explains that we must practice a system that is unmistaken and complete. A practice may be correct, but it is deficient if it does not include all the causes and conditions necessary to reach the desired result. The correct approach is to practice method and wisdom together. Finally, the third topic is the sequence of the trainings and the way to practice them.

i) The reason why you must learn the trainings after developing bodhicitta

We all know that if we do not act upon a decision, nothing will happen according to plan. This holds true even for ordinary matters, for example a journey to a specific place. Before we decide to go somewhere we think about what a wonderful place it is, the benefits of going there, and so on. Finally we conclude, "I must go there for that purpose and for this reason." Then we must start our journey, otherwise we will never get there. It is the same for bodhicitta and the attainment of enlightenment. It is very meritorious to develop the motivation to attain buddhahood for the benefit of other sentient beings, but without doing something more than having a spontaneous desire for it, we cannot achieve our goal of enlightenment. However, with the practice of the right method we can achieve our objective. To elaborate on this point Tsongkhapa quotes several different sutras and commentaries. The great scholar Kamalaśīla's first *Stages of Meditation* says, "Without practice bodhisattvas cannot attain enlightenment."

In the *Condensed Lamrim* Tsongkhapa is a bit more specific:[2]

> Even if bodhicitta arises I will not attain enlightenment
> If I do not train in the three types of conduct.
> Understanding this well, may I be blessed
> To assiduously keep all the bodhisattva vows.

The three types of conduct include all the Mahayana practices. We must practice all of them until they are natural and spontaneous, because without them there is no way to attain perfect enlightenment. The first type of conduct is the prātimokṣa vows taught in the Vinaya. The purpose of the Vinaya is to control one's physical, verbal, and mental activities so that one causes no harm to others; one blocks negative actions such as killing and lying, and attitudes like hatred and attachment. The next kind of conduct is to do virtuous activities. This is a very wide category because to benefit others a bodhisattva engages in almost limitless actions on many levels. The last type of conduct is to directly accomplish the goals of other beings. The main way that bodhisattvas do this is by teaching others the practices that lead to emancipation from suffering. It is difficult to explain a method to others if you do not know it yourself. So the first step toward benefiting other sentient beings is to learn, practice, and become very familiar with all those methods. The *Commentary on the "Compendium of Valid Cognition"* by the great teacher Dharmakīrti says this explicitly:

> In order to destroy suffering, compassionate ones
> Apply themselves to the methods.
> If you don't know the cause for creating a result,
> It is difficult to explain it to others.

Compassionate love is the desire that every being have the highest, everlasting happiness and be totally separate from trouble, misery, and the root cause of suffering. The job for those with great compassion is not just to eliminate others' temporary pain and provide them with short-term pleasure; their objective is to free all sentient beings from the root of all suffering. The bodhisattva deeds are the method to free oneself and then teach others how to destroy their misery and place themselves in true happiness. Bodhisattvas succeed in helping others by teaching and example. Therefore they have to master every aspect of every method themselves. This in brief is the reason why we should practice all the trainings on the Hinayana path even though our own freedom is not our goal. We practice until we are skilled in these methods, because without this expertise we cannot free others.

ii) Demonstrating that you will not become a buddha by learning either method or wisdom separately

Once we decide to take action we must determine precisely what to do because certain practices will lead us to our goal and others will not. No matter how much effort we make, we will not get the result we want if we engage in the wrong approach; no matter how long we pull a cow's horns, we won't get any milk. But even a correct method will not be enough to accomplish one's goal if it does not include all the necessary causes for achieving the desired result. For example, many causes and conditions are required to produce a harvest of grain. Of course the main cause is seed because without seeds no plants will grow. But a pile of seeds is not enough on its own. The seed has to be put into the soil; it needs warmth and moisture to sprout; and then many activities, like weeding, are necessary to foster it. Farmers know that if any one of the complete set of necessary causes and conditions is lacking, they are not going to get a bountiful harvest.

So what are the main causes and conditions for the attainment of perfect enlightenment to help other sentient beings? In *Vairocana's Great Enlightenment Discourse (Mahā-vairocanāsaṃbodhi-dharma-paryāya)*, the Buddha summarized the complete and unmistaken method into three short words: great compassion, bodhicitta, and the perfect method. Great compassion is like a material cause; it is the root from which omniscient wisdom grows. In other words, compassion is the rudimentary cause for enlightenment. Great compassion is not only impartially desiring that all mother sentient beings be totally free from misery, it is also taking on the responsibility to free them. This leads directly to the second and primary cause: bodhicitta. There are two types of bodhicitta in this context: *phenomenal bodhicitta* and *ultimate bodhicitta*. Phenomenal bodhicitta is the wish to attain perfect enlightenment oneself in order to help others. Ultimate bodhicitta is a bodhisattva's direct realization of the ultimate truth, or śūnyatā. Finally, the perfect method completes the set of causes. The variety of methods is divided into six or ten perfections.

Some readers may know what the six perfections, or *pāramitās,* are but because some may not, I will summarize them very briefly before we begin the extensive account of what they are and how to practice them. The six perfections are the perfections of generosity, ethical discipline, patience, perseverance, meditative stabilization, and wisdom. The first three perfections focus on meritorious action; one controls the senses and keeps one's actions pure. Generosity is giving others whatever will help them, whether it is one's wealth or even one's body. The perfection of ethical discipline is to completely avoid harming others directly or indirectly. The third perfection, patience, is the ability to bear others' negative actions. Only with patience can one maintain a virtuous mind and pure conduct when others try to harm one out of greed, hatred, and ignorance. The fourth perfection is perseverance. Perseverance is a special joy when one practices virtue. Even if it is inconvenient or difficult, one happily perseveres because one sees the value and purpose of the practice of virtue and the negative consequences of not practicing this way. The fifth perfection deals with controlling the mind; meditative stabilization is the ability to concentrate on whatever one wishes with complete control for as long as one desires. The mind is stable; it does not succumb to distraction or become dull. One remains alert and one's concentration is clear and vivid. This is important because most of our problems stem from the fact that the mind is wild; every moment it goes off in all directions in an uncontrolled manner. Until we achieve mental stabilization, the mind is weak. We try to do something but immediately get distracted; the mind flies away like a little feather carried off by the wind. The perfection of meditative stabilization has a physical aspect too; because the mind is within the body, when we train the mind we also train the body. Eventually the mind and body harmoniously support each other. One feels a special sensation of pleasure brought about by completely training the mind. We must have this concentrated mental instrument to practice many high spiritual techniques on the path, particularly the sixth perfection: the perfection of wisdom.

Generally speaking, wisdom is any correct knowledge; it properly knows what is correct and what is incorrect. Here, however, wisdom refers to more than understanding right from wrong; it is understanding the nature of truth—śūnyatā—the emptiness of the self and phenomena. When we do not understand things accurately, subjects and objects appear as a real and absolute duality. Based on this incorrect perception, all the delusions arise. The mind is dominated by ignorance; ignorance pushes us to create all kinds of negative karma; bad actions result in internal and external problems. When one concentrates on the true nature of things, one will develop wisdom that directly realizes the truth. This wisdom destroys the poisons of greed, hatred, and ignorance. Wisdom breaks the cycle of karma and suffering. To bring this list of perfections up to ten, we add the perfections of method, prayer, power, and transcendental knowledge.

The combination of the practices of compassion, the two types of bodhicitta, and the perfect method of the perfections comprise a perfect vehicle for carrying one to enlightenment. Another way to categorize the necessary causes for reaching a state of perfect freedom, knowledge, compassion, and power is to divide them into the practices of method and wisdom. The wisdom side of the practice is ultimate bodhicitta: the realization of śūnyatā. The method side is compassion, phenomenal bodhicitta, and the remaining perfections. The profound deep wisdom of ultimate bodhicitta held by compassion and phenomenal bodhicitta is the antidote of all inner obstacles. If we lack either one we will not be able to obtain buddhahood. We would be like a bird without wings, or with only one wing, and so unable to fly. Another example is that a person needs both sight and locomotion to be able to go somewhere. If one has wisdom but lacks the method, it is as if one can see where to go but does not have any means of travel. If one has the method but lacks wisdom one is like a blind person; such a person may be able to walk but cannot see if he or she is on the right path or walking into danger. In short, to get to enlightenment we need all the practices. The *Perfection of Wisdom Sutra in Eight Thousand Lines (Ārya-aṣṭasāhasrikā-prajñapāramitā-sūtra)* says:[3]

> The blind led by the blind
> Do not know the path or have a vehicle.
> Even if they want to go to a special place
> They have no way to enter the desired city.

> If you lack wisdom you cannot see.
> And without the other perfections
> You have no vehicle and leader.
> So how can you reach buddhahood?

Thus it is a misunderstanding to think that a single method or wisdom on its own is enough to lead to enlightenment. Certain Buddhist schools have propounded the idea that there is no need for all these practices. Tsongkhapa explains why this position is wrong using the ideas attributed to the Chinese master Hva Shang Mahayana as an example of the opposing view. Hva Shang was an important figure in the history of Tibetan Buddhism so I will give you a little background.

In the early eighth century King Trisong Detsen and various nobles in central Tibet had some interest in Buddhism, but Buddhism was not widespread through the country as it came to be in later times. Most people, including some high officials surrounding the king, followed the Bon religion. Bon is the ancient, pre-Buddhist religion of Tibet. Its practices included animal and human sacrifice, black magic, worship of tree and water gods, and other such things. To convert his subjects to Buddhism, the King invited Śāntarakṣita, one of the most eminent Indian Madhyamaka masters, to come to Tibet. There was a lot of opposition; the general public was not happy that a foreigner had come to teach an alien religion. A lot of bad things happened that year; there were many big floods, famines, epidemics, and one of the palaces was destroyed by a flash of lightning. All of this happened, said the Bon supporters in high government positions, because the Bon deities did not like the Buddhist proselytizing. Furthermore, the people did not find Śāntarakṣita's emphasis on pure religious conduct and other Mahayana practices attractive. Because he was not successful in his missionary work, Śāntarakṣita advised the king to invite the great tantric yogi Padmasambhava to Tibet so he could counteract these hostile forces with his magical powers. Śāntarakṣita also suggested that after Padmasambhava subdued the demons, the king should invite to Tibet Śāntarakṣita's disciple, the great teacher and famous scholar Kamalaśīla. After assenting to this advice the King suggested that Śāntarakṣita leave Tibet and go to Nepal.

At the same time that Buddhism was coming to Tibet from the west, carried from India by the great teachers Śāntarakṣita and Padmasambhava, the Chinese Buddhist monk Hva Shang Mahayana came from the east. He stopped many places on his journey from China to Lhasa to teach Mahayana Buddhism with a Zen-like emphasis. (Zen is much more profound than this system; do not confuse the two and think I am criticizing Zen.) It does not matter whether the philosophical position ascribed to Hva Shang accurately reflected his view or if the Tibetans misunderstood his teaching. At that time and subsequently the Tibetans maintained that a certain philosophy and method of practice were his, and because they are attractive, but mistaken, Tsongkhapa strongly and firmly rejects them.

Hva Shang teaches that conceptual thought causes sentient beings to create karma, which in turn results in miserable lives in samsara. You may wonder how this works. First, he says, we perceive objects through our senses. Then we believe those things exist as they appear to our perception. Immediately thereafter we judge those things to be good or bad, attractive or unattractive, and so on. Once we make this distinction, desire, hatred, anger, pride, jealousy and the rest of the mental afflictions arise. These emotions impel us to act in various ways considered to be good or bad. Sometimes we think good thoughts and do positive things; sometimes we think bad thoughts and act accordingly. Whether good or bad, all thoughts are karma. Karma is the cause of our misery and suffering in samsara. Therefore, discriminating thoughts are our main problem. Of course there is no need to say anything about bad thoughts and negative actions binding us to samsara, but Hva Shang's view is that good thoughts similarly fetter us. He says that whether thoughts are good or bad is irrelevant; any constructive thought is an obstacle to attaining enlightenment because *all* thoughts are misconceptions. By way of analogy, it does not matter if your feet are bound with gold chain or tied with ordinary rope; it comes to the same thing—you are shackled. It does not matter if a big cloud is white or black; both black clouds and white clouds obscure the sky and block the sun. You will be in pain whether you are bitten by a white dog or black dog. In the same way, any kind of thought makes one experience suffering and misery.

To explain the ultimate nature of the mind and the possibility of attaining buddhahood, Hva Shang relies on passages from the *Essence of the Tathagata Sutra (Tathāgatagarbha-sūtra)*, some other sutras, and many other texts. These scriptures teach that every living being has a pure natural mind that is free of conceptual thought. This original mind can be described by the term *clear light*. This means that just as the sky is naturally without clouds, the mind is naturally free from all innate obstacles. It is light, pure, and thought-free. The original mind is without any kind of perception or object; in other words, it is the wisdom realizing śūnyatā. This wisdom is a special insight of the innate pure mind. When this empty mind comes to the surface one has the perfect realization of emptiness.

The natural state of clear light is enlightenment itself. Hva Shang understands this to mean that the mind is like pure, clear water. Water can be colored and flavored by various things; we can make soup, coffee, something sour, something sweet, or pollute it with mud or poison. But we can separate water from these impurities. Similarly, the mind is naturally pure but is muddied by conceptual thought. Reflections, concepts, and thoughts are impurities because they are the causes of attachment, hatred, and so on. Any kind of thought—good or bad—pollutes the originally pure mind. Separating the mind from impurity therefore means clearing away all thoughts so that the original purity of the mind will emerge.

In short, Hva Shang's understanding of the wisdom realizing śūnyatā is that *empty* means *nothing*. Since his view of the problem is that thoughts create bondage to samsara, he concludes that if we eliminate all constructive thought so that there is nothing in the mind, the mind's original nature will be revealed. The mind not clouded by any type of thought is like a clear mirror. A mirror will reflect any color or shape placed before it; when nothing is placed before it, the mirror's clarity is shown to be its fundamental nature. Hva Shang's teaching, therefore, emphasizes emptying the mind; to think nothing—to wipe out any kind of thought—is the best method for attaining the original pure mind of perfect enlightenment. He instructs his followers that they should think neither good nor bad thoughts. They should try to block every thought.

If you do not think it follows that you do nothing. Deliberate action requires premeditation; one has to think about what one is going to do, how to do it, or even if one should do it. Hva Shang's followers understood that the practice he was urging them to do was, "Think nothing and do nothing." In other words we should not practice generosity, ethical discipline, or patience because they all involve the thinking process. According to Hva Shang, the Buddha taught practices like generosity for people who are unable do the meditation practice on the pure original mind without conceptual thought. It was only to give stupid or inept people something to do that the Buddha taught morality, bodhicitta, and so on. People who can find the real truth through nonconceptual meditation should not do those practices; they are obstacles. Those who can properly meditate should *only* meditate. Hva Shang understands the sutras to mean that when one realizes śūnyatā there is nothing other than śūnyatā. In other words it is not necessary to meditate on compassion or teach the Dharma if one has a realization of śūnyatā. In fact if one were to engage in those practices it would be like the highest king falling down to the level of common people and doing ordinary things. It would be as foolish as someone who has found a real elephant but continues to search for an elephant's footprint. He says that the only method to attain enlightenment is meditation stopping all thoughts. This meditation was thought to be a white panacea: it was all one needed to achieve one's goal. You just do this one thing; there is no need to do many complicated and difficult things for many years or even life after life.

In eighth century Tibet many people were attracted to this method because it does not require complex logic or difficult practices. One just stops thinking and sits in one place doing nothing. This makes one feel peaceful immediately; one eliminates all worries about the future and ceases to recollect the negatives of the past. One relaxes, doing nothing and thinking nothing, and waits for buddhahood. The king, however saw this as quite a serious matter because if you literally accept this teaching, you eliminate all moral and civil conduct. In that sense Hva Shang's teaching is very dangerous. It was also confusing to the King because Hva Shang's teaching of the Dharma was completely opposite that taught by Śāntarakṣita. Śāntarakṣita said that one should do all kinds of meritorious practices, keep various vows, and to obtain realizations one must do rigorous analysis of the Madhyamaka view. King Trisong Detsen wondered, "Which is the best practice to follow?" To resolve this contradiction he decided a representative from both schools of Dharma would debate each other in front of the court at Samye Monastery. The winner's system would be followed from there on. Therefore the king acted on Śāntarakṣita's advice and invited the great teacher Kamalaśīla to come from India to debate Hva Shang.

Hva Shang was already in Lhasa with many followers. When Kamalaśīla reached the Lhasa area, Hva Shang and many others went to welcome him. They waited for him with various high Tibetan officials near the Brahmaputra river, which runs south of the city. Kamalaśīla paused when he arrived on the far side of the river. He had wondered if Hva Shang was very intelligent so from the far side of the river he waved his walking staff in a circle to test him. Kamalaśīla was asking, "What ties sentient beings to this circle of samsara? What makes them cycle?" The great Chinese man on the near side of the river understood. He pushed up his long sleeved yellow robe and slapped his hands together to answer, "Grasping subject/object duality is the cause." So the two great teachers communicated. Kamalaśīla must have been surprised.

During the great debate at Samye both masters cited many scriptures. Hva Shang quoted eighty different sutras and scriptures to prove his thesis. This is important because Hva Shang's views are not imaginary; we can find these ideas in certain sutras. Kamalaśīla rejected this view by drawing from many, many more scriptures and employing valid logic. There are sutra passages that can be quoted literally by both sides. Some sutras say that without practicing all the activities of the method side you cannot achieve buddhahood. Other sutras teach about the disadvantages of conceptual thought. In some sutras wisdom is emphasized and in others the emphasis is on the method. Sometimes people think that because a sutra says something we should accept it. However, we should understand that sutras can have both a direct meaning and an indirect meaning. They may say something explicitly for a certain purpose but their real intent is something else. Obvious examples are passages such as, "Your father and mother should be killed." or " If you kill the king and all his subjects you will become pure." These passages should certainly not be taken literally! *Father and mother* are to be understood as karma and the mental afflictions; *the king and all his subjects* indicates ignorance and the mental afflictions.

The Buddha taught sutras with varying emphases because each was meant for a specific person, engaged in a particular practice, at a certain time, on a specific stage of the path. The great masters with deep understanding of the teachings know that following the literal meaning of some passages is harmful, so they examine the sutras for their implicit meaning. Hva Shang places incorrect stress on various sutras that explain that conceptual thought has to stop. There are certain times when that is true. When one is engaged in meditative direct realization of emptiness, one has no other thoughts. At that time one engages in no activity other than meditation on śūnyatā. Also, not letting the mind waver is part of the practice of mental stabilization. Meditative stabilization is a peaceful and very stable mind. It is complete mental control so that when you set your mind on something, you can concentrate on it as long as you wish without any distraction. When one first tries to concentrate the mind keeps running away like wild elephant. To tame a wild elephant one has to have a big strong pole to hold him in place. In order to stabilize the mind the sutras teach techniques to stop thinking and hold the mind on a single object. Onc should understand these instructions are like a skillful doctor's recommendations to do certain things and avoid other things *at a particular time.* At one point a doctor may say, "You should eat meat to regain your health." But at other times she may warn, "If you eat meat it will make you much sicker and may even kill you." In the same way, simply stopping thought is not the sum total of the method to attain enlightenment. It is not to be followed literally from the beginning as the only thing to do. To sit without thinking for hours and hours is a waste of time and perhaps even damaging. It makes one ignorant from the start. If we accept that the literal meaning of the sutras is that we will attain perfect enlightenment by thinking nothing, then we have to stop doing anything. We would even have to stop eating, because to prepare food requires a thought process and activity.

According to Tibetan historical sources, Kamalaśila won the debate and Hva Shang was sent back to China. Of course, each side has a different version of what happened; we do not know what really occurred. However, Kamalaśila later wrote extensively about these issues in his *Stages of Meditation.* There he proves that method and wisdom in combination are necessary for attaining enlightenment. In particular he shows that Hva Shang's approach completely negates the path to enlightenment because urging disciples to simply stop thinking essentially annihilates the extensive method side of the Buddhist practice. Hva Shang's followers are told to do nothing—neither practice virtue nor avoid nonvirtue. When one denies that the method side is part of the correct path to enlightenment, the wisdom side is also destroyed. Not concentrating on anything, not analyzing, and not doing anything makes reaching a nonconceptual understanding of the ultimate nature of reality far distant. According to the Indian Madhyamaka system, if one does not engage in analysis one will not attain a direct realization of emptiness. No one can realize śūnyatā by stopping thought from the very beginning. The method to come to a direct realization of the truth is to first learn about it. Next one examines and analyzes what one has studied. Through inferential reasoning one gains an understanding that becomes more vivid through meditation. One should use both scriptures and logical reasoning to produce valid knowledge that establishes that all phenomena in samsara and nirvana do not inherently exist. One must logically examine the self and other things in order to come to a direct and nonconceptual realization of their emptiness. This is the way to obtain real insight. In short, it is very destructive to believe that all practices other than meditation are not worth doing and are obstacles to buddhahood.

Even though Kamalaśila explained this so well, Hva Shang's view was still common in Tibet during Tsongkhapa's lifetime. So Tsongkhapa feels it is necessary to remind his readers that both method and wisdom are required. Even today many people think that study and analysis are obstacles to spiritual attainment. They believe that sitting meditation—rejecting any kind of thought—is the highest practice. Tsongkhapa strongly disagrees. He says that one of the worst wrong views is to hold that the mind without thought is the perfect path because that approach reduces one's capacity to remove mental obscurations from the root, develop perfect powers, and attain perfect enlightenment.

Tsongkhapa says there are three related reasons why his contemporaries held Hva Shang's view. First, the teaching of Buddhism had nearly disappeared. Second, there were fewer and fewer great holy teachers with a deep understanding of the path gained through scriptural study and stainless reasoning. Finally, even though people had faith in the Dharma, because they had limited merit the power of their intellect was very weak. As a result some people saw no point to bodhisattva activities such as taking vows, keeping ethical discipline, and doing various kinds of virtuous activity. Following Hva Shang they believed that to meditate on the path meant to cast all these other practices away. Some other people did not reject the method side completely, but in general they believed Hva Shang's philosophical view was better. Others completely ignored analytical wisdom. These three are not too different; there is just a slight disparity between them. The first one wipes out the method side. The other two cast away the analytical wisdom that examines the nature of reality. In all they appear to accept Hva Shang's view that thinking nothing is the best practice.

Those following Hva Shang do not even come close to actually meditating on emptiness. First of all, they mistake the meaning of emptiness. They understand śūnyatā to mean "empty of something else." In general when we say, "the pot is empty," we mean the pot is there but there is nothing inside it; an "empty stomach" means there is no food there. A full pot or stomach contains some other substance. Hva Shang says we should understand the emptiness of the mind in the same way. Thus his followers' interpretation of the emptiness of the mind is that the mind is not filled with any thoughts. Therefore, they say that the highest realization of Buddhism—the profound understanding of śūnyatā—is a completely blank or empty mind. But it is incorrect to think that this is emptiness. All the other Buddhist philosophical systems' ways of explaining śūnyatā are very different and far more complex. (See volume 5 for a more detailed explanation.) In addition, Hva Shang's approach to attain a realization of emptiness is the opposite of what it should be. If you do not think, you cannot understand. Finally, even if Hva Shang had correctly understood the meaning of emptiness and his way of meditating on it was unmistaken, he thinks that there is nothing else to do other than meditate on śūnyatā. His followers say those who realize śūnyatā should not do other activities; only before one realizes śūnyatā should one practice the method side.

So precisely what is wrong with the statement that just one technique is all that is required to follow the path to enlightenment? First of all, it is contradictory to the Mahayana scriptures. It is also completely illogical. One cannot achieve a rich and extensive result from a single cause. Even the small pleasure derived from eating a good meal requires many ingredients, processes, and exertion. Buddhahood is not just a blank mind; it is a combination of many perfect things. The traditional way to say this is that buddhahood is the combination of two perfect bodies or kāyas: the *dharmakāya,* or perfect mental body, and the *rūpakāya,* the perfect physical body. Buddhas are omniscient, their selfishness has been completely destroyed, they have perfect compassion and love, and their power has no bounds. Their external qualities are also perfect. They do not have an ordinary physical body; it is something much more subtle that merely manifests as a physical form. Their bodies have thirty-two major marks and eighty minor marks, their speech has sixty different perfect qualities, and their environment is perfect as well. Such a complex of qualities requires multiple causes. One small, single cause cannot have these results.

In order to understand the consequences of a belief and method such as Hva Shang's, one must understand something about the Mahayana goal. Many Mahayana scriptures use the terms *parinirvana, buddhahood,* or *nonabiding nirvana* for the highest goal. Nonabiding nirvana is the highest peace; it is separate from samsara and the mere peace of nirvana. *Abide* means to exist in one of the two extremes—either in samsara or in mere peace. The Hinayana achievement of nirvana is mere peace—one's own individual emancipation from samsara. Being satisfied with mere peace is an extreme from the Mahayana point of view because one does not engage in compassionate and loving activities for others' sake. Of course, the other extreme is to cycle in samsara because of karma and the mental afflictions.

So what do we need to do to avoid abiding in samsara or mere nirvana? According to the *Ornament for Clear Knowledge:*

> By practicing wisdom you will not abide in samsara.
> By practicing compassion you will not abide in peace.

In other words, we must complete the two accumulations: the *accumulation of merit* and the *accumulation of wisdom.* The profound wisdom part of the practice is aimed at cutting the root of samsara. We are in samsara because of karma and the mental afflictions: ignorance, hatred, attachment, and so on. All karma, both good and bad, is founded on an egotistic view that grasps at a self or soul. This primary ignorance is the root cause of all the varied conditioned lives in the cycle of samsara. Ignorance is destroyed by the profound realization of ultimate reality—selflessness, or emptiness. In short, the function of the accumulation of wisdom is to remove ignorance and the mental afflictions. The result is a perfect cessation. It is the complete purity of mind due to removal of all faults and their causes. The scriptures use many terms for this wisdom: the path based on the ultimate truth, the profound path, or accumulation of wisdom. But by itself this deep meditation on ultimate truth does not lead to buddhahood; mere cessation of one's own ignorance cannot help others. When Hinayana practitioners attain nirvana and become free from samsara because of the accumulation of wisdom, they remain in enjoyment of that state for eons and eons without concern for other sentient beings. Thus buddhahood is not just a mere negation or perfect cessation; it is also a combination of various positive qualities. The method side—also called the accumulation of merit, or the vast path—is the foundation for the positive qualities of buddhahood. When one has perfect compassion, there is no way one could bask in one's own peace. Compassion, love, and bodhicitta will urge one to help other sentient beings all the time. So the two accumulations are the cause for obtaining the two buddha bodies. One must have a direct realization of wisdom to achieve freedom from samsara, to attain the dharmakāya. And the method-side practices—such as generosity, ethical discipline, patience, and so forth—are the causes for one to become a basis of enjoyment for all sentient beings: the rūpakāya.

Bodhisattvas engage in these two aspects of the path over many lives, sometimes for eons. Until one attains buddhahood one cannot practice the two simultaneously. The accumulation of wisdom is meditation on the deep realization of the truth with no dual perception. Any other thought during that meditation would be an interruption, so one ceases all other thoughts and brings the mind completely into profound contemplation on śūnyatā. When one arises from meditation on emptiness, one keeps in mind the understanding that the nature of things is illusory and empty of substantive existence, and engages in various activities to accumulate merit. Practiced together in this way wisdom and method will result in buddhahood. The great teacher Nāgārjuna therefore made this prayer in the *Precious Garland:*

> In order to benefit all beings, from this merit
> May I complete the accumulations of merit and wisdom
> And obtain the two perfect bodies
> That arise from merit and wisdom.

Tsongkhapa quotes from a number of sutras to support the necessity of both wisdom and method. In the *Sutra of Showing the Tathāgata's Inconceivable Secret (Tathāgatā-cintya-guhya-nirdeśa-sūtra)* we find:

> The accumulation of wisdom eliminates all the mental afflictions. The accumulation of merit nurtures all sentient beings. Bhagavan, since this is the case, great bodhisattvas should strive for the collections of merit and wisdom.

The next short quotation is from the *Questions of Sky Treasure Sutra (Gaganagañja-paripṛcchā-sūtra):*

> Knowledge of wisdom removes all the mental afflictions;
> Knowledge of the method will not give up on sentient beings.

The Buddha says in *Sutra Unraveling the Intended Meaning (Saṃdhinirmocana-sūtra):*

> I did not prophesize the unsurpassed perfect enlightenment of one who is not acting to benefit sentient beings and is not engaging in all the [bodhisattva] activities.

And the *Teaching of Vimalakīrti (Vimalakīrti-nirdeśa-sūtra)* makes a similar point:

> What is bondage for bodhisattvas? What is their emancipation? Bondage for a bodhisattva is taking birth in samsara without the method. Taking birth in samsara because of the method is a bodhisattva's [means for] liberation. Bondage for a bodhisattva is taking birth in samsara without wisdom. Taking birth in samsara because of wisdom is a bodhisattva's [means for] liberation. Wisdom not held by the method is bondage. Wisdom held by the method is liberation. Methods not held by wisdom are bondage. Methods held by wisdom are liberation.

The *Teaching of Vimalakīrti* goes into a lot of detail to explain that the method is such overwhelming compassion, love, and bodhicitta that all one's activities go toward helping other sentient beings. If one has this method, even birth in samsara is part of the path toward perfect freedom. But without this method, living in samsara is merely bondage. This not only pertains to the method; it is bondage to be born in samsara without wisdom—the realization of emptiness. This is bondage because it means that one has taken birth because of ignorance and the power of karma. But with wisdom a samsaric birth can be a means to achieve emancipation. Wisdom and method should be combined. Even though the insight of selflessness cuts off the root of samsara, without the skillful method of bodhicitta it is bondage for a bodhisattva because mere wisdom leads one to fall into the Hinayana goal of nirvana. In the same way, compassion, love, or even bodhicitta without a realization of the ultimate truth is bondage for bodhisattvas. If they do not see reality, they do not know and cannot achieve the goal.

Although wisdom and method must act together, when the sutra speaks about *methods held by wisdom* and *wisdom held by the method,* it does not mean that wisdom becomes compassion or that compassion becomes wisdom. *Held* means that, within the mental continuum, the two assist each other all the time. When compassion arises with wisdom, it is not ignorant compassion. Similarly, compassion influences wisdom so it is not just dry wisdom. Together they result in the achievement of the bodhisattva's goal. If either one is lacking we cannot get there. The *Foremost of Gayā* says, "In brief, the bodhisattva path is twofold. What are these two? They are method and wisdom."

Another way to look at this is that we need two causes in order bring about buddhahood, just as in an ordinary sense it takes a man and woman to bring a child into the world. A woman alone cannot conceive a son or daughter nor can just a man create a child. What is the father and mother in the case of enlightenment? Prajñāpāramitā, the wisdom that realizes the ultimate truth, is the mother. The father is the method side: compassion, love, bodhicitta, and skillfully doing various activities to bring these motivations and the realization of wisdom into practice. That is the basic meaning of the line from *Glorious First and Foremost Tantra (Śrī-paramādya-kalpa-rāja):* "Perfection of wisdom is the mother. Skill in means is the father."

Furthermore, in India and Tibet ethnicity was traditionally determined by parentage. Belonging to a particular ethnic group was based on the so-called "bone-lineage" of the father. If a boy's father was Chinese, the child would be considered Chinese no matter who his mother was. If the father was a westerner, the child would be a westerner. A woman could have children fathered by different men; she could have a Chinese child, a western child, and one of any other nationality or race. Similarly, wisdom is a mother common to the śrāvaka, pratyekabuddha and Mahayana goals; the method side is their unique cause. Realization of the truth that cuts out ignorance from the root married to the method of desiring one's own freedom will bring about the Hinayana goal: personal emancipation. This same realization of truth married to the Mahayana method of bodhicitta brings about the highest goal: buddhahood. So if we want perfect buddhahood, we need the wisdom that realizes the truth and, in addition, compassion, love, and bodhicitta.

The Buddha taught Kāśyapa in the *Kāśyapa Chapter* that wisdom assisted by bodhicitta is like a king helped by various skillful ministers. With this assistance the king can do all kinds of activities to help his subjects; but without the support of his staff a king cannot do much. Similarly, a bodhisattva whose wisdom is combined with the skillful Mahayana method can do almost all the activities of the Buddha.

Tsongkhapa pulls all these quotations together in order to critique Hva Shang's position that wisdom is simply the original or natural mind. Because the natural mind does not engage in conceptual thought, it does not include a realization of phenomenal truth. Therefore, Hva Shang concludes that natural wisdom will do everything; we do not need all the complicated mentation or hardships entailed by other practices. Tsongkhapa retorts that when the power of wisdom is praised in the sutras as being able to do everything, it means that wisdom destroys ignorance. However, those passages are not saying that wisdom, or a realization of selflessness, is the only cause for positive results. It is a matter of emphasis. We should do a meditation on śūnyatā that possesses the necessary method. The method must hold the meditation. The wisdom that realizes śūnyatā and has every aspect of the supreme method is the true white panacea; this combination will lead to the Mahayana goal.

To prove this point Tsongkhapa quotes from the *Questions of Crest Jewel Sutra (Ratna-cūḍā-sūtra):*

> The [bodhisattva] should wear the armor of universal love for all beings, abide on the stage of great compassion, and then meditate on the realization of emptiness that possesses all these supreme aspects. What is the *emptiness that possesses all the supreme aspects?* It is not separate from generosity, not separate from ethical discipline, not separate from patience, not separate from perseverance, not separate from meditative stabilization, not separate from wisdom, and not separate from the method.

Even in modern warfare armor is necessary to protect soldiers' bodies. Great love is like armor because it shields us from every fear and worry. When we wear the armor of compassion and love, we cannot be injured by hatred or anger. When soldiers engage in battle they need more than armor; to destroy an enemy they need a powerful weapon. In order to annihilate ignorance we have to have penetrating wisdom: the realization of emptiness. Just as warriors need both armor and weapons to win a war, to succeed we must practice both wisdom and the method. A meditation on emptiness combined with all six perfections is supreme.

The meaning of this sutra is also explained in verse by Maitreya in the *Sublime Continuum:*

> Generosity, ethical conduct, patience, etc.
> Are artists with particular skills;
> The image is emptiness:
> Supreme and complete in every aspect.

Imagine five different artists, each of whom can expertly draw one part of the body but is unable to draw anything else; one can draw the face, another can draw a hand, and so on. You would need all five to create a complete portrait of a king. If you lack one of them, you may end up with a picture that is without an eye or something else. The image of the king is analogous to śūnyatā. The various skillful artists are the perfections—the practice of the method side. If any of the methods is missing, one's deep realization of emptiness will not be complete. It will be like an unfinished portrait—a body without a head or without a hand.

Thus it is a mistake to think that only perfect wisdom should be practiced because the other perfections are worthless and unnecessary. In order to attain buddhahood we need the proper realization of the truth combined with proper activity. No matter how sharp one's wisdom, if it is not conjoined with other methods it cannot cut through ignorance. For example, no matter how much you whet an axe blade, if there is no handle or no one swings it, that well-honed blade cannot cut anything. The sharp blade must be joined to a handle and properly swung to cut down a huge poisonous tree. In the spiritual case, wisdom must be accompanied by the ethical discipline described in the bodhisattva and tantric vows undertaken out of compassion. People who say that only wisdom is necessary do not have ethical discipline or any constraint on their behavior. In the *Sutra Gathering All the Threads (Sarva-vaidalya-saṃgraha-sūtra)* the Buddha said to Maitreya, one of his highest disciples:

> "O Maitreya, some foolish people say that bodhisattvas correctly practicing the six perfections to attain perfect enlightenment should only practice the perfection of wisdom. They say, 'What need is there for the other perfections?' They destroy the other perfections. Maitreya, what do you think? Was it incorrect when the Buddha, born as a king of Kaśī, cut off some of his own flesh to give to a hawk to save some pigeon chicks?"
>
> "No, Bhagavan, it was not," replied Maitreya.
>
> Again the Buddha asked, "Maitreya, when I practiced the activities of a bodhisattva, collecting the roots of virtue connected with the six perfections, do you think they harmed me?"
>
> "No, Bhagavan, they did not," said Maitreya.
>
> Again the Buddha spoke, "Maitreya, you too perfected the practice of generosity over sixty eons. You perfected the practice of ethical discipline over sixty eons. You perfected the practice of patience over sixty eons. You perfected the practice of concentration over sixty eons. You perfected the practice of wisdom over sixty eons. In this regard some foolish people say that only one method is needed to attain enlightenment. What is that method? It is the method of emptiness. Those who say this behave impurely."

Sometimes the sutras and śāstras use words and expressions that, if taken literally, can lead one to make a serious mistake. This is one such dangerous area. According to Tsongkhapa, if people do not understand that the method side is important they may think that whatever they do is okay, as long as they have the correct view of emptiness. They claim bad actions such as stealing, sexual misconduct, and killing will not have negative consequences because they have a realization of śūnyatā. It is wrong, however, to believe that negative actions harm only those who do not have a realization of śūnyatā. Such people do not understand emptiness. Further, this mistaken view discredits the Buddha's activity because it implies that all the difficult tasks the Bodhisattva undertook in many lives before attaining enlightenment occurred before he understood true reality. In other words, generosity and all the other activities are to be practiced—according to this wrong view—only when one does not have a firm realization of śūnyatā; once one has a realization, it is enough and one does not need to do anything else. Śāntideva refutes that a realization of śūnyatā makes actions irrelevant by simply stating:[4]

> There is nothing that bodhisattvas should not train in.
> There is nothing the wise masters do that is not meritorious.

A bodhisattva's primary aim is to help all other sentient beings. Sentient beings have many different needs so there are many ways to assist them. Therefore, even bodhisattvas who have a high realization of emptiness do all kinds of things to help sentient beings attain their temporary and ultimate goals. Tsongkhapa very clearly states that there is no action that even eighth level bodhisattvas will not do to benefit others.

A brief explanation of the bodhisattva levels will help you to understand the import of this statement. On the Mahayana path there are ten different bodhisattva stages *(bhūmi)* that begin on the path of seeing—the first moment of direct realization of śūnyatā. From the first to the seventh level, bodhisattvas reduce the passions of desire, hatred, and the gross levels of self-centered ignorance by gradual degrees. On the eighth level, bodhisattvas target a single enemy: the self-cherishing attitude. It is on the eighth level that, because of their deep realization of śūnyatā free of conceptual thought, they become completely free of all the mental afflictions. Eighth level bodhisattvas have no misconceptions, wrong views, hatred, attachment, jealousy, or pride because all of those things are based on ignorance, and ignorance has now been removed. The only negative things left are some very subtle stains, or predispositions. So the eighth and higher levels of the bodhisattva path are called the *great levels*. The *Sublime Continuum* uses an analogy of the birth of a child to explain the difference between the great levels and the first seven levels. Below the eighth level, mental obstacles bind a bodhisattva just as a fetus in the womb is bound by physical constraints. Once bodhisattvas attain the eighth level, it is as if they are born; they leave their mothers' womb for wide open space. Because the power of eighth level bodhisattvas' wisdom removes all obstacles, their activities and realizations become enormous.

If it were true, as Hva Shang and his followers contend, that someone who has realization of emptiness can do anything with impunity and need practice nothing else, then an eighth level bodhisattva would not need to practice the other perfections. He or she would have everything necessary to attain enlightenment; there would be no need for the practice of the method side. But even bodhisattvas on the great eighth, ninth, and tenth levels need to practice the other perfections in order to attain perfect enlightenment. Tsongkhapa refers anyone who doubts this to the *Sutra on the Ten Levels (Daśabhūmika-sūtra)*. This Mahayana sutra explains in detail the ten bodhisattva stages.

Each of the ten bodhisattva levels is generally taught to correspond to one of each of the ten perfections. On each stage a special confidence and expertise in one perfection is developed; on the first stage a bodhisattva gains expertise in generosity, on the second in ethical discipline, and so on. However, this does not mean that the other perfections are not practiced on that level. All ten perfections are practiced on every level; it is just that a proficiency in a particular perfection is developed at each stage. In fact, every single perfection is combined with all the others. For example, in the explanation of generosity there is the generosity of generosity, the ethical discipline of generosity, the patience of generosity, and so forth. Giving without stinginess is the generosity of generosity. Keeping pure conduct of body, speech, and mind at the time of giving is the ethical discipline of generosity. The patience of generosity comes from understanding the nature of people and their problems. The perseverance of generosity is to be happy making an effort to be charitable even if one is sick and finds it difficult to give. The meditative stabilization of generosity is to be very, very focused on the activity in which one is engaged. The wisdom of generosity is realizing the true nature of the thing that is given, the receiver, and the giver. In short, when we give something to a beggar we can practice all six perfections at once. Each time bodhisattvas on the great levels do this kind of practice they create enormously powerful virtues that remove inner obstacles. Therefore, when one reaches this level attaining buddhahood is not that far away. Maitreya in his five books, Nāgārjuna, and Asaṅga all explain this in the same way.

At the eighth level bodhisattvas have attained the most powerful nonconceptual insight. Because of their profound realization of śūnyatā they are completely freed from the afflictions—they are liberated from samsara. From that point of view they are equal to Hinayana arhats. Śrāvakas and pratyeka-buddha arhats remain in this peace. I will not quote word for word, but Tsongkhapa cites the *Sutra on the Ten Levels* to show that bodhisattvas on the unshakable eighth level abide in a special meditation that could last for eons. There is a slight danger that just like Hinayana arhats these bodhisattvas would forget about being of benefit to other sentient beings and simply enjoy their own peace instead of continuing on the path to buddhahood. But the buddhas do not let them do that. They use a special signal to wake these bodhisattvas up from their meditation and urge them on toward their goal of helping all sentient beings. The buddhas remind them that although they have a high level of attainment, their power, knowledge, body, and environment are not as complete or perfect as those of a buddha. They say, "Well done, well done so far, O noble ones. You have obtained pure peace—freedom from samsara. However, look at these measureless good qualities. Don't you see that you do not have the ten powers, four fearlessnesses, or eighteen unmixed qualities, and so on?"[5]

Ordinary beings cannot see a buddha's pure environment because it is not a place of earth and stone. Buddhas do not depend on material things; their wisdom manifests as a special place called a *buddha field,* or a *pure land.* It is something like an object in a dream; in dreams the mind creates a vast countryside, houses, humans, and many other beautiful things. A buddha's measureless knowledge gives him or her super-powers to do all kinds of things. They can create many thousands of items out of a single object and condense countless things down to one. They can emanate their body in measureless ways throughout countless worlds. When a buddha speaks, he or she can be understood in many different languages simultaneously and different people hear different meanings. When teaching, a buddha can emanate a special light from his or her forehead or heart that extends for miles around.

In addition to exhorting the great level bodhisattvas to compare their qualities to those of a buddha, the *Sutra on the Ten Levels* reminds them, "Look at all the sentient beings who are not in peace. Sentient beings have so many troubles because of the mental afflictions. Like children they discriminate between themselves and others; they hate, harm, disagree, and fight. You bodhisattvas should make a great effort to help them. And, while you are doing that, do not cast away the special realization of śūnyatā called *ultimate patience.*" Usually when we say *patience* it means being able to bear harm without reacting. That is one type of patience, but there are two others. Patience can also mean voluntarily accepting hardship in the course of performing an action. The highest, most powerful patience is the third type: patience due to the realization of the ultimate truth. It is this third type that is referred to here. The eighth level bodhisattva's deep meditation on emptiness is called *ultimate patience.* When one realizes the true nature of things and the self, one can bear many difficulties. Our doubts and fears are due to ignorance.

Prior to a realization of śūnyatā, many things seem incomprehensible or unacceptable. We may have questions that lead to negative thoughts, the nihilistic view, or other problems. However, once we have a realization of śūnyatā and are convinced that emptiness is true, we have a special kind of patience. In terms of śūnyatā this realization is said to be nonarising, unproduced, and empty of truly existing.

Although great level bodhisattvas are vastly superior to ordinary people, they are still not comparable to a buddha. Even though eighth, ninth, and tenth level bodhisattvas' meditations on śūnyatā are almost like those of a buddha, they do not have a buddha's perfect omniscience. These bodhisattvas still have some obscurations that prevent them from fulfilling their primary objective: helping others. The bodhisattvas must maintain their meditation on śūnyatā and in addition practice many other things in order to develop the immeasurable qualities that spontaneously occur when all the gross obstacles and subtle impurities of body, speech, and mind are removed. Reminded of this, the bodhisattvas recognize that they must practice the activities of the method along with wisdom. Therefore, the wise laugh at those who think that having a mind free of all thought and in a very subtle meditation is sufficient to attain buddhahood. If merely a nonconceptual meditation on śūnyatā were enough, then śrāvaka arhats, pratyekabuddha arhats, and eighth level bodhisattvas would all be buddhas because they all have a nonconceptual realization of emptiness. There would be no need to remind them that they are forgetting to practice for the benefit of others.

Well, you may wonder, if Hva Shang was wrong, then what is the wisdom that is required to attain freedom? A brief explanation will be enough for the time being; later I will explain the complicated details. (See volume 5 of this series.) Śūnyatā means that things are empty of any absolute. The nature of everything in existence is empty of, or lacks, being ultimately real. There is nothing that ultimately or inherently exists. When one realizes śūnyatā, one sees everything as relative, dependent, and as illusory as a magical creation. When people see a magic show, they may believe the magical illusions are real and so become afraid or greedy. But when a magician looks at the same object, he knows it is a chimera that exists in dependence upon fooling the audience's eyes. A trick makes something appear to be real, but there is nothing ultimately real there. Similarly those who realize śūnyatā see things completely differently from the way we do. They know that things do not exist in the way that they appear. When one doesn't understand śūnyatā, things appear real even though there is nothing substantive that can actually be found. When one realizes emptiness, one knows that everything that one sees has an illusory nature; in reality all things are empty of that appearance.

The Buddha did not create śūnyatā; it simply is the nature of everything. The Tathāgatha realized that the true nature of all things is a lack of inherent existence, and used many methods with various levels of subtlety to help others understand it.

All of the mental afflictions—attachment, hatred, and so on—arise from holding things to be truly existent. As long as we hold that things truly exist as they appear, attachment, hatred, and so on remain in the mind. A direct realization that appearances are like a magical illusion is the most powerful antidote to ignorance and the mental afflictions. Without a direct realization of śūnyatā we cannot get rid of the cause of samsara. Only a direct realization of śūnyatā can remove ignorance and the mental afflictions and bring us freedom. So, as I said earlier, a direct realization of śūnyatā is not just a special quality of a buddha; every śrāvaka, pratyekabuddha, and bodhisattva must realize śūnyatā in order to attain freedom from samsara. A direct realization comes from repeated attempts to understand śūnyatā. Gradually one's meditation becomes deeper and deeper until finally all discursive thoughts and gross levels of mind cease. A direct realization is nonconceptual; one does not have any sense consciousness, perception, or thought at that time. The only thing that appears is a deep and profound nondual perception of emptiness.

There is also a section of the *Perfection of Wisdom Sutra in Twenty-Five Thousand Lines* that discusses goading eighth stage bodhisattvas to practice:

> Subhūti, bodhisattvas must know every aspect of all the paths: every aspect of the śrāvaka path, every aspect of the pratyekabuddha path, and every aspect of the bodhisattva path.

In the sutra, the Buddha calls on Subhūti to discuss how bodhisattvas should help anyone practicing any aspect of the path. *Helping others* means to explain properly whatever the person needs to know in order to follow the path successfully. To do that a bodhisattva must have personal experiential understanding of every element on every part of the path.

The sutra says that there is one exception to this: remaining in the extreme of peace or nirvana without remainder. When śrāvakas and pratyekabuddhas free themselves from samsara, they still have a body that was created by karma from their prior lives; this is called *nirvana with remainder*. At the time of their death they will be completely freed from any kind of subtle misery associated with a body; this cessation is called *nirvana without remainder*. From then on they will be free from all samsaric qualities and can remain in peace for a long time. Because this cessation of the five aggregates is not helpful to other sentient beings, *nirvana without remainder* is an obstacle for bodhisattvas. It is the only aspect of any of the three paths a bodhisattva should not personally experience. A bodhisattva on the eighth level could relax and enjoy this extreme of final reality; he or she may be tempted to do it, but a bodhisattva never does. There are three promises a bodhisattva must keep before he or she can enjoy this state. Since at the beginning of the Mahayana path bodhisattvas vow to attain perfect buddhahood for the benefit of others, they must reach that goal. Second, they promised to take on the responsibility to free all sentient beings and lead them to perfect enlightenment; therefore they must help all sentient beings mature spiritually. Third, bodhisattvas must create the necessary causes and conditions to produce a buddhafield as did the Buddha Amitābha. Therefore, the buddhas remind them that, until they attain enlightenment, bodhisattvas must practice the accumulation of measureless wisdom and method to fulfill their vows.

There is an ancient analogy in the *Sutra on the Ten Levels* about the difference between eighth level bodhisattvas and ordinary people. Long ago ships did not have motors; to travel a great distance across the ocean they needed to catch the right currents and a favorable wind. Without these one could not go nearly so far, even if one rowed a boat, or dragged a cart overland for years. Similarly, because of their realization of emptiness, eighth level bodhisattvas have enormous power and can take a shortcut on the path to the city of buddhahood. With our limited abilities we could not travel that much of the path even in a million years. But the sutra also says that these bodhisattvas must still practice in order to accomplish all the qualities of buddhahood. This is the opposite of saying that the quick path is to stop thinking or doing anything. Hva Shang Mahayana's view, in contradiction to the sutra, is that all problems are caused by thought. If the mind is blank it will revert to its pure original state—the realization of śūnyatā—and all good qualities will naturally arise. Therefore, all other practices are unnecessary and to do them is wrong. Hva Shang says we do not need to train in the bodhisattvas' activities because simply not-thinking completes the practice of all the other perfections. Take generosity, for example. He says if we do not think, we are not grasping at the giver, gift, or recipient, so we perfect the bodhisattva's special nonperceptual or object-less generosity.

Tsongkhapa's response is that we are deceiving ourselves if we think, "My problems come from thinking, so if I stop all thought everything will be all right." First of all, the correct way to understand *nonperceptual* and *with no object* is that there is nothing inherently real to be grasped by thought. The perception of inherent reality is false. Although there are no ultimately existing objects or subjects, this does not mean there are no subjects and objects at all. The subject and object of any action are relative, dependent, and like illusions. Thus *generosity with no object* refers to understanding that the gift, the giver, and the recipient are empty of inherent existence. If one thinks that the thing one is giving, the recipient, and oneself are real, truly existent things, then attachment will arise. When practicing generosity with a bodhisattva's compassion, one must understand the true nature of these things and not grasp something that does not exist. Practicing giving with a realization of śūnyatā in the back of the mind is *nonperceptual* generosity. It is similar for each of the other perfections: ethical discipline, patience, and so forth. The practice of ethical discipline is to protect oneself by avoiding nonvirtuous actions of body, speech, and mind. To perfect the practice of *nonperceptual* ethical discipline we must understand the lack of inherent existence of the nonvirtuous actions that we are avoiding, who we are protecting, and the objects of our actions. In summary, the bodhisattvas' practice of all six perfections must be based on understanding that the true nature of things is emptiness.

The sutra also says that all six perfections are included in the nonperceptual practice of any one of them. For example, perfect generosity includes the generosity of generosity, ethical discipline of generosity, patience of generosity, joyous perseverance of generosity, meditative stabilization of generosity, and the wisdom of generosity. Some people believe that totally blanking out thought completes the practice of nonperceptual generosity, because when one stops thinking and acting there is no perceptual object. But if *generosity with no object* meant merely "generosity without thinking," we could be extremely generous simply by practicing ordinary single-pointed concentration. Why? Because one does not think during that type of meditation; the gift and so on do not appear in a real ultimate way. Single-pointed concentration would then count as practicing all six perfections. Further, if just doing one practice were sufficient for attaining enlightenment, something like offering the mandala would be enough because we offer in imagination various symbols and substances to complete the six perfections. It is not logical, however, to think that simply because a practice includes all six perfections it is all that we need to do. Practicing each perfection so that it includes all the others must mean more than doing just one practice such as stopping thought. If we stop thinking we may have some peace for a few minutes, but this will not get us anywhere. It will not cut out the root of the passions. Merely not-doing and not-thinking will not result in good qualities; one has to practice the individual perfections. Finally, if not thinking were the criterion for completing the perfections, then all śrāvakas would be practicing the perfections since their direct meditation on śūnyatā has no conceptual thought. They would be Mahayana practitioners and their practice would be the Mahayana path.

So, what is the perfect practice to attain buddhahood? It is the union of method and wisdom. The method side must be practiced, but by itself it is not enough; we need the wisdom that realizes the truth. We must have wisdom, but just comprehending emptiness is not enough; we need to practice the method side of bodhicitta and the perfections.

The union of method and wisdom is described as "method that is held by wisdom" and "wisdom that is held by method." The word *held* makes it clear that one is not the other. The method side practices of generosity, compassion, bodhicitta, and so forth are not the wisdom that realizes śūnyatā. The realization of śūnyatā is not part of the method. The right way to practice is to hold the two together as in the following example. If a woman has only one cherished child, she suffers great sorrow if her beloved child dies. Her sadness is felt so very deeply that it carries over into all her activities; wherever she goes, whatever she does, her thoughts are always influenced by sorrow. She may do many different things and have a great variety of thoughts, but all of them are colored by sorrow. Similarly, whatever bodhisattvas do is imbued with bodhicitta. This means that all their activities are under the power of a compassionate desire to take responsibility to help all others. The power of this method side practice carries over even into a deep meditation on śūnyatā. If a meditation on śūnyatā is preceded by contemplating bodhicitta, then the motivation for attaining a realization of emptiness is to remove ignorance so that one can attain enlightenment and thereby help others. During the meditation session one is only meditating on the profound realization of śūnyatā, and although there is no bodhicitta in the mind, the whole session is empowered by the wish to benefit other sentient beings. That is how bodhicitta influences the single-pointed concentration on śūnyatā. This is what it means for wisdom to be held by method.

When bodhisattvas awake from their meditation on śūnyatā, the power of their realization of emptiness carries over to their practice of the methods of generosity and so forth. They understand that everything is like a magical illusion, so they do not grasp things to exist ultimately. Therefore, whatever method side practice they do—such as making prostrations, reciting mantras, teaching the Dharma, and so forth—is influenced by the powerful wisdom that realizes śūnyatā. At the time they are doing these activities they are not focused on śūnyatā; nevertheless, their activities are influenced by their prior realization of śūnyatā. This is what it means for method to be held by wisdom. This is the connotation of wisdom and method not being separate from each other. This is the way we can do these two practices together without contradiction. This harmony of method and wisdom makes a bodhisattva's activities a superior kind of practice.

We do the opposite. When we are angry at someone, we believe that person is our real, permanent, absolute enemy. If we are in love with someone, we superimpose absolute beauty upon him or her. This is objectifying; we imagine something beyond the object's own nature and then grasp it as real. This kind of hypostatizing leads to attachment, hatred, and all the other mental afflictions. We then act according to our incorrect thoughts and emotions. In contrast, when one understands an object's true nature, one is like a magician who knows that his beautiful or frightening creations are illusions. He knows they are not ultimately real; they are just a relative phenomenal effect of certain causes and conditions. This is a rough understanding of objectless activity.

The expressions *objectless, without object, with no object,* or *nonperceptual* sound awkward in English, but many sutras use these words in phrases such as *compassion without object, nonperceptual bodhicitta,* and *generosity with no object.* If we take the meaning of the words literally, these sutra passages can seem very strange. Generosity with no object does not mean not having a thought to give. Without a thought to give there is no generosity. If it were perfect generosity to have no thought of giving, then we would have perfect generosity all the time; the practice of generosity would be very easy! The correct meaning of objectless or nonperceptual generosity is giving gifts without hypostasizing or superimposing the idea that something or someone exists in an ultimately real way. It is the same for the other six perfections.

Confusion can arise because various sutras use these terms in different ways. Because the Buddha taught for forty-five years after his enlightenment, he taught many different people on different stages of the path. The sutras are therefore on many different levels, with meanings that are implicit or indirect, or explicit or direct or to help various beings attain liberation and enlightenment. If the Buddha had explained only the highest, most subtle point of view, many people would have found it difficult to understand his message. They could easily have misunderstood his intended meaning. So we must examine the scriptures to discern which ones can be accepted literally and which ones require interpretation.

It is worthwhile to raise the question of interpretation with people who are confused, or who pretend confusion. If we leave things vague, uncertainty remains. We need to raise the matter up front and clear away ambiguity. For example, sometimes people are perplexed by sutras that say there is no difference between nirvana and samsara. They are the same because their ultimate truth is the emptiness and purity of the mind. Other sutra passages say meritorious karma will result in a better life in samsara, so it seems that the causes for an ordinary rebirth and the causes for emancipation are the same.

This seems contradictory: does ethical discipline result in a samsaric rebirth or in liberation? The same line of thought leads some people to misconstrue statements such as: "Practicing generosity will result in wealth," "Not harming others will result in a long life," and "Patience results in beauty." These people mistakenly think these statements mean that if we engage in these or any other virtues, we will be reborn in samsara. They think, "Since all of these practices are the causes of samsaric life, we should stop doing them if we do not want to be reborn in samsara." Do not be confused. If these practices are done without skill in method and wisdom, then their results will be a good life in samsara with wealth and happiness. However, if they are done with skill in method and wisdom, then they are the causes for a buddha's perfect body and mind. When method and wisdom hold each other they are causes of emancipation and buddhahood. As Nāgārjuna wrote in the *Precious Garland:*

> O King. In brief, the perfect form body
> Is born from the accumulation of merit.

Many other passages must be interpreted along the same lines. For example, a sutra says, "Grasping the six perfections—generosity and so forth—is evil action." The *Three Heaps Sutra (Tri-skandhaka-sūtra)* says, "You must confess each of the following: giving gifts while falling into objectifying, protecting your own conduct because you hold ethical conduct as superior, and so forth." And the *Sutra Requested by Brahmā (Brahma-paripṛcchā-sūtra)* says, "All activity whatsoever is conceptual thought; the completely nonconceptual is enlightenment." The first passage does not mean that the practice of the six perfections is evil and therefore we should not do them. There is no way we can accept this statement literally because we would have to accept that meditation and wisdom are evil actions because they are perfections. The passage means that it is evil to practice any perfection motivated by a perverted view that holds the self to exist absolutely. There are two aspects to this perverted view: superimposing something absolute upon oneself and grasping *I,* and grasping other phenomena to exist as they appear to a wrong perception. Any action, even the perfections, is evil if it is done with this kind of misunderstanding.

The *Three Heaps Sutra* uses the phrase "falling into objectifying." *Objectifying* is believing that things absolutely exist as they appear to our perception. Things do not objectively, ultimately, or inherently exist; objects do not exist exactly as they appear. The practice of generosity done under the sway of an objectifying view should be confessed. However, this does not mean that the practices of generosity, religious conduct, and so forth should not be done at all. Especially for bodhisattvas, there is pure generosity and impure generosity. Impure generosity is to give with a wrong motivation and incorrect understanding of reality. That is a negative, perhaps even an evil action, that should be purified. If merely practicing generosity were something to confess, the sutra would not need the phrase "falling into objectifying." It could just say, "Giving gifts is sinful." But it does not say that.

As far as correctly interpreting the third passage is concerned—"All activity whatsoever is conceptual thought; the completely nonconceptual is enlightenment"—it is very important to understand how Kamalaśila's third *Stages of Meditation* responds to Hva Shang's ideas. Hva Shang rejected the method side of practice because he incorrectly understood the intent of this and certain other sutras. He is correct to say that grasping things as real should be eliminated. Grasping at an ultimate subject or object is called *grasping at signs*. Signs or labels identify an object, as in the following examples: "This is a man," "This is good and that is bad," "This is the right thing to give to that person," "I am the giver and you are the recipient," and so forth. When we believe these signified things exist as they appear, we grasp at the subject as a self of persons and grasp at an object as a self of phenomena. This wrong view is removed by the profound realization of śūnyatā. With wisdom we reach the signless state. Therefore, according to Hva Shang any thought that holds a signifier is an obstacle to the realization of emptiness. To engage in any of the activities of the method side we need perception and conceptual thought; so whenever we do them we grasp at signs and hold things to be inherently real. For that reason Hva Shang says these thoughts—including everything on the method side—have to be eliminated because they are the opposite of enlightenment, which is signless, wishless, emptiness.

A major logical fault arises if one holds Hva Shang's view literally. If every thought that involved a wish or sign were wrong, then all the teachings on the path would be wide of the mark. It would be a mistake to think about even the good qualities of the teacher, the leisure and fortune of this life, impermanence and death, the misery of the lower rebirths, the truth of suffering, taking refuge, and karma and causality. It would even be wrong to meditate on love for all mother sentient beings, to think about compassion, or to develop bodhicitta. Taking the bodhisattva vows and keeping the precepts purely would be incorrect practices because they require thinking about signs such as how beings suffer, the good or bad aspects of situations, the causes for suffering and freedom, and so forth. Without such thoughts we cannot produce renunciation or bodhicitta. If all these were merely wrong perceptions then people who realize śūnyatā would avoid them. But that is not the case. Yogis work very hard to get rid of hatred, pride, and ignorance. Yet, according to Hva Shang's system, incorrect grasping at phenomena grows greater and greater the more they do this. In fact the opposite is true. The more strongly one holds the explanation of emptiness in Hva Shang's system, the weaker one's understanding of the method side practices and the path system becomes. To such a person the method side practices and the wisdom side seem to be complete opposites, like hot and cold. He or she can never have a strong understanding of both of them. Method and wisdom are not used together; in the view of such a person, one destroys the other.

As mentioned earlier, the goal of enlightenment can be described as composed of kayās, or bodies of the buddha. The wisdom body—the dharmakāya, or mental body—is ultimate and immaculate wisdom; it is the mind that has been transformed beyond all impurity. The form body—the rūpakāya—is various manifestations of perfect wisdom into form. These two bodies are noncontradictory; they are the same nature and are simultaneously obtained. We practice two aspects of the path—method and wisdom—in order to obtain those two results. Wisdom is the realization of śūnyatā: knowing the true nature of all phenomena and the self. It is the realization that nothing—not even the tiniest atom—exists ultimately as it appears. The method side involves analysis of the reasons to abandon negative actions and to do positive ones, and actually putting this understanding of causality into practice.

From a realization of emptiness we understand that things are empty of ultimate existence. From the method side we develop an understanding of causality and phenomenal reality, such as, "This result will arise from this cause," or "This has this fault and that has this good quality," and so forth. Understanding causality and that things do not exist as they appear are not contradictory. This is the fundamental understanding of the two truths: phenomenal truth and ultimate truth. Phenomenal truth is understanding how things exist. Ultimate truth is understanding in what way they do *not* exist. When we understand the two truths correctly we can practice the path properly and the final result, the two kayās, will arise.

Valid understanding of the ultimate truth is knowing that the true nature of subjects and objects is dependent, illusory, noninherently existent. Although things do not objectively exist, relatively there are causes and effects. Certain causes result in a particular effect; other causes do not yield that result. Valid knowledge of phenomena—or conventional knowledge—is understanding the nature of causality. Not only should we see that these two types of valid knowledge do not contradict each other, we should recognize that one helps the other. Because things are really empty of being ultimate, they are relatively existent; because they are relatively existent, they are not ultimately real. So one valid knowledge proves the other one. Someone who understands this has found the real intent of the Buddha. A person who realizes śūnyatā and causality sees everything the way a magician understands that the hundred fearsome elephants he created by means of a magic trick do not exist as they appear. The elephants really seem to be running around; the magical illusion exists but there is no ultimately real, objective elephant there. It is important to understand the two truths because if we think that they contradict each other we cannot practice properly.

Tsongkhapa points out that the passage from the *Sutra Requested by Brahmā* is an analysis of production. The words, "All activity whatsoever is conceptual thought; the completely nonconceptual is enlightenment" are a response to the question, "Do things arise independently and inherently or in dependence on other things?" The sutra explains that properly understanding the nature of the two truths and then engaging in the bodhisattva activities is the perfect practice. Generosity, pure ethical conduct, and so forth are empty of inherent existence; they are relatively or nominally existent. The deed itself, the object, and the doer of the deed do not absolutely exist as they appear to our senses or thoughts; they exist phenomenally or dependently. They lack inherent existence, but from the positive perspective they exist as imputations of name and thought. What we see are mere imputations. *Mere imputation* means that the way something appears to exist is not the actual way it exists. All the things that appear to the mind have some kind of name, definition, or sign. Between the name and the object we impose some kind of absolute. Things are not really that way; they are *imputedly*, or we could say *nominally*, existent. This is the positive perspective; it shows how things exist. The sutra does not mean that generosity and the other bodhisattva practices are wrong, evil, and should not be done. It uses negative phrasing to stress that we should not practice these deeds *with a wrong view*. Refuting the wrong way to do something is not saying do not practice at all.

If we want to attain buddhahood we must train in all the bodhisattva activities. There are almost countless deeds that should be practiced all the time. The essence of all of them is encapsulated in the six perfections: generosity, ethical discipline, patience, perseverance, meditative stabilization and wisdom. We should make a heartfelt effort to accomplish these practices. Begin with the easy ones and do whatever you can. We can admire and wish to be able to do those practices that we are not able to do now. That wish along with trying to eliminate obscurations and building up the collections of merit and wisdom are the causes for being able to practice more difficult things before too long.

If we do not distinguish what these sutras mean, we may wipe out practice and study out of ignorance. To deceive ourselves and lead others that way is very bad; it will cause the excellent teaching of the Buddha to sink like the setting sun. Darkness comes when the sun sets. The teachings enlighten and clear away the darkness of ignorance. If the teachings do not remain in the world, we will be left circling in darkness, not knowing where we are going or how to get out. As Nāgārjuna's *Compendium of Sutras (Sūtra-samuccaya)* states, "It is an evil action to understand the nonconditioned while being annoyed with the virtues of the conditioned." This means that when we try to understand the nonconditioned, which is emptiness itself, we should not be irritated with what is necessary on the method side—accumulating merit and purifying negativities. We destroy the positive side—the method—when we only want to realize śūnyatā. It is also a mistake to practice the method side only, without any emphasis on the wisdom side. Some people concentrate on practices to create merit and forget to do the wisdom side of practice—realizing the lack of inherent existence of all the practices. The *Compendium of Sutras* also says that bodhisattvas who lack skill in the practices of the method side should not practice the profound dharma of śūnyatā. In other words, bodhisattvas who do not understand the method side do not understand śūnyatā properly either. While trying to develop an understanding of śūnyatā they fall into the extreme of nihilism and contradict the method side. A correct understanding of śūnyatā does not hurt the method side of practice. Similarly practicing the method side does not hinder attaining a realization of śūnyatā. There should be a harmonious joining of method and wisdom in practice.

A passage from the *Sutra of Showing the Tathāgata's Inconceivable Secret* shows us the correct way to think:

> O noble one, it is like this example. A fire burns because of its cause, [the fuel]. When the cause is exhausted, the fire is extinguished. Likewise, mental activity arises from an object; without any kind of object the mind does not function. A bodhisattva who is skilled in this method understands through the pure practice of the perfection of wisdom that objects do not really exist, yet they do not cease the roots of virtue as an object. They do not let the mental afflictions arise as an object. They focus on the perfections as an object. Although they understand each of these objects is empty, they see all sentient beings as an object of great compassion.

Our ordinary way of thinking—ignorantly grasping objects and subjects as dual and absolute just as they appear—is not right. Holding unreal things as real, we see them as attractive or unattractive, and from that the mental afflictions of attachment, hatred, jealousy and so forth develop. In contrast, the right way to understand things is that although ultimately nothing is inherently real, in a relative sense there is cause and effect. A bodhisattva does not make the mistake of believing that something that is not real is absolutely real. With a proper understanding of reality, bodhisattvas understand the basis of all the passions and do not allow them to expand. At the same time they foster a practice of meritorious virtues. This is not contradictory. The sutra explains that it is not inconsistent to understand śūnyatā and also see that one particular action should be abandoned while another one should be developed. So clearly it does not mean that all thinking is incorrect.

When we practice giving gifts we should understand the way things appear and what they actually are. Viewed one way, all sentient beings are empty of absolute existence, but we should also see their problems, have compassion and love for them, and want to free them from misery. Tibetans have an expression that encompasses this understanding; it goes, "Your body, speech, and mind should be closed tight. But sometimes you need to loosen the ties that bind the mind." The first sentence refers to a vow to tightly control ourselves; we lock the door so we do not do any negative actions. The second sentence advises us that simultaneously we should loosen the ties of the wrong view—holding the mark or sign of true existence—that fetter the mind. We must understand what should be tied up and what should be loosened. We produce wisdom to free the mind by untying the bonds of hatred, the other mental afflictions, and the ignorance that grasps unreal things to be real. But we should tie mind with vows and various practices to bind it tightly to the virtuous side; we do not let the mind stray to negative actions or ignorance.

One single cause cannot produce the perfection of omniscient buddhahood. However, certain teachers say that we do not need to study many things or do all kinds of practices. To justify their claim that a single practice is enough they say, "A single loud noise can chase away hundreds of birds; similarly, one practice can lead to all the achievements and clear away all the obstacles." Tsongkhapa rejects this assertion. This excellent human life is like a wonderful wish-fulfilling jewel because we can use it to attain the most essential goal. We can do marvelous things, but this one huge misunderstanding may lead us to waste our life of leisure and fortune. Being satisfied with practicing just one aspect of the path shuts the door to the accumulations of merit and wisdom so that at the time of death we will be empty-handed. Someone who tells us not to practice both the method and wisdom sides of the path is a bad friend who encourages us to act in negative ways. Furthermore, one distinction between the Mahayana and Hinayana is the practice to accumulate limitless merit. The Mahayana practice is much wider in scope because the Mahayana practitioner's goal is to free all sentient beings from suffering. The Hinayana practitioners' primary objective is just their own emancipation, not to benefit all other sentient beings. Since they are striving for a lesser goal, their practice of the accumulation of merit is smaller from the point of view of time and object. From the Mahayana point of view, Hinayana practitioners engage in a partial practice.

It is the nature of causality that an effect is in accord with its cause. For even an ordinary result, like tasty food, to be created requires many different causes and conditions, including effort. So there is really no need to say that many, many causes and conditions must be accumulated to achieve the highest supreme goal of buddhahood—complete freedom from all suffering and possession of all perfect qualities. The *Lotus of Compassion Sutra (Karuṇā-puṇḍarīka-sūtra)* says, "A partial cause accomplishes a partial result; a complete cause accomplishes a complete result." In addition, the *Sutra on the Coming Forth of the Tathāgatas (Tathāgatotpatti-saṃbhava-sūtra)* says:

> The arising of the tathāgatas is not from one cause. Why? O bodhisattvas, the causes for accomplishing buddhahood are measureless hundreds of millions. How are these enumerated? They are the measureless accumulation of merit and wisdom, and so forth.

These causes are all listed in the sutra, but Tsongkhapa does not elaborate upon them here. The *Teaching of Vimalakirti* also says that the tathāgata's body arises from hundreds of merits. It is created by all the measureless meritorious virtues of the path.

In the *Precious Garland* Nāgārjuna says:

> Since the causes for the buddha's physical body
> Are as measureless as the causes for the universe,
> So then, in a similar way, how can you count
> The causes for the enlightened mental body?

There are so many different causes and conditions for the external world that we say they cannot be counted. So how can we measure the causes of the form and wisdom bodies? The form body of a buddha is the manifestation of the perfect physical body and environment. The mental body has qualities such as omniscience, perfect compassion, love, and power. The measureless qualities of the form and mental bodies are the result of getting rid of mental impurities and obstacles from the root and accumulating virtuous practices life after life for eons. The perfect form body is primarily the result of the method side of practice. The causes for the mental body are the wisdom side. There is no way to count all these causes; they are incalculable.

In short, both method and wisdom should be practiced fully. The measureless practices of method and wisdom are included in the practice of the six perfections. The six perfections were taught in sutras in order to make it easy to understand what we should practice. Training in these practices is common to both the Sutrayana and Tantrayana. In the great tantric texts the various aspects of mandalas, deities, the deities' implements, etc., represent the qualities of the perfections. The secret meaning of these symbols is that they are the mental qualities of the six perfections, the thirty-seven paths, sixteen types of the realization of śūnyatā, and so forth. For example, Yamāntaka's nine heads are the nine types of teaching; his two horns are the two truths; his sixteen legs symbolize the sixteen realizations of śūnyatā. Every hand, gesture, and implement is a symbol for a special interior quality. Each mandala with its deity is the representation of the results of the complete path from the beginning up to the attainment of enlightenment. Although most of the teachings of the Mahayana path are common to both the Sutrayana and Tantrayana, there are a few exceptions. A few advanced tantric practitioners are taught to use sensual enjoyment on the path. For an ordinary person the use of sensory pleasures such as beautiful sights, sounds, tastes, and sexual enjoyment would increase their obscurations. But when someone reaches a certain level of spiritual realization on the tantric path, these things can be powerful methods of practice. For example, if we ingest a powerful poison we will be harmed or killed. But if that poison is mixed with other medicines, it may become a powerful cure for certain illnesses.

All the preceding explanations of sutra quotations are to make us dissatisfied with the idea that just a single practice or a few limited practices are all that is necessary to attain buddhahood. We must have a firm understanding that both method and wisdom are required for a path to be complete. In order to practice the Mahayana path we need to understand that without many complicated practices there is no way to attain the result. Everyone has the potential to attain buddhahood. At present we are at different levels, but we all have buddha-nature. This latent potential must be developed. It is covered by obstacles, which must be removed, and it must be increased in power. Those who have intelligence should open their minds to find out how this works. They must study and learn to gain a firm understanding. This understanding brings about proper practice. Proper practice is knowing which things should be removed and which should be developed. Doing these practices as much as we can is the way to increase our potential to become enlightened. This is one of the highest activities we can do as human beings.

8

Training in the Mahayana: Precepts and Perfections

iii) Explanation of the process of learning the precepts
    a' How to train in the Mahayana in general
        1' Establishing the desire to learn the precepts of bodhicitta
        2' Taking the vows of the conquerors' children after establishing the
           desire to learn the precepts
        3' How to train after taking the vows
           a" What the precepts are based upon
           b" How all the precepts are included in the basis
              1" A discussion of the main topic: the fixed number of
                 perfections
                (a) The fixed number of perfections based on high
                    rebirth
                (b) The fixed number of perfections based on fulfilling
                    the two aims
                (c) The fixed number of perfections based on perfecting
                    the complete fulfillment of others' aims
                (d) The fixed number of perfections based on their
                    subsuming the entire Mahayana
                (e) The fixed number of perfections in terms of the
                    completeness of paths or method
                (f) The fixed number of perfections based on the three
                    trainings
              2" An ancillary discussion of the fixed order of the
                 perfections
                (a) The order of arising
                (b) The order in terms of inferior and superior
                (c) The order in terms of coarse and subtle

iii) Explanation of the process of learning the precepts

From here to the end of the *Lamrim Chenmo,* Tsongkhapa explains what to practice and how to practice on each stage of the bodhisattva path. This step-by-step explanation has two main subdivisions:

a' How to train in the Mahayana in general (chapters 8–15, all of volume 4, and chapters 1–26 of volume 5)

b' How to train in the Vajrayana in particular (chapter 27 of volume 5)

Tsongkhapa first discusses the general Mahayana practices—the practices that the Sutrayana and Tantrayana have in common. Because many of these practices were discussed before, here we will concentrate upon how to do a daily practice of the six perfections. At the very end of the *Lamrim Chenmo* Tsongkhapa presents a short summary of how to practice the Vajrayana path. The tantric path is a special method to make the Sutrayana quicker and more powerful. Tsongkhapa explains the tantric practices in detail in another text, the *Great Exposition of Secret Mantra (sNgag rim chen mo).*

a' How to train in the Mahayana in general

The general practice of the Mahayana is divided into three topics:

1' Establishing the desire to learn the precepts of bodhicitta

2' Taking the vows of the conquerors' children after establishing the desire to learn the precepts

3' How to train after taking the vows

Without a desire to practice the bodhisattva path one will not bother to do it. So first we have to develop a wish to practice. As a result of this desire one decides to take the bodhisattva vow. We must know what to do once we have taken the vow.

1' Establishing the desire to learn the precepts of bodhicitta

A strong wish to do something is founded upon knowing the benefits of doing it and the disadvantages of not doing it. When one is confident of these things one makes a firm decision to engage in a particular action. Here the action under consideration is taking the bodhisattva vow.

There are three types of vows: the vows found in the vinaya, the tantric vows, and the bodhisattva vows. The bodhisattva vows are not like the other two. Prior to taking the vinaya and tantric vows one is not allowed to learn about the individual precepts or rules. Only after one is given the vows does one study them in detail. There is a special purpose for this way of proceeding: it prevents misunderstanding and/or dislike of the overall system. In contrast, before one takes the bodhisattva vows one is supposed to learn about the precepts' nature, content, purpose, importance, and so on. Then, knowing the value of these precepts, one thinks, "I must take this vow." Only then is one given the vows. Tsongkhapa advises us to come to understand the precepts well because then our practice will be firm. Although sometimes we do not study the precepts in detail beforehand, it is a good approach.

The great Indian teacher Asaṅga makes this clear in the conduct chapter of the *Bodhisattva Levels.* There he says that the bodhisattva vows, the basis of the vows, and the faults incurred by breaking the vows should be explained to those who desire to take them in accordance with the *Summary of the Bodhisattva Fundamentals.* After that students should seriously question themselves, "Is this suitable for me? Can I do this kind of practice? What value does this have for me? And what temporary and final results will I get from this practice?" One will be eager to take the vows when these things are understood. You will not be taking these vows because someone tells you that it will be good for you. Of course, a good teacher will explain the benefits of taking the vow, but you should not take the vows just because he or she says to do it. Traditionally disciples and spiritual teachers worked closely together. Only when both of them felt ready did the guru give the bodhisattva vows. Also one should not take the vows in competition with others. Do not take them because you think, "A lot of people are going to take these, so I should too." It has to be a heartfelt and confident decision based on wisdom.

When one understands the benefits of keeping the vows one will not find it difficult to keep them. Painful external difficulties or others' ridicule will not diminish your joyful practice because you know what you are doing and why you are doing it. Bodhisattvas are steadfast; as long as there will be a benefit to other sentient beings they have no hesitation about doing anything. In contrast, if one takes the vows without any prior assessment, one will always be uncomfortable and find things difficult to do. Without proper understanding one will not have a stable practice. The vows will soon be broken and great misery will result.

There is additional detail about the benefit of taking the vows in the course of the discussion of the perfection of ethical discipline (chapter 11). There we will see that virtuous conduct is one of the main instruments to attain enlightenment and help other sentient beings.

2' TAKING THE VOWS OF THE CONQUERORS' CHILDREN AFTER ESTABLISHING THE DESIRE TO LEARN THE PRECEPTS

Tsongkhapa wrote a commentary on the conduct chapter of the *Bodhisattva Levels,* called the *Basic Path to Awakening,* in which he explains the vows, how to take them, and how to repair a precept if we break it. There are many different degrees of transgressing vows; breaking some precepts is worse than breaking others. All transgressions occur because of the mind; based on ignorance and the mental afflictions one commits faulty actions. For the same reason—the mind—one can reverse this process. In other words, because we create damaging actions based on a negative mental state, we can purify our actions based on a positive mental state—wisdom. When we trip on the ground and fall down, we push ourselves back up again using that very same ground. Because we must learn all this detail before taking the vows and the *Lamrim Chenmo* does not go over the precepts exhaustively, Tsongkhapa refers us to this chapter and his commentary. It would be a good if you could read these works at some point.

3' HOW TO TRAIN AFTER TAKING THE VOWS

The bodhisattva vows include many precepts. The precepts are the activities one promises to do in order to attain enlightenment for the benefit of other sentient beings. In addition, there are actions that one promise not to do. All the bodhisattva deeds are included here. How to practice these is explained in three sections:

a"What the precepts are based upon
b" How all the precepts are included in the basis
c" The process of learning the perfections (chapters 9 and on)

First, Tsongkhapa introduces the principal aspects of Mahayana practice, specifically the six perfections. Next, he demonstrates that all the other Mahayana practices are included in the six perfections. In other words, these six are necessary and sufficient for a proper, integrated practice of the Mahayana path. Last, he explains how to train in each of these six practices one by one.

a" WHAT THE PRECEPTS ARE BASED UPON

If one enumerated every aspect of bodhisattva practice, the list would be limitless. Why? Because there are countless sentient beings and their abilities and behavior are unbelievably varied, bodhisattvas have to do incalculable numbers of things to resolve all their problems and lead them to emancipation and enlightenment. Śāntideva says, "There is no practice that is not done by bodhisattvas."[1] However, all these practices can be divided into categories such as the three trainings, the two accumulations, or the four ways to gather disciples. These abridgements include every necessary activity to attain enlightenment; they do not, however, provide an overview of the entire Mahayana path. The six perfections are special because not only do they encompass the countless practices taught in the sutras and tantras, they give us a wide understanding of how all the trainings fit together. These six—the perfections of generosity, ethical discipline, patience, perseverance, meditative stabilization, and wisdom—include all the other practices and systems of organization. Even detailed explanations of the practices on the five paths and the ten bodhisattva levels can be subsumed into them.

The four ways to gather disciples are a good example to see how this works. The Buddha taught the four ways to gather disciples to enable bodhisattvas to reach out to other sentient beings. In order to lead other sentient beings to higher states like freedom from misery, one first has to bring them together around oneself, otherwise one would be inefficiently running around to meet them individually. The first and simplest way to attract others is to give them what they need—food, clothing, or service. This will make them happy and want to befriend one. The second way to collect disciples is to give them a better type of help—sweet words. This does not mean saying, "You are so wonderful," or anything like that. It means giving step by step Dharma instruction according to the mental capacity of the listeners. These first two methods are part of the perfection of generosity: giving material goods and helpful advice. The third method to gather disciples is to lead sentient beings to do whatever is necessary to reach their goal. This is actually doing something, not just giving an explanation. Actively leading other beings to practice is also part of the perfection of generosity because it is a way of teaching. Fourth, one must follow one's own advice. If a bodhisattva says, "Do this," then he or she should behave this way as well. When we do what we tell others to do, they will be more willing to trust and follow us. This is part of the perfection of ethical discipline. So, as you can see, the explanation of the four ways of gathering disciples can be found within the discussion of the six perfections.

The six perfections are the best summary of the Mahayana path from many different points of view. They are the best way to put in our daily life something so vast it seems impossible to practice. The six perfections are not difficult to recognize. Tsongkhapa explains that if we understand what practices are included in each of the perfections, their function, requirements, benefits, and results, we will understand the entire Mahayana path. Our understanding will lead us to desire to practice the perfections and we will be happy to make a special effort to actually do so. By doing these practices we will complete the Mahayana path. These six practices are not just for bodhisattvas; lower practitioners and tantric practitioners can also do them. A detailed explanation of this topic is therefore very important.

b" How all the precepts are included in the basis

The way the entire path is condensed into the six perfections has two parts:

> 1" A discussion of the main topic: the fixed number of perfections
> 2" An ancillary discussion of the fixed order of the perfections

Everything you need to know and practice to reach enlightenment for the benefit of all other sentient beings is included in the practice of the six perfections. They are sufficient for achieving buddhahood; there is no need for more and you cannot do with less. There is nothing necessary that is not included. This is the reason these six are called the basis. Tsongkhapa will also explain that there is a reason the perfections are explained in a particular order.

1" A discussion of the main topic: the fixed number of perfections

All the Mahayana practices merge in the six perfections the way tributary streams flow from all directions becoming a single river. All other practices are built in to a complete practice of the six perfections. It is important to understand that all current buddhas and all those who will become buddhas in the future follow no other path of practice. When one is completely sure that there is no need to do anything other than practice these six, one will be attracted to them. This leads to a conviction that they are the best practices and one's endeavor to practice them will follow. When a practice is deep and strong the results will be powerful too. In contrast, if one lacks knowledge or strong interest before beginning, one's practice will be shallow. If one's practice is weak the results will be feeble as well.

Because it is so important to understand the six perfections' nature, purpose, the obstacles they eliminate, and the positive results they bring, Tsong-khapa explains them from various angles following Maitreya's six-fold explanation in the *Ornament for the Mahayana Sutras.* In that text the great Maitreya expands upon Buddha Śakyamuni's teachings on the sufficiency of the six perfections found in the *Perfection of Wisdom* and other sutras. Following the *Ornament for the Mahayana Sutras,* the six different ways that all the Mahayana practices fit into the six perfections are:

(a) The fixed number of perfections based on high rebirth
(b) The fixed number of perfections based on fulfilling the two aims
(c) The fixed number of perfections based on perfecting the complete fulfillment of others' aims
(d) The fixed number of perfections based on their subsuming the entire Mahayana
(e) The fixed number of perfections in terms of the completeness of paths or method
(f) The fixed number of perfections based on the three trainings

(a) The fixed number of perfections based on high rebirth

The six perfections are sufficient to fulfill individual sentient beings' spiritual goals. There are two types of religious goals: temporary and ultimate. The ultimate or final goal is complete emancipation and perfect buddhahood. A buddha's excellent qualities are permanent and cannot be destroyed. In a sense, buddhahood is an ever-lasting high rebirth. It is not easy to attain buddhahood; enlightenment is not the result of doing a simple action for a short time now and again. Lots of activities and techniques must be practiced comprehensively to attain perfect enlightenment for the benefit of other sentient beings. Of course, it would be wonderful if you could attain enlightenment in this life, but you may not be able to do it. A few people may attain buddhahood in one life, but they have already progressed to a quite high level through training in prior lives. In general, it takes many lives of practice to reach enlightenment, so for now it is best to focus on building a basis to continue practicing the path in our next life. This is the temporary spiritual goal: a high rebirth while in samsara. Even though higher rebirths are temporary goals, they are important steps toward achieving the final goal.

We lose the opportunity to practice by engaging in negative actions and then falling into the lower realms in our next life. For eons after that most of one's rebirths will be dark, ignorant, and in strange uncomfortable places. In those lives there is no potential to do anything truly worthwhile. One's mind and environment will be completely miserable and one will not even hear about the Dharma. So what could one do at that time? Nothing. One merely experiences suffering. Only rarely will one be reborn in the upper realms. But even rebirth as a worldly god is not useful for reaching enlightenment. The gods have peaceful lives, but they are drunk on that temporary pleasure and make no effort for the future. None of these lives will be helpful for attaining the final goal. Bodhisattvas want a special high rebirth with the conditions that make it easy to practice so that they can proceed without interruption until they reach the ultimate goal of enlightenment. So our temporary goal is a high rebirth and our final goal is perfect enlightenment. Practice of the six perfections enables us to attain them both.

Even in an ordinary sense it is important to choose the best way to go to a desirable far-away place. If we go by foot it will take a long time and be very hard. Going by car would be faster, while a plane covers many miles in just an hour, thereby cutting a lot of time out of the journey. Some sutras say perfect enlightenment is far, far away and it may take many lives—even countless lives—to complete the great practices leading to buddhahood. But enlightenment is not absolutely or permanently far away; one can travel there quickly by using a special vehicle. A human rebirth that supports religious practice is the bodhisattva's time- and distance-cutting vehicle. A human life is the best for working toward the ultimate spiritual goal because humans experience many types of misery and are capable of understanding the causes of their suffering. Through direct experience and inferential knowledge humans can understand causality and take action to solve their problems. Not every human life has the necessary special qualities; practice is much easier if one is intelligent, has no physical limitations, possesses wealth, and has access to the teachings. So Mahayana practitioners strive for a continuum of excellent quality human lives in which they find a teacher, hear the teachings, and have the ability to practice. If we add the practices of the six perfections to a continuum of such fortunate human lives we have enormous potential; we have the opportunity to create the causes—the merits or virtues—to attain our objective of complete buddhahood.

In order to have good quality lives one after another, we have to create the causes in the present life for the next life. During that next life we use our potential to create the causes for the subsequent good one. This makes our practice increasingly powerful and we will attain enlightenment quickly. If we do not make this life meaningful by using our potential to practice meritorious actions, we will lose our fortunate opportunity. Then spiritual progress will become very, very difficult. The yogi Śāntideva says:[2]

If I do not practice virtue when
I have the fortune of great merit
What can I possibly do when
I am ignorant and suffering in low rebirths?

Ordinarily we consider a good life to be one that has things we enjoy. A high rebirth is described as having four excellent qualities. First, one has wealth so that one is comfortable and has no difficulty obtaining food, dwellings, clothing, and so on. Second, one's body and mind are excellent and healthy. Third, the people surrounding one are helpful, friendly, and provide one with exactly what one needs. The fourth quality is to be able to accomplish whatever one tries to do. We consider someone who has these four things to have an excellent, but ordinary, human life. These four qualities are also necessary in a spiritual sense. Even serious religious practitioners need a sufficient amount of material things in order to avoid suffering and interruptions to their practice. Second, one needs a healthy and strong body and mind to practice. Next, the society around one should be supportive to religious practice. Finally, one must be able to finish what one starts.

A life with these four excellent qualities is necessary for someone who has taken on the huge responsibility of attaining enlightenment for others' sake, but it is not nearly enough. One needs two more special qualities. First, one must not fall under the power of the mental afflictions. For many people having the four desirable qualities just listed becomes the condition for negative attitudes like desire, hatred, jealousy, and pride to arise. If one is dominated by passions, one's life will be used the wrong way. When we follow negative impulses and harm others, we are using this excellent vessel of a human life as a garbage bin. Second, we need a special kind of wisdom. We have to understand the value of a human life, that a life like this does not come about without causes, that we have a life like this because we created the causes for it in the past, and if we want this kind of life in the future we must create the causes for it in this life. Knowing these things will make one decide to accumulate merit. As a result of this effort one's next life will be even better. Without this knowledge one may act improperly, and when the present life ends one's experience of the good results of previous karma will be finished. If we use up prior good karma and do not create any new good karma, we will experience the beginning of suffering and misery. We destroy ourselves like a banana tree that dies as soon as it bears fruit. So we should have the wisdom to distinguish good from bad and what should be done from what should be avoided.

These six good qualities do not arise without cause. Causes are related to, or we can say *similar to,* their effects. Some people are born with every necessary condition: they have a suitable environment, wealth, supportive relatives, a sharp mind, and a natural tendency to do virtue. These attributes do not necessarily come from their parents. Parents may be involved in a lot of evil activites but a child may still have a tendency toward wisdom. What are the causes that bring about an excellent life with these good qualities? The concordant causes that result in an excellent life are the six perfections. From the prior practice of generosity, one is born having whatever one needs. Wealth is not an accident of birth; affluence comes from an individual's generosity in a prior life. If we want prosperity in the future we must create the cause for it—the practice of generosity. The practice of ethical discipline results in a beautiful human body and a long life. Ethical discipline is good conduct: not harming others, avoiding negative actions, and keeping the actions of body, speech, and mind pure. The third cause is patience; treating others well even when they try to harm you results in pleasant surroundings and helpful companions. Others will find you attractive if you are patient, always try to smooth things out, and make peace no matter how badly others behave. In the future even when people meet you for the first time they will feel comfortable. In contrast, a lack of patience causes others to dislike or fear you for no reason at all. Perseverance in the past enables one to accomplish whatever task one undertakes in this life. Without it one will be scattered and run around ineffectually. So these four basic good qualities result from the first four perfections.

The fifth perfection, meditative stabilization, results in the ability to restrain the mind from negativity for as long as one wishes; one has the control to subdue the passions and not fall under their sway. One is able to keep the first four good qualities from becoming conditions for the mental afflictions to arise. Yet even having those four excellent qualities together with mental stabilization is not enough; one needs the eye of wisdom that can distinguish what should be abandoned from what should be undertaken. The practice of wisdom results in an interest in learning, an open mind, and a naturally sharp intelligence. One gets this wisdom from listening to teachers, studying scriptures, experience, inferential knowledge, and meditation. The past practice of wisdom enables one to distinguish good from bad so that one does not create the causes of future destruction. In this way the six perfections are the causes for a marvelous high rebirth.

So even if we are not seeking anything higher than a good worldly rebirth, these six practices are necessary and sufficient. If we want these qualities in the future we should prepare by practicing now, not just for one day but again and again. Many of you have an almost perfect life right now: you have a good body, a mind that can understand, sufficient wealth, and you have the capacity to accomplish whatever you make a determined effort to do. From listening to the teachings you can gain a certain kind of mental control and distinguish between virtuous and nonvirtuous karma. This is the most precious type of life. Now that you have it, you should feel ashamed to use it in the wrong way and waste the opportunity. Even if you doubt that there are past and future lives or that your actions will have an effect, just questioning these matters shows great intelligence. You should ask yourself, "Why do some people say that there is just one life? And, how could it be that we have many lives?" Even if you cannot decide, you should think, "Maybe, as the teachings say, there *are* multiple lives. If that is true then I am in trouble! It would be good to do something to ensure my future right now. If I am reborn as a cat or a rabbit I will know how to follow a scent to find food or search out a warm bed, but I will not have much intellectual ability. Only with an excellent human life do I have the correct support for practice."

In summary, when we have this special type of rebirth any kind of practice will be more powerful. Even just a few lives during which we do some practice will result in great improvement. Someone whose goal is to attain enlightenment for the benefit of other sentient beings as soon as possible must look toward that final goal; for the time being he or she should practice the six perfections in order to create the causes to have this excellent kind of life again. This will enable one to make further progress. To have a continuum of high rebirths, one has to create the causes in each life for the next one. How the six perfections are sufficient from the point of view of a high rebirth was concisely explained by Maitreya in a stanza in the *Ornament for the Mahayana Sutras:*

> A high rebirth has excellent qualities:
> Wealth, body, companions, the ability to accomplish actions,
> Never falling under the power of the mental afflictions,
> And properly understanding actions.

(b) The fixed number of perfections based on fulfilling the two aims

The second way to understand how all Mahayana practices are included in the six perfections is that the perfections are sufficient for accomplishing both one's own and others' goals. The *Ornament for the Mahayana Sutras* says:

> Those striving to accomplish sentient beings' goals
> Persist in giving, nonharming, and patience.

Stability and the basis of freedom
Have every aspect for achieving one's own goal.

This stanza does not literally show how the six perfections accomplish the ultimate spiritual goal of others. Maitreya will show how they do so later, but here his point is that the perfections can be divided into two groups: the first three perfections—generosity, ethical discipline, and patience—are the basis for helping others, while the last two—meditative stabilization and wisdom—result in one's own goal of emancipation. Perseverance, the fourth perfection, is included in both groups.

Of course, the ultimate way to help others is to lead them to enlightenment, but in order to entice them to follow us, we first need to help them with ordinary things like food, nursing care, and other necessities. The starting point of a good relationship is to get to know others and generously give them what they need. But giving must be done in the proper way and with a good motivation; it will not make others happy if we give things in a harmful manner. So the second practice to help others is ethical discipline. When we practice generosity we should avoid negative physical actions—killing, stealing, and sexual misconduct—as well as wrong verbal actions—lying, harsh speech, gossip, and slander—and evil mental activities—desire, hatred, ignorance, and so forth. The basis of the bodhisattva vows, prātimokṣa vows, and lay vows are precepts to avoid any action that harms others.

We need patience in order to avoid harming others and to be generous in a proper way. Patience is necessary even when we are motivated to act with compassion and love. If we lack patience we may get angry if others find our generosity unsatisfactory. We may subsequently want to retaliate with similar bad behavior. Then the cycle escalates. If others hit you once, you hit them back. Then they hit you twice. If they say something bad, you say something even worse. In this way we end up destroying any good we have done. There are so many sentient beings all of whom are suffering emotions like jealousy and hatred. If we respond to them in the same fashion, all of us will accumulate negative karma. Instead, we should react in a good way. If we cannot do that, we should at least keep quiet and accept the situation. Patience is armor; it protects our conduct when others attack us. We will not be hurt by what others do to us and we will not hurt them in return. If we do not react with hatred or other negative behavior, they will not get angrier and do additional bad things. They will cool off and find they like interacting with us. Eventually, they will want our help and offer us their friendship. When they become close to us we can lead them to the practice of virtuous activities. In this way patience completes the practices of generosity and ethical discipline. Doing these three together is how to work to benefit others.

One's own goal—personal freedom from all obstacles and obtaining the omniscient wisdom of enlightenment for the benefit of others—is achieved through the perfections of meditative stabilization and wisdom. Stabilizing one's mind and developing wisdom only indirectly benefit others; they directly accomplish one's own enlightenment. The practice of wisdom is the basis of freedom from samsara because a realization of the true nature of reality cuts off ignorance at the root. The highest wisdom cannot be achieved without meditative stabilization because the mind must be in control to meditate on the truth. One has to be able to concentrate for long periods on the object of meditation. The mind is usually out of control; every second it runs to a different object. A wild mind cannot focus long enough to achieve any goal. If one has mental stabilization one can concentrate single-pointedly on an object for as long as one wishes—even days or weeks. With mental stabilization one can gain wisdom by looking at reality.

Wisdom and meditative stabilization have different natures, functions, and results. Nevertheless, some people confuse the two. Earlier Tsongkhapa discussed the problems involved in not distinguishing wisdom from deep, nonperceptual consciousness. It is incorrect to believe that a consciousness that is not engaged in conceptual thought is both meditation and the wisdom realizing emptiness. Nonconceptual concentration is only part of the practice of meditation. In other words, we have to understand the function of each of the six perfections. It is important to know how all the perfections work, how they are related to each other, and how they support each other to bring about a final result. For example, the perfection of perseverance is necessary for accomplishing both one's own and others' goals. Someone who is lazy will not diligently make an effort day and night. If we do not see the benefit of all the perfections we may want to choose just one and forget the rest. Singling out a single perfection as the cause of buddhahood is a mistake. All of them together, not just one or a few of them, bring about buddhahood.

(c) The fixed number of perfections based on perfecting the complete fulfillment of others' aims

In the last section Maitreya showed how the six perfections could be divided into two groups: three perfections to benefit others, two to achieve one's own goal, and one that assists attainment of both goals. Here we examine all six perfections from the point of view of being beneficial to others.

In the next passage of the *Ornament for the Mahayana Sutras* Maitreya shows how all six perfections are necessary and sufficient to achieve others' temporary and ultimate goals:

> By freeing them from poverty, not harming,
> Bearing harm, having no regret for your actions,
> Making them happy, and explaining well,
> You accomplish others' and your own goals.

As in the preceding section, the first three perfections are the best means to temporarily benefit others. First, by giving ordinary things to others we eliminate their poverty. After that, we avoid harming any being in any way. Not only do we not harm others, we must be patiently able to bear any harm they try to do to us. In addition, we should be diligent in our efforts to help others in every way that is meritorious, even if it is physically uncomfortable. Because we see the purpose of the action, the mind will not be swayed by any hardship. So long as something is helpful to others we should have no hesitation doing it. Being joyful in undertaking meritorious actions is the fourth perfection: perseverance.

The first four perfections satisfy others' temporary goals but they are not enough to accomplish the ultimate goal: freedom from samsara. In order to attain liberation sentient beings must cease creating new negative karma and eliminate the possibility that their past negative karma will ripen. The root cause of negative actions is ignorance. To eliminate ignorance and develop the path that removes the other mental afflictions, sentient beings must directly realize ultimate reality. How can we create that wisdom for them? There is no way other than to lead them along a higher spiritual path. We must instruct them about what to do and how to think. In order to teach others successfully we must first get them to listen. To get others to listen we practice the first three perfections and the perfection of meditative stabilization. Through our practice of meditative concentration we gain supernatural knowledge and powers. We become able to do miraculous activities to give our disciples delight and create trust and admiration. With our powers we can ascertain our listeners' capacities and determine what they really need. They will listen to our instruction because they wish to have supernatural accomplishments like ours, such as reading minds and seeing the past and future. Without such accomplishments we may give instruction but others may not have any faith in our words. When someone becomes a good listener we can instruct him or her from the beginning. We can teach different individuals according to their respective levels of development and their unique personalities. We can give different teachings just as doctors give different medicines according to individual patients' sicknesses. Through our teachings we eradicate others' doubts and free them from all sorrow. In order to be able to teach this way we must have wisdom. If we lack wisdom we cannot explain things properly to others.

Thus the six perfections are sufficient to help others temporarily and ultimately to free all others from misery. There is no need for anything more. If we practice them properly we are doing everything necessary to benefit others. This also accomplishes one's own goal; it does not leave the practitioner out. Even though we are not working for our own benefit, by doing these things for others we achieve our own goal. If we lack any one of the six perfections we lack the ability to truly help others and ourselves. Tsongkhapa says that this and the preceding stanza from the *Ornament for the Mahayana Sutras* mean that there is no way to benefit oneself and others other than depending on the six perfections. When we are certain that they are indispensable for benefiting others as well as for achieving our own goal, we will come to respect them. We will really want to practice them even if we encounter difficulties. In this way practice will come naturally.

(d) The fixed number of perfections based on their subsuming the entire Mahayana

Maitreya's fourth point is that all the practices of the Mahayana are included in the six perfections. In other words, the six perfections are a summary of the entire Mahayana path. The Mahayana path is the vehicle that carries one to enlightenment. More specifically it is the stages of mental practice that remove all negative actions, eliminate ignorance, and lead to perfect enlightenment. In short, the Mahayana is the vehicle we ride from the beginning to the end.

Sentient beings are ordinarily caught up in their attachment to wealth; all their energy, thoughts, and actions are directed toward accumulating possessions. Fixated on this they have no means to accomplish their own spiritual goal much less succeed in Mahayana practice. The beginning of Mahayana practice is to reduce our attachment to worldly goods so that we do not spend all our time in pursuit of prosperity. How do we do this? Through the practice of generosity. We share whatever we have motivated by a desire to benefit others as much as we can.

Generosity is not the only way to benefit others; the foundation of not harming others is ethical discipline. However, in order to be able to avoid harming others we must not be so attached to wealth. From an attitude of nonattachment we are able to take and keep the bodhisattva vows. The vows are promises to avoid certain types of behavior. We can maintain ethical discipline without a vow, but with a vow it becomes much more forceful and virtuous. When we keep the bodhisattva vows purely we are able to bear whatever hardships arise from animate or inanimate causes. Nothing will sadden us.

Not being bothered when negative things occur is only part of the practice; the positive aspect of our practice is perseverance: joyfully engaging in any type of virtuous activity. An example that shows both patience and perseverance is reading this heavy book for hours; it can give you a backache, but you bear the pain and enjoy learning nonetheless. Concerning the last two perfections, we should note that most of the time we are swept away by discursive wrong thoughts. By stabilizing the mind with meditation we reach a state of nonconceptual thought; then we can use that stable meditative concentration to attain a deep insight of the truth. A direct perception of ultimate reality is the wisdom that eliminates bondage to samsara. In this way everything from the method and wisdom sides of practice is included in the six perfections.

The *Ornament for the Mahayana Sutras* says:

> Not entranced by wealth,
> Respecting pure conduct, undiscouraged by the two,
> And practicing nondiscursive yoga:
> Here is the end of all the Mahayana practices.

Saying this is "the end of all the Mahayana practices" means that all of these are required and no other practices are necessary. Tsongkhapa therefore says it is contradictory for someone to want to practice the Mahayana but avoid the practice of the six perfections. Tsongkhapa is alluding here to Hva Shang Mahayana's view that the six perfections are unnecessary because they are actions based on conceptual thought. Remember, Hva Shang asserts that all thought is wrong because both good thoughts and bad thoughts are the cause of samsara. Since whatever we do is founded in thought, both virtuous and nonvirtuous practices are destructive obstacles to enlightenment. Tsongkhapa reminds us that remaining in nonconceptual concentration without thinking or doing anything else will not lead to enlightenment.

(e) The fixed number of perfections in terms of the completeness of paths or method

Each perfection has a specific function and a significant purpose. We need to understand how the perfections operate and what they accomplish when practiced together.

Our world is the desire realm. Living here we are distracted by sensual objects all the time. Our physical, verbal, and mental efforts almost always go toward obtaining and enjoying things we find attractive. We are stingy and guard our possessions. We never take the road to emancipation because we are so attached to samsaric wealth, life, and experiences. This attachment is the first obstacle to spiritual practice. The perfection of generosity is the best means to free us from attachment toward the things we already possess.

Although generosity is giving others whatever they need and desire, do not take this to mean that you should give away everything you own right now. It would be foolish to kill yourself just because someone says, "Give me your life!" The antidote to attachment is a mental practice. In the beginning we give only small things, but wish to be able to give much more. As we practice dedicating our wealth, body, and life to others, we gradually come to feel that nothing is ours and everything belongs to others. When that attitude is powerful we will be free from stinginess and attachment. Thus the perfection of generosity does not mean that no one experiences poverty because of one's charitable giving. If it meant that then Śakyamuni Buddha would not have perfected generosity because there are still so many poor people in the world.

We are also consumed with desire for things that we have not yet obtained. We put so much time and energy into the pursuit of temporary pleasure. We fight, kill, steal, or lie to obtain sensory gratification. Attachment takes us away from a peaceful, simple life. We neglect spiritual endeavors because we strive so hard to obtain worldly things like wealth, power, and fame. The method to prevent wasting one's life this way is the second perfection—the perfection of ethical discipline. Our primary goal is beyond this life and its temporary, superficial objectives. Taking and keeping the vows—especially the complete ordination vows for monk or nuns—minimizes one's pursuit of worldly goals and maximizes one's focus on the final goal. The vows help us live in simplicity. They contain rules that help us eliminate the actions of body, speech, and mind that arise from attachment. The essence of all the vows is to avoid any physical, verbal, and mental action that causes harm to others. For the perfection of ethical discipline it is best to take the vows, but even if one does not take them one can practice pure moral conduct with the same purpose in mind—maintaining awareness of the ultimate goal by avoiding all negative actions and keeping one's body, speech, and mind pure.

The practice of patience prevents us from becoming discouraged and dropping the bodhisattva vows. The foundation of all Mahayana activities is compassion, love, and a desire to help others. It is quite serious if a Mahayana practitioner, especially a bodhisattva, gives up and thinks, "I can't do anything for them. I better do something for myself." Once the thought to abandon sentient beings arises we no longer have a Mahayana practice. We may start doing something out of love but give up because we become impatient with hardships that occur. This happens because, even when we try to help others, they may react negatively. Sentient beings act crudely because they have no control over themselves: some are under the power of attachment, others are dominated by hatred, some are principally ignorant, and still others are under the power of all three. If we cannot bear their behavior we may want to give up working for their benefit. The best way to prevent that from happening is the third perfection: patience. Patience comes from understanding the nature of sentient beings and the causes for their behavior. As mentioned before, patience is like armor: when we wear it we do not get upset even if someone strikes us. When we are patient it does not matter what others do or what difficulties befall us; we can be joyful about helping others. At an advanced level of the path bodhisattvas almost welcome difficult situations; because they understand the problems and nature of those trying to hurt them, their love and compassion become even stronger. Their bodhicitta is like a good fire; adversity, like a sprinkling of oil, simply causes the flames to grow stronger.

There are so many Mahayana practices that must be done to attain enlightenment. The best means to increase our meritorious actions over a long period of time is the practice of perseverance. This is not diligence in general; the enthusiastic pursuit of negative activity is not the practice of perseverance. The perfection of perseverance is joy in doing wholesome actions. We become able to continue our virtuous activities because we see the benefit of helping others. Temporary difficulties and hardships recede when we concentrate on the good results for ourselves—and especially for others—that come from our actions. A stable and powerful happiness arises and consequently we are able to stick with any task a long time. Even if bodhisattvas experience pain, cold, heat, or injury, they are joyful because they know that their actions help others. Perseverance combined with patience makes it easy to create the merit necessary for the attainment of enlightenment.

The last two perfections—meditative stabilization and wisdom—are the best way to gain complete freedom from the obstacles that keep us from liberation and enlightenment. There are two obstacles to the final goal: the *obstructions to liberation* and the *obstructions to omniscience*. The *obstructions to liberation* are the mental afflictions; these are the wrong thoughts or wrong perceptions—such as attachment, hatred, jealousy, and pride—that are based on a certain kind of ignorance. We perceive things incorrectly and then latch on to that misperception of an object in a wrong way. This leads to various emotions and actions. The *obstructions to omniscience*—sometimes called the knowledge obstacles—are more subtle. The obstructions to omniscience prevent us from clearly knowing the truth of things as they are. Even if we have rid ourselves of the mental afflictions, we will still have a subtle stain or blockage that keeps us from seeing things as clearly as buddhas see them. This second obstruction must also be removed to attain complete enlightenment.

The practice of the perfection of meditative stabilization helps us deal with the first obstruction. It temporarily suppresses the mental afflictions, but by itself meditative concentration is not enough to eliminate the mental afflictions from the root and completely eradicate their stains. For that we need the wisdom that realizes the true nature of the self and all phenomena. This deep realization is developed stage by stage conjoined with meditative stabilization. Together meditative stabilization and deep insight into reality result in omniscience. Although there is a sutra point of view and a tantra point of view regarding the practices of meditative stabilization and wisdom, the different levels or names of their stages do not matter here; the point is that all of the meditation and wisdom practices of sutra and tantra are included in these two perfections.

In summary, we need all the perfections, from generosity up to and including wisdom, in order to attain enlightenment. A stanza from the *Ornament for the Mahayana Sutras* summarizes the function of the six perfections:

> The path is nonattachment to things,
> Restraint from the distraction of obtaining possessions,
> Not giving up on others, increasing merit, and
> The others that completely purify obstacles.

To paraphrase, the purpose of the practice of generosity is to eliminate being attached to things we already have. Once we have lessened attachment to our possessions, the practice of ethical discipline prevents us from striving for more worthless things. By practicing patience we do not give up our intent to benefit other beings. Perseverance increases our meritorious activity. The last two, meditative stabilization and wisdom, completely eliminate the obstacles to liberation and enlightenment.

(f) The fixed number of perfections based on the three trainings

The sixth and final point drawn from the *Ornament for the Mahayana Sutras* proves the sufficiency of the six perfections in terms of how they complete the three trainings. The Buddha taught the set of three trainings—ethical conduct, meditative stabilization, and wisdom—in many hundreds of scriptures that are generally divided into what we call the three collections: Vinaya, Sutra, and Abhidharma. The Vinaya includes all the scriptures that explain topics such as religious conduct, ethical discipline, and the precepts and vows of the Hinayana and Mahayana path. The second collection accords with the second training; it includes scriptures with an emphasis on the many names, styles, and ways to enter into meditative concentration, or samādhi. Meditative stabilization is the ability to fix one's mind clearly and vividly on an object for as long as one wishes without distraction. Once stabilized the mind can concentrate spontaneously on any virtuous object or activity and one experiences a subtle kind of physical and mental bliss. It is only with a stable, focused mind that we can achieve a deep realization of the true nature of reality. Therefore the Hinayana sutras, Mahayana sutras, and the tantras teach many ways to practice the progressive levels of meditative concentration. The third collection is the Abhidharma; this includes scriptures about the profound wisdom that knows the reality of subject and object, all phenomena, the self, and so forth. In short, all Buddhist scriptures—all the teachings on the three trainings—are included in the three collections.

The vast amount of material in the three trainings is encapsulated in the practice of the six perfections. The practice of the six perfections is not different from the practice of the three trainings. The first three perfections—generosity, ethical discipline, and patience—are included in the first training: ethical conduct. Obviously the training of ethical conduct and the second perfection—ethical discipline—are the same thing. As we have seen, generosity is the foundation of morality because if we have less attachment toward our livelihood, wealth, and sensual pleasure it becomes easy to take the religious vows and keep them purely. The practice of patience makes our ethical conduct firm and prevents it from degenerating. Patience keeps us from becoming disturbed if someone criticizes us to our face, gossips about us behind our back, or gets angry with us. We will maintain our composure and our conduct will remain positive. If we do not have patience we may want to retaliate. If someone says something bad to us we may want to say something nasty back; if someone is angry at us, we may also become angry; if someone hits us, we want to strike back in the same way or even harder. In this sense, therefore, generosity and patience are part of the training in ethical discipline. The latter two trainings, meditative stabilization and wisdom, correspond directly to the last two perfections. Perseverance, the fourth perfection, is part of all three trainings. In short, Maitreya says:

The victorious one taught the six perfections
From the point of the three trainings;
The first one has three, the last two are the other two,
One is part of all three.

In conclusion, Tsongkhapa summarizes Maitreya's explanation that the six perfections include all the practices of the Mahayana. In other words, the perfections can be understood in terms of being the causes for the life required for spiritual practice, the two goals, the vehicle, the method, and the training. First, the six perfections are sufficient causes for the type of life necessary to support religious practice. Second, the six perfections are necessary and sufficient practices for someone to achieve two goals: his or her own liberation and temporarily satisfying others' needs. Third, the six perfections are the vehicle or practice necessary to lead others to their ultimate spiritual goal. The fourth point is that the perfections include all methods and the fifth shows which training is accomplished by each perfection. In short, all the teachings are included and complete in the six perfections.

Clearly then, the practice of the six perfections is not something easy. A list of the six practices may sound simple, but the perfections contain all the essential bodhisattva practices. We should think in detail about the nature of the perfections, how they work, what is involved, what they accomplish, and how they are related. When we understand these points we will feel that the six perfections are precious. We will not want to do anything other than practice them because it will accomplish our own and others' temporary and ultimate goals. We will know what and why we are practicing and will do so joyfully. Without this understanding everything will be difficult and our practice will be unstable. Since this is so important, Tsongkhapa relies on many sources to give us the details necessary to elucidate the sufficiency of the six perfections for the Mahayana path. Up to this point we have looked at his commentary on Maitreya's explanation in the *Ornament for the Mahayana Sutras*. Now Tsongkhapa draws from the great Indian teacher Haribhadra's commentary, the *Long Explanation of the Perfection of Wisdom Sutra in Eight Thousand Lines (Abhisamayālaṃkārālokā)*. Haribhadra, following Asaṅga, explains this in three ways: (1) The sufficiency of the six perfections for eliminating obstacles to practice, (2) the sufficiency of the six perfections for achieving all the qualities of buddhahood, and (3) the sufficiency of the six perfections for helping sentient beings develop spiritually.

Haribhadra's first point is similar to what we have seen before: the six perfections are sufficient for Mahayana practice because each perfection overcomes a specific obstacle to practice. As beginners we face many obstructions to religious practice. We have little interest in looking beyond this ordinary, worldly life. Even though we receive teachings, do some practice, and have some wisdom, it is difficult to find the will to practice to achieve something superior. Why aren't we strongly attracted to emancipation from samsara and the attainment of nirvana or enlightenment? There are two main obstacles: attachment to wealth and attachment to our home. The antidote to attachment to our life as householders is found in the practices of the perfections of generosity and ethical discipline. The practice of the perfection of generosity counters attachment to wealth. The antidote to our attachment to our home and family is to become ordained as a monk or nun, leave home, and live a religious life practicing ethical discipline in solitude. From a positive perspective, ethical discipline is adhering to rules of moral conduct to maintain the purity of one's physical, verbal, and mental actions. From the negative perspective, it is guarding oneself from falling into negative actions. If one cannot take full ordination, even lay vows will make one's practice of ethical discipline stronger and more stable. Whether or not one takes any vow, keeping one's body, speech, and mind virtuous and avoiding the ten nonvirtuous actions is ethical discipline. It counters negative worldly activity.

Even if we reduce our attachment to wealth and home, there are still obstacles to persevering in pure spiritual practice. We may desire to follow a religious path, but give up easily. There are two main causes for not continuing our practice: one is external and the other is internal. The first problem is that, when we try to practice, other sentient beings may make us miserable. We try to help them but, out of ignorance and the mental afflictions, they act badly. Their attitude and behavior may make us depressed and irritable. We know how much we are doing for them, yet it seems every one of their actions is designed to hurt and oppose us. First this one did this, then another one did that, until finally we just cannot take it anymore. The second obstacle is from our own side: we may become discouraged because virtuous practice is difficult and takes so very long. Many people begin virtuous activities but few keep on with their practice. They do it for a little while, but when it does not come easily, or is not comfortable, they give up. They are immediately discouraged by small difficulties and have no pleasure in practice.

The solution is found in the practices of the perfection of patience and the perfection of perseverance. Patience and perseverance are important not only for the practice of the great Mahayana path; they are also crucial at the beginning of a small practice of virtue. If we have strong patience we are able to accept whatever external circumstances befall us. We are not bothered by the dreadful actions of sentient beings; we can joyfully continue helping them. When they do negative things, our practice becomes stronger because we become more concerned for their future. Perseverance is the remedy for discouragement. The nature of perseverance is joy in doing meritorious actions. No matter how much physical discomfort, mental hardship, or inconvenience an activity entails, we joyfully persevere. The ability to bear discomfort and joyfully persevere does not come easily. For joy to arise when one is sad and tired one must understand the benefit of doing the action and the disadvantages of not doing it. One will be encouraged to continue by understanding the details of what one is doing and why one is doing it. Then one's perseverance becomes as strong as a professional boxer; even though he is knocked down, in pain, or almost dead, he gets up to fight because he has a special reason that keeps him going. A religious practitioner, especially a Mahayana practitioner, should do every action for the benefit of all sentient beings. Once patience and diligence are established in the mind, even if one has to do something for a very long time, it feels like just a day. There is no problem and one experiences a special kind of joy.

So the first four perfections solve the problems we face at the beginning of religious practice and break down the obstacles to continuing to practice. However, even while we are maintaining a religious practice, we may waste or diminish the value of what we are doing. There are two things that may make our practices a wasted effort: a distracted, wandering mind that is not constant on its virtuous object, and lacking the wisdom that knows the nature of reality. The last two perfections, meditative stabilization and wisdom, are the remedy. If the mind is not trained, it runs away from the object of meditation after just a few minutes. Śāntideva says that if the mind wanders while one does recitations or any other virtuous activity, that action is almost purposeless. The practice will be ineffective because one was not concentrating. The antidote to mental wandering is meditative concentration. When one achieves real meditative concentration, the mind is able to stay effortlessly on any virtuous object as long as one wishes. It is clear, unwavering, and without distraction or sleepiness.

The Buddha taught for forty-five years in order to help sentient beings get rid of their suffering and free themselves from samsara. His teachings and the commentaries that elucidate them explain how to train the mind on the spiritual path. The subject of these texts is wisdom. Wisdom is knowledge of true reality. Wisdom distinguishes good from bad, discriminates between what should be done and what should be abandoned, understands the methods and goals and how they are related. If we lack this understanding, we may think that wrong things are the correct practice and take them seriously. Or we may think that the right things are incorrect and should be abandoned. We may be confused about even the most basic things. Without wisdom, even if one is diligent and patient, all one's effort may be the wrong track.

The solution is the practice of the perfection of wisdom—understanding phenomenal causality and the true nature of reality. We will attain perfect enlightenment when we develop this wisdom and combine it with the other five perfections—the method side of practice.

Haribhadra's second point shows how the six perfections are sufficient to achieve all the qualities of buddhahood. The qualities of a buddha directly arise from meditative concentration and wisdom. Together these two practices get rid of obstacles from the root and one achieves omniscience and all the qualities of a buddha's body, speech, and mind. The first four perfections—generosity, ethical discipline, patience, and perseverance—are the necessary causes and conditions for meditative stabilization. Generosity is important because one cannot concentrate if one is attached to one's life, wealth, or other objects of desire. The greatest obstacle to meditative concentration is letting the mind fall under the power of desire for sensory objects. When the mind is distracted by gross objects of the senses, one's body and speech also go that way. Ethical discipline eliminates these distractions and keeps the mind in accord with virtue. Patience and perseverance ensure that one is not bothered by external hardships or discouraged by long practice. Upon this foundation one can develop meditative stabilization. Then, with this firm and stable mind, one meditates on emptiness. Without meditative concentration there is no way to have a direct realization of the truth. When one joins meditative stabilization to the special insight realizing emptiness, one is on the way to removing all obscurations from the root and manifesting the perfect qualities of a buddha. Because the other perfections are the pre-conditions for achieving this, Haribhadra says that the six perfections are necessary and sufficient.

Haribhadra's third point is that the six perfections are sufficient for helping sentient beings develop spiritually. Tsongkhapa discussed this above in the context of how the six perfections accomplish others' goals. Haribhadra's explanation is so similar to Maitreya's that there is no need to repeat it.

Now we have finished discussing the sufficiency of the six perfections for the Mahayana path. The topic that goes along with this is the order of the six perfections.

2" An ancillary discussion of the fixed order of the perfections

This topic has three subdivisions:

(a) The order of arising

(b) The order in terms of inferior and superior
(c) The order in terms of coarse and subtle

(a) THE ORDER OF ARISING

The first perfection is the practice of generosity, second is the perfection of ethical discipline, third is the perfection of patience, fourth is the perfection of joyous perseverance, fifth is the perfection of meditative stabilization, and the sixth is the perfection of wisdom. They are in this order because the former produces and/or influences the subsequent one. It is much easier to practice a perfection if we have mastered the preceding one. Generosity is first because, in order to help others, they have to relate to us. The practice of generosity is like waving, "Come here!" We call others with a gesture that indicates we will give them whatever and as much as they need. In his *Commentary on the "Middle Way"* Candrakīrti says:[3]

> Every sentient being wants happiness.
> There is no human happiness without wealth.
> Understanding that wealth come from generosity,
> The Buddha taught generosity first.

Ethical discipline is easier to practice if one is less attached to worldly things. In contrast, if one is strongly attracted to material objects, one wants to accumulate things that one does not have and wishes to keep for oneself whatever one already possesses. To protect one's wealth and accumulate more people lie, fight, steal, and do all kinds of evil things. If one is motivated this way it is hard to take up pure moral conduct. So generosity—the practice of nonattachment—makes it easier to practice ethical discipline.

If one continuously tries to prevent oneself from committing negative actions of body, speech, and mind it is easier to practice patience. Patience is not getting upset about difficulties that occur. When one is patient there will be fewer conditions that cause one to turn away from practice. This helps one to develop perseverance. Perseverance is being able to joyously and diligently engage in virtuous activities day and night. If one has this kind of stability one's mind becomes suitable for the practice of the fifth perfection: meditative stabilization. If one has single-pointed concentration one can see things exactly as they are. One cannot directly realize the ultimate nature of reality through the senses; it takes a deep insight that comes through meditation. So to practice each perfection one needs the help of the preceding one. From this point of view the order of the perfections is due to causality.

(b) The order in terms of inferior and superior

Superiority is another way to understand why the perfections are in this order. The first one is the most inferior, and each successive one is more and more superior. The practice of generosity is inferior to the practice of ethical discipline, patience is a superior practice to ethical discipline, and so forth.

(c) The order in terms of coarse and subtle

"Coarse and subtle," in this context, refer to the difficulty of practice and is similar to saying "higher and lower." The easier practices are coarser and each successive perfection is more difficult to practice because it is more subtle.

Maitreya says in the *Ornament for the Mahayana Sutras* that the order of the perfections is based on these three points of view: causality, superiority, and subtlety.

> They are taught in an order because
> Depending on the former the latter arises,
> Their inferiority and superiority,
> And the coarse are succeeded by the subtler.

This is enough about the six perfections in general. Starting with the next chapter we will look at how to practice each of them one by one.

❧ 9 ❧

The Perfection of Generosity

c" The process of learning the perfections
   1" How to train in the bodhisattva deeds in general
      (a) Training in the perfections that mature the qualities you will have
          when you become a buddha
         (i) How to train in the perfection of generosity
            (a') What generosity is
            (b') How to begin the development of generosity
            (c') The divisions of generosity
               (1') How everyone should practice it
               (2') Divisions of generosity relative to particular persons
               (3') Divisions of actual generosity
                  (a") The gift of the teachings
                  (b") The gift of fearlessness
                  (c") Material gifts
                     (1") The generosity of actually giving material
                        things
                        (a)) How to give away material things
                           (1)) Recipients of giving
                           (2)) The motivation for giving
                               (a')) What kind of motivation is
                                   required
                               (b')) What kind of motivation must
                                   be eliminated

c" THE PROCESS OF LEARNING THE PERFECTIONS

FROM ONE PERSPECTIVE the perfections are difficult and advanced Maha-yana practices, but from another perspective every human with intelligence, leisure, and fortune like ours is able to practice them. Knowing about each perfection is important. If we do not understand what each one is and how to practice it we will not be able to deal with problems that come along. Before we can actually practice we need to learn two subjects:

1" How to train in the bodhisattva deeds in general (chapters 9–15)
2" In particular, how to train in the last two perfections (volumes 4 and 5)

The remainder of this volume covers the first topic. Here Tsongkhapa provides a detailed explanation of the first four perfections, generosity through perseverance, and concludes with a brief overview of the last two perfections: meditative stabilization and wisdom. The second topic, an extensive discussion of the last two perfections, is almost half of the *Lamrim Chenmo*. These important subjects are covered in volumes 4 and 5 of this series.

1" HOW TO TRAIN IN THE BODHISATTVA DEEDS IN GENERAL

The general way to train in the bodhisattva practices has two divisions:

(a) Training in the perfections that mature the qualities you will have when you become a buddha (chapters 9–14)
(b) Training in the four ways to gather disciples that help others to mature (chapter 15)

First we learn how to practice the six perfections with the emphasis on our own spiritual development. This is the process of taming the mind. Once we have trained ourselves we can begin to help others spiritually develop. The way to reach out to help other sentient beings is called the *four ways to gather disciples*.

(a) TRAINING IN THE PERFECTIONS THAT MATURE THE QUALITIES YOU WILL HAVE WHEN YOU BECOME A BUDDHA

The practices to develop the mind and become a perfect buddha are called *perfections* because they are not done only for the accomplishment of one's own goal. If they were just for oneself we would simply call them *practices*.

When they are practiced because one wants to attain perfect buddhahood for the benefit of other beings, they are the perfect essence of the Mahayana path. There are six sections to this topic:

(i) How to train in the perfection of generosity (chapters 9–10)
(ii) How to train in the perfection of ethical discipline (chapter 11)
(ii) How to train in the perfection of patience (chapter 12)
(iv) How to train in the perfection of perseverance (chapter 13)
(v) How to train in the perfection of meditative stabilization (chapter 14)
(vi) How to train in the perfection of wisdom (chapter 14)

(i) HOW TO TRAIN IN THE PERFECTION OF GENEROSITY

The practice of generosity is explained in four subtopics:

(a') What generosity is
(b') How to begin the development of generosity
(c') The divisions of generosity (chapters 9–10)
(d') A summary (chapter 10)

(a') WHAT GENEROSITY IS

We assume that we know what generosity is; we commonly define it as giving or sharing something with others. But the Mahayana practice of generosity is much more. If we do not know what it is and how to practice it, no matter how much we give we may not create much merit, the merit we create may go for some small purpose, or our act of charity may not be meritorious at all. So we need instruction on the kind of attitude to develop, where to place our emphasis, what should be perfected, and so on.

To clarify the nature of generosity Tsongkhapa draws from Asaṅga's *Bodhisattva Levels* to say that it has two aspects: a consciousness that is willing to give, and the physical and verbal actions that are motivated by this attitude. Thus while generosity includes actions of body and speech, the mental aspect is the key and has to be developed first. This special attitude has two parts: its foundation, or essence, is a lack of attachment to one's property and even to one's body. In addition, generosity is a sincere desire to give whatever is necessary to those in need. This is a willingness to give one's wealth—and, if the necessity arises, one's life—without hesitation or stinginess. A time comes in a bodhisattva's practice of generosity when he or she can freely give away his or her body as if it were nothing more than a vegetable. That kind of giving comes later. Before that is possible one has to develop a special attitude.

Once one's attitude is perfect, then giving anything, even one's life, presents no difficulty.

The perfection of generosity is complete when one's attitude is perfect. In other words the *perfection of generosity* does not imply that one has successfully eliminated poverty and made everyone rich. That would be impossible. How could anyone do that? All buddhas have mastered the perfection of generosity and all bodhisattvas are practicing it now, and yet there are still many starving and impoverished creatures in this world. If the perfection of generosity depended upon the elimination of all poor sentient beings in need of charity, then we would have to accept that no one has ever attained enlightenment. As Śāntideva writes in *Engaging in the Bodhisattva Deeds*:

> If the perfection of generosity
> Means that no creature is poor,
> Since there are many in poverty now,
> How have past saviors perfected generosity?

The perfection of generosity is a mind perfectly free of attachment and stinginess that joyfully, without any hesitation, wants to give. Therefore, the most important aspect of the Buddhist practice of generosity is training the mind, not the physical act of giving. The merit created by an act of generosity is determined by one's attitude, not by whether one gives something of greater or lesser value. In order to understand the correct attitude, let's first look at what is incorrect. Ordinary generosity includes the anticipation of getting something back in return later. Its goal is actually one's own benefit. Giving when one wants something back is like a business transaction. It is not a religious practice to think, "I will give this now because later I will get double back." That type of giving is bargaining with no greater purpose than getting something better for oneself. It looks like religious practice, but it is merely an exchange of merchandise. For example, giving to the poor can be done with the attitude that at some point in the future those people will help one in return. Or one could make a charitable donation with the intention of becoming famous when people hear about one's generosity.

Sometimes when people hear about the bodhisattva practice of the perfection of generosity they think it is the only way to practice generosity. That is not correct. Just because one does not have the perfect motivation does not mean it is impossible to practice generosity. There are many levels of practice. One can be generous focusing just on this life because one does not believe in future lives. This creates merit, but not great merit. One could take a longer perspective and practice generosity while thinking about future rebirths; for example, one could practice generosity out of fear of being reborn as a hungry ghost or in some other poor situation. This is virtuous, but it is still not a Mahayana practice because it is done for one's own benefit. Even practicing generosity while wishing that one will thereby become free of attachment and attain emancipation is not the Mahayana practice of generosity; one is giving with the expectation that in the future one will obtain something for oneself.

The bodhisattva's practice of generosity, the perfection of generosity, is giving without any expectation of future reward. *Giving without expectation* is more than a simple willingness to give whatever belongs to you; it means that even the merit created from acts of generosity is dedicated to others. Mahayana practitioners pray that all their past, present, and future merit may cause others to be happy, healthy, free of poverty, attain liberation, and so on. In other words, the perfection of generosity is to give one's merit in addition to other charitable gifts to all beings without any partiality between friend and enemy and without any hope of future benefit for oneself.

In the beginning it is natural to think, "I can't do this. I do not even want to do this." Do not get discouraged. Some people can generate the highest motivation from the start, some begin in the middle, while others start at the lowest level. Bodhisattva practice depends on mental training and this state of mind can be developed. Through repeated training the mind will become accustomed to the perfection of generosity. When this attitude becomes spontaneous one has the perfection of generosity. When the mind is not trained, the perfection does not exist. As the next stanza of *Engaging in the Bodhisattva Deeds* says:

> The perfection of generosity is said to be
> The thought of giving to all beings
> Your possessions and your merits.
> Thus, the perfection of generosity is dependent on the mind.

(b') How to begin the development of generosity

A wish to share everything one has, even one's merit, with all others equally does not arise easily. To generate this wish sincerely from the heart we need a method. Knowing the method and the goal is important. The goal is the perfection of generosity and the method is how to give. Since the nature of generosity is mental, in the beginning we must fight against psychological obstacles. Without mental training even if we give something we may regret it later. However, if we use the method to develop the wisdom to see the essencelessness of things and yet remember their usefulness, even if we are in poverty we can generously share the little we have with others.

The psychological obstacle to generosity is wanting to hold on to things as our own. Thus it includes miserliness, stinginess, and attachment. We are extremely attached to our body and property; and attachment goes much further—to our family, town, nation, and so on. Even if one owns an entire country, consumed by greed one still wants more and does not want to share even something as small as a penny. Dominated by selfishness we want everything for ourselves; we want to fight if someone gets in the way of our attempt to accumulate and hold on to things. We need to consider many examples to convince ourselves that stinginess is like a rope tying the mind. These knotted bonds should be cut off. Think about the many negative consequences of attachment and stinginess. Not wanting to share is the root of many problems throughout the world—from small-scale arguments to murder and warfare. That is what happens in this life, and of course in future lives one will be born into poverty—or, if one has possessions, they may be taken away or destroyed by other people, animals, or impersonal events. Through meditating on the disadvantageous consequences of holding everything for oneself we can weaken greedy attachment.

Destroying miserliness from the root is still not enough to complete the perfection of generosity, because even Hinayana practitioners completely eliminate attachment. Hinayana arhats have not perfected generosity because when they practice they are working for their own emancipation from samsara. Of course, their positive, generous activities to help others create merit. But the most powerful Mahayana practice of the perfection of generosity requires more than just giving having gotten rid of attachment. One needs something positive in addition: great compassion and love for others. One must want others to have freedom and happiness. So, in addition to meditating on the disadvantages of attachment, we contemplate the benefits or good results that come from sharing. It takes repeated analysis of both to develop a spontaneous desire to give.

These disadvantages and advantages are not imaginary; we must truly see them with wisdom. Only when we are completely convinced can we reverse our current patterns of thought and behavior. The first step toward developing the wisdom to overpower ignorance is seeing the reasons to practice. If one knows the goal and understands what one is doing, one can deal with any unpleasant internal and external conditions that may arise as one practices. Concentrating on the benefits of generosity and the disadvantages of miserliness is the antidote to stinginess and will eventually eliminate it. Then we can give with a special kind of joy. If one does not know the benefits, one's practice will not be strong or comfortable. Therefore, the sutras and commentaries extensively explain the advantages of sharing sincerely from the heart and the faults of selfishness. Yogis and practitioners concentrate over and over on these advantages and disadvantages as laid out in the scriptures. Tsongkhapa brings together a number of quotations so that we will clearly see these points and develop a pure practice. As you read and contemplate these examples, think of other instances from your own experience. Gradually your attachment will decrease and you will release your stinginess. Slowly you will come to like sharing and want to help others.

The *Moon Lamp Sutra (Candra-pradīpa-sūtra)* illustrates the many faults of holding things back for oneself:

> This body, which is the nature of filth,
> And life are changing without control.
> They are like a dream or illusion.
> Because the childish are attached to these
> They do very unwholesome actions,
> Unwisely falling under the power of sinful activity
> Until carried off by the Lord of Death
> To the inexhaustible misery of life in the hells.

We do not want to see the true nature of the body; we color it in a nice way and delude ourselves into thinking it is attractive. However, when we look at the body with wisdom, we see it is foul and smelly. The body is more and more disgusting the deeper we look beneath the skin. Tsongkhapa comments that this impure body and life are like water flowing down a steep hill: they change from one moment to the next. The body seems solid but it does not remain the same for even an instant; from birth we change to childhood, adolescents become old, then we die and the body becomes just bones in a cemetery.

Both the body and life are under the power of karma and conditions; there is no self-essence that is independent or free. There is nothing solidly trustworthy about it. Our life is like a dream or an illusion created by our previous karma and the mental afflictions. Those who have directly realized the four noble truths see life exactly as it is: the truth of suffering. Like a magician, they understand the scary illusion they created does not exist in the way it appears. In contrast, we ordinary beings are attached to our illusory body and life. Where does this attachment come from? It comes from ignorance about the true nature of the body and life and the way they are produced. We incorrectly superimpose on them the idea of some substantive reality. To ordinary people impure things seem pure, impermanent things seem permanent, and things that are dependent seem independent. We become deeply attached to this unreal thing and do not want to share any part of it at all. In this sense ordinary people are like children. When anything is in opposition to their thoughts of *me* or *mine,* they get angry. If they see someone with something better, they get jealous. When they have something special, they feel proud. As a result of these emotions they engage in unwholesome actions.

Even between friends and families all kinds of problems come about because of such attachment. Under the power of negative attitudes, and with no skill to get rid of them, we ignorantly go through life until seized by death. Remember the Lord of Death is simply death itself. Where does the Lord of Death take us if we have done negative actions? The karmic result of egotistic selfishness is a bad life. The worst kind of life is to be born into the inexhaustible suffering of hell. Although the hells are not permanent places where one remains forever, the sufferings experienced there are horrible and last for a long, long time. Through meditation one can come to understand things correctly. Understanding the nature of the body is another aspect of the antidote to attachment and the first step toward developing spontaneous generosity from deep in the heart.

The next sutra quotation, from the *Formula That Accomplishes Limitless Methods (Ananta-mukha-nirhāra-dhāraṇi),* gives us another perspective on how to develop this understanding. A *formula,* or *dhāraṇi,* is a type of scripture that gives a method for reciting a mantra in order to get a specific result. For example, we can recite certain mantras for a long life. However, the scripture says the best way to live a long time is not by reciting a mantra; it is through eliminating attachment:

> Certain sentient beings fight;
> The root of this is attachment to oneself.
> Therefore give up what you are attached to;
> Eliminating this craving is the mantra.

If one is attached to oneself, whenever anything unpleasant happens anger, hatred, and jealousy arise. Then one kills and injures others in order to gain or maintain possession of things. Even if one did not do this in this lifetime, one can be harmed as the result of that type of action done in other lives. Either way, the root cause of untimely death is karma motivated by attachment.

The body is changing every moment. Every kind of unclean thing is contained in it and it is the source of polluting filth. In essence this is not something that we would want to touch. However, we usually ignore reality and feel that the body is pure and lovely. The body is impure, but if we use it properly we can turn it into something valuable; we can practice generosity and eliminate attachment. Through the Mahayana practice of mental purification, we can attain the permanent, stainless body of buddhahood. The ordinary body has the capacity to establish a priceless pure thing; it is like trading something bad for something invaluable. So why not exchange this body for that? This is how yogis talk to themselves. We should do the same to generate the desire to remove attachment and share with others. As the *Compendium of Trainings* says:

> Thus my body and mind
> Change every moment.
> So why not trade it for something priceless?
> For this impermanent body dripping filth
> You obtain permanent pure enlightenment.

Thus the method to develop the perfection of generosity includes various ways of thinking. We think about the body's impurity but also consider its use and value for attaining the wish-fulfilling jewel of buddhahood.

To understand the meaning of the next quotation you may need some background information. This passage is from the *Garland of Birth Stories (Jātaka-mālā)*, a collection of stories about Śākyamuni's lives as a bodhisattva before he became the Buddha. The stories illustrate how he practiced the six perfections. In one of those lives he was born as a great prince who had the positive attitude of a bodhisattva. One day the prince went outside the palace for a walk. There he saw a starving and thirsty tigress. She was so weak and miserable that she was about to eat her five cubs. The young prince saw this and felt great compassion for the cubs and their mother. He decided to save them. He thought, "The only thing I have is my body. This body has no independent self. It is always being destroyed by change. It will not stay with me forever; every moment it is on the path of departure. It has no essence; it is nothing more than bones, blood, and impurity. It is simply suffering. It is like a wound, requiring great care and even a light touch can cause it great pain. Even though I have served this body my whole life—feeding it, clothing it, ornamenting it—it does not repay my kindness. All it gives me is problems. It is always impure. So why not use it to save them? If I feed it to the tigress they will all live. The great merit of this action can become the cause for my attaining enlightenment for the benefit of others. Then this body will be very beneficial; this life will become very meaningful. Not to enjoy the opportunity to give a temporary body like this would not be wise." So he said these words as he lay down to let the tiger drink his blood and eat his flesh:

> This ever-changing body lacks a self and has no essence.
> It is suffering, ungrateful, and always impure.
> But this body can be of great benefit to others.
> Not to enjoy this would be unwise.

The prince's action was incredibly courageous. Tsongkhapa comments that no matter how much effort we exert to protect the body, we are caring for it just to throw it away. That is pointless. The prince recognized that if he used his body with a good attitude to create merit, he could temporarily fulfill others' needs and finally attain buddhahood. Although right now we are attached to the body and not able to give it away like the bodhisattva prince, we should mentally practice in order to be able to do this at some future time. Not to train the mind to see the purpose of generosity and the disadvantages of stinginess is ignorant. Therefore, as much as possible, we should try to produce the desire to give our wealth, and even our body, to others.

The great Buddhist yogi Śāntideva says:

> From giving all you attain nirvana.
> I too desire to be free of misery.
> Since everything is given up eventually,
> To give to other sentient beings is best.

There are three reasons why mentally giving to others is an excellent practice. First, the result of the virtue created by giving one's wealth, body, and merits without stinginess is the attainment of nirvana. Second, we want to attain emancipation from the misery of cyclic existence. And third, sooner or later we have to give up every single atom of our wealth and body anyway. No matter how much wealth one has, one will separate from it at death. If we give it away now, while we have the choice, it will be a great achievement; there is no merit in giving up our body and possessions at the time of death when we have no alternative.

The *Compendium of the Perfections* takes this idea further saying:

> When you see that wealth is impermanent
> And great compassion spontaneously arises,
> You understand based on good reasons
> That your possessions stored at home belong to others.

Generosity begins with a mental practice. An understanding of impermanence and spontaneous compassion arise from analytical meditation. When one comprehends impermanence clearly, one knows that at some time one will definitely part from everything that one has stored safely at home. Compassion leads one to think that these things are suitable gifts that can be given to others. When one mentally dedicates these things to others, they come to belong to other sentient beings. One's possessions are no longer one's own; we are merely holding on to them for others. Even one's body does not belong to oneself anymore; it is something to share with others. This is the bodhisattvas' mind-set. Whenever someone needs something of theirs, they think, "OK. This belongs to them anyway." They feel no difficulty parting with things; they do not separate off one part thinking, "I will not give this piece." They have no stinginess or feeling of *mine*. They feel no anger even if thieves steal something precious. Instead they think, "I should be giving this away, so it is wonderful they came here to receive it."

In the beginning we do not actually give things away. Slowly and gradually our mental practice will convince us to actually give. We start small, giving only as much as we can without stinginess—perhaps just a few cents or a few mouthfuls of food. Little by little, as we develop the mind, we increase the quantity and quality of our gifts. When one lacks stinginess and feels no hardship in giving, then naturally the physical action of philanthropy will follow. If one's mind is not trained and one crazily gives something away at the urging of others, a little later one may have long and hard regrets. Then that act of giving will be wasted; it even becomes a negative karma. This is not the way to practice. Mental training—thinking about the faults of stinginess and the benefits of giving—is the key practice in the beginning. After developing the mind one will be happy to give, and then looking back on that action one will be joyful. This doubles one's generosity.

The next stanza from the *Compendium of the Perfections* elaborates on these benefits and disadvantages:

> From giving you become fearless;
> From stashing your wealth you become fearful.
> Dissatisfaction, communality, and always needing protection:
> If you give, these faults will never harm you.

We are always fearful. Where does fear come from? We are afraid of death, bodily harm, and many of our fears are related to our possessions. Once we want to share everything we have with others, however, we no longer dread losing our belongings or having them stolen. One benefit of giving to others purely is that it eliminates this fear. What are the disadvantages of miserliness? For so long as we are stingy we will not be satisfied with what we have. When we have ten we want fifteen; when we have fifteen we want twenty. Even if we have enough stuff for ten lifetimes, we still are hungry for more. We do all sorts of things so that we do not have to share our possessions. We do not want them held in common with others. We become unhappy if even some small thing has to be shared, so we fight to keep it our own whether we need it or not. Trying to protect our possessions is a lot of trouble. Some people even lose their lives trying to protect their property. If one mentally shares with others from the heart then these problems will disappear. Dissatisfaction, fear that your things are going to be held in common, and feeling the need to protect things will not harm us.

The scriptural passage continues:

> Generosity brings worldly and supramundane happiness;
> Not giving brings suffering even in this life.
> Human wealth is like a shooting star:
> Even if you do not give it away it quickly disappears.

Generosity, both mental and physical, is meritorious so it will bring good results that will never harm one. It is easy to see that even in this life the practice of generosity has beneficial results. If we are reborn in samsara, we will have happiness in that life if we practice generosity now. We may be born with wealth or all kinds of advantages will simply come to us. Of course, the supreme wealth is the everlasting happiness of buddhahood, and that too is a result of generosity. The opposite attitude—not wanting to share or practicing only for oneself—brings only suffering. We should concentrate on these advantages and disadvantages because they are real and true.

Possessions are impermanent. They appear and certainly will disappear whether we give them away or not. Disadvantages arise when wealth is an object of attachment. However, if we share our wealth then it will be like having riches all the time. When we sincerely give to others, even if just mentally without any physical action, we create virtuous karma. That karma is like a treasure; it will bring about an enormous result. At present we share what we have, but in the future, in this or other lives, we will receive wealth without begging or working. If we dedicate the merit of our generosity to benefit other sentient beings, the results will be almost inexhaustible. These karmic results will not disappear; sooner or later we will experience them. Not only that, the result will increase almost as if it were capital bearing interest.

The *Compendium of the Perfections* therefore continues:

Wealth not given is impermanent: it will vanish.
Given away it becomes a treasury.
Essenceless wealth becomes significant
When sincerely given to benefit other beings.

Therefore the wise praise generous giving,
But childish people enjoy accumulating things.
Grasping never prevents anything from being lost;
Giving always brings excellent results.

These stanzas repeat the point that wealth does not have an essence: it is impermanent and nothing special or essential. Bodhisattvas know that worldly goods do not bring everlasting peace. Material goods give benefits that are small, temporary, and usually a mixed pleasure; for the most part they bring misfortune. Even though our possessions have no essence, they become very valuable if we give them away motivated by a desire to benefit others. Even a small worthless thing becomes a worthy object, because sharing it with love and compassion creates great merit. Temporarily it benefits others and ultimately it benefits oneself. Therefore, the wise masters always praise generosity. In contrast, ordinary individuals are so attached to accumulating possessions that they are like little children. Children want to keep their play-things; they cry if they lose them. No matter how hard we try to hold on to things, however, there is nothing that we will not be separated from. In contrast, giving without tightfistedness always brings an excellent result. In fact, generosity is the basis of the Mahayana path. Mahayana practitioners dedicate their life and actions to helping all mother sentient beings by leading them to the highest state of enlightenment. How can we help all others? To reach them at first we attract them to us by generously giving material things. Later we can give them the Dharma that will lead to the best supramundane results.

This section of the *Compendium of the Perfections* concludes:

By giving you will no longer hold on to misery;
Grasping is an ignoble path and produces the afflictions.
Those who practice generosity are on the best path;
Other practices, say noble ones, are a bad path.

Hoarding possessions is like clasping misery. Doing something other than the practice of generosity is a wrong course of action that leads to more mental distress. If we eliminate the cause of misery we will not suffer any longer.

Thus anyone practicing generosity is on the path to nirvana or enlightenment. To attain buddhahood we need a vast accumulation of merit and insight. The bodhisattvas' way of practicing generosity accumulates merit quickly because they dedicate the merit of their generous acts to all other sentient beings. Although sometimes they dedicate their merit for some temporary purpose in the world—for example, wishing that others be free from famine, obtain happiness, and so on—they also dedicate their merit for the final goal: that all beings may attain highest bliss and omniscience.

If we practice generosity this way we will create merit as vast as the number of sentient beings. There are even more sentient creatures than there are grains of sand in the banks of the Ganges River. We cannot count that much sand. So if we dedicate to all these beings, the merit gained is also countless. Therefore, even giving little gifts, but dedicating the merit for the benefit of all sentient beings, will quickly complete the accumulation of merit. This is stated in Nāgārjuna's *Precious Garland*:

> If the merit gained from dedication
> Were physical in form,
> It would be more numerous than the sand of the Ganges;
> It would not fit in the realms of the world.
>
> This is what the Buddha taught.
> There is also a logical proof for it:
> There are limitless sentient beings—
> The merit of wishing to benefit them is the same.

Generally the result of a specific action is not something that ordinary beings can know. We can understand the generalities of karma, such as that an effect will be commensurate with its cause, but the specifics cannot be logically proven. For more detail we usually look at what the Buddha taught in the sutras. In this case, however, we do not have to depend on the Buddha's words. It is logical that we gain as much merit as there are recipients to whom we give. Sentient beings are numberless; there are so many that they cannot be counted. Thus if we dedicate our merit to all of them we obtain limitless merit.

How can we increase our practice of generosity? Serious practitioners examine the obstacles to giving freely without stinginess. All of us have things to which we are very attached; just by being there in front of us these things increase our stinginess. These things seem to benefit us but really they are obstacles. They are deceitful, confusing, and like anti-generosity drugs. They poison our practice of generosity and obstruct our progress on the path to enlightenment. Not only do they block the increase of our generosity, they also reduce the thought to give that we already have. The things themselves are neither good nor bad; whether or not they are a problem depends on the person in question. Even the seven precious royal things are not suitable for a bodhisattva if he or she is very attached to them. For this reason bodhisattvas—and ourselves as well—should not hold on to property like this, and even if someone offers it to us we should not accept it.

The *Compendium of the Perfections* says:

> Things that increase stinginess
> Or decrease the wish to give
> Are obstacles that deceive.
> Bodhisattvas avoid all such things.
>
> Whatever hinders generosity
> And obscures the path to complete enlightenment—
> Even the special wealth of royalty, jewels, and so on—
> Is not worthy of bodhisattvas' acceptance.

When we eliminate stinginess and attachment there is no problem with having or getting possessions. No matter how much we have we can use our wealth to benefit others. But until we reach that point it is more difficult to have things that so entrance us.

If we are attached to things we should think as follows, "The Buddha started out in samsara just like me. He had the same kind of troubled life, but he attained enlightenment. Now he is way up there so why am I still down here?" We should recollect that we are trying to emulate the Buddha by taking the bodhisattva vow to attain enlightenment for the benefit of others: "I have promised that my body, life, and wealth are for the assistance of other sentient beings. I am trying to give mentally but I am still attached to the things that I have in my possession. I am like a foolish elephant going in and out of water."

The example just cited may seem odd to you if you are unfamiliar with elephant behavior. In India, where it is very hot, elephants like to go into ponds to cool off. Then they come back on the bank and think, "Oh, I'm all wet," so they throw sand and dirt all over themselves. Immediately they think, "Oh, I'm all dirty and hot," so they go back in the water to wash off. They keep doing this; it is senseless. We engage in the same kind of back-and-forth behavior. We are pulled one way and promise to practice the perfections and give everything to other sentient beings; then we are pulled the other way because we are so attached to our possessions.

To avoid this attachment we should think about the many benefits that come from generosity and the disadvantages of being attached to our possessions. Weigh these side by side. Compare the drawbacks of stinginess—quarrels, enemies, unhappiness, and so on—to the benefits that come from wanting to share with others. You will become excited about giving to others and very afraid of continuing to grasp things. So for generosity to arise naturally there are two thoughts to produce in the mind: enthusiasm for virtue and fear of the repercussions of bad behavior. To increase our generosity we should develop love and great compassion. Further, consider the stories about how the great sages and the Buddha in his former lives developed the practice of generosity. Through these means we can produce the perfection of generosity. Śāntideva wrote about how to do this in *Engaging in the Bodhisattva Deeds:*

> My body, likewise my possessions,
> And all the merit I create in the three times,
> I give without any hesitation at all
> In order to accomplish the aims of all others.

Someone who truly wants to benefit others is a bodhisattva. Bodhisattvas practice generosity. However, this does not mean that beginners have to actually give things physically. It does not mean we should give up our possessions or life for stupid reasons. We have to understand what should and should not be done. Beginners cannot even give small things away, much less their body and life. The sincere and spontaneous thought to give is the mind of generosity. We have to train the mind, trying again and again to create the desire to give. If done from the heart this kind of practice turns away attachment to one's belongings; it reverses the thought holding things as *mine*. When this attitude is strong enough we will have no difficulty in actually meeting the needs of others. We will be able to judge when it is best to give and when it is best not to give. When we choose not to give, our decision will not be based on stinginess; it will be skillful means based on wisdom.

The following passage from the *Compendium of the Perfections* is similar to what has been discussed already:

> "All these things belong to them;
> I have no pride in their being mine."

Thinking this amazing thought again and again
Is emulating the fully enlightened buddhas.
Whoever does this is called a bodhisattva.
This is what the inconceivable, perfect Buddha taught.

When we have possessions we should mentally give them away. We should no longer think, "These are mine." We should not take pride in giving a nice gift because, in actuality, that thing already belongs to the other person. Practice thinking this way over and over again. This is what buddhas did to attain enlightenment. This is how we should practice until we are actually able to give without any hardship. The perfection of generosity is our goal.

Beginners' minds, however, are full of attachment. The root of attachment is ignorance. Attachment and ignorance are mental problems, so the fight against them has to take place in the mind. If we do this mental practice properly, eventually a positive attitude will triumph over the negative. When that occurs one's type of birth changes; one's physical body will be different and one will have no problem giving it away. Now, however, our attitude of generosity is not mature. Even though we may have taken the bodhisattva vow promising, "From now on I dedicate myself to all others," this positive thought is still new and weak. We must gradually accustom ourselves to the thought of giving prior to physically giving things away.

There are many levels of the practice of the bodhisattva vows. Certain things at certain times are wrong actions, but at other times those very actions are appropriate. Correct actions and practices are taught stage by stage. When one is at a lower level, doing the advanced practices can be dangerous. One needs to know what should be done, when it should be done, and how it should be done. Therefore, beginner bodhisattvas practice thinking, "Whatever I have—my wealth, my body, my life—actually belongs to others." Even though they make this dedication with complete sincerity, they do not give these things in actuality. We continue to use our body and property, but we must not forget that we are using them for the benefit of others. We should think, "I am eating this food for the benefit of other sentient beings." Or, "For the benefit of others, I will wear this coat." Giving one's life to others means that from now on one is in their service. We are working to accomplish their goals: freeing them from misery and having them attain the highest achievements. One's life is an extremely important tool for completing this task. We therefore nourish and take care of the body so that we can get our work done. With this attitude there is no problem with using the things that we have mentally given to others.

Although the attitude being described may seem strange, in the past it would have been the attitude of someone who was an indentured servant. These people ate their food and wore their clothes knowing that they were doing so in service to their masters. Perhaps today it is something like a company's giving workers lunch every day for their labor. A bodhisattva's attitude is, "Even though this body and these material goods are not mine, I will use them for the purpose of attaining enlightenment in order to save others."

If bodhisattvas forget this, they incur a downfall and break the bodhisattva vow. There are various types of downfalls: heavy, intermediate, and light ones, with many subdivisions among them. In this case, the serious downfall is to fail to remember others and use things for one's own pleasure stimulated by the poisons of desire, hatred, or ignorance. We create this downfall even if our attachment is directed toward a person other than ourselves—for example, doing something for a beloved relative while neglecting all others. An intermediate downfall is less serious: it is breaking the rules without attachment. An action might not be negative by its very nature, but because it is contradictory to a precept that forbids it, it is a downfall for those who have taken the vow. For example, eating at a certain time or wearing a certain type of clothing is not essentially or naturally wrong; they are, however, incorrect actions if one has promised to abide by certain rules regarding these behaviors. Merely forgetting that one is eating food—or doing something else to nourish the body—for the benefit of other sentient beings is the least type of downfall. Nonetheless, if one has taken the bodhisattva vow, one must be careful in this regard.

How do these contraventions of the bodhisattva vow fit into the prātimokṣa system? There are four major categories of downfalls within the prātimokṣa vows: stealing, killing, lying, and sexual misconduct. According to Śāntideva in his *Compendium of Trainings,* breaking the bodhisattva vows by forgetting that one is using things that belong to others in order to benefit them is stealing. When we dedicate our belongings to others, our perception should be that the things really do belong to them; it is theft to use these things simply for our own benefit.

The *Lamrim Chenmo* contains a discussion of the nature of this downfall, because there are several different opinions regarding what it means to dedicate one's possessions to others but then still use these items. It is a major fault for a bodhisattva to do something out of attachment for him- or herself; some scholars, however, say that this is not a complete downfall. Their rationale is that because one has dedicated one's food or clothes to all sentient beings, each individual sentient being has only a very tiny share of these things. Because the value of what one takes from each one is so miniscule, one incurs only a partial downfall. Others disagree, saying that one has dedicated the entire amount of whatever it is to each and every sentient being; this being the case, the complete crime of stealing has occurred. Some others say that for the full misdeed of stealing to have occurred, the object has to belong to someone else, that person has to be harmed, and he or she must be aware of the situation. The full transgression is not complete, therefore, because even though one has dedicated one's possessions to others, they did not know it and will not be hurt by one's use of the objects.

What is the truth among these positions? The actual meaning of the statement from the *Compendium of Trainings* is that if we dedicate things to some people from the heart, then those things actually belong to them. When those people understand that these things have been given to them and feel that they now own them, we will be stealing if we use those things for our own purposes. Further, if that thing is of some value, then the misdeed will be heavy. However, the *Compendium of Trainings* goes on to say:

> No fault is incurred if you think, "I am protecting this body that is owned by others with these things that are owned by others." Servants work only for their masters' benefit; they have nothing of their own.

In other words, although it may seem wrong to avail yourself of things that you have mentally given to others and they did not give you permission to use, there will be no fault if you think, "I have dedicated everything—my body, life, and so forth—to others. From now on I will use these things only for their benefit." Śāntideva says this is similar to cases where servants' work is completely dedicated to their master, so they do not need permission to do every single task. In particular, it is proper for servants to make decisions about what to do when their master is sick or mentally disturbed. When we dedicate our possessions to all sentient beings we cannot possibly get permission to use a particular item from every single one of them. Because they are not capable of giving us their permission, we have to decide on our own whether and how to use things. As long as we have not mastered the bodhisattva attitude, this is difficult to do, but we will have no problem once we have trained ourselves to dedicate everything to others from the depths of the heart. Until then we have to be careful, because this is a dangerous area.

Another question you may have is, "Isn't this kind of giving meaningless, because we have not actually physically given these things? It almost seems as though bodhisattvas are lying. They think, 'I am giving you this,' but then do not follow through and actually give it. There is no essence to that kind of generosity." This disrespectful attitude arises because we do not see the true nature of reality. Even though we are not giving materially, this thought is not worthless. It is a very special attitude; it is a wonderful, perfect thought. The mental attitude of wishing to give grows into the marvelous thought of giving without expectation or hesitation. There is no doubt about the efficacy of this practice.

(c') THE DIVISIONS OF GENEROSITY

This topic is divided into three:

(1') How everyone should practice it
(2') Divisions of generosity relative to particular persons
(3') Divisions of actual generosity (chapters 9–10)

The first two divisions of generosity are from the point of view of the practitioner. There are different practices for lay practitioners and for those who have taken ordination. However, some practices are common to both, so the first topic is how both laypeople and those who are ordained should practice generosity. The second division explains the differences between how a lay person and an ordained person should practice. The third topic discusses the natural divisions in generosity itself—for example, the generosity of giving material goods, the generosity of giving the Dharma, and the generosity of giving protection.

(1') HOW EVERYONE SHOULD PRACTICE IT

The way that lay and ordained people practice in common has two aspects. The first concerns six superior qualities, and second refers to the way in which the practice of generosity includes all of the other perfections. As for the first, it can be stated in brief that the six superior or holy qualities of the practice of the perfection of generosity are: the support or cause is superior, the material thing that one gives is superior, the purpose is superior, the method is superior and gracious, the dedication is superior, and it involves a special, superior purification. Now I will explain a bit about each of these in turn.

The support or foundation of the perfection of generosity is bodhicitta: the desire to attain enlightenment for the benefit of other sentient beings. With this thought, any practice—generosity, ethical discipline, and so forth—becomes a Mahayana practice. Every bodhisattva practice is grounded in this thought. So even giving a mouthful of food becomes the perfection of generosity if given with this intention. With some other motivation one's generosity will be meritorious but it will not be one of the six perfections. If one has a smaller purpose, no matter how much one gives—even a house filled with gold—it is still not the perfection of generosity.

The second quality is that the material thing that one gives is superior. When practitioners take the bodhisattva vow they dedicate everything that they have to others. So when they give something they think, "This thing belongs to them; I am just returning their property." Remember, this does not mean that they give everything away all at once. It has to be the right time and the appropriate situation. But in general they no longer think, "This is mine." A bodhisattva keeps this in mind while giving particular things to individuals. He or she does not think, "I am giving this specific thing to this particular person." They know that is what they are doing, but they bear in mind that all these things belong to others.

The third quality is the superior purpose for performing an act of generosity. One's goal is to benefit all sentient beings, both temporarily and ultimately. One is trying to give them temporary pleasure, but one's final purpose is to lead them to the highest, everlasting happiness of enlightenment. When one gives things to alleviate others' hunger, misery, or pain, one is giving temporary happiness. That act of generosity does not directly help them achieve ultimate happiness. A bodhisattva knows that, until he or she attains perfect enlightenment, one can only help other beings in a limited way. Therefore, bodhisattvas wish to attain enlightenment quickly in order to be able to save all sentient beings. They dedicate the merit of temporarily helping others so that they may ultimately be able to help others achieve the highest happiness. Nothing about their own purpose is here; their intent is to provisionally and permanently benefit others. This dedication becomes the cause for their accomplishment of the accumulation of merit so that they can really help others.

Understanding the superior, skillful method of the practice of generosity is a bit more difficult. The method is to give with a special type of wisdom. We must realize that all three spheres of the act of giving are empty of inherent existence. We should not grasp the giver, the gift, or the action of giving as real or absolute. Sometimes the three spheres are presented as the gift, the giver, and the recipient to whom you give. In either case, you as the giver, the action, the gift, and the recipient are all illusory in the ultimate sense. They are empty of any inherent subsistence. They are relative in nature. To give skillfully we must have some understanding of this. Higher level bodhisattvas have a special kind of gnosis—a direct realization, not just a conceptual understanding—of emptiness. This realization about the nature of reality gives them a special kind of skill. We beginners do not have this kind of nonconceptual realization of śūnyatā. It is achieved on the āryan stage. However, even now we can imagine this conceptually. We can have a rough understanding that the various spheres of the act of giving are not real in an ultimate sense. We should understand that things do not ultimately exist as they appear.

The fifth quality is the supreme dedication. After we give a superior material thing, we dedicate the merit of that action to others rather than having some expectation for ourselves. In other words, we dedicate the merit of the action to attain perfect enlightenment quickly in order to truly help other sentient beings. By making this dedication we create a particular kind of merit. In contrast, when we give something we usually expect something back for ourselves. If we give with that attitude it will not be a superior dedication.

The last quality is the holy purity of generosity. When we practice the perfection of generosity we try to give with a pure thought. The pure thought is the intent to counter the mental afflictions and the obstructions to omniscience. The mental afflictions are obstacles to liberation; they are the passions such as desire, hatred, jealousy, pride, stinginess, and so on. Even those who have removed the mental afflictions, such as arhats, have still not achieved perfect enlightenment. They are limited because they have knowledge obstacles, or obstacles to omniscience. These more subtle obstructions keep them from being as perfect as buddhas. Eliminating these two obstacles is the holy purification.

If our practice of generosity has these six qualities, it is a bodhisattva practice. It does not matter whether one is a lay person or ordained; because our giving has these six superior qualities, it is a great practice.

The second way that all beings practice the perfection of generosity in common is drawn from Haribhadra's *Long Explanation of the Perfection of Wisdom Sutra in Eight Thousand Lines*. Haribhadra explains that when one practices the perfection of generosity, all the other perfections are included in that practice. Tsongkhapa uses the example of giving the Dharma to elucidate this. *Giving the Dharma* is speaking even just one or two words that lead the audience to peace, emancipation, or even some small ordinary good. The ethical discipline of generosity is to give with good conduct. This is more than ordinary good conduct, such as giving without lying. A bodhisattva's ethical discipline is taking care to avoid the desire for any kind of return for him- or herself. Bodhisattvas must be vigilant at all times in order to refrain from dedicating the merit of their generosity for their own emancipation or happiness. Their ethical discipline is to guard the mind, always making sure that their motivation is to benefit others. The third perfection, patience, is to be able to bear any hardship when one is practicing generosity. Even though others may make one's situation unpleasant by acting disagreeably, one endures it without getting upset or losing one's intent to attain enlightenment for the benefit of all sentient beings.

The next perfection is perseverance, or diligence. It is taking joy in any type of meritorious action. Instead of obsessing about one's own problems, one finds joy in doing things for others. This happiness gives one courage. Within the context of practicing all six perfections as part of the perfection of generosity, the perfection of meditative stabilization does not have its usual meaning of single-pointed concentration. Here one-pointedness is a mental attitude focused solely on the benefit of others. It means that one concentrates on benefiting others by one's generosity, dedicating even the merit of an action for the attainment of enlightenment in order to benefit others, not at all for oneself. The sixth perfection is wisdom. It is realization of the true nature of reality. Understanding the emptiness of the act of giving, of the giver, and of the recipient cuts the root of ignorance. One gives with the understanding that the gift, the giver, and the recipient are like a magical illusion; they are relative, based on thought and on causes and conditions.

Even giving a small gift with all six of the perfections is very powerful. How does this generosity help others? The best way to help others is to quickly become a buddha. We dedicate the merit of an action to quickly attain enlightenment so that we can lead others to ultimate bliss. We are not acting for our own purpose or pleasure; we want to help others. This is the generosity of generosity.

(2') DIVISIONS OF GENEROSITY RELATIVE
TO PARTICULAR PERSONS

Generally the advice given to lay bodhisattvas is to practice generosity by giving material gifts. Because monks and nuns have taken up a simple life in order to fully dedicate themselves to practice, they are not able to give a lot of money or other things. It can take a lot of time and effort to get material goods. If monks and nuns put a lot of sweat and toil into obtaining such things, it could damage their ethical discipline. In any case, gifts of material goods provide only temporary enjoyment and happiness to others. And it is not at all certain that material gifts will result in even temporary happiness. Monks and nuns are therefore instructed to place more emphasis on giving the Dharma than giving material goods.

In addition, the *Bodhisattva Vows of Liberation (Bodhisattva-prātimokṣa-catuṣka-nirhāra)* says that the generosity of giving the Dharma is far superior to giving material things:

> O Śāriputra, the amount of merit created by a lay bodhisattva offer-
> ing as many buddha fields filled with jewels as there are sand grains in
> the Ganges River to each completely enlightened buddha is far
> exceeded by the merit created by an ordained bodhisattva giving even
> a four-line stanza of religious instruction. Therefore, Śāriputra, the
> Tathāgata did not tell ordained bodhisattvas to give material goods.

This sutra seems to say that it is not suitable for ordained people to give material gifts. However, the *Compendium of Trainings* says that we should understand this passage to mean that ordained monks and nuns should not give
material things if it interrupts their analysis, meditation, or other practices. This
does not imply that ordained people should not give anything. Monks and nuns
should not keep what they have, find, or are given. Although they should not
strive to create material wealth, if they have many possessions because of their
previous merit, they can and should give them. Giving religious teachings
results in far more merit than giving ordinary things because one does it so that
others can achieve the highest happiness of liberation and enlightenment. It
would, of course, create great merit if someone gave a world filled with gold to
thousands of buddhas, but even more virtue comes from teaching one short
passage with pure Mahayana motivation. If lay people have knowledge, they
too can share it by teaching others. In other words, the difference is a matter of
emphasis; both lay and ordained people can do both types of giving.

Geshe Sharawa, one of the great Kadampa teachers, said to a disciple, "I
will not tell you about the benefits of generosity. I will tell you about the faults
of stinginess." Sharawa said those who work for material goods in order to
give them away in the practice of generosity did not please him. We should
not go out and break the rules of proper conduct trying to accumulate things
that we can give away as gifts. At the same time, we should not have strong
attachment for the things we already possess. We should meditate to reduce
our attachment.

(3') Divisions of actual generosity

Bodhisattvas want to be the source of all others' enjoyment. Just as water, air,
and the other great elements are the necessary underpinning for the existence
of sentient beings, bodhisattvas want to be the foundation of all living creatures' benefit. Śāntideva writes in *Engaging in the Bodhisattva Deeds:*[1]

> May I always support the life
> Of all boundless creatures,

Just like the great elements
Such as earth, space, and so on.

A bodhisattva puts his or her body, life, wealth, and energy into the service of others.

There are three types of generosity:

(a") The gift of the teachings
(b")   The gift of fearlessness
(c") Material gifts (chapters 9–10)

(a") THE GIFT OF THE TEACHINGS

The gift of Dharma is to teach others with unperverted motivation. One teaches whatever will be to others' benefit—whether temporary or final. The gift of the teachings is therefore not necessarily an explanation of scriptures; it can be experiential advice that leads indirectly to emancipation. Out of love and compassion one can teach in many ways and on many levels to help others who are under the power of hatred, jealousy, attachment, and ignorance. Any instruction that aids others' progress toward bliss and liberation is giving the gift of the teachings.

We should give teachings in a different manner from the way we teach ordinary sciences or technological subjects. We should not teach motivated by a desire for fame, wealth, honor, and so on. Teaching with such an intent can be harmful to oneself and others. It can become a contaminated, negative activity. The right motivation is solely to want to help others. The gift of the Dharma is giving teachings in order to lead others to clear away ignorance and gain the wisdom that leads to emancipation. Giving pure teachings on the prātimokṣa, bodhisattva, or tantric vows, or instruction on how to take and keep the precepts, are ways to truly help others. Leading others to the highest happiness is the best type of giving. Immeasurable benefits arise from teaching to help others stop their negative actions and thoughts.

(b") THE GIFT OF FEARLESSNESS

The second type of generosity is to give others protection from fear. Sometimes people fear other people. They are frightened of punishment, or of being killed or robbed. Sometimes they are afraid of wild animals or inanimate things such as water, fire, or wind storms. Whatever one does to alleviate others' fear is the practice of generosity. So this kind of generosity has many forms. We can keep others from falling down, ease their hunger or thirst, save their lives, shield them from harm, safeguard their wealth, shelter them from danger, and so on. We start with what we can do; even saving an insect is the practice of giving protection. From small and easy tasks we progress to greater ones. There are many opportunities for practice if one is concerned and interested. We can find something to do on some scale every day.

In Tibet we had a good system for practicing the generosity that provides fearlessness. On special holidays like Buddha's birthday, a lot of wealthy lay people would go to slaughterhouses. People would pay to save the sheep and yaks from being butchered. We can do this too whenever we have the opportunity. We can do this daily in a simple way or it can be a very high and complicated practice. If one wishes to practice the Mahayana, one works to alleviate others' fears on many levels, at every moment, all the time.

(c") Material Gifts

Most people consider generosity to be the giving of material gifts. This is elaborately explained here under two headings:

(1") The generosity of actually giving material things (chapters 9–10)
(2") The generosity that is just mental (chapter 10)

Thus the proper way to give has two levels: actually giving and mentally giving.

(1") The generosity of actually giving material things

This section has three subtopics:

(a)) How to give away material things (chapters 9–10)
(b)) What to do if you are unable to give (chapter 10)
(c)) Relying on the remedies for the hindrances to generosity (chapter 10)

(a)) How to away give material things

There are four topics in this section:

(1)) Recipients of giving
(2)) The motivation for giving
(3)) How to give (chapter 10)
(4)) Things to give (chapter 10)

In order to attain enlightenment a bodhisattva must accumulate a vast amount of merit by engaging in practices such as generosity. In that context, those to whom one gives are like a field in which one plants the seeds of virtue that will grow into a harvest of virtue perhaps a hundred times more vast than the original virtue. The first topic explains the field to whom we give. In the second topic Tsongkhapa explains the motivation for generosity. Next is an explanation of the actual way to give: both the proper thought and actions as well as what should not be done. Finally there is a discussion of the things we should actually give.

(1)) RECIPIENTS OF GIVING

We should practice generosity toward all other sentient beings without any discrimination. There are no exceptions. But here we divide sentient beings into ten categories taking account of our usual attitudes toward others. Ordinarily we have a positive attitude toward some and a negative attitude toward others. We see some as our friends, others as enemies, some as beneath us, and others as our superiors. So to clarify how a bodhisattva should practice, we first look at how we commonly divide sentient beings. Once we recognize all these sentient beings as objects of generosity, we consider how to think about them, how to properly give to them, and the manner of dedication. These subjects will follow.

The first three divisions of sentient beings are dear friends who help us, enemies who harm us, and those toward whom we feel neutral because they have done nothing to either help or harm us. Bodhisattvas should not give others gifts reasoning, "These are my friends. They have done so much for me." Nor should they feel anger or fear toward someone to whom they give something. They should also not give carelessly to those about whom they feel neutral. Bodhisattvas have to level out their attitude toward these recipients.

The fourth category are those who have good qualities such as pure moral conduct or excellent knowledge. The fifth group is those who have various faults such as breaking their vows or engaging in other types of unsound conduct. We tend to give more to people we consider good and less to those who appear to be bad. We should not discriminate this way.

The sixth category is a result of our conceit; we look down on those who have fewer good qualities than ourselves. The seventh and eighth categories are also determined by judging others in terms of ourselves; we feel competitive toward those who are our equals, and we are jealous of those who are our superiors. The ninth group are those who have wealth and happiness and last are those who are miserable and poor.

Every sentient being fits into one of these categories. We usually pick and choose among them; we want to be generous to some and not to others. To practice the perfection of generosity we have to develop a nondiscriminatory attitude toward them all. The bodhisattva practice is to give equally, treating all sentient beings with love and compassion.

(2)) The motivation for giving

When practicing generosity one's attitude is the most important factor; it determines whether one's practice is only for oneself or for the benefit of all sentient beings. There are two subdivisions here:

(a')) What kind of motivation is required
(b')) What kind of motivation must be eliminated

Tsongkhapa details the nature of the positive thought, both in general and in particular instances. We will also examine the kind of thought to avoid when practicing generosity.

(a')) What kind of motivation is required

There are three aspects to the positive thought: the purpose of giving, the thing given, and field or recipient. The purpose of every bodhisattva practice is to attain perfect enlightenment in order to help others. When doing any kind of virtuous practice one should have this goal in the back of one's mind. In this case one should think, "I want to become an enlightened buddha because only an enlightened being can truly help others. In order to do that I have to accomplish the accumulation of merit and wisdom. The practice of generosity is a way to do that."

The practice of generosity depends upon one's intent. People have different reasons for practicing generosity; depending on their purpose some acts of generosity are bodhisattva practices and others are not. For example, one could give with the intent to indirectly hurt someone, to get some return in the present, to have wealth in a future rebirth, or to achieve one's own liberation from samsara. If one's purpose is correct, even giving a small thing becomes a great Mahayana practice. Do not be deterred from practicing generosity because you think that you do not have the right attitude. Tsongkhapa is emphasizing the qualifications for bodhisattva practice, but ordinary people who have little compassion for others can still practice generosity. It is not bodhisattva generosity, but it is generosity and it is still meritorious.

Candrakīrti says in the *Commentary on the "Middle Way"*: [2]

Those with hostility and no love for others
May only desire their own benefit,
But their generosity results in future wealth;
They are saved from destitute poverty.

There are so many ways of doing a practice, and the various levels are based on one's intent. For example, wealthy people may give a great deal of money only intending to improve their own position. They may give with harsh words and a hard manner; they have no concern for others and only want a return for themselves. Such giving is mixed. In one way, it is very negative because they have such a poor attitude. However, because their generosity benefits someone else, they are still acting virtuously. The merit from their action will result in samsaric benefit; they will have wealth in the future. In comparison, giving even one small gift without discrimination, wholly for the benefit of all mother sentient beings, creates enormous virtue. The merit is as great as the number of sentient beings. The power of attitude is why bodhisattvas achieve enlightenment so quickly.

The object given is of less significance than why one is giving, but our attitude toward that object is important. The second aspect of a motivation is the way we look at the things we give. From the time of taking the bodhisattva vows a bodhisattva considers that all his or her belongings have already been given to others. In other words, bodhisattvas feel that the things they use are actually on loan from others. It is as if sentient beings have said, "Please hold on to these things. Use them well. If I need them at some time, you can give them back to me then." So when we give we do not think, "I am giving them something of *mine,*" or "I am giving this because they need *my* things."

The third aspect of a motivation is the field or the object of generosity. In order to practice generosity we need someone to receive our gifts. We should think, "I can practice generosity only by giving to these sentient beings. So these people are helping me to create the virtues that are the cause to attain enlightenment. They are truly my spiritual friends." Usually the term *spiritual friend* refers to a religious teacher or a buddha. Here we apply it to sentient beings because they too are a special support through which we attain enlightenment.

There are many detailed explanations about the features of generosity found in the *Questions of Subāhu Sutra (Subāhu-paripṛcchā-sūtra)* and the *Compendium of the Perfections.* The *Compendium of the Perfections* contains a stanza summarizing these three facets of the correct motivation for giving:

When a beggar comes before him, a bodhisattva thinks
About increasing his accumulation of merit to attain enlightenment,

> Is aware that he is returning the others' possessions,
> And perceives the beggar as his spiritual friend.

One aspect of thought applies universally to all the recipients of what we give: we should recognize that they provide us with the opportunity to give; they are therefore the source of our perfection of generosity. In other words, they are the field of our spiritual growth. In addition, we should concentrate on countering the specific wrong attitudes for each category of sentient being. When we give to those we consider enemies because they have tried to harm us, we should feel love. They are the object of our mercy because they are under the sway of a powerful internal enemy that causes them to attempt to hurt us. Out of attachment, ordinary people single out for favor those who have helped them in the past. Instead, we need to feel equanimity for those we have designated as friends. As for those who have superior qualities, such as pure morality, instead of feeling jealous we should admire them. For the poor and miserable we should have a special kind of compassion. We should not be proud that we are better than someone else; instead, we should feel compassionate love for those who are beneath us in some way. And we should not view our equals as competitors. We need to level out this rough, discriminating attitude and regard them all the same way—with love.

It is true that sometimes the field makes a difference. Certain fields have more power to make things grow. Similarly, actions in regard to certain types of people are very powerful; perfect buddhas, āryan beings, and those who have been meditating on love for all mother sentient beings for a long time are particularly potent fields. The results of what we do to such people, whether good or bad, are magnified. Some sentient beings on an ordinary level are powerful fields as well; these include, for example, one's parents or an ordinary person who has given one religious instruction. Someone who wants to have good things in this and future lives, or desires his or her own salvation, may choose to be generous to these types of beings rather than others because of the greater results that will be received. But bodhisattvas are different. They do not discriminate among sentient beings this way. From a bodhisattva's point of view, all these fields are equal. They do not neglect the low ones and give to the high ones so that they get more merit. Bodhisattvas practice generosity out of compassion and love, not for what they can gain in return. They dedicate to others even the merit that comes from their generosity.

Candrakīrti says:

> Having an equal attitude toward all,
> And giving without stinginess

To all whether a good or poor vessel,
Is the pure type of giving.

Giving without any miserliness—
Both material things with love
And the results of giving at the same time—
Is praised as the best by the holy ones.

And an arhat extolled the Buddha in the *Praise of Infinite Qualities:*

You said that if some people see a destitute inferior seeking alms,
But heartlessly look for someone with higher qualities because they
   desire results,
They have a bad attitude. Although they give, they are like a beggar
   themselves.
Therefore, you give to all who ask with great compassion.

(b') What kind of motivation must be eliminated

Because motivation is so important, we should also know what kind of attitudes to avoid when practicing generosity.

1. *Avoid holding a wrong view as superior.* The first wrong view is to believe that no results will come from giving. It is particularly wrong to teach that there is will be no results in a future life. It is also incorrect to think that the practice of generosity includes giving things that are deliberately harmful. Just because one gives a gift, one is not automatically practicing the Dharma. For example, giving a gun to someone who wants to kill is not religious practice. Furthermore, one should not give a gift thinking that good fortune will accrue for oneself. Another wrong view is to hold that merely by practicing generosity all good things—both mundane and supramundane—will result. In other words, it is not correct that the practice of generosity on its own will temporarily suppress attachment while one is in samsara, and that it will ultimately free one from rebirth because nirvana is definitive freedom from attachment. This is not to say that all the last two views are completely wrong; however, a bodhisattva should avoid giving selfishly, looking for his or her own good fortune or liberation.

2. *Avoid conceit.* One should not look down on beggars nor should one give in competition with one's peers. Do not think, "My neighbor gave ten dollars yesterday, so I will give twenty dollars today to show him up." After giving we should not look down on others thinking, "I am a great donor. I gave

so much. I am better than those other people who gave less. They are stingy." Even though one has done something good by giving to those in need, one's merit will degenerate because of this arrogance.

The *Purification of the Obscurations of Karma Sutra (Karmāvaraṇa-viśuddhi-sūtra)* says that ordinary individuals often get angry when they see that others are not as generous as themselves. Anger is a nonvirtue; if one gives in anger one will get a bad result. It becomes an obstacle to the practice of generosity. Similarly, if one is practicing ethical discipline and in anger says bad things about someone who is not acting properly, one ruins one's own morality. Using generosity or moral conduct as a reason to get angry is not right. This may make other people angry with the person singled out for improperly practicing those virtues. They may lose faith, do harmful things, and cause others to do so as well. That will cause many, many bad results, perhaps even rebirth in a lower realm. The same principle applies to the practice of patience; it is not productive to one's practice to become impatient with those who are impatient. This leads instead to many negative actions. Because of conceit, one's practice of the perfections will not be fruitful.

So what kind of attitude should we have? The *Praise of Infinite Qualities* says we should not praise ourselves even when our study and learning have become great. No matter how many excellent qualities we have or how much wisdom we have developed, we should not glorify ourselves. We should be humble; we should respect and hold as superior those with lower qualities. To deflate our conceit we should examine ourselves, not overlooking even the smallest fault. Bodhisattvas always treat other sentient beings as higher than themselves. They view themselves as a servant for others.

3. *Avoid dependency.* Bodhisattvas do not give to others with the thought that it will make them famous.

4. *Avoid discouragement.* To avoid low spirits, bodhisattvas develop joy and happiness prior to giving. Because they are very clear about what they are going to do, they have no regret afterward. We may occasionally regret an act of generosity; we may feel that we should not have given away something. Not only should we not have any remorse, we should admire our generosity afterward. When we hear about the fantastic acts of generosity performed by past bodhisattvas, we should not become disheartened and think such difficult feats will be impossible for us. Do not put yourself down. You will be able to do it. It may take a while before you are ready, and you will have to practice. But you should think, "I have the potential. Even animals and insects have a latent ability to attain enlightenment. If they can do it, why not me? I am a human being—so why can't I do these things? Of course I can do them." Encourage yourself like this.

5. *Avoid turning your back.* We should not have a retaliatory attitude. In other words a bodhisattva does not respond differently to sentient beings no matter how they act toward him or her. Whether they are friendly, adversarial, or neither friend nor enemy, a bodhisattva sees that they all equally want to be free from misery and to have happiness. On this basis there is no difference between them. A bodhisattva therefore treats them all equally.

6. *Avoid expectation of a return.* This is giving with the hope that one will benefit from generosity in this life. We should not anticipate that by giving something as small as a mouse we will gain something as large as a yak. Why is it wrong to give with this expectation? If we give wanting a return, it eliminates the happiness of sentient beings, burns us with the fire of attachment, and we have no power to remove suffering. When we see that this type of motivation only causes suffering, we will give it up and generate the opposite attitude.

7. *Avoid desiring fruition.* We also should not give with the idea that we will get a result in a future life. Bodhisattvas do not practice generosity intending that their actions are seeds that will ripen as prosperity in a future life. That attitude is to want a good life in samsara for oneself. A bodhisattva should see that every aspect of samsaric life has no real essence, is inferior, and mixed with suffering. Instead, bodhisattvas focus on the worth and benefit of highest perfect enlightenment. So bodhisattvas do not give gifts looking for samsaric wealth. Do not misunderstand. When a bodhisattva or anyone else is generous, moral, patient, and so on, the result of these meritorious actions is to be born in an excellent high rebirth. However, a bodhisattva is not looking for these things. This is not contradictory. It is not right for bodhisattvas to view these results as their ultimate goal. They should not be emotionally attached to them and strive to obtain only them. However, rebirth with an excellent body, wealth, and retinue is a suitable temporary goal. It is a vehicle or a means to reach the main goal—perfect buddhahood. Ordinary bodhisattvas—those who have not had a direct realization of emptiness—have to be reborn in samsara. In samsara they need a perfect body and an appropriate environment in order to help others. So we should not reject these results; they are an important, albeit provisional, tool. A bodhisattva should simply avoid putting all his or her effort into achieving a samsaric body and wealth as an ultimate goal.

In the *Compendium of Trainings,* Śāntideva provides details about other attitudes we should avoid when practicing generosity. It is wrong livelihood to think that, when we are charitable, we will be recognized and honored by the mighty and powerful. Also, we should not practice generosity only because we fear experiencing poverty at a later date. This kind of generosity does create virtue and the merit will produce good results, but these results will be limited because the motivation for giving was small. Furthermore, we should not give to the needy with the intent to deceive them. Do not give while feeling dislike, anger, or when distracted by other things. These emotions are indicative of a mind that has no compassion for others' problems and misery. Even when we generously give to beggars purely motivated by love and compassion, the recipients of our gifts may say or do bad things. We should not get upset or angry in reaction. Do not blame them or disparage them. Instead, we should have more compassion and love for them. Situations and emotions like this normally occur. We need to recognize them because, if we do not deal with them properly, they can weaken or ruin our practice of generosity. This is why Tsongkhapa describes various circumstances and the normal reactions that we have.

Finally we should not be swayed by others. Someone may tell us that it is foolish to practice generosity in an attempt to influence us to stop practicing and act in another way. When we understand the nature of generosity, the value of generosity, the types of generosity, the correct motivation, the results of generosity, and so on, nobody can destroy our practice. Such people will not be able to convince us that our actions are wrong. If we do not have a firm understanding of these topics, we will be weak. Then if someone says, "You are stupid," we can lose our practice completely. So, in the beginning, we need to study, think, and concentrate to establish these thoughts firmly in our mind. With this understanding, even when we are doing something small, we will feel joyful before we begin, while we are doing it, and afterward as well.

❖ 10 ❖

How to Give

(3)) How to give
    (a')) How not to give
    (b')) How to give
(4)) Things to give
    (a')) Brief presentation of the things that are and
        are not to be given
    (b')) Detailed explanation of the things that are and
        are not to be given
        (1')) Detailed explanation about internal things
            that are and are not to be given
            (a")) Inappropriate giving from the view-
                point of time
            (b")) Inappropriate giving from the view-
                point of purpose
            (c")) Inappropriate giving from the viewpoint
                of the one who asks for something
        (2')) Detailed explanation about external things
            that are and are not to be given
            (a")) How not to give external things
                (1")) Inappropriate giving from the
                    viewpoint of time
                (2")) Inappropriate giving from the
                    viewpoint of the gift
                (3")) Inappropriate giving from the
                    viewpoint of the person
                (4")) Inappropriate giving from the
                    viewpoint of material things
                (5")) Inappropriate giving from the
                    viewpoint of purpose
            (b")) How to give external things

(b)) What to do if you are unable to give
(c)) Relying on the remedies for the hindrances to generosity
   (1)) The hindrance of not being used to generosity
   (2)) The hindrance of declining fortune
   (3)) The hindrance of attachment
   (4)) The hindrance of not seeing the goal
(2") The generosity that is just mental
(d') A summary

---

(3)) How to give

WHEN BODHISATTVAS have the opportunity to practice generosity their joy is greater than the happiness of arhats who have attained emancipation. Their happy anticipation cannot be measured. Actually giving their wealth, body, and merits to others makes them even happier. As Candrakīrti says in his *Commentary on the "Middle Way":*[1]

> Hearing the words "please give,"
> Produces joy for bodhisattvas
> Greater than the happiness of arhats.
> So what needs to be said about actually giving?

Advanced practitioners have no problem engaging in generosity because they have already developed a skillful mental practice. But beginners are in the dark about what to do when they hear such instructions as, "Everything should be given." Not knowing what to do, how to do it, and what is going to happen makes us anxious. Understanding is like a mirror; in a mirror we can see the dirt on our face and take sensible steps to remove it. Similarly, knowing the details about how to give is important in order to be able to incorporate this practice into our daily life.

Even if we have a good motivation, there is a correct and incorrect way to actually give. Therefore, the discussion of how to give has two subsections:

(a')) How not to give
(b')) How to give

Although Tsongkhapa added some information about particular situations, he drew most of the following information from Asaṅga's *Bodhisattva Levels*.

(a')) HOW NOT TO GIVE

Giving is good, but there are ways to give that are wrong. If we give a lot but give it improperly, harshly, without respect, or make it difficult for others, we will lessen our good qualities and make others dissatisfied. Of course, there are exceptions to any rule, particularly if breaking that rule would be beneficial for the recipient of one's gift. However, without any special consideration of that sort, doing the following would be bad manners and should be avoided:

1) It is not right to make someone wait a long time if we could give something to him or her right away. We should give as soon as we can. If there is a spiritual purpose for waiting, it is okay to postpone our generosity, but it is wrong to delay giving needlessly.

2) We should not make someone suffer or do difficult tasks before we give something. For example, we should not say, "If you want this food you have to do such and such first."

3) We should not make people do something contrary to the Dharma or to ordinary, appropriate behavior in order to receive our charity. For example, it is not proper to say, "Kill that creature, then I will give you some money." This also pertains to animals; for example, we should not make a dog do something wrong before giving it a treat.

4) We should not promise to give a certain amount and then reduce that amount.

5) We should not keep an account of how much we have given or how much someone has received. It is not right to inquire along the lines, "Didn't I do this for you last year?" or, "How much did you get before?"

6) If we are giving a number of things to someone, we should not dole them out little by little if it is suitable to give them all at once.

7) If we become a powerful ruler, it is incorrect to take someone's wife or child and give them to someone else. Such things do happen in the world, so do not dismiss this instruction out of hand.

8) It is wrong to take by force things that belong to our parents, friends, or children and give them to others. This is taking from people without their willingness.

9) Our generosity should not harm someone else. It is wrong to give in a way that hurts either the recipient or anyone else.

10) When one is practicing generosity, it is better to carry out the action oneself, if possible. We create greater merit when we act with the proper thought and in the proper manner, instead of making someone else perform the action for us. There are exceptions, but generally *action* refers to one's own mental, physical, and verbal activity.

11) We should not disturb or discourage the recipients of our generosity by slandering them directly or indirectly, or by saying harsh words prior to giving.

12) Someone who has taken vows should not break those religious rules and then give.

13) It is wrong for a bodhisattva to accumulate things for a long time in order to give them away later. In general, wealth is the foundation of many kinds of disasters and suffering. First, we endure the misery of not being able to acquire it. Then, if we do become prosperous, we have the misery of trying to protect our possessions. Finally, when our wealth decays or is destroyed, we become depressed. Even trying to accumulate wealth in order to give it away leads to various faults. Mental afflictions such as stinginess may arise because we do not want to give anything until we have a certain amount. It is a type of greediness not to want to give something until a certain point in time.

Craving fame, we may try to collect a lot of money to give all at once in order to gain renown for our generosity. We may get angry because we endure hardships preventing others from taking our things until we accumulate a specific amount. Most of the time, before we get to the point of distributing all our material goods, they will be lost or damaged and we cannot accomplish our goal of giving them all at once. Our struggle to deal with these difficulties prevents us from doing other worthwhile activities. Furthermore, there is no particular special merit to saving in order to give a lot all at once. In fact, while we are accumulating things we may be turning away those who need our assistance. Our lack of generosity may make them upset or create other disturbing emotions in them. Not only do we turn away those in need, when we finally do give all this accumulated wealth we may end up giving it to someone who does not need it. Therefore, it is best if bodhisattvas give whatever they have to whoever needs it rather than trying to accumulate wealth to give.

Nāgārjuna writes to his friend the king in the *Friendly Letter (Suhṛl-leka)*:

> Understand that wealth is impermanent and without essence.
> Therefore practice generosity properly and accumulate merit.
> There is no better friend than the practice of generosity.

Worldly wealth is always changing and will not remain. It has no value in and of itself. However, material goods can be used to obtain our essential goal if we give them with love to benefit others. There is no better friend than giving this way. If we are helpful to others no one will rise as our enemy during this life. Even if we are not looking for a friend, our generosity will make us friends. Whether we want to or not we will be born into a future life; that is the nature of things. Our present generosity will lead us to be reborn with wealth, have it throughout our life, and have many helpful friends as well. They will assist us in the same way and even more than we help others now. Generosity is also critical for attaining the final goal of buddhahood. The perfect environment of a buddha field is the result of generosity. A buddha field lacks nothing; it has every physical and mental perfection. So there is no better friend than the practice of generosity from now until enlightenment.

(b')) How to give

If we avoid the wrong ways of giving, our generosity will be helpful to others. Even giving just one cent will create many merits and make ourselves and others happy. So how should we give? We should strive to use our body, speech, and mind in a positive way. When we give we should smile, speak honestly, and not look angry. We should not treat some recipients with more respect than others; we should honor everyone equally. If we possibly can, we should give directly rather than having someone else give on our behalf. We should give at the right time and our gift should not be harmful to others. We should be able to deal patiently with any physical or mental difficulties. We usually give away items of lesser quality and keep the better ones for ourselves. Now we should give the best things and give everything that we had planned. In short, we should practice generosity with patience, joy, respect, and wisdom.

Bodhisattvas do not practice generosity to get the results that come from giving correctly; they give to benefit others. Nevertheless, the *Chapter of the Truth Speaker (Satyaka-parivarta)* says:

> The result of respectful generosity is that others, your relatives and so on, will serve you. From giving with your own hands, others will always honor you. From giving in a timely manner, you will accomplish your goals on time.

Furthermore, the *Treasury of Knowledge (Abhidharmakośa)* says that by giving with our own hands we will obtain extensive wealth. The result of giving in a way that is not harmful to others is that in the future our possessions will not be adversely affected by fire, weather, warfare, or animate beings. This stability is in contrast to the experience of others, who may obtain a lot of wealth only to have it destroyed or lost. If we bear the difficulties that come with actively engaging in giving, in the future people will feel kindly toward us and want to be close to us.

There are always exceptions. Acting in ways contrary to the advice just given is appropriate if it is for the purpose of helping another person. For example, on occasion it is proper to have someone else give on your behalf. To help someone who is much attached to his or her own possessions learn to practice generosity, we can approach this person and respectfully say, "I have a lot of a certain type of item and I want to give them to others so that I can help them." We can then explain the benefits and importance of charity and continue, "For that purpose I need people to whom I can give these things. If you come in contact with anyone in need of them, please bring him or her to me. If they cannot travel, please come yourself and take these things from me to give to them." This person may have never wanted to share anything in his entire life, but since he is not losing anything of his own he may enjoy fulfilling our request. He can help someone else by bringing them to us or by giving them our things directly. In this way we plant a seed to help this person eliminate his or her stinginess. Little by little, this person may come to enjoy helping others. He may become more generous and start giving something of his own. From a small start, non-attachment can be developed; as selfishness decreases, interest in helping others increases until it becomes great.

In a similar way we can help our teachers, students, or friends who are willing to give but have no wealth. With the intention of helping these people practice generosity, we can have them give away our possessions. This kind of bodhisattva practice increases one's merit; not only are we practicing generosity ourselves, we are causing others to give. If bodhisattvas do not have anything to give they can do other activities or teach the practice of generosity. For example, sometimes beggars need things but we have nothing to give them. If we know some faithful and wealthy practitioners, we can tell the beggars, "Go to these people for alms." We could even go along with them to help them get what they need. This helps the rich people use their wealth in a positive way and helps the destitute get what they need. These are some ways to put generosity into practice. They are all part of the bodhisattva practice of forming a close relationship with sentient beings in order to be able to help them spiritually.

(4)) Things to give

Now that we have looked at the motivation for giving, to whom to give, and how to give, we will examine what should be given. This has two subtopics:

(a')) Brief presentation of the things that are and are not to be given
(b')) Detailed explanation of the things that are and are not to be given

(a')) Brief presentation of the things that are and are not to be given

In general, whatever we give should bring pleasure at present, be free from the causes for lower rebirth, and result in the happiness of a higher rebirth. In the long run these things should bring about the ultimate positive result by helping the recipients eliminate sinful actions and leading them to create virtue. Therefore, both from the short- and long-term perspective, the things we give should be meritorious. We can give something that is temporarily unpleasant but ultimately brings blissful happiness. This is similar to a physician's giving a patient an injection: it may be painful but the long-term result is helpful.

If something is harmful both at present and in the future, then it should not be given. Something that is desirable in the present but harmful in the long run also should not be given. For example, wise parents do not let their children have too many sweets in the afternoon because they will feel ill in the evening. In this case, the wise parents are giving their children protection; the very act of not giving is, in this instance, a form of generosity. So we have to know what to give and what not to give because both giving and not-giving can be forms of generosity. Sometimes people hear that generosity has great benefits and crazily jump into giving everything away. That is not correct. We need to understand the motivation, purpose, and method of giving. A more detailed explanation of these points follows.

(b')) Detailed explanation of the things that are and are not to be given

This topic has two subdivisions:

- (1')) Detailed explanation about internal things that are and are not to be given
- (2')) Detailed explanation about external things that are and are not to be given

Internal refers to one's body while *external* refers to one's belongings, food, shelter, and so forth.

(1')) Detailed explanation about internal things that are and are not to be given

A bodhisattva can practice generosity by giving his or her body or life. This includes giving a single organ or one's entire body. How is this done? When should it be done? Tsongkhapa says that if we understand when this is *not* suitable, we will know when and how it *is* suitable. So first I will explain the things that are not permitted, in the following three subsections:

(a")) Inappropriate giving from the viewpoint of time
(b")) Inappropriate giving from the viewpoint of purpose
(c")) Inappropriate giving from the viewpoint of the one who asks
   for something

(a")) Inappropriate giving from the viewpoint of time

From the moment of taking the bodhisattva vows, a bodhisattva dedicates his or her body, wealth, and merits to others. So should a bodhisattva give his or her body whenever it is requested? Although they have mentally given these things, it does not mean that beginner bodhisattvas must physically give them right away. Giving freely and entirely does not mean giving everything all at once. We must be judicious. For example, parents wish to give everything possible to their children, but they hold some things back because the children may not be able to use certain things safely until they are older. Bodhisattvas give like good parents who establish a trust fund for their children. The money in trust belongs to the children; however, they cannot have it right away, even though they might want it. The children need to be protected until they reach a certain stage of development.

A beginner bodhisattva, one who has not directly realized śūnyatā, must be careful not to do too much at the start. Before reaching the first āryan level, we could experience problems if we were required to give whatever was asked of us. For example, we would not be able to freely cut off one of our hands and give it to someone. The misery of giving something like that could make one lose love and compassion for others and think, "If I have to undergo this much hardship to help even one sentient being, I'd better give up." We have an historical example of this sort. Some time after the Buddha's disciple Maudgalyāyana developed bodhicitta, a man came up to him and asked for his arm. So with his right hand Maudgalyāyana cut off his left arm and gave it to him. But that man was not satisfied and when Maudgalyāyana saw that gratifying even *one* person was so difficult, he felt discouraged about being able to help *all* sentient beings. From that point on he slowly lost his bodhicitta. This is a very negative thing. Usually, once one drops the altruistic intention to attain enlightenment, one cannot attain arhatship in that life. However, Maudgalyāyana did become an arhat because his karmic propensities were very strong and he had a solid relationship with the Buddha.

Until one has fully-ripened compassion and a realization of the true nature of reality, one's spiritual strength is undeveloped and one's perseverance is weak. In the beginning we should do only as much as we can do comfortably. Do what you can enjoy and feel good about afterward. It is immature to take on too heavy a task for too long a time. That will cause one to make mistakes, do things incorrectly, and feel great regret afterward. In the long run it can make one give up accumulating the merit to attain complete enlightenment. This would be enormously harmful to other sentient beings in addition to oneself. If you give up your human life before you are properly prepared to do so, you may not be reborn in a state where the complicated practices of the bodhisattva path can be practiced. You could fall to a lower rebirth. You will have wasted the seed of your bodhicitta. If you destroy the seed then of course there will be no harvest. We must be careful not to damage the cause for our goal of saving all sentient beings.

We have to choose how to use our precious human life. Should we save it or destroy it? Saving one's life can benefit others, but giving one's life might also benefit others. According to the *Compendium of Trainings,* even though a bodhisattva has mentally given his or her body to sentient beings, he or she should make an actual gift of it only at the proper time. A bodhisattva has to weigh every situation skillfully to determine when to give. For a long time we should simply exercise the mind and develop a strong wish to give from the heart. In fact, the *Questions of Sky Treasure Sutra* says, "The desire to do something at the wrong time is evil." For example, committing suicide is powered by evil because it destroys one's potential in this life to develop spiritually and thereby help all sentient beings. There are many ruthless and crazy sentient beings; no matter how much we do for them they will continue to act badly. There are so many obstructions to acting in a way beneficial to others. We sometimes call these disruptions *māras*—demons or evil forces.[2]

Śāntideva says in *Engaging in the Bodhisattva Deeds:*

> Until the thought of compassion is completely pure
> You should not give your body.
> In general, in this and other lives,
> You give to accomplish the great purpose.

In the beginning practitioners need to develop compassion and love. Only when they have pure great compassion can they and should they give their body as part of the practice of generosity. For example, in one of the Buddha's past lives he was able to offer his body to a starving tigress. At that time he had already reached a high bodhisattva level. He had no attachment to his body; he could freely give his flesh and bones as easily as we give a vegetable to a beggar. When one's attitude toward one's body is that it is just food, like a vegetable, then what difficulty would one have in giving it away?

We become accustomed to generosity gradually. We should try to give whatever we can; in the beginning, it might be as little as a mouthful of food. After a while our stinginess will lessen and we will want to help others more and more. After long practice, when our generosity has become very advanced, we will be able to offer our own flesh like the bodhisattvas or buddhas in stories. The great teacher Śāntideva succinctly says:[3]

> In the beginning, the great teacher encourages
> The giving of such things as food.
> Later, when accustomed to this,
> You may progress to giving away your own flesh.
>
> At such a time when my mind is developed
> To the point of regarding my body like food,
> Then what hardship would there be
> When it comes to giving away my flesh?

We should do everything possible to lessen our attachment and increase our generosity and compassion for others. All suffering comes from a self-centered attitude. If we do not eliminate selfishness, there is no way to be free from suffering. Attachment increases hatred. We feel animosity toward anything that might prevent us from getting what we desire and fear the possibility of losing what we have already obtained. We do not see others' fear; we have no sympathy for them and only pity ourselves. So many problems and worries come from selfish attachment. Until we drop our self-interested pursuits, we are holding on to the source of pain; if we do not let go of a burning torch, we will get burned. The practice of generosity targets selfishness. Instead of wallowing in egotistical attachment, bodhisattvas develop the desire to share with others. We too can free ourselves of attachment. Gradually one's property and even one's life can become of service to others. When one strongly feels the dearness of others, giving one's body to them produces great joy. We become an object of value.

These instructions are to be practiced in daily life. Desiring to share one's body and one's belongings in order to benefit others is the result of correct practice. Enjoyment of generosity shows we are going in the right direction.

(b")) Inappropriate giving from the viewpoint of purpose

It is not good to give your body to others for an insignificant reason. The body can be used to practice the holy Dharma and thereby help many other beings. In that sense the body is like a wish-granting jewel; if we use it to attain enlightenment we will quickly fulfill the wishes of all sentient beings. That is far more worthwhile than giving up one's life for one person for some trivial reason. So we should carefully examine our motivation all the time. The main reason we do not practice generosity is stinginess. A bodhisattva has no unwillingness to share; however, he or she determines whether giving will be helpful to others or not. Ask yourself if what you intend to do fulfills the wishes of all sentient beings or just one.

(c")) Inappropriate giving from the viewpoint of the one who asks for something

We should not give something if it would harm ourselves or others. There are evil spirits who are always looking to do harm. They injure others for their own enjoyment. Some sentient beings may be under the sway of these demonic forces; in that case a bodhisattva should not accede to their request for his or her body or life. Even though a bodhisattva does not worry about his or her own suffering, giving in such a situation would only enable the requestors to harm themselves. Those other beings have already created negative karma; if we allow them to kill us, they will create even more negative karma. Similarly, we should not give our life to the insane or mentally disturbed if they ask for it. They are not requesting from the heart; their words are just gibberish.

Not giving in these situations is not breaking the bodhisattva vows. In fact, it would be wrong to give in these situations from the point of view of time, purpose, and the requestor. Except for situations like these, when we are prepared we should practice generosity by giving the body. There are two aspects to giving away one's body or life. The first involves giving part now and part later; for example, giving blood at various times during the year. Just remember that whatever and whenever you give, it is permanently given. The second involves temporarily giving others power over one's body to accomplish a religious purpose; an example would be going to work as a servant in a monastery or convent.

(2')) Detailed explanation about external things that are and are not to be given

There are two sections to explain this topic:

(a")) How not to give external things
(b")) How to give external things

(a")) How not to give external things

There are some things that are proper to give and others that are not. Similarly, there are good times and bad times for giving. There can be positive reasons for doing something and negative reasons for avoiding doing that same thing. A positive reason is the purpose or goal of the action; a negative reason details the danger or negative repercussions of performing that action. We have to examine which is greater. If the negative outweighs the positive, we should not do it. If there is a small negative reason, but the positive benefit is greater, then we should do it. We have to be like an intelligent parent. It would be dangerous and stupid to allow children to do everything that they want to do simply because we love them. This is why Tsongkhapa explains in such detail about when to give, what to give, and to whom to give. This discussion has five subtopics:

(1")) Inappropriate giving from the viewpoint of time
(2")) Inappropriate giving from the viewpoint of the gift
(3")) Inappropriate giving from the viewpoint of the person
(4")) Inappropriate giving from the viewpoint of material things
(5")) Inappropriate giving from the viewpoint of purpose

(1")) Inappropriate giving from the viewpoint of time

It is improper to give at certain times. For example, some monks and nuns do not eat after noon, so we should not give them food after that time. Also, it would be inappropriate to offer a meal to someone who is fasting.

(2")) Inappropriate giving from the viewpoint of the gift

A gift may be inappropriate when we consider the recipient. We should not give religious practitioners leftovers or waste scraps of food. This does not mean we should not give this kind of food to anyone; beggars could receive it and enjoy it. I cannot imagine you would even consider this, but the second instruction is not to give food contaminated with urine, snot, vomit, blood, spit, and so on. Further, some people do not consume certain things like meat, alcohol, onions, or garlic, so it would not be suitable to give them those things. If someone is not permitted to eat a specific kind of food because of certain vows, we should not give that person anything made with that particular ingredient.

Tsongkhapa next advises us about a type of giving that occurred occasionally in the past. A long time ago a man might give his family to work in servitude, or a king might give a whole town to another king. It was important in these cases that the donor clearly explains the reason for the gift to the people who were to go. Even if the people affected agreed to go, the gift would be inappropriate if the recipient were unkind, crude, harmful, or did not recognize the kindness of others.

Some food and drink is not suitable for some people. Other items are fit for consumption, but only in specific quantities, or when eaten in specific circumstances. We should ask sick people what they are permitted to eat before we give them food; and sometimes, even if they want something, we should not give it to them. This instruction is especially important for nurses. Some people are very greedy about food; even if we give them enough to fill their stomach, they still want more. Giving to excess is not a fault if we do not know the situation. However, it is a problem if we recognize what is needed and give more than that amount. This practice is the way a mother cares for her dear child; she stops her child at a certain point and does not give him or her any more.

At this point in the *Lamrim Chenmo* Tsongkhapa discusses when it is inappropriate to give Dharma books. Religious scriptures are different from books that have no spiritual value. Other books may contain information that can cause harm to oneself or others, but Dharma books only contain instructions leading to higher rebirth and liberation. They should therefore be honored and respected. As a result, there are times when we should refuse to give a Dharma book. For example, some people ask for Buddhist religious texts merely to find fault with them and publicly refute them. Others see no spiritual value in the scriptures and only want them as a commodity to sell for profit. We should know how to refuse if those with these improper attitudes ask us for scriptures. We should not just flatly say, "No. I will not give this book to you." That could get them angry. We should explain that our refusal is not due to a lack of compassion, but out of love. If we were to give the book to them, they could create negative karma that would injure themselves and others.

We should be careful about distributing some books even to people with good attitudes. Reading particular books may be too difficult or even dangerous for those who are unprepared for the teachings and practices contained in them. We must determine what the people want, why they want it, what we should do, and how to do it. Tsongkhapa says we should follow the guidelines presented in the *Bodhisattva Levels' Compendium of Determinations (Viniścaya-saṃgrahaṇī)*, an extensive chapter in the great Asaṅga's *Bodhisattva Levels*. Asaṅga explains that if we give a religious book to someone begging for it who has childish intelligence, we will be breaking a vow. A childish person has no noble intent; he or she merely wants to play with or sell the text. Bodhisattvas would also incur a downfall if they request others to give religious texts to such people. However, there is no downfall if a bodhisattva thinks, "Even though this person has a poor attitude, I will give this text to him because in this way I will be able to lead him to have faith in the Dharma." Whether the bodhisattva is actually able to inspire the person to have faith in the Dharma is not the deciding factor; if he or she thinks that he or she can do it, then it is appropriate to give.

The chapter also says that bodhisattvas should not give others books that contain incorrect information, books that feign being teachings but are not, or books written by holders of extreme views. Even if bodhisattvas have such books on hand, they should not give them, even to those who have faith in those wrong views. Nor should bodhisattvas commission these types of books to be written or printed. What should bodhisattvas do with this kind of book? They must explain to others why these books are purposeless and not good to read.

There are also special considerations concerning the giving of paper. In the past paper was a rare and valuable commodity, so bodhisattvas had to be careful about giving someone stacks of blank paper. If someone requests a supply of paper, a bodhisattva should ask in return, "What do you want to do with it?" If the person answers, "I need money so I want to sell it," the bodhisattva should give the person some money instead, particularly if that paper was originally intended for the printing of Dharma texts. If the bodhisattva does not have any money, he or she still should not give the paper. The publication of Dharma books will benefit many people; selling the paper will be helpful only to one person. Once again we must compare the benefit of helping one person if we were to give the paper with the broader benefit the greater public will receive if we withhold it. Now, if the paper was not intended for the printing of religious texts, then we can give it away because satisfying someone is an appropriate use of a material possession. We should similarly evaluate giving paper to those who request it in order to publish something they have written. If their work is extremely negative and they want to print it just to make money, there is no fault in refusing to give. A bodhisattva should not give paper even if the person's composition is only slightly bad or simply not so good. In contrast, if some people want to print a sutra or another spiritual text that will be beneficial to other sentient beings, bodhisattvas should assist them by giving whatever they can. In that case not giving the paper would be a downfall.

(3")) Inappropriate giving from the viewpoint of the person

Now we look at what not to give from the point of view of the person who is giving rather than from the viewpoint of the recipient or the object. Again we take the example of religious books and unprinted reams of paper to learn who should and who should not engage in the practice of generosity. Bodhisattvas should consider their purpose in keeping or giving away a spiritual text. There are three purposes to giving religious volumes: to fight attachment, to produce wisdom, and to benefit other sentient beings. Since the primary purpose of giving is to eliminate attachment, if bodhisattvas have a strong desire to keep a particular book, then they should give it away. If you check within and find that you have no attachment, you must determine whether giving away the text would impede your ability to complete your intent for possessing the book in the first place. If you could produce wisdom and benefit other sentient beings without the volume, then it would be right to give it away. However, if you could freely give it away, but without the text could not complete the other two purposes of generosity, there is no fault in keeping it. In order to attain buddhahood quickly for the benefit of other sentient beings, a bodhisattva must accumulate merit and wisdom. The value of a scripture is the information within it; we study books in order to gain knowledge. If a book will serve to edify oneself and increase one's wisdom, then giving it away would diminish one's opportunity to accomplish the accumulation of wisdom. In that case one should not give it away.

Furthermore, we must compare how much benefit there would be to others by keeping the book or giving it away. Does it make sense for us to give a scripture to someone who asks for it but does not know how to use it, while we lose the chance to gain the understanding that would enable us to truly help many others? Which will produce more merit—giving or not giving? If the only thing accomplished by giving a volume is satisfying a single person, then there is not much point in giving it away, especially if one could use it to further one's progress on the path to attain enlightenment for the benefit of all sentient beings. In short, we should evaluate a situation by determining which purposes of generosity are fulfilled and then act accordingly. The *Bodhisattva Levels* gives more detail on how to determine smaller and greater purposes in this regard. The great Śāntideva says in *Engaging in the Bodhisattva Deeds* that if just a small purpose will be accomplished by giving, we should not do it. Because a bodhisattva is like a wish-fulfilling jewel for all sentient beings, giving his or her entire body to satisfy the hunger of a single creature would be a very small purpose. In such a case, not only is there no fault in *not* giving, it would be a much greater error *to* give.

The *Lamrim Chenmo* does not provide additional detail about evaluating the purpose of giving in specific situations, but Tsongkhapa does discuss how to act when we determine that it would be inappropriate to give a religious text to someone. We should not say anything harsh or hurtful like, "I would never give this to you!" We should say whatever is necessary so the person does not get angry and lose faith.

So what would be a skillful thing to say? In answer, let us consider for a moment that portion of the Buddhist ordination ritual that requires monks and nuns to keep certain objects with them. In general, monks and nuns should live very simply, renouncing many things. However, in order to live in samsara, to study, and to practice for the benefit of others, there are a few things that they should not readily give away: the three garments that make up their robes, a begging bowl, and so forth. The ordination ritual instructs sangha members to keep these items with the attitude that they are utilizing these things temporarily, but they really belong to others. At some point it may be beneficial to give them away, but for the present time the monk or nun should use them in order to be able to benefit others.

This way of thinking is analogous to the bodhisattvas' dedication of their possessions but then keeping them for use. From the beginning of the bodhisattva path, practitioners dedicate their possessions, body, and life to all other sentient beings and to the buddhas of the ten directions. These things then belong to others; bodhisattvas have them only on loan. Dedicating to the buddhas or to sentient beings actually come to the same thing; essentially they are saying, "From now on I only will do what the buddhas want—help other sentient beings." So when bodhisattvas judge it better not give, they must explain it in a nice way. They may say, "These things are not actually mine. They belong to others. I am sorry but I cannot give them to you." Returning to the example of someone requesting a volume of scripture for inappropriate reasons, we can say, "I am sorry that I cannot give you this book, but please take more money than it is worth." By acting like this the other person will think, "It is not because this bodhisattva is stingy. He or she simply does not have the authority to give me this book." If one thinks and acts this way, even while accumulating great wealth one can still create great merit.

There is nothing that the buddhas and bodhisattvas would not give to help sentient beings. When faced with an opportunity to practice generosity, we should give if the item is suitable as a gift. That is what the buddhas want. However, if the item is unsuitable, the time is not right, the purpose is wrong, or there is some other valid reason, then even if someone asks us sweetly, we should not fulfill their request. Generosity with wisdom is the skillful bodhisattva practice. Even not giving requires skill and a lot of wisdom. You should know the purpose of generosity, how not to harm others, how to act for a greater purpose, and be able to evaluate various situations. Then your generosity will come out of great wisdom.

(4")) Inappropriate giving from the viewpoint of material things

Certain things are not suitable to give. For example, it is not right to give food and drink that contain many living beings because consumption involves killing many creatures. There may be certain situations, such as part of a surrender treaty, where one has to give away one's servants or relatives. In general, it is not suitable to give away one's family or servants, but one should if they are in miserable circumstances and it would be to their benefit to send them away. However, it is not proper to do so if they do not understand the situation or simply do not like it. During one of the lives of the Buddha before he attained enlightenment he gave away his wife and children in order to attain enlightenment.

Another example of inappropriate material things to give is found in the *Bodhisattva Levels' Compendium of Determinations*. As mentioned before, Buddhist monks and nuns should keep their three garments of ordination. These garments mark them as renunciates. People recognize them because they are not wearing clothes like ordinary people. The robes are a kind of protection and a victory banner indicating that the monk or nun is trying to become free. According to the vinaya, monks and nuns are allowed to keep additional things only if they do not have attachment, if the things are useful for creating merit, and if they are also helpful in doing positive things for others. The key is non-attachment. Generally monks and nuns are supposed to lessen their attachment; they are supposed to live a simple life. Not possessing other things and not giving certain things away are both appropriate so long as they are for the purpose of creating virtue. The *Bodhisattva Vows of Liberation* says:

"Śāriputra! Giving away the three garments principally to satisfy a beggar is not the correct practice for bodhisattvas to lessen attachment."

Giving these away is a downfall; it is breaking the rules.

(5")) Inappropriate giving from the viewpoint of purpose

We should not fulfill the request of someone who asks for poison, weapons, fire, or intoxicants for the purpose of harming others. In addition, it is not right to give something to others if their reason for wanting it is to amuse themselves in a way that will create a cause to be born in a lower realm. For example, there are places where people kill bulls for sport and entertainment, and here in Wisconsin many people enjoy going hunting. In the latter case, if we grant others' request for a gun, we may give them a little temporary pleasure, but because they will use it to harm other beings, it will bring them a great negative result. We have to examine the purpose to which the gift will be put. Giving to someone so he or she can harm animals by archery, trapping, or any other means is not right. We should not instruct people in methods that could harm others' bodies or lives. Sometimes countries cede areas, along with the people living in them, to the winner of a war. But a country's ruler should not give territory to someone whose intent is to harm the residents. This example is on a large scale, but it is a model for how we should behave even in regard to small pieces of property. We should not sell or give real estate if the other party's intent is to destroy the creatures living there. When practicing generosity we are fighting against selfishness and trying to increase our desire to help others as much as possible. We are certainly trying not to harm other sentient beings.

(b")) How to give external things

In the sections above, Tsongkhapa discussed exceptions to the practice of generosity so that we would understand under what circumstances it would *not* be suitable to give. So how *should* we give? According to the vinaya, it is proper to give if it is neither an inappropriate time nor an unsuitable object for that particular recipient. From the point of view of the practitioner, the main purpose of generosity is to reduce stinginess and attachment. If attachment is strong it must be fought. So using the previously explained example of religious scriptures, if we have strong attachment to a book we should give it away to combat our stinginess. If we have two copies of the book, we could give away the extra one. If we do not have additional copies, we could give the book's price in cash. If we have neither the money nor extra copies of the text, we should give away our copy even if we have not finished studying it. A bodhisattva should think, "I am going to give this text away to reduce my attachment. Even if I remain stupid my entire life, it is better than remaining so stingy."

From the point of view of the object, we should give it so long as it is not harmful or dangerous. We can give people things for play and enjoyment if they will not cause them to create negative karma leading to rebirth in the lower realms. Things themselves are not absolutely harmful; it depends on how they are used. So if we are asked to provide them for a positive purpose, it is right to give them. In the proper situation even weapons and poisons are not problematic gifts. In this context, *weapons* can refer to the special knives used by surgeons and *poisons* can be compounded into powerful medicines that cure disease. In summary, if it is not a harmful situation and the things will not be detrimental, it is right to engage in the practice of generosity.

What should we do if two people, one rich and one poor, come to us and ask for the same thing? Sometimes there will be a conflict about what to do, but in general one should decide how to proceed beforehand thinking, "If I can, I will fulfill both their wishes. If I cannot do that, I will help the poor person." In a nice way we can say to the wealthier person, "I am sorry. I have already dedicated this thing to someone else, so I cannot give to you now." This explanation is not a lie; we are helping them to understand.

Learning the details about how to practice generosity is important for beginners who have taken the bodhisattva vows. You can read more about this subject in Asaṅga's *Bodhisattva Levels*. Tsongkhapa drew from that text to explain the practices, vows, and how to keep them. While Tsongkhapa added some information about particular situations, most of his outline about how to practice generosity comes from there.

(b)) What to do if you are unable to give

Up to this point Tsongkhapa has explained what to give, what not to give, in what situations, and at what time. Now he discusses what we should do when we are not able to practice generosity even though all the circumstances are right.

If we are so overpowered by stinginess that we cannot part with an object, we should ask ourselves, "Why do I feel this miserliness? This thing and I are separate. There is no way we can stay together: sooner or later I will have to leave it or it will leave me. This is the nature of things. This object has no real essence: it cannot produce everlasting happiness and it may cause me some problems. However, if I give this thing away it may give someone else some temporary pleasure and free that person from some passing suffering. In addition, this act of generosity will become the cause of my future wealth. So generosity has a real positive essence. Even if I were to die because of giving this thing away, it would not really matter. Sooner or later I have to die anyway. If I am tight-fisted and hold on to my possessions all my life, I will still have to leave them at death. Then I will experience misery and regret my parsimonious actions. But if I practice generosity, I will create merit that will comfort me at the time of death. Wherever I go in my next life, I will bring karmic seeds with me just as a shadow follows a form. Whether my karma is good or bad, it will eventually ripen. So if I give everything away now, when I am dying I will know that I have used everything in a positive way. This will give me great joy."

Let's say you think this through and still find yourself unable to give. In that case, when others seriously ask you to give them something, you have to be able to give them some excuse. The words you use will depend upon the situation, but the meaning you should convey is this: "I am a beginner in the practice of generosity and helping others. I am unable to do this because I am still under the sway of attachment. Bodhisattvas who realize emptiness are able to practice generosity, but I am not like them. I am powerless and controlled by the selfish egotistic view grasping *I* and *mine*. Please excuse me. Have patience and do not be unhappy because I am not able to give this to you right now. Later, I hope to be able to do something that will satisfy you and all other sentient beings." Even though you do not give them the material thing that they requested, your nice way of excusing yourself can please them. This idea comes from the *Questions of the Householder Ugra Sutra (Āryagṛha-pati-ugra-paripṛcchā-nāma-mahāyāna-sūtra).*

According to the *Compendium of Trainings,* this mode of action will prevent people from losing faith in beginner bodhisattvas who are not able to practice generosity even though they have taken the vows. Although it prevents distrust between people, it does not reduce stinginess nor does it avert breaking the bodhisattva vows. Tsongkhapa says that if we do not give material things or teach the Dharma because of tightfistedness, we create the heaviest kind of downfall. Stingy selfishness is so egregious because bodhisattvas are motivated by a wish to benefit others all the time. If they do not give, it should be because they are trying to accomplish something else virtuous out of compassion and love. When ordinary people have a lot of stinginess, it is shameful; it is far more despicable for bodhisattvas to be miserly. If we do not give, but excuse ourselves properly, we lessen the weight of the downfall. We will still be breaking the rules, but because we do it with a regretful, heartfelt apology, it is not as severe. The following stanzas from the *Compendium of the Perfections* make the same suggestions about what to do if we are not able to give:

> If a beggar comes in front of you
> But you are weak and unable to give,
> Without disparaging the beggar
> You should please him with kind words.

> In the future when someone asks for things
> Do not be discouraged and depressed.
> Clear away the fault of stinginess;
> Make an effort to eliminate grasping.

(c)) RELYING ON THE REMEDIES FOR THE HINDRANCES TO GENEROSITY

Asaṅga explained that there are four obstacles to the practice of generosity. Each of these difficulties, along with what to do to counter them, is treated as a subtopic in the *Lamrim Chenmo*. They are:

(1)) The hindrance of not being used to generosity
(2)) The hindrance of declining fortune
(3)) The hindrance of attachment
(4)) The hindrance of not seeing the goal

The first problem is that one is simply not comfortable giving because one never does it. The second hindrance to generosity is poverty; if one is poor one just does not have much to give. The third obstacle is attachment or stinginess. Finally, one may not be interested in giving because one does not recognize the positive benefits that come from generosity or the negative results that come from miserliness.

(1)) THE HINDRANCE OF NOT BEING USED TO GENEROSITY

The first obstacle to generosity is not being habituated to giving. We may have plenty of things that we could share, see many people in need of such things, and parting with a few things would cause us no inconvenience, but we do not even think of giving. Just because we are not used to being generous we should not let that bad habit continue. Think about the benefits of

generosity and the disadvantages of miserliness. Reflect that if we do not create good causes we will not experience good results, and if we do not change
this selfish behavior we will experience poverty in the future. The antidote is
to think, "It must be the case that I am experiencing one of the karmic results
of not being generous in the past. I did not try to give and never became
accustomed to giving. If I do not become used to giving now, in my next life
I will continue to be stingy in the same way. I will never have the joy that
comes from practicing generosity. So now, while I have the opportunity, it is
important to practice generosity."

Once doing something becomes routine, it gets easy. There are many levels of practice. Do not think, "This is way too hard. It is not my kind of thing.
I will just forget it!" Anyone can do this practice. Bodhisattvas were nothing
special at the beginning; they were no better than you or me. They were ordinary human beings and had to train their mind. Give yourself some encouragement; start small and go step by step. Do not jump right into some big
thing without properly training the mind. If we do too much all at once, we
may feel disappointed and discouraged the next day. There is no such thing
as instant spiritual achievement. We need to develop slowly through a gradual and stable practice. Then we will feel happy to practice; we will have no
regrets.

(2)) The hindrance of declining fortune

The second obstacle to generosity is poverty. We may have nothing to give,
or we may have so little that we think that we must keep the few things that
we have to survive. Actually a lack of wealth is not the main reason we cannot practice generosity; the problem is our attitude. Even if we are poor we
can train the mind to be generous. With the right attitude we can practice
generosity.

The antidote for not wanting to share the little bit that we have is to think,
"I am experiencing poverty, not getting what I want, and losing what I have.
These unpleasant experiences are the results of my past miserly karma. If I
had practiced generosity, I would not be in this situation now. But because I
neglected the virtuous practice of generosity in the past, I am still under the
power of stinginess and continue to create the causes of suffering." Then
think in a positive way, "If I help others by being generous now, I may experience some temporary discomfort, but my actions will result in a better
future." The choice is to be a little uncomfortable now and much better off
in the future, or to continue as we are and be miserable later. We should think,
"Everyone dies sooner or later. If I die without having created any merit from

the practice of generosity, I will endure poverty in the future as well. There are so many poor people who are dying of hunger. Instead of turning away those in need, I should give them the few good things that I have. I can survive by picking up some scraps here and there. Even if I should die, it would be better to give because the results in the future will be much better for me and for others. Some temporary distress will create my future happiness." Seeing that we can help those in need, we should want to help them. Bodhisattvas can endure great misery in this regard, but even beginners can deal with a little discomfort when they understand the great benefit to others. Voluntarily accepting discomfort for the purpose of helping many others is part of the practice of patience.

(3)) THE HINDRANCE OF ATTACHMENT

Even if we are habituated to generosity, we may want to keep things that we feel are particularly good or beautiful. It is attachment that prevents us from wanting to give these things to help those who truly are in urgent need. Attachment itself is suffering—it is a miserable feeling of not wanting to let go. Attachment is also the cause of future suffering. The antidote for attachment is to consider its faults. So think, "Attachment is a wrong perception; it is holding a cause of misery to be the source of lasting happiness. This mistaken belief is the cause of a lot of trouble. All during one's life one tries to protect one's property. Sometimes attachment deceives people so much that they are willing to give up their lives to defend their possessions. Even if one manages to hold on to one's property, attachment cannot bring happiness. It only brings misery and sorrow." Understanding that attachment is evil will reverse one's lack of generosity.

(4)) THE HINDRANCE OF NOT SEEING THE GOAL

Humans generally decide to do something based on whether they think the outcome will be painful or pleasant. The last of the four obstacles to the practice of generosity is that one sees neither the beneficial result from giving nor the negative result from not giving. We will be able to give if we remember that our body and wealth are impermanent. They constantly change. We feel that they will be useful forever, but every moment they are disintegrating and we are closer to the separation of death. If we give these things now with the intention of benefiting others, we will help others and ourselves. The supreme result of generosity is perfect buddhahood; buddhas are free from all suffering and are great leaders who truly benefit others. Bodhisattvas attain perfect buddhahood through the practices of the six perfections, the first of which is generosity—being willing to give one's body, wealth, and merit to others. In addition to this ultimate result, there are temporary consequences of the practice of generosity. A better next life—a human rebirth with good circumstances—also depends upon the practice of generosity. Satisfying others will make them grateful; they may assist us even in *this* life.

But thinking merely about one's own enjoyment in this and other lives is not praiseworthy for a bodhisattva. Generosity with these motivations merely yields a simple, worldly result. In his *Four Hundred Stanzas (Catuḥ-śataka),* Āryadeva says:

> Thinking, "I will get a great result
> By giving this gift to him now,"
> Is disparaged as giving and receiving,
> Like trade for profit.

Bodhisattvas wish to free all mother sentient beings from suffering. They recognize that at present they do not have the power to do so, so they think, "For the purpose of attaining buddhahood I am going to engage in virtuous practices such as generosity." Great results come from dedicating the merit from giving even a small gift. If we practice thinking this way we will become accustomed to it. We will come to enjoy it and quickly attain enlightenment to help others.

(2") The generosity that is just mental

The perfection of generosity is to be free from stinginess. In other words, generosity is an attitude. Therefore, even if we are in dire poverty and have absolutely nothing to give, we can still practice generosity. Certain meditators doing yogic practices in caves live on just enough to survive. They do not have any material things to give away but still they practice generosity. We too can work with the mind. Meditating on the wish to benefit others by giving them what they need is an aspect of the practice of love. We can visualize giving others food, shelter, and clothing. This is imaginary, but it is not senseless. We are training ourselves to give many things to many other beings.

Mental generosity does not entail physical hardship, but according to many sutras it can create measureless virtue. Tsongkhapa quotes Asaṅga's *Bodhisattva Levels,* "This is the generosity of bodhisattvas who have great wisdom." Although Asaṅga says bodhisattvas with realizations can do this, it does not mean that others, even those of us without high wisdom, should not do this practice as well. Ordinary people can do this imagination practice. When Asaṅga mentions "bodhisattvas who have great wisdom," it is in the context of the five paths and ten bodhisattva levels. The first two paths are ordinary levels that precede the ten āryan levels. When a bodhisattva has a direct realization of emptiness, he or she attains the first bodhisattva āryan level. This is the first moment of the path of seeing. From that point on through the rest of the ten levels, bodhisattvas are considered wise. Bodhisattvas below the āryan stage may practice mental generosity; they may lack wealth but have great compassion and love. From the first āryan stage onward, there is no such thing as a poor bodhisattva. These bodhisattvas are rich in many ways. They have the superior thought of bodhicitta and can create various things through the power of their concentration.

(d') A SUMMARY

After a person produces bodhicitta, he or she takes the bodhisattva vow. The vows contain many rules specifying what is and what is not permitted at certain times. In other words, the bodhisattva practices of generosity and so forth have lower and higher stages. Each level requires a certain degree of maturity and spiritual development. In the beginning of the practice of generosity we give small things in our imagination. Slowly we develop this mental practice until we can actually give some of our possessions. Gradually we become more skilled and eventually on the higher bodhisattva levels we will actually be able to give our life without any hesitation. We should not try the high level practices right away. For the time being we can wish that someday we will be able to do this, but we must begin in a small way and progress step by step. It requires wisdom and skill to know what should be done and what is not permissible. To avoid doing things in a crazy way we should study the scriptures, listen to teachers, and use our intelligence.

The main purpose of the practice of generosity is the elimination of attachment. There are different degrees of attachment and therefore different levels of the antidote. First we reduce attachment to our possessions so that we can give. After reaching a point where we can freely give our material things, we reduce our attachment to the merit that results from giving. As our attachment decreases our joy in sharing with others increases and we have a greater and greater desire to give.

As we practice we should check to see if we are improving. We should be happy if we find that our attachment has lessened. However, if we discover that we are in the same tight stingy state as before, we should be sad and apply the antidote again. If we do this, the *Questions of Subāhu Sutra* explains that in our next life we will have less difficulty practicing the perfection of generosity. We have all seen people who from childhood had a natural inclination to share their possessions with others. They can do this kind of practice with less difficulty than those who had not accustomed themselves to generosity in a prior life. In contrast, if we allow our habitual stinginess to remain or even increase, we will experience many bad results in this and future lives. Not only that, in our next life we will have no desire to practice generosity. Each lifetime our selfish habits may become worse and worse until finally it will be extremely difficult to begin to practice the bodhisattvas' deeds.

A bodhisattva's every action is done for the benefit of others. This includes taking the bodhisattva vows, all the practices entailed by the vows, and the practice of the perfections. The basis of every perfection, including generosity, is bodhicitta—the desire to attain enlightenment for the benefit of other sentient beings. The *Compendium of the Perfections* says:

> The root of generosity is bodhicitta;
> Do not drop the desire to give gifts this way.
> The Buddha said that wishing to give with this attitude
> Is the best type of generosity in the world.

Without bodhicitta no matter what we do it is not a bodhisattva practice. So whenever we do something we should ask, "Why am I doing this? What am I hoping to achieve?" We should be mindful and make sure that bodhicitta is our motivation. If it is not, we should correct our motivation. Bodhisattvas dedicate their actions with the wish to attain enlightenment quickly. Practicing generosity this way is the perfection of generosity. The very word *perfection* indicates that there are other types of generosity. We should never vary from giving purely with the intention to help other sentient beings. This sums up all the details about this practice explained in the *Questions of Subāhu Sutra.*

The practice of generosity is not finished when you complete reading this section of the book. Now you have to consider and meditate on what you have learned. Are some of the things written here suitable for you? Refer back to what you have read; the second time you read something it becomes clearer. But familiarity with material can be dangerous if you do not put it into practice. When we are first exposed to something we may be moved by what we hear and have an earnest interest. But if we do not follow through with practice, when we encounter that subject again we may think, "Oh, I already know that. It is nothing new." So we pay less attention. Then, if it is presented to us a third time, even if the Buddha himself were teaching this subject right in front of us, we would be tired of hearing it and would not want to listen. The mind grows so tough that the antidote becomes useless. It is similar to misusing a medication and the disease becoming resistant to the drugs meant to treat it. That is why in the lamrim tradition the teachings are given little by little, like a dose of medicine. When students reach a certain level of practice they are given a little more. Therefore, we should apply the teachings by putting them into practice in our daily life. Then, like doses of medicine, the teachings will have great power to change us for the better. It is best if we practice in this way from now on.

❖ 11 ❖

The Perfection of Ethical Discipline

(ii) How to train in the perfection of ethical discipline
    (a') What ethical discipline is
    (b') How to begin the cultivation of ethical discipline
    (c') The divisions of ethical discipline
        (1') The ethical discipline of restraint
        (2') The ethical discipline of gathering virtue
        (3') The ethical discipline of acting for the welfare of living beings
    (d') How to practice
    (e') A summary

(ii) HOW TO TRAIN IN THE PERFECTION OF ETHICAL DISCIPLINE

THE BUDDHA taught the perfection of ethical discipline *(śīla)* right after he taught the perfection of generosity. This is a logical progression. As we have seen, the merit we create from generosity in this life will lead to two or three times more wealth in a future life. But where will that life be? If we harm others by doing things like killing, lying, or stealing, we may be reborn in a lower realm and experience the result of our practice of generosity in a bad rebirth. For example, animals can enjoy prosperity. Think of the pets we have here; they live in a warm house, sleep on their own comfortable cushions, and eat nice food. These are the results of generosity. But once these karmic results are experienced, that is it; they are used up. Animals do not have the chance to accumulate more merit because they do not have the mental ability to practice virtuous actions. Their comfortable experiences are like spending one's capital along with the interest. Once the merit is used up, the only way to go is down. Candrakīrti says in his *Commentary on the "Middle Way"*:[1]

The prosperity arising from generosity occurs in the lower realms
When aspects of one's ethical discipline degenerate.
If one completely uses up the capital as well as the interest,
There will be no further wealth resulting from that generosity.

If, however, we practice ethical conduct, we will have a high rebirth in the future. As a result of our prior generosity, we will have wealth in a life that gives us the opportunity to create virtue. If we use that life properly we can have continuous and inexhaustible good results life after life. In other words, pure ethical conduct is the foundation of all good qualities from here up to enlightenment.

Tsongkhapa explains the second perfection, ethical discipline, in five sections:

(a') What ethical discipline is
(b') How to begin the cultivation of ethical discipline
(c') The divisions of ethical discipline
(d') How to practice
(e') A summary

The purpose of the *Lamrim Chenmo*'s outline is to help us keep all the topics in a sensible order so that we can succeed in practice. In this chapter Tsongkhapa first provides a general overview so we can come to know what ethical discipline is. Next, we consider how to begin to practice religious conduct. We can only do this if we know the types of pure ethical conduct, the third topic. Then we are ready to actually put each of them into practice, so the fourth topic is an explanation of how to practice. With this background our practice will be stable, precise, and effective. If we practice blindly, without understanding all these things, or if we understand the information but do not practice, we will not accomplish our goal.

In this section of the *Lamrim Chenmo* the emphasis is on a bodhisattva's ethical discipline. There is very little explanation of the general nature of ethical discipline and the methods to practice it because Tsongkhapa discussed those subjects earlier in the context of the three trainings: ethical conduct, concentration, and wisdom (volume 2, chapters 11–12).

(a') WHAT ETHICAL DISCIPLINE IS

The nature of ethical conduct is the avoidance of harming others. Unlike schools such as the Vaibhāṣika that say that ethical discipline refers simply to physical and verbal actions that should not be done, Tsongkhapa follows the

Madhyamaka and stresses that ethical discipline is primarily mental. Physical and verbal activities are part of religious conduct, but they are not the most important factor. Ethical discipline focuses on control of the motivations leading to harmful actions. If mental ethical discipline is not present, then a physical action does not have much meaning. Let's take the ethical discipline of avoiding the negative action of killing as an example. Trees do not go around killing people; they simply stand in one place. However, because trees do not have a conscious, reasoned intent to avoid giving harm, we cannot say that trees have ethical conduct. Pure ethical discipline or religious conduct means that a person has made a decision not to harm others. This mental promise motivates one to avoid directly or indirectly hurting others.

The foundation of this decision is an understanding of the benefits of avoiding doing harm to others. Śāntideva explains the benefits of the mental roots of ethical discipline in *Engaging in the Bodhisattva Deeds* as follows:[2]

> All the negative actions
> And misery in the world
> Arise from self-cherishing.
> What use is that demon for me?

We usually point at something external as the cause of our problems, but Mahayana practitioners look for the source of their suffering inside themselves. Past masters have found that all misery and trouble comes from our obsession with our own happiness. Our unhappiness is not caused by an external force; it is caused by our selfish struggles to attain happiness for ourselves. Self-cherishing is like a devil that makes us do all kinds of things to fulfill our desires. A bodhisattva looks inward and asks, "What good is this horrible devil? I should get rid of it!" We can all examine our attitudes and behavior and make a decision about how to use our life. As long as our aim is to benefit ourselves alone, our actions will either directly or indirectly bring suffering. In contrast, if we are concerned with benefiting—or at least not harming—others, our actions will always bring about happiness and peace. Our conduct will be ethical because it is based on compassion and love for all sentient beings without exception.

Watching our attitudes and actions in relation to others is how we keep to the virtuous side and avoid even the tendency to do things that are harmful. In other words, Mahayana ethical discipline can be practiced without taking vows so long as we abstain from anything that would harm what matters most to others: their life, property, and relationships. To this end the vows can be helpful. The vows are a mental promise to maintain awareness and avoid doing actions that harm others. So taking the vows strengthens our intention by making our determination very concrete. Making a promise in front of the buddhas puts us in a position where we feel compelled to act in a specific way. But our attitude and actions will not be perfect immediately upon taking the vows. In the beginning we are inconsistent; sometimes we want to act properly, but there are many other times when we want to engage in harmful conduct. However, when we see negative actions as harmful to others, and even more detrimental to ourselves, we will naturally want to act ethically. We become accustomed to the practice of ethical discipline by concentrating upon the advantages of not harming and the disadvantages of harming others. Gradually, with repeated attempts, the mind will become perfectly disciplined. We will never, not even slightly, want to harm anyone directly or indirectly.

Do not misunderstand. The perfection of ethical discipline does not mean that no sentient being will ever be harmed by anything again. If perfect ethical conduct implied that all sentient beings were safe from injury, then no one would have ever perfected it. Not even the Buddha would have had pure religious conduct, because there are still many living beings who are subject to great wrongs. Of course, it would be wonderful if we could free all sentient beings from harm and place them somewhere safe, but that is not possible. So the perfection of ethical discipline is similar to the perfection of generosity: it is a mind-set. In this case it is a consistent loving attitude that completely overcomes the wish to hurt others. The point is not whether other sentient beings are free from injury; it is whether one truly wants to avoid harming them. Of course, if we could save all beings—or even just some of them—from harm, we should do it. The line of reasoning is that by purifying the mind our verbal and physical activity will follow suit. This idea is summarized in *Engaging in the Bodhisattva Deeds* as follows:

> The killing of fish and others
> Has not been completely eradicated anywhere.
> The perfection of ethical discipline is explained
> As obtaining the mind-set wanting to avoid harm.

Sometimes, when discussing religious conduct, we divide it into three types: prātimokṣa vows, bodhisattva vows, and tantric vows. But conduct in accord with any or all of these vows is just one aspect of a bodhisattva's ethical discipline. The bodhisattvas' practice of ethical discipline has three parts: they avoid harming others by conduct in accordance with the vows; they practice virtue to create the merit necessary to attain enlightenment; and they engage in actively helping others. The first part—a bodhisattva's conduct in accord with the vows—refers to the ethical discipline common to the Hinayana and Mahayana; it is practiced by those desiring their own liberation as well as those striving for enlightenment.

The great Indian master Candrakīrti says:[3]

> Other than pure conduct there is no way
> For ordinary individuals, śrāvakas,
> Pratyekabuddhas, and bodhisattvas
> To attain high rebirth and their final goal.

As you know, practitioners have two types of goals: temporary and final. The temporary goal is a high rebirth having the necessary external conditions for practicing religion. These include special conditions—such as the presence of spiritual teachings, religious teachers, fellow practitioners, and supporters—as well as ordinary ones like food and shelter. We also need positive internal conditions, such as health and intelligence. A high samsaric life is a nice short-term goal, but what we are really after is everlasting peace and freedom. When one completely gets rid of all the mental afflictions one ceases taking uncontrolled rebirth in samsara. Even better than that is the goal of buddhahood. Attaining the temporary and two final goals depends upon pure religious conduct. Of course, the direct cause of the two everlasting goals is a direct realization of the true nature of reality. But in order to achieve this profound realization, one has to control the mind. Ethical discipline is necessary in order to gain control of the mind. Without the practice of religious conduct, our actions fall under the power of selfishness. Selfish actions bring suffering and turmoil. Thus ethical conduct is the basis of taming the mind. One becomes accustomed to what should be done mentally, physically, and verbally. One develops the mental strength and stability to engage in the meditation that joins concentration with highest insight. Regarding this, Nāgārjuna writes in the *Friendly Letter:*

> Pure conduct is the foundation of all the higher spiritual qualities,
> Just as the earth is the foundation of everything animate and inanimate.

Because the goal of Mahayana practitioners is to help others, an excellent first step is to avoid doing things that harm others. It is the prātimokṣa, taught in both the Hinayana and Mahayana scriptures, that explains how to restrain one's body, speech, and mind from actions that cause suffering. The lay vows, vows for novice monks and nuns, and vows for fully ordained monks and nuns all stipulate the elimination of specific actions that are detrimental to others and instruct one to act in the opposite way. These actions can be summarized as restraint from the ten nonvirtues and practice of the ten virtues. These were explained in detail earlier (volume 2, chapter 2), so I will just summarize them briefly here.

The first three nonvirtues are physical actions: killing, stealing, and sexual misconduct. Then there are four ways to injure others verbally: lying (deceiving others through speech), slander (dividing those who are close), harsh speech (because hurtful words can be like poisoned arrows), and idle talk. People like to talk. It is fine if we are speaking in order to help our listeners develop virtue or do something good. But if we just casually talk, talk, talk, it can lead to anger, attachment, jealousy, and pride. The foundation, or causes, of these seven physical and verbal nonvirtuous actions are the mental attitudes of desire, hatred, and wrong views, or ignorance. In other words, for these three physical and four verbal actions to be nonvirtuous, they must be motivated by one of these three nonvirtuous thoughts. Only actions that are motivated are karma. If someone is injured accidentally in the course of one's activity, it is not nonvirtue. For example, in the course of childbirth the infant may die. Because no one had the intention to harm the child, no one accrues the negative action of killing. Similarly, if just by accident we happen not to kill anything, it is not virtuous because we had no positive motivation to avoid killing. We should consciously try to keep away from the ten non-virtues and keep to the ten virtues.

Whether one takes the vows or not, whether one is a Buddhist or not, the nature of the ten nonvirtuous actions is evil. We must be mindful and try not to do things motivated by attachment, hatred, or ignorance. Mindfulness comes from seeing the disadvantages of doing these actions and the advantages of avoiding them. It is not difficult to recognize those ten nonvirtues. We should also become cognizant of the many other actions and attitudes that fit into these ten larger categories. We should avoid all of them and practice good conduct. This is easy to say, but not so simple to do in the beginning. It will become easier; from making an effort our understanding will grow. Wisdom is knowing what should be done and what should not be done. Once we understand we can become aware of our own behavior in light of these standards. If one does not remain aware, even if one becomes a monk or nun, one can even create more negative karma. Understanding and awareness together lead to virtuous conduct.

So we have a lot to practice daily! Sometimes good conduct is given the epithet *obtaining coolness*. Good conduct is like a cool breeze that alleviates the misery of being burned because we have harmed others. It also helps those undergoing misfortune as the result of our actions. Good conduct leads to mental peace for others and for ourselves. Even if we cannot do all ten virtuous actions completely, doing just some of them with mindfulness is beneficial. It is extreme to think that if you cannot do all ten perfectly, you will not do anything at all. Do what you can—some purely and the rest roughly. We should be happy if we can look back at the end of the day and think, "Well I didn't do all ten, but I did seven, or six, or three." We should be glad that we fought against the ten negative actions. In brief, this is the nature of good conduct.

(b') How to begin the cultivation of ethical discipline

A Mahayana practitioner takes the bodhisattva vow solely for the purpose of benefiting other sentient beings. His or her goal is to bring all sentient beings to highest enlightenment. Because engaging in pure ethical discipline will result in reaching buddhahood, a bodhisattva must help others to practice perfect conduct. Successfully encouraging others to practice ethical discipline depends upon practicing it oneself. If one does not have practical experience, one cannot effectively teach others to practice the perfection of ethical discipline. Furthermore, if we act in a negative way we will be born in a lower realm. Because in the lower realms we will endure extremely painful suffering, we will not be able to do anything at all for others. So a bad rebirth is not just losing out for ourselves; it is also a loss for all other sentient beings. In this sense ethical conduct is not merely in one's own self-interest. Keeping our actions virtuous and our body healthy builds the strength necessary to help others. Without it we cannot benefit others, much less ourselves. Therefore, it is important for bodhisattvas to maintain ethical discipline. Nāgārjuna's great disciple Āryaśūra says in the *Compendium of the Perfections* that if we want to help others spiritually, it is very important to practice religious conduct first:

> Those endeavoring to help all living beings
> Attain complete enlightenment adorned with pure conduct,
> Must first practice ethical discipline themselves.
> Pure ethical discipline produces the power to succeed.

> If their conduct degenerates they cannot accomplish their own goal,
> So how could they be able to accomplish the goal for others?
> Therefore those who make an effort to accomplish others' welfare
> Must not slacken proper practice of ethical discipline themselves.

Tsongkhapa says that pure ethical discipline is to do positive activity and turn away from the negative side. The ability to do this depends upon mental strength. In this context *mental strength* means that we protect our conduct as instinctively as we protect our eyes from wind or dust. In Tibetan we say, "Protect it the way a yak protects his tail." This saying may not have much meaning for you if you are unfamiliar with yaks! Yaks are very proud of their tail hair. If a single strand of their tail gets stuck on a thorny bush, they will not pull away; they just stand there because they do not want to lose a single hair. We should always be this watchful of our conduct. This strong awareness keeps us from slipping into any negative behavior.

Most people do not have this mental strength. How do we develop this powerful desire always to do certain things and avoid others? It comes from a firm understanding of what we are doing and why we are doing it. We never do anything unless we understand the purpose and the result of our actions. We want to know what we will get out of doing something. If we clearly see great disadvantages, we are opposed to doing it. If we see immense benefits, then we want to do it. Furthermore, we have to be convinced that these benefits are achievable through our actions. Together these lead to a firmness of mind and our physical and verbal actions will follow. In this case, in order to have the desire to practice ethical discipline, we must recognize the faults of doing nonvirtuous actions and the benefits of doing virtuous ones. That is why we start by examining the disadvantages of each of the negative actions and concentrate on the advantages of avoiding them.

This requires acceptance of karma and the existence of past and future lives. According to Buddhism, all our experiences are the result of our prior actions. If one believes in future lives, then it is easier to accept that our present actions will affect our future. In particular, we believe that if we engage in negative conduct we are creating the causes for trouble later. That conviction makes it easier to maintain pure ethical discipline. It is more difficult for those who do not believe these things. However, even those who do not believe in karma and reincarnation admit that, in an ordinary worldly sense, our actions produce results, or consequences. For example, murderers worry that they will be put in jail or that someone may harm them in revenge. (Of course, in the Buddhist world view, killing someone will have many bad results in one's next life as well.) Merely understanding the details of causality is not enough. We have to think about our negative behavior from the point of view of the suffering we will have when reborn in a miserable life. Then we will be motivated to act ethically. The *Compendium of the Perfections* says:

Seeing the unending fearsome consequences of your actions
Makes you feel it worthwhile to avoid even a small thing
    to be abandoned.

If we do not believe in causality, we continue to do bad things without fear of repercussions. We ignorantly enjoy ourselves because we do not see the disadvantageous consequences of our actions. We usually think fear is a bad thing and do not want to have any worries. But certain types of fear are positive because they prevent us from doing something stupid. Such fears should be produced. Seeing the relationship between nonvirtuous actions and unpleasant consequences will make us afraid of what will happen in the future, and makes us determined to regulate our behavior now. It also makes us try to remedy the negative things that we have already done. Such fear, therefore, is the antidote to many faults. If we avoid certain activities because we are afraid of their consequences, then eventually we will reach the permanently fearless state. Being stupidly fearless, however, is the cause of disaster; with such a wrong attitude we will not avoid negative actions and will not do meritorious actions.

For proper fear to arise we must contemplate the faults of the ten nonvirtues. First we get a general idea; some points may take a long time to become clear while others are easier. The clarity of one's understanding determines how much one practices. A firm understanding results in decisive action. This is the purpose of analytical meditation. The Buddha suggests that we consider how karmic causality is analogous to external causality. A small seed can grow into a tree so large that thirteen wagons can park in its shade; a single karmic seed can result in a rebirth into the lower realms. There is a detailed explanation of karma and its results, both negative and positive, earlier in the *Lamrim Chenmo* (volume 2, chapter 2); here Tsongkhapa just reminds us that ethical discipline will become easy if we see that doing something small may bring about an almost unthinkable experience.

Tsongkhapa also prompts us to remember the benefits of practicing good conduct by explaining a number of stanzas from the *Compendium of the Perfections*:

Heavenly goods, human wealth that gives joy,
Bliss, excellent food, and god-like riches
Are brought about by pure conduct. This is no surprise.
But look, even the excellent qualities of buddhahood arise from it!

It is not easy to be born in the realms of the gods. Such a rebirth is the result of a special purity of conduct. Even human qualities such as an attractive body, inner beauty that everyone finds appealing, wealth, and pleasure are brought about by virtuous conduct. It is no surprise that ethical discipline results in these worldly assets. More wonderful is that ethical discipline also yields the highest pure qualities of buddhahood. There is no way to attain buddhahood or nirvana without ethical discipline; it is the foundation of the entire path. In the beginning, avoiding causing injury to others is based on compassion. This attitude develops into the bodhisattva motivation; bodhisattvas want to do more than just avoid harming others, they want to bring others freedom and bliss. In this way practicing ethical discipline takes one to the level of a bodhisattva. Gradually, every facet of one's mental, physical, and verbal conduct becomes purer; one gets rid of the seeds of negative activity and develops pure wisdom. In the end, every aspect of a buddha's perfect body, mind, and environment arises from the purification of conduct.

There are various poetic images in the *Compendium of the Perfections* praising pure conduct. Ethical behavior that avoids even the smallest non-virtue is called the best ornament we can wear. Usually we drape ourselves in special clothes, lovely colors, and jewelry to make us attractive to others. Ordinary adornments can be nice in some situations, but they look strange in others. Some things look good on young people but are unattractive on someone old; other things are the reverse. Some things are appropriate for women and would look laughable on men. Some things are right for monks and nuns but not for laypeople. All these decorative things, even if they cost hundreds of thousands of dollars, have no essence and are but a sham. But pure conduct is suitable for everyone all the time. It never changes under various conditions. It is the real source of beauty within. It is natural beauty and liked by everyone.

Another example is that unlike the scent of ordinary perfume that follows a breeze in one direction only, the sweet smell of the reputation of ethical conduct pervades everywhere. Another comparison is to scented healing lotions that may be suitable to heal a layperson's burn but its use would break the vows of monks or nuns. In contrast, religious conduct is a salve suitable for everyone; it is the ointment that protects us from the heat of the mental afflictions. Finally, practicing ethical discipline is like possessing wealth. In the world someone who possesses a lot of money is often considered to be better than those who have less. Pure conduct is real wealth; it is superior to any type of property. If all people wore identical valuable garments, they would look the same on the outside; nevertheless, some people are worth more than others. It is the person with ethical conduct who is superior. As stated in the *Compendium of the Perfections*:

Ethical conduct is the path of special attainment,
Making us equal to those who have a compassionate nature.
Its nature brings pure wisdom.
It is the supreme ornament free of faults.

Its delightful perfume pervades the three realms.
It is not inappropriate for even the ordained.
Among those dressed the same, the one with pure conduct
Is the best among men.

Those who practice ethical discipline purely will somehow always have enough to survive. Their needs seem to be met naturally; they always have enough food, shelter, and necessities. Ordinary people and governments sometimes expend a lot of effort to get worldly goods. They may threaten individuals or small countries, "You had better do this or you will be harmed, or jailed, or the army will invade." This can force others to fall in to line, but those with pure conduct never have to resort to such threats. They get what they need without engaging in flattery or coercion because people like to share with those who have pure conduct. They are naturally attractive to others because they have true beauty and kindness. Their relatives and friends of course care for them, but even those unrelated to them, and those they have not helped in the past, like them and want to assist them as soon as they meet them.

People have so much respect for this type of person that they even value the dirt under their feet. You may not have this custom, but in India it is a mark of great respect to touch the ground at someone's feet and bring that dust to the top of your head. It is not that the ground is holy, but pure religious practice has the power to make the place around the practitioner peaceful. People and animals do not have to be compelled to bow down; they naturally incline their heads when someone with pure ethical discipline passes. This does not mean that we should practice good conduct in order to get honor and possessions. It is the nature of religious ethical conduct, however, that these things do happen. This is reiterated in another passage from the *Compendium of Perfections*:

You do not need to use words or labor,
Necessities just come to you.
Without threats all the world is respectful.
You obtain dominance without effort or toil.

If we keep the advantages of ethical discipline and disadvantages of a lack of good conduct in mind, whenever we are tempted to do something negative our knowledge of the consequences of our actions will enable us to stop right away. Until this becomes spontaneous we should try to become more familiar with this topic. This is where the motivation to actually practice comes from. This is the method to enter into the practice of pure conduct. Those who have thought this through are wise, skilled masters.

So what should we do? What is the Mahayana practice of ethical conduct? The *Compendium of the Perfections* says:

> It is not out of attachment to their own happiness
> That bodhisattvas avoid breaking pure ethical discipline worthy
>   of protection.

> With this self control you are happy.
> The wise protect this conduct praised as an ornament.

The wise who are practicing good conduct are not attached to their own enjoyment and peace. This does not mean that practicing to achieve one's own true happiness is not religious conduct. Remember that there are three different levels of motivation on the Buddhist spiritual path. The initial or lowest spiritual level is willingness to practice virtue in order to save oneself from what one fears most—rebirth in the lower realms. A little better is the intermediate level of motivation. This is being concerned with more than a good next rebirth; it is wanting to stop cycling in all of samsara. Both of these reasons for practicing ethical discipline are merely for one's own sake. They are incomplete when compared to the greatest level of motivation for practice: a bodhisattva does everything out of concern for others.

Bodhisattva ethical discipline is perfect because one forgets oneself and acts for the benefit of all others. Here we are talking about ethical discipline on this high level, but do not look down on the other ones. You should not get the impression that practicing that way is almost sinful. It is perfectly correct for beginners to have the first two levels of motivation. The lower goals are valid and important; even bodhisattvas have to equip themselves to work for the benefit of other sentient beings. To do all kinds of things to solve others' problems, we must have a high rebirth with certain kinds of good conditions. Practicing ethical conduct to attain that kind of rebirth as the basis to help others is no problem for a bodhisattva; but to work for that goal for one's own sake is only the general, common form of good conduct. After taking the bodhisattva vow, these lower motivations interrupt a bodhisattva's practice.

The selfish attitude is the main enemy target of the bodhisattva because the primary purpose of Mahayana practice is to benefit other sentient beings. If at any point bodhisattvas think, "I will do this for myself," they are not practicing Mahayana ethical discipline even though their conduct may be meritorious. If they have that attitude they will have gone astray from a bodhisattva's pure conduct.

There is no comparison between the benefit of one hour of a bodhisattva's conduct and many years of good conduct done for one's own enjoyment. We should not have any pride that we are doing this for the benefit of all others. Thinking, "I'm so great because I have that motivation," weakens one's practice. Although the mind usually gravitates to selfishness, we can and should exert control over this tendency. Once we start to think and practice we will be mentally prepared and have power over the mind. We will know what is correct and what is not, and we will do the correct action with confident happiness. This is how to guard pure ethical conduct, say wise bodhisattvas.

According to the *Compendium of the Perfections:*

> One is said to have the perfection of ethical discipline
> By practicing pure conduct for the benefit of the world,
> And wanting to lead all the sentient beings
> In measureless worlds to practice good conduct.

> Clear away your fear of lower rebirths and
> The desire to obtain wealth and high rebirth for yourself.
> Protect perfect stainless ethical conduct and
> Rely on ethical discipline in order to benefit all others in the world.

All the misery of every living creature in the world is a result of not having practiced ethical conduct. To eliminate their problems, all sentient beings must be led to practice ethical discipline. For that purpose we should try to do it ourselves and spread it to others.

In summary, Tsongkhapa says we will practice if we see that our hard work will benefit us. We develop a desire to practice ethical discipline by seeing the negative consequences of acting badly and the positive ones arising from pure conduct. When we are familiar with the consequences of negative behavior, wisdom will direct us away from negative actions. We also must study the benefits of ethical conduct. The highest practice of ethical discipline is practice unconcerned with oneself. It is conduct motivated by the desire to be the great savior of all mother sentient beings. In a stanza of the *Condensed Lamrim,* Tsongkhapa summarizes some of the analogies we have seen before:[4]

Ethical discipline is like pure clean water.
It is the moonlight cooling the heat of the passions.
An ethical person is a mountain among men;
All men bow down before his power.
Seeing that all these good qualities come from pure conduct,
Guard your conduct like noble ones who are wise.

(c') THE DIVISIONS OF ETHICAL DISCIPLINE

The Mahayana practice of ethical discipline is divided into three:

(1') The ethical discipline of restraint
(2') The ethical discipline of gathering virtue
(3') The ethical discipline of acting for the welfare of living beings

The first is the usual type of ethical conduct aimed at avoiding harming others directly or indirectly. This type of ethical discipline is to stay aware and control one's body, speech, and mind. It is the most important aspect of ethical discipline because it is the foundation for the other two. If the mind is negative and one's speech and physical actions are harmful, there is no way one will be able to practice the second and third types of pure religious conduct. The second type of ethical discipline includes a more positive perspective; it incorporates the desire to benefit others. It is difficult to help others if one has not developed the mind, so the second type of ethical discipline is to engage in positive activities to create good qualities in oneself. On the basis of these two types of ethical discipline one can do the third one—actually meeting the needs and desires of other sentient beings.

(1') THE ETHICAL DISCIPLINE OF RESTRAINT

Tsongkhapa says we should understand this aspect of ethical discipline according to the chapter on good conduct in the great Indian text, the *Bodhisattva Levels*. Tsongkhapa does not elaborate on this here because he wrote a detailed commentary on Asaṅga's views in his work titled *Basic Path to Awakening*. If you would like more detail on how to practice bodhisattva morality you can read that text.[5] In brief, the *Bodhisattva Levels* says that this category of pure religious conduct is the prātimokṣa. *Prātimokṣa* refers to the vows of individual liberation. There are seven types of prātimokṣa vows: lay vows of five precepts for men, lay vows of five precepts for women, novice vows for monks, vows of full ordination for monks, novice vows for nuns, post-novice vows for nuns taken for two years, and full ordination for nuns. These vows restrain the three aspects of activity: mental, physical, and verbal. The Tibetan word *vow (sdom pa)* implies shutting a door so that thieves cannot come in. In this sense the vows shut the doors of our body, speech, and mind so that the ten nonvirtuous actions are locked out.

The prātimokṣa vows are called *common* because they are basic elements of all Buddhist practice, both the Hinayana and the Mahayana. A bodhisattva who takes any of these vows—lay, novice, or full ordination—must keep those rules purely. Bodhisattvas are not necessarily ordained. There are even bodhisattvas who have not taken the lay vows. However, all bodhisattvas, even those who do not take any prātimokṣa vows, practice a form of religious conduct common to the Hinayana; they consciously try not to engage in any of the ten nonvirtues. They are always aware of their actions. They see the disadvantages of the negative actions and the advantages of avoiding them, so they try to keep their body, speech, and mind on the wholesome side. In other words, ethical discipline is common to those who take the vows and those who do not. Turning away from negative actions and doing virtuous ones is extremely important in the beginning.

(2') THE ETHICAL DISCIPLINE OF GATHERING VIRTUE

The second type of religious conduct is literally translated as *gathering virtue*. This is a very large category. It is any type of virtuous practice, particularly the six perfections, done daily for the benefit of other sentient beings. We try to bring into being aspects of the practice that we have not yet produced. And we should not lose or let degenerate the virtuous practices that we are already doing. Moreover, we try to increase and improve the positive things we are already doing. This means that bodhisattvas must study the path system, its goals, and how to lead others. They analyze and meditate on these topics. They do many things daily, such as relying on a spiritual teacher, listening to instructions, giving lessons, eating and sleeping properly, practicing generosity, and helping others in many ways. All of these are part of accumulating merit and are included in the bodhisattva vow.

(3') THE ETHICAL DISCIPLINE OF ACTING FOR
THE WELFARE OF LIVING BEINGS

After we have controlled the mind and accumulated merit, we are equipped to actually help others. In general, there is nothing that a bodhisattva does not do to help others. There are so many activities required to help the astoundingly wide variety of sentient beings that they are actually uncountable.

We can, however, categorize all these sentient beings by their needs, attitudes, and mental levels into eleven types:

1. Sentient beings who need immediate and direct help
2. Sentient beings who do not know how to achieve what they desire
3. Sentient beings who need material or spiritual assistance
4. Sentient beings who are in fear
5. Sentient beings who are in misery
6. Sentient beings who are in poverty
7. Sentient beings who need someplace to stay when traveling
8. Sentient beings who want friends or agreeable companions
9. Sentient beings who desire to enter the practice that leads to nirvana or enlightenment
10. Sentient beings who are on a wrong path and need help to reverse direction
11. Sentient beings who need extraordinary, miraculous help

Bodhisattvas must be spiritually wealthy in order to become a wish-fulfilling jewel for all these beings. In other words, they must control their mind and actions as well as create many virtues. Thus the prātimokṣa is of critical importance for bodhisattvas; that is why it is the first aspect of a bodhisattva's ethical discipline. Regarding the ethical discipline of restraint, there are no bodhisattva vows separate and distinct from the prātimokṣa. Like every Buddhist, the Mahayana practitioner must guard the doors of his or her body, speech, and mind. Such practitioners must be aware of what is coming and going so they can keep their vows purely. Because our physical and verbal actions have an impact on others either directly or indirectly, we must avoid those that are harmful. We should investigate the purpose of our actions by asking ourselves, "Are my words meant to help or to harm? Is my action supportive or detrimental?"

In the beginning we will not be able to inspect every action or comment precisely, but we can recognize and try to avoid the most harmful ones. As one's practice becomes more serious, one will become more accustomed to checking what one is doing and what one has done. It will become natural to think, "Oh, I did that again. I should be more aware of that so I do not repeat it." When one cannot help oneself from doing something, one will feel uncomfortable about it. This is a good thing. If you did not know any better, you might do something negative and think that you've done something great. Rejoicing in a bad action makes the negative karma even stronger. In contrast, feeling uneasy that one has done something wrong is part of the antidote. Our practice will slowly become better; first we will be able to eliminate the gross level of wrong action, then the intermediate, and finally the most subtle. The time will come when we will be able to look back at our day and find that we did not do even one nonvirtuous action. That is really wonderful. That is the highest level of practice.

The other two types of ethical disciplines are actually subsets of the first one; it is the first that makes the latter two possible. If the first one is firm, the other two will be easy. If we do not do the first one well, or if we lose the first one, then our bodhisattva vows will also degenerate. We will not be able to make a lot of merit or help others effectively. That is why Asaṅga and other texts say that serious practice of the first type of ethical discipline is the most important in the beginning.

Sometimes Mahayana practitioners think that instructions like, "Do not do this or that" are only for Hinayana practitioners. They think, "Those Hinayana people are beginners. We Mahayana practitioners do not need to worry about that kind of thing. We do whatever we want because we have a great purpose." They think the bodhisattva and tantric vows are different from Hinayana ethical discipline. Tsongkhapa emphasizes that this is incorrect. He says if we think that a bodhisattva should do something other than follow all the rules of the prātimokṣa, we have misunderstood a key point of the bodhisattva practice. It has been said many times in many places that the prātimokṣa—the ethical discipline of restraint—is the basis of the bodhisattva practice. Without restraining our body, speech, and mind from causing harm to others, we have no foundation for further practice. To help others we must first not harm them. Only then can you do something to help them with what they wish or need.

When discussing the ethical discipline of restraint, we distinguish between two categories of negative actions: actions that are naturally wrong and actions that are wrong because they are contrary to rules of ordination. There are over two hundred rules for fully ordained monks and even more for nuns. Some of these are primary and others secondary, but all of them are for the purpose of controlling the sangha members' actions so they do not harm others or themselves.

Many of the secondary rules prohibit actions that are not naturally non-virtuous; these actions are not negative for people who have not taken that vow. For example, there is nothing inherently wrong about eating after noon, touching someone of the opposite sex, sitting on a special seat, or wearing jewelry and perfume. However, because monks and nuns have promised not to do these things, if they do them they are committing a negative action. The purpose of the secondary rules is to help monks and nuns avoid behavior that might lead them into problems with the essential, primary vows. The secondary rules are like a series of protective fences around a special fruit tree. If someone or something breaks the outermost barrier, the fruit tree is still undamaged. If the second fence is broken through, the harmful intruder is a little closer to the tree. If the last protective barrier breaks, the tree is in immediate danger. Similarly, the secondary vows prevent monks and nuns from approaching particular types of negative conduct that break the essential vows. The proscribed actions may not be harmful in themselves, but doing them creates a problematic situation.

A good example of this is drinking intoxicants. Drinking a little bit will not damage anyone or anything. But most people cannot determine exactly how much they can drink before they become drunk. When we get drunk, we lose judgment and control. Once we lose control, we might do anything. There is a story about this from the time of the Buddha. Once a woman came across a monk while traveling on a deserted road. She was in great distress and begged the monk to help her. She said, "I will kill myself here and now if you do not do one of these three things: kill the goat I have with me, drink this jug of wine, or have sex with me." The monk thought, "I should do one of these actions so she does not kill herself. But what should I do? All three are negative karma—but the worst would be to kill and the next worst would be to break my vows of celibacy. The only thing to do is drink the wine." This proved to be a big mistake. After he drank the wine he found the woman to be very attractive and succumbed to lust. After they had sex he was hungry and killed the goat for supper! So he ended up doing all three.

Naturally negative actions are the principal deeds to avoid. They are negative no matter who does them: monks, nuns, laymen, or laywomen. They are wrong whether or not someone has taken a vow. The extent of the negativity differs depending on whether one has taken the vow, but it is always a negative action. Killing another living being is an example of a naturally negative action. There are many, many actions that are naturally so, so many that we could not even conceive of starting to avoid each and every one of them. The Buddha therefore categorized the most serious of them into ten. Ten is a small number; we can handle dealing with ten things. These ten are physical, verbal, and mental actions that we tend to do daily. If we recognize them and try to not do them, we naturally avoid many other lesser negative actions as well. Therefore, avoiding the ten nonvirtues is the essence of the first type of ethical discipline.

Restraining oneself from nonvirtue should be mental, not just physical and verbal. Remember that all our physical and verbal actions are preceded by a motivation; desire, hatred, and ignorance are part of the ten nonvirtues. Not only should we try to avoid the negative actions themselves, we should take countermeasures as soon as a negative motivation arises. Śāntideva says:[6]

> It is best to attentively guard the mind.
> That is the ethical discipline of guarding all conduct.

Take a look at your mind. See if a selfish or other negative intent is there. If it is, what does it make you want to do or say to others? If one's attitude is rotten, even if one's words or actions seem nice, they will be negative. If one's attitude is positive, one's physical and verbal actions will also be wholesome. So we should carefully watch what we are thinking.

Śāntideva advises us to be as vigilantly careful of the mind as we would be of a wound. If we have an injury, we are very sensitive to pain when it is touched. A person with a large wound is very wary of being bumped when walking through a large, wild crowd. Consider the mind to be like a big wound. If it touches a negative attitude, a painful disaster can come about. This is the analogy Śāntideva makes in *Engaging in the Bodhisattva Deeds:*[7]

> Just as I would be attentive and careful of a wound
> When amidst a bustling uncontrolled crowd,
> So I should always guard the wound of my mind
> When dwelling among harmful people.

The *Compendium of the Perfections* says we should restrain all three doors: the body, speech, and mind:

> Do not let the paths of the ten actions deteriorate:
> They are the comfortable path to high rebirth and freedom.
> Someone who abides in these while thinking about benefiting others
> Has an attitude that will yield a special result.

> "Properly restraining your speech, body, and mind
> Is, in brief, ethical discipline," said the Buddha.
> Since pure conduct is the foundation for everything,
> You should train yourself to practice and develop this.

The emphasis in this discussion of ethical discipline is on the first of the three types of ethical conduct: staying away from the ten nonvirtuous actions and performing the ten virtuous ones. It is rudimentary that in order to be able to help sentient beings, we must first keep ourselves from harming them.

This is the groundwork, but it is not enough for a bodhisattva. In addition, bodhisattvas must do many good actions to improve themselves so that they will be able to benefit others. These are the practices of the six perfections. Further, because the Mahayana motivation is to help other sentient beings, bodhisattvas do everything necessary to lead all others to emancipation and enlightenment. They strive to ripen those beings who are not yet spiritually mature. They help those who are a little spiritually developed progress further. Finally, they can lead all others to the final perfect result.

(d') HOW TO PRACTICE

How do we practice the three types of ethical discipline? Just as Tsongkhapa explained earlier in the section on generosity, the practice of any one of the six perfections contains the practice of the other five. In other words, the practice of the perfection of ethical discipline includes the generosity of ethical discipline, the patience of ethical discipline, the perseverance of ethical discipline, the meditative stabilization of ethical discipline, and the wisdom of ethical discipline.

The generosity of ethical discipline is not only to practice the ten virtuous actions, but to do it for the benefit of other sentient beings. The patience of ethical discipline is to be able to bear the hardships and difficulties that attend the practice of ethical discipline. Those who are dedicated to the simple life of ordination sacrifice some temporary pleasure; they may face problems because of the way others act, or their temporary needs may be compromised. However, they can cheerfully bear it because they see the great benefit of what they are doing. The perseverance of ethical discipline is joy in practicing virtue. The meditative stabilization of ethical discipline is to always be aware of one's actions.

The wisdom of ethical discipline is the highest form of ethical discipline. Practitioners of ordinary ethical discipline see the qualities and details of the doer of the action, the object of the action, and the action itself as real and absolute. Their wisdom is the correct *worldly* way of thinking, but the *supramundane* wisdom of ethical discipline referred to here is the wisdom that realizes the emptiness of the three spheres. It is understanding that the doer (oneself), the object (another sentient being), and the action are relative, phenomenal, and dependent phenomena that lack an ultimate nature. There is no such thing as permanent, absolute ethical discipline that is independent of causes and conditions. Realizing the true nature of moral conduct in this way is the wisdom of ethical discipline. Candrakīrti's *Commentary on the "Middle Way"* says:[8]

> The ethical discipline that conceives as existent
> The three—agent, object, and action to be given up—
> Is explained to be a worldly perfection.
> Conduct devoid of attachment to these three is supramundane.

The sutras and the *Ornament for Clear Knowledge* also explain that the practice of any one of the perfections contains all six. Containing everything in one practice makes the bodhisattva method very powerful.

(e') A SUMMARY

Because this is the Mahayana, the motivation for practice is bodhicitta—the desire to attain enlightenment quickly in order to save all mother sentient beings. Until we attain enlightenment, there is no way to have the limitless power and knowledge necessary to help all living beings without any discrimination. Therefore, bodhicitta is essential. It must be developed, reinforced, and increased because only with bodhicitta will we be able to create the many causes resulting in enlightenment. These causes are the bodhisattva deeds such as generosity, ethical discipline, patience, and so forth. Bodhicitta is the root of ethical discipline. It is the supreme way to safeguard pure ethical conduct. Why? Because bodhicitta by its very nature is the best way to avoid harming others. Tsongkhapa therefore advises us to develop bodhicitta. If we have it, he says, we should not let it degenerate and we should try to increase it as much as possible.

In order to engage in the bodhisattva practices, we must know what it means to practice, what the practice is, the nature of it, and so on. If we understand this we can practice all six perfections in many ways every day. There are certain types of conduct practiced on the higher bodhisattva levels that ordinary sentient beings cannot do. For example, the third type of ethical discipline—doing things to benefit other sentient beings—includes the advanced and difficult practice of sacrificing one's body, as mentioned earlier. Although we cannot do that now, we can wish that sometime, somewhere we might be able to do it. It can be a positive goal. We should not think, "I can't do that. It's impossible. I don't even want to start that kind of thing." However, trying to jump right in and engage in the most advanced practices perfectly right at the beginning is a prelude to failure. Seeing what excellence is and wishing that we might be able to do it is important, but we must recognize our present limitations. Encourage yourself by deciding to do as much as you can now while keeping your goal in mind. For example, decide to keep yourself from doing harmful actions fifty percent or even just ten percent of the time.

Then improve yourself bit by bit with joy and awareness. Think, "Before I could only do five percent, but now I can do ten percent." The mind can be developed to an unlimited extent once we start. From a small start we can train ourselves to accomplish something immeasurable.

Beginners must start at the beginning. They must learn what to do and what to avoid. They have to know what actions are negative and decide to eschew them every day. In particular they must understand the two types of negative action: actions that are naturally wrong—such as the ten nonvirtuous actions—and those that are negative merely in connection with breaking the vows one has taken. Ordinary practice is to do whatever one can to restrain oneself from engaging in those actions. It is especially important for those who have taken vows—whether they are prātimokṣa, bodhisattva, or tantric vows—to be aware of the rudimentary downfalls. These are very heavy when broken.

If one has committed actions that are wrong by nature or actions prohibited by the vows one has taken, one should purify them. Purification involves two primary things. One refers to the past: knowing you made a mistake and feeling sorrow about it. The other points to the future: resolving that you will not do that action again. Every day examine yourself; see what you can do and then actually do it. Without that virtuous resolve, even if you do not commit a negative action it is merely a neutral action—neither virtuous nor nonvirtuous. To create virtuous karma you have to have made a resolution, for example, "From now until tonight I will not engage in killing," and then not kill anything the entire day. If you simply happen not to kill anything that day, but had not determined on that course of action, the karma you create is neutral. There is nothing negative about it, but it is not powerful virtuous karma either. To create great merit takes a combination of the mental and physical. Similarly, any action, even if it seems nice on the surface, can be a powerfully negative action if the thought behind it is evil. The motivation, the action, and being satisfied with the action after its completion are all necessary for a rudimentary downfall to occur.

We can be mindful to some extent even in the midst of being busy with other activities. In the morning, or multiple times during the day, think, "Today I will not do such and such." Then at the end of the day check to see what you have done. Did you do that action? If you avoided what you intended to avoid, you should feel happy. Then the next day you will want to continue. This kind of action will yield a positive result even if you cannot accomplish too much in this lifetime. For example, in your next life you will naturally want to act this way without needing to be taught; you will find virtuous practices easy. Then if you receive some teachings, you can develop even more. This is a result corresponding to the cause. Of course, the primary result of deliberately deciding every day to avoid a certain action and then avoiding it will be a fruitional result—a specific type of rebirth.

Right now you have the opportunity to create these positive causes. It would be terrible to carelessly throw it away by not paying attention, not doing positive things, and instead doing heavy negative things. If we continuously act negatively and do not apply an antidote, in future lives we will naturally tend to do the same thing. Our situation will get worse and worse and for many lifetimes we will not be able to train on the excellent path. This can happen. Therefore, from now on we should make an effort to practice. Even if we start small, our positive actions will accumulate.

·12·

The Perfection of Patience

(iii) How to train in the perfection of patience
    (a') What patience is
    (b') How to begin the cultivation of patience
    (c') The divisions of patience
        (1') The patience of disregarding harm done to you
            (a") Stopping impatience with those who harm you
                (1") Stopping impatience with those who prevent your happiness and with those who cause you to suffer
                    (a)) Showing that anger is unjustified
                        (1)) On analysis of the object, anger is unjustified
                            (a')) On analysis of whether the object has self-control, anger is unjustified
                            (b')) On analysis of either adventitiousness or inherency, anger is unjustified
                            (c')) On analysis of whether the harm is direct or indirect, anger is unjustified
                            (d')) On analysis of the cause that impels the harm-doers, anger is unjustified
                        (2)) On analysis of the subject, anger is unjustified
                        (3)) On analysis of the basis, anger is unjustified
                            (a')) Analyzing the causes of harm and where the fault lies
                            (b')) Analyzing your commitment
                    (b)) Showing that compassion is appropriate
                (2") Stopping impatience with those who prevent your praise, fame, or honor, and with those who have contempt for you, or say offensive or unpleasant things to you
                    (a)) Stopping impatience with those who prevent three things: praise, fame, or honor

(1)) Reflection on how praise and so forth lack good
qualities
(2)) Reflection on how praise and so forth have faults
(3)) The need to delight in those who prevent praise
and so forth
(b)) Stopping impatience with those who do three things
to you: have contempt for you, or say offensive or
unpleasant things to you
(b") Stopping both dislike for harmdoers' attainments and delight
in their troubles
(2') The patience of accepting suffering
(a") The reason you must definitely accept suffering
(b") The way to develop acceptance
(1") Rejecting the idea that when suffering occurs it is
absolutely unpleasant
(2") Showing that it is appropriate to accept suffering
(a)) Reflecting on the good qualities of suffering
(b)) Reflecting on the advantages of bearing suffering's
hardships
(1)) Reflecting on the crucial benefits such as
liberation, etc.
(2)) Reflecting on the benefit of dispelling
immeasurable suffering
(c)) How it is not difficult to bear suffering if you gradually
grow accustomed to it, starting with the small
(c") A detailed explanation from the viewpoint of the bases
(3') The patience of certitude about reality
(d') How to practice
(e') A summary

(iii) How to train in the perfection of patience

THE THIRD PERFECTION is the practice of patience. Tsongkhapa explains
this topic by dividing it the same way as he did the earlier ones:

(a') What patience is
(b') How to begin the cultivation of patience

(c') The divisions of patience

(d') How to practice

(e') A summary

In order to practice patience we need to know what it is, so the first subtopic outlines the nature of patience. The second subtopic answers the question, "How do I start practicing patience?" Tsongkhapa explains what we have to do first and how to become interested in the practice. Once we are attracted to the practice we need to know the types of patience; this is the third topic. The fourth topic is an explanation of how to actually practice these sorts of patience. As before, this section includes a discussion of how the other perfections fit into the practice of this perfection. Finally, there is a concluding summary.

(a') WHAT PATIENCE IS

We all know what patience is in a general, vague way but Tsongkhapa says it is important to understand it precisely. Patience has three aspects: being able to ignore the harm caused us by others, the ability to endure mental hardship or physical suffering in the course of what we are doing, and the fortitude to contemplate the ultimate nature of reality. What is the function of each of these three types of patience? What happens if we don't have them? Details about these topics will come later in the discussion of the divisions of patience; here they are just introduced. The first type is the usual way we think about patience: being able to bear any kind of harm, pain, or misery caused by others. The ability not to be bothered by difficulties comes from understanding. We usually get angry when others injure us; we consider someone who harms us, our relatives, or our friends as an enemy. From dwelling on, "This person did this; that is how he did it," and so forth, hatred develops and we want to retaliate. In contrast, patience is accepting whatever happens because we understand the nature of the situation and its causes.

The second type of patience is being able to voluntarily accept hardships such as physical pain or emotional misery as we work toward a goal. For example, students can get very tired studying; farmers endure heat, cold, hunger, and thirst in order to produce a harvest; and bodhisattvas persevere for a very long time to serve all other sentient beings. One's objective must be positive, religious, or helpful if the ability to accept whatever difficulties occur while pursuing it is to be called patience. The problems that arise are not necessarily in relation to an enemy; they include any difficulties that occur when one is trying to help others. When bodhisattvas develop complete bodhicitta, they find even grueling situations enjoyable. Their joy is similar to that of a boxer who relishes his fight; even if he falls down, he gets right back up to box some more. If your patience is strong, no matter how many times you are knocked down you get up to continue working toward your goal. If it is not strong, just one small knockdown is enough to finish you off.

The third type of patience is thinking about the nature of reality: causality and emptiness. Sometimes, when people are unfamiliar with concepts such as karma and śūnyatā, they become impatient or uneasy when the truth is explained. They do not want to hear about the nature of reality because they do not want to learn to think in new ways. This third kind of patience is being able to learn, analyze, and understand the subject, object, and the action of someone harming us from the perspective of ultimate truth. It involves seeing that there is no real ultimate enemy; there is simply a combination of causes and conditions. The action, actor, and object of the action are like an illusory phenomenon. An errorless understanding of emptiness makes uneasiness and fear go away because we see there is no real enemy trying to cause us absolute harm. The true nature of reality is that there is nothing to be angry about. It is all equally empty of ultimately existing. So this kind of patience—knowing the emptiness of things—is a deeper and more subtle form of patience. It is the antidote to our usual incorrect perception of things as truly real. When we realize the true nature of phenomena, anger created by ignorant grasping no longer arises.

There are different levels of this type of patience. In the beginning it is weak, but when yogis reach the first stage of the āryan path their patience becomes irreversible. This is because they have gained a direct realization of the four noble truths and emptiness. No one can shake their understanding by saying, "You are wrong." The *Commentary on the "Middle Way"* says:[1]

> How could anyone, in any way, at any time,
> Injure a bodhisattva who directly realizes emptiness?
> Because he sees all phenomena are like an illusion,
> That very perception brings about patience.

Each of these types of patience has an opposite. The opposite of the first type of patience is hatred. If we do not have the first type of patience, our anger in regard to those we consider enemies will increase. The opposite of accepting hardship in pursuit of our goal is hatred combined with discouragement. We are deterred from doing anything because of difficulties. The opposite of the third type of patience is a dislike or lack of desire to do things.

When we lack the wisdom that realizes the true nature of reality we do not want to engage in difficult activities. In this context anger, discouragement, and dislike are all referred to as impatience. So patience is a bit wider than our usual conception of it. What is the nature of the perfection of patience? It is never allowing the mind to engage in any of these three opposing attitudes. When we are able to apply their antidotes and not let them arise in any situation, then we have perfected patience.

Patience is the destroyer of our true enemy. Harm comes to us because we constantly create the causes for it; our real enemy is our own anger. As soon as anger arises the enemy is there. If we control our internal enemy, no matter how many sentient beings want to harm us for whatever reason, we will be calm and compassionate. This will bring peace and enjoyment to everyone. This arises from inside—it is not a result of eliminating all external enemies. That would be impossible because there are limitless numbers of crude and vicious sentient beings. It is also not necessary. We do not need to subdue or control others; all we have to do is control our own mind. We can accomplish all our goals by doing that. If we conquer anger and develop a loving attitude, there is no one and no thing left to be an enemy. When bodhisattvas perfect patience it is impossible for them to feel hatred because they see all reality with wisdom. Since they understand that there are no absolute enemies, all negative actions that directly or indirectly involve others cease. Everyone becomes an object of their love and compassion. They no longer have any selfishness, so every one of their actions is peaceful. No injury can come from their actions. Their actions result only in happiness, higher rebirth, liberation, and enlightenment. The mental strength not to embrace anger and hatred is the perfection of patience.

So patience is considered one of the most powerful practices, because controlling the internal enemy—anger—is like a victory over all enemies. As Śāntideva says in *Engaging in the Bodhisattva Deeds:*

> You cannot subdue all of the wild,
> Fearsome sentient beings filling space.
> If you destroy your own anger
> It is like destroying all enemies.
>
> How could you find enough leather
> To cover all of the earth's surface?
> Just enough leather to cover your feet
> Is like having enough to cover the entire earth.

Similarly, how can I combat
All external enemies?
All I need to do to repel them
Is to transform my own mind.

What the mind does in connection to others is very important. We produce powerful hatred if we concentrate in a black way thinking, "He is my enemy. He did this and maybe he will do that." This reasoning encourages our fury to grow stronger and stronger. Even if we lie down to sleep on the softest bed, we are uncomfortable because inside we are in turmoil. When someone feels hatred he or she can damage many, many others and perhaps even make him- or herself ill. We should always aim to destroy our anger. Our anger is the enemy target, not something outside. Once we subdue the internal enemy there is no external enemy. The essence of patience is to be free of hatred. It is a way of thinking.

Panchen Losang Chokyi Gyaltsen writes in the *Guru Puja:*[2]

May I be able to accomplish the perfection of patience
So that even if all the beings in the three worlds become angry,
Say harsh things, blame, hit, or even try to kill me,
I maintain calm and respond only to benefit them.

Bodhisattvas develop patience slowly; they practice on many levels until they completely control their anger. Then, even if every living creature rises up as their enemy, it does not bother them. They still feel love for all others. That is the perfection of the practice of patience. That is the goal.

(b') How to begin the cultivation of patience

There are many different ways to develop a feeling of urgency about the necessity to practice patience. The most effective one for us at the present time is to contemplate the benefits of patience and the disadvantages of anger. We will not have much interest in this practice until we are completely convinced about the magnitude of anger's evil and the wonders of patience. We need many reasons to convince ourselves to do anything, so consider, "What kind of effect will patience have on me? What kind of effect will it have on others? What are the destructive effects of not having patience and acting in anger?" Reflecting on these matters again and again while taking into account additional reasons will lead to conviction. The wisdom that comes from thinking logically about the causality of both the positive and negative sides will push us into serious practice. To cultivate patience we must think; patience does not arise simply from getting good at sitting in one place for hours at a time. If we do not consider the reasons supporting the cultivation of patience, there is no way to develop it.

Tsongkhapa quotes Asaṅga's *Bodhisattva Levels* to introduce a discussion about the benefits of patience:

> Bodhisattvas should first look at the many benefits of patience. They should think, "Those who have patience will not have many enemies or any more divisiveness later. Their physical and mental happiness increases. They die without regret and, after this body is at an end, they will be born in the deity realms of the high and happy rebirths." Seeing benefits like this, they express their praise of patience: "I want to practice patience myself and in addition I want to help others to practice patience." When they see someone who has patience, they feel attracted to him or her and are joyful.

This passage answers the question, "What does patience do?" The more people subdue their anger, the fewer enemies they have. No matter what is going on in the world at large, the number of their enemies is naturally reduced until finally there are none at all. A patient person does not experience any more divisive conflict with his or her associates. Close friends are not separated and those already separated go no further apart. With patience people just become closer and closer. For all these reasons, a patient person's physical and mental enjoyment arises and increases. According to Buddhism, our actions in this life will affect our future lives. Most negative actions are in relation to harming others either directly or indirectly. If we are patient, we cease doing anything that harms others. If we do this early in life, we will remain positive, calm, and without regret when we die. And it is definite that we will have a high, peaceful rebirth. Wherever we are reborn we will be loved by others.

There are many details about the benefits of patience in other texts as well. For example, Āryaśūra, a master of poetry, wrote the *Compendium of the Perfections*. Āryaśūra was not a Buddhist but after meeting Āryadeva he became one and earned fame as a great teacher and practitioner. He wrote many praises of the Buddha and his teachings as a spur to practice. If we study his works, our confidence will become stronger and we too will be encouraged to practice patience.

In the *Compendium of the Perfections,* Āryaśūra says:

The Buddha said, "Patience is the holy means
To counter someone desiring to stop altruistic activity."
Anger can destroy the best things in the world,
So protect yourself with patience!

Bodhisattvas need protection from others' bad intent to cut short their practices for the benefit of others. Patience is the best way to deal with such people. If bodhisattvas have patience then no one will be able to stop them. In fact, an attempt to disrupt a bodhisattva causes the bodhisattva to make a special effort to help that person. Anger is counterproductive; it is like a powerful forest fire that burns all growing things. All the excellent things in the world—meritorious virtues and their resulting happiness—can be destroyed by anger. A moment of anger can wipe out the merit it took years to create. Because powerful anger has this fault, we need protection from it. The protection, says Śāntideva, is patience:[3]

There is no vice like hatred.
There is no asset like patience.
Considering these virtues,
I should practice patience in various ways.

Returning to the stanzas praising patience from the *Compendium of the Perfections:*

This is the holy ornament with great power.
It gives strength to those practicing austerities.
It is the stream of water dousing the fire of harmful intent.
Patience clears away harm in this and other lives.

A real ornament of great beauty pleases everyone who sees it. Kings are adorned with lots of jewelry and have the power to grant great assistance or cause great injury. But these royal attributes are not holy or real ornaments. Patience is the true ornament because everyone who sees those with patience wants to be near them, be under their guidance, receive their help, and so forth. The great power of patience pleases everyone because it offers protection and assistance.

Those who want to seriously practice the path give up certain temporary pleasures and luxuries. It can be uncomfortable to practice in solitude with only the simplest food and shelter. Yet sometimes people practicing the most difficult austerities are more peaceful, healthy, and happy than anyone else.

How can they endure these deprivations and practice so joyfully? Patience gives them the power to live an austere life. Without patience they could not do those things for even a couple of days. The source of their patience is the wisdom realizing the advantages of practice and disadvantages of a worldly life.

A hateful mind is like fire. Just as a fire can spread to every tree in a dry area, anger can destroy our virtues and inflame others. If we drench a fire with water we can stop the destruction. Similarly, patience is the stream of water that can put out the fire of anger. If the fire of anger is left unchecked we will create a lot of negative karma. Injuring others, retaliating for our own selfish purposes, and so forth will result in much misery in this and future lives. Patience eliminates these problems. In this life it eliminates our enemies because we do not retaliate against perceived harm. Instead of harming others, we will try to benefit them; as a result we will have nothing to worry about in the future.

The *Compendium of the Perfections* also says:

> Patience is the armor of superior beings;
> It deflects the arrows of wild beings' harsh words.
> Instead flowery praises come from them,
> Becoming a beautiful garland of fame.

People under the power of hatred often shoot arrows of poisonous words. Sometimes words are so powerful they cause pain worse than a beating. Even one sharp word can make us miserable for days or even years. If we do not have patience, then hearing those angry words makes us angry as well. But words like these cannot penetrate the armor of patience. The words do nothing; they are just sound. A patient person smiles and continues to want to make the other person happy. Slowly the angry person will cool down. The furious words will turn into praise. It is as if he or she were tossing flowers. So the term *superior beings* refers to buddhas and, in addition, to bodhisattvas who have produced compassion and love.

Śāntideva also uses a martial analogy to express the benefits of patience in *Engaging in the Bodhisattva Deeds:*[4]

> Great conquerors vanquish hatred and so forth
> That produce all suffering.
> In contrast ordinary heroes
> Slay only corpses that are already dead.

We usually think our enemies are somewhere out there. However, the real enemy—the one who makes you suffer so much—is you yourself. Under the power of anger, jealousy, pride, and so on we strive to destroy those whom we consider to be our enemies. We cannot succeed. There is no need to destroy them anyway; they will all die soon naturally. Thus trying to annihilate external enemies is like beating a corpse. That is not very heroic. In contrast, our inner enemies are always with us. They have been with us since beginningless time; wherever we have taken birth in samsara they have caused us injury and sorrow. These internal enemies throw us into bad rebirths. If we conquer the internal enemy of hatred we are a true hero.

Everyone likes someone beautiful. Patience makes us attractive. In our future lives others will immediately like us. Even beyond that, patience is one of the causes for a buddha's special qualities of form. A buddha's perfect body is not like human flesh and bone; it has a special kind of beauty described as the thirty-two major marks and eighty minor marks. Patience is the artist who makes these beautiful attributes. As it says in the *Compendium of the Perfections:*

> Patience is the artist who creates
> Worldly beauty and the marks of enlightenment.

Do not dismiss these stanzas as simply beautiful poetry. They are describing reality; they are metaphors for the most powerful religious practices. We can see this for ourselves on a daily basis. Think about your anger. What do you do to support and develop it? What kind of actions do you do stimulated by anger? What kind of results come from those actions? Of course they will not be good for others, but will they be good for you either? Seriously think about that and its opposite—patience. If some hate-filled person causes you to have problems, instead of retaliating you can use that person as the object of your patience. They are completely under the power of their internal enemy, so how can you help them to destroy it. What will be the result of acting this way? The benefit of doing this is that it will bring you peace of mind. By teaching this method to others you can bring tranquillity to them and the entire world.

Now Tsongkhapa summarizes the import of these stanzas. Patience gives us the strength never to give up acting for the benefit of others. It becomes impossible for anyone to interrupt a patient bodhisattva's practice. Patience protects us from the enemy—the hatred that destroys many merits. There are so many things that usually bother us or make us angry, but once we have patience we are able to stay calm. Patience is the ornament that makes all who possess it attractive. It is the best austerity because it makes us immune to difficulties, hardships, and suffering. It is like a stream of water that extinguishes the fire of hate. Patience subdues hatred just as a garuda, a powerful eagle, conquers snakes; when a garuda flies above, snakes dare not come out of their holes. Patience is armor that cannot be pierced by an enemy's arrows. It is the method to create the perfect body of a buddha. These are the benefits of patience.

It is important to understand the benefits of patience because practicing patience may entail some temporary difficulties. If we do not see the advantages of doing the practice and disadvantages of not doing it, we could think, "Why should I sacrifice my comfort for that?" We might not even attempt the practice. Or, if we do attempt it, we will not be able to practice with intensity. But when we thoroughly see its benefits, our practice will be strong and stable. Remember, to meditate on patience does not mean to make patience an object of single-pointed thought—it means to actually practice patience.

The great Śāntideva says in *Engaging in the Bodhisattva Deeds:*

> Whoever tries with great effort to overcome anger
> Will be happy in this and other lives.

Tsongkhapa explains that just practicing once in a while will not work very well. However, if we make patience a daily practice, we will always experience joy. Even if we are in physical pain, the mind will be happy. We see this in an ordinary way with people who play sports. Running, boxing, and so forth can cause sore muscles and broken bones, but athletes are joyful because they see a purpose to their suffering. Their goals are limited: perhaps some money or fame. If we see the spiritual benefit we will gain from the practice of patience in this and future lives, not just for ourselves but for all mother sentient beings, then we will truly feel joy that never degenerates. During this life we will always be happy and our future lives will not be in the lower realms. Even if we have to be reborn in the world prior to attaining enlightenment, our rebirths will be special higher states. Good life after good life, we will finally attain the definite high achievement of emancipation or enlightenment. From now until we attain enlightenment, the result of patience is to be continuously peaceful and happy.

It is not difficult to see how, in daily life, negative actions have an effect on others and on us. While some of the disadvantageous results of anger can be seen in this life, others cannot. In other words, there are visible disadvantages and invisible disadvantages. The invisible results of anger—for example, the experience of being reborn in the lower realms—are taught in the sutras and śāstras. We have to trust the explanation of the omniscient ones on this matter because ordinary people like us cannot directly perceive these karmic effects.

Engaging in the Bodhisattva Deeds says:

> All of the merit from wholesome actions,
> Such as generosity or making offerings to buddhas,
> Amassed during a thousand eons
> Will be destroyed by a moment of anger.

Anger is one of the worst mental afflictions. It is like a powerful fire that quickly engulfs and destroys a huge jungle of trees, flowers, and shrubs. Anger is not physically destructive, but it impairs the good potential in one's mental continuum. One moment of anger is so powerful it can destroy the virtues created over one thousand eons.

Not every moment of anger is this strong. There are many different levels of anger. To determine how powerful a moment of anger is we look at the person who is getting angry, how the anger arises, and the object of the anger. An instant of anger is particularly powerful if the object of anger is a bodhisattva. Bodhisattvas have bodhicitta—they have dedicated their lives for the benefit of all sentient beings. They have no selfishness. They see it as their responsibility to free all sentient beings from suffering and lead them to enlightenment. So if we harm a bodhisattva, it is like harming the potential happiness of *all* sentient beings. It is like injuring the president of the United States. Because the president is the representative of all of the American people, harming him wounds the entire population of the country. Thus it is much worse to hate a bodhisattva than to be angry with an ordinary person. Another way to understand the importance of the object is to think about planting a seed in a field. Different fields have different qualities. A field with fertile soil will result in a better harvest than a rocky field with played-out soil. So the person toward whom we act—the field where we plant our virtues or nonvirtues—makes a difference.

There are passages in some sutras and texts by Buddhist scholars that seem to explain this differently. Aśvaghoṣa, who wrote many stories about the Buddha's life and karma, explains this in the same way Śāntideva does—a moment of anger destroys a thousand eons of merit.[5] However, the *Play of Mañjuśrī Sutra* says, "If one becomes angry it destroys the merit created over a hundred eons." Even if one does not act out of anger, one moment of angry thought can destroy a hundred eons of merit. Candrakīrti says the same thing in the *Commentary on the "Middle Way"*:

> If you get angry at a bodhisattva
> For a single moment, you destroy
> The merit of a hundred eons of generosity and ethical discipline.

Tsongkhapa explains that these passages stipulate different amounts of destruction because they are referring to different types of people getting angry. Śāntideva and Aśvaghoṣa are discussing an ordinary person becoming angry with a bodhisattva, whereas the sutra passage and Candrakīrti are referring to a lower level bodhisattva getting angry with a bodhisattva on a higher level.

This is a bit complicated. There are five paths, the three higher of which are divided into the ten bodhisattva stages. At the outset of the first path—the path of accumulation—bodhisattvas are beginners and the buddhas have not yet prophesized their attainment of enlightenment. At a certain point late on the second path—the path of preparation—bodhisattvas are definitely on the way to enlightenment. The buddhas prophesize, either directly or indirectly, that they will achieve enlightenment. So at that point we can say they have achieved the prophesy of attaining enlightenment. The not-yet-prophesized bodhisattvas have not rid themselves of their internal enemy from the root. If they get angry at a higher level bodhisattva—one who has received a prophesy—their progress on the path will be delayed for as many eons as moments they are angry. For example, if they become angry with a higher level bodhisattva for one moment, then even if they were ready to progress to the next stage on the path, they will not progress for one eon.

Not only does anger spoil the causes of happiness, it brings a very bad result of its own. Anger is the cause for a bad rebirth for ordinary beings and for bodhisattvas who have not yet attained a direct realization of emptiness. In *Engaging in the Bodhisattva Deeds,* Śāntideva says that they will remain in lower realms for as many eons as there were moments of their anger:[6]

> The Buddha says, "Whoever has evil thoughts
> About a beneficent bodhisattva such as this
> Will remain in hell for as many eons
> As there were moments of evil thoughts.

If these terrible results come about for a bodhisattva who gets angry at a higher level bodhisattva, there is hardly a need to talk about how awful it is for an ordinary person who gets angry at a bodhisattva. Now, if a higher level bodhisattva gets angry with a lower level bodhisattva, or if a bodhisattva gets angry with an ordinary person, the results will be different. In general, the worst repercussions come from getting angry at a bodhisattva. This is a sensitive area since we have no way of knowing whether someone is a bodhisattva or not. If a person is a bodhisattva and we get angry, all our merit could be ruined! We should therefore strive not to get angry at anyone. No matter who the object is, anger has disadvantageous effects.

The disadvantages for an ordinary person who gets angry at another ordinary person are also taught in the sutras. The *Compendium of Trainings* cites one of the Sarvāstivāda sutras:[7]

> "O monks! Consider a monk who with a pure mind does a full prostration to a stupa containing the hair or fingernails of the Buddha."
>
> "It is so, Reverend One."
>
> "O monks, this monk is said to create the positive potential to become a cakravartin king one thousand times the number of the grains of sand that his body covers down eighty-four thousand leagues[8] to the earth's golden core."
>
> Then the bhikṣu Utpāli stood up, prostrated to the Buddha, and said, "The Conqueror says this monk created a great root of virtue. Is there something that can exhaust, diminish, completely wipe away, or completely extinguish the root of this merit?"
>
> "O Utpāli, I do not see merits like these in someone who has become angry with, injured, or slandered an equal ordinary practitioner. O Utpāli, these great merits are thinner; they are completely wiped away and completely extinguished. O Utpāli, therefore you should not have harmful thoughts toward even inanimate objects, so what needs to be said about anger toward sentient creatures?"

This sutra passage may well be the source of the common Asian practice of circumambulation and prostration to temples and stupas that contain relics or holy objects. The sutra says that one moment of doing humble prostrations with faith in the quality of the Buddha creates enough merit to be born a cakravartin king as many times as there are particles of dirt under one's body going all the way down to the center of the earth. It takes great deal of merit to be born human and even more to be a king. Really powerful merit is required to be reborn as a cakravartin king. A cakravartin king has such special qualities that no one contends with him. He does not have to do anything and yet everyone submits to his rule. He has great wealth and power.

The Buddha's disciple Utpāli asked if something can obliterate the vast amount of merit it takes to yield a result like that. The Buddha said yes; this huge amount of merit can easily be destroyed by getting angry and expressing that anger physically and verbally toward a practitioner of equal advancement—even someone like an ordinary monk or nun. We go back and forth; we can create great merit, but then in the next moment our powerful anger wipes it out. Most of the time our anger is equal to or stronger than our merit, and so we have no positive results. Because anger has such a powerful effect, the Buddha advises us to avoid getting angry even at inanimate objects such as trees or a house. There is hardly a need for him to mention the far worse results that come from getting angry at something that has a mind.

There are several meanings to the phrase *anger destroys merit*. One is that anger can diminish the consequences of a large amount of merit so there will be fewer positive results. It can also mean that anger completely eliminates the merit so that the result of the merit will never occur. Some scholars say that it means that anger causes the experience of the result of the merit to be postponed for a very long time.

Tsongkhapa does not agree that the connotation of *destroy* in this case is that there will be a time lag before the results occur. First, let us look at why some scholars assert that anger does not completely annihilate the virtue, but rather merely delays when the merit will ripen into an effect. They say that if one gets very angry after one has created great virtue, the result of the negative action—the anger—may occur before the result of the meritorious action. Sometime later, however, after the negative results are finished and conditions are suitable, the merit will bring about its positive effect because the seed of the merit is not ruined. They say this because they are comparing the destruction of merit to the suppression of the mental afflictions on the early levels of the path.

The path system is complicated, but in simple terms we can divide the five paths into two levels: the mundane and the supramundane. The first two paths—the path of accumulation and the path of preparation—are mundane paths and the latter three paths—the paths of seeing, meditation, and no further training—are supramundane paths. As a result of long practice of the mundane levels of the path, one can subdue the mental afflictions. One does not get rid of ignorance, attachment, hatred, and so forth from the root, but one temporarily suppresses them. The seeds or roots of the mental afflictions are left in the mental continuum, but for the time being they are powerless. However, since their roots are still there, the mental afflictions can sometimes rise again. The practices on the supramundane level of the path are conjoined with a direct realization of the true nature of reality. This deep insight of the truth removes the mental afflictions from the root so that they never arise again.

We can understand the differences between the mundane and supramundane paths by comparing them to two methods of removing a poisonous tree from our yard. The mundane path is like cutting down the tree but leaving the roots in the ground. We have temporarily eliminated the poisonous tree, but if conditions are right, new poisonous growth can sprout from the roots. In contrast, the supramundane path is like digging out the roots of the tree after we cut it down. No new poisonous growth can sprout from it again. The scholars mentioned before say that anger works on merit the same way the mundane path works on the mental afflictions; it does not destroy the merit from the root. Why? Because anger is a mental affliction based on ignorance, it does not have the power to destroy merits based on the truth. They therefore assert that anger can delay experiencing the results of the merit but not completely annihilate the positive cause. Later, when the right conditions are present, the results of the virtuous actions will occur.

Tsongkhapa says that this line of reasoning is not conclusive. He points out that ordinary individuals—those on the mundane path—can purify negative karma that leads to rebirth in the lower realms through engaging in the practice of confession with the four powers. Confession does not destroy the negative karma; true cessation can only be accomplished by the direct realization of truth on the supramundane paths. However, even though the purification of confession does not extirpate the roots of negative karma, the powerful virtue of the practice blocks the negative karma from *ever* ripening—even if conditions for its fruition are present. Furthermore, once a particular karmic result occurs, then that particular karmic cause cannot yield another result. The ripening of a karma means that in the future, no matter what conditions are present, it will not ripen again. But this is still not the same as getting rid of the mental afflictions from the root.

As one progresses through the four levels of the path of preparation, one gets closer to attaining a direct realization of emptiness. The second and third levels of the path of preparation are called *peak* and *patience,* respectively. These names indicate that the practitioner is close to reaching the supramundane path. At these levels practitioners have an advanced level of mental clarity, but not direct realization of emptiness. When a practitioner attains these levels on the path of preparation, powerful wrong views such as nihilism, doubt, or the opposite of the four noble truths can never occur again, even though they are not yet destroyed from the root. At the level called *patience* the practitioner attains a special confidence that he or she will never be reborn in the lower realms. Again, it does not mean that the negative causes and all their potential have been removed from the root; but such powerful resistance has been acquired at this stage that, even if the conditions are present, these wrong views cannot arise and so there will never be lower rebirths.

It doesn't make much sense to say, "This cause was destroyed," simply because its effect was delayed and another effect was experienced first. We create so many virtues and nonvirtues during our lifetime that lead to good or bad results respectively. At the time of death just one of those karmas will ripen as the next rebirth. It is only one karma that yields the next rebirth; we cannot experience two lives at once. So one karma has to come to fruition before the others. Which one? It will be the heaviest one. If there are karmas of equal weight, the one created closest to the moment of death may ripen first. If there are a few that are equally close, the effect of the action that was more habitual may come first. However, no matter which one ripens first, it does not mean that the other ones are destroyed. One merely yields its result before the others. If *destroy* merely meant this kind of delay then we would have to say that the ripening of any powerful karma, whether virtuous or nonvirtuous, destroys other karmas. In other words, we would have the absurd conclusion that a powerful virtue could destroy another virtue because the powerful one ripened first.

The meaning of *destruction of merit* is that a virtuous action is prevented from ever yielding a result. Regarding this, Bhāvavivika, another great Indian teacher, says that confession with the four powers can destroy negative karma, and powerful wrong views and hatred can destroy merit. If a negative karma has been purified by powerful confession, the negative karma cannot bring its result. Powerful hatred and wrong views destroy merit in a similar way. We can understand this by looking at something familiar, horticulture. If seeds are damaged they will never sprout, even if all the conditions for germination are provided. Tsongkhapa says that these earlier scholars assertion that the result will eventually occur after a delay is wrong. A *delay* is a matter of time, but the meaning of *destroy* is that the seed is so badly damaged it can never bring about a result, even if the conditions for fruition are present.

Different causes have different types of effects, and so there are various levels of destruction. The worst form of destruction is that the primary result of a karma will never occur. This is similar to saying that if a rice seed is destroyed, its main result—a rice sprout and the rice harvest—will not come to pass. Looking at a karmic example, the primary or main result of ethical conduct is a good rebirth and the primary result of generosity is wealth in a future life. Destruction of a particular karmic seed means that a specific life or quality of life will never occur as a result of this individual cause. However, anger —or another destructive mental affliction—does not necessarily destroy every result of a virtuous act or one's entire practice of virtue. The potential for some results may be completely destroyed while some may just be lessened. Anger may destroy the primary result of a karma, but the result corresponding to the cause may not be destroyed. A *result corresponding to the cause* is to enjoy doing a similar type of activity; for example, if you accustom your-self to the practice of generosity, in a future life you will naturally have an inclination to be charitable. Anger can cause various things to happen; some-times the main result is destroyed but the result corresponding to the cause is not destroyed; sometimes the result corresponding to the cause is destroyed but the main result is not destroyed; and sometimes, as mentioned earlier, a new bodhisattva's anger will slow his or her progress on the path. In short, Tsongkhapa says that just as saying, "Confession can purify certain aspects of negative karma" does not mean that all the functions of that negative karma are gone, saying, "Anger destroys merit" does not mean that every function of that merit is made nonexistent.

How much of the root of merit is cut out can only be seen by those with omniscience. We have to depend on our study of the scriptures, our teacher, or the Buddha to understand how much damage is done when those more advanced on the path get angry at less advanced practitioners, or lower ones get angry with higher ones, or equal to equal. Although the subtle details of the disadvantageous results of anger cannot be seen directly, we should under-stand that anger yields very undesirable effects and also destroys the possi-bility of the fruition of the desirable results of other karma.

Some disadvantages of anger are obvious. If one's mind is disturbed by hatred, one will not have any peace or happiness. When we are happy noth-ing seems disagreeable, but if we get angry our enjoyment and peace of mind disappear instantly. If we continue to be angry, not only is our past happiness destroyed, we will not obtain future happiness. We will be miserable and unable to sleep peacefully. People are completely changed when they are angry: the way they look, they way the act, the way they talk, the way they see things, and the way they feel are all transformed in a negative way. If our anger is very strong it may make us completely forget all the kind actions other people did for us in the past. We see those people as enemies and want to destroy them. We may even want to kill our dearest friends. Because of our anger, these kind people will no longer want to be close to us. They will want to get away from our hostility, so they will ignore and abandon us. They will not return even if we try to win them back by giving them lovely presents. We lose those friendships because of anger. Śāntideva says the same thing in *Engaging in the Bodhisattva Deeds*:

> A mind afflicted by hate
> Will never be at peace.
> You will not obtain joy and happiness.
> You cannot sleep and have no stability.

Some people depend on the kind gifts
Of a master's wealth and services.
But even they will attack and kill
Their master if he is hateful.

Your dear friends will ignore you;
They will not stay even enticed by gifts.
In brief, nobody who is angry
Can live in happiness.

We continually see problems caused by anger between friends, family members, students and teachers, rulers and subjects. Once hatred builds up, a past good relationship with someone is all forgotten. All we see is black. It seems impossible, but even our kind parents—who nourished and protected us from the time we were in the womb through our childhood—can seem to be our enemy. An enemy is someone who destroys our happiness. We usually think our enemies are external. Upon consideration, however, it becomes clear that all the problems in the world actually come from within; the real enemy is our own anger. When we see the disadvantages of anger we will not want to be angry for a moment. There is no way that we will be the friend of anger any longer. In contrast, we will see that patience is our best friend because it brings peace and happiness. We will have a great desire to be patient. In short, the development of the antidote to anger is based upon seeing the benefits of patience and the disadvantages of anger.

To reinforce this point Tsongkhapa quotes a stanza from the *Garland of Birth Stories,* a collection of tales recounting the lives of the Buddha before he attained enlightenment. At one time the Bodhisattva was born and raised as a Brahmin. He married, but then took religious vows and began a life of religious austerities. His wife also became ordained and stayed nearby him. The king became aware of this couple seriously practicing yoga. He wondered if the yogi had developed any special power as a result of his religious practice and decided to test him. So the king went to their hermitage and said, "It is dangerous for you and your wife to remain here without any protection. Someone could come and kidnap her. You should not stay here." The yogi replied, "I can destroy my enemies just as a downpour of rain settles the dust."

The king thought, "This yogi has no real power; he is just attached to his wife." So, as a further test, the king sent some men to kidnap the yogi's wife. All through the abduction the yogi sat peacefully. He did not do anything. The king came back and said, "You told me earlier that you had a means to destroy any enemy who came to your hermitage. This was the time to put your plan in action, but you didn't do anything. Obviously you cannot do anything." The yogi replied, "My words were true. I kept my promise and completely destroyed the enemy." Surprised, the king said, "What? If not these men, then who is your enemy?" The following stanzas were the yogi's response. He introduced the king to the idea that the enemy is not external; it is internal anger that destroys happiness:

> The fire of anger will disfigure your face;
> Even ornaments cannot make it attractive.
> Although you lie down to sleep in a soft bed,
> The mind afflicted by anger is in anguish.
>
> You forget those who benefit you;
> Injured by anger you are led down a wrong path.
> You lose your reputation and cannot accomplish your goals.
> Your wealth and glory wither like the waning moon.
>
> Out of anger you fall into a vast abyss
> Of acting badly even toward loving friends.
> You destroy your ability to see what is helpful or harmful;
> Seeing them completely opposite, you make yourself more ignorant.
>
> Anger makes sinful actions habitual,
> So you suffer many hundreds of years in the lower realms.
> What can your most vicious external enemy
> Do other than destroy your flesh and bones?
>
> Anger is the internal enemy.
> Understanding that this is how it is,
> Who can bear
> Its power's increase?

Anger can harm us so much more than any external enemy. In this life it makes us experience many painful losses. When someone is angry, his or her face completely changes. Neither ornaments nor make-up will make the red, quivering face of an angry person attractive even if that person is ordinarily nice looking. Anger makes us lose the ability to distinguish right from wrong. We actually make ourselves ignorant and completely misconstrue situations. Believing things to be the opposite of how they actually are, we act badly, crazily trying to harm others and their property. Because anger destroys everything positive and creates powerful negative karma, we will fall to the lower realms in our next rebirth. Even if we have a good rebirth, such as a human life, the leftover result of anger is to be physically ugly. Our appearance is disagreeable to others; they dislike us simply based on how we look. In contrast, the worst thing the most vicious external enemy can do is kill us, and we will die sooner or later anyway. An external enemy cannot have a negative impact on our future lives if we do not get angry. We have to realize that it is anger that harms us so much more. The great teacher Candrakīrti summarized this in a single stanza in the *Commentary on the "Middle Way"*:⁹

> Anger results in an ugly appearance, leads to low actions,
> Steals away your knowledge of right and wrong,
> And impatience quickly hurls you to a bad rebirth.
> Patience is explained as the opposite: it brings all good qualities.

In general, the Buddhist teachings stress that we should be patient, but we should not be patient with our tendency to get angry. We should be impatient with anger. We should think about anger the way we usually think about an external enemy: "What did he do before? What is he doing to me and my friends now? What can I do to retaliate and destroy him?" Substitute anger for the external enemy. Examine its bad qualities, consider how it has harmed you and others, and look at what it has destroyed. Anger causes so many difficulties; it causes squabbles between parents and children, strife between friends, and wars between nations. As long has we have anger, we have an enemy. When hatred motivates us, we harm others and ourselves. We should meditate on how anger functions and what its results are until we have a very firm understanding of its destructiveness. When one has a spontaneous insight that anger is the real enemy, one will not want to obey it when it rises up. One will seriously think, "How can I fight this? What is the best weapon to destroy anger? Wouldn't it be wonderful to defeat it." This is the key. As a result of meditating like this we will never again be friends with anger; our friend will be patience. We call yogis *great heroes* because they battle the internal enemy that is anger.

Candrakīrti says in the *Commentary on the "Middle Way"*:¹⁰

> Ordinary individuals have anger;
> Bodhisattvas know the benefits of patience and faults of anger.
> The noble ones abandon impatience
> And always quickly try to practice patience so worthy of praise.

Recognizing the faults of anger and the benefits of patience, bodhisattvas always practice the latter. Patience is praised because it always brings peace and virtuous results. Someone who has patience is worthy of praise because his or her actions yield positive consequences. Seeing the detriments of anger and the benefits of patience is the method to enter the practice of patience. It is the practice of the noble ones. *Engaging in the Bodhisattva Deeds* summarizes all that was said above:

> There is no sin like hatred.
> There is no austerity like patience.
> Therefore you should assiduously practice
> Patience in many different ways.

The reason Śāntideva says, "There is no sin like hatred" is explained in Candrakīrti's auto-commentary, the *Explanation of the "Middle Way" Commentary (Madhyamakāvatāra-bhāṣya)*:

> Just as all the water of the ocean cannot be measured with a small scale, we cannot calculate the primary results of anger. There is no negativity greater than a lack of patience in terms of projecting undesirable results and harming virtues.

The main result of powerful hatred cannot be measured. Anger brings an almost incalculable number of terrible rebirths and many horrific misfortunes during those lives. There are many other types of nonvirtuous actions that bring negative results, but anger is considered the most powerful. This is because it has two consequences: it destroys the meritorious karma created during many eons of past lives and causes many bad results of its own. Tsongkhapa says that if anger just brought its own bad results, we would not consider its power to be so great.

Anger is the most destructive, but there are a few other negative actions that also destroy previously created virtue and bring powerful negative results. These include perverted views—such as denying causation—as well as abandoning the holy Dharma, and thinking, speaking and acting in a negative way toward a bodhisattva or a guru out of pride and conceit, and so forth. Concerning the first, it is important to be aware that not all wrong views fall under the category of perverted views. There are many types of wrong views; some hold on to an idea while others deny an idea. Here *perverted views* refer specifically to those that disallow the correct view. For example, denying causation rejects the view that virtues and nonvirtues bring concordant results. This negates the existence of past and future lives as well as the possibility of buddhahood. The other powerful negative views that destroy merit and bring powerful negative results are explained in the *Compendium of Trainings*.

In short, there is nothing more negative than hatred. It is bad for oneself and it is bad for others. It is bad in the short term and in the long term. It is bad spiritually and from a worldly perspective. Hatred is the most destructive influence on past virtues and merits. We therefore need a very strong and powerful antidote to anger. That antidote is the practice of patience. Patience is like a powerful austerity, because if you have it you can bear many hardships. If you practice patience all the time, it brings immeasurable wonderful qualities. Candrakīrti says:[11]

> Patience makes you beautiful, esteemed by the noble,
> Know what is proper and what is improper,
> Take rebirth as a human or god in the next life,
> And it eliminates all sins.

(c') THE DIVISIONS OF PATIENCE

We know roughly what patience is, but the *Lamrim Chenmo* teaches us about the specific types of patience and the many ways to practice them. Patience is mental work; it involves controlling evil attitudes that cause us to act badly. Spontaneous and strong patience can be developed through training the mind; through knowing the categories of patience we will be prepared when particular types of situations arise. There are three major types of patience:

(1') The patience of disregarding harm done to you
(2') The patience of accepting suffering
(3') The patience of certitude about reality

The three types of patience will be explained in detail, but an introductory summary will contextualize the discussion. We usually get angry because we perceive others trying to harm us. We think that they are our real enemy and have many reasons for why they are absolutely bad. We increase our anger by thinking, "He did that to me in the past, he is doing this now, and in the future he will do such and such. He did this to my relatives and friends, he is continuing to do this, and maybe will do so again. And he has been, is, and may be helpful to my other enemies." The first type of patience is countering these nine negative thoughts by seeing that they are wrong perceptions.

We must learn that there is no point in thinking about the cause of harm, the object of our anger, or the reasons for being angry in this way. The main point is to understand that the person trying to hurt us is under the power of his or her internal enemy. Such people perceive things incorrectly and create trouble for themselves and others. Considering things this way makes us able to tolerate whatever others do.

The second type of patience is being able to voluntarily and courageously bear the difficulties that may be experienced in the course of bodhisattva practice. We may even enjoy these difficult situations because we see the purpose of our struggle. For example, a sick person who wants to get well is willing to endure the pain of medical treatment. Bodhisattvas can take on much hardship in order to attain their objective because freeing all other sentient beings from samsara is so important to them.

The third type of patience arises from knowing reality. Until we understand how things really exist, it can be difficult to do certain actions. We have doubts and cannot accept the situation. When we understand reality—the ultimate nature of the harmer, the person harmed, and the action of harming—we can be patient. For example, when people go crazy, do stupid things, and lash out at their doctor, the doctor doesn't get angry because he or she understands what is going on. Fear, anger, and impatience can be removed by realizing the truth. Realization of the truth is the best type of patience because anger usually arises from ignorance.

(1') The patience of disregarding harm done to you

How to practice patience when others try to harm us has two subtopics:

> (a") Stopping impatience with those who harm you
> (b") Stopping both dislike for harmdoers' attainments and delight in their troubles

The first subtopic concerns ceasing our inability to bear it when someone beats us or says something bad about us, our friends, or our relatives. The second topic is about rejecting feeling happy when bad things befall our enemies and feeling unhappy when good things happen to them. Through studying this topic we will learn how to terminate both feeling glad when someone who has harmed us is in pain or suffers a reversal of fortune, as well as feeling impatient when a person we consider to be an enemy has wealth, fame, or other fortunate circumstances.

(a") Stopping impatience with those who harm you

This has two subdivisions.

> (1") Stopping impatience with those who prevent your happiness and with those who cause you to suffer
>
> (2") Stopping impatience with those who prevent your praise, fame, or honor, and with those who have contempt for you, or say offensive or unpleasant things to you

The first subtopic deals with our anger at those who directly harm us by interrupting our present happiness, physical well-being, or peace of mind. We also consider how we are angered when we think about those who prevented our prior enjoyment and spoiled good things we had in the past, and how we get riled up as we worry that they may do the same things in the future. The second topic is about our angry reaction when others engage in a more indirect form of destroying our happiness, such as injuring our reputation or hindering our attainment of wealth, honor, or fame. Our usual way of thinking about the direct and indirect ways we have been harmed increases our anger just as the body is strengthened by consuming nourishing food. If we stop feeding our anger it will die. So we consider why these ways of thinking are incorrect in order to be able to eliminate our anger.

(1") Stopping impatience with those who prevent your happiness and with those who cause you to suffer

This topic has two subdivisions.

> (a)) Showing that anger is unjustified
> (b)) Showing that compassion is appropriate

Here we look at the reasons for why we should be patient even if someone did interfere with our happiness. Not only do we examine why we should not be angry, we see that we should have love and compassion for that person instead.

(a)) Showing that anger is unjustified

Tsongkhapa examines three points of view to show why anger is inappropriate:

> (1)) On analysis of the object, anger is unjustified

(2)) On analysis of the subject, anger is unjustified
(3)) On analysis of the basis, anger is unjustified

The object is the person who is causing us harm. The subject is oneself; here we examine how our emotions, desires, and thoughts can be contradictory. The third subtopic is the base. This refers to the life we have, our very body being the basis for our anger. Just as the stick someone hits us with is the immediate cause of harm, the body is the direct cause of anger.

(1)) ON ANALYSIS OF THE OBJECT, ANGER IS UNJUSTIFIED

Why shouldn't you feel hatred toward someone who is physically hurting you, preventing your happiness, or causing you misery? This first topic is an examination of why it is not suitable to consider this person an enemy. Without thinking deeply about the causes and conditions for our anger, there is no way our patience can become firm and strong. There are four parts to this discussion that must be considered in minute detail in order to overcome anger:

- (a')) On analysis of whether the object has self-control, anger is unjustified
- (b')) On analysis of either adventitiousness or inherency, anger is unjustified
- (c')) On analysis of whether the harm is direct or indirect, anger is unjustified
- (d')) On analysis of the cause that impels the harmdoers, anger is unjustified

(a')) ON ANALYSIS OF WHETHER THE OBJECT HAS SELF-CONTROL, ANGER IS UNJUSTIFIED

First let us look at why we get angry with someone. What triggers our anger? It is thinking, "That person wants to hurt me. He thought about how to harm me. Then he did this and said that. His actions caused me pain and sorrow, so I hate him!" In short, our usual reason for getting angry is that we think that the other person acted with a deliberate intention to harm us, our relatives, or our friends. The key point to question is whether this person is acting independently or whether he or she is compelled to do these things under the power of something else. Are such people acting of their own free will or is there something wrong with them? Upon consideration it is obvious that they have no self-control. Something inside them—like a sickness—dominates their mind. When we understand this we see that it is not right to hate those people; they need our compassion and help because they are in trouble. This line of reasoning is the most effective for developing patience so we will look at it in more detail.

What does it mean to say that people are powerless when they get angry and try to harm you? Anger is not the nature of anyone; people are not born wanting to hurt someone else. No one wants the mental afflictions—attachment, anger, jealousy, and so forth—to rise, but they do as a result of a combination of three causes and conditions. First, there is a predisposition for the mental affliction in the mind. Every time someone feels anger a mental seed is planted and in the future, when the right conditions are present, the person is ready to feel that way again. Just as an ordinary seed needs conditions such as soil, moisture, and sun to germinate, for the propensity of anger to sprout an object must be nearby. In other words, the second necessary condition is that there must be something to be angry at; no one gets angry at nothing. Even if you are angry at yourself, you are there! Third, there is a wrong perception of this object. *Wrong perception* is ignorance projecting something incorrectly on the object, such as seeing impure things as pure, impermanent things as permanent, and so on. Then we perceive the object mistakenly, grasp it that way, and elaborate reasons for our feelings. When these three causes and conditions are complete, the result—anger—will definitely arise. Thus ordinary people have a special potential for anger because the seed of anger is always present. When the other conditions are not there, this potential remains dormant. But as soon as the conditions are there—for example, someone criticizes us and we perceive the situation and the object incorrectly—we immediately get angry. Even though we may not want to get angry, we are powerless to prevent it.

Ordinary people experience these three conditions coming together every day of their lives. Out of ignorance and egotistic selfishness we perceive things a certain way; we worry, doubt, and create all kinds of negative rationales. These thoughts are not founded on the truth; they are based on false perceptions. Nevertheless, they make us feel that we must struggle and fight. These thoughts push us into action; we retaliate and physically injure others or speak harshly to them. This is a chain of causation; one thing leads to the next and we have no power over it. It is like a mental illness that individuals cannot control; their actions are directed by an internal enemy. They have to do whatever that internal enemy says; they are the servant of their hatred. Hatred and ignorance have more power than the person; the individual has no freedom to disobey and is forced by this internal enemy to do actions that are not in his or her best interest. These actions are the cause for future trouble. No one wants to cause misery for him- or herself, but that is the result. As Śāntideva says:[12]

> Those who are disturbed by powerful sickness
> Do not have the strength to do anything.
> Likewise, those disturbed by ignorance
> Do not have the strength to do to anything.

Upon examination we can see that anyone who harms someone else is under the power of his or her internal enemy. To think that this person is bad in an absolute way is false. In reality, it is a pitiful situation—the person who is trying to hurt us is set up and betrayed by his or her own internal enemy. Ignorance creates the anger, hatred compels the wrong actions, and wrong actions will harm him or her. This person does not have the power to choose what to do; his or her actions injure the person as much or more than they wound us. This person is in trouble. He or she totally lacks freedom and the resulting actions are completely outside that person's control.

Physicians do not get angry no matter what their patient does; doctors look for the cause of the abnormal behavior and the cause of the disease in order to cure the sick person. Even when a patient acts like a madman and attacks others with guns or knives, those in a normal state of mind—this person's doctor, parents, relatives, or friends—know that he or she has lost conscious control and is under the power of an illness. They do not treat this person as an enemy, hate him, and try to destroy him or her. They make a clear distinction between the person and the illness. They love that person and want to do whatever they can to free him or her from this evil. They want to destroy the cause of the strange behavior, not the person himself.

We use the same technique here because it is the same situation. When others say the sharpest words they can to destroy our happiness, attempt to physically hurt us, or commit crimes that directly or indirectly injure us, think about how they are not acting of their own free will. There is something wrong with their mind. They are afflicted with mental illness or are possessed by evil spirits. Their evil attitude comes out of ignorance and wrong perceptions; it is not their nature. Treating such people as an evil enemy and retaliating will not help, it will only create more harm. Responding with the incorrect perception that they are the enemy will lead us to act improperly as well. This will add more fuel to their anger and create more misery and suffering for everyone. They need our help, not our hostility. We can reduce their anger by being patient and showing them love and compassion. Then the food of their anger will be exhausted. They may then become stronger and their internal enemy may become weaker. This is the way to practice patience.

A buddha or bodhisattva sees things properly and does not become angry when faced with those under the power of this evil. They feel compassion when others try to harm them. They realize that many things are involved and they try to help people calm the fire of their anger in many ways. They know that love and compassion will settle the immediate situation, but as soon as the necessary conditions are again present, the same problems will arise. So bodhisattvas and buddhas teach others to eliminate anger from the root. Teaching the Dharma is the most beneficial response we can have. This is the way of the Mahayana practitioner.

This is not difficult to understand, but making this way of practicing patience a reality is not easy. Our minds are weak and we are so habituated to the negative side that this way of practicing looks impossible. It is not impossible. Do not give up simply because it is difficult; many people have developed patience this way. The buddhas, bodhisattvas, saints, and wise and noble people of the past were the same as us in the beginning. They were not patient but they chose to develop their minds. The only difference between them and us is that we have not yet chosen to work on this.

Working on this is meditation. We practice mentally so that when a situation arises we can act properly. If we do not practice in advance, when a situation arises we will fall under the power of our internal enemy. So, in a quiet time, we should contemplate this topic. Our insight will develop so that we will understand what is going on. We will be able to keep cool and endure unpleasant circumstances. At the same time, our compassion and love will well up because we know what is going on in the other person's mind. Without training these positive attitudes will not arise spontaneously in our everyday life because we have been accustomed to another way of thinking for a long time. Anger is what comes naturally to us now. We have long obeyed anger and ignorance and believed that other people were our enemies. When the wrong perception arises, we immediately come up with more reasons to support it, and our anger becomes stronger and stronger. If we let these habitual attitudes and actions continue, they will perpetuate a ruinous pattern. We angrily react to someone hostile; the other person reacts antagonistically to us; and together we are like a big fire burning each other. In fear of this the great teacher Gendun Drup prays to Tara for protection:[13]

> Wrong perceptions are the wind
> Inflaming the negative actions
> That incinerate the roots of virtue.
> Please protect me from destruction by the fire of hatred.

We must become habituated to another train of thought. Resistance to meditating on patience occurs because our internal enemy does not want to obey. We should have courage and think, "Now I will act like a bodhisattva. Buddhas do not get angry at people who try to harm them because they know that the bad things people do are compelled by their internal enemy, the mental afflictions. Buddhas and bodhisattvas know that the mental afflictions need to be destroyed, not those afflicted by those passions. The wise know that the mental afflictions can be removed and have worked for many lifetimes to do so. Those under the influence of ignorance and anger have no control and are helpless. I have to do something to help them." If this thought sincerely rises, you will almost magically be able to bring down your anger. This positive way of thinking always works because it is founded on the truth. Once it becomes a habit, it will be continuous and unshakable. It is true practice. Āryadeva summarizes this precisely in his *Four Hundred Stanzas:*

> Because someone angry is seized by demons,
> His doctor is not annoyed at him.
> Similarly, the buddha sees that the demon is the mental afflictions,
> Not the person who has mental afflictions.

This contemplation is one of the most effective methods to reduce anger. What we usually consider to be our enemy is not correct. The source of our problems is not another person; it is anger and the other mental afflictions that come from ignorance. Buddhas and bodhisattvas see this reality and never get angry at other beings. Since the mental afflictions are the source of the problem, buddhas and bodhisattvas lovingly try to help others to eradicate the internal enemies of egotism, ignorance, and hatred. This is how we should treat everyone in the world. For example, when people see their elderly mother doing something harmful, they do not get angry at her. They try to understand her problem. They try to determine what is making her do these things. Because they love her, they try to separate her from the cause of her illness so that she can recover. The great Candrakīrti says:

> Wise people understand,
> "This is not the person's fault;
> The problem is the mental affliction."
> So, they do not fight with others.

This investigation of whether the person is independent or not is the easiest to understand of the many lines of reasoning for the development of patience taught in *Engaging in the Bodhisattva Deeds.* We should concentrate on this because it is a powerful antidote to anger. With this weapon we can become victorious over the mental afflictions, just like great yogis of the past. We will be able to remain calm even when enemies come to harm us. Our response will be peaceful and helpful rather than retaliatory.

Asaṅga develops a similar logical argument in the *Bodhisattva Levels.* He says we should consider a situation where someone gets really angry at us. They tremble with hatred, seize a weapon, and come to kill us. When we look at this person, we perceive an absolute, really evil, bad person. But an independent, real, absolute, so-called *enemy* is not there. The perception of an absolute enemy arises out of ignorance and is a dependent result of causes and conditions. The enemy is empty of inherent existence: it is a mere dharma, a dependent arising, a phenomenon of illusory nature. This is actually the same point Śāntideva makes in *Engaging in the Bodhisattva Deeds* when he says that a person has no independence. Our perception of a completely evil, absolute enemy is wrong because the person is not in control of his or her actions. Our perception of an independent person is wrong because it is like the result of a magic trick—it is really just a lot of causes and conditions coming together. When we understand that there is no real, independent enemy over there, our anger will cease. We should meditate on this until we have a firm understanding. If we become convinced about this now, then we will know what is happening when someone attacks us physically or verbally. We will know that the person has a problem and that we are the right person to help them. The great Śāntideva says it this way:

> In that way they are all under another's control;
> Dependents have no autonomous power.
> Understanding this you have no anger,
> For all things are like an illusion.

This is the patience of understanding of the truth. It is patience based on a more subtle understanding of the emptiness of the action, actor, and object. From a positive perspective we say that one sees that the action, actor, and object exist in a phenomenal, illusory way. Whatever situations we encounter should be understood as dependent products of various causes and conditions. Things appear to us as truly real, but there is no ultimate thing that exists that way. Understanding this will make one happy and at peace. Śāntideva continues:

> When you see something improper,
> Whether done by a friend or an enemy,
> The thought, "This occurs only due to conditions"
> Is the understanding that brings happiness.

Another way to think about this is that no one would suffer unhappiness if he or she were acting freely under his or her own will-power. No one wants misery; everyone wants happiness. So if people had autonomous control, they would not do harmful actions that cause them to suffer. The reason we suffer is because we do not have the independent power to control our experiences. Causes and conditions push us to act and our actions yield all kinds of misery.

When people are moved by powerful hatred or attachment, they injure the person they love most—themselves. Each of us cherishes our self more than anyone else; we grasp our self as the most important thing in the world. But when hatred, attachment, or the other mental afflictions rise out of ignorance, we fall under their power. Under the sway of these mental afflictions, we injure ourselves. We stop eating and drinking, inflict pain upon ourselves with weapons, or hurl ourselves under a train. If under the power of hatred we do not love even ourselves, what needs to be said about antipathy toward other sentient beings? We reject our friends, parents, and children without any self-control. Because people have no power to do otherwise, why should we hate them when they attack us? It does not make sense to get angry and harm them in return. We need to understand this situation in order to stop our anger. On this basis we can develop patience and want to help others. This is religious practice that will benefit all. The following stanzas further explain this point:

> If experiences resulted from free will,
> Then since no one wants to suffer
> There would not be any living creatures
> Who would be miserable.

> When people are under the power of the afflictions,
> They may kill their own dear self.
> Then how could they not
> Cause harm to others' bodies?

In summary, when people come under the power of the afflicted mind, they have no control. They cannot stop harming even themselves. If they harm themselves, how could they not try to harm others? If people truly could choose what they wanted, no one would suffer. Since sentient beings are suffering, thinking that they are acting freely is incorrect. Therefore, treating them as if they had a choice is wrong. The right thing to do is to help them. One will not get angry with others when one understands this.

(b')) ON ANALYSIS OF EITHER ADVENTITIOUSNESS OR INHERENCY, ANGER IS UNJUSTIFIED

Another way to think about the object of our anger is to analyze whether a person's intent to harm us is his or her inherent nature or a temporary, accidental occurrence. The point here is that it is incorrect to be annoyed with someone in either case—whether the person's nature or some passing, adventitious attitude is at fault.

Examine what is actually causing you injury. If it is the very nature of a sentient being to cause harm, why should we be angry? Is there is any point in getting angry at a fire for being hot? The nature of fire is heat; if you put your hand in the flames, naturally you will get burned. Similarly, if it is the nature of certain sentient beings to harm others, we should not get angry at them when they act that way. Neither you nor they can do anything about it. But it is also not right to be angry at others if the harm they cause us is simply due to temporary causes and conditions. For example, does it make sense to get angry at the sky when smoke or dust stings our eyes? The smoke adventitiously occurred; the nature of the sky had nothing to do with it. We should be angry at the smoke, not the sky. Following this analogy, a person's nature is something like the sky and the smoke is like his or her anger. It is not the person but the anger that is the problem. There are just these two choices; there is no other possibility. The following lines from *Engaging in the Bodhisattva Deeds* summarize these points:

> If harming others
> Is the nature of ordinary beings,
> It is not right to be angry at them;
> That is like anger at fire's nature to burn.

> If the nature of sentient beings is pure
> And their faults are adventitious,
> Well then, it is not right to be angry;
> That is like anger at smoke in the sky.

Another way to think to prevent anger is to consider that the nature of sentient beings is like water—it is naturally pure, but it can become muddy. The mud is not the water; it is only temporarily present in the water. This is also the case for ignorance and the mental afflictions in the minds of sentient beings. We respond to situations emotionally because of how they appear to us. With deliberate mental training we can come to understand the difference between temporary occurrences and the nature of things. Wisdom comes from examination. If we do not make an effort, we look at things under the power of ignorance. In contrast, when we analyze situations we see them completely differently. On that basis our feelings and attitudes can change; instead of anger, patience, love, and compassion will arise. Yogis, saints, and so forth changed; they always feel compassion and love even when others act badly out of anger and hatred. No matter what others do, their response is always peaceful. This is the result of meditation.

(c')) On analysis of whether the harm is direct or indirect, anger is unjustified

Another point to consider is whether the harm we experience is directly or indirectly inflicted by someone else. For example, if someone hits you with a stick, you get angry because it hurts. But where should your anger be directed? Should you be angry at the direct or the indirect cause of your pain? If you respond, "I should be angry at the direct cause of the injury," then you should be angry at the stick because it is the direct cause of the pain. But we know that the stick has no power on its own; it is the person wielding the stick that causes the problem. So the way we usually think is that we should be angry at the indirect cause because the direct cause had no independent control. But it is not right to be angry at the person, because he or she has no autonomous power either. If this person had no mental afflictions, he or she would not have hit you. The person has no control and cannot be held responsible; the real harmdoer is hatred or ignorance. This is where your anger should be directed.

It is right to wish to harm anger and ignorance! We should make every effort and use any method we can to destroy them. Anger that comes out of ignorance sees other sentient beings as real enemies; it stimulates harmful thoughts and is always wrong. Wanting to destroy ignorance, anger, and attachment looks like a harmful thought, but it is not negative. Although it is a desire to destroy, it is correct to desire to put an end to the main causes of trouble. When Śāntideva says he is going to cultivate anger, he means this kind of anger; he is practicing to eliminate the source of sentient beings' misery. The main cause of our suffering is indirect; it is ignorance and hatred. How can we make these mental afflictions weaker and weaker until we finally completely get rid of them? It is necessary to analyze them and get angry at them. Śāntideva says:

> Things like sticks and so forth are direct causes.
> If you get angry at the one who uses them,
> Then it is right to be angry with hatred,
> Since hatred is the instigator.

We should not be angry at the person for the same reason we should not be angry at the stick: neither has autonomy; the person is flung around by hatred just as the stick is waved by the person. You may think, "Oh no, these are not the same. People can think and sticks cannot." This is not relevant. When we examine every aspect of the two, we see the person and the stick are exactly the same: neither one has any independence. They both harm us under the power of something else. The stick has no thoughts whereas the person has a mind, and it is a person's thoughts that compel him or her to act. These thoughts are under the sway of ignorance. So it is as if the person is a stick in the hands of ignorance. Such people have no freedom of choice. They do not want to be angry, but hatred arises anyway because of various causes and conditions. In that sense the person is almost exactly like the stick. If it were right to get angry at the stick, then it would make sense to be angry at the person. If it is not right to be angry at the stick, then we should be angry at hatred, not the person who uses the stick. This is an accurate description of reality.

If we practice according to where the truth lies, we can totally defeat the enemy. We must therefore rely on wisdom. Practitioners engage in an internal debate between their wisdom side and their ignorant side. They examine the analogy of a person being equal to a stick until they firmly understand that the person is as innocent of causing them pain as the stick is. But we always go the other way; we go down a wrong path. Relying on ignorance and filled with the internal enemy, anger, we try to defeat our external enemy. Then the other person gets angrier and retaliates. This feeds the fire of our anger. The internal enemy gets stronger and stronger. When ignorance and its branches of attachment, hatred, jealousy, and doubt are dominant, they control a person's actions. Then all kinds of trouble arise.

Yogis think about this for a long time so that, instead of getting angry when difficult situations arise, they immediately realize that the other person has a problem. They feel compassion and desire to help the other person cool down and fight his or her internal enemy. This is the motivation for patience. Those who are dominated by patience will always do virtuous things to create peace and happiness for themselves and others. Meditating on patience means to think; it is an analysis of reality. We think about what makes us angry from many points of view: whether the cause is direct or indirect, whether or not someone has free will, how things are caused, what the point of view of the object is, what our point of view as the feeling subject is, and what things are like from the point of view of life itself. This is a difficult task because we always befriend and obey our internal enemies. Now we have to fight against them. This is the practice of meditation. It is developing wisdom so that patience, not anger, will dominate us.

(d')) On analysis of the cause that impels the harmdoers, anger is unjustified

When we examine what drives someone to harm others, we see that it is not suitable to hate that person. To comprehend the logic of this section we need a general understanding of the Buddhist theory of causality. According to Buddhism, nothing occurs without a cause; every experience—even the smallest pleasure or slightest pain—is the result of a cause. There are two general types of causes: temporary conditions and fundamental causes. In samsara, karma is the fundamental cause for every sentient being's life and experiences within that life. Experiences in one's present life are the result of past karmas: some may have been created in this life, in one's last life, or many thousands of lifetimes ago.

A karma creates a potentiality, or we can call it a seed. Some of these seeds have already ripened into experiences and some of them have not yet ripened. A cause does not yield a random result; a result always accords with its cause. Bad experiences are the result of negative or nonvirtuous actions; good experiences are the result of virtuous or wholesome karma. For any particular experience there is a direct cause and an indirect cause. For example, when someone causes us pain, the basic cause of our unpleasant experience is our previous karma; the other person is a contributing, or indirect, cause of our discomfort. Our prior harmful action ripens as a result such that someone does something hurtful to us. If we had not created the negative karma, we would not have to experience the result. In contrast, buddhas and arhats have destroyed their past negative karma and no longer create any new nonvirtuous karma, so they never experience any more suffering. They only experience peace and happiness. There are many details in the sutras and abhidharma showing which kind of causes yield which kind of results.

Strong belief that whatever we experience is created by the power of karma leads one to stop blaming external circumstances for one's problems. Instead of reproaching others by thinking, "It is their fault; he did this to me and she did that," one thinks, "I am having this experience because I created the primary cause for it at some point in time. These other people are just the contributing cause." At times this is obvious; people may try to harm you in retaliation for something you did in this life. But sometimes it seems as though someone is trying to harm you even though you have done nothing to that particular person. In fact, you *had* done some action in a prior lifetime that harmed that person. If the cause was not created at some point in the past, the result cannot occur. One person's action leads the other person to act; the bad actions go back and forth gaining intensity. Karma created in prior lives causes a chain reaction leading this person to react to you in this life with spontaneous, natural dislike and a desire to cause you harm. In either case—whether or not we know why others are harming us—it is not right to blame them. Our own bad actions affected them; they have a prior karmic relation to us. Whenever harm comes to us, the fundamental cause is our own bad karma. Our karma temporarily forces others to act negatively and we experience the result. Because the harm we experience is primarily the result of a cause we created in the past, instead of blaming the other person we should blame our own previous bad deeds. They are making our problems; they have indirectly caused the other person to act this way toward us.

Experiences are unique to individuals as a result of their karma. External conditions and the entire environment are not unrelated to us. According to the Buddhist sutras, even the worst experiences occur because of the karma one creates. If we have killed, hurt, or burned other sentient beings, we will experience the same kind of result, or even something worse. The amount we suffer is determined by the negative actions we created. After death we could be born in the hells where fearsome hell guardians drag us off for severe punishment. The hell guardians and the terrifying, painful surroundings described in the sutras seem external, but they are manifestations of our own karma. This is much more real than a frightful dream.

Śāntideva goes on to say:

> In the past I caused sentient beings
> Harm of this very sort.
> Therefore it is right that I experience this harm
> Because I had injured this sentient being.

We created the entire situation, so it makes no sense to get angry and blame someone else for it. It is wrong to think, "I have done absolutely nothing! My enemy is absolutely the cause of the damage." Nothing happens like that. In samsaric life the dominant cause for all pain, misery, sensual pleasure, and enjoyment is our own previous karma. We should blame our own past actions for what is happening to us now.

Śāntideva continues:

> The childish do not want suffering,
> But attached to the cause of misery
> They act badly causing themselves harm.
> What is there to blame on another?

Children desire to do some very dangerous things in pursuit of pleasure. They want to eat this or that, touch something they shouldn't, or go somewhere hazardous. They do not want pain, but if they do these things they will suffer. We are like children. We do not want suffering, but the way we act causes us misery. We assume our actions will bring us good things and so we pursue our selfish goals. We get angry and then consciously harm others to get what we want. We do not see that our actions will bring us much greater suffering later. Is there any reason to hate others? No. The cause for our problems is entirely within us: it is our own failings that harm us.

Śāntideva goes on:

> For example, hell guardians
> And the Sword-leafed Forest
> Arise because of my own karma.
> Who else can I be angry with?

The denizens in one particular hell see the appearance of a beautiful arboretum in the distance. When they run there for safety, they find that the leaves of the trees are like sharp knives. These knife-leaves fall down and chop the hell-beings to pieces. There is no external being that plants these trees, throws the weapons, or causes this misery. It is all produced by those sentient beings' karma. So if we are born there, with whom should we be angry? There isn't anyone else besides us.

Not only are our negative actions the cause of our unhappiness, they create the conditions for others' future misery. Ignorance leads us to act. Our action makes the other people angry and do something negative in retaliation. As a result of their actions they will suffer, perhaps falling into a lower rebirth. So didn't we create the trouble for them?

Urged by my karma
Others arise to harm me,
Then they fall to hell.
Didn't I destroy them?

These passages are important. We should put all these ideas together in order to see that we are responsible for our situation. In this sense we are in total control; there is nothing to blame on anyone else. If we do not restrain ourselves, our actions become the cause of a chain of misery for ourselves and others. If we understand things this way, patience naturally arises. The Kadampa Geshe Shawopa said, "When someone says, 'It's not my fault,' this shows that they don't have the slightest Dharma practice." This subject may seem a little difficult; however it poses no problem for someone with faith in Buddhism. When we think about how karmic causality works—that we cannot experience harm without our having created its cause—we are relying on wisdom. Our condemnatory attitude toward others will go away. We will have no more active hatred and anger. We will be patient.

(2)) On analysis of the subject, anger is unjustified

Up to this point we have been examining the object of our anger to see why we should be patient. Now we look at the subject to understand why it is not suitable to be angry. Tsongkhapa uses the term *subject* in a broad way; it refers to our understanding, feelings, attitudes, perceptions, and thoughts. So here we examine how anger in association with any of these mental factors is not logical.

We get angry at others because we are not able to bear the pain that they are causing us. Since we do not want to have any unpleasant experiences, it is contradictory to wish others harm when they cause us misery. Why? Once again the answer is based on the Buddhist understanding of causation. The temporary injury inflicted on us by our enemies is small compared to the misery of hell. If we get angry about relatively minor discomforts in this life, we create the cause for the far greater misery of rebirth in the lower realms. So not wanting pain but continuing to injure our enemies is illogical. It makes no sense if, on the one hand we do not want even the slightest, fleeting discomfort but, on the other hand we do things to create long-term, excruciating pain for ourselves. This is stupid. If we do not want misery, then we should not get angry and harm others. Śāntideva tells himself to think this way to stop anger:

> If I am not able to bear
> This minor misery right now,
> Why don't I stop my anger—
> The cause of the great suffering of hell?

There is a positive way to think about those who cause us harm in this life. When we experience misery we are experiencing the result of previous karma. By experiencing it we finish it off; that bad karma will have no further effect. Thus our enemies are helping us to exhaust some bad karma. If we are patient toward the person who is harming us, not only do we not create new negative karma, we will create great merit. Being patient instead of getting angry will bring us good results such as happiness and peace in the future. So our present enemies are providing us with two things: the exhaustion of previous karma and the opportunity to create positive karma.

Patience, love, and compassion need an object; if there is no fuel there can be no fire. Bodhisattvas think, "This harmful person is actually very helpful in that he (or she) is the object of my patience. Instead of getting angry I should contemplate his kindness in providing me with an opportunity to practice patience." Although it appears that our enemies are trying to harm us, they are kindly giving us the chance to create powerful virtue and solve our problems. They do this by acting improperly without considering the future trouble they will have to endure. By creating a situation for us to practice patience and purify our negative karma, they are creating the causes to destroy their merit and experience future misery. In this light our enemy becomes an object worthy of praise. Who is more deserving of our patience than someone so kind? Rather than getting angry, we should thank them!

There is a story in the *Garland of Birth Stories* to help us understand this rationale. In one of the former lives of the Buddha, when he was a bodhisattva, he was born as an elephant in the jungle. Many small animals attacked the elephant, biting his head and causing him to run here and there in pain. These creatures were actually gods testing the Bodhisattva. Finally, someone asked the elephant, "You are so powerful and have such big tusks. You could smash all these bad little creatures with one blow. Why don't you do it?" The bodhisattva elephant answered with this stanza:

> Without thinking about destroying his own virtue,
> It seems someone is purifying my evil karma.
> If I am not patient with this person,
> What could be less considerate than that?

In the patience chapter of the *Commentary on the "Middle Way,"* Candra-kīrti says:

> It is most desirable to say,
> "The result of prior negative actions is exhausted."
> Since anger and harming others will bring suffering,
> How can you bring yourself to plant that seed?

Right now we are experiencing the result of our prior angry actions. This experience exhausts that particular karmic cause. It is finished and will cause no more harm. However, if we angrily retaliate we create new negative karma that will be the cause for us to suffer in the future. How can we do this to ourselves! How can we want to plant the seeds of even more misery? Patience is mental. We use the mind to consider how even an unpleasant experience is good for us. For example, last week I had an operation: a surgeon cut into my stomach and took out some small thing. It was not comfortable, but I was told that the surgery would prevent great misery in the future. When someone is very ill, he or she will gladly accept the pain involved in surgery, moxibustion, or other therapies if that person believes the treatment will prevent greater pain or danger. We can choose to be patient or impatient with the pain of a cure. If we think, "This will bring me a longer, better life," we are able to bear it. This is the same kind of patience we should have in relation to external harm caused by others. We should look at it in a positive way; there is something beneficial here.

(3)) ON ANALYSIS OF THE BASIS, ANGER IS UNJUSTIFIED

This topic has two divisions:

- (a')) Analyzing the causes of harm and where the fault lies
- (b')) Analyzing your commitment

(a')) ANALYZING THE CAUSES OF HARM AND WHERE THE FAULT LIES

We get angry when someone hits us because of the physical pain that we suffer. There are two supporting factors here: our own and others' bodies. If we did not have a body—say if we were made of empty space—no one could hurt us. However, we do have bodies. They are so delicate; they are like a wound—ready to hurt at the lightest touch. Our enemy has a similar type of body and is afflicted by hatred. So which of the two is to blame for our pain and anger? Usually we think that the enemy is at fault; we are sure we are faultless and did nothing wrong. But Śāntideva examines the situation and says:

> His weapon and my body
> Are both the cause of suffering.
> He brought the weapon and I brought the body,
> So at which should I be angry?

From the point of view of the basis, both one's body and the enemy's striking it with a weapon are the direct cause of the pain. If he did not strike us, we would not experience pain. However, if we did not have this kind of body, we would not feel pain either. Which one should we get angry at? Since both of them are the cause of the problem, both should be the object of our anger.

Śāntideva goes one to say:

> A human body is like an abscess,
> Naturally painful, it cannot bear touch.
> I took this birth blinded by attachment,
> So at whom should I be angry?

Ignorance and so forth cause us to create karma. As a result we are born with a body subject to harm from other beings and the elements. A human body is so fragile that even a tiny mosquito bite causes us grief. So at whom should we get angry when this body is harmed? When we seriously examine the situation, we find that the greater fault lies with us. The primary responsibility for our pain is having taken rebirth in this kind of body. If you have a big wound and go into a crowd of people who are playing around, you may be pushed or bumped; that will cause you a lot of pain. Whose fault is it? On the one hand, there were a lot of people carelessly running around. But on the other hand, you went out into that crowd with a big wound. It is not only the others' fault; you have to be angry at yourself too. In fact, you should be far more annoyed at yourself; if you had not made the mistake of going out there when you were injured, then you would not have suffered additional pain.

There is no basis for your anger with others: the blame lies with you. Understanding this leads to patience with others. We will not get angry at the damage they do because we know that the problem is rooted in having a body that is naturally the basis of harm. We get angry instead at the true cause of our misery: karma and the mental afflictions. In short, if we do not want future pain, we should not grasp a body conditioned to experience misery. This means we have to change the way we act; we must fight against the internal enemy, anger itself, and practice patience so that in the future we will have a completely pure and perfect body, like a buddha's.

Śāntideva continues:

> Out of ignorance some cause others harm.
> Out of ignorance others get angry in response.
> Which of them is acting faultlessly?
> Which of them is acting incorrectly?

Most people are ignorant of the relationship between positive and negative karma and their resultant experiences. Consequently, they think that by harming others they will get what they want; they mistake the cause of happiness and misery. The people that receive the harm get angry and want to retaliate; they are also ignorant about the negative consequences of anger. Both sides are acting in ignorance; neither one is acting correctly. We cannot say that just one side is creating the cause of future harm. In this sense there is no difference between others' actions and our own: both are the cause of our pain. Understanding how things occur is the way to practice patience. When we recognize the causes and conditions for a situation, we can remain calm. We can see that patience is beneficial to us and to those who try to harm us.

(b')) ANALYZING YOUR COMMITMENT

Another way to think about anger is to consider the religious precepts one has accepted. If someone is angry and filled with hatred, he or she will not be able to attain emancipation from samsara. So getting angry with others is not appropriate even for Hinayana practitioners who are seeking freedom for themselves alone. If anger is unjustified for those with an almost selfish motivation for entering the path, it is even more incorrect for those who have taken the bodhisattva vow. The bodhisattva vows start with bodhicitta: a promise to free all mother sentient beings from misery. Bodhisattvas enter the path in order to benefit others. Therefore, there is no need to say that it is not right for them to be angry at anyone else. In contrast, when someone does something detrimental to them, bodhisattvas should want to help that person even more. They are able to bear whatever discomfort or hardship arises by recollecting what they are doing, the purpose for which they entered the path, and their precepts.

The Dharma is the antidote for all misery and suffering in the world; it is the real medicine for all sentient beings because it brings the highest happiness and enjoyment. Bodhisattvas therefore pray that the teachings remain, develop, and spread throughout the world until the end of samsara. This is not a wish that the teachings remain in a library somewhere. The spiritual development of individuals is how the teachings remain. Individuals should understand the teachings, practice them, take the vows, and keep the precepts purely. Then they should share this practice with others. When there is no understanding, the teachings cannot spread; that is when the teachings will have disappeared.

Vasubandhu said something similar in the *Treasury of Knowledge:*

> The holy Dharma is two things:
> Scriptures and realizations.
> Holding and spreading the teaching
> Are the two great practices.

The scriptures are the means for us to learn. They are one part of the Dharma, but the most important part is the realization of the teachings within us. "Holding the teaching" means our own spiritual growth and understanding. We develop the mind following the path higher and higher until we finally attain enlightenment. Individual practice is how to attain realizations and achieve our own goals, but the bodhisattva Dharma is also to spread the teachings to others who do not have this knowledge. The bodhisattvas' goal is to lead others to happiness and emancipation from suffering. The way to achieve this goal is through these two activities: holding the teachings to develop oneself and sharing them with others. This is how the teachings of the Buddha remain in the world.

Regarding this the great Kadampa lama Potowa says:

> The Buddha's teaching is not to do sinful activity. Yet when someone does a small harmful thing, others do not practice patience and then accuse that person saying, "He (or she) is destroying the root of the teachings." Those critical people are giving up their vow; they are destroying the teaching from the root.
>
> We do not have the general Dharma teaching. We break our vows and the teachings decline. We are like a yak catching its tail in the saddle ropes and bucking and kicking. If the yak relaxed, the ropes would loosen and it would be happy. Similarly, we become more unhappy when we do not relax and competitively retaliate to harm done to us.

The essence of the Buddha's teachings is not harming others. The way to practice this has two aspects: the foundation is to avoid doing sinful actions. This means not to harm others in thought or deed. This in itself is meritorious. Practicing not harming others and developing the mind out of desire for one's own emancipation is the Hinayana. The second aspect is Mahayana practice; Mahayana practitioners do activities to benefit others in addition to not harming them. Sometimes, when practitioners see another practitioner doing some small harmful thing, instead of practicing patience they point at that person and accuse him or her of destroying the teachings from the root. Even if others are doing extremely harmful things, such as killing, we should not accuse them of destroying the Dharma, but we should be patient and help them. We may be tempted to say that they are acting against the Dharma, but someone who says that is giving up his or her own vows. The accuser is the person destroying the teachings from the root. If an individual loses his precepts, merits, and virtues, then the teachings are completely destroyed; the Dharma is gone like the setting sun. This is not external destruction; it means that there is nothing left inside that practitioner. For the Dharma to remain, individuals have to have realizations, precepts, and spiritual growth. Destroy these internal things and the Dharma disappears. This is in regard to one as an individual. For the Dharma to remain in the world, it must shine within. It is from the point of view of an individual that the Dharma exists.

Potowa gives an analogy that is culturally specific and so may sound strange to you. When we release the ropes that tie a big load to a yak's saddle, the yak usually tries to get away. Its tail can catch in the ropes and it bucks and kicks the saddle trying to get free. This makes it worse and the ropes tighten. If the yak relaxed, it would be easy to remove the ropes. Similarly, if we relax—if we are patient and do not react too much when someone injures us—we would be okay. If we get impatient and retaliate, however, we will only bring ourselves more misery. Hitting the enemy twice because he hit us once will worsen the situation. The point is that patience will bring happiness and peace. It will bring to an end many harmful, unpleasant situations. Continuing to act in the same angry way to which we are accustomed will just bring us more suffering.

Up to here we have looked at reasons why it is not suitable to become angry with others. Now we will examine why it is suitable to have compassion for those who harm us.

(b)) Showing that compassion is appropriate

Why should we have compassion for others? It is because all of us—every sentient being—has been born in samsara from beginningless time. We have been born together with them all in many types of lives. There is not one type of life in which we have not been each others' father and mother many times. We cannot point to any single living being and say, "This person has never been my mother, my father, my relative, or my dear friend." Each of these lives is impermanent. Every moment life changes; nothing stays as it is. Sentient beings die and then they are reborn. Not only do they experience death: they endure the three types of suffering: the suffering of suffering, the suffering of change, and the suffering of pervasiveness.

The suffering of suffering is ordinary physical pain and mental anguish. The misery of change is that even temporary pleasure is actually the nature of suffering because it is ready to bring us misery. The final type of suffering is that no matter where one is born in samsara, one is subject to misery. Those born in the higher realms of the form and formless deities may not have any mental or physical pain in that life, but they are still under the power of karma and the mental afflictions; therefore, when that life ends they fall down in samsara. Life in the upper realms is only a temporary, slight relief from the suffering of suffering.

All sentient beings are in misery because of being reborn in lives conditioned by karma and the mental afflictions. The mental afflictions drive sentient beings crazy. Everything they perceive, everything they do, and everything they think is under the power of ignorance, desire, hatred, jealousy, doubt, and so on. Perceiving things incorrectly, they act in ways that are harmful to themselves. They do not know if their actions are harmful or beneficial. The mental afflictions destroy the possibility of attaining happiness in this and future lives.

We should recollect this general situation when somebody says or does things to harm us. Consider the nature of the problems endured by this particular person. All such people have an internal enemy that is making them destroy their own happiness. They need our help now. So when others act this harmful way, we should be patient and try to cool them down. If they say cruel things, respond pleasantly. If they try to injure you, try to help them. If we do this, the other person's internal enemy will eventually be reduced and his or her real nature will be revealed. It is very useful for ordinary people like us to think this way sometimes. When we recollect the troubled nature of all sentient beings, we see that we should have compassion and love for them. How could it be right to get angry or retaliate when they harm us?

(2″)Stopping impatience with those who prevent
your praise, fame, or honor, and with those
who have contempt for you, or say offensive
or unpleasant things to you

We typically think that praise, honor, and respect make us happy. We do many things in order to become famous and earn commendation. When others block us from achieving renown, we become angry with them. If they blame us, demonstrate disrespect, or speak harshly, we get irate. Therefore, there are two subtopics in this section:

(a)) Stopping impatience with those who prevent three things: praise, fame, or honor
(b)) Stopping impatience with those who do three things to you: have contempt for you, or say offensive or unpleasant things to you

(a)) Stopping impatience with those who prevent
three things: praise, fame, or honor

There are three parts to the discussion of how to stop getting angry when someone obstructs our attainment of praise, fame, and honor:

(1)) Reflection on how praise and so forth lack good qualities
(2)) Reflection on how praise and so forth have faults
(3)) The need to delight in those who prevent praise and so forth

First, we examine the nature of praise and so forth in order to recognize that they have no significant good qualities. We feel that praise and fame are worthwhile, but actually they are disastrous; all they bring us is a lot of trouble. Therefore, the second topic is a discussion of the faults of praise and so forth. Finally we reduce our anger because we see how those who prevent us from being praised and honored are our benefactors.

(1)) Reflection on how praise and so forth lack
good qualities

Praise is a verbal expression of esteem spoken directly to you. Fame is praise spread abroad; it is not said directly to you, but far away others speak well of you. Both praise and fame have no significant positive attributes. They are empty words; they cannot bring us a long life, freedom from illness, health, or wealth. Not only do they not provide anything of real value in this life, they do not bring us the merit that results in a better future life and good things in that future life. If praise and fame did lead to attaining our goals in a future life, then they would be worth something. But they don't; they have no essentially good quality. Nevertheless, if someone puts an end to our fame and so forth, we get upset and become angry. This is very childish.

There are two stanzas in *Engaging in the Bodhisattva Deeds* that tell how foolishly we are acting:

> Things like praise and repute
> Do not bring merit or a long life.
> Nor do they bring health or freedom from disease.
> They do not even bring any physical pleasure.
> If I understood what would benefit me,
> What good are these things for me?

> When a sandcastle is destroyed,
> A child cries until he is exhausted.
> Similarly, when I lose fame and repute
> I react mentally just like a child.

Children work very hard building sandcastles on a beach. If someone comes along and destroys them, they cry and cry. A sandcastle has no value; it cannot function as a real house and is not useful for anything else. It is a senseless thing, but children feel that it is a most important object. In the same way, we ordinary beings get extremely upset when someone destroys our fame, praise, honor, or repute. These other people are not destroying anything real; nevertheless, we get very angry with them. Thinking that these meaningless things are so critical to our happiness, we get upset when they are interrupted. When we see that these things do not have much purpose, their lack will not matter to us.

Think about this in a positive way. Instead of feeling angry, we should understand that when these things are destroyed, it can actually be good for us. Of course, we do not usually think this way. We are strongly habituated to think otherwise and it seems that there is no way to stop doing so. But practitioners can change; by engaging in concentrated analysis they come to realize that praise, fame, and so forth are hollow. Realizing that there is nothing to get upset about, their feelings of deep attachment will slowly diminish. When they understand the causes and conditions for a situation, their anger will stop. When we meditate this way we will know how to respond as soon as the situation arises.

(2)) Reflection on how praise and so forth have faults

Wise people are not preoccupied with purposeless words of admiration. When ordinary people are praised they start thinking of themselves as something special; they become conceited and attached to their reputation. When someone is completely distracted by fame and conceit, he or she feels happy. For any spiritual practice we must feel sorrow about the misery we and others experience. We have to want our own freedom from suffering, and we have to want to free others from such problems. Without this kind of sorrow we have no spiritual goals; our religious practice will go nowhere. Attachment to fame and praise destroy this very important kind of sorrow. Furthermore, when we are vain about our reputation we become jealous seeing others with praiseworthy qualities or education. Our conceit makes us envious when someone receives more honor than we do. The increase of our self-attachment confuses us, inviting and strengthening the other inner enemies. We become the servant of our inner enemies. We do all kinds of bad things based on pride and so forth. As a result our virtuous activity degenerates. There is no good that comes from that. As Śāntideva states:

> Praise and so forth distract me.
> They destroy my sorrow.
> They make me jealous of others' goodness.
> They destroy all positive things.

Anger, desire, and the other internal enemies have no limbs or intelligence, but we do exactly what they want. If anger orders, "Say something bad," we say it. If anger demands, "Do something—Hit them! Kill them!" we obey. As Śāntideva states:[14]

> The enemies hatred, desire, etc.,
> Have no arms, legs, and so on.
> They have no heroism or intelligence,
> But I act just like their servant.

If we are going to get angry, it should be toward these internal enemies. But we are very patient with our anger. This is the wrong place to be patient. This is what makes so much trouble for us. From this analysis we see that praise, fame, honor, and attachment to them bring us nothing but problems.

We should renounce them. Sincere religious people try to avoid them instead of trying to get them. Yogis and real practitioners do not avoid developing qualities that are praiseworthy, but they are not striving for praise. Furthermore, it is meritorious to admire someone's good qualities. Extolling another person's good qualities will bring us benefit. But the person who is praised should not be attached to those words; that attachment will only strengthen their internal enemy. When we practice patience this way, developing love and compassion becomes much easier. For as long as we lack patience and are under the power of anger, it is very difficult to succeed in the rest of the practices. Seeing this will help us stop anger and impatience.

(3)) The need to delight in those who prevent praise and so forth

We need to stop our habitual attachment to praise because it causes our internal faults to increase. These faults lead us to create bad karma, as a result of which we fall into lower rebirths. When somebody prevents us from feeling misery and pain, we should be grateful. So when others destroy our reputation, we should welcome them from the depths of our hearts thinking, "They are wonderful! I have been so attached to praise and so forth that it seems as if I want to undergo the deepest suffering of the hells. But these people are preventing me from falling into the lower realms; they are helping me cut the bonds of attachment. This is like a blessing of the Buddha!" Thinking this way will bring to an end to our anger. Joy will arise. Meditators analyze each situation, "What is here that is worth something? What is the future benefit of this? If I don't have this, what will happen?" They learn to see situations clearly, with wisdom. They feel happy and calm when someone cuts short their praise and so forth. This happiness leads them to act in a way that helps others as well. *Engaging in the Bodhisattva Deeds* has some verses that make the same point:

> Therefore aren't those closely involved
> In destroying my reputation
> Actually coming to protect me
> From falling into a lower rebirth?

The other person may not actually be thinking in this positive way, but this is how it should look from your side. This is the real antidote to anger in this type of situation.

Śāntideva says:

Since I am striving for emancipation
I do not need the bondage of wealth and honor.
How can I be angry toward those
Who try to free me from these chains?

Wealth, honor, respect, and so forth bind us to samsara because when the mind is caught up with attachment for them we are tied to misery. Since we are working for emancipation from suffering we should want to be free of these ties. We should not hate someone who frees us from these things. We should thankfully enjoy it. Śāntideva then concludes:

I seem to want to enter misery.
But like the blessing of the Buddha,
Someone closes the door, not letting me go.
How can I be angry with that person?

How can we get upset when others prevent us from being praised? How can we be angry with those who keep us from going to hell? We should be happy and grateful.

(b)) Stopping impatience with those who do three things to you: have contempt for you, or say offensive or unpleasant things to you

One can easily become angry when faced with contempt, offensive speech, and unpleasant words. In order to develop patience, the wisdom side of the mind must argue with the ignorant side. We have already dealt with the mistaken idea that we should respond with anger toward those who cause us direct harm. Now the ignorant side of our mind makes another argument by bringing up those who cause us indirect harm. It says, "Others will not like me if someone ruins my reputation." The wisdom side responds, "It does not hurt you if others do not like or respect you. Their affection or dislike is in their minds; it does not harm you, so there is no need to be concerned." Ignorance retorts, "If others do not like me, I will have no friends and I will be unable to become wealthy." When thoughts like this arise we must counter them. It can happen that if others hear bad things about you they will not be friendly and that will block you from getting worldly goods. But if you worry about this and act in damaging ways to become affluent, your prosperity will not be helpful to you. Wealth is only temporary. Even if you are wealthy throughout a long life, when you die all of your possessions are left behind.

All you take to your future life is the karma you accumulated to gain those material things.

Considering this Śāntideva says:

> It is better for me to die today,
> For living long with ill-gotten gains is not right.
> Even if someone like me lives a long life,
> At death these things will be the cause of misery.

Dying is not unusual, and death can come at any time. We should therefore not spend all our time enjoying food, houses, and so forth that have been obtained by actions stimulated by desire, hatred, pride, or jealousy. We may take pleasure in our possessions for a long time, but at death all this stuff becomes the cause of misery. These objects are seeds that sprout negative karma. In this way they lead to suffering. After we die all of our hard-earned wealth is gone. We cannot take a single thing with us.

Śāntideva also says:

> If you enjoy a wonderful long-lasting dream,
> What is there when you wake up?
> If someone dreams of happiness just a short time,
> What is there when he awakes?
> When the two of you are awake
> There is no dream-pleasure left for either.
>
> A short life or long life
> Are both finished at the time of death.
> I may live a long time
> Enjoying the great wealth I obtained,
> But like a great thief, death steals it all;
> I leave destitute with empty hands.

It doesn't matter if a good dream is long or short; when one awakes the pleasurable experience is finished. There is no ongoing enjoyment from a dream. Nothing, not even a small amount of happiness, is left. Similarly, it does not matter whether this life is long or short. Either way the pleasure that arises from food, clothing, houses, and other things is temporary. Whether we have a lot or a little, over a long time or just for a minute, at the time of death it amounts to the same thing. There is nothing we can carry with us. Even if the entire world were in your possession, death is like a great thief who steals it all. You are not left with one single thing. What we take with us are the seeds of the actions we created. Every negative action deposits a negative seed in our mind stream. Those seeds ripen in future lives.

(b") STOPPING BOTH DISLIKE FOR HARMDOERS' ATTAINMENTS AND DELIGHT IN THEIR TROUBLES

In the preceding sections we looked at how to stop anger when someone harms us directly or indirectly. In this section we examine how to stop two other attitudes toward those we consider to be our enemies: our unhappiness when good things happen to our enemy, and our pleasure when they experience difficulty.

The essential goal of Mahayana practice is to liberate all sentient beings from suffering and bring them to a state of the highest bliss. The way to attain this objective is to become perfect in order to be able to help others successfully. If we desire to attain buddhahood quickly for the benefit of other sentient beings, how can we be angry when good things happen to some of them? On one side, we wish that all other sentient beings attain the bliss of enlightenment; on the other side, we are unhappy when they have wealth, honor, or enjoy some small thing. These are completely contradictory attitudes. If our objective is that all living beings be happy, we should be pleased when others experience positive circumstances. We should be assisting them to attain even better situations and more happiness. Seeing this contradiction in ourselves, we should abandon jealousy and rejoice in others' good fortune. Otherwise our bodhicitta, love, and compassion are just words and nothing we do is real Mahayana practice. Śāntideva says:

> Desiring the happiness of all living beings,
> I produce the thought of attaining enlightenment.
> How can I become annoyed
> If some being attains happiness on his own?

> If I desire that all sentient beings
> Become worthy of the honor of the three worlds,
> How can I be pained by jealousy
> If I see them gain some limited respect?

Buddhas are revered as objects of worship in the desire, form, and formless realms. Bodhisattvas want every sentient being to attain that status; they want all sentient beings to attain buddhahood and be worthy of homage. It is inconsistent to want that and also be envious or unhappy when someone else receives a little wealth or honor. When jealousy like this arises, a Mahayana practitioner should immediately say to him- or herself, "How can I have this contradictory attitude? I should be enjoying their happiness." We should be like good parents who care about their children's welfare. If children have wealth, health, and happiness, their parents are happy. They cannot be unhappy because they wish that their children would achieve these things. Śāntideva says:

> Caregivers are responsible for their charges' livelihood.
> If that person I assisted is able to thrive—
> Finding material wealth and a good reputation—
> How can I be disgruntled or annoyed?

Further why should we be unhappy if someone gives something to our enemy? Those material things do not belong to us whether or not our enemy possesses them. If we are unhappy when our enemies have some agreeable experiences, then our wish to help them to attain highest enlightenment is completely false. According to Śāntideva, anyone who is angered or envious of others' success does not have bodhicitta:

> If I do not want even that for others,
> Then what is my wish for their enlightenment?
> How can someone have bodhicitta
> If he is angered by another's good fortune?

> Whether they receive something from someone
> Or it remains in the benefactor's house,
> It is completely immaterial to you.
> How can it bother you if they give or not?

Mahayana practitioners must continuously fight against the enemy of bodhicitta. This enemy is internal: it is unhappiness when someone else has a good experience, and enjoyment when someone else experiences poverty, sickness, or other bad circumstances. It is wishing that bad things happen to our foes—that their property, reputation, or even their life is destroyed. It is happy when even a single person has a problem. This enemy prevents the attainment of great love, compassion, and bodhicitta, and it destroys those qualities once they have been attained. We should therefore always try to stop this negative attitude. Of course, in order to stop feeling this way, we first have to recognize how we usually think about others. Then we consider the negative consequences of this attitude. Wishing that bad things happen to others leads us to engage in actions that destroy others as well as ourselves. Any harm done to others is negative karma that will bring us an unpleasant result in this life or in a future life. We may also experience a negative result right away because the injured person gets angry and retaliates. Maybe this person has many friends and they get angry as well. Evil thoughts are like a fire that starts small but spreads further and further. In addition, there may be far worse consequences in a future life. Even if we do not take action based on this negative thought, we will suffer a negative result. The mental activity is a cause that will have an effect even if nothing directly happens to the person we label *enemy*. If nothing bad happens to this so-called enemy, we suffer because we do not get what we wish. We feel angry, dissatisfied, and unhappy. We simply destroy our own peace of mind.

Śāntideva continues:

> When the enemy is unhappy,
> What is there for you to be happy about?
> Your mere thoughts and wishes
> Will not cause him harm.

> Even if your wish caused the enemy's suffering,
> What is there for you to be happy about?
> If you say, "It gives satisfaction,"
> What is more destructive than that?

> The hook cast by the fishermen, the mental afflictions,
> Is unbearably sharp. Once caught on it,
> It is certain that the hell guardians
> Will cook me in a kettle in hell.

When yogic practitioners use their wisdom to argue with their ignorant wrong attitudes, they sometimes address that wrong side as *you*. So they say, "Why are you happy when your enemy is miserable? You wish bad luck on them, but no matter how much ill will you have, it will not have any harmful effect on them. Even if the wretchedness you wish upon them actually occurs, what is there for you to enjoy? Does it bring you a long life, wealth, or virtue? No, it brings you nothing good." Now the negative side will contend, "Well, it gives me satisfaction; that is good enough for me." But the wish for others to be distressed and feeling satisfaction when they experience it creates powerful negative karma. This attitude is a disaster; it is very destructive. It is a mental affliction that hooks you and throws you into the cooking pot of hell. It is like the desire and hatred of fishermen who catch fish, take them out of the water, and cook them in a pot for supper.

Yogis point to their own actions rather than blaming something external for their unhappiness. There are many reasons for unhappiness. Someone may have harmed us directly or hurt us indirectly by damaging something that makes us happy. We also become unhappy if our friends and relatives do not have good fortune. And if those we find disagreeable have a small amount of pleasure, that also makes us unhappy. We have to know how to deal with all such instances of unhappiness because unhappiness fuels anger, and anger is the most powerful evil in the world. Anger may start small—as when a squabble breaks out within a family—but if no one stops it, unhappiness increases wildly and pushes people this way and that. Even wars begin with an individual's anger. If an antidote is not applied, unhappiness and anger continuously arise. When we are not unhappy, anger does not arise, and neither do the resultant problems. The method to eliminate unhappiness and anger is to understand causal relationships. Without this understanding we have no antidote.

How do we develop firm patience? There is no marvelous secret trick. The only way is to follow the instructions based on the writing of great bodhisattvas like Śāntideva and many others. These yogis developed wisdom using many tools: they used logical reasoning, scriptural resources, and contemplated their own experience. With all of these together they were able to stop unhappiness and hatred. We too must try to gain wisdom by going back and forth between logic, scripture, and experience. We must use all three in our debate against ignorance, pride, jealousy, and so forth. The logical approach is to turn away from unhappiness for our own good. The problem facing us is that our ignorant side places the blame for our problems outside on someone else. Our practice is to look at our ignorant side as the source of our difficulties. We must internalize this view and think this way all the time in order to stop anger. In this internal debate, wisdom will eventually be victorious over negative thoughts.

There are two types of wisdom. Wisdom that is conjoined to mental stabilization penetrates the depths of the truth and is victorious over all the mental afflictions. Prior to this direct realization there is analytical wisdom. Analytical wisdom is thought. It scrutinizes what is happening between us and our internal enemy; it examines the causes for our experiences, and investigates how causal relationships affect each other. When we have a proper understanding of this, we will completely stop hating others and will instead direct our anger at the true cause of suffering—anger itself. We must employ analytical wisdom so that patience will arise naturally. When patience rises based on understanding, it will not be fleeting. It will be strong and stable. Then no matter what anyone does, we can be patient and loving.

Sometimes people have an incorrect understanding about the way to meditate to attain enlightenment. Following Hva Shang Mahayana's view, they believe that every thought is an obstacle to deep realization and enlightenment. According to this view, the pure mind is like empty sky: thinking—both good and bad thoughts—is like clouds that obscure the space of the mind. When these clouds are removed, the pure mind comes forth and the person has attained enlightenment. Holders of this view believe that because analytical wisdom is constructive thought, it should not be done.

Of course, as mentioned earlier, there are some points in spiritual practice when thought is an obstacle. But this is not true all the time; it is true at certain specific times only. For example, when one has a direct realization of śūnyatā, the direct object of one's meditation is only emptiness; the mind perceives only śūnyatā, and nothing phenomenal or relative appears. During that meditation session one will not have thoughts. But this does not mean that at other times practitioners should not think or judge between good and bad. If one's practice is simply to stop thinking, it is like going to sleep. That is laziness. Some people are attracted to this because it is peaceful. They do not need to worry about anything; if anything comes to mind they try to blank it out. It is difficult to vacate the mind at first, but success in this will not get you anywhere. In fact, it is a great barrier to learning, education, and developing wisdom.

Śūnyatā—emptiness—does not mean an empty mind. The emptiness of all phenomena is that they lack, or are empty of, any kind of ultimate reality. A realization of emptiness is seeing how things exist and how they do not exist. Under the power of ignorance we believe phenomena exist as we perceive them. In the beginning of our practice we must gain an understanding of this through analysis, employing inference and logic. This inferential knowledge gradually deepens until it becomes a direct realization. From there it goes even deeper until it is wisdom free of seeing phenomenal things. In short, the realization of śūnyatā requires both analysis and mental stability.

Those who cast away analytical wisdom are throwing out the wisdom side of practice. If one casts away analytical thought, how could one meditate on even fundamental concepts such as the four noble truths? How can one meditate on the truth of suffering without thinking about it? This holds true for all the practices of the method side, such as meditating on impermanence, love, compassion, bodhicitta, and so on. For example, we need many reasons to practice pure religious conduct; we must understand why we should not lie, or kill, and so forth. It is through analysis that we come to an understanding of the disadvantageous consequences of stealing and the other non-virtuous actions. It is this understanding that enables us to stop stealing. Tsongkhapa therefore comments that it is a great obstacle to spiritual development to think that meditating on patience means to keep the mind blank or to focus upon patience as an external object. While the mind is blank we may feel no anger, but as soon as we are faced with an unpleasant situation we will get angry. With analytical wisdom we can fight against anger. Our patience will be very firm and stable. The practice of Buddhism does not come by itself; it requires learning, investigation, and a lot of study.

(2') The patience of accepting suffering

We have already looked at the first type of patience, which is to have no desire to retaliate when others cause us injury. The second type of patience is to voluntarily and joyfully accept whatever problems arise. Instead of seeing a miserable experience as bad and trying to fight it, we should tolerate it. This subject has three subtopics:

(a") The reason you must definitely accept suffering
(b") The way to develop acceptance
(c") A detailed explanation from the viewpoint of the bases

The first topic outlines why we should voluntarily accept suffering. The second explains how to do it. In the third section we will look at detailed examples illustrating how to do this.

(a") The reason you must definitely accept suffering

The reason to willingly accept difficulties is that if we do not do so, the original problem will be magnified and, in addition, we will suffer mental misery.
    Śāntideva says in *Engaging in the Bodhisattva Deeds:*

> The causes for happiness sometimes occur.
> The causes of misery occur very often.

Samsaric life is caused by karma and the mental afflictions. There are many external and internal causes and conditions that continuously result in misery. As a result of the combination of our previously created karma and temporary conditions, pain and misery certainly occur. Sometimes there is mental discomfort, and sometimes there is physical pain; sometimes the misery is rough, other times it is more subtle. From a superficial worldly point of view, religious practice requires an austere life that results in much discomfort. Yogis, ordained men and women, and even serious lay practitioners engage in activities that are not geared to temporal pleasure. Whether or not we are practicing virtue, our karma ripens and we experience problems.

For the time being there is no way to avoid negative karmic results, but we can deal with our experiences in a way that makes them beneficial. We can make negative experiences and our problems part of the path. We must learn how to transform our difficulties and unhappiness so that they help us to attain a higher rebirth, enlightenment, and benefit others. If we do not know how to do this, then we will naturally experience pain and misery.

We often react negatively to the most minor uncomfortable experience. Although the problem is a natural karmic experience, we think of it as bad and worry about it. Our anxiety magnifies the problem and we suffer far more mentally than we did from the discomfort of the original difficulty. Having made the whole situation much more miserable, we become negative, mentally weak, and our enthusiasm for the practice of virtue dies down. Out of this comes anger, destroying the causes for happiness and our ability to continue practicing. However, if we accept whatever happens, a physical problem will not bother us mentally. In fact, a basic acceptance of suffering can turn even intense physical pain into something insignificant. The initial misery cannot be turned away, but because we do not elaborate upon it there is no additional suffering.

Furthermore, if we voluntarily accept suffering we can come to view it as positive. We see this with athletes; they may break their bones or almost die, but they do not necessarily see this as suffering. Boxers, for example, do not consider their sport a punishment. Boxing is painful. If boxers did not view it with a positive attitude, being hit just once would cause a tremendous amount of suffering. But they ignore the pain because they see it as a means to get things that will make them happy. They see their sport as educational, a source of wealth or fame, and as something that makes them heroes. So they have courage and accept their opponent's punches no matter how many times they are knocked down. Theirs is a small purpose; Mahayana practitioners have a goal that is far, far more important—to help all sentient beings attain enlightenment. So just like athletes, it is important for practitioners to be able to use the difficulties they encounter in a positive way in order to persevere in spiritual practice. Bodhisattvas are able to make many painful sacrifices because they feel a special joy when working to benefit other sentient beings.

Their own suffering does not matter to them because they are so determined to help others.

Impatience and anger are always negative responses to hardship, pain, or suffering. If we voluntarily accept these as a means to a positive goal, we can endure them joyfully. The mind can make every circumstance—pain and of course pleasure—part of the path. Even if a bodhisattva has to remain for eons in hell to lead just one sentient being to enlightenment, he or she will do it without the loss of compassion and love. With practice we too can develop this kind of patience.

(b") The way to develop acceptance

Naturally we do not like it when we have problems. We see the situation as bad and this makes us unhappy or irritable. This section discusses how to develop the patience of acceptance in two subsections:

(1") Rejecting the idea that when suffering occurs it is absolutely unpleasant

(2") Showing that it is appropriate to accept suffering

(1") Rejecting the idea that when suffering occurs it is absolutely unpleasant

In general, we become more and more unhappy when we are in pain. However, it does not help to make oneself miserable if it is possible to change the situation. If we can change the situation, we should do something about it instead of dwelling on our problems. Some types of difficulties cannot be resolved, but it is still unproductive to make oneself unhappy. If it is an unalterable situation—for example, an incurable disease—worry and concern will not change things or benefit us. If we are overly sensitive, even the smallest, subtlest thing can be terribly bothersome and difficult to bear. Sensitivity is a mental quality that comes from thinking and worrying too much about oneself. If we are not overly sensitive, we can withstand much greater suffering. We do not turn small problems into giant ones. Śāntideva says the same thing:

> If there is a cure,
> Why be unhappy about it?
> If there is no cure,
> What is the point in being unhappy?

He also says:

> I should not be hypersensitive about
> Heat, cold, rain, wind,
> Sickness, bondage, beatings, and so on.
> Being that way just increases the pain.

Our attitude is the key. The more patience we have, the more we can bear. When you see the benefit of doing something, the difficulty of doing it will not bother you too much. Some people believe that jumping into freezing water will improve their health. Because of this conviction, they are able to take icy baths. Farmers endure heat and cold working outside, but they bear it so that they can reap a rich harvest. In contrast, other people worry, "Going outside on a windy day is very uncomfortable," so even when there is a light breeze they endure great suffering. Until one completely gets rid of the causes for samsaric life there will always be problems. If one has wisdom and develops the patience of acceptance, one can bear all kinds of external problems: from inanimate difficulties such as the weather to tribulations caused by animate sources like people or animals.

(2") Showing that it is appropriate to accept suffering

Suffering can benefit spiritual practitioners because it increases their mental strength. Their love and compassion for others will become much stronger and sharper. Even ordinary people can utilize some of their problems for their own benefit. There are three subtopics discussing various ways to accept suffering:

(a)) Reflecting on the good qualities of suffering
(b)) Reflecting on the advantages of bearing suffering's hardships
(c)) How it is not difficult to bear suffering if you gradually grow accustomed to it, starting with the small

Suffering does not naturally have good qualities, but if we use it properly we can get something good from it. The point is that if we did not have any suffering we could not get what we want—patience. To develop patience we need some type of problem, because patience cannot arise on its own. You may think, "Well, there may be some benefit to suffering, but I can't do this practice. It is too hard." It is difficult, but if you start with something small you will become accustomed to it. Slowly you will increase your ability to be patient. Finally, even a great problem will not be difficult to bear. For example, bodhisattvas are so accustomed to this practice they can give their flesh, bones, even their life without regret. They too started small and developed stage by stage.

(a)) Reflecting on the good qualities of suffering

Suffering has five good qualities:

1. Suffering urges us to strive for emancipation from samsara. Generally when we are in pain, ill, or have problems, we are very conscious of our difficult situation. Clear awareness of misery makes us determined to search for a means to eliminate it. If you believe you do not have a problem, you will not have a desire to be free from it. If you do not have a desire to be free from that problem, you have no incentive to practice the method that leads to its elimination. This is not just applicable to temporal situations; when one is aware of the problems of samsara, it changes the way one thinks about life. One develops renunciation of cyclic rebirth. This stimulates one to search for a religious practice to attain freedom. In the beginning, ignorance conceals the depth of our suffering; we regard our life as unproblematic and fundamentally enjoyable. This can lead us to waste the precious opportunity offered by this fortunate life. Suffering has the valuable attribute of making us determined to achieve its opposite—total emancipation from misery and the attainment of the highest happiness.

2. Suffering eliminates conceit. Pride and conceit are problems for a practitioner because if we think that we are great, we put ourselves above everyone else. Sometimes, out of vanity we take some small positive attribute in ourselves—beauty, wealth, or knowledge—and blow it up hundreds of times. We become puffed up with conceit, like a balloon filled with air—just hollow and empty. Vanity prevents us from seeing the need for further education or spiritual practice. Suffering deflates us and brings us down to the ground. It humbles us. This is a valuable experience.

3. Suffering causes us to be careful about negative karma. The experience of suffering is the result of a karmic cause. If we do not want an experience, we should not create the cause for it. Once one understands that negative karma is the cause of misery, one becomes careful to avoid creating that type of karma. For example, usually we have no hesitation about eating. But once a certain type of food has made us very sick, even if it is very delicious, we try to avoid eating it again. Sometimes people endure sickness or an accident that nearly kills them. If they recognize that terrible circumstance was the result of negative karma, they become very religious; to avoid a similar circumstance in the future they strive to avoid negative actions as much as possible. Thus a positive quality of suffering is that it stimulates our spiritual practice.

4. Suffering makes us have a strong desire for happiness. If we want happiness, we have to create its cause. The cause for happiness is virtue or meritorious conduct. From the experience of misery we become serious about the practice of virtue. We become happy about engaging in wholesome conduct.

5. Suffering causes us to make the inference that others also suffer, and as a result we develop pity, mercy, and love. If we do not feel any discomfort, others' misery would not seem real. In that case our desire to free others from suffering will be weak because their situation seems like fiction to us. In contrast, experiencing misery sharpens our compassion because we can extend our personal knowledge of suffering and its causes to others who continue to wander in samsara. A desire to help others stop the causes of their misery and create the causes of happiness arises from understanding our own suffering situation.

We need to think about these points again and again. You should add examples from your own experience, meditation, and analysis. When one really sees the good results that can come from suffering, the experience of misery will become something good! It becomes something that you desire because you recognize that it leads you to stop unwholesome actions, destroys conceit, leads you to create virtue, develops compassion, and so on. Yogis and bodhisattvas know how to use samsaric suffering to promote their spiritual practice. We too need to learn how to joyously welcome difficulties, physical pain, and hardship. When we suffer we should take advantage of the situation. Śāntideva says to himself:

> Without misery there is no thought of renunciation.
> Therefore, you mind, accept this firmly.

Emancipation is the total cessation of samsaric misery. You have to truly want emancipation, otherwise you will not try to attain it. In order to desire it, you have to recognize how and why suffering is a problem. This will not occur without experiencing suffering. Renunciation of suffering in samsara is not possible unless you accept suffering. Śāntideva's stanza reiterates this point:

> Moreover the benefits of suffering are:
> Sorrow clears away pride,
> Produces compassion for living beings,
> Avoidance of sin, and joy in virtue.

(b)) Reflecting on the advantages of bearing
    suffering's hardships

There are two subtopics to explain the advantages of patiently enduring suffering:

(1)) Reflecting on the crucial benefits such as liberation, etc.
(2)) Reflecting on the benefit of dispelling immeasurable suffering

(1)) Reflecting on the crucial benefits
    such as liberation, etc.

There are worldly benefits to accepting suffering. People, and even some animals, weigh their choices and voluntarily take on some difficulties for future benefit. Students study day and night, sacrificing some pleasure because they know that going out for fun may result in failure. Sick people are willing to take bitter medicine, injections, and even endure amputation in order to get well. In samsara we have done many difficult things, deliberately ignoring the pain, in order to pursue our goals. For the sake of sensual enjoyment or happiness we have done whatever seemed necessary. Thieves and murderers focus on their short-term desire for wealth, property, and power without any concern for the hardships involved in committing those actions, the immediate problems that may result, or the consequent unimaginable suffering in future lives. We have experienced the results of those negative actions many times. We have fallen to lower rebirths and have endured pain there many thousands of times. But none of this had any purpose; we are still in the same situation. We did not achieve true happiness nor did we give everlasting bliss and freedom to others.

Consider it this way, "While in samsara I have been willing to endure suffering to attain small goals such as wealth or fame. From beginningless time up to now I have cycled up and down in many types of lives and experienced measureless suffering all for limited, temporary purposes. I have wasted all that time; all that suffering was of no use—I have not achieved any good, lasting thing." As Śāntideva says:

> In order to satisfy my desires,
> I have burned in hell many thousands of times.
> But that did not accomplish my goals,
> Nor did it bring about benefit for others.

In contrast, accepting suffering as part of a spiritual practice has far greater benefits; it extends life after life, leads to emancipation, and grants one the ability to help all others. We should think, "If I was able to accept so much misery for my trivial goals, I should certainly be able to withstand some difficulty, pain, or suffering for something far more worthwhile." The goal of the spiritual path is for you and all others to obtain measureless happiness and the highest bliss. For such a superior goal we should be willing to undergo great tribulations, so there is hardly a need to say anything about accepting minor difficulties. With an attitude of voluntary acceptance there is no mental discomfort in the face of these problems. With patience we can be happy and bear any hardship. If others try to injure or kill us, we can have sympathy for them and create no negative actions in retaliation. We can accept whatever happens. This is not an unwilling, resigned acceptance; it is a joyful willingness to accept the situation. When you see that your patience benefits both you and others, it gives you great happiness.

Śāntideva continues:

> This mere suffering is not painful,
> Since it accomplishes the great goal
> Of eliminating the misery harming living beings.
> Suffering is something about which to be joyful.

So why not be patient and willing to bear suffering? We can achieve great things if we use this life well; we can obtain better future lives for ourselves and accomplish great benefit for others. Mahayana practitioners see the value of a human life for developing bodhicitta. They recognize that their experience now of heat or cold or discomfort is nothing in comparison to their past experiences in the hell realms. They think about their goal of truly helping others and know that if they are patient and accept the immediate situation, they can accomplish it. In this way any difficulty along the way becomes a source of happiness for them. Try to remember this way of thinking when problems occur in the course of your practice. Therefore, if something troublesome happens, think, "Why shouldn't I be able to bear this problem? I may have difficulties now, but I am still fortunate to be able to work for the benefit of other beings." When we see the purpose of our actions and the value of our goal, we will be far less touchy about insignificant matters. With this kind of attitude you can raise your spirits and be happier.

According to Buddhism if we lack compassion and strive to obtain worldly goals, we are following a bad path. Often we are willing to endure extreme difficulty as we struggle against others to obtain ordinary pleasures. Sometimes we are deceived by bad spiritual teachers who convince us to engage in austere and painful religious practices for egotistic, selfish ends; we may stab ourselves with tridents or sit in the midst of blazing fires thinking it is the path to freedom. Other people take on a life of severe austerities for a greater purpose. Buddhist yogis can be healthy and joyful because of their mental attitude. Their wisdom gives them great strength. It provides them far more peace and happiness than the satisfaction of an extremely rich person with a worldly attitude. Those with selfish, limited goals can own a great deal, but the slightest difficulty makes them incredibly unhappy. Bodhisattvas' joy never diminishes because they practice for a higher goal than selfish happiness or the temporary elimination of misery. This assessment will give you the courage to accept suffering voluntarily. It is not easy to do, but you should not fear it. It is nothing compared to what you have endured for far lesser goals. Try to have a fearless attitude.

(2)) Reflecting on the benefit of dispelling immeasurable suffering

The second benefit of accepting hardship is that this type of patience can turn away immeasurable misery. This is the case in ordinary as well as spiritual situations. For example, in certain places there is capital punishment for criminal activity: if you kill someone you will be put to death. However, if your death sentence is reduced to amputation of a finger, you would be very happy. You will happily accept the small punishment because it is so much less severe. Śāntideva says:

> Isn't it fortunate if a man condemned to death
> Is released with just an amputated hand?
> Isn't it wonderful that accepting human suffering
> Frees you from the suffering of hell?

When we experience problems it is the result of previous karma. In previous lives we created negative actions and as a result we have a great deal of trouble and suffering in this life. We have a choice: we can accept what happens, or we can get angry and blame others for our difficulties. The injury we experience now is the fruition of a karmic seed. That karma is exhausted by our experience, but our negative reaction to the injury creates new causes for future suffering. If we become impatient and retaliate when someone harms us, our problems escalate and we will never have any peace. Our present situation will deteriorate, and for eons our lives will get worse and worse. But we can stop that from happening by accepting the hardships we encounter in this life. We can use the present situation to create virtue. If we accept our misery right now, thinking, "If react with hostility, I will create the causes for misery a thousand times worse and far more lasting than this. In a way, experiencing this difficulty is a good thing because it exhausts the former karma. I will not have to endure far worse suffering in the lower realms. Also by using this opportunity to be patient, compassionate, and loving toward others, I can create the causes for future happiness." This is the way that accepting difficulties cuts off the causes and conditions for misery in future lives. In other words we can choose temporary suffering or long-term misery. Shouldn't it make us happy to see that almost unimaginable future suffering can be stopped by accepting our present problems?

This is how yogis and bodhisattvas think about their lives. Sometimes the practice of the spiritual path is difficult because it requires practitioners to sacrifice worldly enjoyment. Due to external circumstances, it can be austere and at times painful. Mahayana practitioners know that if they act with patience and acceptance, they can improve the temporary situation for themselves and others. Even more importantly, they always recollect the reason they are engaging in difficult yogic practices: only if they eliminate the seeds of samsara, cease taking rebirth propelled by ignorance and karma, and attain omniscience will they be able to truly benefit other sentient beings. To achieve the altruistic goal of bodhicitta, we should joyfully accept any problems that come our way. Understanding this will help us now and turn away many difficulties in our future lives. It will give us courage and help us create virtue. As we become accustomed to this way of thinking we will gradually be able to practice patience. When our entire life is used to create the causes for everlasting freedom and happiness there will be a great result.

The mind is the main thing. We can look at things in a foolish way and create gigantic amounts of misery. Or we can look at a giant problem in a special way—seeing its advantages and disadvantages, now or in the future— and act in a way that creates great merit. Because the patience of accepting some temporary suffering during this short human life can achieve a great purpose and stop the misery of future lives, shouldn't we feel wonderful about it?

(c)) How it is not difficult to bear suffering if you gradually grow accustomed to it, starting with the small

Everything becomes easier though practice. In the beginning of the practice of patience you cannot endure great hardship. But if you gradually develop the intention to be patient, and then actually train your mind in the type of practices presented here, you will eventually develop this ability. Through training the mind, starting with small problems, eventually big things will not be so difficult to bear. Śāntideva says:

> There is nothing at all
> That does not become easier through practice.
> Therefore, from accepting small problems
> You will be able to bear great difficulties.

When soldiers go into battle they wear armor for protection. Our mind needs protection in a similar way. Mental armor is an attitude. Putting on mental armor is deciding to take on voluntarily every internal and external hardship because of a special objective. It is thinking, "Because I must quickly attain buddhahood to fulfill my desire to help other sentient beings, I must be able to bear whatever difficulty occurs along the way. So when this type of thing happens, I will never do *that* again. I will do *this* instead." If we develop this attitude in advance, it will be in place when needed. At first our ability to accept suffering will be mixed; some things will bother us and some we will be able to tolerate. But gradually our ability to accept suffering becomes stronger. The *Compendium of Trainings* says that if we become accustomed to enduring small problems, later we will be able to deal with the most difficult ones. When bodhisattvas reach a certain level they have no difficulty sacrificing themselves for the benefit of others. They even enjoy helping others this way. We cannot do this the beginning. We start small, go step by step, and eventually we can achieve great things.

Every day we suffer in samsara. Sometimes we do not even realize it because we are so accustomed to our misery. In our confusion we think that something that is inherently faulty is wonderful and the basis of happiness. Because we see the samsaric world as attractive and enjoyable, we do not want to leave it. This is a very different perspective from that of yogis who have realized the truth of suffering and the truth of the cause of suffering. By practicing patience we can change our perceptions to be more like those realized beings. We can come to understand that suffering is not happiness. However, misery can be the cause of happiness because if we accept it we can exhaust the results of prior negative karma and create great merit. Understanding this will make one feel comfortable and even enjoy taking on difficulties.

The *Questions of the Householder Ugra Sutra* explains how to do this, saying, "You should separate yourself from a mind that is like cotton fluff." Cotton fluff is very soft and delicate. When practicing patience the mind should be firm, not easily swayed, stirred up, or defeated. In other words, we should not be so sensitive that small things easily bother us. The *Array of Stalks Sutra* exhorts us similarly, "Daughter, in order to overcome all the mental afflictions, you should produce a mind that is difficult to victimize." This is particularly relevant to Mahayana practitioners because a mind that is easily disturbed is an obstacle to being able to dedicate one's life to helping others. It takes firmness of mind to get rid of the mental afflictions and other more subtle mental obstacles.

Tsongkhapa says we should be heroic. Ordinary heroes do not get discouraged if they see their own blood during a battle. Instead, their aggression becomes stronger and they fight even more bravely. Worldly heroism may involve conflict and killing, but heroic bodhisattvas have the strength of mind to be loving, compassionate, and unshaken by any hardship or difficulty. That is true power. Wearing the armor of patience makes the mind stronger when problems arise and protects us in our struggle to help other beings. If we develop this mind-set, hardships increase the power of our perseverance. Difficulties become helpful; they are like fuel added to the fire of our practice. For example, if bodhisattvas feel hot, they become even more determined to help those who are experiencing far greater misery from scorching temperatures. This increases bodhisattvas' ability to bear their own discomfort.

When new practitioners first hear about the great austerities of spiritual life they may think, "Some people may be able to do that, but I am not that kind of heroic person. I could never do that kind of thing." We are belittling ourselves if we think that such things are impossible for us, and consequently simply wish to avoid hardship. By convincing ourselves that we are incapable, we close ourselves off from these practices. That is a big obstacle. It puts us far away from the practice. When some small difficulty occurs we are persuaded, "I cannot continue to do this. This is unendurable." This is cowardly—the opposite of heroism. Those who are weak and easily upset will not be able to fight a battle. As soon as they see blood, even if it is someone else's blood, they get so frightened that they faint. As it says in *Engaging in the Bodhisattva Deeds*:

> When some people see their own blood
> It makes them even more courageous.
> When some people see someone else's blood
> They faint and fall down.

Why does this happen? It isn't that one person is physically strong and the other one is weak; it isn't that one battle is fierce and the other isn't; it isn't that one person has a sharp weapon and the other doesn't. All these exterior factors are irrelevant. It is the nature of the mind that differs. Those with a heroic mind have strength; they can go on even if they see themselves bleeding. The others are easily shaken; even though nothing has happened to them yet, they are easily discouraged.

(c") A detailed explanation from the viewpoint of the bases

Tsongkhapa answers the question, "What kind of suffering should we accept voluntarily?" with a list of difficulties based on eight foundations. This list of problems is a summary of the issue presented in greater detail by the great Asaṅga in his *Bodhisattva Levels*.

The first type of suffering we should accept is related to our dwelling place and necessities of life. In order to survive everyone requires various things such as food, clothing, medicine, and so on. If we do not have these things, our delicate bodies may perish and we would lose this precious life. Serious spiritual practitioners who strictly keep vows in order to use this life to attain buddhahood should not be bothered if they do not have more than the minimum of necessities. They should not be upset if they do not get all kinds of special things, if they receive bad things, or get only a small amount of what they need.

In ancient times monks and nuns would beg for alms and live on whatever they received. Sometimes lay people would give them good food, sometimes bad; sometimes they would receive a lot, and sometimes a little. Even now those striving to live a spiritual life—especially monks, nuns, or yogis—should be able to bear certain things that would seem difficult to an ordinary person. Their strength comes from a firm understanding of the goal, the practice, and the general social situation. There are so many things that can vex us if we have a small mind; these include, for example, being disparaged for wearing religious garments, being made to wait, or treated disrespectfully by those giving alms. If such things make us unhappy, we will become discontented, discouraged, and want to give up serious practice. Instead, we should be patient. These hardships have a benefit: they help us get rid of some obstacles and create merit. The hardships can be treated as a method of practice.

The second type of suffering we should accept arises from worldly concerns. People absorbed in the world feel that nine things are the cause of unhappiness: to lose wealth, not to have fame, to be blamed, pain, disintegration, the exhaustion of things, aging, sickness, and death. Avoiding these nine comprise the goals of ordinary people. We should not be upset if we encounter these difficulties. From the perspective of spiritual practice it does not matter if people gossip about us, if we are in pain, if our resources are destroyed or used up, if we age, get sick, or die. We should examine these circumstances, think about them, and through wisdom accept them voluntarily.

The third type of difficulty to accept comes from our basic daily activities. We usually say there are four fundamental activities: moving, standing, sitting, and lying down. Walking and sitting are the two primary activities in the practice of meditation. Spiritual practitioners are trying to purify the mind day and night. The main obstacles to this practice are sleepiness and distraction. If we feel sleepy, we should get up and walk back and forth to wake up. If we are too distracted, we should sit down to concentrate. When obstacles arise, we should accept them. For example, it may be painful to sit a long time, so we want to take it easy and lie down. Lying down at the wrong time is laziness. We should not try to arrange our seats simply to make ourselves comfortable.

The fourth type of suffering to accept arises in connection with religious practices such as taking refuge in the Three Jewels, honoring one's spiritual teacher though service, memorizing scriptures, teaching what one has memorized to others, raising one's voice in recitation, residing alone and concentrating on meditation, and developing meditative concentration along with deep insight. When we are doing these things we should joyfully persevere no matter what problems arise.

Fifth is the suffering that arises in regard to earning a living. This is not referring to the difficulties involved in ordinary professions where one works to create wealth and obtain luxuries. This is referring to the suffering that may come up in a yogic life of austerities, when one gives up ordinary work and lives on the simple things one receives as alms from others. A pure life like this is uncommon nowadays. But in ancient times monks and nuns completely renounced worldly life and lived in solitary places. The original monastery was an isolated hermitage, not an institution. When solitary practitioners got hungry or cold, they would go to a place where faithful lay people would provide them with necessities.

Sangha members and laypeople have a special relationship. The laypeople know they need to create spiritual merit; that is the reason they give alms, not just to help poor people. The spiritual practitioners dedicate their merit so that they can help the laypeople. Even now, serious practitioners are committed to their practice and are not concerned about accumulating possessions. Their sustenance is dependent upon receiving things from others. It is not comfortable to depend on others for basic necessities: some people may dislike you, some people do not believe in you, some people are disrespectful, and others may say bad things to you. Nevertheless, monks and nuns should not worry about the next ten to fifty years: instead of trying to accumulate a lot of possessions, they follow the teachings. They are strangers to worldly conventions; they voluntarily make themselves unattractive by shaving their heads and wearing clothing that is deliberately unappealing in color and made up of cut-up pieces of cloth. Furthermore, because they have abandoned sexual activity, they have turned away from one of the main pleasures in life. Dancing and singing for recreation are also abandoned. Loved ones and dear childhood friends are no longer close. To those who do not know the Dharma, their behavior seems crazy.

If you want to be like other people, look nice, and have sensory pleasure, this kind of life will bother you. If you try to live this austere life, you may become agitated and regretful because you want these worldly things and are not able to have them. Each of them, any of them, may bother you if you lack patience. However, if you understand what you are doing and have the patience to accept doing without these worldly pleasures, you will have no difficulty. With patience these hardships are not a form of poverty or misery; they are almost a decoration. Enduring them makes you peaceful and happy. You can remain firmly dedicated to your spiritual practice one hundred percent of the time. There is no falling into a half-worldly and half-spiritual lifestyle. It is not easy to live this way. It has to come gradually.

The sixth suffering is the weariness that comes from hard work and diligent activity. The physical and mental hardships of the practice of virtue can make us fatigued. When we sit, walk, or do prostrations for a long time, we become worn-out physically. It is emotionally exhausting to deal with those who dislike us even though we are striving to practice generosity or nurse the sick. We should not easily lose heart and instead accept these circumstances.

The seventh type of difficulty arises when we strive to accomplish the goals of other sentient beings. We can think of the practice of patience from two perspectives: first, we can consider the disadvantages of anger and the advantages of patience in terms of their future results; second, we can think about patience as a way to take refuge in and please the buddhas. The buddhas are our best friend. Ordinary friends are fickle: sometimes they are our friends and sometimes they turn away from us and become enemies. Buddhas never change; they are a perfect friend—always supporting us, loving us, and helping us. All buddhas' activities are directed to temporarily and ultimately benefiting sentient beings. How can we repay their immeasurable kindness? What can we do to please them? There is no better way to repay the kindness of the buddhas than to practice what they teach: controlling our prideful egos, becoming humble, ceasing to attack and harm others, and serving the eleven types of sentient beings.[15] Similar to parents' appreciation when someone takes care of their beloved child, anything we do to satisfy sentient beings will make the buddhas happy. The line between pleasing and displeasing the buddhas is whether we save sentient beings from suffering. Even when others crazed by desire, hatred, and ignorance attack us, there is no need to react negatively. Escalation of the situation will only bring more misery. If we stay calm, however, their anger and so forth will eventually cool down. Even though they had been in the grip of their inner enemies, we will be able to rescue them from engaging in further negative actions. If we want to make offerings to the buddhas we should think, "From now on I will not retaliate even if many sentient beings trample on my head or try to kill me. I will control myself and train myself to become the savior of the world. This is how I will please the buddhas."

Finally, the last type of suffering we should be able to bear consists of difficulties related to ordinary activities. There are many things that require us to be patient. Every moment necessitates patience because we live and interact with other people in social situations. In other words, patience is a special attitude we can practice every day in the course of every activity, not just when someone says nasty things or hits us. Being patient—in other words, calm, compassionate, and loving—is one of the most beneficial practices for others. Our patience can put out others' internal fire of anger. If we are impatient, the fire can spread to our relatives, then to their friends, and so on; it just grows and grows. First, there is fighting between individuals and then it spreads further and further until there are wars. The practice of patience brings peace to oneself, to others, and to the whole world.

Candrakīrti says that Buddha taught the first three perfections—generosity, ethical discipline, and patience—with particular emphasis for laypeople. According to Nāgārjuna:[16]

> The practice of charity results in future wealth.
> The practice of morality results in future happiness.
> The practice of patience results in radiance.

In an ordinary human life the result of the practice of patience is that everyone finds us likeable. Patience brings about a physical body with a kind of beauty that everyone finds attractive. Furthermore, someone with patience is a holy person because he or she skillfully judges what is correct and what is incorrect. Unlike ordinary people who usually misjudge and attack others, someone with patience has a special ability to see what is actually going on. When one perceives situations correctly, one takes appropriate action based on that understanding. In addition to the results experienced in this life, patience results in a high rebirth. Birth in the lower realms is a result of negative karma. Negative karma is causing harm to others and patience restrains us from those actions. Patience is also one of the causes for perfect buddhahood. According to the Sutrayana system, the first three perfections are the cause for the Buddha's physical form: the rūpakāya. In particular, patience is the cause of the Buddha's beauty and radiance. No one can dislike the Buddha's perfect form.

(3') THE PATIENCE OF CERTITUDE ABOUT REALITY

The third type of patience is mental clarity about reality; it is understanding causation. When we do not know something, we have doubts about it. That makes us feel negative. Not liking a practice, not wanting to do a practice, or—even if we do it—feeling uncomfortable and having reservations about the practice, are all aspects of impatience. In order for religious practitioners to be comfortable and inspired to practice, they must understand the causes, the nature, and the results of each practice. So in this context *mental clarity* means faith, or we could say a trust without any negative reservations, or a pure motivation for doing a practice. Patience is using wisdom to see the reality of the Dharma. This enables us to hold religious practices in a positive light. We will admire them, like them, and become able to do them. Drawing from Asaṅga's *Bodhisattva Levels,* Tsongkhapa briefly goes over a list of eight areas to be certain about. In Asaṅga's work you can find a more extensive explanation of these topics.

The first object of certitude is the positive qualities of the Three Jewels. In order to take refuge in the Buddha, Dharma, and Sangha we must trust them. To have faith we must know what they are, what their individual qualities are, what they mean to us, and what is involved in our relationship to them. The strength of our trust is a function of our understanding. If our comprehension is vague, or if we have no grasp at all, then taking refuge is meaningless. So truly taking refuge requires learning about the Three Jewels, thinking about them, and then understanding them.

The second area of certitude is the object of direct realization. The best type of patience is achieved on the path of seeing when one has a direct realization of the two truths. The object of realization on the path of seeing is the two types of selflessness—the emptiness of the person and of phenomena. Of course, this is difficult. Right now we do not have an understanding of the nature of phenomenal or ultimate reality. Until we have a direct realization of these, we feel uncomfortable accepting certain truths. The first time you hear someone say that there is no self, you immediately become impatient.

Prior to having a direct realization we must study and try to understand śūnyatā conceptually. One's impatience diminishes as one studies. When one completely understands selflessness then all one's impatience is gone. At that time a special kind of faith arises in the mind.

The object of desire, the third object, is the goal we wish to attain: the great mental and physical powers of a buddha. Buddhas can emanate their body countless times, their knowledge of the past, present, and future is comprehensive, and they can do miraculous things. They have six supernormal knowledges,[17] the six perfections, and other special powers. When we first hear about these qualities, we may want them but at the same time have some doubts about them. If one has misgivings it will be difficult to have enough trust to try to attain them.

The fourth and fifth objects are presented together. One object of certainty is what should be taken up to attain a desirable goal, and the other is what should be cast away in order to avoid a miserable result. Here we need to gain confidence about which activities are good and which are sinful, because they are the causes for desirable and undesirable results respectively. To do this we must study karma and its results and the four noble truths: the truth of suffering, the truth of the cause of suffering, the truth of cessation of suffering, and the truth of the path to cessation. We have patience about the Dharma when we have no uneasiness about these topics.

The next two are also discussed as one object with two facets. First, we are trying to achieve a goal by practicing meditation; the objective goal of our meditation is the enlightenment of a Buddha or one of the two Hinayana goals. Second, there is the way to aspire to these goals; it is the method or path that leads to the attainment of liberation and enlightenment. Certitude about both the goals and the paths leading to them are the objects here.

Last is the object that we pursue though hearing and analysis. This refers to understanding the objects of study and learning. In other words, these are the objects of knowledge. The teacher Drolungpa says this means understanding things in general by an analysis of whether they are impermanent or permanent, happiness or unhappiness, virtue or nonvirtue, and so forth. In contrast, the *Bodhisattva Levels* identifies this object as an understanding of the meaning of the twelve branches of scriptures. Buddhist texts can be divided into various categories: sometimes there are twelve groups, sometimes nine, and the most abbreviated and common division is into three classes— the Tripiṭaka. Tsongkhapa agrees with the second interpretation; in other words, all the scriptures should be heard, analyzed, and examined. Patience is feeling comfortable and inspired about these subjects rather than feeling uneasy. The more knowledge we integrate into the mind, the more stable, calm, and patient we become. As our understanding of all the scriptures grows our internal agitation and impatience will diminish because those problems come from ignorance.

(d') How to practice

Practicing patience is similar to the practice of the other perfections in that the practice of each of them incorporates six superior qualities and the six perfections. When the six superior qualities are integrated with the practice of patience it becomes a perfect bodhisattva practice. The six superior or holy qualities were explained more fully in the context of the perfection of generosity, but I will summarize them here as a reminder.[18]

The first holy quality is that the support of the practice of a perfection is bodhicitta. When a practice has a foundation of bodhicitta, it is a bodhisattva deed. If patience is practiced out of selfishness or for some other purpose, it is not a bodhisattva activity. The second superior quality is the area of action. In the context of generosity it refers to the object that one gives; when practicing patience it is the object of one's patience. Third is the superior purpose of benefiting others, not just oneself. Fourth is the superior method of practice. This refers to recognizing emptiness while doing the practice. Although usually we say meditation on śūnyatā is the wisdom side of practice, in this context the superior method refers to practicing the perfection while contemplating the emptiness of the practitioner, the action, and the object of action. The fifth superior quality is a holy dedication: one dedicates the merit of the practice for a great purpose—the liberation or enlightenment of others—not some small purpose of your own. The last superior quality is purity. The practice is done with a pure intention that it will be the antidote to, or purifier of, the two kinds of obstacles: the mental afflictions and the obstructions to omniscience.

As mentioned before, the practice of one perfection incorporates all the other perfections. So the bodhisattva practice of the six perfections has thirty-six aspects because each of the six perfections has six facets. Therefore, when practicing patience there is the generosity of patience, the ethical discipline of patience, the patience of patience, the perseverance of patience, the meditative stabilization of patience, and the wisdom of patience. The generosity of patience is helping others to practice patience. It is giving them patience in the sense that one is teaching them how to practice it, not that one is giving one's patience to them. The ethical discipline of patience is following pure conduct of body, speech, and mind while practicing patience. The patience of patience is accepting the difficulties of practicing patience. Developing patience is hard to do; here one accepts, even welcomes, those hardships. It is double patience! The perseverance of patience is a special diligence. The meditative stabilization of patience is being mindful and focused when practicing patience. The wisdom of patience is becoming strong in one's practice of patience because of knowing the nature of reality.

(e') A SUMMARY

The foundation of all the bodhisattva deeds is bodhicitta—wanting to attain enlightenment in order to lead all sentient beings to be completely free of all their mental afflictions and obstructions to omniscience. The elimination of the internal obstacles and their stains is the highest patience: it is the mind of the buddha, completely at peace, in harmony with all other sentient beings, and without any animosity or hatred. It is therefore important for Mahayana practitioners to produce bodhicitta and then recollect it mindfully while doing all other practices. When we have bodhicitta, whatever we do is based on the desire to lead all sentient beings to this highest goal.

The strength of bodhicitta develops gradually. First we must produce it and then work to increase it. The patience of bodhisattvas who abide on the higher stages is such that even if all the beings of the three realms came to kill them, their response would be, "What can I do to help these troubled beings?" We cannot do that right now, but we can aspire to such a high level of practice. We can pray to be able to do that someday. There are things that beginners can do. There are teachings for beginners that explain what we should do and how we should think in situations where we would ordinarily get angry. There is a lot of advice about the best way to respond, and how and why to keep calm. These teachings will open our eyes to new paths of action. By keeping these instructions in mind, we train ourselves to act properly when difficult situations arise. This will not come all at once; but step by step we can train ourselves in the practice of patience.

Many people have taken the bodhisattva vows and promised to keep various precepts. If practitioners break one of these rules—for example, if they become uncontrollably angry—they should take countermeasures as soon as possible. They should confess or acknowledge what they have done, regret it, purify it, and develop a strong intention to not do such a thing again. To be careless and not pay attention to that broken vow is an additional powerful negative action. If we do not watch what the mind is doing, we will continue to act in negative ways. In this life we will become absorbed in negative actions and soon our mind will become completely covered with negativity. In future lives also it becomes much more difficult to engage in the great bodhisattva practices. In contrast, if we are careful we can look out for our future; we can try not to do certain things and, if we do them, we can confess them to prevent continuously accumulating negativity. Even if we are not perfect, by paying constant attention we plant positive seeds in the mind.

We must understand the crucial aspects of the bodhisattva path. Then we can try to accomplish those things that we are capable of doing right now, and pray to be able to do other practices that are beyond our abilities for the time being. If we train ourselves to desire to do these practices, we will be able to accomplish the practice of patience in the future. In future lives practicing patience will become easier and easier, gradually taking less effort, becoming familiar and comfortable, until it is completely natural.

This is the end of the chapter on patience. You may have finished reading it, but your effort to practice what was taught here must continue.

❖ 13 ❖

The Perfection of Perseverance

(iv) How to train in the perfection of perseverance
    (a') What perseverance is
    (b') How to begin the practice of perseverance
    (c') The divisions of perseverance
        (1') The actual divisions
            (a") Armor-like perseverance
            (b") Perseverance of gathering virtue
            (c") Perseverance of acting for the welfare of living beings
        (2') The method of developing perseverance
            (a") Eliminating unfavorable conditions that prevent perseverance
                (1") Identifying factors incompatible with perseverance
                (2") Employing the methods to eliminate the incompatible factors
                    (a)) Stopping the laziness of procrastination
                    (b)) Stopping attachment to ignoble activities
                    (c)) Stopping discouragement or self-contempt
                        (1)) Stopping discouragement about the goal
                        (2)) Stopping discouragement about the means to attain the goal
                        (3)) Stopping discouragement because wherever you are is a place to practice
            (b") Gathering the forces of the favorable conditions
                (1") Developing the power of aspiration
                (2") Developing the power of steadfastness
                (3") Developing the power of joy
                (4") The power of relinquishment
        (c") Based on the elimination of unfavorable conditions and the accumulation of favorable conditions, being intent on joyously persevering

    (d") How to use perseverance to make the mind and body
     serviceable
  (d') How to practice
  (e') A summary

(iv) How to train in the perfection of perseverance

Just as before, the perfection of perseverance is explained through five subtopics:

  (a') What perseverance is
  (b') How to begin the practice of perseverance
  (c') The divisions of perseverance
  (d') How to practice
  (e') A summary

(a') What perseverance is

Before we begin a practice we have to want to do it. This desire comes from knowing the nature of the practice and the benefits of doing it. The nature of perseverance is joy in doing virtuous activity. Joy does not arise on its own; it needs an object. For ordinary joy we have to eat something tasty, hear something pleasant, or see something attractive, and so on. For spiritual joy the object is wholesome activity that benefits one's future lives or helps other sentient beings. If we must force ourselves to do an activity, we do it reluctantly and will not accomplish it very well. However, if we feel joyful, even if we encounter many problems, we will be determined to accomplish the task. Joy makes any practice easy to do continuously and vigorously. The perfection of perseverance is a special kind of happiness that keeps one going no matter what difficulties occur. Śāntideva succinctly says, "What is perseverance? It is delight in virtue."

Feeling delight in doing something negative is not joyous perseverance. Patience and enthusiasm in the course of nonvirtuous activity are, in fact, aspects of laziness. Laziness is one of the main enemies of religious practice. It is the feeling that other things are more important so we do not want to start a spiritual practice. Even if we wish to attain a positive goal, if we are lazy we procrastinate beginning. If we do begin a practice, because of laziness we cannot accomplish our goal. Laziness is also taking pleasure in improper activities. That is why joyous perseverance—the opposite of laziness—is very important; it is the mental energy necessary to do any religious practice. From seeing the benefits of doing a practice and the disadvantages of not doing it, we take joy in wholesome activity directed toward a positive goal. With this kind of enthusiasm we can continue to practice. As the result of practice, the knowledge that comes from the study of the scriptures and learning from others, as well as the realizations that come from putting that understanding into practice, will increase. Whatever the goal, we can attain it with firm and irreversible perseverance. The *Lamrim Chenmo* puts a great deal of emphasis on this practice because it is necessary for accomplishing the Sutrayana and Tantrayana.

(b') How to begin the practice of perseverance

The way to begin is to become interested in the practice. It may be a false conclusion, but we only do things if we think there is a distinct advantage in doing it and a disadvantage in not doing it. The amount of determination we bring to an activity is based on how vividly we see these advantages and disadvantages. So we must examine the benefits of practicing joyous perseverance and the disadvantages of not practicing it from many different angles. Why is it important to practice? What advantages come from the practice of perseverance? What happens when we are lazy? When the answers to these questions are clear, we will seriously want to practice perseverance and eliminate laziness. To develop this conviction we should look at explanations in the scriptures, listen to teachings, and also bring to bear our own experience.

The first advantage is that obtaining anything of value is a result of perseverance. This is explained both in the *Exhortation to Wholehearted Resolve Sutra (Adhyāśaya-saṃcodana-sūtra)* and the *Ornament for the Mahayana Sutras*. The sutra says:

> One should always rely upon that
> Noble perseverance that is praised by all buddhas
> As being the basis for freedom from lower rebirths
> And the remover of all suffering and confusion.

> Every mundane activity and
> Every supramundane activity
> Begun with perseverance is completed without difficulty.
> By the power of perseverance, what wise person is discouraged?

> Whoever sets forth to attain a buddha's enlightenment,
> I have advised of this:
> Seeing the faults of lethargy and sleepiness,
> Always joyously persevere with diligence.

And Maitreya says in the *Ornament for the Mahayana Sutras:*

> Perseverance is supreme among virtues
> Because you obtain results by relying upon it.
> Perseverance brings immediate temporal happiness,
> Supramundane and worldly spiritual attainments.

> Through perseverance we obtain what we desire in samsaric life.
> Perseverance leads us to have pure conduct.
> Perseverance frees us from the view to the perishable aggregates.
> Perseverance perfects supreme qualities and purifies all obstacles.

Those who enjoy samsaric happiness obtain what they wish by diligent practice of wholesome activity. Wealth, fame, and praise are immediate, although temporary, results of the practice of virtue. But if we look a little further we find greater, more lasting results that come from the practice of virtue. The *lamrim* teachings explain three spiritual goals for different types of spiritual practitioners: a high rebirth with special qualities, complete freedom from samsara, and absolute enlightenment in order to benefit all sentient beings.

To obtain the goal of a person with the lowest spiritual capacity—rebirth in a high samsaric realm—we must practice pure conduct. Perseverance in pure religious conduct, in other words avoiding the ten non-virtuous actions, is the cause for a happy and long life free from the lower realms. In addition, it leads to both worldly and supramundane spiritual attainments. Worldly spiritual attainments—for example, the five supernatural knowledges—are good qualities achieved in common by non-Buddhists, Buddhists, āryan, and ordinary individuals. The supramundane spiritual attainments are beyond these ordinary worldly accomplishments; they are freedom from samsara and the even higher state of enlightenment.

The first supramundane goal—complete freedom from all of samsara—is the desire of those of intermediate spiritual capacity. These practitioners are concerned with more than avoiding the lower realms in their future lives; they see all rebirths, wherever they are in samsara, as miserable. Karma is what ties us to samsara. The cause of karma is the mental afflictions. The root cause of the mental afflictions is the egotistic view: grasping a wrong perception of *I* and *mine.* In the sutras this wrong view is called *the view of the perishable aggregates.* The object of this wrong view is the group of the five aggregates that make up one's continuum of body and mind. This combination is not a singular independent unit; it is a combination of many things that change every moment and finally disappear. But we perceive this transitory collection as something desirable, ultimate, and real. We feel that we will live forever and so we work hard for wealth, fame, friendship, and so on throughout life. But all this effort is based on an ignorant misunderstanding. When we understand that the self is empty of any ultimate existence, we eliminate this egotistic view. When that misunderstanding is gone, the rest of mental afflictions can be removed and the creation of impure karma ceases. Only perseverance carries us all the way to emancipation from samsara.

Those with great spiritual capacity are bodhisattvas. Their goal is greater than their own emancipation; they wish to lead all living creatures to the highest enlightenment of buddhahood. In order to do this they must first become buddhas themselves. It takes great perseverance to remove all obstacles and develop supreme realizations, powers, compassion, and knowledge.

In his *Ornament for the Mahayana Sutras,* Maitreya explains that there is no way to attain any of these spiritual goals without perseverance. In another part of that text Maitreya says:

> If you have perseverance wealth cannot overcome you.
> If you have perseverance the mental afflictions cannot defeat you.
> If you have perseverance discouragement will not overcome you.
> If you have perseverance attainments will not defeat you.

The first line of this stanza refers to the lowest level of spiritual practice because the minds of ordinary beings are dominated by a desire for wealth. Many obstacles come from craving affluence; sometimes in our pursuit of material goods we forget our religious practice, and sometimes having riches overthrows our practice. If we have perseverance, it is unimportant if we are rich or poor. We will not become distraught if we lack wealth, nor will we be completely absorbed in enjoying the material goods that we do have.

The second line refers to the intermediate spiritual goal: one's own emancipation from cyclic existence. To become free from samsara we have to defeat the inner enemy—the mental afflictions of desire, hatred, jealousy, and so forth. Only with perseverance can we conquer these passions.

It takes even more effort to accomplish the bodhisattva's aspiration to place all sentient beings in a state of the highest happiness and freedom. The most difficult obstacle to attaining this goal is discouragement, mentioned in the third line of the quotation. Sometimes it is difficult to help a single individual because even with the best goodwill, things can go wrong. For example, one day a beggar requested some flesh from one of the Buddha's disciples. Out of desire to help the poor man, the practitioner immediately cut off one of his fingers and gave it to the beggar. But the beggar became angry because he wanted more. The disciple thought, "This is too hard. I can't even satisfy one person, so how can I possibly help all sentient beings?" Becoming disheartened like this is losing bodhicitta. This is where we need the protection of joyous perseverance. If our perseverance is strong enough we will not be discouraged by anything.

Through diligent practice we can develop spiritual attainments and progress to certain spiritual levels. Yet there is a danger even here; we could become conceited or simply relax and enjoy what we have accomplished. In that sense our attainments defeat us, as indicated in the fourth line of the stanza, because we stop actively wanting to help others. But this will not happen if we have joyous perseverance.

The *Bodhisattva Levels* says that perseverance is the principal cause for accomplishing the good qualities of bodhisattvas because it is behind everything they do. A bodhisattva's diligence is beyond our usual understanding. A way to come to comprehend it is to recite passages from the *Guru Puja,* or from other prayers that mention the development of the perfection of joyous perseverance. We pray that we will have the diligence to be able to take rebirth in the worst hell if that will enable us to save just one sentient being. We pray that even if we have to remain for eons in a blazing fire, we will not be discouraged. We will be joyful because of our great compassion and love. This kind of perseverance can sound like a fantasy to those who have never studied, practiced, or experienced it. However, it is not imaginary. This mental power can be developed.

The *Compendium of the Perfections* says that perseverance makes everything, including the highest enlightenment, possible:

> If you have great perseverance completely free from discouragement,
> There is nothing that you cannot accomplish or attain.

The same text continues, saying that if we have perseverance conjoined with patience, "Humans and non-humans are happy to assist us." Why? Because if we take joy in working so that others can enjoy happiness, they will want to help us in return. Further, the text says that it is through perseverance that we can attain the many different types of meditative stabilization. Perseverance makes one's life meaningful:

Day and night will be fruitful.
One's good qualities will not diminish.

Not only will continuous perseverance prevent the lessening of good qualities, it will lead to their increase. They will proliferate the way water lilies spread over a huge lake:

Qualities superior to ordinary human traits
Will spread like Utpala flowers.

Since perseverance is necessary to accomplish any goal, worldly or otherwise, it is disadvantageous to be without it. The *Questions of Sāgaramati Sutra* says that enlightenment is very far away from someone who lacks perseverance, because laziness creates obstacles to the accomplishment of the six perfections. Laziness prevents us from accomplishing our own goals, and so of course we cannot do anything for others.

The *Mindfulness of the Excellent Teaching (Sad-dharmānusmṛty-upasthāna)* says:

The sole foundation of the afflictions
Is laziness. Whoever has it—
Anyone who is lazy—
Will not have any Dharma.

The term *afflictions* can be used in a general way to refer to both to the mental afflictions—greed, hatred, ignorance, and so forth—and their results—various types of misery. The basis of the mental afflictions and their resultant suffering is laziness. Humans have the capacity to comprehend causality and put that understanding to practical use. Unfortunately, laziness can lead us to live an empty life. When we are lazy we do not use our potential; we do not follow through on our understanding and do something. Or if we do take action, it is without joy and resolve. This sutra says that if we do not have perseverance, we have its opposite: laziness. When we are under the power of laziness, we will engage in very few wholesome practices. As a result, we will not have even the most basic spiritual qualities, much less the superior ones. We lose the opportunity to attain the temporary goals of happiness, wealth, a long life, health and so on, as well as the final goals of liberation and enlightenment. If we lack the cause then, of course, we will not gain the results. We will be poor in this respect. Laziness makes us rich only with black, unwholesome activities and qualities.

In brief, these are the benefits of perseverance and the detriments of its absence. Practitioners must think about these two topics in order to build up strong perseverance. The sutra passages above do not give a lot of detail. Later in this chapter we will examine the advantages of joyous perseverance and the disadvantages of a lack of perseverance through quotations from Śāntideva's *Engaging in the Bodhisattva Deeds*.

(c') The divisions of joyous perseverance

Now that we have become convinced that perseverance is important to have, we examine what types of perseverance should be developed. There are two subtopics in this section:

> (1') The actual divisions
> (2') The method of developing joyous perseverance

(1') The actual divisions

There are three subtopics to explain the divisions of joyous perseverance:

> (a") Armor-like perseverance
> (b") Perseverance of gathering virtue
> (c") Perseverance of acting for the welfare of living beings

The *Lamrim Chenmo* discusses these three types of perseverance for Mahayana practitioners, but keep in mind that any type of Dharma practice requires all of them. Joyous perseverance is the armor that protects us in the battle to vanquish all the causes of suffering. In ancient times soldiers wore armor to protect themselves from knives and spears. If soldiers had unpierceable armor they could win on the battlefield. Bodhisattvas need strong armor to survive the many attacks of the internal enemy on the way to their goal. Spiritual practitioners must fight hard against laziness so they will not give up their practice. The unyielding armor of joyous perseverance is the courage to stay with the practice all the way through to the goal.

The second and third types of perseverance continue this martial analogy. After bodhisattvas have prepared their own protective gear, they have to ready their other equipment and associates. In ancient times kings mustered foot soldiers, horse cavalry, elephant divisions, and so on. Here, in order to remove negative thoughts and actions and their roots, we need a positive force; we become powerful by putting our body, speech, and mind into virtuous activity by practicing the bodhisattva deeds. After arranging for our own protection and gathering an army, we have to battle for victory on a situation by situation basis. The third type of perseverance is taking action, concentrating on the benefit of other sentient beings.

(a") ARMOR-LIKE PERSEVERANCE

Mahayana practice is like a war against one's selfish attitude and activities. When we gain victory over these enemies we will have peace. However, bodhisattvas do not fight for themselves alone; they wage this war to lead all mother sentient beings to perfect enlightenment and emancipation from samsaric misery. Perseverance is the armor to put on prior to going into battle. This armor is mental preparation. "Wearing the armor of perseverance" means having courage. Without it we can easily become discouraged and give up trying to attain our goal. To achieve our wish we have to be able to bear hardships without getting upset; we cannot waver in the face of large or small difficulties. If we train the mind to be compassionate and combine our compassion with joy in the practice of virtue, no matter what happens we will feel joy because we are acting for the benefit of other sentient beings. We will never be sorrowful.

Joyous perseverance is not just a religious accomplishment of bodhisattvas. Whether we call it joyous perseverance or not, this attitude exists even in a worldly context. If a young person wishes to accomplish a huge goal—say, to become president of the United States—he or she may inquire, "What do I have to do to attain this?" The person may then be told, "That is not easy. First you will have to study hard. You will have to give up this type of activity and make many sacrifices. You will have to do so much of this and even more of that." Hearing this could be discouraging. To combat dismay, the ambitious young person must think about the advantages of becoming president. When we are cognizant of the value of the result, as well as of the difficulties of the method to attain it, we develop the ability to accept those hardships with joy. Little by little, more and more, we enjoy the work involved in reaching our goal, even if it is demanding. Eventually, we will be able to accept the most difficult things with courage. When our courage is strong, the challenges we face become helpful to us. Nothing is too difficult. We solve each problem quickly and attain our goal.

I enjoy talking about world-class athletes in this regard. Even though their goal is ephemeral—perhaps just some fame or some money—they are convinced it would be wonderful. They think, "I've got to have that championship ring. I will do whatever it takes to get it." Soon they learn of the difficulties of training—how many times they must fall down, the blood that is shed, perhaps even death—but if their desire for the goal is strong enough, they are not deterred. Their injuries almost seem like an ornament; they are a mark of being a great competitor. This is ordinary mental armor.

The bodhisattva's mental armor is extraordinary. The sutras use some very large numbers and long periods of time to explain the nature of bodhisattvas' joyous courage while working for the benefit others. To simplify a bit, we'll call the Indian length of time, a *kalpa,* an eon. Even longer than an eon is a countless eon. *Countless* here does not mean incalculable; it is the name of a number. We are familiar with counting from one to a hundred, then multiple hundreds, thousands, tens of thousands, hundreds of thousands, millions, billions, trillions, and so forth. Each time we increase by the power of ten. In the Indian system, ten to the sixtieth power is called *countless.*

To calculate the duration of a countless eon we start with the length of one of its days. A single day of a countless eon is as long as a thousand eons composed of our twenty-four hour days. Then we put thirty of these thousand-eon-long days together to get a month. Twelve of those months equal one year. Add year upon year to create an eon. According to the sutra system, after the historical Buddha became a bodhisattva it took him three countless eons to accumulate enough merit to reach buddhahood.

Just hearing about this length of time makes us tired. When someone tells us we have to work this long in order to attain buddhahood, we become discouraged. We would consider the request to practice so long to be completely unrealistic. We would never even try to attain enlightenment if that were necessary. But a bodhisattva wearing the mental armor of perseverance is not disheartened even if it takes this long to accumulate the merit to help a single sentient being. A bodhisattva would think it was worth it to live in the worst hell twice, three times, or even a thousand times longer than this if he or she could attain enlightenment. If bodhisattvas would not give up knowing it would be so hard and take this long, then of course they would never give up on a shorter, easier task. Whether or not it takes a bodhisattva this long to attain enlightenment is not the point. The vast length of time simply illustrates the necessary level of commitment. Asaṅga says in the *Bodhisattva Levels* that a bodhisattva with joyous perseverance is never discouraged when working to attain enlightenment for the benefit of other sentient beings. No hardship or austerity is difficult; everything becomes easy. This irreversible courage is a bodhisattva's special armor.

We are not this disciplined. We want to achieve something in a few days, months, or at most a couple of years. It is likely that when we hear about this type of perseverance we think, "Who could possibly be so determined? Who could act with such diligence?" It is completely beyond our mental scope, so we reject it. That is why the Buddha said that simply admiring or having faith in this kind of perseverance is wonderful. It is actually a kind of perseverance to think, "Maybe it is possible for something so amazing to be true. I wish I could do it. Someday I *will* do it." This thought creates great merit. Heartfelt admiration is the seed that will sprout into measureless joyous perseverance. If merely wishing for perseverance is special, then there is no need to say much about how extraordinary it is to actually have this courage.

Tsongkhapa comments that we too can develop this type of courage if we train the mind. All sentient beings have the potential to become perfectly enlightened buddhas. We all have the capability to develop a bodhisattva's courage to do anything to help other beings without hesitation. At present our potential is latent. It has been covered over by negative attitudes such as ignorance, attachment, hatred, jealousy, and pride for a long time. It is as if we have been asleep. We cannot do much when we are sleeping, but when we awake we have the potential to do hundreds of things. The practice of perseverance will wake up our potential. Accomplishing this may take one's entire life. Even if it does not take that long, if we resolve, "I will do this until I die," then all our activities will be forceful and fruitful. Therefore, Tsongkhapa says we should train ourselves this way.

The *Compendium of the Perfections* makes a similar point:[1]

> In as many eons as there are drops of water in the ocean,
> Eons in which the years are composed
> Of long, drawn-out days and nights equal in duration
> Even to the temporal limits of cyclic existence,
>
> You produce supreme bodhicitta just once.
> Though you likewise have to accomplish every other collection,
> You do not become disheartened because of your compassion,
> And undiscouraged you achieve sublime enlightenment.
>
> To generate this immeasurable steadfast armor
> While disregarding your suffering in cyclic existence
> Is declared the first proper undertaking
> For the disciplined hero possessed of compassion.

The unsurpassable armor of perseverance is similarly explained in the *Teachings of Akṣayamati Sutra.* The time-span from beginninglessness to the end of samsara is so long it is beyond calculation. Nevertheless, imagine that a single day lasts as long as that time period. Then put thirty of these days together to make a month, and use these months to make up a year. Maybe, if we practice for a hundred thousand of these years, we will be able to produce one moment of bodhicitta and be able to see a single buddha. Maybe, if we practice for as many hundreds of thousands of years as there are grains of sand on the banks of the Ganges river, we will be able to completely comprehend the mind and behavior of one sentient being. Such an ability is important because to help someone without error we must understand him or her. Just as physicians must know their patients' problems and the causes of those problems before they can treat their illnesses, bodhisattvas must know a sentient being's nature to be able to lead him or her to emancipation. Neither doctors nor bodhisattvas can successfully cure others just by giving them some expensive medicine and saying, "Eat this." It takes a very, very long time to create enough merit to achieve the level of knowledge necessary to prescribe errorless spiritual medicine to just one sentient being. It is therefore unthinkable how long a bodhisattva must practice to understand each and every sentient being.

Because of their compassion for others, bodhisattvas wearing the armor of perseverance feel joy even when faced with the necessity of practicing such an incredibly long time. Bodhisattvas are true heroes. They are far more courageous than ordinary heroes who disregard their personal welfare to fight an enemy on behalf of their relatives or their country. Ordinary people postpone or avoid doing a task if it seems that it will entail difficulty. However, sometimes even ordinary people are willing to go to extraordinary lengths to achieve a goal. For example, parents will sacrifice themselves if it is necessary to help their beloved children. That is small-scale courage when compared to a bodhisattva's determination to practice to benefit all other sentient beings.

It is not necessary to start with the amazing perseverance of a bodhisattva. That may be too much, so we gradually train the mind to want to undertake the enormous practices for the long, long time it takes to benefit others. We begin by simply wishing that we could do it. We aspire to have the compassion that results in joyfully doing anything necessary to help others. First think, "I want to be the leader of all sentient beings. I want to free them all from suffering. I want to help them attain bliss." Then remind yourself, "It is most difficult to attain enlightenment for the benefit of other sentient beings. It takes a long time; one has to sacrifice a lot and endure much hardship." Picture yourself confident, happy, and with no reservations, even if you have to practice for so long. No matter how much difficulty you imagine, your mind still says, "Okay. No problem. I am happy to do it." This kind of preparation gives the mind enormous power. It is armor made of something precious and strong; nothing can pierce it and it can deflect every obstacle. If we train ourselves this way, our enthusiasm will gradually become as firm as a bodhisattva's diligence.

It is important to train the mind this way because it will make every practice much easier. If we are able to produce this kind of thought even for a moment we will have the courage to face every difficulty we encounter while helping other sentient beings. This heartfelt enthusiasm in itself creates more merit than years and years of practicing generosity and other virtues. In addition to accumulating a limitless amount of merit, perseverance purifies innumerable obstacles and negative karmas.

Nonvirtuous karma is physical, verbal, and mental activities that harm others. Physical and verbal actions are motivated by one of the three poisons: desire, hatred, or ignorance. In other words, the primary creator of negative karma is the mind—primarily the ignorant, egotistic, self-centered view. A powerful opposing mental attitude is therefore needed for purification. The antithesis of ignorance is joyous perseverance. It is the supreme cause of an irreversible practice. On early stages of the path to enlightenment we may lose heart and turn back. But at a certain point practitioners will never give up. According to some sutras, the sharpest practitioners reach this irreversible point even before the path of seeing, while attainment of this path marks this point for most practitioners. The very slowest of bodhisattvas do not become irreversible until the eighth bodhisattva level. But that is the very last point; by the eighth bodhisattva level every bodhisattva has reached the point at which he or she will not reverse. No matter when it is reached, training in perseverance is the cause for this irreversible stage.

If we are joyful and unafraid to spend a long, long time practicing to attain enlightenment, we will reach our goal much more quickly. Some bodhisattvas attain enlightenment in just one lifetime. Others may do so in a few lives, some take sixteen lifetimes, and others practice for countless lives. But all of them have the mental strength to take eager delight in practicing for however long it will take. The opposite also holds true. If we want to attain enlightenment in the easiest way in the shortest amount of time, it will take much, much longer because we have no real enthusiasm for engaging in the limitless deeds necessary to benefit other sentient beings. As soon as we see some small difficulty we think, "I don't want to go through that. I want something less complicated and quicker." Because we want to avoid adversity and practices that take a long time, we cannot muster the energy to do much of anything. Everything becomes a hardship and hindrance. That is a sign that enlightenment will not be achieved for eons.

Remember that the mind has incredible potential. If we train it properly we can attain a great goal. When we see that it is possible to develop this kind of courage, we can do it. That is why the armor-like perseverance is so important. As Tsongkhapa says in the *Condensed Lamrim:*[2]

If you wear the strong armor of diligence,
Good qualities increase like the waxing moon,
All your activities become meaningful,
And you attain whatever goal that you wish.

(b") PERSEVERANCE OF GATHERING VIRTUE

Once a warrior has prepared his armor he gathers up his weapons. It is similar here. Now that we have the armor that prevents discouragement, we must engage in the practice of virtue to create the causes and conditions necessary for the attainment of enlightenment. The practice of the six perfections brings together everything necessary. It includes all the practices of virtue that must be accomplished and the antidotes to remove all the obstacles. Doing these activities with delight and without hesitation is the practice of the perfection of joyous perseverance. We start with small, easy practices and gradually become able to do the most demanding ones without difficulty.

(c") PERSEVERANCE OF ACTING FOR THE WELFARE
OF LIVING BEINGS

There are so many activities that can be done to help the astoundingly wide variety of sentient beings. These can be condensed into eleven varieties of activity based on categorizing sentient beings based on their needs, attitudes, and mental levels.[3] The third type of joyous perseverance is to take pleasure in doing all these things.

(2') THE METHOD OF DEVELOPING PERSEVERANCE

Joyous perseverance is one of the most important perfections because it is needed to produce, maintain, and increase the accumulations of method and wisdom. Candrakīrti says in *Explanation of the "Middle Way"*:[4]

All good qualities follow perseverance.
It is the cause for the two accumulations of merit and wisdom.

Joy in virtuous activity is necessary in the beginning, middle, and end of practice on the path. If we do not have joyous perseverance in the beginning, we will not have the courage to commence producing good qualities. If we initiate developing these qualities but do not have perseverance in the middle, we will lose our practice because of laziness. Finally, we may maintain a certain level of development, but without continued joyous perseverance we will not be able to maximize our good qualities. Perseverance is like the water farmers depend upon to grow their crops: in the beginning, seeds must be moistened in order to germinate; in the middle, there must be water for the plants to thrive; and finally, the plant needs moisture in order to be able to produce a fruit. In spiritual practice perseverance is needed to produce a quality initially; it is important in the middle so that quality does not degenerate; and it is necessary at the end to increase that quality for a result to be attained.

The amount we will be able to practice depends upon how much joy we take in wholesome activity. Tsongkhapa says that his explanation of how to produce joyous perseverance follows the instructions the great master Śāntideva laid out in *Engaging in the Bodhisattva Deeds.* This advice is easy to understand and put into practice. Every aspect of what we must do to eliminate laziness is explained. There is nothing left out because Śāntideva describes the practice just as he engaged in it on a daily basis. This method to develop joyous perseverance has four subtopics:

(a") Eliminating unfavorable conditions that prevent perseverance
(b") Gathering the forces of the favorable conditions
(c") Based on the elimination of unfavorable conditions and the accumulation of favorable conditions, being intent on joyously persevering
(d") How to use joyous perseverance to make the mind and body serviceable

Basically there are two aspects to the practice of joyous perseverance: getting rid of the hindrances to perseverance—in other words, eliminating laziness—and, on the positive side, developing the necessary conditions for perseverance.

(a") ELIMINATING UNFAVORABLE CONDITIONS THAT PREVENT PERSEVERANCE

There are two sections that explain how to eliminate obstacles to perseverance:

(1") Identifying factors incompatible with joyous perseverance
(2") Employing the methods to eliminate the incompatible factors

(1") Identifying factors incompatible with perseverance

There are two things that prevent us from beginning to practice, and then make our practice degenerate if we have begun to follow the path. The first obstacle is that although we know that the result is worthwhile and attainable, we still do not want to pursue it. This is a form of laziness. The second hindrance is another type of laziness—discouragement. This is thinking, "How could I possibly accomplish this? I cannot do it. I am just a such and such." Actually, there is a third obstacle that bars us from entering the path that is not explained here: it is to never even consider whether or not the result is attainable. But the assumption here is that we have thought about the path and are striving for emancipation and enlightenment, so this third impediment is not relevant. We still, however, have two problems: not bothering to practice and thinking that someone like us cannot do such a great thing.

The first obstacle—the laziness of seeing that the goal could be attained but not wanting to pursue it—has two divisions. The first is procrastination: we understand the value of the goal, learn about the path to attain the goal, and recognize that we can accomplish the goal through this method, but we delay. We think, "This is great. It can and should be done. I'll do it later." The second obstacle is not deliberately postponing practice, but being attached to inferior activities in pursuit of ordinary rewards such as wealth, health, praise, or fame. *Engaging in the Bodhisattva Deeds* describes these obstacles as follows:

> The factors opposing perseverance are:
> The laziness of attachment to low things,
> Procrastination, and belittling oneself.

Śāntideva explains that each of the three types of laziness is a serious hindrance to a bodhisattva's practice. We must be able to recognize which kind of laziness is arising and apply the appropriate antidote. If we know who the enemy is, where he is, and when he is coming, we can counter and defeat him. On the other hand, if we do not know who the enemy is, we will be overwhelmed.

The first type of laziness is attachment to low things; *low* because they are inferior to bodhisattva practices. We pursue sensual enjoyment by going to the theater, playing sports, drinking, going fishing, or doing other such things. We are willing to do just about anything to gain wealth or fame. Out of attachment to nonspiritual things we do many nonvirtuous actions. We have no concern about how our activities may injure others. We do not even start a spiritual practice because we are overcome by a desire for temporary pleasure. This is called the laziness of attachment to ordinary activity.

The second and third types of laziness arise when we have some desire to engage in the practice of wholesome activity. The second type of laziness is the common understanding of the word: we just have no energy to do something. We see what is good, we would like to do it, and even though we are not attached to low activity, we postpone doing that positive action. We think, "This is a good practice to do at some point. I should do it, but not now. I have lots of other things that I must do first." The worst way to think is, "I'll do it when I get old." Not quite as bad is, "Not this year, I'll do it next year. Not this month, next month. Not this week, next week." We think, "I'm supposed to do this in the morning, but I'll do it later in the evening." Then in the evening we think, "I'll do it tomorrow morning when I am refreshed." Even a person right on the brink of death can think, "I still have a bit of time; I won't die right this moment." This attitude always makes us put aside our practice in favor of something else.

The third type of laziness is to belittle ourselves. We want to do virtuous activity and do not have the problem of procrastination, but we think, "I'm stupid. I'm untalented. This goal is so noble; it is meant for intelligent people, not for the likes of me. These practices are hard to do; there are so many steps, so many rules, so much learning is required, and so forth. I cannot do it. It is not for me." We discourage ourselves by self-denigration. The result is that we have no enjoyment or enthusiasm in our practice.

Śāntideva says that there are four causes of laziness:

> Laziness arises from:
> Indolence, attachment based on
> The taste of pleasure, sleep, and
> Not being disgusted with the suffering of samsara.

This stanza is not describing laziness in regards to the ordinary activities we are supposed to do. For example, if we promised our friends that we would go hunting with them, but do not get up in time to go with them in the morning, others would call that laziness. But that is not laziness in this context. Here laziness is anything that prevents or discourages joy in performing wholesome actions. First, because of attachment to inferior activity, we postpone doing proper work. Second, we are attached to the taste of ordinary pleasure, such as sitting comfortably or eating delicious food. Third, we enjoy sleeping. And fourth, we lack revulsion to cyclic existence. If we do not see any faults in samsara and our situation seems wonderful, naturally we will be attached to it. This is a hindrance, because if we are not revolted by the problems of samsara, we will not want our own emancipation nor will we feel the need to attain buddhahood out of concern for other sentient beings. Commenting on this stanza, some people say that indolence and attachment to pleasure and sleep are *forms* of laziness rather than *causes* of it. But this is not an important distinction.

(2") EMPLOYING THE METHODS TO ELIMINATE THE INCOMPATIBLE FACTORS

There are three methods to eliminate the obstacles to perseverance—one to stop each kind of laziness.

    (a)) Stopping the laziness of procrastination
    (b)) Stopping attachment to ignoble activities
    (c)) Stopping discouragement or self-contempt

(a)) STOPPING THE LAZINESS OF PROCRASTINATION

Procrastination is knowing the benefit of Dharma practice but not wanting to do it right at this moment because some other activity seems important to do first. This laziness is based on the idea that we will always have time later. There are three steps to prevent the mind from straying to this misconception: meditating that we will definitely die, that it is uncertain when we will die, and that at the time of death nothing helps except Dharma practice. Tsongkhapa discussed these three topics in great detail when he explained the practices for a person with limited spiritual capacity (volume 1, chapter 9), so he does not go into depth again here. However, because it is important to use these meditations in this context, I will briefly outline the basic concepts. Note that for this type of meditation to be effective, one has to consider the many details presented earlier.

    The first meditation is to contemplate impermanence, in particular that the body we have right now will not last forever. The antidote to thinking, "This year I'm too busy; I'll do the practice next year," is to ask ourselves, "How do you know that you will be alive next year? If you die before next year, you are in trouble." Continue by thinking about procrastinating until next month, next week, or tomorrow. Do you have any assurance that you will definitely wake up tomorrow morning? It is our negative mind, laziness, that says, "Tomorrow will definitely come." We come up with many reasons to put things off such as, "Right now I'm healthy. Even if I were to get sick, there are medicines to cure me. I have lots of friends to help me. I'm powerful." None of these are grounds for certainty. A person healthy today could die tonight. As for wealth, power, and friends, these are irrelevant; they are powerless to ward off death.

The second meditation focuses on the fact that while death is certain, the time of death is uncertain. We all know we are going to die, but we usually do not think about when it will happen. Death is at the door and ready to come in. It cannot be put off; nothing can stop it. Until it arrives, our time is precious because we can make use of it to accumulate merit. It is similar to preparing for a long journey. If we do not make preparations the trip will be very difficult. If we wait and try to do something right at the moment of death, it will be too late. There is nothing to do then except experience the results of the karma we have created. Unless we have attained a high spiritual level, we are under the power of karma and the mental afflictions; we have no control over how long we will live, the kind of death we will experience, or our next rebirth. We should not look at others to see if they are high bodhisattvas; we must examine ourselves. If we have created a lot of negative karma, we will suffer greatly at the time of death and then be reborn in a lower realm. Therefore, before we die we should purify some of our negative karma and create some good karma to benefit our future. We must use wisdom to fight the feeling that we can take care of these concerns later and attend to something else first. We have to think seriously about death in order to be willing to give up temporary pleasures that will not benefit us in our future lives. If we were really convinced that death could come at any time, we would prepare for it right now. So the second meditation is also a powerful motivator. Śāntideva says:[5]

> Death will come quickly and soon;
> Until then I must accumulate merit.
> To avoid laziness at the moment of death
> Is pointless; it is too late to do anything.

At this point we may rationalize, "Okay, after death I may have a bad rebirth, but eventually that will end and I will be reborn once more in a good situation." Although no rebirth is permanent, karma can result in the most miserable conditions in which we experience extreme physical pain and mental anguish for a long time. It is true that when the karmic cause is exhausted that experience will end, but the prospect of such misery occurring in our next life should make us very frightened. Furthermore, falling into the lower realms is like losing a wish-fulfilling jewel. A human life has incredible potential.

Humans have the intelligence to comprehend the difference between good and bad and the relationship between cause and effect. If we are born as an animal, we will not be able to see beyond immediate events. Because animals tend to negative activity, their next rebirth will be even worse. It is like a rock tumbling down the side of a ravine from a high mountain peak; it is most difficult to stop and bring back up. Once in a low rebirth we may experience many, many lives stuck way at the bottom. It is foolish to think that we will be reborn as a human very soon. In other words, the third antidote to laziness is to meditate on how rare it is to obtain an excellent type of life, the causes that are necessary for a human rebirth, how difficult it is to create these causes even in a human life, and how much harder it is to create these causes in the lower realms. After studying, analyzing, and concentrating on this subject we will see that once we are born in the lower realms, we will be there for millions upon millions of lives. This conviction leads us to see how crucial it is to do something positive in this life. We decide not to waste even a moment today because tomorrow we could fall to the lower realms.

The more we are afraid the less lazy we will be. Fear convinces us that nothing is certain beyond this point in time, and that this moment is extremely useful. If, however, we are only slightly concerned—perhaps experiencing a vague nagging feeling in the back of the mind without much conscious anxiety—then we will procrastinate. When the correct view dominates the mind, laziness has no power to induce us to postpone practice. If we are truly afraid of what will happen after we die, we will want to do whatever we can to help ourselves in our next life. The most advantageous thing we can do is practice virtue. As the final section of the meditation on impermanence emphasizes, other than the Dharma nothing can help at the time of death; wealth, friends, military, or political power are all useless. The only thing that will benefit us are the seeds of virtuous karma.

The degree to which we meditate on these three topics determines our ability to prevent procrastinating because we think we have time later. This is how yogis practice; they do not waste a single instant because they believe that they will have no time in the future. They know that this is their only chance. It is a wonderful opportunity and once it is gone nothing will be possible. They see the disadvantages of unwholesome actions and develop a negative attitude toward them. These thoughts cause them to practice virtue joyfully all the time. The Buddha said that among animals the elephant leaves the biggest footprint. Similarly, among meditations the understanding, "I may die before tomorrow" makes the greatest mark on the mind. It causes us to prepare for our next rebirth by engaging in Dharma practice right now rather than leaving it for tomorrow.

(b)) Stopping attachment to ignoble activities

The second type of laziness is to be attached to temporary happiness. Sensual gratification is held to be the highest type of pleasure by those who are convinced life is only what we see. But those who take a wider view believe in future lives and karmic causality. They recognize that the happiness we enjoy now is short-lived, but that everlasting happiness can be obtained if we create the causes for it now. So, from a religious perspective, playing, joking around, and sensual pleasure are considered to be distractions because they do not bring unending peace or lasting happiness. These diversions keep us from doing something meaningful with this life. Not only do they damage our desire to pursue enlightenment, they produce desire, jealousy, and so on, all of which result in future suffering. Knowing these faults, how could we be happy engaging in these activities? Śāntideva says:

> How can you take pleasure in distractions
> And laughter—the causes of suffering—
> While abandoning the cause of happiness—
> The supreme joy of limitless holy teachings?

When we see these disadvantages we will try to stop this form of laziness. We will desire to engage in Dharma practice because it is the cause of limitless happiness. Even in this life virtue brings us temporary enjoyment. Rebirth in a higher realm is also the result of spiritual practice. Finally, the everlasting peace of freedom from samsara and enlightenment follow from the practice of Dharma. The more we study, concentrate, and analyze these distractions and their opposites, the stronger our wisdom will be. The wisdom that comes from understanding ten reasons is stronger than that which comes from understanding only two or three reasons. Gradually, the wisdom that comes from analytical meditation will dominate the mind, ignorance will become less active, and our practice will become strong.

(c)) Stopping discouragement or self-contempt

It is not enough to eliminate the first two types of laziness. Even though we no longer procrastinate and are not attracted to ordinary activities, we may still find ourselves unable to practice because we think we are incapable of doing these wonderful things. Sometimes we are discouraged because the goal seems impossible to attain. Sometimes we are discouraged because the method to achieve that goal seems incredibly difficult. The lamrim method outlines the bodhisattva practice for the achievement of buddhahood in order to benefit other sentient beings. To be able to liberate all sentient beings we must be perfect. Many practices must be mastered to become a perfect buddha. It takes a tremendous amount of work to accomplish the path. A practitioner has to endure much hardship and give up so much over a very long period of time. As a result we may think, "Someone like me cannot do this." This is the laziness of self-contempt. We need courage to engage in all the difficult practices over many lives until we attain enlightenment. We need to change our discouraging self-disparagement into the positive attitude that thinks, "Why can't I do this? Everyone can do it. All the buddhas and bodhisattvas who have attained the highest achievements were previously just the same as me. Of course I can do it too."

There are three countermeasures to discouragement:

(1)) Stopping discouragement about the goal
(2)) Stopping discouragement about the means to attain the goal
(3)) Stopping discouragement because wherever you are is a place to practice

(1)) Stopping discouragement about the goal

A buddha has gotten rid of all faults. He or she has no mental obstacles, no misery, and no worldly trouble because all the mental afflictions and their stains are eliminated. In addition, from the positive point of view, a buddha has completely developed every possible good individual and environmental physical quality, as well as the mental qualities of compassion, love, omniscience, and power. There is nothing lacking in a buddha's total cessation of faults and accomplishment of positive qualities. We may become discouraged because we think, "I have difficulty getting rid of even one fault, so how can I get rid of all of them? I find it challenging to maintain just a few imperfect positive qualities, so how could I possibly achieve all of them?" A negative attitude about oneself is dangerous for those who have taken the bodhisattva vow. It is losing bodhicitta to think you cannot attain this goal. We should block this train of thought as soon as it begins, well before we reach the conclusion, "Forget it. I cannot do this." We need a skillful way to promote the confidence that it is possible to become a great savior of all mother sentient beings by attaining enlightenment. We have to fight against any hindrance to this attitude.

Tsongkhapa explains the method to stop discouraging thoughts by citing some stanzas by Śāntideva and a few sutra passages. Śāntideva developed a remedy for self-contempt so that he could meditate on bodhicitta day and night, even when lying on his bed. First of all, he says, look at the Buddha. He has achieved perfection and eliminated all faults, so he is the highest authority. Whatever he says is true; he would not be deceitful, lie, or teach something perverted. The Buddha teaches that every sentient being has the same potential to attain buddhahood that he had. Before attaining enlightenment, the Buddha had many, many lives: sometimes he was a human, sometimes an animal, sometimes an insect, and so on. All those who have become buddhas started out just like us. They were not buddhas from the beginning. They obtained a special human life, came in contact with the teachings, and seriously practiced them over a long period of time. Slowly their mental afflictions and ignorance decreased and their spiritual qualities increased. With a great deal of effort and courage they attained enlightenment. Because all living creatures have the same potential, all of them can attain enlightenment if they meet with a proper method, have enough courage, and exert enough effort. Right now flies and insects have an inferior physical body and mind, so for the present they cannot produce these qualities, but they have the potential to do so someday. Śāntideva advises us to ask ourselves, "Since even animals can attain buddhahood, why can't I do it?"

Unlike animals or other unfortunate beings, we have a wonderful opportunity to accomplish enormous things. It is easy to see this by comparing spiritual development to an arduous physical task. Our ability to complete the task is severely compromised if we have to do every part of it by hand. If we have the right machine, the work will be accomplished easily. Similarly, in samsara the human life we now have is best equipped for accomplishing our ultimate goals. Humans have the intelligence to understand the benefits and disadvantages of virtue and nonvirtue, to deduce from present circumstances what type of causes we created in the past, and infer from our present actions what will happen in the future. With this kind of mental aptitude, of course we can attain enlightenment if we persevere with courage. We should encourage ourselves with this type of praise. Śāntideva summarizes this reasoning as follows:

> I should not be indolent,
> Saying, "How can I attain buddhahood?"
> Because the Buddha who says what is true
> Has spoken this truth:

> "Even flies, bees, mosquitoes,
> And other types of insects
> Can attain the highest enlightenment so difficult to attain
> If they exert powerful effort."

Someone like me, born as a human,
Is able to distinguish benefit from harm.
Why couldn't I attain enlightenment
If I don't give up the bodhisattva practice?

The Buddha taught in the *Cloud of Jewels Sutra* that we should encourage ourselves by thinking about the many sentient beings who have attained buddhahood. A thousand founding buddhas will appear in this eon: there have been many in the past, Śakyamuni is considered the present Buddha, and there will be future buddhas. All these buddhas were initially ordinary beings like us; it is not correct to think that they were always perfect, or that there is no way we can ever become like them because we are very different types of people. We should think instead that the difference between buddhas and ordinary beings is like one of the significant differences between adults and children: their ability to differentiate short- and long-term benefits. Unlike mature adults, children may choose something temporarily pleasurable that will be harmful in the long run. But children can grow up and ordinary beings can become buddhas. Bodhisattvas encourage themselves by thinking, "They were the same as me. They attained buddhahood, so why can't I? I am the same category of being. I will attain perfect enlightenment by following the same method that past, present, and future buddhas followed in order to benefit all other sentient beings." We should think this way as well.

Tsongkhapa draws on the *Praise of Infinite Qualities* to encourage us to compare our present life to some of the ordinary lives Śakyamuni and other buddhas had prior to becoming enlightened. They had many miserable lives, but because they did not become discouraged or fall into self-contempt, they eventually attained buddhahood. Our present situation is much better in comparison. We should not run down our abilities. If we deride ourselves we will become discouraged.

True discouragement does not arise until we recognize the nature of enlightenment and how difficult it is to attain. Buddhas have limitless positive qualities. These qualities are the outcome of an immense number of causes, because every result comes from a specific cause. The path to enlightenment therefore entails almost limitless practices to create virtue and countless methods to eliminate faults. When we think about ourselves in relation to this goal and what must be done to achieve it, we may readily become depressed. When we do not fully understand the practices necessary, we do not get discouraged. Out of ignorance it may look as though buddhahood is easy to attain. When a mountain is far away it appears small and we think,

"It will be easy and fun to scale that peak." As we get closer the mountain looks bigger. When we are at the foot of the mountain we think, "How can I ever get up there!"

When true discouragement arises it is important to apply the antidote. However, it is a mistake to encourage yourself by thinking that all you must do is perfect a single method. Such a thought may give you confidence, but this lack of depression is not a good sign. It indicates that you have only a vague understanding of one part of the path and are not even deeply involved in that practice. You have a false notion that the path is easy because you think that perfecting just one method will yield the limitless qualities of the result. If you have this misunderstanding, you will not get discouraged. But that confidence in a single method will not work. It is like trying to put up a tent by hammering all the tent stakes in one spot and tying all the support ropes to one of them. When we have little understanding and are not actively practicing the multitude of methods, we can be quite surprised when a teacher shows us a broad outline of the path system. We kept discouragement at bay because of a wrong notion, and when we see what it actually will take to do a thorough practice, we give up. The great siddha Sharawa says:

> To someone who has not entered into practice, a bodhisattva's activities seem as easy as shooting an arrow is for an expert archer. They won't even be slightly discouraged. Now our understanding of the Dharma is incomplete. We have not reached the stage of discouragement or self-contempt. When we completely understand, there is the danger of discouragement.

When we see an expert archer shoot at a target, it seems effortless. His arrow easily hits the bull's-eye. But when we try it, it isn't so easy! Similarly, we will not be discouraged until we know the nature of the goal, the path to attain the goal, the requirements we must meet, and have actually begun to practice. That is the time to apply the antidote to discouragement.

(2)) STOPPING DISCOURAGEMENT ABOUT THE MEANS TO ATTAIN THE GOAL

Once we are convinced that achieving enlightenment is an excellent goal and that ordinary people like us can attain it, the question becomes, "What do I have to do to attain perfection?" In order to become buddhas we must master the six perfections: generosity, ethical discipline, patience, joyous perseverance, meditation, and wisdom. The sutras explain that generosity means being totally without stinginess. Bodhisattvas have no feeling of *mine;* if someone wants their possessions, money, or even their life, they are happy to give it away to make others happy. This may discourage us. We may feel, "Theoretically, everyone can do this, but it is too difficult for me. I cannot even give away a little bit of my food, so there is no way I could give the limbs of my body." Because of our egotistic self-cherishing, we always see things we are unaccustomed to from the negative side.

To encourage ourselves we should think about how much suffering we endure in the course of our everyday lives. From beginningless time we have created all kinds of karma in our attempt to have happiness and avoid suffering. As a result of our selfish actions we have been born, aged, gotten sick, and died many times. Sometimes we were born in hell, and sometimes we were born as humans or deities, but there has been wretchedness everywhere as we went up and down, and around and around in samsara. Life after life we have been stabbed, burned, cut apart, cooked, and eaten. Yet, despite this unimaginable suffering, we have not accomplished anything. If all this pain had been worthwhile, by now we would have attained real happiness and eliminated misery. However, we are still in the same situation, and it will continue just as before.

The hardship involved in the practices to attain enlightenment is nothing in comparison. It may look like bodhisattvas have to endure all kinds of adversity for a long time, but these difficulties are short-term. Because bodhisattvas understand that these difficulties are helping them attain the great goal of enlightenment for themselves and others, such experiences do not feel very onerous to them. Enlightenment is a permanent state; undergoing some temporary pain to achieve it is therefore not viewed as a hardship. Their experience of suffering cannot be compared to ordinary misery. As Śāntideva says:

> Thinking, "Nevertheless, I am afraid
> Of having to give up my limbs"
> Is fear caused by ignorantly
> Failing to distinguish between heavy and light.

Heavy and light, difficult and easy—these are all relative. When we have not practiced something, it seems difficult. People can do unbelievable things, like walk on a high wire, if they work at it for many years. But it can be hard to stand up on a table if you have never practiced it. Similarly, we can train ourselves gradually to give. As we become more accustomed to it, what is easy to give changes. We will have advanced so far mentally that when the time to give up our limbs arrives, there will be no difficulty doing so. We will be able to do it with a special kind of confidence and joy. There is no need to be discouraged simply because you cannot do such things now.

Śāntideva continues:

> For many countless eons,
> Innumerable times I have been cut,
> Stabbed, burned, and flayed,
> But I have not attained enlightenment.
>
> There is a limit to the suffering
> For me to attain enlightenment.
> It is like the pain of an operation
> To remove a deep and harmful disease.

The hardship required to attain enlightenment can be measured; it has a limit. We may experience this much, but no more. It can go on for a certain length of time, but no longer. In contrast, ordinary samsaric suffering is immeasurable. It makes sense then to willingly go through a certain amount of pain in order eliminate limitlessly more misery. This is analogous to being willing to undergo a painful cure for a dangerous illness. We accept the misery of surgery, injections, and bitter medicines because we know that by enduring this unpleasantness we will get rid of something much worse. We do not worry about the pain of the treatment; in fact, experiencing the pain makes us happy, because we know it will cure us. Likewise, bodhisattvas feel a special joy when they engage in the most difficult practices because they know that they are accomplishing something very beneficial for others. They have no difficulty enduring the hardships necessary to clear away all suffering from the root. As Śāntideva says:

> Even ordinary doctors' treatments
> Are unpleasant cures for disease.
> Therefore I should be able to bear minimal discomfort
> In order to overcome the many sufferings of all.

It takes a special kind of wisdom to reach this level of practice. We start slowly and do things little by little. There are limitations to what we can and should do in the beginning. For example, in general we start to practice generosity mentally. Even later, we will be breaking our vows if we give at the wrong time or give something without practicing mentally first. Mastering the practices of the bodhisattva path is similar to learning to fly a plane.

Novice pilots have to practice basic techniques on the ground. If they break the rules and fly a plane before they are ready, it can be very dangerous.

Ordinary physicians order their patients to undergo difficult tests and therapies whether they are ready or not. In contrast, Buddha prescribes steady, measured steps to cure the disease of limitless suffering and its cause. The bodhisattva practices look impossible to us now, but at the appropriate time they will be easy because we will be prepared to do them. Right now we are afraid to practice the perfection of generosity because, under the power of self-centered egotism, we are attached to our body and life. While we have this fear, we should not give up part of our body. We will reach that higher level of practice someday, but Buddha said in the beginning that we should give only what we are able to give willingly, respectfully, and without stinginess. At first we might not want to give much at all. We give only things we feel comfortable giving—small amounts of food, clothing, or money. With that attitude the gift of even a spoonful of food creates great merit. Our practice of generosity will progressively develop in small increments. As we become accustomed to giving, we may find we can happily give one-third of something and keep two-thirds for ourselves. Later, we may want to give two-thirds and keep only a third. In order to progress, we have to see the purpose and benefit of generosity. As we develop great compassion, love, bodhicitta, and an understanding of śūnyatā, we will come to enjoy practicing generosity and be more and more willing to give. Eventually our selfish attitude will be completely gone; we will feel it is much more important to do a favor for others than to cherish ourselves.

When the strength of our compassion for others is so extensive that we love them more than ourselves, we turn away from attachment to the body. Only at that point—and only if we determine that giving a part of our body to others will to serve a greater purpose than keeping it—should we do it. This is not something done unthinkingly: bodhisattvas have to see that it would be meaningful to help others this way. The measure of this level of practice is being able to give your body or life as easily as giving a vegetable. As Śāntideva says:

> The supreme physician does not employ
> Ordinary remedies such as these.
> He cures incalculable illnesses
> With very gentle techniques.
>
> Our guide instructs us at the start
> To give such things as vegetables.

After we become accustomed to this,
In stages we progress to giving our flesh.

When my attitude toward giving my body
Is just as if I were offering a vegetable,
At that time how could it be hard
To give my flesh and so forth?

Mahayana practice is divided into the Sutrayana and Tantrayana. The tantric path is quick and short, whereas it can take three countless eons to reach buddhahood following the path explained in the sutras. Some people therefore say that the Sutrayana is too difficult, because practitioners have to give up their bodies and lives many, many times over such a long period of time. These people do not accurately understand the practice of the perfections. Śāntideva's stanzas clearly say we should not give, even if we are tempted to do so, before we are ready. For as long as we see something as a fearful or frightful, we do not do it. *Perfection* of any practice indicates mental excellence. The perfection of generosity is a total lack of stinginess so that there is no hardship in giving. It is not the perfection of generosity to give everything you have in the world while feeling uncomfortable about it. Only when we have completely eliminated attachment to the body can we give it away. We should therefore not worry about being unable to do this practice at present. The difference between us and high level bodhisattvas who can do this practice now is the training. Once we have trained our mind, we will be able to do it as well.

(3)) Stopping discouragement because wherever you are is a place to practice

In addition to being discouraged about the goal and method to attain it, we may become disheartened about the difficulties concerning where we must practice. We may think, "To accomplish buddhahood I have to take rebirth in samsara almost countless times. It might take eons and there are so many problems and so many things can hurt me. Life in samsara is very difficult in itself, much less in combination with all the things that must be done to practice the path. Practicing the path in a peaceful place where no one bothers me and there are no difficulties might be okay. But I do not think that I can practice the path while enduring the hardships of this world."

To reverse this self-defeating attitude we should think along the following lines. Suffering in samsara is the result of negative karma. Negative karma—

harming others to gain our own ends—is founded on ignorance. Powerful self-centered attachment to our body and possessions leads to jealousy and the other mental afflictions. These in turn impel us to do many negative things to others. Bodhisattvas completely change this pattern. In the past they cherished themselves, but now they have great compassion, love, and a spontaneous desire to attain enlightenment in order to benefit others. Bodhicitta leads them to dedicate everything they do to benefit other sentient beings. As a result not only do they not create negative karma, all their actions are virtuous. Since there is no cause of suffering, there is no suffering result. Wholesome karma brings a fortunate life of happiness, peace, and enjoyment. Even though bodhisattvas may appear to be ordinary human beings, because of their wisdom and compassion they do not experience samsaric suffering in the same way we do. Even when bodhisattvas experience the results of earlier negative karma, it does not matter to them; they are careless of themselves and careful of others.

There are two basic types of suffering: physical and mental. The physical suffering of life in the human, animal, hell realms, and so forth is the direct result of negative actions done to others. Mental suffering, such as agitation and regret, is the result of ignorance. As long as we are dominated by egotistical self-cherishing, we firmly hold to *me* versus *everyone else*. We believe that others are ultimately and inherently the enemy because they do things that harm us. We worry about what they have done and what they may do. Not knowing what will happen, worry, and uncertainty are all forms of mental suffering. Not understanding reality makes us almost crazy and, as a result, we do all kinds of negative things.

Bodhisattvas do not do this because they understand the causal relationship between actions and their results. They understand that all things lack an inherent nature and are like a magical illusion. They see that the wrong view of egotistical self-cherishing does not have a real object. Wisdom understanding the illusory, empty nature of phenomena pushes down the wrong view. All the mental agitation and suffering experienced by ordinary people goes away. Bodhisattvas are ornamented by joy: they are confident, happy, and peaceful. They have no physical suffering. Since bodhisattvas are physically and mentally at ease, it doesn't bother them to remain in the world. It gives them great pleasure to help sentient beings. Having gotten rid of samsaric problems and their causes, they regard even a long span of time as short, and difficulties become easy. They do not feel frustrated no matter how long they have to stay in samsara to help sentient beings. Śāntideva says it like this:

There is no physical suffering because sin is eliminated.
There is no unhappiness because one is wise.
Wrong understanding brings mental suffering.
Sinful actions will harm the body.

Merit results in physical comfort.
Wisdom results in mental peace.
What compassionate person has reason to regret
Remaining in samsara for the benefit of others?

It can be difficult to cross a vast desert on foot. Nowadays we have cars and planes to make going long distances easier, but when Śāntideva wrote the most efficient mode of transportation was a horse. He therefore used the horse as an analogy for the vehicle that will carry bodhisattvas to buddhahood. All bodhisattvas ride the powerful attitude of bodhicitta. Wanting to achieve enlightenment in order to benefit others carries all their actions. Dominated by love and compassion, there is no way for bodhisattvas to create the cause of misery. Motivated by bodhicitta, they do positive actions continuously. Every moment of their activity leads to peace and happiness. Every action takes them closer and closer to enlightenment. Knowing this, they are not indolent; they are happy doing anything and everything:

Thus riding the horse of bodhicitta
Clears away all hardship,
And goes from happiness to happiness.
What sensible person would be lethargic?

When we are bound by the egotistical self-centered attitude, not only do we worry about having to go somewhere unpleasant, we are anxious about how long we may have to stay there. The sutras talk about eons and eons of time that we should practice in samsara. But, just as the place itself is not necessarily the cause of misery, neither is the length of time we remain there. In general, if great suffering lasts even a short time, it is extremely troubling, but we have no problem with happiness lasting a long time. We would like it to last even longer. Therefore, we should not be discouraged by the duration of the path. Nāgārjuna's *Precious Garland* says:

Suffering even for a short time is difficult to bear,
So there is no need to talk about a long time.

If you have no suffering and are happy,
What is the problem if it lasts a long time?

They have no physical suffering.
They have no mental pain.
Out of compassion for the world's misery
They remain as long as necessary.

Therefore saying, "buddhahood is far away"
Does not discourage those who are wise.
We should always make an effort
To eliminate faults and obtain good qualities.

When we do not know what is going on, we imagine an impossible situation. Out of ignorance, we perceive a little bit here and a little there, and mix it all together. Śāntideva therefore recommends that we understand the specifics of a situation in order to eliminate discouragement. How do we do this? He says we should make an effort to eliminate faults. This refers not just to our own faults; it includes the faults of all sentient beings in the world. The cause of all sentient beings' misery is their faults. These faults can be eliminated with a special method. When they are completely gone, sentient beings will have the highest, perfect qualities of enlightenment. We should try to achieve that goal for ourselves and help others attain it as well. In order to attain perfect enlightenment we have to create the causes for it; this means completing the accumulations of wisdom and merit. The prospect of eons upon eons of work to accumulate merit and wisdom can be discouraging. However, there is no need to be disheartened. Although a measureless accumulation of wholesome activity is needed, with proper understanding we will see that it too is not difficult.

Accumulating merit and wisdom becomes easy when we are motivated by impartial, universal compassion for all sentient beings. When we are dedicated to easing the suffering of all others, we search for the best means to lead them to emancipation. It takes a buddha—someone who has eliminated all faults and has attained perfect omniscience, compassion, love, and power—to be able to do this. Seeing our present limitations, we will desire to attain buddhahood quickly in order to save sentient beings. Motivated by bodhicitta, we think, "I will do whatever it takes, for however long it takes, go anywhere necessary, and endure any difficulty in order to achieve the qualities of buddhahood." This goal is for ourselves, but we are motivated to attain it so that we can benefit limitless others. Taking the bodhisattva vow in front of all the buddhas with this motivation makes every action purely for the benefit of other sentient beings. Even the most personal actions, like eating and sleeping, are for the benefit of other sentient beings, because only by nourishing themselves can bodhisattvas continue to do so much for others. Furthermore, if bodhicitta is spontaneous, it persists even when we do not have a conscious intention to attain enlightenment for the benefit of others. Our virtue increases every moment no matter what we are doing, because we are subconsciously motivated by bodhicitta. It does not grow just one merit at a time; it increases by the number of other sentient beings. When we think about it this way, creating a lot of merit is not so difficult! Again from the *Precious Garland:*

> We say that just as in every direction
> There is a limitless amount
> Of space, earth, water, fire, and air,
> There are countless suffering sentient beings.

> Bodhisattvas look with compassion
> On all those countless sentient beings.
> In front of the buddhas they promise
> They will lead them from suffering.

> Those who remain resolute like this,
> Once they have taken the vow,
> Whether sleeping or awake,
> Even if their mind is somewhere else,

> Continuously collect merit as limitless
> As the number of limitless sentient beings.
> Since their merit is limitless,
> Limitless buddhahood is not difficult to attain.

Accumulating all the merit necessary to attain enlightenment is therefore discouraging only when we cannot get beyond our egocentric view. As long as we are subject to selfish concerns, it seems impossible to do anything for all sentient beings. But if we develop bodhicitta, we will not feel worried or be overcome by adversity. In every moment we will accumulate as much merit and purify as much negative karma as there are sentient beings. There are four immeasurable things: time, sentient beings, the highest realizations of the goal, and wholesome actions. With these four incalculable things don't you think that we can attain enlightenment in not too long a time? As Nāgārjuna says:

> Willing to remain for measureless time
> For the benefit of measureless sentient beings,
> Wishing to attain measureless enlightenment
> By practicing measureless wholesome deeds—
>
> With these four measureless things in combination,
> Even though enlightenment is limitless,
> Why will we not attain this state
> Without it taking very long?

We must distinguish between the various reasons for wanting enlightenment as soon as possible. It is correct if it is for the benefit of other sentient beings. The essence of the Mahayana attitude is to want enlightenment quickly, because only by becoming a buddha can we alleviate sentient beings' suffering. We want the quickest possible path to enlightenment because sentient beings have been suffering from beginningless time and cannot wait any longer. This attitude will bring enlightenment quickly. This mind-set is a marvelous thing; it is what we should strive to cultivate.

But Tsongkhapa comments that usually our motivation for reaching buddhahood quickly is nothing like this. We see a long, long period of incalculable work. Worrying about our own difficulties, we look for something easier, a shortcut for ourselves. This selfish attitude hinders us from accomplishing our goal because it indirectly damages aspirational bodhicitta and directly spoils active bodhicitta. Not wanting to try something that appears so difficult keeps us from starting to develop bodhicitta. It is the precise opposite of active bodhicitta—taking the bodhisattva vow and actually doing things to benefit incalculable beings for a vast length of time. In sum, wanting a quick result in order to make it easy on ourselves reduces our potential to practice the Mahayana path and pushes enlightenment far, far away. It is contrary to the proper way of developing bodhicitta, increasing it, and expanding it. It keeps us from starting to practice, and, if we do start, it blocks us from continuing. It is counter to Buddha's teaching of the Mahayana as explained by Nāgāruna, Asaṅga, and others.

If we wallow in discouragement, we will not try anything. It is not good for us, nor is it of any benefit to others. Not only is it not helpful, it only makes us more and more dispirited. The fact that so many different methods are explained so extensively in the sutras can cause us to become downhearted.

It can be difficult to know how they all work together. If we understand how the methods work, we will be happy to engage in something even if it is difficult. We need to praise and encourage ourselves. If we take joy in practicing, these goals are right in our hands.

The following stanzas from the *Garland of Birth Stories* exemplify the power of encouraging oneself to practice:

> Discouragement is not helpful for freeing you from misery.
> Therefore, without wallowing in sorrow,
> Rely on wise ones to attain the necessary goal.
> Then what seems difficult becomes easy.

> Therefore, without fear or a lack of joy,
> Accomplish what is necessary with the correct methods.
> Blessed by relying on the brilliance of the wise,
> The achievement of all goals is in our hands.

In one of his lifetimes before he became enlightened, Buddha was a trader. He went across the ocean with many other merchants to buy and sell jewels and other precious things. On their return voyage a dangerous storm came up; there was a huge wind and their boat was about to sink. Everyone was very scared. The Bodhisattva had compassion, love, and bodhicitta, so he wanted to calm their fear. He said, "Since I made the vow to attain buddhahood for the benefit of sentient beings, I have not harmed anybody. All my actions have been for the purpose of saving others. By the power of the truth of these words, may all these people be freed from fear." The power of truth made the wind suddenly drop and everyone was saved. The point of the story is that we should encourage ourselves to practice and rely on a skillful spiritual friend. If we do both these things, what seems hard becomes easy. We can become free from suffering and free others as well.

Even in a worldly context, the higher the goal the more preparation, effort, and hardship it takes to acquire it. This can be discouraging, but if we give up we will not get anywhere. We put ourselves in a position to get worse and worse; we can get stuck at the bottom. If we value the goal, understand the method, expect the hardships, and accept the difficulties, we can enjoy working toward our goal. Tsongkhapa reminds us of Asaṅga's advice that, in this regard we need two approaches: we should not be discouraged about the extensive training required of bodhisattvas, and we should not be satisfied with a few inferior qualities. The first piece of advice is to learn about the Mahayana practices taught in the sutras so that we know what to practice, where, and when. This prevents the discouragement that keeps us from starting to practice, or, if we do start, that causes us to fall back. The second piece of advice is to not be satisfied with just a few virtuous qualities. Self-satisfaction can make us not want to pursue anything better. We may have one or two good qualities, but they are just a small portion of the many that exist. If we conceitedly think we have done everything necessary to attain enlightenment, we will be very disheartened when someone who really knows the path shows us that we have not done nearly enough to reach the highest goal. Hearing that we have to develop many more high qualities and reduce numerous negative qualities can make us want to give up. Again and again Asaṅga says that no matter what wholesome qualities we have already developed, we must look forward; we must be eager to learn more, to develop more, and to master the limitless perfections of buddhahood.

(b") Gathering the forces of the favorable conditions

In order to develop joyous perseverance, we must fight the hindrances and develop the necessary conditions. In the sections just concluded, we learned how to fight against discouragement regarding our pursuit of the right things and enthusiasm for the wrong things. In this section, we learn about the positive conditions we must develop. There are four subsections:

- (1") Developing the power of aspiration
- (2") Developing the power of steadfastness
- (3") Developing the power of joy
- (4") The power of relinquishment

(1") Developing the power of aspiration

To aspire means to desire or want something. Many times the word *desire* refers to a mental affliction. But while such thoughts as wanting to attain enlightenment and wishing to free all sentient beings from misery are desires, they are not part of the afflicted mind. For that reason, we often use the term *aspiration* to denote a *wholesome desire*. As used here, *aspiration* means to have a natural liking for a wholesome goal, and to be inclined to act in a positive way in order to achieve that goal. A desire to do something wholesome is necessary for practitioners, because if we lack interest in a spiritual practice, we will not do it. If we do something without much desire, we will not get much of a result. In contrast, if we really desire something, we will enthusiastically persevere in attaining it. Śāntideva explains this in *Engaging in the Bodhisattva Deeds* as follows:

> In the past and in the present
> I have lacked desire for the Dharma,
> So I am in this poor situation.
> Who would give up desire for the Dharma?
>
> The Buddha taught that this desire
> Is the root of all virtuous things.

In this stanza "desire for the Dharma" means wanting to do something virtuous. Because in the past and even now we have lacked interest in a spiritual practice, we are in a very unfortunate situation. In a worldly sense, being poor is associated with many problems and a lot of misery. The suffering associated with spiritual poverty is aging, death, rebirth, not obtaining what we desire, coming in contact with undesirable things, and so on. Since a lack of aspiring for the wholesome leads to so many difficulties, someone with intelligence would never give up his or her interest in the Dharma. This aspiration, or enthusiasm, is the foundation of the path leading to a spiritual goal. The intensity of our desire determines how much we will practice. A little desire leads to a little practice, while more desire leads us to do more to reach our goal. In this sense desire is the root of all virtues. Every positive result—from a high rebirth within samsara to the final goals of freedom from samsara or full enlightenment—is dependent upon this desire to practice. So aspiration is like a pillar holding up our perseverance in virtuous activity.

How do we produce this aspiration? Śāntideva continues:

> Its root is constant meditation
> On fruitional results.

The way to develop a desire to practice the Dharma is to learn about karmic causation. True understanding does not come easily. We cannot perceive the relationship between cause and effect with our sense consciousnesses; it is not like seeing a color or hearing a sound. We have to think about the difference between wholesome and unwholesome activities and about their respective results. The first step toward understanding is faith. This is not *blind faith*, however. In order to aspire to Mahayana spiritual practice, we have to develop the *faith of conviction* that unwholesome causes lead to negative results and that wholesome fruit comes from positive causes.[6] The faith of conviction in causality is founded on studying the scriptures, learning logical proofs, and investigating experiential and historical examples. Clearly seeing the relationship between causes and their results will make us want to eliminate the negative side and achieve the positive side.

Tsongkhapa is not simply saying that we should understand karma and its results in general; he says we should particularly examine causality in regard to each of the bodhisattva practices. Our aspiration to practice the Dharma will be as strong as our desire for a particular positive result and our understanding of the virtuous causes that lead to it. Bodhisattvas' firm faith in causation completely shatters their tendency to act selfishly, because they see the unwholesome results that come from breaking their promise to help all sentient beings. Taking the bodhisattva vow is not a small thing; once we have made that vow our actions affect all sentient beings. Someone with the bodhisattva vow is similar to the official ambassador of a big country like the United States. If he or she promises to do something good, there will be much positive gain. But if this ambassador does something wrong then, because it is on behalf of the entire country, the results will be a big disaster. The deeds of a bodhisattva are similar; because they are on behalf of all sentient beings, their benefits are great and the disadvantages of not doing what was promised are enormous.

Achieving enlightenment in order to benefit all other sentient beings is a great project. To persevere in working toward such a goal we need strong enthusiasm for every aspect of the method. When we have no energy to engage in practice, it seems that we do not have even a small part of the perseverance necessary to clear away our negative traits and develop positive qualities. To encourage ourselves we should think, "Beginning bodhisattva practice means promising to eliminate all the misery endured by myself and others. It means that in order to help others I will develop every good quality from the beginning stages of the path to those of highest buddhahood. It may take eons to completely remove each inner fault from the root and clean away the stains left by the predispositions for these faults. But if I compare this to how long I have been familiar with the negative side, it is not really long at all. Life after life from beginningless time I have been habituated to desire and the other mental afflictions. What have I done? What am I doing now? What are my thought processes, my physical and verbal actions? All of these have caused and will cause great hardship. None of them help me attain my goals. From now on I will not act this way. I will make my life meaningful."

Śāntideva says:

I will destroy all the measureless faults
That belong to me and others.
To finish off each of those faults
May take an ocean of eons.

I cannot see in myself even a part
Of the effort needed to eliminate those faults—
The source of measureless misery.
Why doesn't this break my heart?

Śāntideva calls misery and the causes of misery *faults*. Bodhisattvas vow to eliminate all their own and others' faults, even though it may take a very, very long time. If we do not resolve to do this, all our physical, verbal, and mental activities are ordinary karmas that are potentially the causes for immeasurable suffering. The yogi Śāntideva asks himself, "Why doesn't this worry me? Why do I continue to do such pointless things that cause me so much trouble? Why doesn't this break my heart?" He continues this thought in the following stanzas, reminding himself that bodhisattvas also promise to acquire good qualities to benefit themselves and others. He examines himself and sees that he has the type of life needed to achieve this goal. It seems miraculous, a rare stroke of luck. Not everyone has this opportunity: not all humans come in contact with the Mahayana teachings, have the desire to practice, or take the bodhisattva vow. He thinks, "I have not created any good habits, so where could a life like this come from? Now that I have such a rare opportunity, how astonishing it is to not make any effort to achieve a wholesome goal to benefit myself and others. What a waste of such a life."

I will develop many good qualities
For myself and others.
To cultivate each of those good qualities
May take an ocean of eons.

I have never accustomed myself
With any part of these good qualities.
It is truly incredible that I am wasting
This life that came I know not how.

Seeing the situation in this light makes one desire to do more from now on. We decide that from this day forward we will be more serious. We become enthusiastic and put more effort into our practice.

(2") Developing the power of steadfastness

Strong aspiration is not enough on its own to carry us through to the end. We need to be resolute. In the context of the practice of perseverance, being *resolute* or *steadfast* is to complete an undertaking without giving up. Sometimes we start a project without considering whether we are really able to do it or not. We make a snap decision to jump in because an activity seems interesting. So we begin, but soon find it is not as easy or as enjoyable as we thought. So we drop it and begin something else. We are always looking for something new to replace our current activity. Before committing ourselves to a new endeavor, we should determine whether it will be possible for us to complete the task. If it seems impossible, then for the time being we should not undertake it. We should leave it for later; after we progress more we can re-examine it in light of our improved abilities. It is better not to start something than to begin and drop it in the middle. On the other hand, we should begin—even if a task seems difficult—if it is possible and beneficial to complete it. Once we begin we should really try to accomplish our objective.

This quality of fortitude is important even in worldly situations. People make decisions to enter upon difficult journeys, endure hardships, or go to battle based on an analysis of the benefits of the goal, the difficulty of obtaining it, and their ability to achieve it. It is even more important to do this kind of examination in regard to spiritual endeavors. Without this analysis we will continually promise to do one thing or the other, only to give up later. This is a very bad habit. It is the cause for us to have a similar lack of stamina in our future lives: we will never complete what we begin. Furthermore, if we promise to engage in virtue and do not follow through, we will accumulate negative karma. Because our negative karma in this life will increase, so will our suffering in future lives. In addition, because we will feel obligated to go back and fulfill our first promise, we will be prevented from completing other virtuous practices; as a result we will drop them as well. Because we keep starting new things, nothing gets done properly. We do not finish any virtuous practices, so the results of our activities are inferior. To summarize, the dangers of not carrying through on a promise to do something are as follows: we become unable to bring any task to completion; we do not get the results we desire; our initial promise hinders us from doing other things; and the stability of our other vows and precepts is weakened. As Śāntideva says:

> Examine an activity at the outset
> As to whether to begin or not.

If unable, it is better to not start.
But having begun, I will not reverse.

That habit carries over into other lives.
Negative karma and suffering increases.
Also at this time other actions and their results
Will be poorly done or not done at all.

It is important to develop the power of resolve. The way to become able to follow through on what we begin is to cultivate pride. Pride is generally considered to be a mental affliction; and certainly smug arrogance is something to be abandoned. But certain religious practices are called *pride* because, in some respects, they look similar to ordinary pride. However, the religious practice of pride is positive, wholesome, and something we should develop.

Śāntideva says that there are three types of such pride, and they are explained in relation to action, ability, and afflictions. As for the first, the *pride of action,* this means that when we make a promise to engage in a virtuous practice, we should not rely on others to do it for us. We have to complete it ourselves. Śāntideva puts it succinctly as follows:

Saying, "I will do this alone,"
Is the pride of action.

We have to practice the path, get rid of mental afflictions, and develop higher qualities all on our own. Spiritual growth comes from within, not from someone else. Someone else's meditation practice eliminates his or her mental afflictions, not ours. We cannot expect someone else to take responsibility for our liberation. We cannot expect someone else to take the responsibility for others' liberation either. Freedom and enlightenment depend entirely on one's own practice. Nāgārjuna also makes this point in his *Friendly Letter:*

Emancipation depends upon me.
It never occurs because of others' help.

Statements like, "I will do this myself. No one else can be depended upon to do this. I alone am responsible," sound similar to the mental afflictions of pride and conceit. It seems as though we are so egotistic that we feel that we have to do something ourselves in order for it to be done correctly. It appears that even if we do need some help, we will refuse it out of conceit. But a bodhisattva's pride of action is similar to ordinary pride only in that it is an intention to accomplish the action oneself. The motivating force of Mahayana pride, however, is not self-centered arrogance. It is compassion and love.

As for the *pride of ability,* this is to be confident of our capacity to accomplish the path. Afflicted, self-centered pride is to see oneself as better than others; it is raising oneself up while putting others down. It is the thought, "I am such and such and they are not. I can do such and such and they cannot." But here the attitude is not to belittle others; it is acknowledging that we are in a much better position to accomplish our goals than most sentient beings. The hell denizens, hungry ghosts, animals, and most humans are completely under the power of hatred, desire, ignorance, and the other mental afflictions. They are suffering, incapable of accomplishing what they desire, and so of course they cannot achieve anything for others. In contrast, we have all these special opportunities: we have physical, mental, and verbal good qualities enabling us to practice like bodhisattvas; we have met with the Dharma; we have taken the bodhisattva vow, and so forth. In short, we have all the necessary conditions to attain enlightenment quickly. We can help all other sentient beings accomplish their goals. This comparison encourages us to practice seriously. We decide, "I can and will accomplish the goals for their sake." As Śāntideva says:

> Worldly beings under the power of the afflictions
> Are not able to accomplish their own goals.
> Those beings cannot do what I can do.
> Therefore, I will do this.

We should practice continuously. When hardships or complications tempt us to stop, we should compare our difficulties to how much others suffer trying to achieve small goals such as sensual pleasure, food, or a small amount of money. For example, farmers work day and night, uncertain whether they will reap the harvest they want. Even if they do get it, the result they are working for is limited, temporary, and can be the cause of more suffering. It cannot give them supreme pleasure or everlasting peace. Nonetheless, they vigorously pursue their inferior goal without cease, no matter what difficulties they encounter. Sometimes they even give up their life in their endeavors. Think, "If they don't give up, why should I? I should be working even harder than they are because I am striving for a different, far superior result— the attainment of everlasting peace and the highest happiness of enlightenment in order to benefit others." After thinking this way conclude, "So why am I giving up? Why am I not working seriously? I have the ability to accom-

plish this colossal goal. There is no way for me to stop trying to achieve it."
Śāntideva says this is the way to think:

> If others do inferior actions,
> How can I just sit here doing nothing?

Do not get confused because at one point we were told to eliminate pride
and here we are told to develop it. We should never increase afflicted pride.
When engaging in this practice we should not have afflicted pride which is
conceited and looks down upon others. It is self-important arrogance to lack
compassion and think, "They are low, no good, and incapable, whereas I am
superior and can do this." We should not practice with that attitude. The
nature of the pride encouraged here is different. We should look at others the
way parents view their young children—with love and compassion. Until
children are able to do things on their own, their parents do whatever they
can to help and protect them. Parents do not do this out of pride in their own
abilities; they do it because they love their children more than themselves. We
should practice pride without mixing in self-centered conceit. We should
think, "I will do whatever is necessary because they are not capable right now.
If something must be eliminated, I should eradicate it. If something is needed,
I should provide it." Śāntideva summarizes:

> I do not do this out of pride.
> It is best not to be proud of myself.

Mahayana practice is the antidote to the selfish egotistic attitude. The third
pride, the so-called *pride of the afflictions,* is a heroic attitude that views ignorance, desire, hatred, jealousy, and so forth as the enemy. These mental
afflictions are the source of every sentient beings' misery in this or other lives.
Dominated by the afflictions, sentient beings are compelled to create many
other negative actions that yield disastrous consequences. Therefore, the
mental afflictions are the target that all practitioners try to destroy. The usual
antidote to pride is to be humble, compassionate, and without haughty, self-
satisfied contempt for other sentient beings. However, we should never
extend this attitude toward the mental afflictions! In regard to the afflictions
we should think that we will never allow them to control us. We should always
try to subdue them, conquer them, and never let them arise. We should extirpate them as much as we can. They should not be allowed to exist. We should
look down on them as bad. In short, we should be proud of our courage to
push the afflictions out and develop wisdom and compassion.

We will have the mental power to really practice when we have determined that we are capable of fighting whatever difficulties may arise. As Śāntideva says:

> I will be victorious over all.
> None will be victorious over me.
> As a child of the victorious lions
> I will abide in this pride.

Buddhas are not called *victorious ones* because they triumph over other people, but because no mental affliction can rise up in their minds again. Buddhas have no more problems and nothing can defeat them because they have destroyed all internal enemies. Buddhas are compared to lions because lions exemplify fearlessness and pride. No other animal can successfully fight a lion. Bodhisattvas are youngsters in the lineage of lion-like buddhas. They have the pride that they too will be victorious. We should have this kind of pride also.

Mahayana practice is not easy. It takes a special kind of bravery and strength to take responsibility for the welfare of other sentient beings. We need positive pride to fulfill our vows and precepts. If we lack it we will be weak. The slightest predicament will overwhelm us. Our minimal enthusiasm and courage will evaporate. As Śāntideva says:

> When they see a dead snake,
> Crows act like garuḍas.
> If I am so weak,
> Even small downfalls will harm me.
> Has anyone become free from suffering
> If he was easily discouraged and gave up?

Garuḍas are the mythical kings of birds. They are extremely powerful; no other bird can compete against them, and they can kill and eat any kind of snake or nāga. In contrast, crows are usually cowardly, but they have no fear of a dead snake. If we are easily disheartened by small inconveniences, we are acting like a fearful crow. We pretend to be brave when things are easy but let ourselves become overwhelmed and dissuaded from virtue when faced with minor problems. In this way small problems can bring much greater negative results. How could someone who gives up his or her practice so easily ever be freed from the misery of poverty, and so forth? No one attains freedom by giving up quickly.

The Kadampa lama Sharawa says that sometimes people begin Dharma practice, but when they encounter difficulties or deprivation, they give it up in order to enjoy themselves. Although in this life they may have some pleasure, it is a temporary, so-so happiness, no better than what they had before. Giving up the Dharma will bring limitless suffering in the future. We may not try to destroy the afflictions, but they will have no mercy on us in return. They will take advantage of us as much as we allow them to do so. If we let anger arise and grow, things will always end badly. The other afflictions are the same. The reality is that we must make an effort to apply the antidote to the mental afflictions. Just saying the words, "I will complete this virtuous practice to benefit others," will not help. It is a mistake to expect that the buddhas and bodhisattvas will save us without any effort on our part. They are perfect, but no matter how powerful they are, they cannot save us if we do not take refuge and make an effort to practice. Buddhas are like a big hook that can lift things up. We must become something that they can hook on to. Practicing pride properly will give us the strength and enthusiasm to think in a positive way. It will prevent discouragement, even when we have big problems.

Śāntideva goes on to say:

> With the perseverance produced by this kind of pride,
> It is difficult for even big obstacles to overwhelm me.
> Therefore, with a steadfast mind,
> I shall overcome the downfalls.

The "obstacles" that Śāntideva refers to in this stanza are breaking the vows we made to benefit other sentient beings. If we break our promise and ignore the precepts, negative actions will be the victor. The afflictions will overpower us. In that situation, wise people would laugh if they heard us say, "I want to be the victor over the mental afflictions of the three worlds." It is important to have the courage to continually fight against these internal enemies. To be courageous we need to be confident that we are able to overcome the mental afflictions.

The meditation practice to produce courageous pride requires analytical reasoning. Just blanking out thoughts will not help us here. Quieting the mind is necessary to achieve mental stabilization, but once we can focus the mind we must use its power in analytical meditation in order to fight against the mental afflictions. If we do not prepare ourselves with analytical meditation, we may be able to sit calmly for a long time, but once we get up the afflictions will take over. We will become angry as soon as someone says, "You are incompetent." We will become inflated with pride if someone says, "You are so wonderful and beautiful." Or we will become jealous if someone says, "That person is much better and prettier than you." We have no ability to counter these afflictions because we did not develop the antidote in analytical meditation. We must prepare ourselves to fight against each mental affliction by developing wisdom. Then the afflictions will not be able to take over in situations where they ordinarily would. Tsongkhapa says that although certain commentators on *Engaging in the Bodhisattva Deeds* explain *pride of the afflictions* a little bit differently, the explanation above is correct.

In summary, how do these first two powers—aspiration and steadfastness—develop joyous perseverance? Aspiration creates a desire and enthusiasm for doing practices to benefit other sentient beings. The power of steadfastness, or pride, enables us to establish that determination so that we never give up that newly formed resolve. Steadfastness begins with wanting to do the job ourselves. We give up relying on somebody else to take care of it. We produce the courage to take responsibility for others who are unable to help themselves; then we develop confidence in our ability to do this. We think like a great hero who, knowing that others cannot do what he can, does it for them out of compassion. Once we want to take responsibility to do this ourselves and develop the confidence that we can do this, we actually go to battle against the mental afflictions. We are always careful and resolute because we will not be able to help all other sentient beings if the afflictions overcome us. We stand up to the afflictions vowing, "You will never take advantage of me again." We promise ourselves, "I will never let them destroy me. I will annihilate them."

We should contemplate again and again the disadvantageous consequences of giving up a task in the middle; then we will be determined to complete whatever we decide to do. We decide what to do after examining the goal, its benefits, the required method to attain it, and our ability to fulfill those requirements. If we decide to begin, it will be with the firm attitude: "I will not give up until I have completed this." Out of wisdom we will not do things halfway. This is the power of steadfastness.

(3") DEVELOPING THE POWER OF JOY

The first two powers, aspiration and steadfastness, are important when we have not yet produced joyous perseverance. The third power—the power of joy—helps us after we have initially developed perseverance. The power of joy works in two ways: we are happy to begin an activity, and doing the activity gives us so much pleasure that we want to do it continuously. The power of joy makes us insatiable. No matter how much happiness we experience as a result of our practice, it is never enough. Looking for more and more happiness until we reach the highest bliss makes us tireless in creating the cause of happiness. Śāntideva says that the power of joy is like children's enthusiasm for play; they never want to stop. Bodhisattvas' perseverance is similar; their wish for the fruit of the path makes their desire to practice the path unquenchable:

> Like a child enjoying the happy fruits of play,
> A bodhisattva is attracted to whatever action
> He is engaged in at the time.
> His joy in the activity is never satiated.

In other words, not being easily satisfied leads us to make a special effort. It is a hindrance to be satisfied with a small accomplishment. If we are contented with a minimal result, we will not strive for more. We see this even in ordinary situations. Śāntideva says we should train our mind until we feel this way because it will make our practice fruitful:

> Even though we work for the sake of ordinary happiness,
> There is no assurance whether we will be happy or not.
> But some actions definitely bring happiness;
> How can I be happy if I do not do these actions?

Śāntideva gives another reason why we should not be easily satisfied by a little bit of spiritual practice:

> If my desire is not satiated
> Licking honey off a sharp knife blade,
> How can I be satisfied with virtues
> That result in happiness and peace?

We usually look for enjoyment in the objects of the senses. These worldly pleasures bring us superficial, temporary enjoyment. If we are not satisfied and want more and more pleasure, things will get worse until we are in pain. The more we pursue these pleasures, the deeper the suffering. Śāntideva gives the example of the sweet taste of honey giving us a little bit of pleasure. But if we want more of that taste so badly that we lick the remaining honey off a sharp knife, we will cut our tongue. Our desire for a sweet taste will have ended in suffering, not happiness. This is the case with any kind of ordinary pleasure. The degree of pleasure will not increase as we drink more or eat more. When we are hungry, eating seems to make us feel happy. In actuality, eating simply reduces the misery of hunger a little bit; it is not the cause of real happiness. If we eat more hoping for more happiness, we will overfill our stomach, and then we will be miserable.

All happiness in the desire realm is the reduction of some other kind of misery; too much of anything is the cause of another type of suffering. But ordinary people are never satisfied; they work all the time for this kind of pleasure. They will even sacrifice their life for these things. Yogis realize that sensory objects are not the source of pure bliss; they know that virtuous activity is the cause of real happiness in this life and the next. We too should always want more true happiness; there is no need to say that we should truly enjoy persevering in activities that bring us everlasting peace and the elimination of all suffering. This is where we should not be satisfied with some small achievement. We should want to do more and more Mahayana practice because it brings limitless, faultless, and unadulterated temporary and everlasting happiness to ourselves and all others.

Tsongkhapa says many times that the nature of perseverance is joy in doing wholesome actions. He compares the special joy from completing the virtuous actions that we begin to the happiness of hot and thirsty elephants who play in a cool pond covered with lotus flowers. We have been scorched by the heat of misery and now we have the great pleasure of diving into a cool lake of happiness. We should train the mind never to slacken in joyous effort to benefit others. Śāntideva says:

> In order to perfect this action
> I should continually engage in it,
> As an elephant suffering the midday heat
> Rushes into every cool pond he encounters.

(4") THE POWER OF RELINQUISHMENT

The general advice we are given when practicing perseverance is to work continuously and fervently. But sometimes too much effort can become a problem. If we push to an extreme, the body and mind can collapse from exhaustion. This can make us sad, annoyed, and averse to engaging in that activity again in the future. We are beaten by our overexertion. To prevent this from happening, we have to rest a little bit occasionally. Relaxing for a short time until we recover is the power of relinquishment. Once we recuperate we should immediately resume trying to accomplish what we had started. And when we reach our initial objective, we should begin our next project without delay. Even though we have accomplished something, it is important that we should want something even better. It is not good to be satisfied with attaining a rudimentary good quality because self-satisfaction hinders us from striving to attain a higher goal. There are many intermediate goals on the way to buddhahood. We should pursue each successively higher objective in the same way: taking a break when necessary but resuming as soon as we can. We should not be completely satisfied until we have attained buddhahood. Śāntideva says:

> When I lose my physical and mental strength,
> I take a short break in order to resume in future.
> When I complete something, desiring the next,
> And then the next, I abandon complete satisfaction.

The power of relinquishment is how to practice perseverance; we should not be too tight, nor should we be too relaxed. It is extreme to work too hard, but it is also extreme to indulge in too much leisure. We must know exactly how far we should go in either direction to remain in the continuous river flowing between the extremes. We have to be diligent in our activity, but rest when it is necessary.

Aśvaghoṣa praised this quality of the Buddha's perseverance in a beautiful poem which says, in part:[7]

> When you strove for perfection
> You never overdid exertion or relaxation.
> Therefore your many good qualities
> Are not distinguished by degrees of higher and lower.

When the Buddha was a bodhisattva working toward buddhahood, he never fell to the extremes of working too intensely or being too relaxed. As a result his enlightened body, mind, and environment are equal and perfect in every respect. We cannot say that after he attained enlightenment certain qualities were bad but became better later, or were higher earlier and lower later, or some traits are better in comparison to others, or that he can do some things and not others. Degrees of past and present, high and low, and so forth do not apply to the qualities of a buddha.

Tsongkhapa looks to the great Kadampa geshe and yogi Potowa to help us understand how to practice the power of relinquishment. The sayings of the Kadampa geshes are sometimes difficult to understand because they use culturally specific analogies. To make sense of their examples you have to know something about Tibet. Here Potowa compares how people from two places—the far northern part of Kham and central Tibet—dealt with thieves who rob a caravan's property and animals. When this happened to northerners, they did not react hastily. They would carefully prepare to retake their possessions. They accumulated horses, brought together their friends, and arranged for assistance to chase the robbers. The northern people acted slowly but, because they were constant and steady, they were able to overcome the thieves completely. In contrast, central Tibetans wanted to get things done quickly. They were quick to start after the robbers but sometimes were not able to accomplish their task. Potowa therefore tells us not to be like someone from central Tibet—we must work slowly and carefully for a long time like northerners who successfully catch thieves:

> The pursuers from Semodru never arrive. The pursuers from the north are unhurried at the beginning. They follow the robbers until they get there. Similarly, we must practice without rushing for a long time. For example, a louse arrives quickly by going without rushing or stopping. A flea stops with each jump and doesn't arrive.

Potowa's second example is similar to the western story of the race between the hare and the tortoise, but Potowa uses fleas and lice to make the same point. If you do not have many changes of clothes and only wash them once a year, you will get lice and fleas. The insects make you very itchy, so you shake out your clothes to get rid of them. Lice crawl slowly, but they get back on you faster than the quickly jumping fleas. A louse is hard to get rid of because it slowly, diligently crawls back. Fleas jump, but then they have to stop to pump their legs in order to jump again. So the slow and careful louse gets back to you whereas the quick jumping flea may never get there at all.

Another great teacher, Gungthang Tenpay Dronmay, sent his students some advice on how to study while he was away. He warned them that they would accomplish nothing if they went to extremes:[8]

> Some students work so hard they forget to eat all day.
> But after three days they totally relax, forget, and go wild.
> This kind of student will not complete anything.
> Therefore your effort must be like a continuous river.

The power of relinquishment is practicing the middle way—never being satisfied with a lesser goal in order to move on to higher and higher goals until we reach the final goal of complete enlightenment.

(c") BASED ON THE ELIMINATION OF UNFAVORABLE CONDITIONS AND THE ACCUMULATION OF FAVORABLE CONDITIONS, BEING INTENT ON JOYOUSLY PERSEVERING

Up to this point we have established the basis for the practice of perseverance. First, we learned to recognize the three hindrances to perseverance: the three types of laziness. Then, we saw how to apply the antidote to each kind of laziness in order to decrease those hindrances. Following that, we found out how to use the four powers to create the necessary conditions to produce perseverance that was not there before and maintain the perseverance that we already have. To bring about perseverance initially, we must have the power of aspiration. Once we produce perseverance, we use the power of steadfastness to keep it from degenerating. While we are in the middle of working on a practice, we use the power of joy to keep from giving up. The fourth power, the power of relinquishment, shows us how to rest for a little while when we are tired and then immediately go back to work when we are refreshed.

Now that we know how to avoid hindrances and accumulate the necessary conditions by mastering all four powers, the next topic is how to actually practice spontaneous joyous perseverance. Śāntideva says we should act like an experienced warrior to eliminate the things that should be abandoned: the mental afflictions of anger, desire, pride, jealousy, ignorance, and so forth:

> As an experienced warrior engages the enemy
> With superior swordsmanship in battle,
> I shall carefully avoid the weapons of the mental afflictions
> And skillfully overcome the enemy mental afflictions.

A soldier with a lot of experience knows that he must do two things when fighting a battle: engage in defensive actions to protect himself from his enemy's weapons, and simultaneously try to defeat his opponent. It is similar for religious practitioners fighting the internal enemy of the mental afflictions. We have to be skillful so that while we take offensive actions to destroy the afflictions, we also carefully defend our mind from them.

The army of mental afflictions is very rich and organized. It has a lot of power and many devious attributes. When we try to conquer one affliction, other afflictions arise to destroy another part of our virtues. When we try to do meritorious actions, equally strong negative attitudes rise up in our mind that make positive improvement very difficult. For example, in order to do a Dharma practice properly, it is important to understand the goal, the fault to be removed, the antidote, how to apply the cure, and so forth. It is therefore good to value learning because that clears away the hindrance of ignorance. However, studying without putting what we have learned into practice can result in the increase of faults. If knowledge of the Dharma is used only for worldly gain, it fans the flames of the mental afflictions instead of dousing that fire. Education used for the wrong purpose can contaminate our mental continuum and lead us to act under the power of pride or conceit. On the other hand, some people go to the opposite extreme. They think that controlling the mind is the only thing of importance. They therefore just meditate to develop single-pointed concentration; they almost make the mind a prisoner in solitary confinement. Because they do not study they are not aware of their ignorance and, as a result, that enemy becomes even stronger. Because they refuse to learn, they are completely ignorant of what to do and what to avoid after they take precepts. They destroy their mental continuum with downfalls.

Returning to Śāntideva's martial example, Tsongkhapa says that when soldiers fight they are careful to hold on to their weapons, because without them they would be in great danger. If they happen to drop their weapons, they pick up them up again quickly in fear of losing their life. When we are battling the inner enemy, one of our most important weapons is mindfulness. Mindfulness, or recollection, is to recall precisely what one should be doing, what one should not be doing, and the exact object that one should concentrate upon. Yogis should always use this weapon; it is dangerous to be without it because negativities will then occur. The consequence of losing mindfulness is to be reborn in the lower realms. Mindfulness is our protection from this disaster. Śāntideva says:

> If you drop your sword in battle,
> Out of fear you quickly pick it up.
> Similarly, if I lose the weapon of mindfulness,
> Out of fear of hell I quickly take up recollection.

Someone taking up the battle against the mental afflictions must make an effort to maintain his or her mindfulness of what is to be abandoned and what is to be done. It is mindfulness that protects us in the fight against our internal enemy. If we should lose it even for a short period, we should immediately take action to pick it up again. Mindfulness is an essential Dharma practice. It is the highway that all the buddhas of the past, present, and future travel upon to reach enlightenment. There is no way to attain enlightenment without it. Without mindfulness the mind will wander like a wild elephant and do all kinds of crazy, dangerous things. All meritorious actions will be destroyed if we are not careful. Nāgārjuna makes this point in his *Friendly Letter:*

> O great powerful one! The tathāgatas taught
> Mindfulness is the one path to follow.
> You must hold and securely guard this
> Because all Dharma is destroyed by mindfulness' decay.

We can recollect and be mindful only something that we know. If we do not know anything, what can we be mindful of? In other words, mindfulness does not have its own independent object; mindfulness is remembering an object previously understood by wisdom. Wisdom distinguishes what is good from what is bad, right from wrong, reality from mistaken perception, and the poison and its antidote. In short, we must first study to come to understand something correctly, and then we can apply mindfulness to that object. You may wonder, "What particular objects should we understand?" In general, the objects of wisdom are the topics taught in the scriptures—what we should practice and what we should avoid. In particular, we should comprehend the vows and precepts we have accepted as our Dharma practice; these include lay vows, the prātimokṣa vows of monks and nuns, bodhisattva vows, and tantric vows. The vows outline what actions are to be abandoned and what actions should be done. Mindful of these precepts as standards of proper behavior, we can examine an activity to determine if it is appropriate.

Along with mindfulness we should practice introspection. Introspection is a part of the mind that spies on what we are doing, what is coming up, what is present, and what is not there. In short, introspection is awareness of what the mind is doing at the present moment and what it is likely to do next. If we practice mindfulness on the entirety of the Dharma and introspection of ourselves together, we can continually check our practice. Only by using these two tools together can we complete a perfect practice. Without these two, as we try to do something in one area, we may destroy some other aspect of practice. We build up one thing, but neglect something else. We must be like a skillful warrior who is aware of his situation, holds on to his weapons, and thinks through a sequence of events and their potential consequences so he can act and react quickly and properly.

Quick action depends upon sincere fear. This fear comes from a deep understanding that knows, "If I lose my mindfulness, my mind will be overcome with hatred, jealousy, desire, and the other negative attitudes. This will kill the possibility of a good and happy life, much less emancipation. I could be cast into the miserable lower rebirths." A deep-seated fear comes from understanding the relationship between karma and its results. We have to learn what virtuous karma is and the results it will yield. We must know what nonvirtue is along with its results. We must concentrate on these relationships until they are central to our thoughts and the focus of our practice. Then we will be afraid of what we should fear and confident in regard to the right areas. If we do not understand karmic causality, losing mindfulness of the Dharma will not seem too important to us. We will not perceive the danger, because we do not know the consequences of our actions. We act carelessly without any fear. This is a stupid kind of fearlessness. It will not protect us. A yogi always has sincere fear and continually protects him- or herself with the weapon of recollection.

We do not pay enough attention to this deep and profound teaching. If we think that the instruction about karma is unimportant, our spiritual qualities will not grow. Understanding of karmic causation is the basis of the path; without it we have cut away the roots of good qualities. If, however, we fear the results of even a small negative activity, we will immediately stop doing it. A small nonvirtue is like being slightly wounded by a poisoned arrow. The wound is small but the poison will get into the bloodstream and quickly spread throughout the body. Of course we take care not to be wounded in the first place, but if we are struck we take immediate action to prevent the poison from spreading. Similarly, practitioners of virtue try from the start to avoid being wounded by the mental afflictions. When, through introspection and mindfulness, we notice that emotions like hatred, jealousy, pride, and so forth have arisen even slightly, we immediately try to cut off their continuation. If we leave them alone they will quickly become bigger and stronger and pervade the mind. If we do not take the antidote, they will not become smaller by themselves. Śāntideva says we should always be alert and act at the right time to prevent faults from occurring:

> Poison pervades the body
> Borne on the blood.
> Likewise, if given the chance,
> Faults pervade the mind.

According to Śāntideva, practitioners who want victory over the mental afflictions should practice mindfulness and introspection in the same way the arhat Kātyāyana did. There is a story in a sutra about an Indian king at the time of Buddha. This king lived far away from where Buddha taught, so he requested that a special practitioner come to teach in his country. The great arhat Kātyāyana and his disciple set out. As they neared this distant kingdom, the king arranged a lavish welcome ceremony to honor Kātyānana on his arrival. The road was filled with singers, beautiful dancers, and many attractive offerings. When they reached the palace the king asked Kātyāyana how he liked the welcoming ceremonies. But Kātyāyana did not know anything about them; it was as if he had not seen anything. Someone explained to the king that the monks and nuns do not look at such things because they are constantly trying to be mindful of their vows and checking their body, speech, and mind in light of these standards.

The king wondered, "How could someone not be aware of such a scene all around him?" To test whether this degree of mindfulness and introspection were truly possible, he gave an order: "Give a full bowl of oil to one of my subjects. Make him walk in front of a man with a sword along a street where the same kind of exhibition is going on. Tell the man with the bowl that if he spills one drop of the oil, his head will be cut off by the man behind him." Of course, the man carrying the bowl of oil concentrated intently on his task. He did not see any of the sights because he was trying to protect the oil in fear of his life. After this experiment the king believed that mindfulness and introspection were indeed possible. Śāntideva's summary of this story is as follows:

> Practitioners must be as careful
> As someone walking in front of a man wielding a sword,
> Who is threatened with loss of his life
> If he spills a drop from a vessel full of sesame oil.

Practitioners fearing the karmic consequences of lower rebirths should always hold on to the weapon of mindfulness tightly. This is especially important for beginners because we can be distracted from our practice so easily. There are so many attractive diversions that can be dangerous to the mind. In general, we should try to avoid any kind of faulty activity. In particular, we should forestall the causes of laziness because when we are lethargic we lose our alertness, strength, and mindfulness. Serious yogis try to thwart the tendency to indulge in sleep and other pleasures. Enjoying nonsensical pleasures, wanting to eat too much, liking wrong things, and so on, are indirect causes of laziness; they make us sleepy, or they make the mind unclear, or make us disinclined to engage in meritorious actions. So Śāntideva says that instead of letting sleepiness overcome us, we should wake up right away:

> Just as you would quickly jump up
> If a snake slithered into your lap,

If sleepiness and laziness come,
Quickly chase them away.

This is how real spiritual practitioners persevere one hundred percent of the time. They recognize all the possible consequences of dangerous actions and immediately apply the proper antidote. They understand the hindrances, know which antidote to apply, and have the power of all the necessary conditions. We too should understand in advance what actions are correct, what actions are wrong, and their consequences. Then, when situations arise, we can instinctively act properly, never giving the mental afflictions an opportunity to overcome us. If we are careful and keep the mind away from certain areas and focus on others, we will never have much of a problem. This is the strength of perseverance.

Just stopping improper activity is not enough. In addition to ceasing faulty activity as soon as we become aware of it, we should be unhappy that those flaws arose. We need to develop a negative attitude toward those faults. We must strongly regret the negative things that we have done because we see how bad the consequences of those actions will be. The strength of our dismay will determine if we can prevent those faults from rising in the future. To produce this regret we should think, "Until now I have been wandering in the misery of samsara because I did this and that. In particular, I acted contrary to the bodhisattva precepts." Regret is part of purification. The other part is to develop a determination to never again do those faulty actions in the future. When we regret our past faults and determine never to repeat them, we can prevent future downfalls and purify the earlier ones. As Śāntideva says:

Whenever a fault occurs
I castigate myself and
Think for a long time,
"I will never do that again."

Even if we cannot promise, "I will *never* do that action again," at least we can recognize that what we have done is improper and will have negative consequences. Then we can try to avoid doing it as much as possible in the future. The root of this practice is mindfulness. This is not something we should do intermittently; we should practice mindfulness all the time. Mindfulness does not arise of its own accord. We need outside conditions to help us produce and maintain it. The primary helpful condition for mindfulness is to associate with holy friends, such as spiritual teachers who can show us the proper way to act. We know that even our ordinary, worldly friends influence us in many ways. Here what we need is a dear friend who will influence us in a spiritual way. Watching and listening to such a friend will reinforce our mindfulness naturally. In addition to maintaining our perseverance, we must study and listen to teachings about causality. Again Śāntideva says:

> "In all situations whatsoever
> I shall practice mindfulness."
> With this motivation as a cause I will aspire
> To meet spiritual friends and engage in proper actions.

Tsongkhapa brings this particular section of the *Lamrim Chenmo* to a close by summarizing the importance of studying the bodhisattva practices in order to know what we should do and what we should abandon. We have to open our eyes to see the import of the precepts and vows. If our eyes are shut, we cannot see what is good, what is bad, what is dangerous, the antidote, and so forth. Once we have learned these things, we must be mindful of all these topics all the time. We have to compare what we know to what we are actually doing with our body, speech, and mind. Do our actions accord with the precepts? If we see that we are acting in contradiction to the vows, we bring ourselves back into proper alignment. Thus it is important not to lose sight of where we should place our efforts. We have to strive in the right direction because if we make an effort to do the wrong things, our entire life will be wasted.

(d") How to use perseverance to make the mind and body serviceable

The result of mastering the practice of perseverance is that the body and mind become workable and easy to control. They will do whatever we want them to do. Right now even if one part of the mind says, "I should do this," another part of the mind does not want to. Most of the time a negative attitude is more powerful and leads us away from virtue. Furthermore, we may want to do something but do not have the physical ability to carry it through. With perseverance our body and mind become suitable for practice.

Śāntideva explains in the chapter on conscientiousness in *Engaging in the Bodhisattva Deeds* that for the body and mind to harmoniously follow our direction, it is necessary for us to train in the bodhisattva practices. That chapter details how we should control the mind and body. It explains that there will be grave negative consequences if we do not act in accordance with the precepts once we have taken them. We are reminded in many passages that the mental afflictions are much more dangerous than an ordinary enemy. People or animals may hurt our feelings, hit us, or even kill us, but that is the worst they can do. Even killing us is not so serious, because we all have to die sooner or later. The internal enemies do not just kill us once; they have the power to injure us life after life. They cause our rebirth in the most miserable realms and bring about many disastrous experiences. They have done this from beginningless time. They have never been our friend. We can bring this situation to an end by destroying these enemies completely. However, attaining this freedom seems far, far away—almost endlessly in the future. So the inner enemies have had power over us for a period of time that seems to have no beginning and no end.

We are reluctant to work right now because we do not want to experience any mental or physical hardship. We think, "I'm tired. I cannot do this now. Maybe I will do it later." Even if we want to do something, our body and mind are tough and resist obeying. When we see how dangerous the internal enemy is, however, we will not view the hardships that come from fighting it as a burden. Instead, we will enjoy the inconveniences, pain, hunger, thirst, or loss of reputation because they are part of the means to get rid of the inner enemy. Seeing difficulties as beneficial produces mental strength. Our mental and physical recalcitrance dissipates when we see that the hardships of Dharma practice permanently do away with our most harmful enemy. The mind and body will eventually become soft and light; they will say "yes" to whatever we ask. Instead of uneasy reluctance we are able to do anything to benefit others. We jump right in without any hesitation just as a child hops right up to play. No longer are we like an old man who is too stiff, tired, and physically impaired to go to the store to purchase the food he wants to eat. Śāntideva says that bodhisattvas and yogis experience no unhappiness when faced with difficulties; their body and mind amicably follow direction. He adds:

> In order to have strength for everything,
> Before engaging in any action
> I will recollect the advice on conscientiousness.
> Then I will joyfully rise to the task.

The result of the practice of perseverance is that the body and mind go where we direct them as easily as a piece of cotton fluff goes where the wind takes it. There are different levels of perseverance. As our joy in doing wholesome action becomes stronger and stronger, we will have more and more control over our body and mind. When we have complete control, we have attained the perfection of joyous perseverance. With the perfection of perseverance we can accomplish the accumulations of merit and wisdom. In other words, it will become easy to completely assemble all the causes and conditions necessary for the attainment of buddhahood. Śāntideva says:

> The coming and going of the wind
> Carries cottonwood fluff along.
> Likewise, the power of joy in virtue
> Completes everything in this way.

It is easy to say, "If you do this, then that will be easy to accomplish." When we actually try to do something, however, we may think, "This is too hard. It is too difficult for me." Do not think that way. A task may look impossible, but if we start small and go step by step, we can accomplish it. Even if something is difficult, we should try. We should not dwell on the physical and mental hardships involved in attaining enlightenment. Remember, in the beginning Buddha was the same as we are now. He made an effort to practice and didn't give up over the course of three eons. He did these practices, gradually overcoming all the obstacles, and finally became the victorious one. Aśvaghoṣa praises this quality of the Buddha:

> Without undertaking hardships,
> One cannot attain a state difficult to achieve.
> To attain that, without any self regard,
> You increased your joyous perseverance.

(d') How to practice

According to the *Ornament for the Mahayana Sutras,* all the perfections should be practiced in a similar way. They all should have six special qualities: the supreme basis, thing, aim, skill in means, dedication, and purity. The *basis* is our motivation—bodhicitta. We do not undertake these practices for selfish temporary pleasure; we do them in order to attain enlightenment for the benefit of other sentient beings. From this foundation comes the *thing* itself. In the case of perseverance, this thing is the practice we are diligently pursuing. The *aim* or purpose of all the perfections is to attain enlightenment for the benefit of other sentient beings. The *skilled method* is the wisdom that realizes śūnyatā. The method is to act without grasping things as real and absolute. It is knowing the object, doer, and act itself as they really are—

empty of inherent existence. Supreme *dedication* is committing the merit that comes from perseverance to the attainment of enlightenment. *Purity* is the clearing away of all obstacles.

Furthermore, the practice of each of the perfections contains the practices of all the others; when we practice joyous perseverance, it is not merely the practice of diligence. Implicit in the practice of perseverance is the generosity of perseverance, the ethical discipline of perseverance, the patience of perseverance, the concentration of perseverance, and the wisdom of perseverance. For example, the generosity of perseverance is to diligently give others instruction so that they too can practice perseverance. Including all the perfections in the practice of any one of them makes our actions multifaceted. They become great practices.

(e') A summary

The basis of Mahayana practice—the bodhisattva deeds—is bodhicitta. We engage in these practices because out of compassion and love we desire to attain buddhahood for the sake of other sentient beings. Thus when we do the practice of joyous perseverance, we cannot forget our bodhicitta motivation. Bodhicitta is why we are doing this. We must keep it in mind all the time: in the beginning, the middle, and the end. We dedicate the merit we create so that we can attain enlightenment and lead others to practice the perfections.

It is therefore important to increase and develop our practice of bodhicitta while we practice joyous perseverance. On the highest bodhisattva levels the perfection of perseverance is an object of their prayers. The upper-level bodhisattvas know the nature of perseverance and how to practice it, but still they cannot do it perfectly. They fervently wish that they will be able to do it. We beginners certainly cannot do everything that has been explained all at once. We have to start small; cognizant of our abilities, we do as much as we can. Beginners should fight against the laziness of discouragement. Discouragement, remember, is putting oneself down. We must become courageous and enthusiastic about the attainment of enlightenment. A joyful attitude when undertaking the hardships necessary to accomplish the happiness of all sentient beings is the armor of perseverance. With this attitude that comes out of wisdom, nothing can destroy our practice.

There is so much that must be done to attain perfect buddhahood, but we can do the almost measureless tasks because, if we perfect perseverance, just one moment of one action accomplishes countless things simultaneously. At that point perseverance in and of itself has great benefit. According to the

Questions of Subāhu Sutra it creates a great wave of merit that can purify many negativities. It accumulates a mountain of virtues.

If we do not develop perseverance, we will not strengthen our ability to attain buddhahood. We all have one of the special causes necessary to attain enlightenment: buddha nature. Right now our buddha nature is so dormant it almost seems as though we do not have it. Our buddha nature has to be woken up and strengthened. If we are always lazy and discouraged, not only can't we bring out our buddha nature, but additional faults will bury it even deeper.

Even small things are hard at first, but the next time we try them they are easier. However, if we are immediately discouraged and put everything aside, every further step will be blocked. In addition, if we do many negative things in this life, it will be difficult to train ourselves in other lives. So even if we are not able to practice joyous perseverance exactly as Tsongkhapa explains it, we should aspire toward doing it. We should wish for it and make an effort to begin. If we just take some small steps, our perseverance will continue to increase. If we fight against discouragement, set our sights on joyous perseverance, and try to improve as much as we can, we will develop spiritually. If we practice in this life, the same activity will come much more easily in the next life. Eventually, we will accomplish the perfection of joyous perseverance. When we have great joy in the practice of virtue we will want to engage in practices that we have not yet done and our current practices will grow stronger. With joyous perseverance all the other practices can be accomplished and our goal attained.

⁂ 14 ⁂

The Perfections of Meditative Stabilization and Wisdom

(v) How to train in the perfection of meditative stabilization
    (a') What meditative stabilization is
    (b') How to begin the cultivation of meditative stabilization
    (c') The divisions of meditative stabilization
    (d') How to practice
    (e') A summary
(vi) How to train in the perfection of wisdom
    (a') What wisdom is
    (b') How to begin the generation of wisdom
    (c') The divisions of wisdom
        (1') Wisdom that knows the ultimate
        (2') Wisdom that knows the conventional
        (3') Wisdom that knows how to act for the welfare of living beings
    (d') How to practice
    (e') A summary

(v) How to train in the perfection of meditative stabilization

IN THE *Lamrim Chenmo* the bodhisattva activities are explained one by one. So far we have looked at the first four perfections. The last two perfections, meditative stabilization and wisdom, are such profound subjects that to deal with them adequately, Tsongkhapa gives a brief overview before going into detail on each of them. This general explanation appears in this volume. The details on how to practice meditative stabilization are in volume 4 of this series and volume 5 contains the complete explanation of the perfection of wisdom.

As with the explanations of the earlier perfections, the training in meditative stabilization has five sections:

(a') What meditative stabilization is
(b') How to begin the cultivation of meditative stabilization
(c') The divisions of meditative stabilization
(d') How to practice
(e') A summary

(a') What meditative stabilization is

Meditative stabilization is a virtuous mind that single-pointedly abides on its object without being distracted to other things. Asaṅga explains in the *Bodhisattva Levels* that in order to focus on something single-pointedly we have to know the object thoroughly. Knowing the appropriate objects on the bodhisattva path necessitates studying the scriptures and listening to explanations of them. Then we have to analyze and try to understand what these teachings mean. Only with study and analysis can we develop a virtuous mind that abides single-pointedly on an object. Asaṅga says:[1]

> It is the one-pointed state of mind—stabilized on virtue, and either mundane or supramundane—of bodhisattvas who have first studied and reflected on the bodhisattvas' scriptural collections. Whether it is oriented toward meditative serenity, toward insight, or toward both as the path that conjoins them, understand that this one-pointed state of mind is the bodhisattvas' meditative stabilization.

There are two kinds of meditative stabilization: a mundane level and a supramundane level. Meditative stabilization can be associated with three objects: single-pointed concentration, wisdom, or a union of the two. Before we attain perfect single-pointed concentration or superior insight, we focus on them individually and progress through various stages of development. After we develop meditative stabilization that calms the mind and a special kind of wisdom knowing the nature of reality, we can combine the two. In each case a mind that can stay single-pointedly on its object without distraction is the nature of the bodhisattva's meditative stabilization.

Śāntideva says:

> After producing joyous perseverance in this way,
> I set my mind in meditative concentration,
> Because those whose minds are distracted
> Sit between the fangs of the mental afflictions.

The mental afflictions—desire, hatred, jealousy, pride, and so forth—are like sharp teeth in a predator's jaws. If we get distracted, those jaws will snap us up. We will be destroyed by whichever mental affliction grabs us. To prevent this we need meditative stabilization; it enables us to concentrate on whatever method we need to practice.

(b') How to begin the cultivation of meditative stabilization

The way to begin is the same for all six perfections: we have to understand the benefits of doing the practice and the disadvantages of not doing it. If we are sure about the advantageous results of the practice, we will be interested in doing it even if there are hardships involved. If we do not see the benefits, we will not want to bother. This is similar to what businessmen do: before they take a risk, they have to understand the potential for profit and the negative consequences of not taking the opportunity. In this case we have to know the nature of meditative stabilization, the benefits of developing it, and the drawbacks of not developing it. The advantages of practicing meditative stabilization and the disadvantages of not practicing it are presented in detail in volume 4 of this series.

(c') The divisions of meditative stabilization

As alluded to in the above passage from the *Bodhisattva Levels,* if we examine its nature, meditative stabilization can be divided into two types: mundane and supramundane. If we look at meditative stabilization from the point of view of its object, we divide it into three: meditative concentration, wisdom, and their union. The first is concentrating one-pointedly without any analytical content. The second focuses primarily on wisdom without much emphasis on stabilization. Before we develop complete meditative stabilization and superior insight, we do these practices separately; at a more advanced level, however, the two can be united. This path of union is the third object.

We can also divide meditative stabilization into three from the point of view of its function or result: meditative stabilization that produces physical and mental peace, meditative stabilization that accomplishes good qualities, and meditative stabilization that accomplishes the benefit of other sentient beings. The first type of meditative stabilization is mundane; it focuses on this life. The mind is usually distracted; wandering discursive thoughts dominate our lives. With the first type of meditative stabilization we control the mind. We are no longer distracted and can easily focus upon any object for as long as we wish. This power calms the mind, and because the mind and body are connected it also influences the body. Thus by controlling the mind, its vehicle—prāṇa, or air—is also tamed. Mundane meditative stabilization brings mental and physical peace and bliss in this life.

The second type of meditative stabilization yields a number of mental achievements. These attainments are not particular to bodhisattvas; Hinayana practitioners, both śrāvakas and pratyekabuddhas, also obtain these qualities when they practice meditative stabilization. When a person develops meditative stabilization in combination with certain techniques, he or she obtains the first mental achievement: the six supernormal knowledges. The first five types of supernormal knowledge are: the divine eye, the divine ear, knowledge of others' thoughts, miraculous powers, recollection of former states, and knowledge of death and rebirth. With these powers a person can see things that someone with ordinary eyes cannot see. They can hear subtle things from far away. They can read others' minds. They can do miraculous things like fly through the sky like a bird, delve deep into the earth, or walk on water as if it were solid ground. Although these powers describe physical attributes, because they are based on mental practice they are not considered to be external qualities. These five powers can be mundane or supramundane achievements. The sixth supernormal knowledge—knowledge of the extinction of mental afflictions—is only supramundane.

Another mental achievement is called *liberation*. Here liberation does not refer to emancipation from samsara; it is, instead, a meditation practice with that name. This is a complex practice that I will not go into here. In brief, one uses meditative stabilization to focus on the elements progressing on eight levels through three doors of liberation. For example, to develop an understanding of the impurity of samsaric life, we start by focusing on a small bone and gradually expand further and further until the entire world seems filled with skeletons. Another achievement coming from this type of meditative stabilization is being able to suppress the mental afflictions. This is done by using meditative stabilization to compare better and worse, beauty and ugliness, and so forth. Through this comparison we come to understand that these qualities are not the ultimate nature of things; they are relative and determined by our perspective. This enables us to make small things big, big things small, ugly things attractive, attractive things ugly, and so forth. In short, it makes it easier to reduce our attachment.

The third type of meditative stabilization is involved when we take steps to meet the needs of the eleven types of sentient beings.[2] There is a particular meditative stabilization associated with each activity because we need the ability to focus, and we must discern the object, goal, and appropriateness of each action.

This is a very brief outline of these achievements. There is much more detail on these topics in volume 4 of this series.

(d') How to practice

Just as with the other perfections, when we practice meditative stabilization there are six supreme qualities and all of the other perfections are included in the practice. There is no need to go over this again because it has been discussed previously. In short, when we are practicing meditative stabilization, we also engage in generosity, ethical discipline, patience, and so forth. The generosity of meditative stabilization is to share what we have mastered so that others can practice it as well. The rest of the perfections are easy to understand.

(e') A summary

Bodhicitta is the basis of every bodhisattva activity. The purpose of every bodhisattva action, including meditative stabilization, is to benefit other sentient beings by freeing them from misery and leading them to enlightenment. In order to lead others to this state, we have to have reached it ourselves. We must remind ourselves again and again that our effort to develop meditative stabilization is not for our own peace and emancipation; it is for the benefit of other sentient beings. Even at the beginning of our practice we keep focused on our goal of liberating others. We practice the lower levels of meditative stabilization wishing to achieve the higher levels as soon as possible so that we can help them. Our practice must include this motivation in order to be Mahayana practice. If we are aimless or focused on something like temporary peace, we will not be practicing the great vehicle. We should not meditate without conscious intent. Before beginning we must think about its purpose, how to do it, its benefits, the disadvantages of not doing it, and so forth. Then we will work joyfully to the best of our ability for as long as we have time.

Those of us who have taken the bodhisattva vows should try from time to time to train in meditative stabilization. If we do not, we incur the faults of breaking the precepts. Furthermore, if we have promised to train the mind continuously, but later just let it go, we develop a bad habit. This negative predisposition will make it difficult for us to succeed in overcoming our faults in this and other lives. In contrast, if we continue to make an effort to develop meditative stabilization, even if it looks like there is no possibility of success, there will be benefits in this and future lives. In this life the mind will become more stable, distractions will become fewer, and the power of the distractions will diminish. Because the mind will be more settled when we engage in meritorious activity, the merits we accumulate will be more powerful. The *Questions of Subāhu Sutra* says that as a result of this practice we will be reborn with a body and mind that are naturally more peaceful and happy. In that next life the practice of meditative stabilization will be easier to accomplish.

Once again, this is a very brief explanation. Because much more detail will come in the next volume, I will not expand upon it here.

(vi) How to train in the perfection of wisdom

The perfection of wisdom is almost half of the *Lamrim Chenmo*. Before beginning such a vast topic, Tsongkhapa gives us a general introduction to contextualize the perfection of wisdom among the other perfections. So while volume 5 of this series deals solely with the perfection of wisdom, here we look at it briefly using the same outline we have applied to the earlier perfections:

(a') What wisdom is
(b') How to begin the generation of wisdom
(c') The divisions of wisdom
(d') How to practice
(e') A summary

(a') What wisdom is

In general, wisdom is a consciousness that distinguishes the nature, quality, and particular attributes of existing things. Wisdom is what enables us to distinguish one thing from another. According to the Madhyamaka school, things seem to have their own identity and names, but actually they have no ultimate, inherent existence. Existing things—functional things—are nominally existent; they are imputed. Because wisdom makes analytical distinctions between imputed objects, sometimes wisdom can be understood as a *view*. Even if we incorrectly make a distinction, by definition it can still be considered part of wisdom. For this reason, the abhidharma literature explains that the five wrong views are part of wisdom. In other words, there is a big difference between supramundane wisdom and low or ordinary wisdom. Supramundane wisdom correctly understands actual reality.

Asaṅga says in the *Bodhisattva Levels:*

> Know that the nature of a bodhisattva's wisdom is understanding all
> phenomena—objects of knowledge that one perceives and objects of

knowledge that one has perceived—through a complete analysis of the five forms of knowledge: Buddhism, logic, medicine, language, and technology.

Wisdom differentiates phenomena through five sciences. The first of the five, Buddhism or the inner science, is to know and actualize the stages of spiritual realization. It is distinguishing the internal signs of following the stages of the path from the beginning up to attaining enlightenment. This is the highest form of knowledge. The second science, logic, is particularly helpful if someone is confused by dogma. We can use logical reasons to prove something and show the negative consequences of a wrong view. Medical knowledge is skill in curing sickness through knowing the signs of disease and their cures. Language is important because if we cannot express what we know, our knowledge cannot help others. For example, understanding grammar or how language functions enables us to teach others the Dharma. We could teach with gestures, but it is more efficient and effective to explain things verbally. Last is knowledge of the technology employed to make material things. To do anything skillfully we must have the common-sense wisdom of knowing how to do it.

Asaṅga makes a distinction between the wisdom of ordinary bodhisattvas and those who have had a direct realization of śūnyatā. After a bodhisattva has a direct realization of the ultimate truth, he or she is considered a superior, or noble, person on the first of ten āryan bodhisattva stages. Prior to the āryan level, every bodhisattva is an ordinary individual. Accordingly, there are two bodhisattva practices of wisdom: there are practices to develop the wisdom of ordinary individuals and practices for āryans who have already gained a direct realization of emptiness. In the passage quoted above from the *Bodhisattva Levels*, the *objects of knowledge that one perceives* refer to wisdom prior to attaining the first āryan stage, and *objects of knowledge that one has perceived* refer to one's wisdom after becoming an āryan bodhisattva.

There are many levels to both common and spiritual types of wisdom. We should develop these through the five sciences for our own benefit and in order to be able to benefit others.

(b') How to begin the generation of wisdom

Wisdom does not arise naturally or spontaneously on its own; we have to make an effort to develop it. As we have seen, to become interested in producing any good quality, including wisdom, we must see the benefits of having it and the disadvantages of not having it. We all know that even in a worldly sense, there is an advantage to wisdom; our interest in getting an education derives from seeing how knowledge will benefit us in this life. Someone who desires higher spiritual states definitely needs wisdom. To practice the six perfections seriously and continuously we must be firmly convinced that our goal is so important that the difficulties of practice are worth it. This is wisdom. Blindly doing the practices without wisdom is ineffective. Many of you may never have done some of these practices and some of you may never even have heard of them before. If that is the case, then out of uncertainty one's practice will be weak. When we have a strong understanding, no matter what problems we encounter, we will not feel insecure or confused.

The difference between wisdom and ignorance is as great as the difference between someone who is blind and someone who can see. Recognizing this takes a great deal of thought and consideration of various points of view. Only when we know the details about the advantages of wisdom and the disadvantages of ignorance will we be interested in producing wisdom. We usually are not interested in cultivating supramundane wisdom because we do not see the disadvantages of lacking it. The more reasons we have for how bad it is to be stupid and ignorant, the more urgency we will feel about developing wisdom. The more reasons we have to value wisdom, the more enthusiastic we will be to develop it. If we understand these reasons, we will become convinced that we must develop wisdom to achieve our temporary and ultimate goals.

The wisdom that leads directly to enlightenment is the highest type of wisdom. The wisdom that destroys the root of all obstacles to omniscience is the realization of ultimate reality—śūnyatā, emptiness, the selflessness of persons and phenomena. It is important to understand in detail the benefits of having this particular kind of wisdom and the disadvantages of lacking it. Tsongkhapa will go into this in depth in the volume on highest insight. Here he discusses the benefits of wisdom in general. First of all, wisdom is the root of all wholesome qualities in this and future lives. If we want good qualities in this life we must have wisdom. This same wisdom will lead us to have superior qualities in the future. Ignorance is the opposite.

Nāgārjuna says:

> Wisdom is the root
> Of all visible and invisible good qualities.
> Therefore to accomplish both of these
> We must have wisdom.

All good qualities develop in the mind on the foundation of wisdom. We can see this particularly easily with education. As infants we have very little knowledge, but as we receive an education our common sense grows. We come to know whether things are good or bad and we can understand why certain things happen. It is obvious, or we could say *visible,* to us that we must have wisdom in order to achieve the good things we desire. Other things are invisible to us; we cannot see them with our ordinary senses. Our tendency is to deny the existence of things we do not see; for example, many people do not believe in rebirth and karma because they cannot see them. It is not obvious that practicing virtue in this life will result in a better rebirth or spiritual development. We cannot see with our eyes the type of life we will be born into as a result of doing particular actions now.

There are other things that are invisible to us as well. We cannot see many types of sentient beings that may be right in front of us such as ghosts, malevolent spirits, gods, or hell beings; we cannot see into other peoples' minds or directly perceive certain subtle aspects of their character; and we cannot see the many high spiritual qualities of a buddha. However, just because we do not perceive these things with our ordinary faculties, it does not mean that they do not exist. Many things exist that we have never seen, known, or experienced. Through employing special methods we can clear negative qualities from the mind and develop a higher type of wisdom. Then, just like the buddhas, bodhisattvas, yogis, and certain other beings we will be able to see these previously hidden things with our wisdom. All the positive invisible qualities, from a higher rebirth up to liberation and enlightenment, depend upon wisdom.

Dignāga and Dharmakīrtī explain *visible* and *invisible* more specifically. All objects of knowledge—everything that can be known—are included in three categories: obvious phenomena, phenomena that are slightly hidden, and very hidden phenomena. The first category includes things that ordinary beings can directly perceive through their physical senses, as well as some objects that they can perceive with their mind. These are things that we can know without having higher knowledge, without resorting to scriptures, logic, or relying on what someone else says. We establish these things by relying on direct perception; for example, we can tell that a particular flower is yellow simply by looking at it.

The mental and physical senses of ordinary beings are not perfect. With the information that we gather through the instrument of our sensory faculties, we can know a specific thing; this, however, this is a very narrow type of knowledge. There are many additional things that we ordinary beings know through logical reasoning. We do not see or hear these things with our senses, but we confidently accept them as true through inferential reasoning. Objects of inferential knowledge fall into the second category: slightly hidden phenomena. An example is momentary impermanence. Even though things look permanent, we can logically prove that they are impermanent and change every moment.

There are other things that are beyond ordinary perception and their existence cannot be established with direct logical proof. These fall into the third category: very hidden phenomena. They are so subtle that the only way ordinary beings can know them is by relying on indirect authority. We take these things on trust. There is a faint connection to logic because we make analogies to similar things, but our belief in them is based on faith in some authority such as scriptures or a trustworthy person.

A great deal of scientific knowledge is in this category of very hidden phenomena. In past centuries there were many things that people did not know; even the existence of whole continents full of people were unknown. If someone proposed certain scientific theories, everyone else considered him crazy. Later scientists proved many of these theories and discovered even more by using scientific instruments, mathematics, and experimental methods. We ordinary people trust scientists to verify things for us. We rely on their superior training and knowledge, the fact that many things scientists have explained before are true, and that they have no reason to lie to us. So even though we do not see these phenomena for ourselves and do not have logical proof for them, we are so sure they exist that we teach our children about them with confidence. A clear example is our understanding of medicine and disease. We go to a doctor to complain about certain symptoms. If the doctor has worked for many years to become proficient, he or she can see causal relationships that we cannot. He may say, "You have such and such a problem." The next day we can say, "I know I have this disease." We do not know from our perception or from a logical proof; we are relying instead on the doctor's authority for our knowledge.

There are three types of valid knowledge related to these three categories of phenomena: perceptual valid knowledge, inferential valid knowledge, and the valid knowledge of trust. Things that can be known through the first two types of valid knowledge—perceptual and inferential valid knowledge—are considered *visible objects*. The objects of valid knowledge based on trust are considered to be *invisible objects*. Some scholars say only objects of perceptual valid knowledge are visible and the other two types of valid knowledge focus on invisible objects. No matter how we divide them, however, everything that exists is included in these categories. Until we attain enlightenment we have many layers of mental obscurations, so we rely on these three types of knowledge. Buddhas and the highest level bodhisattvas do not have three different types of valid knowledge and their respective objects; for them everything is obvious because they have removed the mental afflictions and the obstacles to omniscience.

Very hidden phenomena is the broadest category of phenomena. Direct perception is very limited; we cannot see beyond the walls of our room. The mind can know a little more through the use of inference and logic; however, this too is quite limited. For example, we can know a few superficial things about each other from direct perception, such as the color of someone's eyes and hair. Through inference we can know that others are upset if we see them cursing or crying. But their actual thoughts and emotions cannot be known to us. Most things are completely hidden from us. How do we explain why some people have good fortune and others have less? Why do five children born into the same family, sharing equally in the same home, possessions, and parental love, end up with such different characters and life circumstances? We cannot come up with convincing logical reasons to explain the causal relationships for these are very hidden things.

Who should we trust to explain and validate these very hidden phenomena? It should be someone dependable who has special knowledge far superior to our own. As we develop, we should find that many of the things this person taught us are true. For ordinary things, people rely on their parents, doctors, or scientists; for the spiritual path and goal we can rely upon Buddha. In general, the spiritual path and the goal of buddhahood are slightly hidden phenomena because they can be proved by logic, but the details are very hidden phenomena. We read in the sutras that when Ānanda, Śāriputra, or another disciple asks Buddha why a person is experiencing a particular event, Buddha explains in detail what that person did in a prior life to have this very good or very bad experience. Although the actions may have been done hundreds or thousands of lifetimes ago, Buddha can tell us that person's name, his parents' names, where he lived, and what he did to cause a particular rebirth, or the subtle remaining effects of that action now that he is born as a human. On an ordinary level there is no way to verify what Buddha says about that person. It is completely beyond our sensory perception and there is no way to logically prove it. If pressed we have to say, "I don't know." We accept these things based on our faith in Buddha. We cannot deny them just because we do not see them.

We cannot do even ordinary things without wisdom; even something as simple as making a meal requires that we know what ingredients to purchase, how to mix them, and how to cook them. There is no way to realize higher spiritual states or discover these hidden objects and their relationships without wisdom. Wisdom fights against ignorance. As ignorance lessens we can see further and further, and more and more clearly. Finally, our vision is completely unobstructed; our ability to see is unlimited from the point of view of space, time, the nature of things, and the relationship of cause and effect. We can see the obscurations, how they block us from certain goals, and the method to use to eliminate the obstructions and attain each goal. In other words, in order to attain positive qualities and higher spiritual states, we must create their causes. In order to create the causes, we have to know what the causes are; we must understand what will bring us good results and what will bring bad results. We need to know the method and how to employ it. We start small; then gradually our wisdom extends and we develop more good qualities. All of them—visible common achievements and the uncommon, superior spiritual achievements—are rooted in wisdom.

Nāgārjuna continues:

> Knowledge is the most important source
> For desired worldly goals and emancipation.
> Therefore, first with great respect,
> Take hold of the great mother wisdom.

Our world is called the desire realm because ordinary beings try to achieve happiness primarily by satisfying the desires of the senses. We want a good life filled with attractive sights, smells, tastes, wealth, fame, and so on. We seek these things continuously, even though they provide only temporary happiness. To attain these worldly goals we need wisdom; we get nowhere if we remain ignorant. There are, however, higher goals than these fleeting sensory pleasures. The highest goal is freedom from all misery and mental obstacles and attainment of the highest enlightenment. The most important source for all spiritual goals is wisdom. To attain emancipation from worldly misery we must properly understand the goal, the method to reach it, and the causal relationship between actions and good or bad effects. If we lack wisdom, we will produce the wrong causes and an undesired result will follow. Nāgārjuna therefore says that from the first we should produce wisdom.

The name *great mother* is given to wisdom as a sign of respect. A mother is the source of life; she produces children. Wisdom is like a mother because when we know things properly, all good qualities—both temporary and ultimate—are produced. A woman alone cannot do everything; she needs a man to conceive a child. Similarly, the sutras teach that wisdom alone is insufficient; the method side of practice is also necessary. Just as a father and mother join together to produce a child, we unite method and wisdom to achieve spiritual goals. Other practices will be successful only if based on wisdom. This image of parents—especially a mother as a source to meet all her children's needs—is used often in the Mahayana and especially in the tantric teachings. Nāgārjuna describes wisdom as the great mother because he is referring to the foundation for all the causes and conditions necessary to achieve enlightenment in order to benefit all sentient beings.

Mahayana practitioners can think about the bodhisattva practices in two categories: the first five perfections and wisdom. We need all six to travel to the city of buddhahood. The first five perfections are the vehicle in which we will travel; wisdom is the eyes we need to see the road. Without wisdom, the other five are blind. They will fumble around, unskillfully trying to attain the goal.

The *Verse Summary of the Perfection of Wisdom in Eight Thousand Lines* says:

> When completely held with wisdom,
> They acquire eyes and obtain this name.
> For example, a painter's work may be done except for the eyes;
> But until he draws in the eyes he cannot obtain his fee.

The example in the final two lines of this stanza refers to an ancient Indian custom. When people commissioned a painting, they did not pay the artist until the eyes of the figure were painted. The artist may have done all the other details of the work, but without the eyes, which were traditionally done last, the painting was not complete. The import of this stanza is that any practice connected to wisdom is called a *perfection;* without this wisdom, it does not "obtain this name."

There are two aspects to the meaning of *perfection* in regard to bodhisattva practices. First, the goal of the practice is faultless; buddhahood is completely perfect. Second, the practices resulting in perfect enlightenment are also given the name *perfection.* The difference between generosity and the perfection of generosity is wisdom. The perfection of generosity does not refer to generosity at the time of buddhahood. It is to give with our eyes open; we are giving with the realization of the emptiness of the three spheres: the person to whom we give, the giver, and either the gift or the act of giving. Even a small thing, if given with this understanding, will be a perfect gift. When we give with a misperception of reality, we are acting blindly. There are many impure types of generosity: giving out of attachment to oneself, or attachment to others, or to achieve a selfish goal such as fame, or out of expectation of a return. These are generosity but not the *perfection of generosity.* All a bodhisattva's generosity is motivated by love and compassion. For love and compassion to be pure, they must not be under the power of egotistic self-centeredness. The antidote to attachment, conceit, and egotism is the realization of śūnyatā.

Every religious practice should be held, or combined, with this special wisdom. For example, when we engage in ethical discipline—such as not stealing, not killing, or taking a vow—we need wisdom for it to be the perfection of ethical discipline. Engaging in the same conduct with the wrong motivation or understanding is still meritorious, but it is not the perfection of ethical discipline.

Perfection is what goes beyond the ordinary. If we decorate an ornament of pure gold with expensive stones, it will be even more beautiful than before. Similarly, adding wisdom that is able to distinguish what is right from what is wrong to each of the practices from generosity to meditative stabilization makes them great. Decorated with wisdom, they become fine, pure, and special. Spiritual practices should not be done blindly; they should be done knowing why and how, seeing the nature of things in general and in particular. If we lack wisdom, these practices will not be unadulterated or perfect. It is similar to how, when making decisions, we use the mind to complement our senses. We do not make decisions simply on the basis of sense perception. Our senses perceive objects, but they cannot judge right and wrong. We have to add the wisdom of the mental consciousness to make a decision about our perceptions. If we determine the object is faulty, we can turn away; we can also do the opposite if we determine the object is trustworthy. This is how we control our actions. Wisdom is like a guide for the blind senses. Nāgārjuna's disciple, the great Indian pandit Aśvaghoṣa says:[3]

> Wholesome actions, generosity, and so on
> Become powerful with wisdom as their guide.
> Similarly, beautiful gold objects
> Shine more when ornamented with jewels.
>
> This wisdom makes vast
> Each of these qualities' ability to accomplish its goal.
> Similarly, objects perceived by the sense organs
> Are more clearly understood by the mind.

With wisdom as our guide, we can practice generosity and other meritorious actions properly. Wisdom directs our purpose, sees the nature of the goal, its advantages and disadvantages, the obstacles to reaching it, and how to accomplish it. Without wisdom, our practice could be wrong or without much power. To attain any goal we must therefore first study to develop the proper wisdom. Mahayana practitioners need a special impetus to engage in serious and hard work to save others. The support of this motivation is the wisdom seeing the advantages and disadvantages of the practice. The *practice of wisdom* means we are trying to gain wisdom. When we see the benefits of wisdom and the many disadvantages of lacking wisdom, the difficulties we experience on the way to gaining wisdom become less and we develop a sense of urgency about our practice. If we do not know the benefits and disadvantages, we quickly become exhausted and give up when something becomes difficult. Wisdom is like a wonderful, stable friend. It makes us confident. It gives us enjoyment and makes us peaceful. This is why we find a lot of discussion about the benefits of wisdom in the sutras, commentaries, and instructions of great teachers and yogis.

Tsongkhapa now gives us a sample of these comments about the benefits of this perfection. First he quotes Aśvaghoṣa, who says in the *Compendium of the Perfections:*

> Wisdom is primary among faith and the other powers,
> Just as the mind is primary among the other senses.
> Having knowledge of faults and good qualities as a guide
> Makes one skilled in the methods to eliminate the afflictions.

In the teachings on the thirty-seven practices to attain enlightenment there are five powers, or organs, for the practice of virtue: faith, diligence, mindfulness, concentration, and wisdom. Wisdom is the principal among these. It is the support of the others. For example, there are three types of faith. We begin many practices with an earnest, almost blind faith. As we progress our faith becomes trust based on reason. Finally, the wisdom behind our faith is so strong we wish to attain the state of being the object of our faith. As wisdom increases our faith becomes less and less shaky until it is irreversibly firm.

Bodhisattvas have to have wisdom in order to practice the six perfections to attain enlightenment to save other sentient beings. Wisdom gives us the confidence and skill to eliminate the mental afflictions and increase our good qualities. For example, when bodhisattvas reach a high spiritual level, they do not only give ordinary things. Because they have wisdom that distinguishes good from bad, the goal, and the true nature of reality, even if a beggar with an injurious attitude were to demand his right arm, a bodhisattva can give his flesh as easily as if he were cutting a branch off a tree. Just as a tree does not think or feel anything, a bodhisattva has no negative thoughts; he or she is neither discouraged nor conceited. He does not think, "Giving my arm makes me so superior." Nor does she think, "I cannot do this. If I did, they would do this or that...." Everything bodhisattvas do is motivated by wisdom and compassion, so there are only wholesome results. Their gifts are like medicine; they benefit the recipients by bringing them temporary peace and satisfaction. With wisdom, whatever is given is curative and helpful.

Ethical discipline is also based on wisdom. It can be difficult to avoid causing harm to all others, but if a bodhisattva has wisdom, these practices become enjoyable. There are many levels of wisdom and hence many stages of the practice of pure religious conduct. At first, we may not even want to engage in ethical discipline; out of self-centeredness we may think, "If I do this, it will hurt." Or we might engage in positive conduct for worldly purposes thinking, "If I do this, I will be respected and honored." The behavior looks good, but it is based on a selfish concern with this life. If we do not understand the misery and causes of samsara, we will not see any faults in the four stages of existence: birth, the state after birth and before death, death, and the intermediate state. Birth is unpleasant, and of course after we are born and before we die we experience aging, sickness, undesirable experiences, and so forth. Death and the intermediate state are also miserable suffering. As we gain a little wisdom about the disadvantages of these four existences, and see that there is a method to prevent them, we may be motivated to engage in ethical conduct.

Wisdom enables us to enjoy practicing ethical discipline because we see the prospect of good future lives and our emancipation from all misery. This is the practice of ethical discipline, but it is not the perfection of conduct because it is for a selfish purpose. In addition to seeing the faults of samsara, Mahayana practitioners develop the wisdom that sees the faults of attaining just their own emancipation from it. The perfection of ethical discipline is religious conduct conjoined with the wisdom knowing the true nature of self and phenomena. It knows the disadvantages of a self-centered view and motivation. It knows that actions motivated by a desire to benefit other sentient beings create enormous merit. With wisdom, our conduct will not be motivated by selfish egotistic desires; instead, based on solid understanding, it will be purely for the benefit of others. Wisdom enables us to practice these things for the benefit of other sentient beings without becoming discouraged or upset.

The pure practice of patience also depends upon wisdom. Because other sentient beings are under the power of delusive attitudes such as desire and hatred, they may respond to our favorable actions negatively—cursing us, causing us physical pain, and so forth. If we get impatient with their actions, we may become miserable and retaliate. We can make peace for ourselves and others if we understand that these unpleasant experiences are a result of our prior karma, and that if we try to exact revenge on those who harm us we will just bring ourselves more misery. Wisdom enables us to control the mind.

Seeing the benefits of patience and defects of impatience leads to compassion and love for those who try to harm us. We become peaceful, others cannot disturb us, and we will not experience misery.

Wisdom is the basis for joyous perseverance as well. Wisdom enables us to complete whatever we start without difficulty. Clearly understanding why we are undertaking an activity gives us a reasoned foundation for our goal. Without wisdom, we may put in a lot of effort and get less work done. Wisdom makes our work on the path effectual.

And it is wisdom that makes meditative stabilization powerful and pure. Single-pointed concentration joined with the realization of ultimate truth is superior, or supramundane, insight. This union of meditative concentration and wisdom gets rid of all the causes of misery from the root. It also eliminates the obstructions to perfect enlightenment. Meditative stabilization on its own is not able to do this. Combined with wisdom it becomes *perfect* meditative stabilization, and that state brings our mind and body into harmony. This mental and physical suppleness yields a special kind of mental and physical pleasure no matter how many hours we remain in meditation. The body does not interrupt the mind and the mind does not disturb the body. Without wisdom, sometimes the body can be still but the mind has gone somewhere else, or the mind wants to stay still but the body acts up. Furthermore, meditative stabilization joined with wisdom eventually produces the best physical pleasure and mental happiness of all: the everlasting peace and complete freedom from misery of full enlightenment itself.

In the following stanzas Aśvaghoṣa goes over the various ways in which wisdom guides all of the perfections:

> If the clear eye of wisdom is wide open,
> A bodhisattva gives even his own flesh.
> Like a medicinal plant he has no thoughts;
> Neither conceit nor discouragement arises.

> Not practicing ethical discipline for their own goals,
> Intelligent ones see samsara as a faulty prison
> And wish all sentient beings were free from it.
> So of course they are not practicing for worldly aims.

As Aśvaghoṣa does here, the scriptures sometimes call bodhisattvas *intelligent ones* because they possess wisdom. Wise bodhisattvas regard samsara like a horrible jail in which all sentient beings are imprisoned. They therefore wish that all sentient beings would become free. Since they are not practicing religious

conduct just for their own benefit, there is no need to say that they are practicing to gain something ordinary, such as a high rebirth or sensual pleasure.
Moreover:

> Those who possess wisdom have the quality of patience:
> They do not retaliate against those who do them harm.
> They are like excellent, well-trained elephants,
> Able to endure doing all sorts of labor.

Bodhisattvas have the pure quality of patience that is produced by wisdom. They are without anger and can accept whatever others do. Instead of seeking to retaliate, their patience and love become even stronger toward destructive beings. In this way they are like a well-trained elephant. Elephants are so big that they could squash a human being who demands they do unpleasant things. But a well-trained elephant will do whatever it is told. Most of us have seen how they perform in shows: standing up, walking on two legs, or doing heavy work.
Aśvaghoṣa continues:

> Exhaustion is the result of perseverance alone.
> Assisted by wisdom, diligence accomplishes great things.

It takes a great deal of effort to achieve worldly goals; spiritual goals are even more difficult to accomplish. If we work hard, guided by wisdom, we will complete something of great benefit. When we try to do something without wisdom, we act stupidly and expend a lot of energy in the wrong task. The end result of misdirected work will be suffering or exhaustion. Furthermore, when we do things incorrectly, we develop negative attitudes and then engage in nonvirtuous actions. Relying on faulty logic or wrong methods results in doing everything in the wrong way; it can cause us to miss the correct path completely. How could someone who incorrectly perceives situations and always does the wrong thing accomplish single-pointed concentration or anything else for that matter? As Aśvaghoṣa asks:

> How can the best happiness and joy of meditative concentration
> Be accomplished in the mind of low beings
> Who rely on means of incorrect reasons
> On a path of accumulated faults and polluted with sin?

Wisdom distinguishes what is right from wrong, so even in confusing situations someone with wisdom acts without contradiction. For example, if someone becomes a wealthy and powerful ruler over vast continents, from a worldly point of view he or she has attained a very high position. The power, wealth, and sensory pleasures of such a position should bring happiness. If such rulers lack wisdom, they may become conceited about their wealth, attached to their possessions, jealous of anyone who has equal attainments, and eager to destroy anyone who has anything better. They fall under the sway of attachment or pride and their possessions end up controlling them. But bodhisattvas with wisdom will never fall into a negative attitude or a wrong practice. They are like a king with an excellent minister who perfects his ruler's commands and cares for all the subjects of the realm. This bodhisattva's minister is not a person—it is perfect wisdom. Wisdom produces compassion, love, and bodhicitta, so all that wealth and power are used to benefit others.

Worldly attachment and ordinary love can look like pure love, but they are not the same. For ordinary beings, love and attachment are difficult to separate, but with wisdom there is not the slightest mixing of the two. Attachment is wanting to possess an object or not wanting to separate from an object, under the power of a wrong perception. It is important to understand that worldly attachment is based on a misperception or incorrect thought. Four things are usually given as examples of incorrect worldly misperception: seeing impure things as pure; identifying something that has the nature of suffering as something that has the nature of happiness or peace; perceiving something that is impermanent as real or permanent; and holding something that is empty of self as having a soul or true identity. These wrong perceptions are rooted in ignorance. Wisdom is the opposite. It sees the truth—recognizing impure things as impure, suffering things as suffering, impermanent things as impermanent, and empty things as empty. Wisdom sees sentient beings properly; it is knowing that because there is ignorance, hatred, and desire in the mind of each sentient being, all of them are subject to pain and trouble. Based on wisdom, real love—wishing that all sentient beings would have peace, happiness, and enjoyment—arises spontaneously all the time. So there is a vast difference between ordinary love and a bodhisattva's love because of the absence or presence of wisdom.

The Mahayana scriptures teach that the difference between love and compassion is their object. Love is wishing very strongly that sentient beings have happiness and the other good things that they lack. Compassion is wanting sentient beings to be separate from all their pain and the causes of future misery. The bodhisattva's practice of compassion is spontaneously finding others' suffering so unbearable that he or she wants to fight to free them from misery all the time. In contrast, when ordinary people see that someone they love has a serious problem, the concern they feel—which stems from their attachment—can cause them to become so beaten down by sorrow that they are rendered incapable of any action. It is almost as if their sadness makes them lazy. Bodhisattvas never have this problematic reaction. Their love and compassion is not a burden under which they suffer. They do not become discouraged. No matter how much suffering they see, they never weaken; their courage and joyous commitment to work for sentient beings' benefit only increase. They can practice because of wisdom.

Altruistic joy and equanimity are measureless practices in the same way that love and compassion are. Because of wisdom bodhisattvas can easily engage in these practices without challenge from an opposing attitude. Bodhisattvas reach a spiritual level where they experience a special kind of joy and peace. This joy is not like ordinary happiness. Ordinary happiness is mixed with suffering. When suffering is at a high level, we label it misery; when this misery is a little bit reduced, we call it happiness even though it is still a condition of suffering.

A disadvantage of ordinary happiness is that we get completely distracted by it. We abandon any serious effort to do other things. When we have a problem we want to practice, but when we are happy we completely give up our practice. Bodhisattvas' happiness is conjoined with great equanimity. Here *equanimity* means not going to extremes; they do not do something intensely all day and all night for a few weeks and then suddenly stop doing it at all. Bodhisattvas stay level and stable; neither good nor bad conditions cause them to change their level of activity. Wisdom enables them to have the equanimity of constant practice. Wisdom mixed with compassion and love produce mental ease without any misery. Even though they have superior joy, they do not become distracted and spend their life senselessly. They strive to help all other sentient beings every moment.

Wisdom keeps us from falling to the negative side. We stay stable and positive. Wisdom makes our practice beautiful. As the *Compendium of the Perfections* says:

> Bodhisattvas who rule kingdoms,
> Possessing assets like those of heaven,
> Do not fall into misperception of their nature.
> They have the power of wisdom as their minister.
>
> Their love is one with their desire to help others;
> It is completely devoid of the stain of attachment.

Their compassion finds others' suffering unbearable;
They never fall low to laziness burdened by other's misery.

Possessing supreme joy, they absolutely never waver.
Great impartiality is never apathetic about others' needs.
Great wisdom beautifies these good qualities
And blocks all their opposites.

The *Praise of One Worthy of Honor (Varṇāha-varṇa-stotra)* says:

Ultimate reality is not cast away;
It is harmonious with conventional existence.

It appears to ordinary people that conventional truth and ultimate truth are contradictory. The ultimate truth is that every phenomena lacks inherent, or ultimate, existence. The highest wisdom is the realization of this emptiness; it is understanding śūnyatā, or suchness. From the perspective of the ultimate truth, things are merely imputed; they only nominally exist. Conventional, or phenomenal, truth is how things appear to an ordinary mind. We see things as real; they appear to exist in their own right. There is a subject and an object; there is cause and effect; there are actual qualities such as good and bad; and they ultimately exist. This conventional understanding seems to be the complete opposite of the ultimate truth—that everything is empty of being real, true, or inherently existent.

When we are first taught that nothing, not even the smallest atom, inherently or ultimately exists, the two levels of truth seem totally incompatible. To ordinary people it seems that if we believe in emptiness, then conventional things such as causality, qualitative differences, and so on are simply imaginary; or, if we accept conventional truth, then ultimate truth could not possibly be valid. We are accustomed to things appearing as real. We perceive them to be real, grasp them as real and, based on that, we feel attachment or hatred.

Emptiness cannot even appear to the ordinary worldly mind. We develop wisdom gradually through investigation and analytical meditation. First, we develop inferential understanding of the two truths, and eventually we have a direct, yogic realization of śūnyatā. When we have a direct realization of emptiness, the contradiction between the two levels of truth is completely resolved. We know that there is no internal or external base that exists inherently, ultimately, or independently. At the same time, we can accept internal and external causality—that a distinct cause produces an individual effect, such as good karma yielding good experiences and barley seeds producing barley sprouts. Yogis with exalted wisdom do not have to cast away ultimate truth in order to accept conventional truth. They understand the illusory nature of phenomena and causality. They are not like ordinary people to whom it seems that things inherently arise, and therefore cannot possibly be empty.

The *Praise of One Worthy of Honor* counters another apparent contradiction, this time in regard to the rules of pure ethical conduct:

> Regarding proscriptions and prohibitions,
> Your word in some places is solely definitive.
> In other places it is not definitive.
> But there is no contradiction between these.

The Mahayana and Hinayana are quite different in terms of what actions are permitted for a practitioner and what actions are to be rejected. A Hinayana sutra and a Mahayana sutra can seem completely contradictory; one says, "You should not do this," and the other says, "You should do this." Even within the Mahayana there are differences between the actions allowed or prohibited in the Sutrayana and Tantrayana. Yet all of these can be taught to one person—it is a matter of recognizing that different situations require different approaches at different times.

The situation is similar to the way a doctor may give two seemingly contradictory prescriptions to a patient. At an early stage in the treatment the physician may say, "Do not eat meat; if you do, you will die." But later, when certain symptoms are subdued or others arise, the doctor may say, "You must eat meat; if you do not, you will die." The doctor's different instructions are equally important, so we must understand when it is appropriate to put into practice a specific directive.

The Buddhist teachings are similar. They may appear to be contradictory because they are instructions for different purposes at different times in our spiritual development. For example, before we begin to practice the Dharma, we are totally under the power of the self-centered view. Because of our ignorance, we are swayed by desire or hatred every moment. Just about every thing we do is directly or indirectly harmful to others, because our actions are founded on selfishness. So at first we are told not to do many things, because they are dangerous to our spiritual development. There are many rules, both major and minor, that function like a series of fences to protect us from our own actions. There are rules about what to eat, what to wear, how to behave, and how to earn a living.

As we train the mind we gradually subdue the power of selfish egotistic view. On a higher level of the path, a practitioner is under the power of compassion and love for others. Then one's actions are purely for the benefit of other sentient beings, not for some selfish goal. In order to benefit other sentient beings bodhisattvas are allowed to do many things that were prohibited earlier. For example, earlier we are told we should never kill any living creature because killing will bring us great suffering in the future. We reject this behavior out of concern that we could fall into hell or another lower rebirth. But for a bodhisattva there may be a situation when killing is permissible.

Consider a situation where someone dominated by the three poisons is about to kill thousands of people. If a bodhisattva sees that there is absolutely no other way to save all those people other than to kill this person, then he or she is allowed to do so. The bodhisattva must meet many requirements before he or she can do this. The bodhisattva must have a high level of wisdom, great skill, and be dominated by compassion and love. He or she must have no self-centered egotistic view regarding this action; he can have no concern that the negative karma of killing this person will cause him to fall into hell or that it will bring praise or renown. The deed must be done purely, joyfully, and out of pure love for all others—to save the lives of the intended victims, to prevent all the intended victims' relatives and friends from getting angry and acting in revenge, and to prevent the perpetrator from doing something that would cause him eons of suffering in the future. When we reach an advanced level like this, not only are we allowed to do things that were clearly prohibited earlier, we *must* do them. If we do not do them, we are breaking our promise.

So, in this case, we are told first that we should never kill because it will make us worse. Then we are told that we must kill, because if we do not we would be very bad. An ignorant person would see these instructions as completely contradictory. Skillful masters have wisdom, and so they see no inconsistency. They know how to understand these statements and when to follow them. They can distinguish the levels of meaning of a teaching and know when instructions are explicit and when they have an implicit meaning. They have the wisdom to discern properly what is truly love and what is not. Without wisdom we mix things up and are unclear about what to do. Out of confusion, when we try to do something we do it incorrectly. Saying that an ordinary person does not have wisdom, does not mean that such people have no wisdom at all; after all, everyone has some ability to distinguish objects. But we say *they have no wisdom* from the point of view of spiritual, or higher, wisdom. They are not able to understand the compatibility of the two truths, or the higher and lower scriptures explaining what is permitted and what is forbidden. One of the best benefits of wisdom is understanding that there is no contradiction in the intent of the Buddha's teachings.

Those who understand the benefits of wisdom strive hard to attain it. Those who see less benefit, or do not see any reason to develop wisdom at all, work far less hard. So it is important to understand the benefits of wisdom. The *Compendium of the Perfections* says that all good qualities arise from wisdom:

> Wisdom is like a child's loving mother,
> But how much more amazing are the great things it provides.
>
> The perfect strength of the ten powers of buddhahood,
> All incomparably superb activities,
> And all perfect qualities without a lack,
> Arise in dependence upon wisdom like that as their cause.

A mother provides for her child in every possible way. She produces the child in her womb, and then nourishes, raises, and protects the baby after he or she is born. She is a child's first and kindest friend. A mother gives her child many good things, but what is unusual about that? Wisdom does far more for us than our mother. Spiritual life and growth is produced by wisdom. Wisdom provides protection from the negative side. It nourishes spiritual development so that good qualities increase. Through wisdom we gain a special realization of the two truths, develop along the spiritual path, remove mental obscurations, and finally achieve buddhahood with ten powers, supreme activities, and perfect qualities of body, speech, and mind. All the perfections are the result of wisdom. The following stanza from the same text gives a little more detail:

> A supreme treasury of the worlds' skills,
> All the discerning sacred instructions that exist,
> Protective knowledge, magical spells, and so forth,
> Knowledge of the varied qualities of phenomena and their arrangements,
> The many doors to emancipation and freedom,
> Every aspect of this and that which are helpful to sentient beings,
> A bodhisattva's ability to do great things—
> All of these arise from the power of wisdom.

If we were at a sporting event where we judged a buddha's performance in comparison to others, we would see that buddhas are unsurpassable. They are perfect. They have every skill. Buddhas are like a treasury containing every mundane and supramundane item of value. Wisdom is the basis of all these good qualities. It is the source of all scriptures and their explanations that help us to see reality. Wisdom is the foundation of all protection, such as medicine and defensive spells and mantras. Wisdom is knowing the various aspects and connections between events. It is also the substrate of the meditative concentrations called the *doors of emancipation and freedom.* There are eight levels of this meditation, but from the point of view of the realization of śūnyatā, there are three meditation techniques employed after achieving single-pointed concentration to reduce specific types of attachment. In brief, these three techniques are to produce physical manifestations, hide things, or compare things. Other than to say all of these arise from wisdom, this is not the right place to go into these methods. We have to recognize these benefits of wisdom in order to take joy in the effort to produce it.

There is a commonly quoted stanza from the *Verse Summary of the Perfection of Wisdom in Eight Thousand Lines* about the disadvantage of not having wisdom. If we lack wisdom, the other five perfections, from generosity through meditative stabilization, are blind. Blindly working at any practice will not lead to success:

> The multitude of blind people without a leader
> cannot see the route, so how can they enter the city?
> If the first five perfections have no wisdom,
> They are sightless, so they are unable to reach enlightenment.

The blind need a guide because they cannot see what is right in front of them. They do not know if a step forward will be on the path or if they will fall into a ditch. They cannot see the correct way to go, so without assistance how can they find their way along a complicated route to a city? Similarly, if we want to go to enlightenment, we have to know what is in front of us. We must know the obstacles and the fundamental practices to remove them. If we do not know the basics, how can we attain a higher result? The first five perfections are like a vehicle that can carry us to enlightenment. But without wisdom we are driving blind. Wisdom is the eye that can see where we are going. We need both a vehicle and the vision to direct it in order to be able to go where we desire. With wisdom the practices of generosity and so forth become the direct cause of perfect buddhahood. Without wisdom these practices might not be the correct path.

The *Commentary on the "Middle Way"* makes a similar point:[4]

One person with sight can easily lead
Many blind people where they want to go.
Similarly here, wisdom is seeing the qualities
To take up to go to buddhahood.

All the misery in the world comes from ignorance—incorrect perception, understanding, and action. In contrast, wisdom understands what is good and what is bad, knows what should be attained and what should not, and distinguishes the right method to attain our goal from an incorrect one. With wisdom we can judge things properly and follow a correct course of action to achieve the goals we desire. This is true in a worldly sense, in terms of spiritual practice in general, and from the profound Mahayana point of view and motivation. We need wisdom to make the practices of generosity and so forth pure. *Pure* refers to the correct way to understand generosity: its purpose, the way to give, what to give, to whom we give, and the giver. Giving with right understanding is the pure practice of generosity. If we incorrectly grasp the object, the recipient, the manner of giving, and the giver, we may have an unethical motivation and do everything mistakenly. We need wisdom to generate the bodhicitta motivation and to understand the lack of subject/object duality. Tsongkhapa shows how wisdom makes all the other perfections pure by quoting the *Compendium of the Perfections:*

If those striving for a good result lack wisdom,
Their practice of generosity will not become pure.
It is said giving for the benefit of others is supreme;
The rest are activities just to increase wealth.

There are many selfish reasons to be generous, such as desiring praise, fame, or something in return. Our generosity is an impure worldly activity if we give with the intent to gain something for ourselves, or if we view the gift, the giver, and the recipient as existing ultimately or inherently. With wisdom, even if we give something very small, our generosity is a superior, Mahayana practice.

We need wisdom to understand the goal of the practice of ethical discipline, the nature of the practice, and how it benefits others. If we engage in religious conduct out of ignorance, the three poisons dominate the way we keep the precepts. Without the eye of wisdom, we may think we are practicing religious conduct if we do not eat for a day, but it could merely be attachment to our body, anger about food, or something else. It is just ordinary activity:

If darkness is not dispelled by the light of wisdom,
Ethical conduct will not come to have purity.
Most ethical conduct done without wisdom
Is contaminated by the afflictions because of mental faults.

Patience requires wisdom in the same way generosity and ethical discipline do:

If the mind is disturbed by the faults of incorrect views,
We do not even wish to have the good qualities of patience.
Incorrectly judging right and wrong, our manner
Is like the fame of a king who lacks good qualities.

If we have wisdom, we can be patient because we truly pity people who act badly under the command of their anger or delusions. Wisdom makes us want to help them and bring them peace and happiness. If we lack wisdom we perceive things in a negative manner and continuously misjudge situations. When others cause us trouble, we think it is smart to retaliate and harm them more than they harmed us; if they hit us once, we hit them back twice. This way of thinking simply serves to increase our anger and the other person's hatred. It leads to a negative manner of action, prevents patience from arising, and negative results will occur. If a political leader does not have good judgment or the other good qualities of wisdom, he may be well-known for a short time but his fame quickly fades away.

And further:

Nothing other than subtle and profound wisdom
Is highly praised by the skillful masters.
Without wisdom we do not go on the straight mental path
That is unobscured by the faults of desire.

Wisdom is the most subtle and profound good quality in the world. Someone with wisdom sees things as they truly are. Such wise people do not stray onto a wrong path because of desire, attachment, wrong views, or misperceptions. They do not make incorrect judgments. They are earnest, direct, and straightforward. Wisdom removes ignorance—the cause of suffering. Seeing the benefits of wisdom, great yogis spend their entire life—some spend many lives—in a long struggle to develop wisdom.

As the light of wisdom becomes brighter, the darkness of ignorance fades away. Eventually ignorance will be completely removed:

> Like the great light of the rising sun,
> The great power of the increasing light of wisdom
> Clears away all the darkness covering sentient beings' minds,
> So all that is left is the mere name.

Ignorance is the root of desire, hatred, and all the other mental afflictions. The darkness of ignorance clouds the minds of sentient beings. When the light of great wisdom dispels ignorance completely, only the word *darkness* or *ignorance* is left. In other words, there is no obscuration left; the mind shining on all objects is omniscient. Therefore, like great spiritual practitioners we too should practice long and hard to gain wisdom.

Now that Tsongkhapa has presented the disadvantages of lacking wisdom and the advantages of wisdom, he discusses the causes of ignorance and wisdom. The *Compendium of the Perfections* says:

> Laziness, indolence, reliance upon bad friends,
> Overcome by sleep, an unanalytical nature,
> Having no interest in the supreme wisdom of the Buddha,
> Asking questions compelled by improper pride,
> Not having the faith to rely upon wise men
> Because of self-denigration and attachment to self,
> And the wrong views, the great poison of wrong thought—
> Are all taught to be the causes of ignorance.

There are external and internal causes of ignorance. Bad companions influence us to hold wrong views, engage in bad activities, and go the wrong way. Some internal causes of ignorance are laziness, enjoying the leisure of doing nothing, liking to sleep, and not wanting to examine things. Tsongkhapa mentions many times that believing we should not have any conceptual thoughts is a wrong view that perpetuates ignorance. Similarly, not liking the various practices of the method side is a cause of ignorance. Having pride, thinking we know everything when we do not, leads us to ask questions only to show off our own knowledge or point out others' ignorance. We are not really trying to learn anything, so our questions will not yield wisdom. Other people put themselves down out of attachment and become discouraged. They feel so inferior that they do not want to try to learn anything from others. Wrong views are like powerful poison. The many wrong views—thinking that there is no causation, that there is no such thing as the path and the fruit of the path, nihilism, and so forth—are all causes of ignorance.

The same text points out the conditions and causes for wisdom. It advises practitioners as follows:

> Follow and respect a spiritual teacher worthy of trust,
> And strive to listen in order to obtain wisdom.

The traditional way to master something is to start by learning about it from someone who has the proper information. Before the age of mass-published books and computers, the only way to learn something was to listen to a teacher. In our case, we should try to find a spiritual teacher who has the qualities that we want to develop in ourselves. When we come across a worthy and suitable guru, we should study with him or her to the best of our ability. If we do not pay attention to what our teacher says, we will not gain the wisdom that rises from listening. Next, we need to think about what we have heard. We have to examine it and consider its meaning. Once we have the understanding that comes from analysis, we meditate on it. We become more and more familiar with it until we reach a high realization. The wisdom that arises from meditation removes ignorance. In order to get that wisdom we need the former two kinds of wisdom. Without them we will not know what to meditate upon, so any meditation we do will be fruitless. We should therefore go wherever we need to go, near or far, to find a skillful teacher. If we pay attention to our teacher's instructions, we will gain the wisdom that arises from listening. This will give us plenty to think about. Through analysis we can come to understand many things. With the wisdom that arises from analysis we can meditate properly because we will know what to meditate upon, the order of the topics we should meditate on, and so forth. Then we will develop deep and extensive wisdom from meditation.

The great teacher Aśvaghoṣa says:

> With little study we are blind; we do not know how to meditate.
> If we lack that, what can we think about?
> Therefore, from the cause of making an effort to study,
> Meditation in accord with analysis yields vast wisdom.

Spiritual practitioners want to go to a state of perfect emancipation and enlightenment. We cannot get there by walking; it is a mental path. We progress to our destination by increasing our wisdom step by step so as to remove mental obstacles. In order to achieve the wisdom of highest realizations, we have to do various kinds of meditation. We first must study subjects such as the purpose of meditation, what is to be negated, how to meditate and skillfully employ other methods, how these methods work, and so forth. Just hearing about these topics is not enough. We need to analyze what we have heard to understand them on our own. When we are confident about an obstacle and its antidote, we can meditate. The power of increasing familiarity gradually rids the mind of all ignorance. The vast wisdom of the great sages comes from meditation. When yogis reach the higher levels of the path, their wisdom is not confined to one narrow thing. They have wide understanding from the point of view of the true nature of phenomena, the obstacles, the goal, the antidotes, and so forth.

There are two major obstructions to attaining perfect enlightenment: the mental afflictions and knowledge obstacles. The mental afflictions are ignorance, attachment, anger, jealousy, pride, and other delusive consciousnesses. These gross level obstructions are sometimes called passion obstacles, or delusions. All these mental afflictions are misperceptions, incorrect understanding, and grasping of things.

Knowledge obstacles are more subtle. They remain in the mind even after we have rid ourselves of the mental afflictions through meditation. Arhats— those who have attained liberation from samsara—have no wrong conceptual thoughts, wrong views, attachment, hatred, and so forth. However, even though they have eliminated all the mental afflictions, there are still subtle obstacles left that prevent an arhat from seeing things as clearly as a buddha or doing things as perfectly as a buddha. These hindrances are not a consciousness; they are a subtle potential. They are predispositions that keep them from attaining omniscience.

To understand the two types of obstructions, imagine something very dirty and smelly wrapped in cloth for a long time. If we throw away the thing that was filthy and impure, the gross object is gone, but there are still stains and smells left on the cloth. To get rid of this more subtle impurity, we have to clean the wrappings. Similarly, we first eliminate the gross levels of ignorance, attachment, and hatred from the mind. But even after we separate these afflictions from our consciousness with the techniques of meditation, there are subtle stains left. We will have attained emancipation, but it is not buddhahood because there are obstructions to omniscience remaining. Until we remove the knowledge obstacles we cannot reach buddhahood.

From a literal point of view, because the mental afflictions are also obstructions to higher knowledge, they too are knowledge obstacles. However, the Prāsaṅgika Madhyamaka school separates the grosser mental afflictions from the more subtle obstructions to omniscience.[5]

Ārya Maitreya presents the Yogācāra Svātantrika-Madhyamaka viewpoint regarding the two obstructions in the *Sublime Continuum:*

> All ordinary conceptions of the three spheres
> Are asserted to be obstacles to omniscience.
> Conceptions like miserliness and so on
> Are asserted to be mental afflictions.

The Svātantrika-Mādhaymika school divides the obstacles in a way that differs from the Prāsaṅgika presentation. They say that the gross level mental afflictions stem from ignorance—the egotistic view of a permanent, absolute self. For example, miserliness is wanting everything for our self, jealousy comes from seeing that someone has something better than we do, anger and hatred arise if we perceive something harmful to us, and so forth. According to this school, the knowledge obstacle that remains even after the mental afflictions are removed is a dualistic conception that subject and object are inherently different.

In many Buddhist texts this dualistic conception is explained in the context of three spheres: the subject, object, and action. For example, in the case of an act of generosity, the three spheres—the person to whom we are giving, the thing that is given, and the giver—seem to inherently exist as they appear—as intrinsically different entities. Until we have a direct realization of śūnyatā, we believe that the duality that we perceive essentially or ultimately exists as it appears.

We usually do not see any problem with our perception that everything is as real as it seems. We will admit that a few things are false—a mirage, for example—but everything else is real and true. Because the conceptual thought that perceives and grasps subjects, objects, and actions to exist dualistically is a subtler and more difficult obstacle to remove than the mental afflictions, it is considered to be a knowledge obstacle in this lower Madhyamaka school. For the higher Prāsaṅgika Madhyamaka, however, this dualistic conception is a mental affliction. An extensive explanation of this point will be presented in volume 5; here it is sufficient to say that *all* the obstacles are targeted by yogis seeking the high spiritual goals. There is no way to attain the goal without removing all the obstructions. And the only way to remove the obstructions is to develop wisdom.

The same text continues:

> Other than wisdom there is nothing
> That causes elimination of these obscurations.
> Therefore wisdom is supreme.
> Its foundation is learning. So study is supreme.

Wisdom is the direct antidote to ignorance; there is no other way to eliminate wrong conceptions of the three spheres. A direct realization of śūnyatā—knowing that things do not exist as they appear—is therefore supreme. Where does this wisdom come from? Its source is study. Without learning, we cannot open ourselves to wisdom. Without studying, we do not even know what wisdom is much less how to attain it. So the foundation for gaining wisdom—listening and studying—is extremely important.

The first step is searching for the right religious teachings. Without that, successive levels of development are difficult to attain. Śāntideva says in his *Compendium of the Trainings in Verse (Śikṣā-samuccaya-kārikā):*

> Be patient, search for learning,
> Then stay in a forest, and
> Persevere in meditative equipoise.

It can be difficult to find and then study with a proper teacher. So in the beginning patience is important for us. Although it is of critical importance, the wisdom that arises from listening is a superficial overview; we need to delve deeper by analyzing and then meditating on these things in a quiet place such as a forest or cave. The *Questions of Nārāyaṇa Formula (Nārāyaṇa-paripṛcchā-dhāraṇī)* also calls on practitioners to study so that wisdom will arise:

> It is like this, child of good family: if you have listened, wisdom will arise. If you have wisdom, the mental afflictions will be pacified. If the mental afflictions are no more, evil has no opportunity to harm you.

Here I am translating the Sanskrit word *māra* (Tibetan, *bdud*) as *evil* rather than the more common *demon,* because the real evil is not an external spirit; it is inside us. Religious texts talk about four types of evil demons. Three of these are internal. The principal one is the mental afflictions—ignorance, desire, hatred, and so forth. The activity of the mental afflictions creates karma, which results in the five aggregates of the body and mind. Thus the second internal evil is the skandhas, or aggregates, of personality. Once we are born under the power of the mental afflictions, the body and mind are the locus of misery, problems, pain, and destruction. So the third demon is the evil of death. A life caused by karma and the mental afflictions has a great many faulty mental, physical, and environmental aspects. Because our body and mind are impure, weak, and the subject of conditions, external forces such as spirits or devils can easily interfere with us. The fourth evil is these spirits of harm. As long as we have the three poisons of desire, hatred, and ignorance, the other evils arise. Once the mind is completely free of the gross obscurations of ignorance and so on, none of these evils can harm us. It is wisdom that destroys the mental afflictions and wisdom starts with study.

Tsongkhapa comments that all these quotations prove once again that wisdom is the vital life of the path to enlightenment, and that the most important first step for those who want to attain high spiritual goals is to listen to and study the teachings. The information we need to attain wisdom is in the faultless scriptures and their commentaries. These texts explain things without error, so we must hear explanations of these teachings many times and in full detail. Just hearing one part is not enough. It is not easy to attain a high spiritual goal. It is like trying to go to a mysterious faraway place that is unknown to most people; to get there we need good directions that clearly describe every landmark. Nevertheless, some people think that because a direct internal realization of the truth is gained through meditation, all this learning is unnecessary. They believe that meditation is non-conceptual, so all the details learned from study and analysis are useless for spiritual development. They say that the kind of wisdom gained from study is only for the purpose of teaching classes, arguing, or giving public presentations.

This idea is still in circulation and continues to fool people. Those who want achieve a superior goal must abandon this idea as if it were poison, because the opposite is actually the case; we need the analytical wisdom that arises from study and deliberation when we meditate. It is true that during direct yogic realization of śūnyatā all conceptual dualistic thought ceases, but this does not mean that throughout our entire practice we should abandon thoughtful analysis. There are certain places for certain things. Both analytical and stabilization meditation are necessary. Sometimes we need analytical wisdom and sometimes we need to fix the mind single-pointedly on an object. Practitioners need to know what to think, when to think, how long to think, and for what purpose. Without wisdom we would be practicing blindly without complete information. Only with wisdom can we make correct decisions regarding how to practice properly. To think otherwise is false.

The early Kadampa yogis also say that analytical meditation is necessary to see the two truths clearly. Their sayings make it clear that wisdom means distinguishing details precisely. It is not vague. Therefore, there are many things that we must study and examine. Naljorpa Chenpo says:[6]

> Jowowa, in order to attain buddhahood that is omniscient, what kind
> of teacher would rely on a scripture that fit in the palm of his hand

while disregarding a dzo-load of texts? With just that kind of effort you will not get anywhere.

A dzo is a cross between a cow and a yak. Such animals are very strong and are used to carry loads and pull plows. I do not know how many pounds they can carry, but it is certainly a lot more than you could lift with one hand. So Naljorpa Chenpo's point is that if we just study one small text, we will not know enough to attain enlightenment. Another Kadampa teacher named Puchungba says:

> I keep these great scriptures open near my bed. We must always study. Even if I cannot look at everything, I keep them here out of sincere respect. If someone says, "Practice without knowing the teachings," how could you practice?

Following Tibetan custom, some resident monks accompanied the great Kadampa Geshe Potowa a little distance when he departed after a visit to Chengnawa. Potowa's farewell advice to them includes a reference to craving for something tasty so much that your mouth waters. The story goes:

> When Potowa departed, the monks of Chenga accompanied him a short way. He said, "You are so fortunate," to them three times. "You don't have to salivate over other teachers because you have my spiritual teacher who covers the entire earth like the sky. You don't have to work hard to find teachings because there are scriptures and commentaries everywhere you look. Your minds are at ease because you don't have wrong views about karma and its results. You are satiated by each tantric practice that achieves its result.

Everything was there for these monks. They had every resource needed for their spiritual practice to attain enlightenment: teachers, scriptures, and a suitable environment to gain wisdom.

Geshe Sharawa was also a famous yogi. He says that until we become enlightened there is always something we have to develop, so there is always something new to learn:

> Until you attain perfect enlightenment there is no end to what you must study. When you become a buddha it is done.

In the same vein the great Kamapa says:

Those who have studied little will degenerate if they think, "What need is there for knowledge when practicing the Dharma?" It is dangerous to say, "If you practice assiduously what need is there for knowledge?" If you are persistently practicing the Dharma you must have knowledge. You should think, "Since I will not complete this in my short life, I must continue to learn throughout an uninterrupted line of future lives of leisure and fortune.

It is contradictory to think we can practice the Dharma without knowing what to practice, how to practice, the purpose of practice, the obstacles to practice, how these things are causally connected, what is right and wrong, and so forth. Because we cannot know everything and complete all there is to do during this short human lifetime, we need a sequence of lives during which we can practice until we reach the goal of perfection. We have to create the causes to ensure that our next life will be even better. Right now we have the chance to practice, but if we do something wrong, our next life will be in a lower realm. Then we may stray farther and farther away, cutting off the opportunity for further learning and practice.

Kamapa continues:

> Some think, "Meditators do not need to study; those who teach need to study." Actually, learning is more necessary for meditators; teachers may just incur the fault of explaining something incorrectly.

Meditators put the Dharma into practice. They are following instructions for progressing on the path, not just explaining them intellectually to others. It is most dangerous for meditators to lack wisdom, because without it they run the risk of losing their way. In short, wisdom is the most important element for spiritual development. Without knowledge gained from learning there is no way to acquire wisdom.

Real spiritual practice requires that we meditate. To meditate we have to know what to do. To know what to do we need to study. We must be certain about this relationship. If we are not absolutely sure that analytical meditation is necessary at the time of practice, we cannot progress. This does not mean that *only* analytical meditation is necessary. The point is the importance of wisdom and the connection between wisdom and study. Sometimes even those with a great scriptural education do not understand this and desire to be better known as meditators than scholars. They think the subjects of the great scriptures are not the true focus of meditation practice; they view the explanations in the scriptures as a big mountain that should be put in the background of a landscape, not something to actually apply in the foreground of practice. In other words, they think we should divide Buddhists into those who hold Buddha's teachings and those who practice them. They believe a holder of the teachings maintains and spreads the tradition and therefore needs to study a lot, whereas those who want to quickly attain enlightenment need to practice meditation. This is an utterly nonsensical and contradictory distinction.

It is true that the teachings can be divided into two: teachings as scripture and teachings that have been put into practice. However, Tsongkhapa points out that these are not in conflict. The scriptural teachings provide the information for how and what to practice. After we understand what we have read and studied in the scriptures and commentaries, we put those instructions into practice. So these two types of teachings are very closely related; one is the cause and the other the effect. In order to do a practice correctly, we have to study it, analyze it, and examine it. Study and meditation are not separate things; they must be done together. We can only practice what we have learned; meditation does not work if we forget what we have learned. We should not study, and then practice something unrelated. If we have not yet learned anything, we should strive to study to the best of our ability. We should not get discouraged and give up thinking, "Oh, I don't know anything about any of this."

Bodhisattvas must rely on a set of practices that encompass the entire path. There are many things to learn and put together. If we do not have extensive mental power at the start, we should become accustomed to a complete but brief set of practices. Then, as our wisdom becomes greater and stronger, our practice can become more extensive. This is the methodology of the lamrim teachings. In contrast to hundreds of volumes of scripture that explain particular topics in great detail, even the shortest lamrim text contains the essence of all the key points of the sutra and tantra and the higher and lower vehicles necessary for the attainment of enlightenment. It provides all the information we need in the most abbreviated and easy-to-follow format. For a while we follow this short lamrim and do what we can. As our wisdom increases, we can absorb more detail from additional scriptures. There are other lamrim texts of varying length. The great *Lamrim Chenmo* lays out the complete sequence of practice from the beginning up to enlightenment. In contrast, if we rely on a teaching that explains only a single aspect of practice, we may become confident of that particular method, but we will not gain a complete understanding of the entire practice of the path. So satisfaction with an incomplete teaching is unwise.

The foundation of proper practice is therefore to rely on a wise spiritual teacher and promising to practice pure ethical discipline. Not only should we listen to teachings from our spiritual friend again and again, we should divide our twenty-four hour day into four parts and during each part do a session of analysis and meditation on the subjects we have heard. In addition, we should accumulate merit by making special prayers to our spiritual teacher and meditational deity, making offerings, paying homage, taking refuge, and so forth. We should also purify our negativities by confession. If we do all the elements of a complete practice on a daily basis our positive qualities will naturally increase. Our wisdom will grow until finally the most profound realizations will arise. In short, Tsongkhapa's advice follows that of earlier holy teachers:

> Gracefully hold in your mind all of what you studied earlier. Then you must consider these things, measure, and examine them again and again. If you forget what you have learned, meditating on the mind itself is not helpful. The best meditator is the best teacher. A middling meditator is a middling teacher. In order to become greater, you must understand the teachings to the same extent that you meditate. When you have a definite understanding from thinking like that, you do not listen when bad friends say, "All virtuous and nonvirtuous thoughts are conceptualizations and are to be abandoned." Instead you think, "The scriptures do not say anything like that. My virtuous spiritual friends do not explain it like that." However, if you do not have this [understanding], but have some faith without wisdom, you can be directed to go anywhere as easily as water because you believe whatever is said to be true. You cry when you see others crying. You laugh when you see others laughing.

It is often the case that people with religious faith lack the wisdom that distinguishes right from wrong. Because they do not have much judgment, they blindly follow others. They are like the animals in the story of Chicken Little. The chicken thought the sky was falling and everyone else believed him and ran away too. The Tibetan analogy is to say someone is like a droplet of water on flat surface which can be pushed in any direction.

In summary, the benefit of wisdom is that it enables us to attain whatever we want—from the most ordinary worldly goal all the way to perfect enlightenment.

(c') The divisions of wisdom

There are three divisions of wisdom:

(1') Wisdom that knows the ultimate
(2') Wisdom that knows the conventional
(3') Wisdom that knows how to act for the welfare of living beings

Wisdom is usually divided into realization of ultimate truth and realization of conventional truth. In the practice of the Mahayana, knowing how to benefit other sentient beings is so important that it is discussed separately.

(1') Wisdom that knows the ultimate

According to Buddhism, the ultimate truth is selflessness, or emptiness. This is the teaching of śūnyatā. It is such a complex and deep subject that almost all the rest of the *Lamrim Chenmo* is devoted to explaining it. Simply put, the wisdom that knows the ultimate truth is the realization of selflessness. There are two ways to realize śūnyatā. The first is understanding an image of selflessness with discursive thought. In the beginning, we understand selflessness from study, reasoning, and analysis. When somebody describes something to us, we get an image in our mind. We can consider this image and come to understand it. Emptiness does not appear directly to inferential wisdom; only through meditation do we gain a direct realization of emptiness that does not depend upon a mental image. The second way of understanding the ultimate truth is direct perception.

(2') Wisdom that knows the conventional

Those who are striving for perfect enlightenment must realize both ultimate truth and conventional truth. There are five important areas of conventional knowledge. The *Ornament for the Mahayana Sutras* says:

> Without striving to master the five sciences,
> Even the best noble beings will not become omniscient.
> Therefore they must make an effort in these
> To defeat others, care for others, and know everything.

The purpose of studying these five sciences is to benefit other sentient beings. The reason that these five types of knowledge are mentioned in particular is because they assist bodhisattvas achieve their aim to help other sentient beings by leading them to emancipation or complete enlightenment. Each of the five sciences—language, logic, technology, medicine, and the inner science of Buddhism—has its own purpose, but the common function of all of them is to attain buddhahood.

In order to free other beings from suffering, a bodhisattva must be able to help them to eliminate the wrong views that cause them to act badly. The first two sciences, language and logic, are the means to defeat sentient beings' internal negative obstacles. For example, if others strongly hold on to a wrong view, they will not listen to you if you just say, "That is not right. You should not believe that." To overcome their destructive wrong view, we have to understand the profound meaning of the scriptures. For this we must understand various aspects of language, including grammar and so on. Once we understand the scriptures' import, we need to master logic in order to show others the faults of their viewpoint and the validity of the teachings. Logic is necessary to understand things that we cannot perceive directly through our senses. Those who hold wrong views cannot be easily taught without those first two sciences.

Bodhisattvas also offer help to those who do not hold wrong views. Some sentient beings have more affinity for the correct view, and we can introduce them to the path to freedom. To that end we offer them ordinary, temporary benefits. We help them with the third science—making things, such as art or buildings—and the fourth science—medicine. People respond positively when we help them in these temporal ways. They will like us and become willing to follow us. After developing that type of relationship, we can move on to our main objective—showing them the spiritual path. This is the fifth science, the inner science—knowledge of the spiritual practices, their objectives, their obstacles, and the methods and techniques of meditation on all the levels of the path. This also includes knowing karma and its results and the four noble truths. From conceptually understanding and then practicing all the practices of the path starting from the beginning, we attain various experiential realizations. Gradually, as our wisdom grows, our ignorance is cleared away until we attain omniscience. Then we have the real wisdom necessary to teach all of the scriptures that explain the Hinayana and Mahayana paths. That is the purpose of inner science.

(3') WISDOM THAT KNOWS HOW TO ACT FOR THE WELFARE OF LIVING BEINGS

This is the wisdom of knowing how to help sentient beings attain their objectives. There are two general categories of goals: temporary and ever-lasting.

Another way to put this is to say that there are goals for this life and goals for future lives. Bodhisattvas need to know how to help sentient beings in their present life with many temporal types of assistance. Benefiting them for their future lives includes knowing how to help them avoid falling into a lower rebirth and assisting them to continue to spiritually develop so they can eventually reach complete enlightenment. With this kind of wisdom and skill we can really help others.

(d') How to practice

Just as with the other perfections, when we are practicing to develop the three types of wisdom we do so in relation to the six superior qualities. Furthermore, the practice of wisdom is also connected with all the other perfections.

(e') A summary

We seek perfection for ourselves in order to help other sentient beings flawlessly. Without bodhicitta, not even wisdom is a bodhisattva activity. Compassion and love must be practiced continuously while we develop the different levels of wisdom. Without wisdom we cannot help others, so those who take bodhisattva precepts must strive to produce wisdom day and night in order to fulfill their promise to benefit all other sentient beings.

When we first enter the Mahayana path, we are nowhere close to the ten āryan bodhisattva levels. The wisdom of the higher bodhisattva stages is the object of our wishful prayers, because it gets rid of ignorance from the root. But merely wishing for these types of wisdom does not make them arise. The method to complete the accumulation of unsurpassable wisdom is to produce the three types of wisdom that were explained earlier. We have to study and make an effort to understand what these types of wisdom are, their function, their benefit, and the means to attain them. We will develop if we strive to learn; if we do not, we deliberately put ourselves in the dark. We will not know what is right and what is wrong. We may take the bodhisattva vows, but because we will not know what actions are contradictory to the vows, we will break them. When we create powerful negative karma, unpleasant circumstances may occur in this life, and of course after death we will fall down to the lowest kind of miserable rebirth. That is what it means to be destroyed by faults. And if in this life we do not desire to learn in order to produce wisdom, we create the karmic tendency to be unable to train in the bodhisattva practices in our future lives. Not wanting to listen or understand now makes our future ability to learn very weak. The opposite is also the case. Making a great effort to produce wisdom shields us from the downfall of breaking the precepts and creates a powerful predisposition for practicing the perfection of wisdom in our future lives. Future practice and development will come easily to us if we make a concerted effort to practice now. It will seem almost as if we know the practices already.

The key support of every sutra and tantric system of practice is the six perfections. Although the sutras and tantras explain the perfections differently, there is nothing in either system that is outside of the six perfections. Even the many mandalas and deities in the tantras are symbolic manifestations of the six perfections. We need confidence in our practice of the perfections to make successful progress on the path to enlightenment. During Tsongkhapa's time many people had a wrong idea about the critical elements of practice. Then, just as now, people liked to sit quietly and meditate, not doing other things or learning much. Even now, those who go off to caves to meditate often do not have much education or knowledge. Not fully understanding the meaning of the scriptures, they think that because the pure mind is free of all thought, all conceptual thoughts are wrong. They think the mind should be like a mirror without any reflection. They believe they should simply stop thinking, so study is unnecessary. With this attitude the practices of the five perfections other than meditative stabilization disappear. To help them understand that in order to attain complete enlightenment we must practice all six perfections, Tsongkhapa explains the perfections in detail with many scriptural citations. So far Tsongkhapa has extensively explained generosity, ethical discipline, patience, and joyous perseverance. He just quickly and briefly went over meditative stabilization and wisdom because these will be comprehensively discussed in the next two volumes.

Every bodhisattva who attains buddhahood does so in dependence upon practice of the six perfections. Asaṅga definitively says this in his *Bodhisattva Levels* at the conclusion of his explanation of each perfection. The practices of the six perfections are the single highway that leads to buddhahood for the bodhisattvas of the past, present, and future. The practice of the six perfections is like an ocean of Dharma. Just as the ocean is the source of various precious jewels, the six perfections are the source of all spiritual qualities, from the beginning of the path of accumulation to the attainment of buddhahood. Asaṅga says:

> Bodhisattvas who attain unsurpassed perfect enlightenment through these six perfections are known as a great river of good qualities and a great ocean of good qualities. Generosity [and so forth] is the precious cause of every marvelous quality for every sentient being. Thus these

and nothing else complete the immeasurable accumulations of merit and wisdom and their accordant result of unsurpassable perfect enlightenment.

Bodhisattvas see the needs of other sentient beings. They recognize that the best way to help them is to free them from misery and lead them to the highest goal. They know that before they can help others they have to be equipped to do it. They have to attain perfect enlightenment in order to help others perfectly. They therefore decide to attain the highest goal of buddhahood quickly. Perfect buddhahood consists of the highest perfection of body and mind—the rūpakāya and the dharmākaya. The causes of physical and mental perfection are the accumulations of merit and wisdom respectively. The way to accomplish these two accumulations is the practice of the six perfections. All the necessary activities to generate merit and wisdom are contained in these six. The six together are a cause perfectly accordant with the accomplishment of perfect enlightenment. So when we look for the best method to perfect ourselves, we will find only the six perfections; there is nothing outside of them. They are the best for ripening the mental continuum. There is no cause other than these six perfections.

Now our subject changes from how to perfect ourselves to how to best help others. The way to ripen the mental continuum of other sentient beings is our next topic.

❧ 15 ❧

Helping Others to Mature:
The Four Ways to Gather Disciples

(b) Training in the four ways to gather disciples that help others to mature
    (i)   What the four ways to gather disciples are
    (ii) The reason they are stipulated as four
    (iii) Their functions
    (iv) The need for those who gather a following to rely on them
    (v) A somewhat elaborate explanation

(b) Training in the four ways to gather disciples that help others to mature

THE GOAL OF MAHAYANA PRACTITIONERS is to help other sentient beings by freeing them from misery and leading them to perfect enlightenment. To achieve this goal we first have to make ourselves capable of benefiting others. We must attain perfect buddhahood because only someone with omniscience, perfect love, and compassion equally for all can truly benefit all others. So how do we become a perfect buddha? We remove our mental obscurations and mature our mental continuum through the practices of the six perfections. Then we are ready to help free others from the mental afflictions and obstructions to omniscience so that they too attain perfect knowledge, the highest compassion, and love.

Bodhisattvas have a sincere desire to help others. However, simply teaching the path out of compassion and love is not enough. Bodhisattvas need wisdom to know the best way to reach other sentient beings. It can take many steps to reach those who have never heard of spiritual matters and are oriented in a very different direction. There are hundreds of ways to help others because there are so many sentient beings experiencing so many varieties of samsaric misery. All of them need our help, but before we can do any-thing for any particular one, we have to develop a close relationship with them. If they are running around busy with their own affairs, we cannot teach them the methods to escape from misery. We need to draw others to us so that we can help them on a temporary or ultimate basis. There are four key methods to collect or gather sentient beings that are explained in five subtopics:

(i) What the four ways to gather disciples are
(ii) The reason they are stipulated as four
(iii) Their functions
(iv) The need for those who gather a following to rely on them
(v) A somewhat elaborate explanation

(i) What the four ways to gather disciples are

The four ways to gather disciples are: generosity, pleasant speech, using the instruction's meaning, and acting consistently. This is the way that bodhi-sattvas practice in relation to others. It is not too complicated. We need a foundation of friendship before we start giving spiritual teachings. To create a positive relationship we try to help others as much as possible with their immediate needs. So the first method, generosity, is obvious: we share things with others to make them happy. By giving we befriend others. They will come to like and trust us. This, however, is not ordinary generosity. Com-monplace, worldly generosity is giving something in hope of a return. A bodhisattva's purpose in giving is not self-centered; he or she gives ordinary things now because it enables the bodhisattva to give the person something so much greater later. Generosity is like waving to others to entice them to come over and join you at a picnic. If we have the opportunity to give oth-ers a little money or serve them in some way, we should do it to establish a relationship with them. After a while we can begin to offer them some spir-itual instruction to help them change their destructive habits.

Once we have a developed a close relationship with others, we employ the second method: speaking suitably and pleasantly. The Tibetan term literally means "to say pleasing words." This connotes giving good advice in a nice way. We give whatever guidance is necessary; it can be instruction regarding a temporary, ordinary goal, but of course the point is to give others the instruction they need to follow the path to freedom from misery and the attainment of enlightenment. People need to learn why they should practice, what to practice, how to practice, and so forth. The way to help people spir-itually is to educate them so they can actually practice. Our advice gives them the knowledge that will eliminate their ignorance about the problem, the goal, and the path to the goal.

Instruction alone is not enough to really help others. Once they understand the words and concepts, the third method is to help them utilize that instruction by putting it into practice. A doctor prescribes medicine and explains a course of therapy to a patient, but to be cured the patient has to follow the prescription. In this case, we explained the perfections and how to practice them; now we actually lead others to physically, verbally, and mentally practice according to the instructions. We lead them to utilize the teachings.

To effectively lead others to engage in spiritual practices, we have to practice those things ourselves. If we do not, it seems that we have no belief in the efficacy of the practices and others will not be comfortable following our advice. It is ineffective to tell others, "You should do this and you should not do that," if we do the opposite. But when people see us acting in accordance with our instruction they will trust us, because we are doing exactly what we suggest that they do. We inspire confidence in others when we gain experience and realizations by following our own advice. They will believe what we say. It is particularly important for a Mahayana practitioner to personally use every method he or she teaches to others.

Maitreya explains these four methods in verse in the *Ornament for the Mahayana Sutras:*

> Generosity is the same. Teaching that, making them take it up,
> And following the instruction oneself
> Are accepted as pleasant speech, utilizing the meaning,
> And acting according to the meaning respectively.

(ii) The reason they are stipulated as four

The buddhas and bodhisattvas help sentient beings in countless ways, but all these methods can be subsumed into these four practices. The primary way to achieve happiness is to engage in a spiritual practice that clears away ignorance, wrong views, doubts, and so forth. In order to engage in practice, we need to know how to do it. To learn how to do it, we need instruction regarding the proper path. To benefit from instruction, we have to find the teacher likeable and his or her advice worth following. If we are not happy to be around someone, we will go away and that person will have no way to help us. Thus to help others attain true and everlasting happiness, we first give them some material things to please them. Even Christian missionaries engage in this practice; they give food, medical care, and other forms of charity as a basis for offering spiritual help. In fact, these four methods to help others spiritually mature are sometimes translated as the *four conversions*. You may not like that phrase because of its connotation in association with other religions, but generosity does function that way here. In order to be able to lead others to engage in virtuous activity, our first task is to establish a positive relationship with them through generosity.

Once people like us, the real way to help them is to lead them to the spiritual path. We give them advice. To benefit from this advice they need encouragement to practice. If we do not do what we teach them to do, they will think, "Why are you telling me this? You are not doing it. You need somebody to make you do it!" They will not listen to us. However, if we engage in those practices, others will too because they think, "This will be beneficial because my teacher is doing it too." New students will enter the path, and those already practicing will become confident and secure. The *Ornament for the Mahayana Sutras* says:

> A method to benefit others,
> Causing understanding, causing involvement,
> And acting in accordance oneself
> Should be understood as the four ways to gather.

(iii) Their functions

What do these four methods to gather others do for the disciples? There are many purposes of generosity, such as fulfilling others' temporary needs by easing their hunger and so forth. Although material goods do not last forever, they do give others temporary satisfaction. However, that kind of fulfillment does not provide any ultimate benefit. Of more importance here is that generosity makes people like their benefactor. Generosity makes people willing to listen to religious instruction given by their supporter. In short, generosity makes someone a suitable disciple.

The function of the second method, pleasant speech, makes disciples enthusiastic about the subject explained. Through instruction they come to understand the details of the practices. This cuts away their doubts and they become determined to attain the goal of everlasting happiness and peace for all sentient beings. If we teach while desiring to become famous and surrounded by many followers, our activities are self-centered. Externally our actions look the same as a bodhisattva's activities, but the motivation is very different. If one's motivation is pure compassion, even if one's external action is rough, the result will be great. If the motivation is selfish, even what looks like the most beneficial and peaceful activity is not part of real practice. It is difficult to know what is going on by judging just the surface; we must train the mind so it does not fall into egotism and is always subject to love and compassion for others.

Once others want to engage in the practices to attain a spiritual goal, they need help putting the instructions into practice. The function of the third method is to help them practice in order to attain their goal. The function of the fourth method—the teacher engaging in the practices that he or she teaches to others—is that disciples will not turn away from the path and will become more grounded in their practice. Again Tsongkhapa refers to a stanza from the *Ornament for the Mahayana Sutras:*

> The first makes a suitable vessel.
> The second makes them aspire.
> The third makes them practice.
> The fourth makes them train.

(iv) THE NEED FOR THOSE WHO GATHER A FOLLOWING TO RELY ON THEM

The buddhas taught that these four methods are the best for accomplishing the goals of others. We should therefore rely on these methods if we are gathering disciples so that they can achieve their goals. The *Ornament for the Mahayana Sutras* says:

> Those who are gathering disciples
> Should properly rely on this method.
> This method will accomplish the goal of all.
> It is praised as the excellent method.

(v) A SOMEWHAT ELABORATE EXPLANATION

Now Tsongkhapa provides a little bit more detail on three of these four methods. He does not elaborate on generosity here because it was discussed in detail in the explanation of the perfection of generosity. (See chapters 9 and 10 of this volume.) We begin with pleasant speech. This is giving whatever advice is needed. Not everybody needs the same advice; every teaching is not suitable for everyone at the same time. We have to teach according to the level of the person receiving the instruction. In general, pleasant speech has two divisions: the lower part is ordinary, worldly advice and the higher is spiritual teaching about the path to enlightenment. A bodhisattva can give advice to help other sentient beings succeed in ordinary situations. Even this type of common instruction has to be done in the proper way for it to be helpful. We must follow common sense and good manners so that others come to trust us and listen to us. For example, we should smile and say nice things like, "How are you?" to make others feel comfortable.

The second facet of pleasant speech is to give religious instruction to benefit other sentient beings temporarily and ultimately. Remember, instruction on any topic—such as faith, ethical discipline, study, generosity, and wisdom—should be at a level that is suitable to the listeners. We begin with easy things and later give more complex advice. For example, in the beginning some people do not even believe in the existence of the spiritual goal, moral causality, future lives, the Three Jewels, the path leading to emancipation, and so forth. Instructing these people on faith is in order to directly or indirectly bring them closer to having a pure interest in these topics. It is not explaining *faith* itself; it is helping others understand various subjects so that trust will arise in their minds. To those who already have some faith but do not engage in proper conduct, we teach the details of karmic causation and the benefits and nature of ethical discipline. In the beginning, most people do not want to study or listen. We must give them various reasons to study and open their minds. Generosity and wisdom are examples of the various subjects on which we give instruction.

Some people are easy to teach: they find us agreeable and want to be helped. We have to learn how to instruct the more difficult ones. We need to practice in our imagination how to act and what to say in even the worst situations. For example, it is not easy to deal with people who are so full of hatred that they want to kill you. A bodhisattva immediately recognizes that such people have no control over their emotions. Bodhisattvas know that killing and injuring others will cause the perpetrator problems in this life and in the future will cause disastrous rebirths. A bodhisattva's compassion is so strong that instead of responding harshly, he or she says kind words to calm someone like this down. The speech of such bodhisattvas is like cool water poured on a blazing fire; they know what to say to stop that person from hurting others.

We also must work at developing an ability to teach those who always misbehave and are very slow to learn. There are some people who never seem to understand, no matter what we say and no matter how many times we try to explain something. Instead of giving up, we should joyfully take on the hardship of teaching. We should have patience because we recognize that this person needs so much more help than an ordinary person. We should encourage ourselves to work even harder to help this person learn. Some other people are so deceitful that they even try to mislead their spiritual teachers. They are not earnest. We should not get angry when we come in contact with such people. Compassion and love should make us desire to help them correct their behavior and eliminate their ignorance. In summary, it is not easy to instruct others. We will not be able to do everything perfectly right away. We work a little bit here, try hard to do something else, and at some point we will succeed.

There are many levels of instruction, from ordinary advice regarding polite behavior in social situations all the way up to teachings that lead to freedom from all samsara and the perfect bliss of enlightenment. What we teach depends upon the level of maturity of the disciple. There are sentient beings whose mental continuums have not developed in the religious sense. They lack knowledge and are under the power of ignorance and attachment to the pleasures of this life. All their actions are directed toward accumulating wealth, fame, or sensual pleasure. They engage in wrong conduct because they are unable to control themselves. They get angry when they do not get what they seek; they become jealous when they see that others have something better. Such people have no interest in the spiritual path or accumulating merit in order to have a good rebirth. To these people we should teach the practices of generosity and ethical discipline so that in their next life they will have a high rebirth with every requisite type of wealth. These are not deep or profound topics; they are something that ordinary people can do in a simple way in the course of their daily lives. They can practice generosity by giving to the poor, serving the sick, tending animals, and so forth. They can practice ethical conduct by avoiding killing, lying, or other negative actions. A simple practice of these—even without meditation, great realization, or a vow—will bring a good rebirth and reduce obscurations. It is very important at the beginning of religious practice.

Those who are more spiritually advanced are not attached to worldly sensual pleasure. They have a spiritual focus; they are looking beyond this life. They have somewhat reduced their obscurations and are enthusiastic about practice. Such people have the capacity to stay simply and quietly, meditate, and develop realizations. These people can be shown more advanced teachings on the practice of the path that frees them from the causes of suffering—such as the four noble truths, for example. Some people, whether lay or ordained, are careless and wild. They are not serious about religious subjects. To these people we give teachings to urge them to be conscientious about their practice. Other people may be serious about practice but have a lot of uncertainty; they need us to discuss various topics in great detail to relieve their doubts.

The third method is helping disciples use the instructions. Leading others to practice has two parts: ripening the minds of those who are not yet spiritually matured, and teaching those who are already mature the practices leading to liberation. The latter can be divided into three types. The first is a beginner—someone who is interested in religious practice but is still involved in this life. This type of disciple is not able to completely give up his or her concerns about survival, prosperity, and pleasure. Such disciples devote time and energy to collecting, protecting, and increasing their wealth and other sources of sustenance. Even these activities can be done with a motivation that is harmonious with the Dharma. We can show them how to live without cheating, killing, or any other negative action. Their worldly pursuits can be virtuous, or at least neutral, actions. Their accumulation of wealth can be used for positive religious purposes.

The second type of disciple is not attached to this life; he or she is more enthusiastic about practicing for the benefit of future lives. Therefore, the emphasis in our instruction is how to use this life for future benefit rather than how to live in this life. Instead of accumulating wealth in this life, we show them how they can live very simply, perhaps even by begging. In this country begging is culturally unacceptable; in Asia, however, in ancient times begging symbolized a life of simplicity and being satisfied with whatever one had. Even nowadays we lead this type of person toward a religious life, especially toward ordination. Many vows and some hardships come with ordination because monks and nuns give up fancy clothes, entertainment, and so forth. We show these disciples that staying somewhere quietly to do religious practice will not make them unhappy or have problems when they are focused on future rebirths. This type of lifestyle may not make this life particularly pleasant, but it will definitely bring happiness in the future.

We help the third type of disciple, whether lay or ordained, achieve aims in both this life and future lives. We help such a disciple practice to become free from ordinary mundane attachment and uncommon supramundane attachment. The first practice is to become temporarily free from the mental afflictions, particularly attachment to self, wealth, and name. The second practice, that of the supramundane path, gets rid of attachment from the root so that it is gone forever. Both of these require special meditation practices. The details are complicated so I give a brief explanation only.

To understand the method to become temporarily free of ordinary attachment, one has to know the structure of the universe according to Asian cosmology. There are three realms of samsara: the desire, form, and formless realms. We live in the desire realm. The highest part of the desire realm is the heavenly abodes of the gods. Above the gods of the desire realm are four heavenly concentration levels of form realm deities. Even beyond that are the four mental absorptions of the formless realm. We cannot be reborn in even the first and lowest level of the form realm if we have attachment to the desire realm. The abhidharma literature says that if we want to reduce our attachment to this world temporarily, we should learn about the superior qualities of the first level of the form realm. Then we compare our current situation— a short life with an ugly, dirty physical body that experiences pain, needs food to survive, and must eliminate waste—to the first concentration level of the form realm, where life is long and peaceful and the body is light. When we contemplate this comparison with single-pointed concentration, we will want those better qualities. Our attachment to the desire realm will be eliminated and we will achieve the first concentration of the form realm. Doing this type of comparison—comparing the disadvantages of the level we are on to the advantages of next higher one—we can go up through the eight levels of the form and formless realms.

Achieving these higher stages does not require practicing Buddhism; any yogi with single-pointed concentration can do it. The process is similar to a familiar psychological experience; if we have a strong sexual attachment to someone, but then see someone who seems to be a hundred times more attractive, we start to compare these two people. When we see that our former lover is no match for our new friend, our attachment for the first person fades away. Although our attachment to the first person is eliminated, we have not gotten rid of the seed of sexual attachment to others. Similarly, our sharp present attachment to the desire realm can be removed by a comparison meditation, but it yields only temporary freedom from lower states because it does not remove attachment from the root. In order to completely eliminate the root of attachment we need the higher practices of the supramundane path. The cause that eliminates attachment forever is a realization of selflessness. The practices of the supramundane path therefore include meditation on the four noble truths and emptiness. Without meditating on emptiness we will not be able to permanently get rid of misery because self-centered egotism creates all the problems and suffering in the world.

Practitioners who engage in the mundane and supramundane practices to eliminate attachment attain a special mental and physical bliss in this life. While they meditate their bodies feel light and all unpleasantness is gone. In addition, these practices free them from future suffering. During a life in the first concentration of the form realm one has no physical or mental suffering. However, the problem with the form and formless realms is that when that life is over, one can be reborn into the desire realm. If we engage in the supramundane practices to eliminate attachment we can attain the everlasting freedom of nirvana and enlightenment. We should encourage and assist others to do these practices that lead to happiness in this and future lives.

Some people are easy to lead, but it may seem almost impossible to help others put the teachings into practice. It is very difficult to help those who do not have much inclination for religious practice because they did not create much merit in this or their past lives. Although they have big obstacles to learning, we should try to teach them to do meritorious things. It is also a challenge to encourage those who have a lot of wealth to undertake a religious practice. The rich are happy in an ordinary samsaric sense—they have few obvious problems, so it is difficult for them to have an interest in eliminating suffering. It is also a lot of work to assist those who dogmatically hold to the world-view of another religion. They are so accustomed to their beliefs that they have a negative view about karma, emancipation, and the path system. Although it is difficult, we should be compassionate and strive to help them change their incorrect opinions. In all these cases we begin by giving those with limited wisdom instructions that are easy to follow. As they become better, we give them the intermediate level instruction. Only when their wisdom is more extensive do we give them the profoundest teachings.

It is important for religious teachers to practice what they encourage others to do. The teacher must believe, understand, and live according to those practices for his or her instruction to be effective. A bodhisattva's primary aim is to benefit other sentient beings. Training oneself is an essential part of this, because it is the only way to successfully lead others. Before he attained enlightenment, even Buddha Śakyamuni had to discipline himself; in other words, he practiced for many lives. The *Praise of Infinite Qualities* lauds the Buddha for this consistency of behavior:

> "Someone who has not disciplined himself may give correct instruction,
> However he cannot tame others because he acts contrary to his own
>   words."
> Knowing the meaning of this you kept all sentient beings in mind,
> And endeavored to control those aspects of yourself that were not tamed.

Even though we discuss four ways of gathering disciples, there are really just two methods: attracting people with material goods and attracting people with religion. The first of the four methods—generosity—is the former. The other three—giving advice, helping others practice according to that advice, and behaving in harmony with what we teach—are ways to gather disciples with the Dharma. From the perspective of how these three help people spiritually, we can understand them as teaching the objects of instruction, giving advice on what and how to practice, and accomplishing purification and development by putting the former two into actual practice.

These four ways to help others have been used by the great bodhisattvas of the past, present, and future. This is how all former buddhas have helped others. Future buddhas will do it this way. And this is how buddhas right now are practicing. It is the route that everyone follows because it leads to the benefit of others. The *Ornament for the Mahayana Sutras* says:

> Those who have gathered, will gather,
> And are gathering right now,
> All do it like this.
> Therefore this is the way to mature sentient beings.

The actions of great Mahayana practitioners are beyond measure because bodhisattvas do not help just one or two sentient beings; they dedicate their actions to benefit all sentient beings. They do not offer just temporary help; bodhisattvas want to give everyone the most perfect, highest peace. To be able to do this they must have those high qualities themselves. There is nothing more to the bodhisattva path than training oneself to help others and then helping others. Thus all of the millions upon millions of bodhisattva practices can be summarized into the six perfections and the four ways of gathering disciples. The six perfections are for the purpose of achieving enlightenment oneself in order to help others. The method to help others once we have the supreme qualities of buddhahood is the four ways of gathering. Asaṅga says in the *Bodhisattva Levels:*

> The six perfections completely ripen the qualities of my buddhahood.
> The four ways of gathering disciples completely mature all sentient beings. You should know that these two are the sum of all bodhisattvas' virtuous actions.

For more detail on these two aspects of practice you can read the *Bodhisattva Levels.*

Atiśa explains how to practice these four ways of gathering disciples both during a meditation session and in between sessions:

> From the path of accumulation onward,
> During meditation and upon arising,

> Yogis practice the bodhisattva practices:
> The vast waves of the six perfections

From the beginning of the bodhisattva path—the path of accumulation—bodhisattvas practice the six perfections. There is nothing beyond these six; all a bodhisattva's activities, whether during meditation or between meditation sessions, are included in the perfections. Some of the perfections are practiced during meditation and some are practiced when not meditating. We practice the perfection of meditative stabilization primarily during meditation. The aspect of the perfection of wisdom known as superior insight—the wisdom of meditating on ultimate reality—is practiced during meditation. The first three perfections—generosity, ethical discipline, and patience—are practiced primarily between meditation sessions. Of course, every action has to be done with proper understanding of what we are doing, the object, the doer, and the action, so an aspect of the perfection of wisdom is practiced at this time too.

The perfection of joyous perseverance applies to both what is practiced during meditation and subsequent to meditation. Patience also can be understood to have two aspects. We usually think of patience as a practice engaged in when not meditating; however, one type of patience is a deep and profound realization of the truth. This realization is called *patience* because it is attained by meditating on something that we usually do not want to accept. Ultimate reality is the opposite of what we ordinarily perceive. It is something way beyond our usual understanding. This aspect of patience is a special kind of peaceful confidence that arises during meditation and helps us when we arise from meditation. Atiśa says this in verse as follows:

> When you have arisen from meditation
> Think of the eight similes for illusion.
> By meditating on the right view of all phenomena
> You purify your subsequent conceptions.

There are eight similes to help us understand how nothing exists as it appears: a magician's illusory creation, dreams, mirages, reflections in a mirror, shadows, echoes, reflections of the moon in water, and emanations. During meditation we may have a deep understanding of śūnyatā, but when we arise from meditation everything appears in the opposite way. Things seem to be real, independent, dualistic, and so forth. We usually accept things as they appear and then become attached to them. During meditation, however, we have now recognized that everything is illusory, even though appearing to be real. We also need to remember this when we are not in meditation sessions in order to train the mind to cease wrong grasping.

If we practice this way life after life, thinking in this manner will become spontaneous and natural. If we do not even try, because we think we cannot succeed, then we will never be able to do it. We will drift further and further away from the path. The positive way to practice is to want to do certain things even though we cannot do them now. With that willing attitude, we will eventually be able to get there. The following quotation from the *Praise of Infinite Qualities* describes how the Buddha did this:

> Even you were not able to practice for a long time
> Certain actions that were painful for the worldly to hear about.
> From practice over time these deeds became natural;
> If you do not practice, these good qualities remain difficult.

Buddha Śākyamuni was not always a buddha. In the beginning he was like us; there were many things he could not do. Achieving certain things requires a lot of diligence and a positive attitude over a long period of time. The future Buddha had the courage to try. Even though he was not able to practice many things at the start, eventually he became perfect.

If we do not practice we will not become accustomed to superior qualities and they will always be difficult. Therefore, there is no way for those who have taken the bodhisattva vow to not train in these methods. The vows are a promise to help other sentient beings. However, this does not mean that we will be able to do everything right from the start. There are many things that we will not be able to do right away. But we should aim toward them. The only way to become able to do them is to practice.

Many people have not ritually taken the bodhisattva vow, but they can still make an effort to train the mind through study and practice. Through learning about the benefits of these qualities they will develop a positive desire to do these practices. They will eventually become happy to do them and will joyfully take the vows. However, we should not take the vows blindly. Before we do something like this we should carefully examine their purpose. When we determine, "I really want to do this," then we are ready to take the vows. Once we take the vows, we should try to follow them and practice as much as possible. Taking the vows in this way will make our practice become firm and stable.

This concludes the general explanation of the path for persons of great spiritual capacity. It includes training on both aspirational bodhicitta—wanting to attain perfect buddhahood in order to help all sentient beings—and, after that motivation has been developed, engaging in the actions to attain buddhahood quickly—taking the vow and acting accordingly. By taking the vow we become a child of Buddha—that is, a bodhisattva—and engage in the bodhisattva activities: the six perfections to train ourselves and the four methods to gather disciples to help others.

The explanation of the practices for Mahayana practitioners is not yet complete. In the next two volumes of this series the perfections of meditative stabilization and wisdom will be explained in detail. These profound subjects are treated separately because they are so profound that they require a great deal of explanation.

Appendix: Outline of the Text

THE OUTLINE USED in the commentary was created by Tsongkhapa to organize his massive text. We have used the same outline so that readers of this commentary can refer to the relevant sections of the original Tibetan and the English translation of the *Lamrim Chenmo.* To make it as easy as possible for readers to use this commentary along with the English translation of the *Lamrim Chenmo,* The Lamrim Chenmo Translation Committee and Snow Lion Publications graciously gave us permission to use their format of the outline headings. We also follow their practice of including the outline for each chapter's content at the beginning of the chapter. While our translation of some terms differs from the English translation of the *Lamrim Chenmo,* these differences are minimal and should not cause any confusion.

In this appendix, two sets of numbers follow each outline topic. The first number refers the reader to the page on which this topic is discussed in this commentary. The second number refers the reader to the page in the edition of the Tibetan text published by the People's Press, mTsho sngon, Xining, 1985, and reprinted in Dharamsala, 1991. To find the page number in the English translation of the *Lamrim Chenmo, The Great Treatise on the Stages of the Path to Enlightenment,* the reader should refer to appendix 1 of that work.

CHAPTER 1
THE STAGES OF THE PATH FOR PERSONS OF GREAT CAPACITY

3) Training the mind in the stages of the path for persons of great spiritual capacity [17, 281]
   a) Showing that developing bodhicitta is the only entrance to the Mahayana [18, 282]
   b) How to develop bodhicitta [33, 289]
      i) How bodhicitta depends on certain causes to arise [33, 289]
         a' The way to produce bodhicitta depending on four conditions [33, 289]
         b' The way to produce bodhicitta depending on four causes [38, 291]
         c' The way to produce bodhicitta depending on four powers [38, 291]

CHAPTER 2
COMPASSION, THE ENTRANCE TO THE MAHAYANA

CHAPTER 3
THE SEVENFOLD CAUSE-AND-EFFECT PERSONAL INSTRUCTIONS

CHAPTER 4
EXCHANGING SELF AND OTHER

CHAPTER 9
THE PERFECTION OF GENEROSITY

CHAPTER 10
HOW TO GIVE

Chapter 11
The Perfection of Ethical Discipline

CHAPTER 13
THE PERFECTION OF PERSEVERANCE

CHAPTER 14
THE PERFECTIONS OF MEDITATIVE STABILIZATION AND WISDOM

CHAPTER 15
HELPING OTHERS TO MATURE:
THE FOUR WAYS TO GATHER DISCIPLES

Glossary

Abhidharma *(chos mngon pa)*. The Abhidharma, one of three major sections of the Buddhist canon, contains texts that systemize and classify the essence of the Buddha's teachings found in the sutras. This body of commentarial texts is encyclopedic in that it deals with Buddhist ontology, psychology, cosmology, the operation of karma and affliction, the path to liberation, and the nature of its stages and attainments. *See also* Tripiṭaka.

absorption of cessation *(dgog pa'i snyoms 'jug)*. A level of meditative absorption, similar to but higher than the absorption of nondiscrimination, that arrests the mind and mental factors. By cultivating this absorption one will be reborn in the Peak of Existence, the highest level of the formless realm.

active bodhicitta *('jug pa'i sems bskye)*. *See* bodhicitta.

affectionate love *(yid 'ong byams pa)*. The feeling that all other sentient beings are dear and appealing.

afflictions *(nyon mongs)*. *See* mental afflictions.

anātma *(bdag med)*. The emptiness *(śūnyatā)* or lack of an independent, inherently existent self. *See also* śūnyatā.

arhat *(dgra bcom pa)*. A person who has attained nirvana, the final goal of the Hinayana path.

ārya *('phags pa)*. A person who has achieved a direct realization of emptiness *(śūnyatā)*, the true nature of all phenomena. Literally, *ārya* means "noble" or "superior" being. *See also* ordinary individual.

aryan stage *('phags pa'i lam)*. Stages of the path including and subsequent to the first moment of the path of seeing, where one achieves a direct realization of emptiness, the true nature of all phenomena.

aspirational bodhicitta *(smon pa'i byang chub kyi sems)*. *See* bodhicitta.

Avīci *(mnar med pa)*. The lowest level of the eight great hot hells, in which there is the greatest suffering.

bardo *(bar do)*. Intermediate state between death and the next rebirth.

bhikṣu *(dge slong)*. Fully ordained monk.

bhikṣuṇī *(dge slong ma)*. Fully ordained nun.

bhūmi *(sa)*. Bodhisattva stages.

bodhicitta *(byang chub kyi sems)*. The altruistic mind of enlightenment. The desire to become a buddha in order to benefit other sentient beings caught in the misery of samsara. The term *bodhicitta* is used in multiple contexts. It can be divided into aspirational bodhicitta and active or engaging bodhicitta. Aspirational bodhicitta *(smon pa'i sems bskye)*, the spontaneous and continuous desire to attain complete enlightenment in order to benefit all other sentient beings, is the entrance to the Mahayana path. After developing aspirational bodhicitta, one practices engaging bodhicitta *('jug pa'i sems bskye)* by taking the bodhisattva vow and actively engaging in the bodhisattva deeds. Bodhicitta can also be divided into phenomenal and ultimate bodhicitta. Phenomenal bodhicitta is the altruistic mind of enlightenment, while ultimate bodhicitta *(don dam sems bskyed)* is the bodhisattva's direct realization of the ultimate truth, śūnyatā.

bodhisattva *(byang chub sems dpa')*. A person who has entered the Mahayana path. Such beings have a continuous, spontaneous wish to attain enlightenment in order to benefit other sentient beings.

body-mind continuum. *See* five aggregates.

Bön *(bon)*. The religious tradition that dominated Tibet before the advent of Buddhism.

cakravartin king *('khor lo sgyur ba'i rgyal po)*. World emperor.

cyclic existence *('khor ba)*. *See* samsara.

desire realm *('dod khams)*. One of the three realms of existence in which beings in the samsaric world live. The three realms are the desire, form, and formless realms. Each realm is dominated by particular types of afflictions; the predominant affliction in the desire realm is desire or attachment—in particular the craving for the sensual pleasures of sex and food.

deva *(lha)*. Deities or gods. In Buddhism, those beings called gods have extremely pleasurable and long lives, but they are still caught in samsara. Their lives are not permanent, and they do not have the power to end their own or others' cycle of misery.

Dharma *(chos)*. The teachings of the Buddha and his followers.

Dharma of realization *(rtogs pa'i chos)*. The realization of the teachings of ethical conduct, concentration, and wisdom in the practitioner's mind.

Dharma of scripture *(lung gi chos)*. All the texts in the Tripiṭaka.

dharmadhātu *(chos kyi dbyings)*. Sphere of phenomena; in other words, emptiness.

dharmakāya *(chos sku)*. One of three *kāyas,* or bodies of the buddha, which are the goal of enlightenment in the Mahayana. The three *kāyas* are the dharmakāya, saṃbhogakāya, and nirmāṇakāya. The dharmakāya—the wisdom body—is ultimate and immaculate wisdom; it is the mind that has been transformed beyond all states of impurity. The latter two bodies—the saṃbhogakāya and the nirmāṇakāya—are together called the form body of a buddha. These are manifestations of perfect wisdom in various forms.

dhyāna *(bsam gtan)*. One of four levels of meditative concentration of the form realm, each higher than the last. *See also* meditative stabilization.

downfall *(ltung ba)*. An action that might not necessarily be negative if performed by a layperson who has not taken any vows, but is negative if it involves breaking a vow one has taken. *See also* misdeed.

eight vows of individual liberation *(so thar rigs brgyad)*. The eight types of prātimokṣa vows. *See also* prātimokṣa vows.

eight worldly concerns *('jig rten chos brgyad)*. Also known as the eight worldly dharmas. Preoccupation with gain and loss, pleasure and pain, praise and scorn, and fame and ill repute. These four pairs encapsulate the concerns of ordinary people, who desire to attain the first in each pair and avoid the second.

eighteen unmixed qualities *(ma 'dres pa bco brgyad)*. The eighteen unmixed or unique qualities are qualities that only a buddha possesses and that demonstrate his attainment of perfection: (1) a buddha is without error in physical activities; (2) he does not cry out excitedly (as when one has lost one's way); (3) he never forgets the appropriate time for a particular action; (4) he is always in a state of meditation; (5) he does not have diverse conceptions such as "samsara is misery, nirvana is peace"; (6) he does not neglect beings through inattentiveness; (7) he is unfaltering in his aspiration to act on behalf of beings; (8) he is unfaltering in his fortitude; (9) he is unfaltering in his recollection that he is committed to the goal of aiding all sentient beings; (10) he is unfaltering in his one-pointed concentration that focuses on the ultimate nature of all things; (11) he is unfaltering in the wisdom that knows beings' minds and knows what Dharma to teach them; (12) he never wavers from deliverance (i.e., the desire to deliver all beings from suffering); (13) all his bodily acts are preceded by and in agreement with transcendent wisdom; (14) all his verbal acts are preceded by and in agreement with transcendent wisdom; (15) all his mental acts are preceded by and in agreement with transcendent wisdom; (16) his wisdom perceives the past without obstruction or impediment; (17) his wisdom perceives the future without obstruction or impediment; and (18) his wisdom perceives the present without obstruction or impediment.

eleven activities for others' welfare *(gzhan don bya ba bcu gcig)*. The actions of a bodhisattva to fulfill the eleven needs of sentient beings on both a temporary and ultimate basis. *See also* eleven types of living beings. The way to help others is the third type of ethical discipline. *See also* ethical discipline.

eleven types of living beings *(sems can rnam pa bcu gcig):* (1) Sentient beings who need immediate and direct help, (2) Sentient beings who do not know how to achieve what they desire, (3) Sentient beings who need material or spiritual assistance, (4) Sentient beings who are in fear, (5) Sentient beings who are in misery, (6) Sentient beings who are in poverty, (7) Sentient beings who need some place to stay when traveling, (8) Sentient beings who want friends or agreeable companions, (9) Sentient beings who desire to enter the practice that leads to nirvana or enlightenment, (10) Sentient beings who are on a wrong path and need help to reverse direction, (11) Sentient beings who need extraordinary, miraculous help.

emptiness *(stong pa nyid; Skt: śūnyatā)*. Suchness; the final nature of all phenomena: their absence of inherent existence.

energy channel *(rtsa; Skt: nāḍī)*. The "veins" of the psychic nervous system through which the energy wind, or energy breath, flows. *See also* energy wind.

energy wind *(rlung; Skt: vāyu).* The subtle energy that flows through the subtle nervous system and carries consciousness.

engaging bodhicitta *('jug pa'i sems bskye). See* bodhicitta.

enlightenment *(byang chub).* The ultimate spiritual goal for Mahayana practitioners: the state of buddhahood. A buddha's mind is purified of all obstacles and their causes, and is omniscient—knowing every aspect of reality.

environmental results *(bdag po'i 'bras bu).* Karmic results that manifest as one's external environment, possessions, and material circumstances.

equanimity *(btang snyoms).* There are three different uses of the term *equanimity* on the Buddhist path. The first is in the context of developing single-pointed concentration *('du byed btang snyoms),* and refers to leaving the mind alone when it is functioning properly. The second use of the term is when discussing the three basic types of feeling: unhappiness, happiness, and a neutral, equanimous feeling *(tshor ba btang snyoms).* The third type of equanimity is in the context of the preparatory practice of the four immeasurables: equanimity *(tshad med btang snyoms),* compassion, love, and joy. Immeasurable equanimity means being even-minded, free from attachment or hostility toward living beings.

ethical discipline *(tshul khrims; Skt: śīla).* Pure ethical conduct; the first of the three trainings and the second perfection. There are three aspects to a bodhisattva's ethical discipline: the ethical conduct of the vows *(sdom pa'i tshul khrims),* the ethical conduct of practicing virtue to create the merit to attain enlightenment *(dge ba'i chos 'jug gi tshul khrims),* and the ethical discipline of actively helping others by taking action with one's body, speech, and mind *(sems chen thams cad gi tshul khrims).*

exchanging self and others *(bdag gzhan mnyam brje).* A method to produce bodhicitta developed and explained by Śāntideva in *Engaging in the Bodhisattva Deeds.*

extreme of existence *(srid mtha'). See* extreme of samsara.

extreme of peace *(zhi mtha').* The state of nirvāṇa, where one remains in enjoyment of one's own liberation from samsara without concern for other sentient beings. The extreme of peace and the extreme of samsara must both be avoided by bodhisattvas. *See also* extreme of samsara.

extreme of samsara *(srid mtha')*. Uncontrolled rebirth due to karma and the mental afflictions. *See also* extreme of peace.

extremely hidden phenomena *(shin tu lkog tu gyur pa)*. One of the three types of objects of knowledge. The first two are phenomena that can be known directly through the senses and those that can be inferred using logic to examine evidence. Extremely hidden phenomena are those that are too subtle for ordinary beings to know by either of these two means. To know these phenomena one must put trust in the statements of the Buddha until one attains the realizations that bring direct knowledge. *See also* objects of knowledge.

faith *(dad pa)*. There are three levels of faith. The first is clear or pure faith *(dang ba'i dad pa)*, a sincere, but rather superficial, trust and happiness to practice the Dharma. The second and stronger type of faith is the faith of conviction *(yid ches kyi dad pa)* founded on some background knowledge, seeing the logic of the matter, and bringing personal experience to bear. As our logical and experiential understanding increases, we produce the third and strongest kind of faith, irreversible faith *(phyir mi ldog pa'i dad pa)*.

five aggregates *(phung po lnga)*. Form, feeling, discrimination, formative activity, and consciousness. Ignorance causes us to grasp at these impermanent collections as a unitary, inherently existent self. This self-grasping is a fundamental cause of our perpetual suffering in cyclic existence.

five paths *(lam lnga)*. The five consecutive paths leading to or culminating in enlightenment. These consist of: (1) the path of accumulation *(tshogs lam)*, during which one begins to amass the accumulation of merit and wisdom that will ripen in enlightenment; (2) the path of preparation *(sbyor lam)*, so named because (apart from Hinayana ārya beings or arhats who enter into the Mahayana paths later) practitioners are preparing for a direct realization of emptiness, during which they progress through four levels as their conceptual understanding of emptiness becomes more and more subtle: heat, peak, patience, and supreme dharma; (3) the path of seeing *(mthong lam)*, during which one sees emptiness directly and nonconceptually for the first time and ceases to be an ordinary individual, becoming an ārya being (This description does not apply to practitioners who become āryas or arhats on the Hinayana paths and later enter into the Mahayana paths. Such practitioners have already realized emptiness directly on the Hinayana paths; from the first bodhisattva ground up to and including the seventh, those arhats are engaged in fulfilling the accu-

mulation of merit and thereafter in removing the knowledge obstacles);
(4) the path of meditation *(sgom lam)* during which one repeatedly famil-
iarizes oneself with the emptiness that was initially and directly cognized
on the path of seeing, thereby gradually eliminating the obstacles connected with each stage of development; and (5) the path of no further
training *(mi slob lam),* in which there is no longer any need to abandon
further obstacles or develop new realizations. At this point the final fruit
of the different spiritual journeys is achieved; those who have followed
the Mahayana path of the bodhisattva attain perfectly complete buddhahood, while those who have followed the Hinayana path attain arhatship.

five sciences *(rig gnas che ba lnga).* The traditional list is: Buddhism, grammar, logic, the arts, and medicine.

form body *(gzugs sku; Skt: rūpakāya).* The saṃbhogakāya and nirmāṇakāya
are together called the form body of a buddha. They are manifestations
of perfect wisdom in various forms. *See also* saṃbhogakāya; nirmāṇakāya.

form realm *(gzugs khams).* Along with the desire realm and the formless realm,
one of the three realms of samsaric existence. Its basic divisions are the
four concentrations *(dhyāna).* Each of the first three concentrations has
three levels, and the fourth concentration has eight levels; a particular type
of "form-realm god" resides on each of these seventeen levels.

formless absorptions *(gzugs med snyoms 'jug; Skt: samāpatti).* The four formless absorptions are advanced states of meditative concentration. When
an individual attains one of these four progressive absorptions and then
passes away, he or she is born into one of the formless realms.

formless realm *(gzugs med khams).* Along with the desire realm and the form
realm, one of the three realms of samsaric existence. Beings in this realm
do not possess material form; the formless realm is without a physical
dimension. *See* formless absorptions.

four concentrations *(bsam gtan bzhi).* The four levels of existence in the form
realm. From the first through the fourth concentration *(dhyāna),* beings
abide in increasingly subtle levels of meditative absorption. *See also* form
realm.

four Dharma conclusions *(phyag rgya bzhi).* The understanding that: (1) all
composite phenomena are impermanent, (2) all contaminated things are
suffering, (3) all phenomena are selfless, and (4) nirvana is peace.

four fearlessnesses *(mi 'jigs pa bzhi)*. A buddha's self-confidence regarding having attained these qualities: (1) the full realization of all dharmas; (2) the knowledge that all his own mental afflictions have been terminated; (3) the ability to declare what things represent obstacles; and (4) the ability to declare what represents the path to emancipation.

four immeasurables. *See* four limitless thoughts.

four limitless thoughts *(tshad med bzhi):* (1) compassion—thinking how wonderful it would be if all sentient beings were free from all forms of misery; (2) love—thinking how wonderful it would be if they all possessed the highest happiness; (3) equanimity—thinking how wonderful it would be if they all were harmonious, having equanimity toward each other, without hatred or attachment; and (4) joy—thinking how wonderful it is that some beings have already obtained the highest happiness, some have intermediate happiness, and some at least have some small pleasure, and rejoicing in their happiness and good fortune. The virtue of this way of thinking is measureless, or limitless.

four noble truths *('phags pa'i bden pa bzhi)*. The principal subject matter of Buddha's first discourse: (1) the truth of suffering, (2) the truth of the cause of suffering, (3) the truth of the cessation of suffering, and (4) the truth of the path to cessation.

four ways to gather disciples *(bsdu ba'i dngos po bzhi)*. Generosity, pleasant speech, using the instructions' meaning, and acting consistently.

fourfold condensation of the teachings. *See* four Dharma conclusions.

fruitional result *(rnam smin gyi 'bras bu)*. The main result of the ripening of a karmic seed. The fruitional result is the type of rebirth you take and is distinguished from the *environmental results* and *results corresponding to the cause,* which together determine the variety of experiences one meets while in that particular type of rebirth.

garuḍa *(mkha' lding)*. The mythic king of birds who destroys poisonous snakes, which are symbolic of anger.

generosity without expectation or hope *(re ba med pa'i sbyin pa)*. The practice of generosity in which one dedicates even the merit generated by one's actions for the benefit of other sentient beings.

Gelug *(dge lugs)*. The school of Tibetan Buddhism founded by Tsongkhapa and his disciples.

geshe *(dge bshes)*. A contraction of *geyway sheynyen (dge ba'i bshes gnyen),* which means virtuous friend, spiritual friend, or guru. In the Gelug school of Tibetan Buddhism it is the title bestowed on those scholars who complete the course of study at one of the three great monasteries.

giving and taking *(gtong len)*. A core practice in the method to develop bodhicitta by exchanging self and other. Here one mentally gives others all one's possessions, including even one's merit, and takes all the misfortune and misery of others onto oneself.

great compassion *(snying rje chen po; Skt: mahākaruṇā)*. The desire to take responsibility to free all sentient beings from suffering.

Hinayana *(theg dman; Skt: Hīnayāna)*. The Vehicle of smaller scope, leading to the attainment of nirvana, personal liberation from suffering.

irreversible bodhisattva *(phyir mi ldog pa'i byang chub sems dpa')*. An aryan bodhisattva who has experienced a particular sign that he or she will never drop his or her practice of the Mahayana path.

ignorance *(ma rig pa)*. A lack of realization of the final nature of all phenomena; the innate belief that things exist as substantial, independent, self-sufficient entities.

intermediate state *(bar do)*. The state one enters after death and before one's next rebirth.

introspective awareness *(shes bzhin)*. A mental factor that, like a spy, constantly observes what is happening within one's mind-body continuum.

Jātaka tales *(skyes rabs)*. Homiletic stories about the previous lives of the Buddha when he was a bodhisattva on the path to full enlightenment.

kāyas *(sku)*. Bodies of the buddha: dharmakāya, saṃbhogakāya, and nirmāṇakāya, also known as the wisdom, enjoyment, and emanation bodies. These three can be coalesced into two: the dharmakāya or perfect mental body and the rūpakāya or the perfect physical body. The rūpakāya includes the saṃbhogakāya, and nirmāṇakāya.

Kadam *(bka' gdams)*. The school of Tibetan Buddhism established by followers of Atiśa.

kalpa *(bskal pa)*. Four billion, three hundred and twenty million years, commonly referred to as an eon.

Kangyur *(bka' 'gyur)*. The collection of Tibetan translations of the Buddha's teachings.

karma *(las). Literally,* "action." There is the contaminated action of sentient beings and the uncontaminated action of buddhas. Every contaminated action of body, speech, and mind plants a seed of potential on the mental continuum that will eventually ripen into experience. Virtuous action (i.e., virtuous karma) ripens into pleasant experience, and nonvirtuous action ripens into unpleasant experience.

kleśa *(nyon mongs). See* mental afflictions.

knowledge obstacles *(shes sgrib; Skt: jñeyāvaraṇa). See* obstructions to omniscience.

lamrim *(lam rim).* Literally, the "stages of the path." The lamrim method is a progressive system of teachings and meditations organized to lead the practitioner from the very beginning of the spiritual path, through the middle phase, and ultimately all the way to buddhahood.

league *(dpag tshad; Skt: yojana).* A free translation of the Sanskrit "yojana," a unit of distance measuring four thousand arm-lengths, about four and a half miles.

māras *(bdud).* Demonic forces. According to the *Ornament for Clear Knowledge (Abhisamayālaṃkāra),* the four māras are (1) the contaminated aggregates, (2) the mental afflictions, (3) death, and (4) the Divine-Youth demon, which represents the obstacles preventing one from overcoming the other three.

Madhyamaka *(dbu ma).* A Mahayana school of philosophy based on the writings of Nāgārjuna. It is called the Madhyamaka ("Middle Way") school because it teaches the doctrine of emptiness *(śūnyatā)* as a middle position between the extremes of nihilism and inherent existence. The Madhyamaka school is divided by Tibetan scholars into Prāsaṅgika Madhyamaka and Svātantrika Madhyamaka subschools. The Svātantrika is further subdivided into the Sautrāntika-Svātantrika-Madhyamaka and Yogācāra-Svātantrika-Madhyamaka.

Mahayana path *(theg chen gyi lam; Skt: mahāyāna).* An outline of the essential methods leading to the goal of perfect buddhahood. The Mahayana disciple wishes to become a buddha so that he or she can help free all other beings from suffering. In contrast, the goal for the followers of the Hinayana path is liberation from suffering for themselves alone.

mandala *(dkyil 'khor; Skt: maṇḍala).* In the tantric context *mandala* refers to the pure abode of a meditational deity. The term is also used to denote the traditional Buddhist representation of the physical universe as a circle of four continents surrounding Mount Meru. *See also* Mount Meru.

meditational deity *(yi dam)*. A tantric form of a buddha that a practitioner worships and strives to become. The deity, or *yidam,* guides the practitioner along the path to enlightenment; the practitioner's subsequent enlightenment will be experienced in the form and nature of that yidam.

meditative concentration *(ting nge 'dzin; Skt: samādhi)*. A correct fixation: a mental factor that holds the mind single-pointedly and continuously on an examined functional thing or mental object. Within the Buddhist path it is a virtuous mind that is single-pointed, abiding on its object without distraction to other objects. *See also* samadhi.

meditative stabilization *(bsam gtan; Skt: dhyāna)*. The mind remaining single-pointedly without distraction, unmixed with the stains of the mental afflictions. Also, a general term encompassing a wide variety of meditation practices and levels of concentration. It is the fifth perfection.

mental afflictions *(nyon mongs; Skt: kleśa)*. Obscuring mental states, such as desire, hostility, and ignorance, that are the obstacles to emancipation. These nonvirtuous mental states obscure the mind from seeing reality in its true nature and motivate actions *(karma)* that cause one to continue to be born in cyclic existence. Other translations of this term include "disturbing emotions," "afflicting emotions," "afflictions," and "negative mental states." *See also* obstructions to liberation.

mind training *(blo 'byong)*. A lineage, along with its literature and oral tradition, that expounds the method to develop bodhicitta called *exchanging self and others* among other topics.

mindfulness *(dran pa)*. A mental factor that functions to hold the mind to its object, not letting the mind forget about it or move away from it. Mindfulness is the quality of mind that does not forget which objects are suitable to engage in and which should be avoided.

misdeeds *(kha na ma tho ba)*. There are two categories of misdeeds or negative actions: those that are naturally bad *(rang bzhin gi kha na ma tho ba),* and those that are negative only within the context of breaking the rules one has promised to uphold as a result of taking vows *(bcas pa'i kha na ma tho ba)*.

mundane path *('jig rten pa'i lam)*. A method of temporarily subduing the afflictions through the practice of single-pointed concentration and meditating on the faults of the level of existence one is trying to transcend. This method is common to both Buddhists and non-Buddhists and can lead to the highest levels of meditative absorption and rebirth in higher realms, but it does not eliminate afflictions from the root.

nāga *(klu)*. Demigods with the head and upper torso of a human and the lower body of a snake who generally live underground or in lakes and rivers. They are sometimes considered to be part of the animal realm.

nirmāṇakāya *(sprul sku)*. The saṃbhogakāya and the nirmāṇakāya are together called the *form body (gzugs sku)* of a buddha. These are manifestations of perfect wisdom in various forms. The nirmāṇakāya—the *emanation body*—takes various forms that can be perceived by our limited senses. It is the emanation body that we see as the Buddha in our world. Various qualities of enlightenment manifest as thirty-two major marks and eighty minor marks adorning the emanation body of a buddha.

nirvana *(mya ngan las 'das pa; Skt: nirvāṇa)*. Liberation from samsara; freedom from all suffering; the attainment of an arhat.

nirvana with remainder *(phung po lhag ma dang bcas pa'i mya ngan las 'das pa)*. When as a result of their practice śrāvakas and pratyekabuddhas free themselves from samsara, they still have a body that was created by karma from prior lives; the rest of that lifetime is called *nirvana with remainder*. This is the last vestige of a Hinayana arhat's connection to samsara. *See also* nirvana without remainder.

nirvana without remainder *(phung po lhag ma med pa'i mya ngan las 'das pa)*. At the time of death, śrāvakas and pratyekabuddhas who had attained nirvana in their lifetime are completely freed from any kind of subtle misery associated with a body. From then on they will be free from all samsaric qualities and can remain in peace forever unless stimulated to practice the Mahayana path for the benefit of other beings. *See also* nirvana with remainder.

nominally existent *(gdags pa'i dngos po)*. Functional things that exist as posited by name and thought.

objects of knowledge *(shes bya)*. All things that can be known are included in three categories: obvious things *(mngon 'gyur)*, which can be observed directly with the senses; objects that are slightly hidden *(cung zad lkog gyur)*, which cannot be detected with the senses, but can be logically inferred based on sensory information; and very hidden phenomena *(shin tu lkog gyur)*, which can neither be observed directly nor inferred from ordinary beings' observations, but must be provisionally believed in out of faith in higher beings' perceptions.

obstructions to liberation *(nyon sgrib)*. One of two types of obscurations that must be removed in order to obtain buddhahood. The obstructions to liberation are the obscuring afflictions preventing one from attaining liberation from cyclic existence; when they are removed one attains arhatship. However, as the result of previous habitual engagement in the ignorance of cyclic existence, one still possesses subtle obscurations. In order to obtain complete buddhahood, one must remove these subtle obstructions to omniscience *(shes sgrib)* as well. Once these are removed one obtains omniscience, or buddhahood. *See also* obstructions to omniscience.

obstructions to omniscience *(shes sgrib)*. Subtle propensities for self-grasping that remain after the removal of the mental afflictions. *See also obstructions* to liberation.

ordinary being/ordinary individual *(so sor skye bo)*. A being who has not reached the state of an ārya, or superior being.

pāramitā *(phar phyin)*. *See* perfections.

Paramitayana. *See* perfection vehicle.

parinirvāṇa *(yongs su mya ngan las 'das pa)*. Final nirvana, the state entered when an arhat or buddha "passes away" at the end of his or her life.

path of accumulation *(tshogs lam)*. *See* five paths.

path of meditation *(sgom lam)*. *See* five paths.

path of no more learning *(mi slob lam)*. *See* five paths.

path of preparation *(sbyor lam)*. *See* five paths.

path of seeing *(mthong lam)*. *See* five paths.

path of no further training *(mi slob lam)*. *See* five paths.

perfection vehicle *(phar phyin theg pa; Skt: pāramitāyāna)*. The vehicle of the bodhisattva, emphasizing the practice of the perfections over a long period of time as the path to enlightenment. *See also* perfections.

perfections *(pha rol tu phyin pa; Skt: pāramitā)*. The activities of practitioners on the Mahayana path after they have developed bodhicitta. The perfections are commonly listed as six: generosity *(sbyin pa)*, ethical discipline *(tshul khrims)*, patience *(bzod pa)*, perseverance *(brtson 'grus)*, meditative stabilization *(bsam gtan)*, and wisdom *(shes rab)*. An additional four perfections are occasionally added to this list: method, prayer, power, and transcendental knowledge.

prāna *(srog)*. The vital energy wind in the body. *See also* energy wind.

prātimokṣa *(so so thar pa)*. The "vows of individual liberation" laid out in the Vinaya and forming the basis of Buddhist ethics. There are eight types of prātimokṣa vows: lay vows for men and women, novice vows for monks and nuns, vows for probationary nuns, full ordination vows for monks and nuns, and one-day ordination vows for laypeople.

pratyekabuddha *(rang sangs rgyas)*. Solitary realizers, so called because in their last lifetime prior to attaining liberation they stay alone—they do not interact with a teacher. Prior study and practice over many lives enable them to be silent and solitary during their last life, in which they attain the state of a Hinayana arhat.

preceptor *(mkhan po)*. A senior monk or learned teacher who gives vows to junior students.

pūjā *(mchod pa)*. To worship, to do what pleases the buddhas and bodhisattvas.

pure land *(dag zhing)*. A buddhafield; an environment of unimaginably excellent qualities, far beyond our ordinary conception, attained as the result of the accumulation of merit.

renunciation *(nges 'byung)*. Intense interest in attaining freedom from suffering.

results *('bras bu)*. *See* environmental results; fruitional results; results corresponding to the cause.

results corresponding to the cause *(rgyu mthun gyi 'bras bu)*. A karmic result that is similar to the cause that produced it. For example, the result that corresponds to killing is a shortened life.

rūpakāya *(gzugs sku)*. The form body of a buddha, composed of the saṃbhogakāya and nirmāṇakāya. *See also* nirmāṇakāya; saṃbhogakāya.

saṃbhogakāya *(longs sku)*. The enjoyment body of a buddha. This is the perfected form in which a buddha attains enlightenment, the ultimate physical body, completely absorbed in enjoyment of the Mahayana Dharma. It is always present but is only perceptible to advanced-level bodhisattvas. *See also* rūpakāya.

samādhi *(ting nge 'dzin)*. A state of undistracted concentration or meditative absorption on a particular object. The second of the three trainings. *See also* meditative stabilization.

śamatha *(zhi gnas; Skt: śamatha)*. Calm abiding. Single pointed concentration; calming the mind, being at peace.

samaya *(dam tshig)*. Tantric vows; particular commitments.

samsara *('khor ba; Skt: saṃsāra)*. The uncontrolled taking of rebirth under the force of karma and the afflictions. The six realms of samsaric existence consist of three lower realms—those of hell beings, hungry ghosts, and animals—and three higher realms—those of humans, demigods, and gods.

Sangha *(dge 'dun; Skt: saṅgha)*. Assembly, community. Conventionally, this refers to a group of at least four fully ordained monks or nuns. Ideally, it refers to anyone, lay or ordained, who has attained a direct realization of the ultimate nature of reality.

sangye *(sangs rgyas)*. Tibetan for *buddha*.

Sarvāstivāda *(thams cad yod par smra ba)*. One of the four root schools of early Buddhism, the other three being Mahāsaṃghika, Sthaviravāda, and Saṃmitīya.

śāstras *(bstan bcos)*. Independent works explaining religious topics and commenting on the sutras. Refers primarily to the works of the classical Indian masters.

Sautrāntika *(mdo sde pa)*. One of the four schools of Buddhist tenets.

sevenfold cause-and-effect method *(rgyu 'bras man ngag bdun)*. A method to produce bodhicitta transmitted by Atiśa.

śīla *(tshul khrims)*. Ethical discipline. The first of the three trainings and the second of the six perfections.

single pointed concentration *(ting nge 'dzin; Skt. samādhi)*. *See also* meditative stabilization.

six superior qualities *(dam pa'i drug)*. Six holy qualities that should be included in the practice of each perfection. They are: superior support or cause, superior object or area of action, superior purpose, superior gracious method, superior dedication, and special superior purification.

spiritual attainment *(dngos grub; Skt. siddhi)*. Special powers that result from both Buddhist and non-Buddhist spiritual practices. With effort even ordinary people can achieve these powers. There are four primary spiritual attainments: the power of pacification *(zhi ba)* of such things as sickness or injury; the power of extension *(rgyas pa)* of life and other things; the power of wrath *(drag po)* that protects one from evil; and the power of control *(dbang)*.

śrāvaka *(nyan thos)*. Literally, "hearers"; practitioners striving for their own liberation from samsara. They receive this name because—unlike pratyekabuddhas—they rely on listening to their teachers' instructions through the course of their spiritual practice.

suffering *(sdug bsngal; Skt: duḥkha)* The three basic types of misery: the suffering of suffering *(sdug bsngal gi sdug bsngal)*, the suffering of change *('gyur ba'i sdug bsngal)*, and the suffering of pervasiveness (*khyab pa 'du byed kyi sdug bsngal*).

sugata *(bde bar gshegs pa)*. An epithet of a buddha meaning "one who has reached the highest bliss" and "the one who is gone well."

superior thought *(lhag bsam)*. An exceedingly powerful type of compassion and love that takes full responsibility to free others from misery and lead them to the highest positive goal of happiness. A state of mind immediately preceeding the development of bodhicitta. *See also* bodhicitta.

supramundane path *('jig rten las 'das pa'i lam)*. The method of practice, unique to the Buddhadharma, leading to the direct realization of emptiness, which destroys karmic seeds from the root.

supernormal knowledge *(mngon par shes pa)*. The six supernormal knowledges are: miraculous powers, the clairaudience, the knowledge of others' thoughts, recollection of former states, knowledge of death and rebirth, and knowledge that the mental afflictions have been terminated.

śūnyatā *(stong nyid)*. Suchness, or emptiness; the final nature of all phenomena; the absence of inherent existence.

Sutra *(mdo; Skt: sūtra)*. One of three major sections of the Buddhist canon, containing the general discourses (sutras) of the Buddha, largely dealing with topics of meditation. *See also* Tripiṭaka.

Sutrayana *(mdo'i theg pa; Skt: sūtrayāna)*. The general Mahayana path, whose doctrines and practices are held in common with practitioners of the Vajrayana. *See also* Perfection Vehicle.

tantra *(rgyud).* Any one of the texts containing the instructions of the Vajrayana, or tantric path, which is a subsection of the Mahayana. In addition to the practices of the Sutrayana, the Vajrayana includes advanced meditation techniques to speed up progress to buddhahood.

Tathāgata *(de bzhin gshegs pa).* The term the Buddha used to speak of himself after his enlightenment. It means "He who has gone thus on the path of all the buddhas."

ten powers *(stobs bcu).* (1) Knowing what is correct and incorrect (about the workings of karma—i.e., that virtue yields favorable results and not unfavorable ones); (2) Knowing (in all its subtleties) the maturations of karma; (3) Knowing the various wishes (of beings); (4) Knowing the various classes of things; (5) Knowing which (beings') faculties are superior and which are inferior; (6) Knowing where all paths lead; (7) Knowing the afflicting and non-liberating qualities associated with the meditations, deliverances, forms of one-pointed concentration, and states of composure; (8) Knowing (one's own and others') prior lives; (9) Knowing when all beings will die and where they will be reborn; and (10) Knowing that the mental afflictions have been terminated.

three collections *(sde snod gsum).* *See* Tripiṭaka.

Three Jewels *(dkon mchog gsum).* The Buddha, Dharma, and Sangha to which all Buddhists go for refuge.

three realms *(khams gsum).* *See* desire realm; form realm; formless realm.

three trainings *(bslab pa gsum).* Ethical discipline, meditative stabilization, and wisdom; these three together constitute the fourth noble truth, the truth of the path. *See also* four noble truths.

trichiliocosm *(stong gsum gyi stong chen po'i 'jig rten gyi khams).* A one billion world system. The universe contains many of these according to Buddhist cosmology.

Tripiṭaka *(sde snod gsum).* The Buddhist canon, consisting of the three "baskets" *(piṭaka)* of Sūtra, Vinaya, and Abhidharma.

two accumulations *(tshogs gnyis).* The accumulations of merit and wisdom, which are the causes to attain enlightenment. The accumulation of merit comes from the practice of bodhicitta and the first five perfections. The accumulation of wisdom, which is the practice of the sixth perfection, derives from direct realization of the ultimate nature of reality.

two truths *(bden gnyis)*. Reality can be accurately viewed from two perspectives: phenomenal or relative truth *(kun rdzob bden pa)* and ultimate truth *(don dam bden pa)*. The former pertains to understanding causation and the latter to understanding emptiness.

ultimate bodhicitta *(don dam sems bskyed)*. *See* bodhicitta.

Vaibhāṣika *(bye brag smra ba)*. One of the four schools of Indian Buddhist tenets.

Vajrayana *(rdo rje theg pa; Skt: vajrayāna)*. The tantric vehicle. *See also* tantra.

view of the perishable aggregates *('jig tshogs la lta ba)*. A wrong view that equates the self with the perishable five aggregates.

Vinaya *('dul ba)*. One of three major sections of the Buddhist canon, containing the scriptures dealing with ethical conduct. *See also* Tripiṭaka.

vipaśyanā *(lhag mthong)*. Superior wisdom; highest insight.

vows of individual liberation *(so sor thar pa'i sdom pa)*. *See* prātimokṣa.

wisdom *(shes rab; Skt: prajñā)*. Perfect wisdom is realization of the final nature of all phenomena; it is direct comprehension of emptiness *(śūnyatā)*, the lack of inherent existence of self and phenomena. Wisdom is the third of the three trainings and the sixth perfection.

worldly concerns *('jig rten chos brgyad)*. *See* eight worldly concerns.

Yama *('chi bdag gshin rje)*. The Lord of Death, a personification of death itself.

yidam *(yi dam)*. *See* meditational deity.

yoga *(rnal 'byor)*. Spiritual discipline, control.

yogi *(rnal 'byor pa)*. An assiduous Dharma practitioner. Because they put the various teachings into strict daily practice, yogis and yoginis (the feminine form of the word) often adopt an ascetic lifestyle.

Yogācāra *(rnal 'byor spyod pa)* Literally "Yoga practice," is the proper name of the so-called "Mind-only" school, one of four schools of Indian Buddhist philosophical tenets. It is a school that focuses on the nature and functions of consciousness.

yojana *(dpag tshad)*. *See* league.

Notes

Notes to the Introduction

1 The full Tibetan title of the *Great Treatise on the Stages of the Path to Enlighten-ment* by Tsongkhapa (Tsong kha pa Blo bzang grags pa, 1357–1419) is *sKyes bu gsum gyi nyams su blang ba'i rim pa thams cad tshang bar ston pa'i byang chub lam gyi rim pa.* It is commonly known as the *Lamrim Chenmo* and will be referred to by this short Tibetan title throughout the present work.

2 The *Lamrim Chenmo* is available in English translation in three volumes. Tsong-Kha-Pa, *The Great Treatise on the Stages of the Path to Enlightenment* (Ithaca NY: Snow Lion Publications, 2000–2004). This volume of Geshe Sopa's commentary explains volume 2 of the translation.

Notes to Chapter 1

1 See volume 1, chapter 8 of this series for an extensive discussion of this topic.

2 *Lamp for the Path to Enlightenment (Bodhi-patha-pradīpa),* v. 5.

3 Tibetan scholars attribute authorship of the *Compendium of the Perfections* to Aśvaghoṣa while contemporary Western scholars say that Āryaśūra was the author. Some Tibetan scholars say that the two names refer to the same person.

4 *Engaging in the Bodhisattva Deeds (Bodhisattva-caryāvatāra)* 1.36.

5 *Sugata* is an epithet of a buddha meaning "one who has reached the highest bliss" and "one who is gone well."

6 Sonam Rinchen, *The Thirty-Seven Practices of Bodhisattvas (rGyal ba'i sras kyi lag len sum cu so bdun ma),* by rGyal sras Thogs med bzang po, v. 12. This is the tenth practice, or tenth stanza subsequent to two stanzas of homage.

7 *Engaging in the Bodhisattva Deeds:* 3.31cd, 3.32ab.

8 *Engaging in the Bodhisattva Deeds:* 1.27.

9 Tsongkhapa, *Condensed Lamrim (Byang chub lam gyi rim pa'i nyams len gyi rnam gshag mdor bsdus te brjed byang du byas pa.)* The colloquial title of this work is the *Lam rim bsdus don.*

10 The Mahayana goal of enlightenment can be described as composed of three *kāyas,* or bodies, of a buddha: the dharmakāya, saṃbhogakāya, and nirmāṇakāya. The dharmakāya—the wisdom body—is ultimate and immaculate wisdom; it is the mind that has been transformed beyond all states of impurity. The latter two bodies—the saṃbhogakāya and nirmāṇakāya—are together called the form body of a buddha. These are manifestations of perfect wisdom in various forms. The saṃboghakāya—the enjoyment body—is the perfected form in which a buddha attains enlightenment. It is the ultimate physical body, completely absorbed in the enjoyment of the Mahayana Dharma. It is always present, but only perceptible to advanced level bodhisattvas and does not transform into any other form. The nirmāṇakāya—the emanation body—takes various forms that can be perceived by our limited senses. It is the emanation body that we see as the Buddha in our world.

Notes to Chapter 2

1 *Engaging in the Bodhisattva Deeds:* 5.58.

2 *Engaging in the Bodhisattva Deeds:* 1.11.

3 *Engaging in the Bodhisattva Deeds:* 6.20.

4 Phur lcog Byams pa tshul khrims, *Source of Happiness (bDe legs kun byung ma).*

Notes to Chapter 3

1 See volume 1, chapter 5 for a discussion of the preliminaries for a meditation session and volume 1, chapter 8 for an explanation of the three types of spiritual persons.

2 All beings in the samsaric world live in one of three realms: the desire, form, or formless realms. Each realm is dominated by particular types of afflictions; the predominant affliction in the desire realm is desire or attachment—in particular the craving for the sensual pleasures of sex and food. The basic division of the form realm are the four concentrations *(dhyāna).* Each of the first three concentrations has three levels, and the fourth concentration has eight levels; a particular type of "form-realm god" resides on each of these seventeen levels. When an individual attains a meditative absorption of the formless realm and then passes away, his or her four mental aggregates are born into one of the four levels of the formless realm, called the four formless absorptions. Because the beings in this realm do not possess obstructive form, the formless realm is without a physical dimension.

3 *Friendly Letter (Suhṛl-leka).*

4 Pan chen Blo bzang chos kyi rgyal mtshan, *Guru Puja (Bla ma mchod pa'i cho ga).*

5 *Friendly Letter.*

6 *Engaging in the Bodhisattva Deeds:* 8.129.

7 According to Abhidharma cosmology our universe is a *trichiliocosm*—what is known as a *great thousand world.* This is calculated on the basis of a single world system like our own: the four continents, the rings of mountains and seas surrounding Mount Meru, along with the sun and the moon. Multiply this world system by one thousand and the result is a *small thousand world.* One thousand of these small thousand worlds equal one *medium thousand world:* a universe of one million world systems. Multiply that by one thousand again and you have a *great thousand world.* So this universe is made up of one thousand cubed, or one billion, world systems.

8 *Engaging in the Bodhisattva Deeds:* 1.11.

9 See volume 2 of this series for a detailed explanation of the various types of suffering in samsara.

NOTES TO CHAPTER 4

1 Pan chen Blo bzang chos kyi rgyal mtshan, *Guru Puja.*

2 (dGe bshes) 'Chad kha ba Ye shes rdo rje, *Seven-Point Mind Training (Blo sbyong don bdun ma).*

3 *Engaging in the Bodhisattva Deeds:* 8.134.

4 Pabongka Rinpoche, *Liberation in Our Hands (rNam grol lag bcangs),* Day 17: Contemplating the many faults resulting from self-cherishing. Richards 590, Engle III.158.

5 *Engaging in the Bodhisattva Deeds:* 8.155.

6 *Engaging in the Bodhisattva Deeds:* 8.132.

7 *Engaging in the Bodhisattva Deeds:* 8.135.

8 Sonam Rinchen, *The Thirty Seven Practices of Bodhisattvas,* by rGyal sras Thogs med bzang po, v. 11.

9 Pan chen Blo bzang chos kyi rgyal mtshan, *Guru Puja.*

10 Sonam Rinchen, *The Thirty Seven Practices of Bodhisattvas,* by rGyal sras Thogs med bzang po, v. 36.

Notes to Chapter 5

1   *Engaging in the Bodhisattva Deeds:* 1.8.

2   *Prayer of Samantabhadra,* stanza 56:

> I dedicate all my root virtues
> In whatever way all the tathāgatas
> Of all three times praised as best.
> I dedicate them toward these noble deeds.

3   There are two types of obscurations that must be removed in order to attain buddhahood. The *obstructions to liberation (nyon sgrib)* are the mental afflictions preventing one from attaining liberation from cyclic existence. When they are removed one attains arhatship. However, as the result of previous habitual engagement in the ignorance of cyclic existence, one still possesses subtle obscurations. In order to attain complete buddhahood, one must remove these *subtle obstructions to omniscience (shes sgrib)* as well. Once these are removed one attains omniscience or buddhahood.

Notes to Chapter 6

1   *Engaging in the Bodhisattva Deeds:* 8.107.

2   The four opponent powers are: remorse, the power of the antidote, restraint, and reliance. For a detailed discussion of the four powers of confession see volume 2, chapter 3 (148–74) of this series.

Notes to Chapter 7

1   *Engaging in the Bodhisattva Deeds:* 4.1.

2   Tsongkhapa, *Foundations of All Good Qualities (Yon tan gzhir gyur ma).* This prayer was composed as part of *Byang chub lam gyi rim pa'i brgyud pa rnams la gsol ba 'debs pa'i rim pa.* It is now commonly recited as a prayer in the *Preliminary Practices (sByor chos: Byang chub lam gyi rim pa'i dmar khrid myur lam gyi sngon 'gro'i ngag 'don gyi rim pa khyer bde bklag chog bskal bzang mgrin rgyan).*

3   *Perfection of Wisdom Sutra in Eight Thousand Lines (Ārya-aṣṭasāhasrikā-prajña-pāramitā-sūtra).*

4   *Engaging in the Bodhisattva Deeds:* 5.100 .

5   According to Pha bong kha pa Byams pa bstan 'dzin 'phrin las rgya mtsho, *Liberation in Our Hands: Part 1,* page 151, notes 95–97, the ten powers *(stobs bcu)* are: (1) Knowing what is correct and incorrect (about the workings of karma—i.e.

that virtue yields favorable results and not unfavorable ones); (2) Knowing (in all its subtleties) the maturations of karma; (3) Knowing the various wishes (of beings); (4) Knowing the various classes of things; (5) Knowing which (beings') faculties are superior and which are inferior; (6) Knowing where all paths lead; (7) Knowing the afflicting and non-liberating qualities associated with the meditations *(dhyāna)*, deliverances *(vimokṣa)*, forms of one-pointed concentration *(samādhi)*, and states of composure *(samāpatti);* (8) Knowing (one's own and others') prior lives; (9) Knowing when all beings will die and where they will be reborn; and (10) Knowing that the mental afflictions *(āsrava)* have been terminated.

The four fearlessnesses *(mi 'jigs pa bzhi)* are a buddha's self-confidence regarding having attained these qualities: (1) the full realization of all dharmas; (2) the knowledge that all his own mental afflictions have been terminated; (3) the ability to declare what things represent obstacles; and (4) the ability to declare what represents the path to emancipation.

The eighteen unmixed qualities *(ma 'dres pa bco brgyad)* are qualities which only a buddha possesses and which demonstrate his or her attainment of perfection. They are (1) a buddha is without error (in bodily activities); (2) he does not cry out excitedly (as when one has lost one's way); (3) he never forgets (the appropriate time for a particular action); (4) he is always in a state of meditation; (5) he does not have diverse conceptions (such as "samsara is misery, nirvana is peace"); (6) he does not neglect beings through inattentiveness; (7) he is unfaltering in his aspiration (to act on behalf of beings); (8) he is unfaltering in his fortitude; (9) he is unfaltering in his recollection (that he is committed to the goal of aiding all sentient beings); (10) he is unfaltering in his one-pointed concentration (which focuses on the ultimate nature of all things); (11) he is unfaltering in the wisdom (that knows beings' minds and knows what dharma to teach them); (12) he never wavers from deliverance (i.e. the desire to deliver all beings from suffering); (13) all his bodily acts are preceded by and in agreement with transcendent wisdom; (14) all his verbal acts are preceded by and in agreement with transcendent wisdom; (15) all his mental acts are preceded by and in agreement with transcendent wisdom; (16) his wisdom perceives the past without obstruction or impediment; (17) his wisdom perceives the future without obstruction or impediment; and (18) his wisdom perceives the present without obstruction or impediment.

Notes to Chapter 8

1 *Engaging in the Bodhisattva Deeds:* 5.100.

2 *Engaging in the Bodhisattva Deeds:* 4.18.

3 *Commentary on the "Middle Way": (Madhyamakāvatāra)*, 1.10.

Notes to Chapter 9

1   *Engaging in the Bodhisattva Deeds:* 3.25.

2   *Commentary on the "Middle Way":* 1.11.

Notes to Chapter 10

1   *Commentary on the "Middle Way":* 1.14.

2   I often translate the Sanskrit word *māra* (Tibetan, bdud) as *evil* rather than the more common *demon,* because the real evil is not an external spirit, it is inside us. Religious texts talk about four types of internal evil demons. The primary evil is the mental afflictions—ignorance, desire, hatred, and so forth. The activity of the mental afflictions creates karma which results in the five aggregates of the body and mind. Thus the second internal evil is the skandhas or aggregates of personality. Once we are born under the power of the mental afflictions, the body and mind are the locus of misery, problems, pain, and destruction. So the third demon is the evil of death. A life caused by karma and the mental afflictions has many faulty mental, physical, and environmental aspects. We have so many weaknesses; our life can be easily injured and destroyed. Because our body and mind are the subject of conditions, external forces such as spirits can interfere and harm us. The fourth evil is harmful spirits or devils. As long as we have the three poisons of desire, hatred, and ignorance, the other evils arise.

3   *Engaging in the Bodhisattva Deeds:* 7.25–26.

Notes to Chapter 11

1   *Commentary on the "Middle Way":* 2.4.

2   *Engaging in the Bodhisattva Deeds:* 8.134.

3   *Commentary on the "Middle Way":* 2.7.

4   Tsongkhapa, *Condensed Lamrim, (Lam rim bsdus don)* is the coloquial name for *Byang chub lam gyi rim pa'i nyams len gyi rnam gshag mdor bsdus te brjed byang du byas pa.*

5   Tsongkhapa's commentary on the chapter on how to practice bodhisattva morality in the *Bodhisattva Levels (Byang chub sems dpa'i tsul khrims kyi rnam bshad byang chub gzhung lam)* is available in English under the title *Asaṅga's Chapter on Ethics with the Commentary of Tsong-Kha-Pa, The Basic Path to Awakening, The Complete Bodhisattva* Mark Tatz trans., Studies in Asian Thought and Religion, 4 (Lewiston/Queenston: The Edwin Mellen Press, 1986).

6 *Engaging in the Bodhisattva Deeds:* 5.14cd.

7 *Engaging in the Bodhisattva Deeds:* 5.19.

8 *Commentary on the "Middle Way":* 2.9.

NOTES TO CHAPTER 12

1 *Commentary on the "Middle Way":* 3.3.

2 (Pan chen) Blo bzang chos kyi rgyal mtsan, *Bla ma mchod pa'i cho ga, zab lam bla ma mchod pa'i cho ga bde stong dbyer med ma.*

3 *Engaging in the Bodhisattva Deeds:* 6.2.

4 *Engaging in the Bodhisattva Deeds:* 6.20.

5 Tibetan scholars identify this scholar as Aśvaghoṣa while Western scholars say it is Āryaśūra.

6 *Engaging in the Bodhisattva Deeds:* 1.34.

7 The Sarvāstivāda *('phags pa thams cad yod par smra ba)* was one of the four schools of early Buddhism: Sarvāstivāda, Mahāsaṃghika, Sthaviravāda, and Saṃmitīya.

8 The term *league* is used here to translate the traditional Buddhist measure of distance *yojana* (Tibetan: *dpag tshad*). This distance is based on the arm-span of the Buddha (Tibetan: *zhing 'dom*). The Buddha had a wider arm-span than most of his contemporaries; it was perhaps similar to a large American's today. Five hundred of these arm-spans is a length called a *krośa* (Tibetan: *rgyang grags*). Eight krośa is a yojana.

9 *Commentary on the "Middle Way":* 3.7.

10 *Commentary on the "Middle Way":* 3.9.

11 *Commentary on the "Middle Way":* 3.8.

12 *Engaging in the Bodhisattva Deeds:* 5.24.

13 dGe 'dun grub, *Praise and Requests to the Twenty-One Taras (The Well Written).*

14 *Engaging in the Bodhisattva Deeds:* 4.28.

15 The eleven types of living beings are: (1) those who need help, (2) those who are confused as to the proper method, (3) those who have given help, (4) those afflicted by fear, (5) those afflicted with sorrow, (6) those poor in goods, (7) those who want a dwelling, (8) those who want mental harmony, (9) those who

proceed correctly, (10) those who proceed wrongly, and (11) those who need to be disciplined by supernormal powers. LRCM II: 265, note 238.

16 *Precious Garland.*

17 The six supernormal knowledges are: miraculous powers, the divine ear, the knowledge of others' thoughts, recollection of former states, knowledge of death and rebirth, and knowledge that the mental afflictions have been terminated.

18 See pages 272–5 of this volume.

Notes to Chapter 13

1 Translation from *The Great Treatise on the Stages of the Path to Enlightenment,* vol. 2, page 185.

2 Tsong kha pa Blo bzang grags pa, *Condensed Lamrim.*

3 For an explanation of the eleven types of sentient beings, see pages 329–34 of this volume.

4 *Commentary on the "Middle Way":* 4.1.

5 *Engaging in the Bodhisattva Deeds:* 7.7.

6 There are three levels of faith based on reason. The first is clear or pure faith. This is a natural trust without much basis in logic. It is simply being happy to enjoy the Dharma, worship God, or do a practice. This can be very sincere but it can be lost quickly because it is a bit superficial. The second type of faith is a little stronger. It is the faith of conviction based on reasoning. This level of trust is founded on some background knowledge, seeing the logic, and bringing personal experiences to bear. As the reasons we understand and our experiential understanding increase, we may produce the third kind of faith, irreversible faith. This irreversible trust makes our desire to practice very firm.

7 Some scholars identify this author, dPal ldan Ma khol, as Mātṛceṭa. Other scholars identify him as Aśvaghoṣa. dPal ldan Ma khol literally means *servant of the mother.* On occasion he was also called pa khol, or *servant of the father,* because he was very respectful of his parents.

8 Gung thang bstan pa'i sgron me, *Jewel Garland of Instruction (bSlab bya nor bu phreng ba).*

Notes to Chapter 14

1 Translation from *The Great Treatise on the Stages of the Path to Enlightenment,* vol. 2, page 210.

2 For an explanation of the eleven types of sentient beings, see chapter 11, section (3') The ethical discipline of acting for the welfare of living beings.

3 The author of this text is sometimes identified as Āryaśūra. Tibetan scholars state that Āryaśūra is another name for Aśvaghoṣa. The connection between Nāgārjuna and Āryaśūra/Aśvaghoṣa is a subject of debate by Western historians.

4 *Commentary on the "Middle Way":* 6.2.

5 The Madhyamaka school is divided by Tibetan scholars into the Prāsaṅgika Madhyamaka and Svātantrika Madhyamaka. The Svātantrika is further subdivided into the Sautrāntika Svātantrika-Madhyamaka and Yogācāra Svātantrika-Madhyamaka. Some of the key ideas that distinguish these subschools are their views about phenomena, the obstacles to liberation, and the obstructions to omniscience. The Prāsaṅgika-Madhyamaka hold that phenomena do not possess intrinsic identity ultimately or conventionally whereas the Svātantrika-Madhyamaka hold that phenomena do possess intrinsic identity conventionally but not ultimately. The Prāsaṅgika and Sautrāntika-Svātantrika-Madhyamaka agree that the external world is a separate entity from the mind whereas the Yogācāra Svātantrika-Madhyamaka agrees with the Yogācāra school that the physical world is the same entity as the mind. These and many other differences between the schools are complex subjects that will be extensively dealt with in volume 5.

6 Many of the Kadampa yogis are called by names that evoke their meditation place or personal qualities. It is similar to referring to someone as the "New Yorker" or "Smarty." In this case the yogi is called by the epithet "Great Yogi."

Bibliography

Classical Works Cited

Advice to the King Sutra
Rājāvavādaka: Ārya-Rājāvavādaka-nāma-mahāyāna-sūtra
'Phags pa rgyal po la dgams pa zhes bya ba theg pa chen po'i mdo
P887, vol. 35

Array of Qualities in Mañjuśrī's Buddha-realm Sutra
Ārya-Mañjuśrī-buddha-kṣetra-guṇa-vyūha-mahāyāna-sūtra
'Phags pa 'jam dpal gyi sangs rgyas kyi zhing gi yon tan dkod pa zhes bya ba
   theg pa chen po'i mdo
P760, vol. 23

Array of Stalks Sutra
Gaṇḍa-vyūha-sūtra
sDong pos bkod pa'i mdo
P761, vol. 26

Basic Path to Awakening
Byang chub gzhug lam: Byang chub sems dpa'i tshul khrims kyi rnam bshad
   byang chub gzhug lam
author: Tsongkhapa

Bodhisattva Vows of Liberation
Bodhisattva-prātimokṣa-catuṣka-nirhāra-nāma-mahāyāna-sūtra
Byang chub sems dpa'i so so thar pa chos bzhi sgrub pa zhes bya ba theg pa
   chen po'i mdo
P914, vol. 36

Bodhisattva Levels
Bodhisattva-bhūmi: Yoga-caryā-bhūmau-bodhisattva-bhūmi
rNal 'byor spyod pa'i sa las byang chub sems dpa'i sa
author: Asaṅga
P5537, vol. 110

Bodhisattva Levels' Compendium of Determinations
Viniścaya-saṃgrahaṇī: Yoga-caryā-bhūmi-nirṇaya-saṃgraha / Yoga-caryā-
   bhūmi-viniścaya-saṃgrahaṇī
rNal 'byor spyod pa'i sa rnam par gtan la dbab pa bsdu ba

author: Asaṅga
P5539, vol. 110–11

Chapter of the Truth Speaker
Satyaka-parivarta
bDen pa pa'i le'u
P813, vol. 32

Cloud of Jewels Sutra
Ārya-ratna-megha-nāma-mahāyāna-sūtra
'Phags pa dkon mchog sprin ces bya ba theg pa chen po'i mdo
P897, vol. 35

Commentary on the "Compendium of Valid Cognition"
Pramāṇa-vārttika-kārikā
Tshad ma rnam 'grel gyi tshig le'ur gyas pa
author: Dharmakīrtī
P5709, vol. 130

Commentary on the Difficult Points of the "Lamp for the Path to Enlightenment"
Bodhi-mārga-pradīpa-pañjikā
Byang chub lam gyi sgron ma'i dka' 'grel
author: Atiśa Dipaṃkaraśrījñāna
P5344, vol. 103

Commentary on the Kāśyapa Chapter
Kāśyapa-parivarta-ṭīkā: Ārya-mahā-ratna-kūṭa-dharma-paryāya-parivartta-śata-
    sāhasrika-kāśyapa parivarta-ṭīkā
'Phags pa dkon mchog brtsegs pa chen po'i chos kyi rnam grangs le'u stong
    phrag brgya pa las 'od srungs kyi le'u rgya cher 'grel pa
author: Sthiramati
P5510, vol. 105

Commentary on the "Middle Way"
Madhyamakāvatvāra
dBu ma la 'jug pa
author: Candrakīrti
P5262, vol. 98

Compendium of Knowledge
Abhidharma-samuccaya
Chos mngon pa kun las btus pa
author: Asaṅga
P5550, vol. 112

Compendium of the Perfections
Pāramitā-samāsa-nāma
Pha rol tu phyin pa bsdus pa shes bya ba
author: Āryaśūra or Aśvaghoṣa

P5340, vol. 103

Compendium of Sutras
Sūtra-samuccaya
mDo kun las btus pa
P5330, vol. 102

Compendium of the Teachings Sutra
Dharma-saṃgīti: Ārya-dharma-saṃgīti-sūtra-nāma mahāyāna-sūtra
'Phags pa chos chos yang dag par sdud pa shes bya ba theg pa chen po'i mdo
P904, vol. 36

Compendium of Trainings
Śikṣā-samuccaya
bsLab pa kun las btus pa
author: Śāntideva
P5336, vol. 102

Compendium of the Trainings in Verse
Śikṣā-samuccaya-kārikā
bsLab pa kun las btus pa tshig le'ur byas pa
author: Śāntideva
P5335, vol. 102

Daughter Like the Finest Moon's Discourse Sutra
Ārya-candrottama-dārikā-vyākaraṇa-nāma-mahāyāna-sūtra
'Phags pa bu mo zla ba mchog lung bstan zhes bya ba theg pa chen po'i mdo
P858, vol. 34

Engaging in the Bodhisattva Deeds
Bodhisattva-caryāvatāra
Byang chub sems dpa'i spyod la 'jug pa
author: Śāntideva
P5272, vol. 99

Essay on the Spirit of Enlightenment
Bodhicitta-vivaraṇa
Byang chub sems kyi 'grel pa
author: Nāgārjuna
P2666, vol. 61

Essence of the Tathāgata Sūtra
Ārya-tathāgatagarbha-nāma-mahāyāna-sūtra
'phags pa de bzhin gshegs pa'i snying po zhes bya ba theg pa chen po'i mdo
P924, vol. 36

Exhortation to Wholehearted Resolve
Ārya-adhyāśaya-saṃcodana-nāma-mahāyāna-sūtra
'Phags pa lhag pa'i bsam pa zhes bya ba theg pa chen po'i mdo

P760.25, vol. 24

Explanation of the "Middle Way" Commentary
Madhyamakāvatāra-bhāṣya
dBu ma la 'jug pa bshad pa zhes bya ba
author: Candrakīrti
P5263, vol. 98

Flower Ornament Sutra
Avataṃsaka: Buddhāvataṃsaka-nāma-mahā-vaipulya-sūtra
Sangs rgyas phal po che shes bya ba shin tu rgyas pa chen po'i mdo
P761, vol. 25–26

Foremost of Gayā
Ārya-gayā-śirṣa-nāma-mahāyāna-sūtra
'Phags pa gayā mgo'i ri zhes bya ba theg pa chen po'i mdo
P777, vol. 29

Formula That Accomplishes Limitless Methods
Ārya-ananta-mukha-nirhāra-dhāraṇi / Āryānanta-mukha-sādhaka-nāma-
    dhāraṇi
'Phags pa sgo mtha' yas pa bsgrub pa zhes bya ba'i gzungs
P808, vol. 32

Four Hundred Stanzas
Catuḥ-śataka: Catuḥ-śataka-śāstra-kārikā-nāma
bsTan bcos bzhi brgya pa zhes bya ba'i tshig le'ur byas pa
author: Āryadeva
P5246, vol. 95

Friendly Letter
Suhṛl-leka
bShes pa'i spring yig
author: Nāgārjuna
P5682, vol. 129

Garland of Birth Stories
Jātaka-mālā
sKyes pa'i rab kyi rgyud
author: Āryaśūra or Aśvaghoṣa
P5650, vol. 128

Glorious First and Foremost Tantra
Śrī-paramādya-nāma-mahāyāna-kalpa-rāja
dPal mchog dang po zhes bya ba theg pa chen po'i rtog pa'i rgyal po
P119, vol. 5

Heart of the Middle Way
Madhyamaka-hṛdaya

dBu ma'i snying po'i tshig le'ur byas pa
author: Bhāvaviveka
P5255, vol. 96

Heart Sutra
Prajñapāramitā-hṛdaya
Shes rab kyi pha rol tu phyin pa'i snying po
P160, vol. 6

Intense Power of Faith Sutra
Śraddhā-balādhānāvatāra-mūdra-sūtra: Ārya-śraddhā-balādhānāvatāra-mūdra-
nāma-mahāyāna-sūtra
'Phags pa dad pa'i stobs bskyed pa la 'jug pa'i phyag grya zhes bya ba theg pa
chen po'i mdo
P867, vol. 34

Kāśyapa Chapter
Ārya-kāśyapa-parivarta-nāma-mahāyāna-sūtra
'Phags pa 'od srung gi le'u zhes bya ba theg pa chen po'i mdo
P760.43, vol. 24

King of Concentrations Sutra
Samādhi-rāja-sūtra: Sarva-dharma-svabhāva-samatā-vipañcita-samādhi-rāja-
sūtra
Chos tham cad kyi rang bzhin mnyam pa nyid rnam par spros pa ting nge
'dzin gyi rgyal po'i mdo
P795, vol. 31

Lamp for the Path to Enlightenment
Bodhi-patha-pradīpa
Byang chub lam gyi sgron ma
author: Atiśa Dipaṃkaraśrījñāna
P5343, vol. 103

Letter to a Student
Śiṣya-lekha
Slob ma la springs pa'i sprong yig
author: Candragomin
P5683, vol. 129; P5410, vol. 103

Levels of Yogic Deeds
Yoga-caryā-bhūmi
rNal 'byor spyod pa'i sa
author: Asaṅga
P5536, vol. 110

Life of Maitreya
Ārya-maitreya-vimokṣa
'Phags pa byams pa'i rnam par thar ba

See: *Flower Ornament Sutra*
P761, vol. 25–26

Long Explanation of the Perfection of Wisdom Sutra in Eight Thousand Lines
Abhisamayālaṃkārālokā: Ārya-aṣṭasāhasrikā-prajñāpāramitā-vyākhyā-
abhisamayālaṃkārālokā
'Phags pa shes rab kyi pha rol tu phyin pa brgyad stong pa'i bshad pa mngon
par rtogs pa'i rgyan gyi snang ba zhes bya ba
author: Haribhadra
P5189, vol. 90

Lotus of Compassion Sutra
Ārya-mahā-karuṇā-puṇḍarīka-nāma-mahāyana-sūtra
'Phags pa snying rje chen po'i pad ma dkar po zhes bya ba theg pa chen po'i mdo
P779, vol. 29

Mahayana Compendium
Mahāyāna-saṃgraha
Theg pa chen po bsdus pa
author: Asaṅga
P5549, vol. 112

Mindfulness of the Excellent Teaching
Ārya-sad-dharmānusmṛty-upasthāna
'Phags pa dam pa'i chos dran pa bye bar gzhag pa
P953, vol. 37

Moon Lamp Sutra
Candra-pradīpa-sūtra
zla ba sgron ma'i mdo
see: *King of Concentrations Sutra*
P795, vol. 31

Ornament for Clear Knowledge
Abhisamayālaṃkāra; Abhisamayālaṃkāra-nāma-prajñāpāramitopadeśa-śāstra-
kārikā
'Phags pa shes rab kyi pha rol tu phyin pa brgyad stong pa'i bshad pa mngon
par rtogs pa'i rgyan
author: Maitreya
P5189, vol. 88

Ornament for the Mahayana Sutras
Sūtrālaṃkāra: Mahāyāna-sūtrālaṃkāra-kārikā
Theg pa chen po'i mdo sde'i rgyan gyi tshig le'ur byas pa
author: Maitreya
P5521, vol. 108

Perfection of Wisdom Sutras
Prajñāpāramitā-sūtra

Shes rab kyi pha rol tu phyin pa'i mdo
P730ff, vol. 12ff

Perfection of Wisdom Sutra in Eight Thousand Lines
Ārya-aṣṭasāhasrikā-prajñāpāramitā-sūtra
'Phags pa shes rab kyi pha rol tu phyin pa brgyad stong pa
P734, vol. 21

Perfection of Wisdom Sutra in Twenty-Five Thousand Lines
Pañca-viṃśatisāhasrikā-prajñā-pāramitā-sūtra
Shes rab kyi pha rol tu phyin pa stong phrag nyi shu lnga pa
P5188, vol. 88

Pile of Precious Things Collection
Ratna-kūṭa: Ārya-mahā-ratna-kūṭa-dharma-paryāya-śata-sāhasrika-grantha
dKon mchog brtsegs pa chen po'i chos kyi rnam grangs le'u stong phrag
    brgya pa
P760, vol. 22–24

Play of Mañjuśrī Sutra
Ārya-Mañjuśrī-vikrīḍita-nāma-mahāyāna-sūtra
'Phags pa 'jam dpal rnam par rol pa zhes bya ba theg pa chen po'i mdo
P764, vol. 27

Praise in One Hundred and Fifty Verses
Śata-pañcāśatka-stotra
brGya lnga bcu pa shes bya ba'i bstod pa
author: Mātṛceṭa, Aśvaghoṣa
P2038, vol. 46

Praise of Infinite Qualities
Guṇāparyanta-stotra
Yon ten mtha yas par bstod pa
author: Triratnadāsa
P2044, vol. 46

Praise of the Perfection of Wisdom
Prajñā-pāramitā-stotra
Shes rab gyi par rol du phin ma'i bstod pa
author: Nāgārjuna
P5340, vol. 103

Praise of One Worthy of Honor
Varṇāha-varṇa-bhagavato-buddhasya-stotra-śakya-stava
Sangs ryas bcom ldan 'das la bstod pa bsngags par 'os pa bsngags pa las bstod
    par mi nus par bstod pa
author: Āryaśūra, Mātṛceṭa
P2029, vol. 46

Prayer of Samantabhadra
Samantabhadra-caryā-praṇidhāna
bZang po spyod pa'i smon lam
P761, vol. 26

Precious Garland
Ratnāvalī, Rāja-parikathā-ratnāvalī
rGyal po la gtam bya ba rin po che'i phreng ba
author: Nāgārjuna
P5658, vol. 129

Purification of the Obscurations of Karma Sutra
Ārya-karmāvaraṇa-viśuddhi-nāma-mahāyāna-sūtra
'Phags pa las kyi sgrib pa rnam par dag pa zhes bya ba theg pa chen po'i mdo
P884, vol. 35

Questions of Crest Jewel Sutra
Ārya-ratna-cūḍā-paripṛcchā-nāma-mahāyāna-sūtra
'Phags pa grsug na rin po ches zhus pa zhes bya ba theg pa chen po'i mdo
P760.47, vol. 24

Questions of Nārāyaṇa Formula
Nārāyaṇa-paripṛcchā-ārya-mahāmayā-vijaya-vāhinī-dhāraṇī
Sred med kyi bus zhua pa 'phags pa sgyu ma chen mo rnam par rgyal ba thob
    par byed pa zhes bya ba'i gzungs
Not found in P
D134:Na92b2

Questions of Sāgaramati Sutra
Sāgaramati-paripṛcchā-sūtra: Ārya-sāgaramati-paripṛcchā-nāma-mahāyāna-
    sūtra
'Phags pa blo gros rgya mtsos zhus pa shes bya ba theg pa chen po'i mdo
P819, vol. 33

Questions of Sky Treasure Sutra
Ārya-gagana-gañja-paripṛcchā-nāma-mahāyāna-sūtra
'Phags pa nam mkha' mdzod kyis zhus pa zhes by ba theg pa chen po'i mdo
P815, vol. 33

Questions of Subāhu Sutra
Subāhu-paripṛcchā: Ārya-subāhu-paripṛcchā-nāma-mahāyāna-sūtra
'Phags pa lag bzangs kyi zhus pa zhes bya ba theg pa chen po'i mdo
P760.26, vol. 24

Questions of the Householder Ugra Sutra
Ārya-gṛha-pati-ugra-paripṛcchā-nāma-mahāyāna-sūtra
'Phags pa khyim bdag drag shul can gyi zhus pa zhes bya ba theg pa chen po'i mdo
P760.19, vol. 23

Questions of the Householder Vīradatta Sutra
Ārya-vīradatta-gṛha-pati-paripṛcchā-nāma-mahāyāna-sūtra
'Phags pa khyim bdag dpal byin gyi zhus pa zhes bya ba theg pa chen po'i
    mdo
P760.28, vol. 24

Questions of Upāli Sutra
Upāli-paripṛcchā-sūtra: Ārya-vinaya-viiścaya-upāli-paripṛcchā-nāma-sūtra
'Phags pa 'dul ba rnam par gtan la dbab pa nye bar 'khor gyis zhus pa zhes bya
    ba theg pa chen po'i mdo
P760.24, vol. 24

Stages of Meditation
Bhāvanā-krama
sgom pa'i rim pa
author: Kamalaśīla
P5310–12, vol. 102

Stages of the Activities of the Guru
Guru-kriyā-krama
Bla ma'i by ba'i rim pa
author: Atiśa Dipaṃkaraśrījñāna
P5374, vol. 103

Sublime Continuum
Uttara-tantra: Mahāyānottara-tantra-śastra
Theg pa chen po rgyud bla ma'i bstan bcos
author: Maitreya
P5525, vol. 108

Sutra Gathering All the Threads
Ārya-sarva-vaidalya/vaipulya-saṃgraha-nāma-mahāyāna-sūtra
'Phags pa rnam par 'thag pa thams cad bsdus pa zhes bya ba theg pa chen po'i
    mdo
P893, vol. 35

Sutra of Showing the Tathāgata's Inconceivable Secret
Tathāgatā-cintya-guhya-nirdeśa-sūtra: Ārya-tathāgatā-cintya-guhya-nirdeśa-
    nāma-mahāyāna-sūtra
'Phags pa de bzhin gshegs pa'i gsang ba bsam gyis mi kyab pa bstan pa shes
    bya ba
P760, vol. 22

Sutra of the Aupicious Eon
Ārya-bhadra-kalpika-nāma-mahāyāna-sūtra
'Phags pa tshangs pa khyad par sems kyi zhus pa zhes bya ba theg pa chen po'i
    mdo
P762, vol. 27

Sutra of the Golden Light
Suvarṇa-prabhāsa-sūtra: Ārya-suvarṇa-prabhāsottama-sūtrendra-rāja-nāma-
    mahāyāna-sūtra
'Phags pa gser 'od dam pa mdo sde'i dbang po'i rgyal po shes by ba theg pa
    chen po'i mdo
P176, vol. 7

Sutra on the Coming Forth of the Tathāgatas
Tathāgatotpatti-saṃbhava-sūtra
De bzhin gshegs pa skye ba a'byung ba'i mdo
P761, vol. 26

Sutra on the Magic of Final Peace
Praśānta-viniścaya-prātihārya-sūtra: Ārya praśānta-viniścaya-prātihārya-
    samādhi-nāma-mahāyāna-sūtra
Rab tu zhi ba rnam par nges pa'i cho 'phrul gyi ting nge 'dzin ces bya ba theg
    pa chen po'i mdo
P797, vol. 32

Sutra on the Ten Levels
Daśa-bhūmika-sūtra
Sa bcu pa'i mdo
P761, vol. 25

Sutra Requested by a Lion
Ārya-siṃha-paripṛcchā-nāma-mahāyāna-sūtra
'Phags pa seng ges zhus pa zhes bya ba theg pa chen po'i mdo
P760.37, vol. 24

Sutra Requested by Brahmā
Ārya brahma-viśeṣa-paripṛcchā-nāma-mahāyāna-sūtra
'Phags pa tshangs pa khyad par sems kyi zhus pa zhes bya ba theg pa chen po'i
    mdo
P827, vol. 33

Sutra Unraveling the Intended Meaning
Ārya-saṃdhi-nirmocana-nāma-mahāyāna-sūtra
'Phags pa dgongs pa nges par 'grel pa zhes bya ba theg pa chen po'i mdo
P774, vol. 29

Tantra Bestowing the Initiation of Vajrapāṇi
Vajrapāṇi-abhiṣeka-mahā-tantra: Ārya-vajrapāṇi-abhiṣeka-mahā-tantra
'Phags pa lag na rdo rje dbang bskur ba'i rgyud chen mo
P130, vol. 6

Teaching of Vimalakīrti
Ārya-vimalakīrti-nirdeśa-nāma-mahāyāna-sūtra
'Phags pa dri ma med par grags pas bstan pa zhes bya ba theg pa chen po'i mdo
P843, vol. 34

Teachings of Akṣayamati Sutra
Ārya-akṣayamati-nirdeśa-nāma-mahāyāna-sūtra
'Phags pa blo gros mi zad pas bstan pa zhes bya ba theg pa chen po'i mdo
P842, vol. 34

Three Heaps Sutra
Ārya-tri-skandhaka-nāma-mahāyāna-sūtra
'Phags pa phung po gsum pa zhus pa zhes bya ba theg pa chen po'i mdo
P950, vol. 37

Treasury of Knowledge
Abhidharma-kośa-kārikā
Chos mngon pa'i mdzod kyi tshig le'ur byas pa
author: Vasubandhu
P5590, vol. 115

Vairocana's Great Enlightenment Discourse
Mahā-vairocanāsaṃbodhi-vikurvitādhiṣṭhāna-vaipulya-sūtrendra-rāja-nāma-
    dharma-paryāya
rNam par snang mdzad chen po mngon par rdzogs par byang chub pa rnam
    par sprul pa byin gyi rlob pa shin tu rgyas pa mdo sde'i dbang po'i rgyal
    po zhes bya ba'i chos kyi rnam grangs
P126, vol. 5

Verse Summary of the Perfection of Wisdom in Eight Thousand Lines
Ārya-prajñapāramitā-ratna-guṇa-saṃcaya-gāthā
'Phags pa shes rab kyi pha rol tu phyin pa sdud pa tshigs su bcad pa
P735, vol. 21

Verses from the Nāga King's Drum
Nāga-rāja-bherī-gāthā
Klu'i rgyal bo rnga sgra'i tshigs su bcad pa
P991, vol. 39

OTHER WORKS CITED

Blo bzang chos kyi rgyal mtshan. 1983. *Guru Puja (Zab lam bla ma mchod pa'i cho ga
    bde stong dbyer med ma),* published under the title *bLa ma'i rnal 'byor dang yi
    dam khag gi bdag bskyed sogs zhal 'don gces btus bshugs.* Dharamsala, India: Tibetan
    Cultural Printing Press.

'Chad kha ba Ye shes rdo rje (dge bshes). 1993. *Seven-Point Mind Training, Blo sbyong
    don bdun ma.* Dharamsala, India: Tibetan Cultural Printing Press.

Das, S.C. 1981. *A Tibetan-English Dictionary.* Kyoto: Rinsen Book Company.

Davenport, John T., trans. 2000. *Ordinary Wisdom: Sakya Pandita's Treasury of Good
    Advice.* Boston: Wisdom Publications.

dBang phyug blo gros, *Sayings of the Holy Kadampas.* Bka' gdams kyi skyes bu dam pa rnams kyi gsung bgros thor bu.

dGe 'dun grub. 1976. *Praise and Requests to the Twenty-one Taras (The Well Written.)* sGrol ma nyer gcig gi bstod pa dang 'dod gsol (legs bris ma). Dharamsala, India: Tibetan Cultural Printing Press.

Gen Lamrimpa (Lobsang Jampal Tenzin). 1999. *Realizing Emptiness.* B. Alan Wallace, trans. Ithaca, NY: Snow Lion Publications.

Gung thang bstan pa'i sgron me. *Jewel Garland of Instruction.* bslab bya nor bu phreng ba.

Hopkins, Jeffrey. 1998. *Buddhist Advice for Living & Liberation: Nāgārjuna's Precious Garland.* Ithaca, NY: Snow Lion Publications.

'Jam mgon Mi pham rgya mtsho. 2002. *Introduction to the Middle Way: Chandrakirti's Madhyamakavatara with Commentary by Jamgön Mipham.* Padmakara Translation Group. Boston and London: Shambhala.

Kloetzli, Randy. 1983. *Buddhist Cosmology.* Delhi: Motilal Banarsidas.

Ngag dbang chos 'byor. 1984. *Jor chö: The Six Preparatory Practices, bla ma'i rnal 'byor.* Losang C. Ganchenpa and Karma Lekshe Tsomo, trans. Dharamsala, India: Library of Tibetan Works and Archives.

Pabongka Rinpoche, Byams pa bstan 'dzin 'phrin las rgya mtsho. 1977. *Collected Works of Pha bong kha pa, vol 5* (Rnam grol lag bcangs su gtod pa'i man ngag zab mo tshang la ma nor ba mtshungs med chos kyi rgyal po'i thugs bcud byang chub lam gyi rim pa'i nyams khrid kyi zin bris gsung rab kun gyi bcud bsdus gdams ngag bdud rtsi'i snying po). New Delhi, India: Chophel Legdan.

————. 1990. *Liberation in Our Hands: Part One: The Preliminaries.* Sera Mey Geshe Lobsang Tharchin with Artemus B. Engle, trans. Howell, NJ: Mahayana Sutra and Tantra Press.

————. 1991. *Liberation in the Palm of Your Hand (Rnam grol lag bcangs su gtod pa'i man ngag zab mo tshang la ma nor ba mtshungs med chos kyi rgyal po'i thugs bcud byang chub lam gyi rim pa'i nyams khrid kyi zin bris gsung rab kun gyi bcud bsdus gdams ngag bdud rtsi'i snying po, Pha bong kha pa Byams pa bstan 'dzin 'phrin las grya mtsho).* Michael Richards, trans. Boston: Wisdom Publications.

————. 1994. *Liberation in Our Hands: Part Two: The Fundamentals.* Sera Mey Geshe Lobsang with Artemus B. Engle, trans. Howell, NJ: Mahayana Sutra and Tantra Press.

————. 2001. *Liberation in Our Hands: Part Three.* Sera Mey Geshe Lobsang Tharchin with Artemus B. Engle, trans. Howell, NJ: Mahayana Sutra and Tantra Press.

Phur lcog Byams pa tshul khrims. 2006. *Source of Happiness (bDe legs kun byung ma). Bla ma'i rnal 'byor dang, yi dam khag gi bdag bskyed sogs zhal 'don gces btus zhes bya ba zhugs so.* Bylakuppe, India: Sera Mey Library.

Robinson, Richard H. and Johnson, Willard L. 1997. *The Buddhist Religion.* 4th ed. Belmont, CA: Wadsworth Publishing Company.

Śāntideva. 1987. *A Guide to the Bodhisattva's Way of Life.* Stephen Batchelor, trans. Dharamsala, India: Library of Tibetan Works and Archives.

————. 1997. *A Guide to the Bodhisattva's Way of Life.* Vesna A. Wallace and B. Allan Wallace, trans. Ithaca, NY: Snow Lion Publications.

Sonam Rinchen, Geshe and Sonam, Ruth. 1994. *Yogic Deeds of the Bodhisattvas*, commentary by Geshe Sonam Rinchen. Ruth Sonam, trans. and ed. Ithaca, NY: Snow Lion Publications.

————. 1997. *Atisha's Lamp for the Path to Enlightenment.* Ruth Sonam, trans. and ed. Ithaca, NY: Snow Lion Publications.

————. 1997. *The Thirty-Seven Practices of Bodhisattvas.* Ruth Sonam, trans. and ed. Ithaca, NY: Snow Lion Publications.

————. 1999. *The Three Principal Aspects of the Path.* Ruth Sonam, trans. and ed. Ithaca, NY: Snow Lion Publications.

————. 2000. *The Bodhisattva Vow.* Ruth Sonam, trans. and ed. Ithaca, NY: Snow Lion Publications.

Speyer, J.S., trans. 1982. *The Jātakamāla of Garland of Birth-Stories of Āryaśūra.* Delhi: Motilal Banarsidas.

Suzuki, D.T., ed. 1955–61. *The Tibetan Tripitika*, Peking Edition. Kyoto, Japan: Otani University.

Thurman, Robert A.F., ed. 1982. *The Life and Teachings of Tsong Khapa.* Dharamsala, India: Library of Tibetan Works and Archives.

Tsong kha pa, Blo bzang grags pa. *A Brief Account of My Spiritual Life (Rang gi rtogs pa brjod pa mdo tzam du bshad pa).* P6061 vol. 153.

————. *Applying the Advice of the Three Jewels (Bla na med pa'i rin po che gsum gyi gtam gyi sbyor ba).* P6062 vol. 153.

————. *Byang chub lam gyi rim pa'i nyams len gyi rnam gshag mdor bsdus te brjed byang du byas pa* (Condensed Lamrim). P6061, vol. 153.

————. *Foundations of All Good Qualities (Yon tan gzhir gyur ma in Byang chub lam gyi rim pa'i bryud pa rnams la gsol ba 'debs pa'i rim pa "Lam mchog sgo 'byed" shes bya ba).* P6003, vol. 153.

————. *Great Exposition of Secret Mantra/The Stages of the Path to becoming a Great Conquering Overlord Vajradhara that Reveals the Essential Points of all Secrets (rGyal ba khyab bdag rdo rje 'chang chen po'i lam gyi rim pa gsang ba kun gyi gnad rnam par phye pa).* sNgags rim chen mo. P6210, vol. 161.

———. 1977. *Tantra in Tibet: The Great Exposition of Secret Mantra Vol. I.* Jeffrey Hopkins, ed. and trans. London: George Allen & Unwin.

———. 1986. *Asaṅga's Chapter on Ethics with the Commentary of Tsong-Kha-Pa, The Basic Path to Awakening, The Complete Bodhisattva (Byang chub sems dpa'i tsul khrims kyi rnam bshad byang chub gzhung lam).* Mark Tatz, trans, Studies in Asian Thought and Religion, 4. Lewiston/Queenston, NY: The Edwin Mellen Press.

———. 1991. *The Great Treatise on the Stages of the Path to Enlightenment (sKyes bu gsum gyi rnyams su blang ba'i rim pa thams cad tshang bar ston pa'i byang chub lam gyi rim pa).* Dharamsala, India: Ganden Bar Nying.

———. 2000. *The Great Treatise on the Stages of the Path to Enlightenment.* Vol. 1. The Lamrim Chenmo Translation Committee, Joshua W.C. Cutler, Editor-in-Chief, trans. Ithaca, NY: Snow Lion Publications.

———. 2004. *The Great Treatise on the Stages of the Path to Enlightenment.* Vol. 2. The Lamrim Chenmo Translation Committee, Joshua W.C. Cutler, Editor-in-Chief, trans. Ithaca, NY: Snow Lion Publications.

Index

About Wisdom

WISDOM PUBLICATIONS, a nonprofit publisher, is dedicated to making available authentic works relating to Buddhism for the benefit of all. We publish books by ancient and modern masters in all traditions of Buddhism, translations of important texts, and original scholarship. Additionally, we offer books that explore East-West themes unfolding as traditional Buddhism encounters our modern culture in all its aspects. Our titles are published with the appreciation of Buddhism as a living philosophy, and with the special commitment to preserve and transmit important works from Buddhism's many traditions.

To learn more about Wisdom, or to browse books online, visit our website at www.wisdompubs.org.

You may request a copy of our catalog online or by writing to this address:

Wisdom Publications
199 Elm Street
Somerville, Massachusetts 02144 USA
Telephone: 617-776-7416
Fax: 617-776-7841
Email: info@wisdompubs.org
www.wisdompubs.org

THE WISDOM TRUST

As a nonprofit publisher, Wisdom is dedicated to the publication of Dharma books for the benefit of all sentient beings and dependent upon the kindness and generosity of sponsors in order to do so. If you would like to make a donation to Wisdom, you may do so through our website or our Somerville office. If you would like to help sponsor the publication of a book, please write or email us at the address above.

Thank you.

Wisdom is a nonprofit, charitable 501(c)(3) organization affiliated with the Foundation for the Preservation of the Mahayana Tradition (FPMT).

STEPS ON THE PATH TO ENLIGHTENMENT
A Commentary on the Lamrim Chenmo

Volume 1
The Foundational Practices
608 pages, cloth,
ISBN 0-86171-303-6, $29.95

Volume 2
Karma
556 pages, cloth,
ISBN 0-86171-481-4, $29.95

Volume 3
The Way of the Bodhisattva
556 pages, cloth,
ISBN 0-86171-482-2, $29.95

FORTHCOMING
Volume 4: Calm Abiding
Volume 5: Special Insight